CORMORANTS,
DARTERS, AND
PELICANS
OF THE WORLD

Paul A. Johnsgard

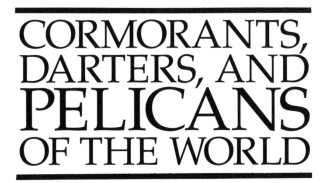

CORMORANTS, DARTERS, AND PELICANS OF THE WORLD

SMITHSONIAN INSTITUTION PRESS

WASHINGTON AND LONDON

© 1993 by the Smithsonian Institution

Editor: Matthew Abbate
Production Editor: Jack Kirshbaum
Designer: Linda McKnight

Library of Congress Cataloging-in-Publication Data

Johnsgard, Paul A.
    Cormorants, darters, and pelicans of the world / Paul A.
  Johnsgard.
        p.   cm.
    Includes bibliographical references and index.
    ISBN 1-56098-216-0 (acid-free paper)
    1. Cormorants. 2. Pelicans. 3. Anhingidae. I. Title.
  QL696.P4745J64   1993
  598.4'3—dc20   92-31997

British Library Cataloging-in-Publication data available

Color illustrations printed in Hong Kong by South China
Printing Company. Text manufactured in the United States
of America
96 95 94 93 5 4 3 2 1

♾ The paper used in this publication meets the minimum
requirements of the American National Standard for Permanence
of Paper for Printed Library Materials Z39.48-1984.

Jacket illustrations
Front: Brown pelican. Photo by Thomas D. Mangelsen/
Images of Nature.
Back: A double-crested cormorant, prebreeding adult of the race
albociliatus. Photo by Kenneth Fink.

For permission to reproduce any of the illustrations, please
correspond directly with the sources. The Smithsonian Institution
Press does not retain reproduction rights for these illustrations
individually or maintain a file of addresses for photo sources.

Contents

PART TWO: SPECIES ACCOUNTS
Cormorants and Shags (Phalacrocoracidae)

Preface

Occasionally serendipity plays a role in the genesis of a book. For example, until 1989 I had no plans whatever to write a book on pelecaniform birds, but while recuperating from heart surgery that year I decided that I should begin to work on a new avian monograph that might require some two or three years of research and writing. A few years previously I had been urged by a long-time English friend, Christopher Marler, to consider writing a book on the pelicans of the world. He was then developing a collection of live birds that ultimately was to include all of the world's species, and was initiating a Pelican Trust to encourage research on and conservation of that group. My first thought at that time had been that the technical ornithological literature on pelicans was probably too limited, especially for the non–North American species, to facilitate writing a major book dealing fully with the Pelecanidae. However, as I mulled over the matter of potential book projects, I wondered if it might not be possible to add one or two more pelecaniform families of rather radically different foraging behavior and ecologies, to provide for a coverage having a greater general taxonomic, ecological, and ethological interest than one dealing with the pelicans alone.

I began a thorough literature search and decided that a book-length coverage of pelicans, cormorants, and darters was feasible in terms of an adequate world literature base, and confirmed furthermore that none of the three groups had been monographed in any comprehensive fashion. For a time I considered also including one or both of the other heretofore unmonographed pelecaniform families as well, namely the frigatebirds and tropicbirds. However, I soon decided that adding these groups (both of which appear to be only peripherally related to the others) would strain my capacity to complete the work in the amount of time that I had set out for myself as reasonable. Additionally, the technical literature on these highly pelagic birds seemed relatively scanty as compared with that available for the other three families, most of whose species are much more accessible for study or are economically more significant and have thus attracted much more research attention from ornithologists.

Besides the great enthusiasm for and help with the project that was immediately offered by Christopher Marler when I first told him my ideas, I also consulted with Elizabeth A. Schreiber over the desirability of writing a book dealing with the world's pelicans. I assumed that she and her late husband Ralph had been intending eventually to write a monograph on pelican biology, and I didn't want to intrude on any plans that they might have made. She not only encouraged me to take on the project but also invited me to search through Ralph's reprint files in the Los Angeles County Museum of Natural History for any useful reference materials. During the summer of 1991 I was also able to spend some time observing pelicans in various European collections, including Christopher Marler's Pelican Trust near Olney, England, the Tierpark Berlin, and Vogelpark Walsrode.

Manuscript writing for this book was completed during 1991, which represents the general deadline for the addition of new literature citations. With regard to literature, it might be noted that there are no complete published bibliographies for the Pelecaniformes. Apparently only two single-species bibliographies exist, one for the brown pelican that contains about 900 references (Schreiber and Schreiber, 1980) and one for the Dalmatian pelican containing about 250 references (Crivelli, 1987). A fairly large technical literature also exists for the American white pelican, double-crested cormorant, and great cormorant, but for most other species the literature is extremely limited, with sometimes fewer than a dozen relatively useful references. The literature cited in this book approaches 900 titles. Although I have reviewed the primary literature wherever possible, I have sometimes necessarily used secondary sources when primary sources were not available to me, most often in the case of the recently published and superb *Handbook of the Birds of Australia, New Zealand and the Antarctic* (Marchant and Higgins, 1990), and less frequently the *Handbook of the Birds of the Western Palearctic* (Cramp and Simmons, 1977).

The taxonomic sequence used here for the Phalacrocoracidae follows that proposed by Siegel-Causey (1988), although his nine proposed genera have been reduced to subgeneric components of only two genera, the latter corresponding to his subfamilial limits. In a few cases the species limits used here also diverge from his. These cases involve the "blue-eyed shags" of the subgenus *Notocarbo*, of which he recognized four allopatric species, whereas I have followed many prior authorities in admitting only a single polytypic species *atriceps*. As an indication of the still-fluid state of cormorant taxonomy, it might be noted that the recent Australian handbook (Marchant and Higgins, 1990) recognized all six allopatric populations of blue-eyed shags occurring within its area of geographic coverage as full species, but nevertheless accepted only a single all-inclusive genus of phalacrocoracids. I have, however, reluctantly followed both of these sources with regard to species limits in the "New Zealand shags" of the subgenus *Euleucocarbo*, which similarly consists of a confusing array of five entirely allopatric and insular populations exhibiting varied levels of apparent speciation. From my own taxonomic perspective these five forms might well have been likewise treated as a single polytypic species, especially inasmuch as the criteria for their recognition are largely limited to adult breeding condition traits, but I have yielded to contemporary opinion on this point. This distinctly differential taxonomic treatment accorded the two subgenera *Notocarbo* and *Euleucocarbo* is thus unfortunate and somewhat inconsistent, but seemingly unavoidable.

In accepting only two species of Anhingidae, my treatment follows that of most modern classifications. However, the current taxonomy of darters is clearly still quite unsatisfactory and perhaps four allospecies may eventually have to be recognized, as was tentatively done by Sibley and Monroe (1990).

In my view there are also no entirely suitable modern taxonomies of the Pelecanidae, including that of Sibley and Monroe (1990). Thus, I have generally adopted both the sequential arrangement and the species level classification (except for the nonrecognition of *roseus*) that was used by Peters (1931), which in turn is a minor variant of a taxonomy that was originally proposed by Ogilvie-Grant (1898).

English vernacular names used for all pelican and cormorant species are essentially those that were proposed by Harrison (1983), with alternate names as used by Sibley and Monroe (1990) shown parenthetically in section headings. However, "shag" has been substituted as necessary for "cormorant" to conform with the primary taxonomic subdivision of the phalacrocoracids recommended by Siegel-Causey (1988), a convention that had been earlier adopted by van Tets (1976a). Additionally, I have at times found it convenient to refer collectively to all the extant pelican species other than the brown pelican as "white pelicans," which is thus intended as a convenient inclusive term for all species comprising the subgenera *Pelecanus* and *Cyrtopelicanus*.

Following Sibley and Monroe (1990) I refer to the three Old World populations as the African, Oriental, and Australian darters, but tentatively consider them as representing subspecies rather than allospecies. I have also used the collective vernacular term "darters" in the generic sense (= *Anhinga* spp.) to refer inclusively to the three forms of Old World darters plus the New World anhinga. The latter is simply called the anhinga, rather than the American anhinga as was done by these authors.

Unless otherwise indicated, all anatomical measurements are given in millimeters, and weights are in grams or kilograms. Estimated fresh egg weights have been determined by a method used in earlier books (Johnsgard, 1972). Such estimates are frequently supplemented by actual reported egg weights, although substantial weight declines occur during incubation, and sometimes these estimates appear to be more reliable than the reported actual weights. Various dimensional or areal measurements that originally appeared in the literature as pounds, inches, acres, etc. have been converted in the text to their metric equivalents, usually showing the original measurements parenthetically. Chinese geographic spellings are given in their modern pinyin form, with the earlier Wade-Giles form included parenthetically as deemed necessary. Some additional alternative terms for geographic areas or political entities that have recently undergone name changes are also similarly included parenthetically to help avoid possible confusion. The species distribution maps show political boundaries of 1989.

I have based many of my plumage descriptions on those of Ogilvie-Grant (1898), although these have been considerably modified and supplemented, especially with respect to predefinitive plumages and softpart colors. A few comments on age and plumage terminology also seem appropriate here. I have adopted the following descriptive age category terminology: nestling or chick (for unfledged young), juvenile (for fledged young still mostly or entirely in juvenal plumage), immature (for early or relatively brief transitional stages between juvenal and definitive plumages), subadult (for later predefinitive plumage stages, especially in individuals at least two years old), and adult (for birds in definitive plumage). For a few species that attain their definitive plumage in a single year the "immature" plumage is obviously simply a variable mixture of juvenal and definitive feathering, but more clear-cut immature stages can be recognized for those species taking more than one year to attain definitive plumage. At least in some such slowly maturing species, breeding may sometimes occur among individuals not yet in definitive plumage, namely while they are still "subadults" according to this age terminology.

Settling on a consistent and logical use of terms related to seasonal plumages and molts was considerably more difficult than adopting one for age groups, inasmuch as molting patterns and sequences in pelecaniform birds are highly complex and still only relatively poorly understood. The molts are known to include such features as a complex and sometimes nearly continuous molting of the rectrices, with the primaries usually exhibiting two or more temporally overlapping and wavelike molt cycles (*Staffelmause*), making distinctions between successive plumages based on wing and tail molt cycles impossible. Furthermore, because of similar body molt complexities it is also seemingly impossible to define any single plumage phase as the "nuptial" or "breeding" plumage. For simplicity, I have thus used the term "prebreeding adult" for the overall definitive plumage aspect and related soft-part appearance of potentially breeding individuals in their peak reproductive state, which typically occurs over a relatively short period between the "courtship" phase of nesting and the start of egg laying. However, molt into the postfertilization plumage phases may begin quite soon afterward, namely during the incubation period. This plumage sequence is evidently initiated by a relatively limited "supplemental" molt, and results in a "nesting aspect" of the plumage and softparts among incubating birds. This is then followed by a brief "nestling" aspect (lasting through the chicks' fledging period) that in turn is followed by a prolonged "nonbreeding" aspect (Schreiber et al., 1989). Since this latter plumage may often be carried for more than half the entire year it cannot in my view logically be termed a "winter" plumage, and in the species accounts I have instead collectively referred to all these postfertilization plumage aspects as the "postbreeding adult" condition, in the full knowledge that this represents a considerable simplification of the actual plumage and molt situation.

Acknowledgments

In addition to the aforementioned great assistance of Elizabeth Schreiber and Christopher Marler, Wolfgang Grummt, of Tierpark Berlin, personally helped me greatly with this project, as did Steffen Patzwahl, of Vogelpark Walsrode. Douglas Siegel-Causey, Marion Jenkins, and Pamela Rasmussen, all of the University of Kansas, helped me greatly with locating certain technical literature on pelecaniform birds, as did Lloyd Kiff of the Western Foundation of Vertebrate Zoology. Other substantial assistance with my literature searches or requests for information came from William Andelt, Neil Bernstein, Charles Brown, Brian Chudleigh, Dave Friis, Scott Hatch, Takashi Hiraoka, Philip R. Millener, Don Paul, Elizabeth Schreiber, and Micheal Taylor. Additionally, at the request of Elizabeth Schreiber, her father-in-law, Dr. William Schreiber, translated much of a long German paper on pelican biology for me.

Use of the library and/or museum facilities at the British Museum (Natural History), the Zoological Society of London, the University of Nebraska, the University of Kansas, the Los Angeles County Museum, and Oxford University's Edward Grey Institute is also gratefully acknowledged. Specimen data were also helpfully provided me by staff at the U.S. National Museum of Natural History, Washington, D.C., the Museum of Vertebrate Zoology, Berkeley, California, the Royal Ontario Museum, Toronto, and the Yamashina Institute for Ornithology, Chiba, Japan. Assistance with various specimen measurements by Thomas Labedz of the University of Nebraska State Museum is also appreciated, and Pamela Rasmussen very helpfully read and substantially improved my plumage descriptions of cormorants. Various parts of the manuscript were critically reviewed by David Duffy, David Ainley, and Elizabeth Anne Schreiber, to all of whom I wish to express my appreciation.

With regard to color illustrations, I must as usual acknowledge with great pleasure the photographic assistance of my long-time friend Ken Fink, who has again allowed my use of his superb collection of bird photographs, helped with my literature search, and hosted me on my photographic trips to the San Diego area. My thanks must additionally and especially include Frank Todd, Jr., of Ecocepts International, San Diego, who not only initially strongly encouraged me to undertake this project, but also generously gave me full access to his extremely large collection of seabird transparencies for possible use in the book. Although not all of them could be used, additional photographs were helpfully offered to me by Neil Bernstein, Brian Chudleigh, Yuzo Fujimaki, Michio Fukuda, Don Haddon, John Janovy, Jr., Gary Lingle, Tom Lowe, Tom Mangelsen, Raphael Payne, Peter Steyn, Warwick Tarboton, Trevor Taylor, and B. Tollerman.

CORMORANTS,
DARTERS, AND
PELICANS
OF THE WORLD

PART ONE

COMPARATIVE BIOLOGY

Nesting female Oriental
darter.

CHAPTER 1

Phylogeny, Taxonomy, and Zoogeography

Fossil History of the Pelecaniformes

In her major review of the fossil evidence for avian evolution, Howard (1950) stated that the Cretaceous form *Elopteryx* is the earliest known possible pelecaniform bird, and might not only be ancestral to the Pelecaniformes, but even intermediate between the modern gannetlike birds (Sulidae) and the cormorants (Phalacrocoracidae). This fossil, however, is now considered to be nonavian (Olson, 1985). Two additional genera (*Eostega, Actiornis*) that were mentioned by Howard as apparently linking these two groups occurred in Europe during the Eocene epoch. However, *Eostega* is possibly nonpelecaniform and needs additional material to be more certainly identified, and *Actiornis* is likewise of distinctly uncertain affinities (Olson, 1985).

Howard furthermore stated that the families Pelecanidae and Anhingidae were represented in Eocene deposits by *Protopelecanus* and *Protoplotus* respectively, although more recent authors have suggested that both forms are only very questionably members of these two families. Thus, *Protopelecanus* is perhaps not a pelican, and *Protoplotus* may actually represent a new avian family (Olson, 1985; Becker, 1986; van Tets, Rich, and Marino-Hadiwardoyo, 1989).

Although *Protoplotus* can therefore no longer be regarded as the oldest known darter, Becker (1986) recently reidentified *"Phalacrocorax" subvolans* as an early Miocene species of *Anhinga*. He suggested that the darters have thus evidently been separated from the cormorants for at least 30 million years, and thereby perhaps the two groups warrant familial separation. In addition to *A. subvolans* from the lower Miocene, two other relatively early darter species (*A. pannonica, A. grandis*) are known from the very late Miocene.

The cormorant family Phalacrocoracidae has fossil members that extend back to the Eocene-Oligocene boundary (Mourer-Chauviré, 1982), making the cormorants the oldest known group among the families considered in this book. However, there is an even older apparent frigatebird (*Limnofregata azygosternon*) from the lower Eocene of Wyoming (Olson, 1985). This fossil is evidently the oldest that can confidently be assigned to any of the modern families of pelecaniform birds.

As noted above, the oldest reputed pelican, *Protopelecanus*, known only from a femur and a scapula, is probably not a pelican and perhaps is instead a primitive sulid or perhaps even a pelagornithid, an extinct group of gigantic marine long-billed gliding birds with toothlike processes on their mandibles. The earliest certain fossil pelican, *Pelecanus grandis*, dates back to the early Miocene, and two additional Old World pelicans occur in Miocene deposits, while a third Miocene form *P. tirarensis* has been found in Australia (Olson, 1985).

The sulids and their relatives are well represented in the fossil record, with the oldest known sulid being *Sula ronzoni* of the early Oligocene, based on a fragmentary fossil that has also been assigned to the Phalacrocoracidae. Other species of *Sula* and *Morus* have been found in Miocene and Pliocene deposits, and several additional genera have been described from these general time periods. Additionally, a related group of flightless birds apparently derived from the suborder Sulae has been discovered (Olson, 1985). These rather penguin- or alcidlike birds had greatly reduced and paddle-like forelimbs, although their hindlimbs show distinct similarities to those of the darters!

A summary of the currently known fossil species of cormorants, darters, and pelicans is provided in table 1.

Taxonomy of the Extant Pelecaniformes

On the surface at least, few orders of birds can be more succinctly and uniquely defined than can the Pelecaniformes: they are the "totipalmate or steganopode swimmers," in which all four toes are connected by webbing, although this webbing is much reduced in the frigatebirds. Apart from this, few if any inclusive traits unquestionably link all 55 living species (Dorst and Mougin, 1979)—for example brood patches are uniformly lacking, and although unfeathered gular pouches of varying size are typically present, the throat is feathered and definite gular pouches are lacking in the tropicbirds (Phaethontidae). All species have an oil (uropygial) gland, although it is very small in the frigatebirds. Furthermore, although the oil gland is well developed in the cormorants and darters, their body feathers are not water-resistant, and indeed rather rapidly absorb water. Pelicans have more water-resistant feathers, but they too tend eventually to become waterlogged. In all pelecaniform birds the tongue is surprisingly small, indeed is often rudimentary, and the hyoid structure is variably reduced. However, the hyoid musculature is important in facilitating evaporative cooling through the opened mouth, by means of "gular fluttering."

A number of biological traits also help to unite the Pelecaniformes. All of the pelecaniform birds live largely on fish or other aquatic vertebrates or invertebrates, which not only limits them to waters rich in such foods but also tends to promote colonial breeding wherever the food base will support such sociality. In most species (excepting the tropicbirds) the usually chalky-surfaced eggs are incubated by transmission of heat from the foot webs, since brood patches are lacking. This nearly unique incubation method makes a one- or two-egg clutch perhaps the optimum number for efficient incubation, and may limit maximum clutch size. In all species the young are hatched in a highly altricial state, blind and usually naked (but down-covered in the tropicbirds), and are dependent upon their parents for food and protection throughout a prolonged nestling period. In nearly all groups (again excepting the tropicbirds), older chicks take food directly from their parents' gullets. Because of prolonged parental dependency by the young, usually persisting

TABLE 1   Fossil Genera and Species of Cormorants, Darters, and Pelicans

	Phalacrocoracidae	Anhingidae	Pelecanidae
Pleistocene	*P. pampeanus* *P. gregorii* *P. vestustus* *P. macropus* *P. tanzaniae* 1979 *P. macer* *P. rogersi* *P. owrei* 1984 *Stictocarbo kumeyaay* 1990	*A. parva* *A. laticeps* *A. hadrensis* 1982	 *P. aethiopicus* 1976 *P. novaezealandiae* 1981 *P. cadimurka* 1981 *P. halieus*
Pliocene	*P. golentensis* 1965 *P. chapalensis* 1977 *P. sericensis* 1984 *P. idahoensis* *P. destefani* *P. kennelli* *P. leptopus* *P. wetmorei*		 *P. odessanus* *P. sivalensis* *P. cautleyi*
Miocene	*P. intermedius* *P. brunhuberi* 1980 *P. ibericum* 1963 *P. lautus* 1972 *P. femoralis* *P. mongoliensis* 1971 *P. reliquus* 1976 *P. marinavis* *P. anatolicus* 1978 *P. littoralis* *Phalacrocorax* *Nectornis mioceanus* 1984	*A. grandis* 1975 *A. pannonica* *A. subvolans*[1] *Anhinga*	*P. intermedius* *P. fraasi* *P. tirarensis* 1966 *P. grandis* *Pelecanus*
Oligocene	Still-undescribed genus approaching *Pha-* *lacrocorax*[2]		
Eocene		*Protoplotus*[3]	*Protopelecanus*[3]

NOTES: Any species not found in Brodkorb's (1963) summary is distinguished by the year of its description. The validity of these new taxa is not known to me. Several taxa in Brodkorb's checklist have subsequently been reevaluated (Olson, 1985) and have been excluded here. Also excluded are *Valenticarbo praetermissus*, a very doubtful Pliocene cormorant, and *Goliatha andrewsi*, which has been recently assigned to the Pelecanidae (Harrison, 1979) but very probably does not belong there (Olson, 1985).

[1] Transferred from *Phalacrocorax* (Becker, 1986).
[2] Cf. Mourer-Chauviré (1982) and Olson (1985).
[3] Family allocations of these Eocene fossils are very uncertain; *Protoplotus* has recently been placed in a separate family (van Tets, Rich, and Marino-Hadiwardoyo, 1989).

for a time after fledging, and their high food requirements, severe limitations are placed on the number of young that can be reared. As a result of these several breeding limitations, the reproductive potential of pelecaniform birds is fairly low, monogamous mating is typical of all species, and in most species sexual maturity usually does not occur until at least the second and often the third or fourth year, assuring that breeding will be done only by the older and more experienced birds.

The genus *Pelecanus* was erected by C. Linnaeus in 1758, but at that time he included nearly all (excepting the tropicbirds) of the pelecaniform birds known to him in this single taxonomic unit. However, the pelecaniform assemblage was apparently first recognized as a distinct order (the Steganopodes) by Johann K. Illiger in 1811. The first fairly comprehensive anatomical monograph on the pelecaniform group was apparently that of Mivart (1878). He examined the axial (postcranial) skeletal anatomy of representatives of *Pelecanus, Sula, Phalacrocorax,* and *Plotus* (= *Anhinga*), all of which he considered as related component members of his large family "Pelecanidae." However, he excluded both *Fregata* and *Phaethon* from this group for a number of reasons, among the more important of which was the fact that they have only 12–13 cervical vertebrae, and these vertebrae are not specialized in such a way as allows for a sigmoid neck shape and a corresponding thrusting or spearing ability.

In his landmark *Key to North American Birds* (fourth edition), Coues (1894) regarded the Steganopodes as a "definite and perfectly natural" group, consisting of six families. Besides the critically shared condition of totipalmate feet, he also noted the generally shared characteristics of minute to abortive nostrils, a gular pouch, and a bill that can be opened widely and usually has a long mandibular groove or sulcus on its upper mandible as well as a hooked tip. With the fifth edition of this book in 1903, Coues suggested that three suborders might be recognized within this order, with the Phaethontidae and Fregatidae each differing "as much from each other as both do from the other four [families]."

An important contribution was made by Pycraft (1898), who examined the skeletal anatomy of the available specimens of birds in the British Museum (Natural History). He concluded that indeed the "Steganopodes" are a natural group. He furthermore concluded that (1) they are all closely related, (2) they cannot be easily subdivided into groups of equal taxonomic value, (3) they must be regarded as a single entity or as a subdivision of some larger group, and (4) that they cannot consistently be merged as a whole with that larger group. He also believed that the characteristics of the skull provided the strongest evidence of phyletic relatedness, with *Phalacrocorax* and *Plotus* sharing the first and most primitive skull type, *Phaethon* and *Pelecanus* a second type, while *Sula* and *Fregata* comprise a third type. Pycraft considered the differences between *Phalacrocorax* and *Plotus* to warrant only a subfamilial taxonomic separation, while the other four genera were each given familial distinction. In a phyletic diagram he indicated that the Phaethontidae and Fregatidae were the most divergent of the included families, and that the Phalacrocoracidae, Pelecanidae, and Sulidae were about equally divergent from a hypothetical ancestral type.

When Ogilvie-Grant (1898) contributed the Steganopodes section in the comprehensive catalogue of birds in the British Museum, he was certainly strongly influenced by Pycraft's work. He likewise recognized the Steganopodes as an order, and placed them in sequence after the "Herodiones" (herons and relatives) and prior to the "Pygopodes" (loons and grebes). Like Pycraft, he considered the darters to represent a subfamily of the Phalacrocoracidae. Ogilvie-Grant's proposed "most natural arrangement" of families was as follows: tropicbirds, pelicans, cormorants and darters, gannets, and frigatebirds.

Subsequent to Mivart's and Pycraft's work, the contributions by Shufeldt on the comparative osteology of the pelecaniform birds are of special significance. One might especially note his 1889 and 1902 papers. In the former study he dealt mainly with *Sula* and only briefly with *Phalacrocorax* and *Pelecanus.* However, in the latter study he described in detail the cranial and postcranial osteology of *Phaethon, Fre-*

gata, Sula, Anhinga, Phalacrocorax, and *Pelecanus.* He accepted the then-current classification of the American Ornithologists' Union for the group, namely as representing six families (Phaethontidae, Sulidae, Phalacrocoracidae, Anhingidae, Pelecanidae, and Fregatidae) within the single order Steganopodes.

Although this feature is perhaps of questionable phyletic significance, Chandler (1916) observed that the microscopic feather structures of *Pelecanus, Phalacrocorax, Sula,* and *Fregata* fall into one group, that of *Anhinga* into a second, and that of *Phaethon* into a third. The distinctive feathers of darters were regarded by him as distinctly similar to those of the New World vultures (Cathartidae). The genus *Phaethon* was considered by him to fall outside the pelecaniform limits on the basis of its feather structure, its nearest affinities apparently being with the gulls (Laridae). However, Lowe (1926) argued for retention of *Phaethon* in the Steganopodes, stating that its quadrate has traits shared not only with the more typical pelecaniform genera but also with penguins and some of the procellariiform birds.

Among complete world taxonomies of birds, the Pelecaniformes were regarded as a natural group by both Stresemann (1927–34) and Peters (1931), the former considering the darters as a subfamily of the cormorant group, the latter maintaining these as separate families. Similarly, Grassé (1950) recognized the order "Pelecaniformes or Steganopodes," with five included families, the darters being considered as a subfamily of the cormorants.

A review of both extant and extinct forms of the pelecaniform birds was provided by Lanham (1947). He agreed with Coues that the frigatebirds and tropicbirds each differed widely from the rest of the pelecaniform stock, and suggested that three suborders should be recognized. He believed that *Phaethon* and *Fregata* show distinct phyletic affinities to one another, are progressively more distantly related to the remaining pelecaniform groups, and more remotely still to the procellariiform birds. He suggested that the Pelecaniformes have been derived from a primitive procellariiform stock, most probably in Cretaceous times. His proposed classification of the extant families was as follows:

> Suborder Phaethones
> > Family Phaethontidae
> Suborder Fregatae
> > Family Fregatidae
> Suborder Pelecani
> > Superfamily Pelecanides
> > > Family Pelecanidae
> > Superfamily Sulides
> > > Family Sulidae
> > > Family Anhingidae
> > > Family Phalacrocoracidae

Later, van Tets (1965) did a comparative behavioral study of pelecaniform birds that, although not taxonomically directed, tended to support Lanham's proposed taxonomy. A few years previously Cottam (1957) had suggested that on the basis of some osteological traits the African shoebill (*Balaeniceps rex*) actually belongs with the pelicanlike birds rather than with the storklike birds (Ciconiiformes) with which it has traditionally been associated. Unfortunately, van Tets had not included the shoebill in his behavioral study, and later observations have indicated that a generally storklike array of social displays are typical of the species (Brown,

Urban, and Newman, 1982). Thus, little credence has been placed in Cottam's arguments until very recently, when Sibley's DNA-DNA hybridization studies have strongly supported the possibility that pelicans and the shoebill may be closely related.

The classification of the pelecaniform birds was seemingly essentially stabilized by the middle of the twentieth century, as exemplified by Wetmore's (1960) proposed classification of the group. Although this was rather distinctly similar to Lanham's taxonomy, Wetmore preferred to sequentially separate the tropicbirds and frigatebirds, pointing out that, whereas tropicbirds have down-covered young and a cushioning layer of subcutaneous air cells, the frigatebirds are nearly naked at hatching and lack such air cells. Like Lanham, Wetmore preferred to retain the cormorants and darters as separate families, noting the highly specialized thrusting mechanism in the neck of darters, the unusual pyloric lobe of the darter stomach, which is lined with unique hairlike processes, and their single rather than double carotid arterial condition. Wetmore's taxonomy of the extant pelecaniform birds is as follows:

> Suborder Phaethontes
> > Family Phaethontidae
> Suborder Pelecani
> > Superfamily Pelecanoidea
> > > Family Pelecanidae
> > Superfamily Suloidea
> > > Family Sulidae
> > > Family Phalacrocoracidae
> > > Family Anhingidae
> Suborder Fregatae
> > Family Fregatidae

Using the results of electrophoretic analyses of egg-white proteins, Sibley and Ahlquist (1972) judged that the darters and cormorants exhibit a close relationship to one another, and that the sulids' electrophoretic patterns resemble those of the cormorants. Those of pelicans were more distinct, but all of the pelecaniform groups studied were judged to have electrophoretic patterns representing modifications of a single ancestral type, which has diverged considerably over the group's long evolutionary ancestry.

In a major (and subsequently highly criticized) revision of avian taxonomy, using cladistic approaches and reasoning, Cracraft (1981) suggested that the pelecaniform and procellariiform birds are sister groups, and that both are distinctly, if more distantly, related to the penguins and loon-grebe assemblage. Cracraft also generally accepted Lanham's taxonomic arguments concerning the intraordinal affinities of the totipalmate birds, but said that the characters Lanham used to unite the tropicbirds and frigatebirds are primitive rather than derived traits, and thus that the two groups properly belong in two separate suborders. In a later (1985) paper he provided details of his conclusions regarding the Pelecaniformes, which can be taxonomically summarized as follows:

> Suborder Phaethontes
> > Family Phaethontidae
> Suborder Steganopodes
> > Infraorder Fregatae
> > > Family Fregatidae

Infraorder Pelecani
    Superfamily Pelecanoidea
        Family Pelecanidae
    Superfamily Suloidea
        Family Sulidae
        Family Phalacrocoracidae
            Subfamily Phalacrocoracinae
            Subfamily Anhinginae

The only other major recent contribution to pelecaniform taxonomy comes from the biochemical work involving DNA-DNA hybridization techniques by Charles Sibley and his associates. Their revolutionary taxonomic conclusions for the entire class Aves were initially summarized by Sibley, Ahlquist, and Monroe (1988), and were more fully discussed and documented by Sibley and Ahlquist (1990) and Sibley and Monroe (1990). Their results have effectively resulted in a more thorough dismemberment of the traditional order Pelecaniformes than has ever previously been suggested. However, all of the order's original parts still remain within a relatively large "Infraorder Ciconiides," an abbreviated relevant summary of which follows, with groups outside the traditional Pelecaniformes shown parenthetically:

Parvorder Phaethontida
        Family Phaethontidae (1 genus, 3 species)
Parvorder Sulida
    Superfamily Suloidea
        Family Sulidae (3 genera, 9 species)
        Family Anhingidae (1 genus, 4 species)
    Superfamily Phalacrocoracoidea
        Family Phalacrocoracidae (1 genus, 38 species)
Parvorder Ciconiida
    (Superfamily Ardeoidea)
    (Superfamily Scopoidea)
    (Superfamily Phoenicopteroidea)
    (Superfamily Threskiornithoidea)
    Superfamily Pelecanoidea
        Family Pelecanidae
            Subfamily Balaenicipitinae
            Subfamily Pelecaninae (1 genus, 8 species)
    (Superfamily Ciconioidea)
    Superfamily Procellaroidea
        Family Fregatidae (1 genus, 5 species)
        (Family Spheniscidae)
        (Family Gaviidae)
        (Family Procellariidae)

As may be readily seen, little remains of the traditional order Pelecaniformes in this classification; not only have the darters been well removed from the cormorants, but also the African shoebill is regarded as more closely related to the pelicans than are any of the other traditional members of the pelecaniform order! It is too early to evaluate this proposed taxonomic arrangement, and only future independent research is likely to do so. However, given this new information, it is now obviously very difficult to argue persuasively that any previous classification of the Pelecaniformes is any better than any other, or even that the Pelecaniformes can continue to be recognized as a natural taxonomic group. Considering this confused state of affairs, it is premature to argue about possible interfamilial relationships among the pelicans, cormorants, and darters, or to dwell on their possible relationships to the frigatebirds, tropicbirds, and sulids, and instead it may be more profitable to simply concentrate on intrafamilial phylogenies and taxonomies.

Taxonomic Relationships of the Cormorants

In his taxonomic treatment of the cormorants, Ogilvie-Grant (1898) recognized only a single genus *Phalacrocorax*, and his linear sequence of the 36 species was seemingly one of convenience, based on the construction of his identification key. Thus, little value is gained by discussing it in detail, and instead one may pass on to the widely adopted classification by Peters (1931). In addition to *Phalacrocorax*, Peters

TABLE 2   Representative Taxonomies of the Cormorants
and Shags of the World

Van Tets (1976)	Dorst and Mougin (1979)	Siegel-Causey (1988)
Leucocarbo	*Phalacrocorax*	Subfam. Phalacrocoracinae
Subgenus *Leucocarbo*	Subgenus *Phalacrocorax*	*Microcarbo*
L. (L.) bougainvillii	P. (P.) carbo[2]	M. africanus
L. (L.) atriceps	P. (P.) capillatus[2]	M. coronatus
L. (L.) albiventer	P. (P.) nigrogularis	M. pygmaeus
L. (L.) carunculatus	P. (P.) varius	M. niger
L. (L.) chalconotus	P. (P.) harrisi	M. melanoleucos
L. (L.) onslowi	P. (P.) auritus	*Compsohalieus*
L. (L.) ranfurlyi	P. (P.) olivaceus	C. perspicillatus
L. (L.) colensoi	P. (P.) fuscicollis	C. penicillatus
L. (L.) campbelli	P. (P.) sulcirostris	C. harrisi
L. (L.) verrucosus	P. (P.) penicillatus	C. neglectus
L. (L.) fuscescens	P. (P?) capensis[1]	C. fuscescens
L. (L.) capensis	P. (P?) neglectus[1]	*Hypoleucus*
L. (L.) neglectus	Subgenus *Stictocarbo*	H. olivaceus
L. (L.) nigrogularis	P. (S.) punctatus	H. auritus
L. (L.) penicillatus	P. (S.) aristotelis	H. fuscicollis
L. (L.) harrisi	P. (S.) perspicillatus	H. varius
Subgenus *Stictocarbo*	P. (S.) urile[2]	H. sulcirostris
L. (S.) punctatus	P. (S.) pelagicus[2]	*Phalacrocorax*
L. (S.) featherstoni	P. (S.) gaimardi	P. carbo
L. (S.) aristotelis	Subgenus *Leucocarbo*	P. capillatus
L. (S.) urile	P. (L.) magellanicus	Subfam. Leucocarboninae
L. (S.) pelagicus	P. (L.) bougainvillii	*Leucocarbo*
L. (S.) gaimardi	P. (L.) atriceps[2]	L. nigrogularis
L. (S.) magellanicus	P. (L.) albiventer[2]	L. capensis
Phalacrocorax	P. (L.) carunculatus	L. bougainvillii
Subgenus *Phalacrocorax*	P. (L.) campbelli	*Notocarbo*
P. (P.) carbo	P. (L.) fuscescens	N. verrucosus
P. (P.) capillatus	Subgenus *Microcarbo*	N. atriceps

accepted *Nannopterum* as a monotypic genus for the flightless cormorant, and generically separated four species of very small, short-billed cormorants as *Halietor*. Although accepting a considerable number of now-discarded subspecies, he admitted a total of only 30 species in the entire family.

Van Tets (1976a) provided what might well be regarded as the first biologically meaningful classification of the cormorants as part of a zoogeographic analysis of the family's probable origins (table 2). Van Tets subdivided the family into two approximately equal genera, *Phalacrocorax* ("cormorants") and *Leucocarbo* ("shags"), with a total of 34 extant species exclusive of the extinct Pallas' cormorant, which he didn't take into account. Van Tets offered a number of morphological and biological criteria for his generic separation, which are summarized and somewhat supplemented in table 3. He furthermore divided each of these two genera into a total of five subgenera, the shags consisting of two subgenera (*Leucocarbo* and *Stictocarbo*), and the cormorants consisting of three (*Phalacrocorax, Hypoleucus,* and *Microcarbo,* with the last-named subgenus corresponding to Peters's genus *Halietor*.

The most recent and by far the most fully documented of the available classifi-

TABLE 2 (Continued)		
Van Tets (1976)	Dorst and Mougin (1979)	Siegel-Causey (1988)
Subgenus *Hypoleucus*	*P. (M.) melanoleucos*	*N. bransfieldensis*
P. (H.) varius	*P. (M.) niger*[3]	*N. georgianus*
P. (H.) auritus	*P. (M.) pygmaeus*	*Nesocarbo*
P. (H.) olivaceus	*P. (M.) africanus*	*N. campbelli*
P. (H.) fuscicollis		*Euleucocarbo*
P. (H.) sulcirostris		*E. carunculatus*
Subgenus *Microcarbo*		*E. chalconotus*
P. (M.) melanoleucos		*E. onslowi*
P. (M.) niger		*E. colensoi*
P. (M.) pygmaeus		*E. ranfurlyi*
P. (M.) africanus		*Stictocarbo*
		S. magellanicus
		S. pelagicus
		S. urile
		S. aristotelis
		S. gaimardi
		S. punctatus
		S. featherstoni
Genera 2	1	9
Subgenera 5	4	0
Species 34[4]	29	37

[1] Subgeneric allocation uncertain; possibly part of *Stictocarbo*.

[2] Identified as component members of superspecies groups.

[3] Considered as possibly conspecific with *pygmaeus*.

[4] Exclusive of *perspicillatus*, which was not considered by van Tets. Comments in a recent handbook (Marchant and Higgins, 1990) indicate that van Tets now admits five genera in two subfamilies (*Phalacrocorax* and *Microcarbo* in the Phalacrocoracinae, plus *Nannopterum, Stictocarbo,* and *Leucocarbo* in the Leucocarboninae). His genus *Phalacrocorax* thus encompasses Siegel-Causey's *Hypoleucus,* and his genus *Nannopterum* includes most of the forms separated by Siegel-Causey as *Compsohalieus, Notocarbo, Nesocarbo,* and *Euleucocarbo*. The remaining three genera correspond to van Tets's prior subgenera as listed above. Sibley and Monroe (1990) accepted 38 species, all included in *Phalacrocorax*.

TABLE 3   Some Comparative Traits of Typical Cormorants and Shags

Trait	Cormorants (Phalacrocoracinae)	Shags (Leucocarboninae)
Climatic distribution	Mostly warm waters	Mostly cold waters
Adult foot color	Black in all species	Usually not black
Black underparts	In 16 of 17 species	In 5 of 17 species
Average adult mass	ca. 0.4–6.0 kg	ca. 1.3–3.5 kg
Tarsal scutellation	Usually one vertical row	Two vertical rows
Ecological distribution	Inland and coastal	Entirely coastal
Nasal salt gland size	Small	Large
Flying ability	Relatively poor	Relatively good
Tail:wing ratio	Mostly >50%	Mostly <50%
Twig and wire perching	Not reported	In some species
Outer:middle toe ratio	ca. 1.3 : 1	ca. 1.4 : 1
Diving method	Normal diving typical	Jump diving typical
Nuptial crests	On nape only	On forehead and/or nape
White nuptial patches	On thighs (3 spp.)	On back or flanks (5 spp.)
White alar stripes	Absent	In several species
Facial caruncles	Absent	In several species
Male gargling	In a few species	In most species
Male wing waving	In most species	In a few species
Nest substrates	Ground, shrubs, and trees	Ground or cliff ledges
Nest composition	Of woody materials	Of soft materials

TABLE 4   Taxonomic and Vernacular Equivalents of Cormorant and Shag Taxa

Van Tets (1976)		Siegel-Causey (1988)	
Phalacrocorax	Cormorants	Phalacrocoracinae	Cormorants
Microcarbo	Microcormorants	*Microcarbo*	Microcormorants
Hypoleucus	Mesocormorants	*Hypoleucus*	Mesocormorants
Phalacrocorax	Macrocormorants	*Phalacrocorax*	Macrocormorants
(considered part of *Leucocarbo*)		*Compsohalieus*	Marine cormorants
Leucocarbo	Shags	Leucocarboninae	Shags
Leucocarbo	King shags	*Leucocarbo*	Guano shags
Leucocarbo	King shags	*Notocarbo*	Blue-eyed shags
Leucocarbo	King shags	*Nesocarbo*	Campbell Is. shag
Leucocarbo	King shags	*Euleucocarbo*	N. Z. blue-eyed shags
Stictocarbo	Cliff shags	*Stictocarbo*	Cliff shags

cations of the Phalacrocoracidae is that of Siegel-Causey (1988), which is based on a cladistic analysis using quantitative osteological characters. His resulting proposed classification accepts 37 species and bears a considerable number of similarities to that of van Tets. However, instead of dividing the family into two genera, he accepts two subfamilies, the overall compositions of which are very similar (table 2), and also recognizes a total of nine genera. In several cases these genera correspond to the subgenera of van Tets, but the large subgenus *Leucocarbo* as proposed by van Tets was subdivided by Siegel-Causey into five genera. A comparison of these two important classifications, showing both their vernacular and taxonomic equivalents, is presented in Table 4.

The revision of the Phalacrocoracidae by Dorst and Mougin (1979) may be thought of as a compressed variation on that proposed by van Tets (table 2). These authors reduced van Tets's proposed genus *Leucocarbo* to a subgenus and accepted only 29 species, all within *Phalacrocorax*. Sibley and Monroe's recent (1990) taxonomy of the cormorants accepted 38 species, all of which they likewise included within the single genus *Phalacrocorax*. Sibley and Monroe further reported that Sibley's DNA hybridization results do not support a "diversity of relationships" such as the two subfamilies and nine genera proposed by Siegel-Causey, although they did adopt his suggested sequence of species.

In this book I have adopted the proposed sequential classification and most of the species limits of Siegel-Causey (1988). However, instead of accepting all nine of his genera, I have followed van Tets (1976a) in recognizing only two, in the belief that Siegel-Causey's subfamilies can be reduced to genera, and his genera similarly reduced to subgenera, without obscuring any of his proposed relationships. In my view this procedure avoids introducing a plethora of generic names that are relatively unfamiliar and thus far have not been generally adopted. Furthermore, I have consistently used the term "shag" in the text to refer to all species here recognized as part of *Leucocarbo*. I have also at times used the term "typical cormorants" when referring to those species collectively placed in the genus *Phalacrocorax*, but otherwise have used "cormorants" as a convenient inclusive vernacular term for all the phalacrocoracids.

Taxonomic Relationships of the Darters

It has already been stated that one major argument relative to the darters concerns whether they should be considered a subfamily of the Phalacrocoracidae, as treated, for example, by Ogilvie-Grant (1898), Dorst and Mougin (1979), Grassé (1950), Mayr and Amadon (1951), and Cracraft (1985). However, Peters (1931), Wetmore (1960), Brodkorb (1963), Vaurie (1965), Owre (1967), Storer (1971), and others have maintained the two as distinct families, sometimes (e.g., Olson, 1985; Becker, 1986) offering specific reasons for this distinction. Additionally, recent DNA-DNA hybridization data (Sibley, Ahlquist, and Monroe, 1988; Sibley and Ahlquist, 1990) suggest that the darters may actually be more closely related to the sulids than they are to the cormorants. Given this situation, I have elected to maintain them as separate families in this book.

Apart from the continuing arguments concerning the degree of phyletic relationships between the darters and cormorants, the only remaining taxonomic question concerns the number of extant darter species that should be recognized and how these are related to one another. In reviewing the fossil darters, Olson (1985) stated that, although the living Old World darters may constitute a superspecies, the New World anhinga has too many osteological differences to be considered a part of that assemblage. Similarly, Vaurie (1965) suggested that the anhinga appears to be the most distantly related of the extant darters, and furthermore that among the Old World darters *novaehollandiae* appears to be the most distinctive, whereas *rufa* and *melanogaster* are apparently the most closely related. However, he did not suggest how many species of darters should be recognized. Recently, Sibley and Monroe (1990) tentatively accepted four species of darters, but said that the whole complex might actually represent a single species.

Although the taxonomic significance of variations in middle ear structure has been questioned, Saiff's (1978) study rather surprisingly suggested that the anhinga and Oriental darter are essentially identical in this regard, whereas the middle ear of the African darter is unique in four traits. The Australian darter was unfortunately not included in his study.

In table 5 a historic summary of representative darter taxonomies of the past century has been provided, showing that few advances have apparently been made during that time in understanding the phyletic relationships of the darters. Indeed, perhaps the least successful of those listed is the most recent (Dorst and Mougin, 1979). This classification inexplicably merges *novaehollandiae* with *rufa*, the two Old World forms that appear in their morphological respects to be the most unlike one another.

By way of comparative summary, table 6 illustrates some of the morphological features that variously serve to discriminate or associate the four populations of darters. No clear lessons can be drawn from it, other than perhaps to force a conclusion that any taxonomic mergers in the absence of new data would seem distinctly premature at this time. Thus, in this book I have followed a conservative course in classification, by maintaining the anhinga as a distinct species and by recognizing all three populations of the traditionally accepted forms of the Old World darter as component races of a second species. In recognizing that this latter group

TABLE 5   Representative Taxonomies of the Darters of the World

Ogilvie-Grant (1898)	Peters (1931)	Dorst and Mougin (1979)
Phalacrocoracidae	Anhingidae	Phalacrocoracidae
Subfamily Plotinae	*Anhinga*	Subfamily Anhinginae
Plotus	A. anhinga	*Anhinga*
P. rufus	A. rufa	A. anhinga[1]
P. melanogaster	A. melanogaster	A. melanogaster[1]
P. novaehollandiae	A. novaehollandiae	A. m. melanogaster
P. anhinga		A. m. rufa[2]

[1] *melanogaster* and *anhinga* were regarded as a superspecies.
[2] Including *novaehollandiae*.

TABLE 6   Comparative Morphological Traits of the Darters of the World

Trait	Anhinga	African Darter	Oriental Darter	Australian Darter
Male with "mane"	Yes	No	No	No
Tail white-tipped	Yes	No	No	No
Sexual dimorphism	Strong	Slight	Slight	Strong
Female underparts	Black	Black	Black	White
Secondary covert outer web color	Silvery	Chestnut	Silvery	Silvery
Scapular length	Intermediate	Very long	Long	Short
Natal down[1]	Pale buff	Rust to buff	White	Rust to buff
Middle ear anatomy[2]	As in Oriental	Unique in four traits	As in anhinga	Unreported

[1] Some individual down color variability has also been reported.
[2] Based on observations of Saiff (1978).

might eventually have to be further subdivided, I have diverged from my normal treatment of using a single collective vernacular name for the species, and have consistently referred to each of these three races using separate vernacular names.

Taxonomic Relationships of the Pelicans

Perhaps the first relatively comprehensive taxonomic survey of the Pelecanidae as they are now generally recognized was that of Elliot (1869). He regarded the group as comprising a subfamily of a more inclusive family Pelecanidae (collectively including the present-day phaethontids, fregatids, anhingids, pelecanids, sulids, and phalacrocoracids). Elliot recognized only a single pelican genus *Pelecanus*, consisting of nine species that were divided into two subgroups on the basis of the shape of the feather edging at the front of the forehead. The first subgroup, with the feathers forming an acute point on the forehead, includes only *onocrotalus* plus two additional taxa that are now considered synonyms of this species. In the remaining forms the forehead feathering takes the form of a concave line. Interestingly, Elliot concluded that *rufescens* and *philippensis* could not be considered as separate species, since "the differences that are claimed as sufficient to separate them are very slight," and he believed might even be the result of age differences. He recognized the South American brown pelican as a separate species, which he regarded as differing "chiefly in its larger size."

Some three decades later, Ogilvie-Grant (1898) recognized nine species of pelicans, collectively comprising a single genus within a separate family Pelecanidae. However, he provided no specific opinions as to presumed intrageneric relationships except for those implicit within his key and its associated sequence of species. He followed Elliot in recognizing two species of brown pelicans, and additionally separated *roseus* from *onocrotalus* as representing a smaller and more southerly species, and specifically separated *philippensis* from *rufescens*.

Another three decades thereafter, Peters (1931) offered his taxonomy of the Pelecanidae, which recognized eight species and three subgenera of *Pelecanus*. Peters largely adopted the species limits of Ogilvie-Grant except for the merging of *thagus* with *occidentalis*, but he additionally separated the American white pelican and brown pelican as monotypic subgenera. In their more recent revision of Peters's taxonomy, Dorst and Mougin (1979) further considered *roseus* as synonymous with *onocrotalus*. This decision was justifiable on the basis of African studies (Brown, Urban, and Newman, 1982). However, they also relegated *crispus* and *philippensis* to the rank of subspecies, with *philippensis* having taxonomic priority. This latter taxonomic change evidently resulted from their decision to accept a surprisingly unchallenged and questionable opinion of Delacour and Mayr (1945) to the effect that, apart from their size differences, the spot-billed pelican and Dalmatian pelican are "very similar in all characteristics."

The only recent contribution to pelican taxonomy has been that of Sibley and Ahlquist (1985, 1990), who included five species of pelicans (*occidentalis, conspicillatus, onocrotalus, rufescens,* and *erythrorhynchos*) in their DNA-DNA hybridization experiments. Briefly, they found *occidentalis* to be the most distinctive on this basis, followed in turn by *conspicillatus* and *onocrotalus*, with *rufescens* and *erythrorhynchos* differing least from one another. In particular, the last of these findings seems quite unexpected and perhaps warrants further attention. Later, Sibley and Monroe (1990) recognized eight extant species of pelicans, with *thagus* considered distinct from *occidentalis* as a separate allospecies. Rather surprisingly (in view of the DNA-DNA hybridization results), they kept both *onocrotalus* and *rufescens* well separated in linear sequence from *erythrorhynchus*, and considered *crispus* and *philippensis* to comprise a superspecies.

A summary of three major stages of pelican taxonomy since 1898 is presented in table 7. Table 8 provides a summary of some possibly significant biological differences among the extant pelican species, with the taxa organized into groups that perhaps reflect their actual phyletic relationships to some degree. Brown, Urban, and Newman (1982) suggested that three pelican superspecies could be recognized on the basis of variations in their fishing strategies (plunge diving, solitary, or communal) and nesting behaviors (small, loose tree colonies or large, packed ground colonies), which would correspond in large measure to the classification shown here. However, much more information is needed before any new species level classification of the pelicans can be seriously proposed.

TABLE 7   Representative Taxonomies of the Pelicans of the World

Ogilvie-Grant (1898)	Peters (1931)	Dorst and Mougin (1979)
Pelecanus	*Pelecanus*	*Pelecanus*
P. *onocrotalus*	Subgenus *Pelecanus*	Subgenus *Pelecanus*
P. *roseus*	P. *onocrotalus*	P. *onocrotalus*
P. *crispus*	P. *roseus*	P. *rufescens*
P. *philippensis*	P. *rufescens*	P. *philippensis*[1]
P. *rufescens*	P. *philippensis*	P. *conspicillatus*
P. *fuscus*[2]	P. *crispus*	Subgenus *Cyrtopelicanus*
P. *thagus*	P. *conspicillatus*	P. (C.) *erythrorhynchos*
P. *erythrorhynchos*	Subgenus *Cyrtopelicanus*	Subgenus *Leptopelicanus*
P. *conspicillatus*	P. (C.) *erythrorhynchos*	P. (L.) *occidentalis*
	Subgenus *Leptopelicanus*	
	P. (L.) *occidentalis*	

[1] Includes *crispus*.
[2] Equals *occidentalis* (excepting *thagus*) of more recent authorities.

TABLE 8   Comparative Biological Traits of the Pelicans of the World

	Foraging method	Nesting site	Down color	Age at maturity	Modal clutch
Spot-billed	Surface-solitary	Tree	White	3	3
Pink-backed	Surface-solitary	Tree	White	3	2
Dalmatian	Surface-social	Marsh/ground	White	4	2
American white	Surface-social	Ground	White	4	2
Eastern white	Surface-social	Ground	Black	4	2
Australian	Surface-social	Ground/bush	White	3–4?	2
Brown	Plunge diving	Variable	White	3	2–3

NOTES: The spot-billed and pink-backed may perhaps represent allospecies, as may the American white and eastern white. Ages of maturity and modal clutch sizes may exhibit intraspecific variations.

Ecological Zoogeography of Extant Cormorant, Darter, and Pelican Species

The present distribution of the extant species of cormorants, darters, and pelicans is obviously a dynamic one, in which individual species' ranges may be in the process of expansion or contraction. Though present distribution is the product of historic and prehistoric changes in geography (even continental displacement), climate, ecology, and the like, it is not the purpose here to try to discern such effects (although the distributions of groups such as the genera *Anhinga* and *Pelecanus* may pose attractive questions of this type). Rather, I will compare the species in each term with respect to their conditions of current sympatry and potential competition with related species, and with the present-day distribution of major food resources, especially marine resources.

The overall breeding distribution of the interiorly nesting pelican species (all but the brown pelican) is shown in figure 1. The southeastern Asian portion of the map indicates the spot-billed pelican's known historic range there, rather than its present-day, highly limited range, whereas the rest of the map more accurately depicts present-day conditions. It may be seen that only in Africa does any significant degree of breeding sympatry exist, which is between the eastern white and pink-backed pelicans. These two species differ very considerably in size, foraging sociality, and foraging locations (see details in chapter 4), and thus probably are not serious competitors with one another. The only interior area of the world now totally lacking in pelicans that might seemingly support them is South America, where the Argentine pampa marshes and perhaps also some of the Andean lakes such as Titicaca might offer suitable breeding habitat. Africa or southern Asia may represent the original source of pelicans, which seemingly colonized northern Asia and then spread eastward into western North America to produce the American white and brown pelicans, and also southeast into Australia to produce the Australian pelican. This line of reasoning would suggest that the brown pelican is a derived form of pelican rather than a sole survivor of an earlier and more primitive line.

The collective breeding distributions of coastally nesting cormorants and shags (including the coastal-nesting populations of the great cormorant) plus that of the brown pelican are also shown in figure 1, which indicates a high level of taxonomic concentration in the Australia–New Zealand region. Van Tets (1976a) has already argued the position that Australia probably represents the center of origin of the Phalacrocoracidae, since it is the only region supporting all five of the subgenera he recognized, and more total extant species occur there than in any other single zoogeographic region. According to him, one large group of marine-adapted shags and cormorants (*Leucocarbo* plus *Compsohalieus*) may have spread from Australia around the southern oceans to the Americas and the Persian Gulf. The cliff shags (*Stictocarbo*) also spread around the edges of the Pacific to colonize coastal portions of eastern Asia, western North America, western Europe, and North Africa.

After this early dispersal, the marine shags became especially abundant in areas of nutrient-rich cold-water currents, such as along the western coasts of South America and North America and the southwestern coast of Africa. Latitudinally organized ocean zones based on surface water temperatures are also shown in figure 1, after Ashmole's (1971) delineation. These zones are important in understanding seabird distributions because of their relationship to areas of primary oceanic productivity and related zooplankton abundance. Generally, except for shallow-water coastal areas fertilized by nutrients from adjacent land masses, the

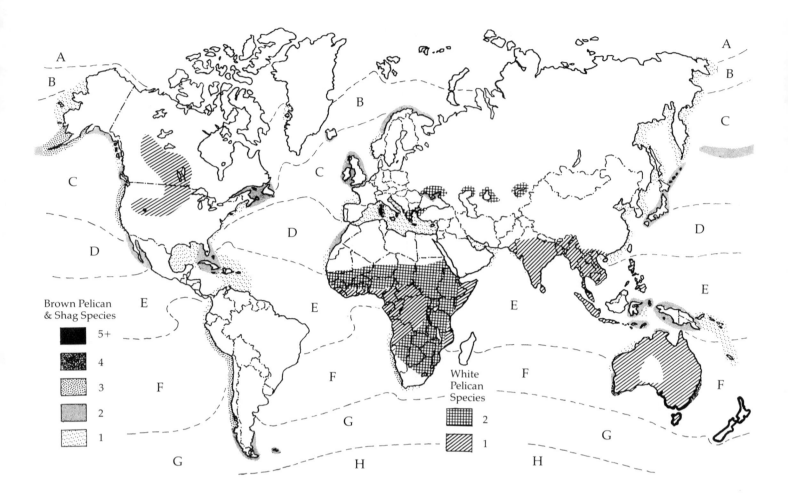

Figure 1. Species density map of coastally nesting cormorants and shags plus the brown pelican (stippling and inked), and of the six interiorly nesting pelican species (hatching and cross hatching). Also shown are oceanic zones (after Ashmole, 1971), including high arctic (A), low arctic (B), boreal (C), northern subtropic (D), tropic (E), southern subtropic (F), subantarctic (G), and antarctic (H).

more productive ocean areas are cold-water zones of the arctic and antarctic latitudes. Productivity is especially high around regions of cold-water upwellings or at boundaries of unlike water masses. In the antarctic, the cold waters of the subantarctic zone circulate from west to east in a nearly unbroken fashion. These eastward currents encounter those of the warmer southern subtropic zone at the subtropical convergence, which is a dynamic area of turbulent mixing and of sinking colder waters. Similarly, the meeting of the subantarctic zone and the antarctic zone farther south produces an antarctic convergence with mixing and sinking of even colder waters. The blue-eyed shags are a group that is closely associated zoo-geographically with the antarctic zone and these oceanic convergences.

The macrocormorants (*Phalacrocorax*) apparently originally spread from Australia to Japan, South Africa, and eastern North America, according to van Tets (1976a). The mesocormorants (*Hypoleucus*) likewise dispersed from the Australian region to southern Asia and the Americas, and the microcormorants may have reached South Africa via southeast Asia and India. These interiorly breeding cormorants have a rather different species density breeding distribution than do the coastal forms, as shown in figure 2. The overall geographic pattern is somewhat like that of the pelicans, but in this case South America has been fully colonized, presumably from an ancestral North American population of the olivaceous cormorant.

Major areas of sympatry among the interiorly nesting cormorants occur in Af-

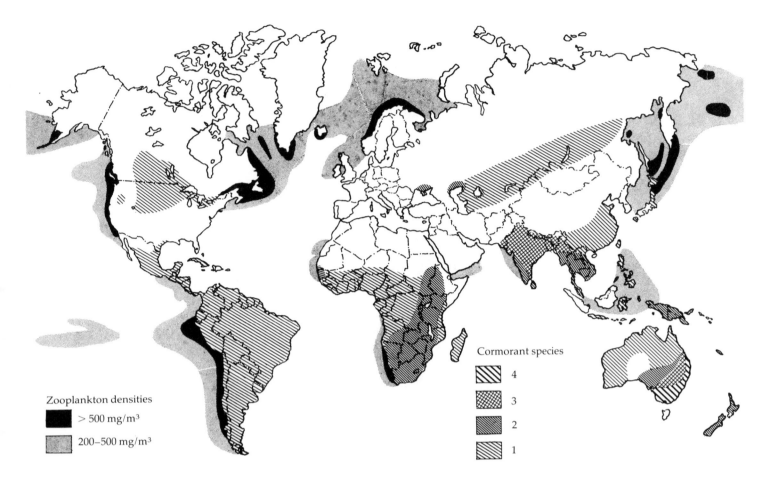

Zooplankton densities
- ■ > 500 mg/m³
- ▨ 200–500 mg/m³

Cormorant species
- 4
- 3
- 2
- 1

rica (between the long-tailed and great cormorants), in India and southeast Asia (among the great, Indian, and Javanese cormorants), and in Australia (among the great, pied, little pied, and little black cormorants). Studies in Africa and India indicate that considerable ecological segregation in foods and foraging behavior exists among the sympatric species of these regions, and more limited studies in Australia suggest similar ecological segregation may occur there, at least between the little pied and little black cormorants, as described in chapter 4. Areas of significant sympatry of three to five species of shags and cormorants likewise occur along several coastlines, especially those where adjoining cold currents produce nutrient-rich upwellings, such as along the Pacific coasts of South America and North America, the southwestern coast of Africa, and the southern coasts of Australia and New Zealand. Presumably these sympatric species are similarly segregated ecologically, but less information is available for the coastal cormorants on the possible foraging adaptations that would favor such segregation.

Figure 2. Species density map of inland-nesting cormorants and shags (hatching and cross hatching), plus the distribution of oceanic areas having high (stippled) to very high (inked) densities of zooplankton. Adapted from the *Atlas of the Living Resources of the Sea* (FAO Fisheries Department, 1981).

CHAPTER 2

Comparative Morphology and Anatomy

General Morphology and External Characteristics

As noted in chapter 1, the term "totipalmate" rather effectively defines the foot condition of most of the pelecaniform birds, although the webbing of frigatebirds is so reduced as to weaken the effectiveness of this as a definitive trait of the Pelecaniformes as a whole. Nevertheless, all of the species of cormorants, darters, and pelicans have feet with substantial webbing that extends to the well-developed hind toe (figure 3). This toe is placed at the same level as the three front toes and is oriented sufficiently far posteriorly to allow for reasonably good perching capabilities, especially in the darters. The anhinga's claws are also relatively long and curved as compared with the double-crested cormorant's, and the webbing between the first and second digit is slightly incised, all of which features are apparently related to the greater arboreality of darters as compared with cormorants (Owre, 1967).

In pelicans the third (middle) and fourth (outermost) toes are of approximately equal length, whereas in darters the fourth toe is about 10 percent longer, and in typical cormorants (*Phalacrocorax*) it averages about 30 percent longer. Among the marine-oriented shags (*Leucocarbo*) the outer toe averages about 40 percent longer than the middle toe. This elongated outer toe is also typical of many other diving birds such as loons (Gaviidae) and various diving ducks (Aythyini, Mergini, and Oxyurini), and probably is associated with maximizing the stroking effectiveness of their laterally oriented feet during underwater swimming. By this criterion, the shags should represent the most effective divers of all the species in these groups.

In all the species of cormorants, darters, and pelicans the nail of the third toe is somewhat modified for scratching or preening. Especially in the darters, and to varying degrees in the cormorants, this nail has a comblike (pectinate) medial surface and clearly is adapted for feather combing. A pectinated middle claw also occurs in the frigatebirds, but not in tropicbirds. In pelicans and sulids this claw tends to be more flangelike, and at least in the latter group it seems to serve for general scratching and perhaps some feather combing (Nelson, 1968). The presence of a pectinated claw is unusual if not unique among swimming birds. This type of claw is usually associated with such distinctly terrestrial birds as the barn-owls

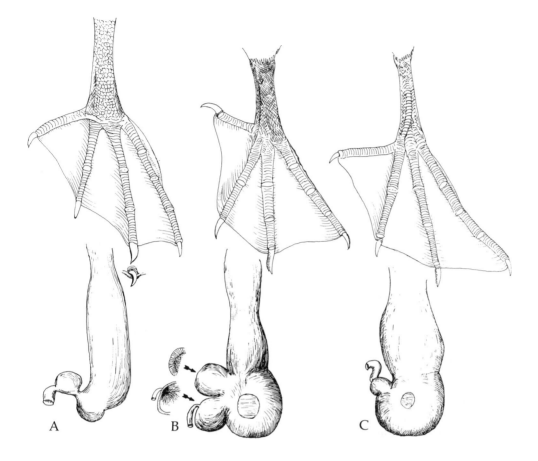

(Tytonidae), pratincoles (Glareolidae), and goatsuckers (Caprimulgidae), plus a few wading birds including the herons (Ardeidae) and crab-plover (Dromadidae). In barn-owls it is certainly used for "combing" their remarkably soft and relatively airy plumages, thus perhaps facilitating the virtually silent flights of these owls. In caprimulgids the pectinated middle claw is apparently used for combing and removing debris from their usually well-developed rictal bristles. In herons it is apparently used for scratching away adherent fish slime that has first been absorbed by talcumlike powdery materials obtained from their powder-down feathers (Simmons, 1964).

A relationship might exist between the pectinated claw and the water-absorbent and relatively noncohesive condition of the contour feathers of darters and cormorants, the claw helping to maintain the relatively noncoherent condition of these feathers' barbs. Thus, in the anhinga the "teeth" of the pectinated claw average about 0.4 mm apart, which is almost identical to the actual average spacing of the barbs on this species' breast feathers in a few specimens that I have measured. Rijke (1968) estimated a similar average barb spacing of 0.39 mm for the breast feathers of the African darter. In the double-crested cormorant the correspondence is less close, as the claw's teeth are spaced at about 1.0 mm intervals, but the barbs of its breast feathers are only about 0.25–0.3 mm apart. Finally, the teeth on the pectinated claw of the American white pelican are very shallow and average about 0.5 mm apart, or about twice as far apart as the spacing of its contour feathers' relatively coherent barbs.

Figure 3. Comparison of the feet and stomachs of the brown pelican (A), anhinga (B), and double-crested cormorant (C). In part after drawings by Audubon (1840–44); otherwise from specimens. Internal views of darter stomach are also shown. Scale adjusted for uniform visual comparisons.

The bill structures of these birds are highly specialized. In all, the bill tends to be as long as or longer than the head, especially in pelicans, where it becomes grotesquely elongated with respect to the rest of the head and body (see figure 6). In pelicans and cormorants the bill is further characterized by two distinct dorsal grooves that pass from the rudimentary opening of the nostrils forward along the length of the maxilla to the posterior tip of the nail. At least in some of the marine-adapted species, these grooves evidently serve to drain away salt-rich exudations from the nostrils. It is now well established that not only cormorants but also the marine-dwelling brown pelican are able to excrete via the bill a highly concentrated salt solution (Schmidt-Nielsen and Fange, 1958). In some pelicans and cormorants this solution simply flows from the nostrils down the grooves in the upper mandible until it reaches the tip and drips off. However, in species such as the brown pelican and those cormorants that lack external nostrils it flows down through the internal nares into the oral cavity, and from there passes outward along the roof of the mouth.

Maxillary grooves are completely lacking in the darters, which rarely if ever venture out on salt water and therefore presumably lack extrarenal salt excretion mechanisms. However, like cormorants, adult darters have fully closed-over external nostrils. The elimination of the external nares in these groups certainly is an adaptation that prevents water from entering the nasal cavity while the birds are submerged. In the plunge-diving brown pelican the external nares have likewise been completely closed over by skin (Richardson, 1939). In these species, as well as in the plunge-diving gannets, breathing while the bill is closed is achieved by the use of "secondary nares" that are located at the angle of the gape (MacDonald, 1960). Furthermore, the external ear openings are distinctly reduced in these groups. In pelicans they are small but still fairly visible, at least among unfeathered nestling birds (see figures 32 and 34). In darters they are reduced to a small slit (see figure 10). In cormorants they are almost invisibly tiny, no doubt in correlation with the fairly deep dives that cormorants often make.

All pelicans and cormorants have smooth-edged mandibles and maxillas that are relatively useless for grasping slippery fish, but well-developed mandibular nails at their tips are important in helping to grasp or kill prey. In darters, which lack recurved mandibular nails (which would spoil their spearing ability), the edges of the acutely tapered bills are finely serrated like those of herons, which similarly help to hold slippery fish in the bill. Unlike herons, however, the axis of the eyes is tilted forward and the visual axis is oriented in line with the bill, rather than tilted downward and oriented below head level, in correlation with their different hunting methods.

In most cormorants and pelicans as well as in darters the lores (the area above the maxilla and in front of the eyes) are featherless in adults, but the Australian pelican is distinctive in that its eyes are fully surrounded by feathers. The lores of juvenile birds are also typically feathered. Featherless facial areas are often quite colorful among birds in peak breeding condition, especially when bright caruncles or papillae develop seasonally, and in many species the iris may also be brightly colored or the bare eyelids may develop a colorful "eye ring." In the eastern white pelican the bare forehead skin of both sexes develops a fatty enlargement that is also indicative of peak breeding condition. The American white pelican is similarly notable for the unique knoblike bill horn that develops on the culmen of adult birds each year prior to the breeding season. This remarkable rhamphothecal structure is both horny and fibrous, and it is molted during the middle of the nesting period sometime after the onset of incubation. Since it is fully developed only among sexually active birds and is dropped early in the nesting period, it has been postulated that it may function as a sexual signaling device (Schaller, 1964). However, it more probably provides a relatively safe shock-absorbing "target" for deflecting aggressive bill jabs from other adult pelicans (Knopf, 1975).

The last highly conspicuous feature of the bills in these birds is the featherless gular pouch, a feature that—except for the nearly pouchless tropicbirds—defines the order Pelecaniformes almost as well as their totipalmate condition. In the pelicans this pouch is extraordinarily large; for example in the brown pelican it can be temporarily expanded to hold as much as 10 liters (or about 2.6 gallons) of water during the capture phase of foraging (Schreiber, Woolfenden, and Curtsinger, 1975). The gular pouches of cormorants and darters are progressively smaller and less conspicuous. However, in many species they are distinctively colored and presumably take on important roles as species-specific display structures (Pierotti, 1987), as is probably also the case with pelicans.

The eye structure of cormorants might be mentioned in relation to their anatomical foraging adaptations (see figure 8). The double-crested cormorant's eye is of only moderate relative size but is notable for its extremely thick and internally flattened cornea, the structure of which may somewhat influence the cornea's light-refraction characteristics (Sivak, Lincer, and Bobier, 1977). The cormorant's eye also exhibits unusually well-developed muscles associated with the iris. These muscles not only regulate the size of the pupil as in all other vertebrate eyes, but evidently also function in a sphincterlike manner on the lens, thus markedly altering its shape and facilitating underwater accommodation, which is highly developed in cormorants (Hess, 1910; Grassé, 1950).

Unlike the double-crested cormorant (and presumably other cormorants as well), the brown pelican evidently lacks an ability to compensate for the loss of the refractive effects of its external corneal surfaces when its eyes are emersed, and as a result it suffers from extreme hyperopia (farsightedness) when its head is submerged (Sivak, Lincer, and Bobier, 1977). The corresponding anatomy and optical characteristics of darters' eyes have apparently not yet been described, but they are likely to show more similarities to those of cormorants than to pelicans, inasmuch as detailed close-up subsurface vision must be very important to darters during their underwater foraging.

Integumentary Anatomy and Feathers

Although these differ somewhat in relative sizes, all the species of these three groups have feather-tufted uropygial glands (or "preen glands") at the dorsal base of the tail. At least the uropygial glands of some pelicans and cormorants secrete a sebaceous fluid that is chemically very similar to that produced by procellariiform birds, and that may serve to help keep the feathers supple and perhaps also to help waterproof them (Jacob and Ziswiler, 1982). However, Snow (1966) noted that a live Galapagos cormorant did not exude oil when its uropygial gland was rubbed. Although both cormorants and darters occasionally spend time not only preening but seemingly also oiling their plumage, this behavior is obviously not related to any need for maintaining feather waterproofing. On the other hand, pelicans spend a great deal of time preening and oiling their plumage.

The contour feathers of all species of pelecaniform birds normally lack aftershafts (but see Schreiber et al., 1989). At least in pelicans and cormorants the developing contour feathers do not grow out from the same follicles as those that produced the prior natal down (Cramp and Simmons, 1977); perhaps as in the sulids the follicles that produce the first generation of natal down subsequently generate the juvenal contour feathers, whereas the second down generation remains as an insulating undercoat below these developing contour feathers (Nelson, 1978). In brown pelicans the total collective weight of the dried skin and feathers was found to represent slightly less than ten percent of the carcass mass (Schreiber et al., 1989), or somewhat more than that of the skeleton.

In addition to any true down feathers that may persist in adults, the downlike bases of the contour feathers and especially of the abundant semiplumes are extremely luxuriant and certainly provide a great deal of insulation. Elongated and hairlike feathers (filoplumes), which often form a conspicuous white or very pale buff contrast to the black contour feathers, frequently occur in both sexes of sexually mature darters and cormorants. These feathers are often held for only a brief period prior to and during pair bonding, and occur mainly on the head and neck, either as relatively scattered feathers or forming clustered tufts or streaks, especially behind the eyes. Among cormorants they also frequently occur in other areas, such as on the back and thighs, where they form distinctive color patches early in the breeding season contrasting with the otherwise dark feathering.

Melanin pigments occur not only in the skin but also commonly in the feathers of all groups, especially in the dark-colored cormorants and darters. Even in the whitest of pelican species the primary feathers are invariably black or fuscous, these feathers thus gaining the advantages of wear resistance provided by the melanin granules embedded in the feather barbs. The almost uniformly blackish coloration of the upperparts of darters and cormorants may also be functionally related to the heat-absorbent qualities of black plumage coloration in direct sunlight (Siegfried et al., 1975), as will be discussed in the next chapter. Juveniles and immatures of all groups generally show less intense melanization of the body feathers, and often also present a more gradual gradient of melanistic pigmentation between dorsal and ventral body surfaces.

Iridescent plumage coloration is totally absent among the pelicans but is well developed in the adult plumages of cormorants and darters, with tones of bronzy green, blue, and purple being common, especially on the upperparts. Green, blue, and purple skin tones (of apparently unknown structural or physiological bases) may also occur on the bare faces of cormorants and darters, and in at least the Australian darter an area of bare skin on the underside of the wing is a bright indigo-blue in breeding females (Marchant and Higgins, 1990).

Carotinoid pigments are wholly lacking in the feathers of cormorants and darters, although adults of most species of pelicans acquire a golden yellow cast on their anterior upper wing coverts, breast, or head feathers during breeding, which tones most probably are derived from carotinoids. It is presumably these feathers, which somewhat resemble dried and sun-bleached blood, that gave rise to the ancient myth that the female pelican feeds her young from blood she has extracted from her own breast. Thus the pelican came to represent an important medieval symbol of Christian self-sacrifice, and as such was commonly depicted in church-associated architecture and artwork (Fawcett, 1970; Rowland, 1978). Other pink feather tints are sometimes associated with secretions of the uropygial gland (Brown, Urban, and Newman, 1982); these presumably carotinoid-based pigments may produce bright pinkish tones on the feathers of the head, neck, back, and belly

(Schreiber, 1985). Bright red and yellow colors (presumably associated with subcutaneous capillary networks) are also common on the bare facial skin, gape, and elsewhere on the head in various species of all these groups.

One feather-related feature of the cormorants and darters that is of special interest is their relatively wettable plumage. Indeed, the contour feathers of four species of African cormorants and the African darter have been reported to possess barbs having spatial characteristics that apparently allow water readily to penetrate the feathers, rather than to accumulate and pearl on their surfaces (Rijke, 1968, 1970). However, this explanation (which is based on textile waterproofing data) for their wettability was tested and rejected by Elowson (1984). As noted earlier, the barbs of darter contour feathers are unusually widely spaced. Elowson found that the average spacing of the barb rami of darter (0.18 mm) and anhinga (0.16 mm) breast feathers was exceeded only by those of the pied-billed grebe (*Podilymbus podiceps*) among the 14 species studied, but these distances proved to be highly variable when different feather areas were compared. The breast feather barbules in all these relatively wettable species are relatively long and hairlike, rather than being coherently interlocked by hooklet-like hamuli. Casler (1973) also noted that the breast feathers of the anhinga are almost devoid of hooklets, which probably allows for their thorough penetration by water when submerged. However, those of the double-crested cormorant lack hooklets only in the distal parts of their vanes. This feature probably helps the bird to retain a thin layer of air immediately around its skin, and thus may avoid wetting the skin and subjecting it to resultant heat loss (Hennemann, 1982).

Mahoney (1984) judged that the plumage of the anhinga is on average about three times more wettable than that of the double-crested cormorant (based on the bird's weight when dry as compared with its weight after it has been held underwater for a time, reflecting the relative amount of water held by its plumage). Additionally, the body plumage of the anhinga is substantially more wettable than are its wing and tail feathers, so that the latter remain water-resistant while the bird is submerged, and as a result the anhinga is able to take flight while its body plumage is still soaked. The plumage of the double-crested cormorant is uniformly more water-resistant (Rijke, Jesser, and Mahoney, 1989). Mahoney (1984) also noted that both species are more wettable when in worn plumage than after they have recently molted (when the hooklets on the newly grown barbs are probably more effectively functional and their vanes thus more coherent).

Both sexes of adult darters also exhibit the unique feature of having regularly spaced transverse flutings or ribs on the outer vanes of their central pairs of rectrices (figure 4). Similar flutings occur on the longest pair of ornamental scapulars, which some authors have described as "tertials" and others as "subscapulars." Owre (1967) speculated that these flutings might perhaps serve as sound producers during tail shaking, but judged that they more probably function as visual signaling devices because of their light-reflective characteristics. The latter role seems to offer a much more promising hypothesis than the former, but no actual observational evidence seems yet to exist supporting either possibility.

The rectrices of pelicans are numerous but are short and not especially remarkable, whereas those of darters and cormorants are adaptively modified for underwater locomotion (figure 4). In the double-crested cormorant the tail length is roughly 20 percent of the total bill-to-tail length, whereas the comparable ratio of the anhinga is nearly 30 percent. The overall surface area of the anhinga's tail is about 2.5 times as great as that of this cormorant, in spite of the fact that their adult

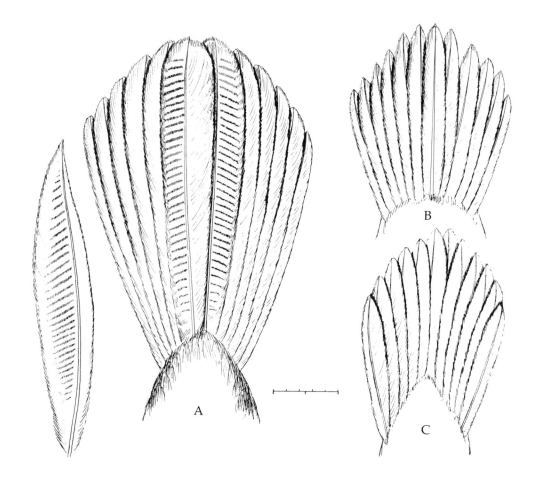

Figure 4. Comparison of the rectrices of the African darter (A) and the double-crested cormorant, the latter shown in dorsal (B) and ventral (C) views. A remixlike, fluted scapular of the darter is also shown. From specimens.

weights are quite similar (Owre, 1967). Owre hypothesized that, whereas the tail feathers of the cormorant are probably used for underwater steering (see figure 16), those of the anhinga are more flexible and thus do not appear to be highly suitable for this role. He suggested that the anhinga's tail may instead function as an airfoil, as well as an aerial elevator, rudder, and brake. The anhinga's very large tail is perhaps even more important in providing additional surface area while soaring and gliding than during flapping flight, and it contributes significantly to the species' relatively low glide-load ratio (Hartman, 1961). However, the tail is often spread while the bird is partly or entirely submerged (see figure 91), and it seems possible that underwater steering could be one of the tail's important functions in darters. Owre judged from its caudal vertebrae that the anhinga is perhaps capable of greater lateral tail movements than is the cormorant, but that it probably has less powerful tail muscles.

Wing Shapes, Wing Loadings, and Aspect Ratios

The wings of cormorants, darters, and pelicans (figure 5) are notable for their considerable length as well as their breadth, the single exception being the rudimentary wings of the flightless Galapagos cormorant. In pelicans and darters the wingtip profile is rounded, with the longest primaries the second or third from the outermost functional primary (in all groups a rudimentary eleventh primary is present). Cormorants tend to have considerably more pointed wings than do dart-

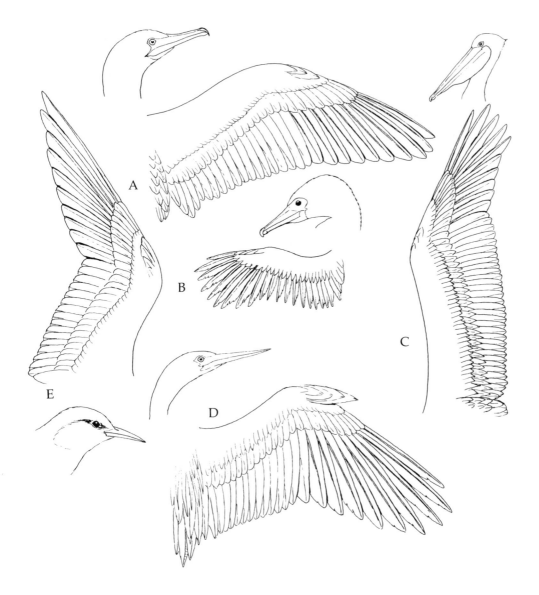

ers and pelicans, although they scarcely compare with the highly pointed wings of tropicbirds, frigatebirds, and gannets.

For their body weights, darters and pelicans exhibit extraordinarily large wings, and this reduced relative wing loading (an index of the relative lift required for maintaining flight) no doubt accounts for their remarkable soaring abilities. Owre (1967) reported a simple (nonlinearized) wing-loading estimate (or ratio of body mass to wing area during flight) of 0.74–0.84 grams/square centimeter for eight anhingas (four of each sex). These figures were about three-fourths of his calculated average wing loadings (1.00–1.08 grams/square centimeter) for a similar sample of eight double-crested cormorants. Similarly, Hartman (1961) calculated a mean wing loading of 1.03 grams/square centimeter for 11 double-crested cormorants, 0.93 grams/square centimeter for 7 Neotropic cormorants, and 0.84 grams/square centimeter for 12 brown pelicans.

Hartman also calculated a "buoyancy" index, which is a more useful relative wing-loading statistic than a nonlinearized wing-loading index because it avoids

Figure 5. Comparative wing shapes and proportions of adults of the double-crested cormorant (A), Galapagos cormorant (B), brown pelican (C), and anhinga (D). A tropicbird (E) is included for comparison. The heads are all drawn to similar linear (bill tip to occiput) scale, and the wings are shown proportionally in dorsal view.

the mathematical problems inherent in evaluating a ratio based on estimated wing surface area (a two-dimensional variable) relative to estimated body mass (a three-dimensional variable) among species of markedly different sizes. Hartman reported his adjusted (or "linearized") buoyancy indices as 4.22 for the brown pelican, 3.7 for the anhinga, 3.4 for the double-crested cormorant, and 3.27 for the Neotropic cormorant—the higher figures in these cases representing lower actual wing loadings. Such indices suggest that the brown pelican should be a more effective soarer than the anhinga, and that it furthermore should have about 80 percent of the theoretical soaring ability of the magnificent frigatebird (which has a buoyancy index of 5.28). Similarly the anhinga has a buoyancy ratio that is 70 percent that of the frigatebird, and the two cormorants average 62–64 percent of the frigatebird's estimated buoyancy.

Apparently all pelicans are able to soar easily under appropriate updrafts (thermal or declivity winds), and probably they together with the largest of the cranes, condors, and albatrosses represent the heaviest bird species that regularly engage in soaring. Pelicans have wings with notably high aspect ratios; indeed these ratios are sometimes nearly as high as those of the classic seabird soarers, the albatrosses and their long-winged near relatives (Pennycuick, 1987). For example, aspect ratios were calculated for several pelecaniform species by Hartman (1961). Using a simple index ratio of maximum wingspread to median wing width, Hartman determined that the brown pelican has an aspect ratio of 3.9, the double-crested cormorant 2.86, the Neotropic cormorant 2.68, and the anhinga 2.69. This numerical sequence corresponds with the relative lengths of the ulna in these four species. Aspect ratios have also been reported by Pennycuick (1972, 1983) for the eastern white pelican and the brown pelican. However, his ratios were calculated differently (using the square of the species' wingspread relative to its total extended wing area), and thus are not directly comparable to Hartman's figures. He also noted (1987) that, although pelicans have somewhat lower aspect ratios, their broader wings also result in lower wing loadings than in procellariiform birds, allowing pelicans to glide at relatively low speeds.

In association with their very long wings, pelicans also have a remarkably large number of true secondary feathers (comparable even to those of albatrosses, which possess the longest wings of all extant birds). These secondaries frequently exceed 30 per wing, exclusive of any so-called tertial feathers associated with the humerus rather than the ulna. A sample of 34 brown pelicans had 27–33 secondaries (Schreiber et al., 1989) and six eastern white pelicans had 30–35 secondaries (Schreiber, 1985), suggesting that a very high degree of intraspecific variation exists in this trait among pelicans.

Plumages and Molts

The plumages and molts of pelecaniform birds exhibit a number of complexities that are beyond the scope of this book and for most species still remain to be studied. Plumages and molts of the North American species have been described in detail by Palmer (1962), those of the Palearctic species by Cramp and Simmons (1977), and those of the Australo-New Zealand region by Marchant and Higgins (1990). As noted in the preface, no single available terminology of molts and plumages seems completely suitable for these birds, and that used for the species accounts in this book is somewhat eclectic. Generally it follows the terminology used by Cramp and

Simmons and by Marchant and Higgins rather than that employed by Palmer, which is essentially the one proposed by Humphrey and Parkes (1959). It is summarized in its simplest form in table 9, with some of the terms used by Palmer or others shown parenthetically. This summary assumes a two-year period to the adult (definitive) plumage and breeding condition, but recognizes that this period can be either shorter or longer in various species.

Wing Molt Patterns and Periodicities

In all these pelecaniform groups the primaries are sequentially replaced in a regular, serially descendent (proximal to distal) order. For example, in the brown pelican the juvenal primaries are molted in such a sequence during the bird's first year of life. However, in subsequent years the primary molt proceeds in two simultaneous "waves," with the outer primaries (from the fifth or sixth to the tenth) molting outwardly during the same period that the inner five or so primaries are similarly undergoing their molting sequence.

   This unusual molting pattern, with multiple simultaneously active molting loci present in the primaries, has caused some problems of interpretation. Stresemann and Stresemann (1966) believed this molting pattern resulted from an interrupted primary molt during the first year, so that during succeeding annual molts two feather generations were involved, with the outer primaries representing a plumage that is ontogenetically one feather generation (or annual plumage cycle) removed from the inner ones. They called this multistage remix molt pattern a *Staffelmause*. Nelson (1978:18) similarly reported that among the sulids (and generally in the Pelecaniformes) the wing molt is semicontinuous, serially descendent, and staged, with primaries representing three feather generations typically present in older birds. However, Schreiber et al. (1989) believed the first-year primary molt of the brown pelican to be complete, and that the primary molt during subsequent

---

TABLE 9   Terminology Used for Plumages and Molts of the Pelecaniforms

Age	Plumage	Molt
Nestling	Natal	Postnatal molt (= first prebasic molt)
Juvenile	Juvenal	Postjuvenal molt (= first prealternate molt)
Immature[1]	Immature[1]	Prenuptial molt (= second prebasic molt)
Adult	Definitive	
	Prebreeding (= "nuptial") plumage	
	Courtship aspect (= definitive alternate plumage)	Supplemental molt
	Nesting aspect (= definitive supplemental plumage)	Postbreeding (= "postnuptial") molt
	Postbreeding (= "winter" or definitive basic) plumage	Prebreeding (= "prenuptial") molt

[1] "Subadult" age categories and plumages may occur in immature birds when more than two years are required for sexual maturity and attaining the definitive plumage. Additionally, some species of cormorants evidently pass directly from a juvenal plumage to their definitive plumage, and thus lack definite immature plumages.

years simply begins at two points simultaneously, so that the two groups of primaries that are being replaced actually all represent those of the same feather generation.

In the eastern white pelican the primaries are reportedly molted in serially descendent pattern, with as many as three active molting centers present in the wing (Cramp and Simmons, 1977). A descendent primary *Staffelmause* apparently also exists in the Australian pelican (Marchant and Higgins, 1990). Only a few observations have been made on the molt of the American white pelican, based on a single male and female that were raised in captivity. The first (postjuvenal) molt of the primaries began in the spring following hatching and was terminated by the next December. However, at least the male retained his juvenal tenth primaries until June of the next year. This pair of feathers was replaced well after the onset of the second annual primary molt cycle, suggesting that an interrupted or staggered wing molt pattern may also exist in this species. In both birds the secondaries, tertials, and axillars were molted annually after the first year, over a prolonged spring-to-winter period. Finally, the rectrices were molted more or less continuously beginning in the first fall of life, and thereafter rectrix molt cycles occurred yearly (Lingle, 1977).

Secondary molt in the brown pelican begins at about the same time that the primaries begin molting, or at about a year of age in the case of the postjuvenal primary molt and generally during autumn months among subadults and adults. Unlike the wavelike and descendent molting pattern of the primaries, the secondaries are molted in a rather irregular pattern, although the molt begins with the inner (proximal) juvenal secondaries and generally proceeds toward the more distal ones. Only rarely are any individual flight feathers held for more than twelve months, although the tenth juvenal primary is evidently carried until the birds are about 22 months old (Schreiber et al., 1989).

Like pelicans, cormorants shed their flight feathers gradually, in a descendent (outward) pattern, with most of the molt occurring during the late summer and autumn months. In contrast, the flight feathers of darters are molted nearly simultaneously, producing a still-undetermined flightless period (Friedmann, 1930; Owre, 1967), which is unique among pelecaniform birds.

Potts (1971) described the pattern of primary molt in the European shag, noting that the juvenal primaries begin to be replaced in outward sequence at about eight months after hatching, with the successive feathers being dropped at intervals of about 17 days. However, a second wing molt cycle begins in autumn with the replacement of the recently acquired innermost primaries at about the time that the first molting cycle has reached the eighth juvenal primary. Both molting centers then soon pause during the winter. Successive primary molt cycles begin each fall so that eventually, although the flight feathers are replaced approximately annually, most older birds will retain feathers representing from two to as many as four earlier feather generations, the species thus exhibiting a typical staggered or wavelike *Staffelmause*.

Wing molt patterns in cormorants other than the European shag are less well studied, but at least the crowned, long-tailed, and Cape cormorants evidently have similar complex wavelike or *Staffelmause* patterns. In the crowned cormorant the primaries are initially replaced in simple descendent sequence during the initial (postjuvenal) wing molt, but during later life there are a series of "wave molts," until the feather replacement mode of the primaries eventually becomes highly confused (Crawford et al., 1982). The great cormorant apparently also has a similar serially descendent postjuvenal primary molt and subsequent wavelike primary molts, with two or three active molt centers simultaneously present in each wing among older birds. In the African race of this species adults can thus be recognized by the presence of two or more waves of molt in the primaries (Brooke et al., 1982). The tenth juvenal primary is persistent and may be retained until the spring of the bird's fourth year (Cramp and Simmons, 1977). In all nine of the Australian and New Zealand species of cormorants so far examined there is evidently a descendent *Staffelmause* pattern of primary molt, although few details are yet available (Marchant and Higgins, 1990).

Tail Molt Patterns and Periodicities

The same general molt pattern and periodicity that occurs in the brown pelican's flight feathers also applies to its rectrices. Juvenile birds show a gradual and almost continuous tail molt during their first year or so after fledging, so that by the time they are 18 months old most of the rectrices are probably being replaced for a second time. In young brown pelicans the tail molt pattern is generally bilaterally symmetrical (although in no clear inward or outward sequence), but in adults this symmetry becomes less apparent. Although much tail molt occurs during the autumn months among older birds, the molting cycles of these feathers is relatively prolonged and some rectrices are in molt virtually continuously (Schreiber et al., 1989).

In cormorants the rectrices are gradually shed over an extended period. In the double-crested cormorant the molting pattern of the rectrices is apparently irregular (Owre, 1967). The tail molt patterns of the European shag and the great cormorant are also seemingly irregular (Cramp and Simmons, 1977). The molting pattern is likewise apparently irregular in the little black and little pied cormorants, but the tail molt pattern has been described as "outward" (centrifugal) for the Australian race of the great cormorant as well as for the pied and black-faced cormorants (Marchant and Higgins, 1990). In contrast, crowned and long-tailed cormorants seem to exhibit a basically inward (centripetal) postjuvenal tail molt pattern, although with advancing age this basic molt pattern becomes progressively obscured (Crawford et al., 1982). Clearly, the tail molt patterns of cormorants cannot yet be easily interpreted and summarized, given the somewhat contradictory available information.

In the anhinga the rectrices are molted nearly simultaneously and at about the same time that the flight feathers are molting, which in Florida occurs during winter (Owre, 1967). However, in the African darter a gradual and irregular tail molt pattern (starting with the central pair, followed by the two or three outermost pairs) apparently occurs (Friedmann, 1930). A published photograph of an adult male Australian darter (in Frith, 1977) suggests that a similar gradual tail molt also occurs in that population of darters, since this bird's central and outermost pairs of rectrices are in early stages of growth while it is still carrying several of its other more faded and obviously older tail feathers. A gradual tail molt has been independently attributed to this species on the basis of similar (or perhaps the same) photographic evidence (Marchant and Higgins, 1990).

Oral Cavity and Respiratory System Anatomy

As noted earlier, the tongue is rudimentary in all the groups being considered here (see figures 10 and 12). It is located almost directly below the comparably small and similarly shaped palatal opening of the internal nares. The associated hyoid apparatus (figures 8 and 9) supporting the tongue is correspondingly relatively small, and has apparently lost its original function of tongue manipulation (Korzun, 1982). In pelicans a thin band of muscles extends forward from the hyoid to the anterior tip of the lower mandible, by contraction of which the pouch is tightened and the lower mandible is bowed open in the manner of a fisherman's landing net. In all three groups the hyoid apparatus also plays an important role as an evaporative cooling mechanism during gular fluttering, when the gular sac is rapidly contracted and relaxed. The hyoid is additionally important in the "kink-throating" display of cormorants and darters, during which this structure is depressed so as to produce a distinct bulge or "kink" in the outline of the gular sac. This display is often associated with a vocalization, which the enlarged gular sac perhaps helps resonate, or the sac may simply be made more visually apparent by the hyoid's displacement.

In the brown pelican, which plunge-dives for its food from some height, the adaptations for reducing the physical shock associated with striking the water are similar to those typical of gannets and, to a more limited extent, tropicbirds. A relatively superficial extension of the air sac system, or "air mattress," is widely distributed over the subcutaneous ventral body area, including the neck, the feathered parts of the head, and much of the proximal wing (reaching the tip of the second digit) (Richardson, 1939). The only apparent air passage connecting this system with the rest of the respiratory system is provided by an axillary diverticulum from the interclavicular air sac. Once inflated, this structure is capable of holding a surprising amount of air. According to one early report, an "inflated" pelican weighing about four kilograms was thus able to support 10.5 kilograms without sinking! As might be expected, the deep-diving Brandt's cormorant completely lacks such an air mattress, as presumably do all other cormorants and darters. Curiously, although the surface-foraging American white pelican possesses open external nostrils, its air mattress was found to be even more highly developed than the brown pelican's. That is, the average measured increase in respiratory system volume was determined to be about 57 percent for two American white pelicans with inflated air sacs, as compared with 35 percent for a similarly inflated brown pelican (Richardson, 1943). This condition may simply assist in its overall buoyancy during swimming, and perhaps also improve its thermoregulatory cooling efficiency.

The air sac systems of the American anhinga and double-crested cormorant are quite similar to one another, but the associated air volume in the anhinga is appreciably less in relation to its body size, and the air sacs penetrate no bones. The anhinga may also increase its specific gravity by expelling air before it submerges, and additionally may drink water before submerging to provide ballast (Casler, 1973).

Syringeal Anatomy and Vocalizations

In all species of Pelecaniformes the vocal organ or syrinx, located at the junction of the trachea and bronchi, is evidently of relatively simple structure, although it remains undescribed for most species. At least in pelicans the tracheal tube is seemingly unmodified for facilitating vocal resonance, nor is the syrinx obviously modified for sound production. There are no apparent flexible tympaniform membranes associated with the syrinx in the American white pelican (figure 9), which produces only grunting or croaking sounds during breeding. However, the eastern white pelican reportedly has at least five different adult utterances, one of which is distinctly low and resonant and somewhat resembles mooing or humming (Brown and Urban, 1969; Cramp and Simmons, 1977). It is possible that acoustic resonation by the gular sac may help acoustically modify these sounds.

With respect to cormorants, the adult European shag produces only hissing and throat-clicking utterances, both of which might well be of nonsyringeal origin. However, some cormorants such as the great cormorant utter as many as seven different adult calls (Cramp and Simmons, 1977), and the pygmy and Javanese cormorants are also notably noisy species. As with other pelecaniform groups, the comparative syringeal anatomy of cormorants is still unstudied.

The syringeal tympaniform membranes are very poorly developed in the darters (figure 10), which are perhaps the loudest and most vocal birds of the three groups considered here. Adult darters produce a variety of rattling, hissing, and grunting notes. The kink-throating display of darters and at least some cormorants typically has an associated utterance; the limited enlargement of the gular sac by means of hyoid depression during this display may perhaps produce some acoustic modifications by providing a small resonating chamber between the syrinx and the opening of the oral cavity.

It is of related interest to note that in male frigatebirds the gular pouch has apparently been adapted to serve both as an inflatable resonating chamber and also as a colorful visual signaling device. It requires about 20–30 minutes for its complete inflation, which is accomplished without visible effort (Nelson, 1968). The anatomical mechanism for its inflation has long been reputed to depend on an air passage connected to the anterior respiratory air sac system, in a similar manner to the inflatable air mattress of pelicans. However, this point apparently still needs confirmation (Murphy, 1936). In any case, vocal resonation in frigatebirds may not depend on any direct air communication with the syrinx or its associated respiratory air sacs, but may instead be indirect and dependent on the lower mandible touching the inflated sac during calling (Nelson, 1975). Apparently no unusually low-pitched and highly resonated calls are uttered by male frigatebirds; rather they produce rattling sounds similar to those of a fisherman's reel, and they also utter a high-pitched falsetto warble (Nelson, 1968).

These observations suggest that the primary signaling function of the inflated neck sac in male frigatebirds is probably visual rather than acoustic, inasmuch as the primary acoustic advantage of channeling vocalizations through this large sac would be the resonance of very low-pitched sounds. The frigatebirds are also unique in that the typical pelecaniform tendencies toward strong territorial defense of nest sites, nest site fidelity, and year-to-year mate retention are virtually absent, apparently in response to their generally low and highly erratic food supplies. This situation makes it necessary for the birds to breed opportunistically whenever and wherever the situation demands. Such breeding uncertainties also favor the evolution of highly effective species-specific and sex-specific signals in the group that result in the rapid attraction of any available females and eliminate any selective value in retaining pair bonds or nesting territories from year to year (Nelson, 1968).

Skeletal Anatomy

As might be expected, the skull and skeleton of cormorants, darters, and pelicans are variously modified in conjunction with their foraging differences. In all three groups the jaws can be opened to a surprising degree, which is an important generalized pelecaniform trait that at least in part must be related to their relative prey-

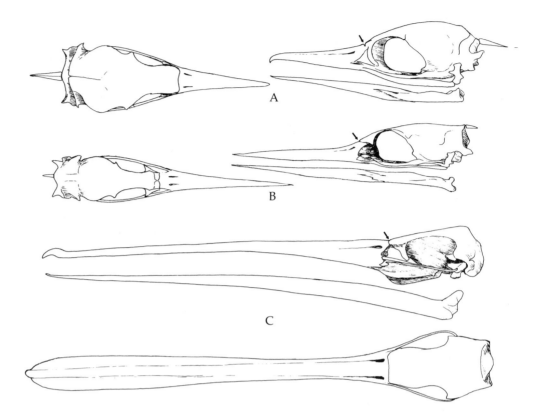

Figure 6. Comparative skull anatomy (lateral and dorsal views) of the double-crested cormorant (A), anhinga (B), and American white pelican (C). Arrows indicate the nasal-frontal hinge. Drawn to scale from specimens.

swallowing requirements (see figure 12). This jaw-opening ability in pelecaniform birds is to some degree facilitated by their additional ability to bend the mandible upward at the hingelike junction of the nasal and frontal bones. The cranial junction at the base of the upper maxilla is noticeably thin and flexible in most of these birds. The resulting nasal-frontal hinge is perhaps best developed among cormorants, but is also well-developed in darters. It is generally less highly developed in pelicans, which nevertheless are also able to gape widely by virtue of their very long bills (figure 6).

A second notable skull feature is provided by the occipital style, an acutely pointed and medially situated bone that is somewhat flexibly attached to the occipital crest in cormorants and darters but lacking in pelicans. It is considerably larger in cormorants than in darters, where it is sometimes mostly cartilaginous. Since the posterior part of the mandibular adductor muscle attaches to it, it certainly functions in increasing the bird's relative grasping ability. This ability, together with a sharp maxillary nail, is obviously important for prey grasping by cormorants. It is of little apparent significance for present-day darters, although in ancestral darters a grasping ability may have been more important (Owre, 1967).

In all of the groups under consideration here the sternum is relatively broad and not very deeply keeled, particularly in pelicans (figure 7). The sternum of pelicans is furthermore notable in that it is completely fused with the furcula, a feature that certainly adds rigidity to the pectoral girdle and has been suggested as perhaps improving a bird's soaring abilities. A similarly fused furcula and sternum occur in frigatebirds and also in all *Grus* cranes, which are likewise adept at soaring (Johnsgard, 1983). However, darters are able to soar nearly as well as pelicans, but together with cormorants lack this skeletal feature. Possibly the combination of unusually

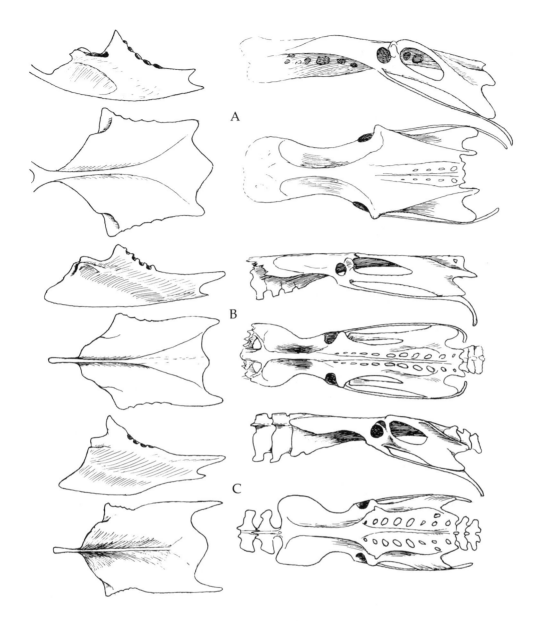

long and broad wings and relatively small pectoral muscle mass makes an unusually sturdy sternal anchor especially important for pelicans. The furcula and sternum are similarly fused in barn-owls (Tytonidae), and these birds likewise exhibit
the combination of relatively small breast muscles and relatively low wing loading
(Johnsgard, 1988). However, in contrast to pelicans and darters, owls apparently
never engage in soaring.

The combined pectoral muscles (pectoralis major and supracoracoideus) that
are associated with primary wing flexion during flapping flight are relatively small
in all three of these pelecaniform groups. They must be extremely small in the
flightless Galapagos cormorant, which has an essentially keelless sternum (Shufeldt, 1915). In six male and two female brown pelicans, these muscles comprised
an average of 13.2 percent of the total carcass weight. By comparison, in combined-
sex samples of 11 double-crested cormorants they averaged 12.6 percent, in 7 Neotropic cormorants 12.7 percent, and in 13 American anhingas 14.4 percent (Hart-

Figure 7. Comparative sternal (lateral and ventral views)
and synsacral (lateral and
dorsal views) anatomy of
adults of *Pelecanus* (A), *Phalacrocorax* (B), and *Anhinga*
(C). In part after Mivart
(1878); otherwise from specimens. Scale adjusted for uniform visual comparisons.

man, 1961). These figures show about the same proportional pectoral muscle mass as occurs in some of the larger North American owls (Johnsgard, 1988).

By comparison, the sternal muscles of an adult frigatebird (*F. aquila*) reportedly may represent up to a quarter of its total carcass weight (Murphy, 1936), which would place it near the maximum reported for all flying birds except hummingbirds. Hartman (1961), however, reported that frigatebirds have an average pectoral muscle mass representing about 15 percent of total body weight, placing them virtually in the same range as the groups under consideration here.

The sterna of darters and cormorants are quite similar, although that of the American anhinga is nonpneumatic. Additionally, its cairina (keel) extends farther posteriorly in the anhinga than in the double-crested cormorant, a condition that has been correlated with the two species' relative soaring capabilities (Owre, 1967).

In both darters and cormorants the coracoids are unusually long. In the American anhinga and double-crested cormorant the coracoids are of the same relative length. However, in the anhinga the coracoids are apparently more capable of lateral and ventral movements (Owre, 1967), a point of uncertain adaptive significance with regard to flight. In pelicans this bone is highly pneumatic and thus very light (Shufeldt, 1902), suggesting that it is probably not subjected to great stresses during flight.

The pelvic girdles (synsacra) of these three groups are also similar, although those of pelicans are relatively broader, shorter, and less "streamlined" than those of darters and cormorants. Thus, in pelicans the synsacrum is about twice as long as it is broad, whereas in darters and cormorants it is about three times as long as broad (Pycraft, 1898). The postilial dorsal surfaces are extremely broad in pelicans, and the preilium is of approximately comparable width. In darters and cormorants the postilial dorsal surface is much narrower, especially in cormorants, and the preilium is greatly enlarged anteriorly (figure 7). The elongation of the postacetabular portion of the pelvic girdle relative to its preacetabular component is associated with swimming adaptations. The posterior component is relatively greater in cormorants than in either darters or pelicans, both of which are about equal in this regard. Generally, however, the pelvic proportions of cormorants and darters are very similar, suggesting that rather comparable adaptations probably exist for muscular foot propulsion while swimming and diving. They also show some distinct pelvic similarities to those of the similarly foot-propelled and even more highly specialized divers, the loons and grebes (see illustrations in Johnsgard, 1987). The lower-extremity muscles of the brown pelican represent only about 4.5–5.5 percent of the total body weight. This compares with 6 percent for the American anhinga and about 10–12 percent for Neotropic and double-crested cormorants (Hartman, 1961), suggesting that cormorants must be considerably more powerful swimmers than are darters, and both of these more powerful than pelicans.

The relative pneumaticity of the appendicular skeleton is also quite variable among these three groups. Overall skeletal pneumaticity is greatest in the pelicans, is reduced in cormorants, and is virtually lacking in darters (Shufeldt, 1902), no doubt in association with increasing diving tendencies in this sequence of groups. Murphy (1936) noted that the dried skeleton of a female magnificent frigatebird (*Fregata magnificens*) weighed only 103 grams. Compared with a presumably comparable adult of the same race that had a carcass mass of 1,587 grams, the skeleton probably represents about 6.5 percent of the overall mass in this species. By comparison, the weight of the feathers alone of a related frigatebird species (*F. aquila*) represented 22 percent of the total carcass weight, and Murphy calculated that in

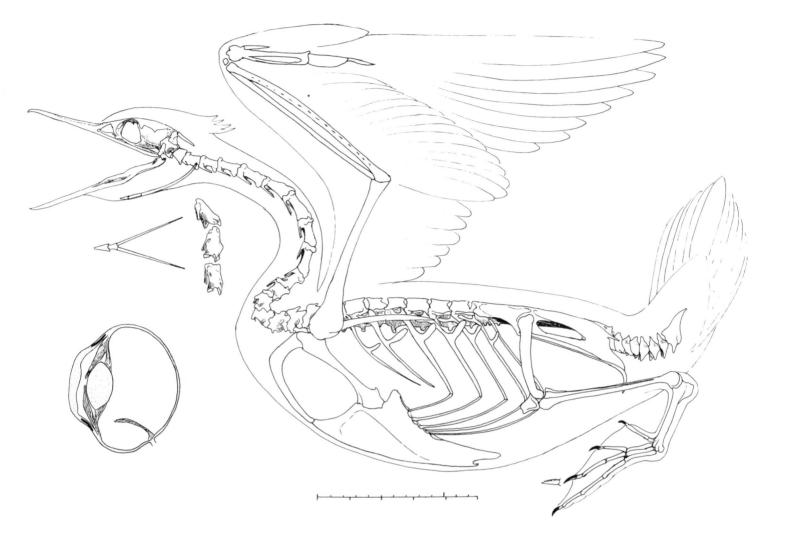

frigatebirds the combined weights of the plumage and pectoral muscles probably comprise almost half of a frigatebird's total adult weight.

Like frigatebirds, pelicans exhibit highly pneumatic skeletons. Four American white pelican skeletons in the Royal Ontario Museum averaged 307 grams, or 7.4 percent of their actual carcass weights (James Dick, pers. comm.), and seven skeletons of this species in the Nebraska State Museum averaged 363 grams (Thomas Labedz, pers. comm.), or about 6–7 percent of the species' average adult weight. Cormorants show an intermediate amount of pneumaticity, with the humerus, ulna, and to some degree also the radius all being moderately pneumatic (Owre, 1967). The skeleton of a double-crested cormorant in the Nebraska State Museum represented 7.1 percent of its 1,680-gram carcass weight (Thomas Labedz, pers. comm.). Another skeleton in the Royal Ontario Museum represented 6.2 percent of its 1,698-gram carcass weight, while single skeletons of three other cormorant species in the Royal Ontario Museum had skeletons averaging 5.7 percent of their carcass weights (James Dick, pers. comm.). In darters the skeleton is nearly nonpneumatic, with only a very small cavity present in the humerus, and all the skeletal elements of the wing are relatively heavy (Shufeldt, 1902; Owre, 1967). The mean weight of 19 African darter skeletons in the Royal Ontario Museum was 95.8

Figure 8. Skeletal anatomy of a typical cormorant (*Phalacrocorax*). Also shown are the hyoid apparatus (dorsal view), the seventh to ninth cervical vertebrae (lateral view), the eye (sagittal view), and the pectinated middle claw. Eye details adapted from Sivak et al. (1977); otherwise from specimens. The eye is shown at approximate 6× scale.

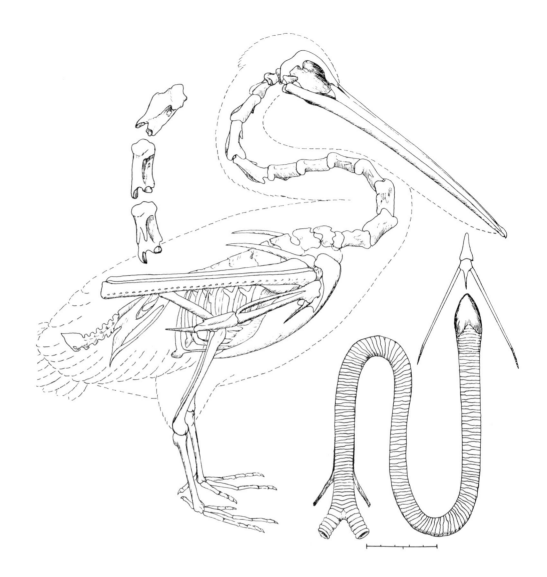

Figure 9. Skeletal anatomy of an Australian pelican. Also shown (at 2× scale) are the seventh to ninth cervical vertebrae (lateral view), and the trachea and hyoid of an adult male American white pelican (ventral view). From specimens.

grams, or 6.8 percent of the carcass weights of these birds (James Dick, pers. comm.). It would appear that no significant differences exist in relative overall skeletal weights among these groups, in spite of their greatly differing degrees of pneumaticity.

Several additional skeletal specializations are evident in the appendicular skeletons of these groups (figures 8 and 9). Cormorants and darters have well-developed patellas, probably similar in function to those of various other foot-propelled diving birds such as loons and grebes. However, at least in cormorants the patella is reputedly of dual embryonic origin, seemingly consisting of a true separate sesamoid patellar component as well as a portion of the cnemial crest of the tibo-tarsus (though this composite origin has been disputed by Lewis, 1929). In any case, the patellas of cormorants and darters are rather different in shape from one another, and in darters the dorsal patellar surface is quite small, suggesting that important differences may exist in the leg musculature and muscle functions among the two groups (Owre, 1967). The femur is also proportionately longer in darters than in cormorants and not so distinctly bowed in shape, which is perhaps related to the darters' fine climbing abilities. Darters, frigatebirds, and sulids are

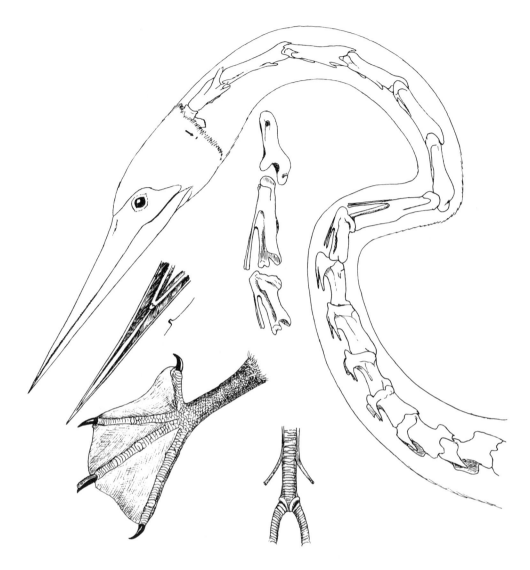

notable in that the fibula is complete in these genera (Shufeldt, 1894), a trait of uncertain adaptive significance other than in perhaps helping generally to strengthen the lower leg. In pelicans and cormorants the fibula is also unusually well developed and it is occasionally complete in individual cormorants (Shufeldt, 1889, 1894).

The very long (high aspect ratio) wings of pelicans are primarily the result of their unusually long forearms (ulna and radius). In pelicans the ulna is distinctly longer than the humerus, approximating the proportions typical of various long-winged procellariiform birds. This ratio contrasts with the proportions of the ulna to the humerus in cormorants, in which these bones are similar in length, and in darters, in which the humerus is considerably longer than the ulna. As noted earlier, there is a correlated substantial difference in the number of secondary feathers present in these three groups, with pelicans having up to nearly twice as many as are present in darters.

Adaptive differences in the crania, bills, and sterna among the three groups have already been noted. The remainder of the axial skeleton is generally less obviously modified in these birds, although the rib cage of cormorants is relatively stur-

Figure 10. Anatomical features of darters, illustrating thrusting adaptations of the cervical vertebrae (the seventh to ninth also shown separately), the rudimentary tongue (in dorsal and lateral view), the totipalmate foot and pectinated claw, the syrinx (in enlarged ventral view), and the location of the external auditory meatus (arrow). In part after Garrod (1876) and Beddard (1892); otherwise from specimens.

TABLE 10   Morphological Traits of Cormorants, Darters, and Pelicans

Trait	Cormorants	Darters	Pelicans
Outer : middle toe length	130–140%	ca. 110%	ca. 100%
Pectinated middle claw	Present	Present	Reduced
Maxillary nail	Hooklike	Absent	Hooklike
Maxillary groove	Present	Absent	Present
Bill edges (tomia)	Smooth	Serrated	Smooth
Nostrils closed in adults	In all species?	In both species	In one species
External ear opening	Very small	Slitlike	Small
Gular pouch size	Intermediate	Smallest	Largest
Tongue development		Rudimentary in all groups	
Uropygial gland		Present in all groups	
Feather aftershafts		Lacking in all groups	
Brood patches		Lacking in all groups	
Feather wettability	Intermediate	Greatest	Least
Nuptial filoplumes	Usually present	Present	Absent
Iridescent feathers	Present	Present	Absent
Tail length : total length	ca. 20%	ca. 30%	ca. 10%
Total rectrices	12–14	12	22–24
Rectrix molt (duration)	Gradual	Variable	Gradual
Rectrix molt (pattern)		Irregular in nearly all species	
Total functional primaries		10 (+ 1 vestigial) in all volant species	
Total secondaries	15–23	16–18	27–35
Remix molt (duration)	Gradual	Simultaneous	Gradual
Primary molt (pattern)	Descendent	Simultaneous	Descendent
Secondary molt (pattern)	Irregular	Simultaneous	Irregular
Primary *Staffelmause*	Present	Absent	Present
Occipital style	Large	Small	Absent
Nasal-frontal hinge		Present in all groups	
Cervical vertebrae	18–20	19–20	17
Thrusting neck mechanism	Poorly developed	Highly developed	Rudimentary
Furcula fused to sternum	No	No	Yes
Ulna : humerus length	Very similar	Ulna shorter	Ulna longer
Ossified patella	Well developed	Intermediate	Absent
Bone pneumaticity	Intermediate	Least	Greatest
Inflatable "air mattress"	Absent	Absent	Present
Esophageal crop		Absent in all groups	
Filiform pyloric stomach	Absent	Present	Absent
Intestinal caeca	Very small	Tiny or lacking	Small

dy and thus obviously well adapted to withstanding the water pressures associated with submergence. Certainly the most remarkable remaining aspect of the axial skeleton of these birds is the varying degrees of neck specialization for facilitating bill thrusting, which especially involve modifications of the seventh to ninth cervical vertebrae. This trait is not apparent in the cervical vertebrae of pelicans (figure 9) but is clearly evident in cormorants. It reaches its extreme form in the darters, in which these three vertebrae take on configurations that might cause one to doubt that they came from the same species, to say nothing of actually being adjacent vertebrae (figure 10). The details of the remarkable cervical anatomy of darters have been described by several authors (e.g., Garrod, 1876; Mivart, 1878; Shufeldt, 1902). The critical points involve the eighth vertebra, which has its lower articulating surfaces oriented posteriorly, whereas its upper ones are oriented anteriorly. This produces a Z-shaped kink in the neck that is very similar to that found in herons (Ardeidae), though in those birds it centers on the sixth cervical vertebra. Other adaptations of darters for thrusting involve the presence of long tendons extending up from muscles that are associated with lower neck vertebrae and attach to the elongated ventral spines of the eighth through the eleventh cervical vertebrae, providing the power for the thrusting stroke. The convergent anatomical similarities between the cervical musculatures and osteologies of herons and darters are probably worthy of study.

Digestive System Anatomy

These and apparently all pelecaniform birds lack enlarged esophageal crops, but the esophagus is highly dilatable in all and allows for the swallowing of surprisingly large fish or other similar prey. Additionally their stomachs lack a thickened muscular gizzard component, and in common with many other nonvegetarian birds the entire stomach wall is instead relatively thin and saclike (figure 3). The stomach is divided into two major components, the anterior cardiac or proventricular portion, and a smaller, more posterior pyloric component. However, in darters the proventricular glands, rather than occurring as a band around the lower end of the esophagus, are located at the side of the anterior stomach as a globular sac (Audubon, 1840–44). Furthermore, in darters the pyloric stomach is lined with bristly, hairlike (filiform) papillae that form a dense mat that surrounds and seemingly protects the pyloric valve. The papillae apparently serve as a sieve to prevent fish bones and the like from entering and possibly damaging the small intestine (Garrod, 1876). Pebbles often occur in the stomachs of some marine cormorants, but probably function as ballast rather than to provide grinding surfaces. The caeca at the junction of the small and large intestines are very small or rudimentary in all these birds, which is not surprising considering that very little vegetable material is normally ingested.

By way of summary, table 10 provides a comparative listing of some of the significant morphological similarities and differences among cormorants, darters, and pelicans.

CHAPTER 3

Egocentric and Locomotory Behavior

The egocentric behaviors of birds involve those maintenance activities that are needed in order to keep them alive, healthy, and presumably comfortable, irrespective of their social environment. Some involve the maintenance of basic life support systems, including drinking and swallowing behaviors as well as elimination or evacuative behaviors such as regurgitation, salt excretion, and defecation. "Comfort" activities often involve care of the feather and body surface, such as preening, oiling, and bathing, as well as local muscular adjustments or exercises, including a variety of stretching, flapping, and shaking movements.

Egocentric behaviors also include a species' nonsocial locomotory behaviors, which in the groups considered here include walking, swimming, and flight. However, these activities may be done in company with other conspecific birds and thus merge with flock-related social interactions, such as social flying and social foraging. Among the most important of any animal's survival-related locomotory activities are, of course, its foraging strategies and food-catching capabilities. Foraging behaviors of these birds will be discussed together with niche-related feeding ecologies in chapter 4.

Still other very important behaviors are those social interactions that are directly or indirectly related to successful reproduction, such as agonistic encounters (attack-escape and related behaviors associated with dominance and submission), sexual interactions, and parental activities. These will be considered in chapter 5.

By far the most comprehensive study of the maintenance behaviors of any of the pelecaniform birds is Schreiber's (1977) account of the brown pelican. An earlier description of pelican maintenance activities was provided by Meischner (1958, 1962), although this account is comparatively incomplete. Schaller (1964) also provided a few comments on the maintenance activities of the American white pelican. Among the cormorants, the important early paper by Kortlandt (1940) on the great cormorant is especially worthy of note, and those of Lewis (1929) and Mendall (1936) on the double-crested cormorant are also very useful. Additionally, van Tets (1959) has described maintenance and locomotory behaviors of the pelagic shag and the Brandt's and double-crested cormorants. He also (1965) described locomotory behaviors among all the groups of pelecaniform birds in the context of their role as a source of ritualized communication signals (social displays). Little has been written on the maintenance behavior of darters, although Vestjens (1975) provided some observations of comfort activities in the Australian darter. Additionally, a good deal of attention has been paid to possible feather-drying and/or body-warming functions of wing-spreading behavior in darters and cormorants (e.g., Clark, 1969; Schreiber, 1977; Rasmussen and Humphrey, 1988).

Resting and Sleeping Behavior

Pelicans may stand or rest on their bellies while sleeping. They typically sleep on land, or while perched in trees in the case of tree-nesting species, but at times have been seen sleeping or dozing in shallow water as well. Sleeping cormorants generally stand on both legs. Although cormorants and darters typically sleep on land or in trees, Lewis (1929) believed that under some conditions cormorants might sleep at sea. Especially during cold weather, but also at other times, one foot is often raised and tucked into the flanks while the bird remains standing on the other foot.

While incubating, brooding, and resting, birds of these groups either simply lower the head on the breast with the bill directed forward, or twist the neck and rest the head on the back and shoulders. When sitting on the ground, pelicans may rest or sleep with their heads directed forward, especially during hot weather, but usually they tuck their bills backward into the scapular feathers. Darters typically sleep while perched in trees, usually with the bill inserted into their scapulars. Cormorants also often place their bill underneath the leading edge of one of the wings while sleeping. Although Lewis (1929) regarded this as the normal sleeping posture of cormorants, van Tets (1959) believed it was primarily associated with cold weather.

Body Care, Exercise, and Comfort Activities

After awaking, all these birds often perform a variety of body care and related activities. Schreiber (1977) recognized a total of 14 muscle-exercising and/or comfort-related (shaking, flapping, and stretching) or body care (scratching, preening, oiling, and bathing) activities among brown pelicans. With minor modifications these may be inclusively summarized for species of all three groups as follows:

Shaking. In brown pelicans shaking takes two forms, a wing shake with the wings somewhat lifted but still folded, and a less common general body shake, with the wings either raised or not. The purpose of both is apparently feather re-arrangement, and Schreiber found no evidence of behavioral ritualization for communication purposes. Similar shaking behavior also occurs in most if not all other species of pelicans, as well as in cormorants and darters. More restricted shaking movements, such as head shaking, may serve to remove fluid or debris from the bill. Backward foot shaking while the bird stands on the other leg has also been observed in cormorants (van Tets, 1959), and probably occurs in the other groups as well.

Tail wagging. Lateral tail shaking is a common comfort or maintenance activity in cormorants, darters, and pelicans. At least in the brown pelican it does not seem to serve any additional communication role, according to Schreiber. However, Meischner (1958) discussed pelican tail spreading and tail shaking (in eastern white, pink-backed, and Dalmatian pelicans) at some length, and considered this activity to have unspecified "psychological" functions in social situations. Tail shaking is a common activity in nearly all water birds, and may serve to remove water from the tail as well as to straighten the tail or tail covert feathers. It often occurs after defecation, then serving a possible sanitary function. It also often occurs after various other comfort activities such as wing flapping and leg stretching (Schreiber, 1985). It perhaps additionally has some generalized social significance, such as indicating a certain level of excitement or unease. It is certainly common during social displays in various waterfowl (Anatidae), often occurring before or after major male displays, but does not itself appear to be specifically ritualized.

Wing flapping. Wing flapping occurs in the context of bathing and also as an apparent exercise activity, not only in nestling birds but also in adults. Schaller (1964) included this type of wing flapping in his "stretching" category. Wing flapping is a common activity of standing or swimming pelicans, which Schreiber believed may serve as an ambivalent preflight activity among disturbed birds. He noted that it may be used to help maintain balance while perching and to shake water from the plumage, and suggested that it may have other less apparent functions, such as helping in swallowing or rearranging the alimentary tract when swallowing fish. He found no indication that it may serve as a ritualized signal. The wing-waving displays of cormorants and darters are, however, perhaps derived from wing-flapping or pretakeoff movements, although they are now certainly highly modified. Wing flapping is a very common exercise in nestling pelicans as well as nestling cormorants. This activity begins even before the flight feathers start to appear, and probably provides for strengthening of muscles in preparation for later flight. In cormorants (and probably also the other groups) wing flapping invariably follows bathing, and may last three or four minutes before the bird finally begins to dry its wings (Snow, 1963).

Wing and leg stretching. This is one of two types of wing-stretching movements that are widespread among many orders of birds. In this type one of the wings and the corresponding leg are stretched backward while the bird is standing or sitting. The other wing may be opened slightly at the same time, perhaps to help maintain balance. Van Tets (1959) calls this the "one-sided stretch" in cormorants, and Snow (1963) illustrated it in the European shag. Vestjens (1975) observed it in the Australian darter while an adult was sitting on the nest, and also noted (1977a) that in the Australian pelican it can occur while the bird is in either a standing or sitting position. It does not appear to function as a ritualized signal in these groups of birds, nor in galliform, anseriform, charadriiform, or gruiform birds, based on my own observations of these additional groups.

Both-wings stretch. Schreiber observed this simultaneous overhead wing-stretching movement only once while watching brown pelicans, but it is a widespread activity in most species of birds, and Schaller (1964) reported it as a common form of stretching in the American white pelican. In the European shag it has been called "wing-stretching with neck forward" (Snow, 1963), and van Tets (1959) refers to it as the "upwards wing-stretch." It has also at times been called the "full stretch." Like the previous stretching movement, this is a widespread behavior but is not obviously ritualized in this group. However, it does expose the undersides of the wings temporarily, and serves as an effective visual signal among boobies as well as various sandpipers such as the wood sandpiper (*Tringa glareola*) (Johnsgard, 1981).

Body up-down. This is a rapid rocking body movement that Schreiber observed among brown pelicans and thought might serve functionally to stretch the leg mus-

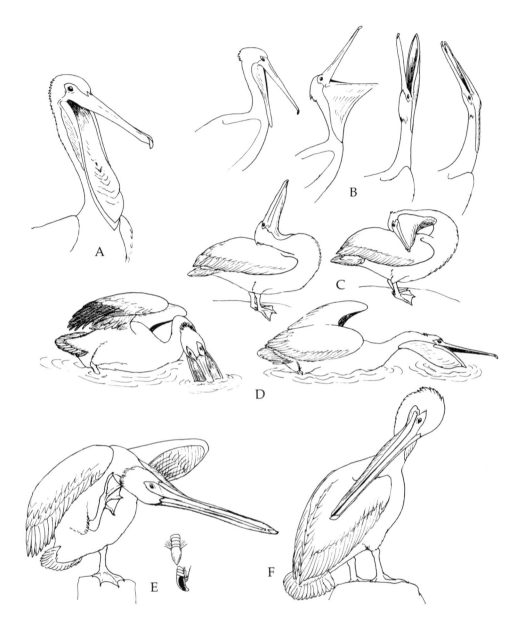

cles. He was unsure of its possible signaling significance, and found no reference to it in other pelican species. It is difficult to relate to comparable activities in other species, but seems to be a rather general and unritualized muscle-stretching movement.

Bill tossing. In brown pelicans this action involves a rapid upward bill-tossing movement to about the horizontal, with the bill slightly open and the gular sac taut, apparently serving to dislodge materials stuck in the pouch or perhaps loosening dried pouch skin. Schreiber found no reference to this behavior in other pelicans, although Meischner (1958) described an energetic vertical swinging action with opened bill and associated beating action of the gular pouch that seemingly served to remove residue. Considering the small sizes of their gular pouches, it is rather unlikely to occur in cormorants or darters.

Bill plunging. This activity as performed by brown pelicans consists of an energetic dipping and lateral thrashing of the open bill in the water, with the lower

Figure 11. Egocentric behavior of the brown pelican, including glottis exposure (A), sequential stages of bill throw (B), head rubbing (C), bill plunging (D), head scratching (E), with the modified middle claw also shown in dorsal and lateral view, and preening (F). After sketches in Schreiber (1977).

mandible widely spread (figure 11D). It may serve not only to obtain water for drinking but also to moisten and cool the pouch, with moistening and cooling perhaps the primary functions (Schreiber, 1977). A somewhat similar behavior in the Australian pelican (Vestjens, 1977a) may also serve to moisten the pouch. It has apparently not been observed in cormorants and darters, although a similar bill-dipping or "displacement diving" activity has been described for the long-tailed cormorant in association with fear or escape (see figure 36).

Glottis exposure ("yawning") and bill throw. Glottis exposure has only been observed in pelicans. It consists of a yawnlike opening of the bill while lowering the widely bowed lower mandible on the neck, thus exposing the glottis and hyoid areas (figures 11A and 12C). Glottal exposure is often associated with bill throwing (figure 11B), in which the bill is rather rapidly raised to the vertical and returned, the entire process usually lasting about one second in brown pelicans (Schreiber, 1977). Vestjens (1977a) described as "upward-pouch-stretching" what Schreiber termed bill throwing; the former term is probably more functionally descriptive. Schreiber believed that both glottis exposure and bill throwing are comfort movements concerned with throat and pouch stretching. Disturbed birds often perform the bill throw, and the behavior is relatively infectious in a flock. As such it may serve as a flight intention signal or help coordinate flock departure (Schreiber, 1977, 1985). Schreiber believed that the bill throw behavior of brown pelicans probably corresponds to the "yawning" described by Schaller (1964) for American white pelicans, and judged that Schaller's description of pouch stretching corresponds to glottis exposure. Similar apparently comfort-related activities were described (as yawning and throat stretching) by Meischner (1958) in captive eastern white, Dalmatian, and pink-backed pelicans. Apparently true yawning as well as jaw-stretching movements also occur in cormorants (Lewis, 1929; Millener, 1972; Marchant and Higgins, 1990), during which the upper mandible is noticeably raised, the head is usually tilted upward, and the gular region is often expanded (figure 12B). Yawning movements have not been specifically reported for darters, although their jaws can be very widely opened during the swallowing of prey.

Bathing. Bathing by pelicans, in common with that of most water-adapted birds, involves a sequence of energetic head-dipping and wing-thrashing movements while swimming (Schreiber, 1977). According to Meischner (1958), bathing as performed by pelicans involves four separate movements, including an oscillatory wing beating (rotary movements of the entire wing), forearm beating (lateral movements of the humeri), head and neck dipping, and head and neck rubbing. Apparently the bathing behavior of cormorants is very similar (van Tets, 1959; Snow, 1963), although it has been suggested that among cormorants, unlike pelicans, bathing may serve as a cooling mechanism (Vogt, 1942; Meischner, 1958). Bill-dipping and head-dipping movements related to bathing movements may also occur in cormorants when they are alarmed (see figure 36), apparently as a kind of "displacement" activity (Bowmaker, 1963). The bathing bouts of cormorants are relatively brief, lasting an average of only about a minute in the case of the Cape shag (Siegfried et al., 1975). Apparently no good descriptions of bathing in darters are available.

Head rubbing and oiling. In this behavior, the bird methodically rubs its head over the area of the uropygial gland and then passes it over other parts of its body, which probably serves to spread oil from this gland over the contour feathers (figure 11C). Brown pelicans may use the tip of the bill to squeeze oil from their uropygial gland, whereas in the eastern white pelican the gland is mostly mas-

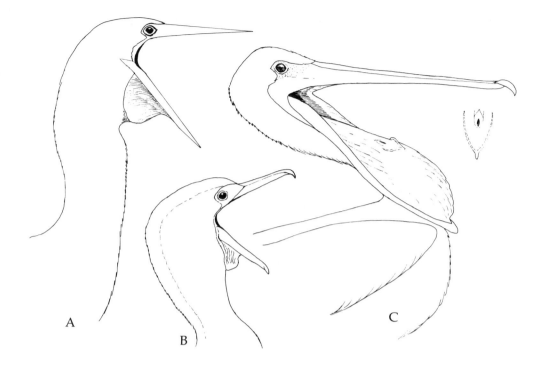

Figure 12. Gaping (or yawning) of the anhinga (A), pied cormorant (B), and brown pelican (C, during glottal exposure). The inset sketch shows the relative locations and appearance of the tongue, hyoid apparatus, and glottis in pelicans. After published photos and specimens.

saged with the side of the bill (Schreiber, 1985). Van Tets (1959) noted that among cormorants both the bill and the back of the head are used in applying oil gland secretions to the feathers. Darters also have functional uropygial glands, and presumably oiling by them is done in a comparable manner. The European shag may perform oiling behavior with or without first obtaining oil from the uropygial gland; it is sometimes used as an apparent appeasement gesture in that species (Snow, 1963). The flightless Galapagos cormorant performs head-rubbing and oiling behavior in the same manner as do more typical cormorants, although its modified and hairlike feathers are structurally unsuited for waterproofing, and the adult's oil gland may actually be nonfunctional (Snow, 1966).

Preening (including feather nibbling and feather stroking). Like head rubbing, preening may also be used to spread oil from the uropygial gland, but preening may additionally serve to rearrange feathers and maintain their condition. Pelicans typically preen with a delicate nibbling action of the upper mandible, but a second type of preening, called "lateral biting" by Schreiber, is also infrequently used. In this method, the feathers are squeezed by a biting action of the upper and lower mandible. Somewhat similar biting behavior was described for pelicans by Meischner (1958), who observed that when the bird is completely wet after a rain or bathing, water may be roughly stripped away from the feathers using the closed bill. Similar but more gentle feather stroking along the feather axis from the base toward the tip, using the pressure of the nearly closed bill, is widespread among birds during normal preening. Such preening probably not only helps to dry the feathers but also tends to restore the normally interlocked condition of the barbs of the contour feathers. Meischner also observed typical preening ("nibble-polishing") of the feather bases during feather care by pelicans. Among American white pelicans preening was by far the most common self-care activity observed by Schaller (1964). Schreiber believed that self-preening in brown pelicans may also be performed as a ritualized display. In at least some cormorants mutual preening (allopreening) is performed as a pair-bonding display. A nibbling type of preening is also typical of cormorants (Lewis, 1929). Preening behavior among cormorants may extend to the legs and feet, which may be similarly nibbled on their callous parts (van Tets, 1959). In the European shag, parents regularly preen their young, and paired adults often preen one another during social interactions (Snow, 1963). Seemingly comparable mutual bill-nibbling behavior also occurs among paired darters (Vestjens, 1975).

Scratching and combing. Localized scratching with the claw of the middle toe (figure 11E), especially in the head and neck region (those areas that cannot be reached through preening), is a common avian activity. It occurs among pelicans (Schreiber, 1977), cormorants (van Tets, 1959), and darters (Vestjens, 1975), and is done without simultaneous lowering of the same-side wing. Scratching includes not only simple, brief scratching activities but also the more prolonged and delicate manipulation of feathers in a more comblike fashion, using the variably pectinated claw of the middle toe. The very presence of pectinated claws in these highly aquatic birds presents a problem; these are apparently the only web-footed birds that have them. Among other pelecaniform groups, only the frigatebirds also have well-pectinated claws, but they also have nearly webless toes and very small uropygial glands. Frigatebirds also avoid landing on water, since their plumages are no more waterproof than are those of darters, and they very quickly become waterlogged when wet. It might be tentatively hypothesized that feather combing with the pectinated claw by darters and cormorants helps to maintain the barb spacing that allows water to penetrate the feathers of these highly submarine birds. Contrariwise, the rudimentary pectination of surface-swimming pelicans may be related to their opposite need to maintain the water resistance of their plumage. Clearly, some comparative observations on the precise use of pectinated claws among the species of these groups are needed.

Temperature-Regulating Behaviors

Wing spreading. The bilateral wing-spreading behavior of cormorants and darters is extremely well developed and a familiar activity (figure 13) but of somewhat questionable function. The birds typically orient themselves toward the sun during this activity, and feather drying is perhaps the function most commonly attributed to wing spreading among these birds (Owre, 1967; Clark, 1969; Bernstein and Maxson, 1982; Hennemann, 1984; Rasmussen and Humphrey, 1988). However, at least in some situations, wing spreading may additionally or alternatively serve to regulate heat loss or gain (Clark, 1969; Curry-Lindahl, 1970; Hennemann, 1988). Finally, Jones (1978) has suggested that wing spreading in the long-tailed cormorant may have acquired an additional social function, namely as a ritualized signal indicating fishing success. Schaller (1964) described a posture that he called "wing-drying" in the American white pelican that involved partial wing spreading and that was performed following a heavy rain. Although mentioned both by Meischner (1958) and by Clark (1969), bilateral wing spreading in pelicans is evidently relatively rare and was never observed by Schreiber (1977) during his extended observations of brown pelicans. Among pelicans, wing spreading apparently often takes the form of wing drooping (see below) and is typically accompanied by a ruffling of the scapular feathers.

Wing drooping. Among brown pelicans, wing drooping typically occurs on hot,

Figure 13. Wing drooping (with gular fluttering) by imperial shag (A, after Rasmussen and Humphrey, 1988), wing spreading (with feather erection and gular fluttering) by Australian darter (B, after a photo by Michael Morecombe), wing spreading by reed cormorant (C, after a photo by Peter Steyn), and wing drooping by brown pelican (after Schreiber, 1977).

windless days and in direct sunlight (Schreiber, 1977). In cormorants it also often occurs during warmer periods and in conjunction with gular fluttering (Rasmussen and Humphrey, 1988). Wing drooping is commonly performed by adult cormorants while brooding or shading their nestling chicks (see figures 14 and 30).

Gular fluttering. This activity, sometimes called "panting," is common among all three groups considered here. At least among pelicans (Bartholomew and Dawson, 1954; Bartholomew, Lasiewski, and Crawford, 1968) and cormorants (Lasiewski and Snyder, 1969), gular fluttering has been shown to be a significant evaporative cooling mechanism, especially during warm and windless conditions. Gular fluttering is performed with the head somewhat raised and the bill slightly opened, by adult birds as well as by both feathered and featherless nestlings (figure

Figure 14. Gular fluttering by a nestling American white pelican (left, after various photographic sources), and gular fluttering ("panting") with feather erection and wing drooping by the European shag (right, after a photo by Martin B. Withers).

14). Perhaps because of the need to swallow large prey, the hyoid apparatus of cormorants (and doubtless also pelicans) has lost its original tongue control functions and been adaptively modified for facilitating throat ventilation (Korzun, 1982). Millener (1972) estimated a gular flutter rate of 120 per minute for the pied cormorant under moderate heat stress. He once observed a bird flying with an open gape and judged that this behavior might also have a cooling function.

Feather ruffling. During this behavior a sitting or standing bird ruffles its body feathers, especially its back and scapulars. Feather ruffling often occurs in Australian pelicans after a sandstorm or a rain shower, and probably serves to help dry or clean the feathers. General ruffling of the body feathers and even the upper wing coverts is especially evident in darters and cormorants during bilateral wing spreading as well as during gular fluttering.

In conjunction with temperature-regulatory behavior, a comment on the possible adaptive relationship between plumage color and temperature regulation may be in order. It has been speculated by Simmons (1972), Löfgren (1984), and others that the white undersides of various seabirds may be adaptive in improving their foraging efficiencies by making them less visible to their prey, or making them less visible to still larger marine predators hunting them from below ("hunting camouflage"). Schreiber and Clapp (1987) questioned whether this explanation could account for plumage color variations in pelecaniform birds, and suggested that temperature regulation should instead be considered as a possible selective force, as had first been proposed for African cormorants by Siegfried et al. (1975). These authors observed that among adults of four endemic African cormorants, which range from skillful solitary foragers (*neglectus, coronatus,* and *carbo lucidus*) to highly social and cooperative foragers (*capensis*), only one of the four species (*carbo*) exhibits partially white underparts. The rest are all essentially uniformly black above and below. Black-plumaged birds are evidently able to supplement their body heat by absorbing the energy of sunlight through their plumages, and thus have an effective means of compensating for the loss of metabolic heat resulting from plumage waterlogging during submergence. On the other hand, the rate of heat loss from black objects through radiation in cool environments is also greater than that from white ones, which might place all-black birds at a physiological disadvantage in cold climates.

The cormorants and shags provide the best comparative basis among the pelecaniform birds for judging a possible relationship between plumage color and internal temperature regulation. Among the five smallest species (the microcormorants), which should be the most susceptible to temperature loss, all but one are uniformly black above and below and thus should be highly efficient in absorbing sun energy. To a large degree they forage on rather slow-moving invertebrates, and so probably have little need for effective hunting camouflage. They also generally occur in warm climates, where there should be no great disadvantage in being entirely black. The exceptional little pied cormorant is dimorphic, with both black-bellied and white-bellied morphs present over its relatively large geographic and climatic range. Possible ecological reasons for its plumage dimorphism are obscure.

The remaining variably larger species of cormorants and shags can be classified as follows: 21 are temperate (their ranges mostly lying beyond the tropics of Cancer and Capricorn), 6 are tropical (their breeding ranges mostly lying between these latitudes), and 2 are intermediate (their ranges about equally divided between tropical and temperate latitudes). The two species with intermediate climatic ranges (the great and little black cormorants) both have black underparts. Of the six predominantly tropical species, only one (the guanay shag) has white underparts. Of the 21 species with temperate ranges, 10 have white underparts, 9 have black underparts, and 2 (the spotted and Pitt Island shags) have gray underparts. This breakdown suggests that the presence of white underparts in cormorants and shags may be as much related to possible adaptations associated with body temperature regulation as to providing effective hunting camouflage. Whereas black or dark-colored upperparts are the most effective means of exploiting the sun for feather drying or heat absorption, white underparts not only provide underwater countershading but also probably help to retain metabolic heat in cold climates. It is thus not surprising that about half of the temperate and subarctic cormorants and shags have a strongly bicolored, black-above, white-below adult plumage pattern, much like those typical of most penguins and alcids (which also are submarine foragers and are similarly cold-adapted). On the other hand only one tropically oriented cormorant species (which lives along a cold current) exhibits this distinctly countershaded plumage pattern. The generally pale-colored legs and feet typical of subarctic cormorants and shags, as opposed to the usually black legs and feet of warm-climate cormorants, perhaps can be similarly explained primarily on the basis of thermal adaptations rather than species recognition.

Among the pelicans, all the species are sufficiently large that enough body heat should be easily retained to avoid requiring any supplemental energy from the sun, and none apparently use wing-spreading or wing-drooping behavior to supplement their metabolic heat. Not surprisingly, all the pelican species that utilize surface foraging are predominantly white to grayish white, which presumably makes them somewhat less visible to prey fish below, and only the plunge-diving brown pelican is dark-colored. As to darters, both of these tropically oriented and generally dark-colored species probably use their black upperparts as a means of both drying their plumages and absorbing solar energy during bilateral wing spreading, as has been proven for the anhinga (Hennemann, 1982).

Ingestive and Eliminative Behaviors

Normal drinking behavior in all groups is done by dipping the open bill in the water and then quickly raising the head, causing water to flow down into the throat (see figure 36). A functionally related behavior in pelicans is "water collecting." This behavior was not observed in brown pelicans by Schreiber, and so far has only been described for the desert-adapted Australian pelican (Vestjens, 1977a). It consists of the bird sitting at the nest during rain showers with its upper mandible raised about 60 degrees from the horizontal, and the lower one horizontal and widely bowed. The bird may remain in this position for up to 16 minutes and collect up to 270 milliliters of water in its lower mandible.

Elimination of wastes or other bodily contents by these three groups of birds occurs in several forms, and they generally might be considered a consequence of homeostatic maintenance requirements.

As mentioned earlier, some water is lost by these birds from their respiratory surfaces (lungs and air sacs) through evaporation during gular fluttering, as well as through evaporation from these surfaces during normal breathing. However, like birds in general they are highly resistant to excessive water and salt loss through surface evaporation inasmuch as they completely lack the integumentary (sweat and scent) glands that are so characteristic of mammals. Thus their daily water needs are fairly low, and at least in many species of cormorants and probably also pelicans can be accommodated through the drinking of sea water. The sense of taste is seemingly almost totally lacking in cormorants (Lewis, 1929); it is apparently not known whether they discriminate between fresh water and salt water when obtaining water for drinking.

Excess salts associated with drinking salt water are largely eliminated from the body through the activity of the lateral nasal (or "salt") glands, which are paired secretory glands located just above each eye (Schmidt-Nielsen, Jorgensen, and Osaki, 1957). These glands extract from the blood and subsequently secrete a salt-rich fluid that typically passes out the nostrils and flows down the grooved upper mandible to its tip, from which it may simply drip away, or be flicked away by the bird with lateral bill-shaking movements. Millener (1972) observed in the pied cormorant that the rate of dripping was about once per ten seconds, and a captive bird exuded 2.0 cc of liquid soon after being fed 220 grams of saltwater fish. Salt glands are known to function in marine-dwelling cormorants and also at least the marine-adapted brown pelican, but are unlikely to be functional in darters.

Defecation of their relatively fluid feces may be done by these birds either when on water or on land, or even while flying. When on water, cormorants defecate backward, after which they rapidly paddle forward, leaving behind them a whitish cloud in the water. On land, they always defecate downhill (van Tets, 1959). Defecation typically occurs immediately around the nest in cormorants and pelicans. As soon as they have sufficient strength (at about ten days or so), nestling cormorants begin to defecate in such a way that the excrement falls outside the nest cavity (Lewis, 1929). Under climatic conditions where they are not constantly washed away by rains, these materials and those of their parents gradually generate a ring of dried feces. The same is true of ground-nesting pelicans, but not of darters or arboreal-nesting pelicans and cormorants (which however often kill their nest-supporting trees through the high salt accumulations in the soil below them). In some extremely arid areas, such as along the coasts of western South America and southwestern South Africa, buildup of sun-dried feces over a long period of time produces guano at the rate of about an ounce per bird per day among breeding cormorants. Its high uric acid content (about 13–20 percent nitrogen in fresh guano plus similar amounts of phosphorus) provides an extremely valuable natural fertilizer and also a source of nitrogen and phosphorus compounds for other industrial purposes (Coker, 1919).

Regurgitation occurs in two forms in these birds. Recently ingested prey that is temporarily held in the esophagus is easily regurgitated, especially by adults that are feeding nestlings. However, recently ingested prey may also be regurgitated by threatened or harassed birds, as an apparent defensive mechanism. Additionally, in cormorants the mucous membrane of the stomach is occasionally shed, enclosing a pellet of pebbles, fish bones, crustacean cuticles, and the like. Such pellets are subsequently coughed up and ejected through the mouth. One captive nestling pied cormorant regurgitated a pellet with undigested plant seeds a few days after being fed materials containing these seeds (Millener, 1972). The presence of pebbles in such pellets may be the result of accidental ingestion, as pebbles are not needed for digestive grinding purposes. However, in the black-faced cormorant they are also purposefully swallowed at times, presumably to provide ballast and thus help overcome the difference in this species' buoyancy in sea water as compared with fresh water (van Tets, 1976b). Even nestling cormorants may have considerable quantities of pebbles in their stomachs, these presumably having been ingested while feeding from their parents' regurgitations (Lewis, 1929).

Locomotory Behaviors

Locomotory activities can be conveniently subdivided into those occurring on land (walking, climbing, hopping or jumping, and terrestrial takeoffs), those occurring in the air (flapping flight, gliding, soaring, formation flying, flexed gliding, and landing), and those occurring on or under water (surface swimming, diving, submerged swimming, and aquatic takeoffs).

All of the species considered here have relatively short legs, and walking on land is done with a ducklike waddling gait. The wings are sometimes partially opened to help maintain balance, especially among tree-perching pelicans and to some degree also among darters. When moving up steep inclines a cormorant may use the hook on its beak, its lower mandible, or even its entire head as a grapnel, especially in the case of juveniles. Young cormorants also have relatively sharp claws, and may even use their stubby wings as an aid in climbing. Thus, young birds can readily scramble up trees or other precipitous inclines, pulling themselves along with the aid of their neck muscles (Lewis, 1929; van Tets, 1959).

When moving from rock to rock or perch to perch, nearly all these birds may use short two-legged hops or jumps, except perhaps the most heavy-bodied pelicans. Hopping is commonly performed by cormorants, especially when moving over uneven ground, and in the heaviest of the living cormorants, the flightless Galapagos cormorant, the birds emerge out of the water and onto the rocks in a hopping manner not very different from that of some penguins. Hopping from branch to branch is also common in darters. In cormorants the hop often serves as a symbolic flight, and may be preceded and followed by distinctive postures (prehop or pretakeoff, and posthop and postlanding) that provide important social signals.

Hopping by pelicans is only regularly used while they are taking off from land. Then they orient themselves against the wind and begin a series of strong hopping movements, pushing backward with both feet simultaneously, and with accompanying synchronized wing flaps. They often need a rather long runway before finally becoming airborne if no headwind is present. Takeoffs from level land by pelicans are probably made more difficult because of their unusually long wings. Cormorants also perform a comparable series of hopping movements combined with strong wing flapping when taking off from level ground, but generally require less runway room than do pelicans. In one observed case a double-crested cormorant required five hops, covering a distance of about four meters, before mounting into the air, and a pied cormorant may require up to three or four thrusts. When taking flight from water, these birds may need a horizontal distance of 10 meters or more if not much wind is present (Lewis, 1929), and up to 30 meters after prolonged fishing and under still conditions (Millener, 1972).

Pelican and cormorant takeoffs from water are always done against the wind if any significant breeze is present and, like takeoffs from land, involve a series of simultaneous rowing movements by the feet that are coordinated with synchronized wingbeats (figure 15). Takeoffs from land by darters are normally achieved simply by jumping off from an elevated perching site, but on the seemingly rare occasions when the bird takes off from water it apparently launches itself rocketlike into the air from below the water surface, using its feet for initial propulsion (Owre, 1967).

A leisurely flapping flight and an associated relatively slow air speed are typical of all three groups. Flight speeds are particularly slow in pelicans. In brown pelicans the estimated wing stroke rate per second ranges from about 1.5 (Palmer, 1962) and 2.3–2.5 (Coker, 1919) to 3 (Pennycuick, 1990), and their flight speed averages about 40–48 kilometers per hour (25–30 mph) (Schnell and Hellack, 1978). Pennycuick (1983, 1990) calculated air speeds of 33–36 kilometers per hour (20–22 mph) for brown pelicans during flapping and gliding flight. The air speed of American white pelicans usually averages about 45–50 kilometers per hour (Palmer, 1962), and the eastern white pelican likewise flies at about 48–56 kph (Feely, 1962). Pennycuick (1972) noted that a flock of eastern white pelicans averaged 45 kilometers per hour over a distance of 110 kilometers.

No measured flight speeds seem to be available for darters, but the wingbeat rate of the anhinga has been reported as averaging about 4 (Palmer, 1962) and 5.1 (Pennycuick, 1990) strokes per second. Coker (1919) estimated an average wingbeat rate of 4.2–5 per second for the red-legged shag. Pennycuick (1990) estimated wingbeat rates of 5.03 per second for the double-crested cormorant, and 5.35 for the European shag. Meinertzhagen (1955) reported a rate of 3.3–4.4 per second for the great cormorant, and 4.0–5.5 for the European shag. Pennycuick (1983, 1990) calculated average air speeds of 50–55 kilometers per hour during flapping and gliding flights of the Neotropic and double-crested cormorants and the European shag. Millener (1972) determined a sustained flight speed of 55–65 kilometers per hour for the pied shag.

Not surprisingly, the relatively long- and heavy-billed pelicans tend to fly with their necks retracted and the lower mandible and pouch resting on the breast. However, cormorants fly with fully outstretched (sometimes slightly curved) necks and darters with distinctly kinked necks (figure 15). In all of them the feet are tucked in below the tail and are apparently not used as flight controls except during

Figure 15. Takeoffs by double-crested cormorant (A) and American white pelican (B), and diving by anhinga (C) and Neotropic cormorant (D) (after photos). Also shown are in-flight profiles of darters (E), typical cormorants (F), shags (G), and pelicans (H).

landing, when they are lowered and the webs fully spread, presumably to help reduce air speed. The long tails of darters are often somewhat fanned in flight and probably serve well as aerial brakes or rudders. The smaller cormorants also have unusually long tails that probably serve as useful flight controls.

The long and distinctly slot-tipped wings of pelicans are shaped very much like those of such soaring birds as storks, vultures, and cranes, but are notable for their unusually high aspect ratios (Pennycuick, 1972, 1983). The wings of darters are scarcely slotted, but have remarkably large alulae ("bastard wings") extending from the wrist that are variously raised or extended away from the wing in flight. These feathers presumably function to improve flight efficiency, perhaps by preventing stalling during slow-speed gliding or soaring, as seems to be their function in raptors. The wings of cormorants lack both the high aspect ratios typical of pelicans and the large alular feathers typical of darters, and thus appear to be adapted primarily for normal flapping flight.

Among the three families, only the darters ever become seasonally flightless during the molt of their remiges; the other two groups have very gradual if not virtually continuous wing molts and are never subjected to a flightless condition. Perhaps the darters can afford to endure a flightless period inasmuch as they are generally sedentary and usually do not need to fly in order to reach their foraging grounds. By virtue of their very sharp bills and lightning-fast stabbing ability, darters can readily defend themselves even when flightless. Darters tend to have unusually long breeding seasons, and by compressing their wing molt into a minimal period they can perhaps more quickly recycle back into breeding condition. They can perhaps also more effectively engage in thermal soaring by not having significant gaps in their flight feathers, although pelicans also thermally soar without any apparent difficulty in spite of their prolonged molting schedule.

Soaring is well developed among both pelicans and darters, using the lift provided by warm-air (thermal) updrafts, which most typically occur over warm land masses but sometimes also develop over warmed surface waters. Thermal soaring has not been reported in cormorants. However, van Tets (1959) did observe declivity soaring (slope soaring) by double-crested cormorants and less frequently by the Brandt's cormorant and pelagic shag. This occurred only when strong winds struck the breeding colony cliffs, producing powerful updrafts that could be exploited by these birds. Soaring by pelicans is obviously an energy-effective method of migrating, and additionally the birds often soar in summer thermals, wheeling lazily about for no apparent purpose except perhaps the gaining of high-altitude visual perspectives on their surroundings. Pennycuick (1983) reported that the soaring flight speed in the brown pelican averages only about three percent slower than ordinary flapping-gliding flight, and about 20 percent slower than gliding flight. He noted (1972), however, that soaring is not an energetically free activity, inasmuch as some energy is necessarily expended in holding the wings horizontally outstretched.

Formation flying is regularly performed by pelicans and cormorants, especially when the birds are traveling at considerable height and for some distance, such as on long foraging flights or during migration. At least in some pelicans, formations may be maintained even while the birds are engaged in soaring (Pennycuick, 1972). Formation flying has apparently not been observed in darters, which are mostly sedentary and have only limited migrations in a few regions subjected to cold winters. Formation flying has been found to be aerodynamically more efficient than solitary flying in the American white pelican (O'Malley, Brian, and Evans, 1982a,

1982b). Single birds spent about 77 percent of their time flapping and the remaining time gliding. This compares with 60–70 percent flapping time among birds flying in formation, except for the lead bird, which is not able to exploit the updraft produced by the eddying and vortexlike air currents produced immediately behind and to the side of a neighboring bird's wings during flight. Thus, the lead bird occupies the aerodynamically least favorable position, and consequently does the least amount of energy-conserving gliding. Brown pelicans often fly just barely above a line of cresting ocean waves, apparently riding the associated "bow wave" of turbulent air, in a similar manner to the method used by porpoises when they are playfully surfing in the bow wave produced by a moving ship. Additionally, all pelicans are prone to flap and glide in synchrony while in formation flight, which perhaps further enhances their flight efficiency, by simultaneously reducing air turbulence during gliding.

Pelicans and darters are very prone to alternate flapping flight with short periods of gliding, which result in slightly higher air speeds and reduced energy consumption at the cost of some altitudinal loss. Cormorants only rather infrequently intersperse gliding with their wing flapping, except when they are losing altitude to land. Steep aerial dives, or "flexed glides," involve a nearly vertical or plunging descent, with the leading edges of the wings flexed backward more or less in line with the body. Such gannetlike dives are typical only of the brown pelican among the species considered in this book, and they are used exclusively as a foraging technique. As such, they will be discussed in the next chapter.

When cormorants and pelicans land on the water surface they typically do so only after a long and very gradual gliding descent into the wind, followed by skidding along the surface with their feet while their wings are beat backward to help reduce their speed. Landing on ice or on open, level ground also results in a gradual rather than sudden stop. Backstroking by the wings is especially evident in the birds when they are approaching a tree nest, cliff ledge, or some other solid and similarly restricted landing site. The tail is also fully spread and may be flapped up and down over a 90-degree arc to reduce air speed. The spread feet may also play a role in reducing speed; their surface area is about half that of the tail (Millener, 1972). Cormorants will typically approach such sites from slightly below the actual landing point. Then at the last moment they must swing upward to land, with gravity thus assisting them in reducing their flight speed (Lewis, 1929).

When pelicans, cormorants, and darters are swimming on the water surface, their feet are stroked in alternate (not simultaneous) sequence, producing a rather slow rate of movement through the water, especially among the relatively heavy-bodied pelicans. Meischner (1958) suggested that the swimming rate of pelicans has become so slow that they have had to resort to social foraging, although it should be noted that all of the smaller species of pelicans typically forage solitarily. Owre (1967) judged that the anhinga's characteristic head-bobbing movements while swimming on the surface or when partially submerged may be the result of a simultaneous foot-stroking action, but this trait might also simply reflect a stop-and-go sequence of head movements for maximizing visual awareness of the surroundings while continuously on the move.

Diving from a floating position on the water surface is performed only by cormorants and darters. Apparently the momentum is provided by a single simultaneous stroke of both feet (figure 15C), which especially in the case of the smaller species of shags and cormorants tends to push them almost out of the water prior to submerging. It is generally true that cormorants hold their wings tightly against

Figure 16. Underwater swimming by the Brandt's cormorant (adapted from a cover photo of the *National Geographic*, July 1969). Also shown (upper left) is diving by a double-crested cormorant (upper right, after a photo by the author), and underwater swimming by a little pied cormorant (lower right and lower left, after photos by G. van Tets).

Figure 17. Diving by the darter, showing apparent use of the wings while diving, and the use of the tail as a rudder (after a photo by B. Grzimek in Roedelberger and Groschoff, 1967). Also shown (insets) are anhingas swimming with captured fish (after published photos).

the body during submerged swimming, and employ only their feet for propulsion (see figure 16). When submerged they use a dolphinlike simultaneous foot-stroking action (Lewis, 1929; van Tets, 1959). Submerged cormorants hold their feet well out from each side (Lumsden and Haddow, 1946), which probably facilitates their additional use as underwater rudders. Lewis (1929) concluded from a literature survey that cormorants may at times use their wings for underwater propulsion, although

TABLE 11   Ethoecological Traits of Cormorants, Darters, and Pelicans

Trait	Cormorants	Darters	Pelicans
Social roosting		Typical of all groups	
Usual roosting sites	Land or trees	Trees	Land
Bilateral wing spreading	Well developed	Well developed	Inconspicuous
Gular fluttering		Typical of all groups	
Parental regurgitation		Typical of all groups	
Defensive regurgitation	Present	Uncertain	Present
Marine habitats used	Frequently	Rarely	In one species
Extrarenal salt removal	In marine spp.	Unreported	In one species
Pebble eating	In marine spp.	Unreported	Unreported
Underwater progression	Rapid	Slow	Absent
Underwater foot stroking	Simultaneous	Uncertain	Absent
Tree-climbing ability	Poor	Good	Lacking
Hopping takeoff	Common	Rare or absent	Common
Typical air speed	ca. 80 kph	Unreported	ca. 45 kph
Typical wing flap rate	2.5–5/sec.	ca. 4/sec.	1.5–2.5/sec.
Soaring flight	Rare	Common	Common
Formation flying	Common	Unreported	Very common
Migration tendencies	In a few spp.	Slight or none	Often strong
Major prey species	Fish and invertebrates	Fish and invertebrates	Fish
Prey capture method	Biting	Stabbing	Scooping
Plunge-dive foraging	Rare	Never	In one species
Foraging depths	To ca. 30 meters	A few meters	Surface
Cooperative fishing	In some species	Unreported	In four species
Feeding territoriality	In some species	Unreported	Unreported

he never personally observed it among either double-crested or great cormorants, and Millener (1972) did not observe it in several New Zealand species. Millener also stated that the tail and feet are both used for underwater steering. Partially submerged swimming along the water surface has been observed in some microcormorants such as the long-tailed cormorant, which often forages in very shallow water with only its head and neck completely below the surface.

Unlike cormorants, darters are prone to enter the water by dropping directly down from their overhead perches or nests, or they may occasionally swim out from shore. At times they slip silently and submarinelike completely below the surface (figure 15C), but commonly swim snakelike with only their head and upper neck visible, and periodically peer into the water. There is some uncertainty about whether darters regularly use their wings for propulsion when swimming under water, although they evidently typically hold them somewhat spread when diving (figure 17). They apparently keep their wings partially opened throughout the time that they are submerged (see figure 91), and the partially opened wings may then be used for underwater steering (Marchant and Higgins, 1990). It has even been suggested that by partially spreading their wings while under water, American anhingas may give the illusion of providing a shady retreat and thus might attract small fish (Palmer, 1962). Like cormorants, darters apparently use simultaneous foot strokes while swimming under water, and normally remain submerged for 30–60 seconds (Brown, Urban, and Newman, 1982; Marchant and Higgins, 1990).

By way of summary, an overall comparison of primarily behavioral traits among cormorants, darters, and pelicans is provided in table 11.

CHAPTER 4

Feeding Behavior and Foraging Ecology

It is in their foraging behavior that the cormorants, darters, and pelicans diverge most strongly from one another behaviorally, and it is these differences that have shaped many of their anatomical and ecological features that are of greatest interest to biologists. In his review of feeding ecology, Nelson (1979) stated that seabirds obtain their foods through six primary ways, including (1) surface feeding while flying, (2) surface feeding while swimming, (3) plunge diving, (4) surface diving followed by underwater pursuit, (5) food piracy, and (6) scavenging and other types of innovative feeding. The species included in this book primarily utilize three of these foraging types (2 through 4), although scavenging of dead fish has occasionally been observed among a few species of pelicans and cormorants.

The feeding ecology of the primarily marine species of pelecaniform birds was reviewed and summarized recently by Schreiber and Clapp (1987). Among other topics, they examined interspecific variations in diets and feeding behaviors, discussed the possible influences of age and sex on relative foraging success in pelecaniform birds, and considered the evidence that plumage color variations might be adaptively related to feeding behavior and foraging success. The possible ecological significance of plumage color variations among cormorants has already been discussed in the previous chapter. Here, foraging and prey capture differences among cormorants, darters, and pelicans, the important ecological question of possible interspecific foraging niche segregation among sympatric species, and the related question of possible intraspecific (age and sex) differences in prey choice among species of these three groups will be addressed.

Prey-Catching Behavior of Pelicans, Cormorants, and Darters

Darters often drop down from their perch and may then directly dive below the surface to capture prey, although these dives are not made from any great height. A few observations have been made of European shags and olivaceous cormorants plunging directly into the water to capture fish, in a manner something like that of gannets or brown pelicans (King, 1972; Humphrey, Rasmussen, and Lopez, 1988). Guanay shags reportedly hover in the air above schools of fish prior to landing and making their concerted attacks, and the Socotra shag has been reported to fly low over the water, with "birds plunge diving into the sea at regular intervals" (Bundy, Conner, and Harrison, 1989), but gannetlike plunge diving is evidently not typical foraging behavior of either cormorants or shags.

Foraging Techniques of Pelicans

Diving directly from the air into water to capture prey is virtually unique to and also is by far the most common method of feeding by brown pelicans. Plunge diving has also been observed in the American white and Dalmatian pelicans (van Tets, 1965), and also in the Australian pelican (Marchant and Higgins, 1990). This is evidently a highly demanding foraging technique, the efficiency of which depends in part upon experience. Orians (1969) determined that relative hunting success (proportion of dives resulting in captured prey) is age-dependent, with adults being almost 1.5 times more successful than birds in immature plumage. Even adults had hunting success rates that only averaged from about 55 percent (during the breeding season) to 69 percent (outside the breeding season) of the total dives that he observed. Similarly, Brandt (1984) determined that adult brown pelicans were significantly higher in their hunting success rates than juveniles, bringing up fish in 82.5 percent of 206 attempts, compared with a success rate of 49.3 percent among 426 attempts by juveniles.

The behavioral elements of plunge diving by brown pelicans have been studied and analyzed photographically by Schreiber, Woolfenden, and Curtsinger (1975), and are worthy of brief summary here. Plunge diving consists of a complex sequence of events, starting with the overhead sighting and visual selection of prey, which apparently means the selection of individual fish, even when the bird is searching in a school of fish. As it starts to dive it progressively retracts its wingtips by bending them at the wrist while keeping the humeri well forward. The head is also withdrawn and the legs are brought forward (figure 18). This wing flexing increases the bird's diving speed and also provides elevatorlike controls, so that it can easily correct its vertical trajectory by moving its wingtips up or down. It has no comparable lateral controls, however, and to correct for right or left movements it rotates its entire body, but not its head, by raising one wingtip and lowering the other. During the dive the bird may attain a speed of 65 kph (18 meters/second) (Ruppell, 1975). The bird may enter the water at a variety of angles, but upon initial bill contact the neck is outstretched and the legs and wings are quickly thrust backward, thus enhancing the streamlining of the bird's profile and perhaps accelerating its emersion speed. As noted earlier, brown pelicans have evolved inflatable diverticula from the cervical air sacs in the upper breast and neck areas that evidently help to cushion the shock produced when striking the water, whereas fish swimming as far as two meters below the surface are perhaps momentarily stunned by the bird's impact (King, 1979). However, in contrast to the deep plunge dives typical of gannets and boobies, no fish are captured that are beyond the approximately meter-long reach of the pelican's extended neck and bill.

As the pelican's bill enters the water its gular pouch is contracted but its bill is opened, so that the fish may become positioned between its upper and lower mandibles. Once it is properly positioned, the rather narrow upper mandible closes fairly rapidly toward the widely bowed rami of the lower mandible, which are opened by muscular pouch contraction, forming an oval "landing net" with a maximum area of about 500 square centimeters. The gular pouch quickly becomes great-

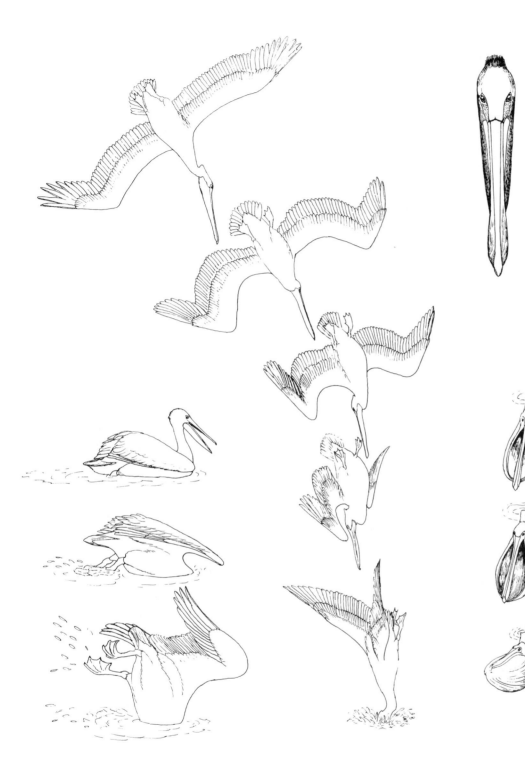

Figure 18. Aerial foraging dives of the brown pelican (middle), and fish-catching behavior when under water (right), as compared with bill plunging by a swimming American white pelican (left). Also shown is a dorsal view of a brown pelican's head, to show relative binocularity. After various photographic sources, including Schreiber, Woolfenden, and Curtsinger (1975).

ly distended with water, holding up to a maximum of about 10 liters. The trap is shut as the lower mandibular rami return to their unbowed position and close to meet the upper mandible, with the pouch remaining full of water. As the bird's head is raised above the surface the water begins to flow out of its pouch, leaving the fish inside. At that point the bird can lift its bill back out of the water. The entire process of capture typically takes less than two seconds from the point of initial water contact to capture, although up to a minute may be needed to drain the pouch fully and swallow the fish (Schreiber, Woolfenden, and Curtsinger, 1975). In the Australian pelican the pouch may be emptied by a tucking of the bill against the breast, thus contracting the pouch and forcing water out along the sides of the gape (Nelson, 1979).

Although prey catching by brown pelicans is essentially an individualized activity, flocks of brown pelicans often dive almost simultaneously into a school of fish, perhaps thereby confusing or panicking the fish. Such a concerted attack may increase the probabilities of individual catching success, although this possibility does not appear to have been investigated yet. Additionally, groups of brown pelicans will occasionally gather in areas of fish abundance and scoop-forage on the surface in the manner of white pelicans. Curiously, in the same area of the Gulf coast where group surface foraging has been reported for brown pelicans, American white pelicans were observed foraging solitarily (Gunter, 1958).

Prey-catching behavior of the other species of pelicans is quite different, and involves bill thrusting while swimming on the surface (figures 18, 19, and 94). In species such as the pink-backed and spot-billed pelican foraging typically occurs solitarily, whereas in most or all others of the non-brown pelicans it is more commonly performed socially. In either case, it can be conveniently subdivided into four stages (Din and Eltringham, 1974b). The first stage consists of searching. When performed by single birds this consists of swimming with the neck raised and the bill pointing forward and downward, its tip near the water. When done socially the group of birds initially spreads out into a semicircle or sometimes into a V formation, with their bills mostly under water and presumably open. The trapping phase consists of the bird suddenly thrusting its bill forward and under the water, with the head often held sideways. During the catching phase the head and eyes are entirely under water, sometimes with the neck immersed to the shoulders. The wings are partially opened and raised, and the two feet momentarily project backward out of the water. The bill is then slowly retracted sideways, so as to allow water to drain from the pouch. If a fish has been captured the bill is raised to about a 45-degree angle, and a series of up to eight muscular contractions of the pouch force it down the bird's throat. If socially foraging, the group then reforms and begins to move forward again.

The relative efficiency of solitary foraging by the pink-backed pelican, versus the mostly social foraging of the eastern white pelican, has been studied in the same Uganda location by Din and Eltringham (1974b). They reported a 20 percent individual success rate in the eastern white pelican, versus a 46 percent success rate in the pink-backed pelican. However, the solitary pink-backed pelican captured smaller-sized fish, and thus needed to catch fish more frequently than did the socially foraging eastern white pelican. Australian pelicans often forage socially, and sometimes form long lines across a stream. At times fish may also be driven by the birds into shallow waters and a feeding frenzy may ensue, with the birds half-running, half-flying over the water with their lower mandibles immersed (figure 20). This intermediate behavior between flying and swimming perhaps represents a development stage toward the brown pelican's spectacular aerial plunge diving.

Foraging Techniques of Cormorants and Shags

Little detailed information seems to be available on specific hunting techniques among cormorants. Before diving, the bird often submerges only the bill and head

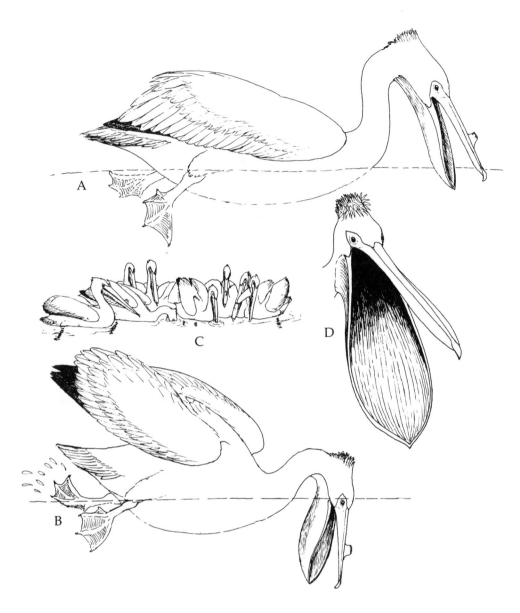

in the water, probably thus avoiding water surface reflections while looking for possible prey. Bowmaker (1963) reported that the relatively small long-tailed cormorant dives with a slight "flurry" of the wings, which perhaps helps in its diving efficiency. This species swims very rapidly under water, but nonetheless is only able to catch the more slowly moving or "lurking" types of fish. These are gripped by the hooklike tip of the upper mandible but not actually impaled by it, although in some cormorant species with better-developed nails impaling is certainly typical. Apparently fish are individually chased and captured by cormorants, whose eyes have been modified to allow a remarkable accommodation capability that is in the range of 35–40 diopters, thus allowing for near-focus abilities under water (see chapter 2).

Lumsden and Haddow (1946) noted that small fish are usually swallowed by the European shag while it is still under water. Indeed, several small fish may be successively caught and swallowed before the bird returns to the surface, making capture rates seemingly impossible to determine for relatively small prey. Larger

Figure 19. Food-related behavior of surface-feeding pelicans, including bill-plunging behavior of the American white pelican (A, B), a foraging group of American white pelicans (C), and gaping with mandible spreading by the Dalmatian pelican (D). After photos by the author and in Hanzák (1967).

Figure 20. Aerial bill scooping by the Australian pelican (left, after a photo by Michael Morecombe) and gaping by the eastern white pelican (right, after a photo in Nicolai, 1974).

fish are typically brought to the surface before being swallowed. After bringing their prey to the surface, these birds often shake or hammer it on the water, apparently to help subdue it. When crustaceans such as lobsters are caught, their legs and antennae are also shaken off. Then the prey is thrown in the air and caught again, thus positioning it for head-first swallowing.

When piracy by gulls or other birds is a problem, the fish are likely to be swallowed by cormorants while they are still submerged (Cooper, 1985b). Thus, Cooper noted that on only two of 157 observed foraging dives did bank cormorants bring prey to the surface, and that gull piracy was a very serious problem for this species. In an area where gull piracy was evidently not a problem, Lumsden and Haddow (1946) observed that six medium-sized fish were brought up during seven dives by one European shag, while another shag brought up three fish during four dives. Van Tets (1959) saw a pelagic shag appear with a fish after 4 of 17 dives. Considering the possibility of underwater swallowing, these figures probably have little significance as estimates of foraging efficiency.

Some species of cormorants and shags regularly feed in integrated social foraging groups. Among North American species, the Brandt's cormorant is perhaps the most social forager. This species often forms great rafts of foraging birds above schools of fish; they have been seen diving away from fish schools but suddenly coming up under the fish, forcing them to the surface where they might be readily captured (Palmer, 1962). Hubbs, Kelly, and Limbaugh (1970) described such behavior by foraging Brandt's cormorants near San Diego. Bartholomew (1942) noted that very large foraging flocks of double-crested cormorants sometimes similarly aggregated in San Francisco Bay. However, this species is not a regular social forager, and the flock's foraging dives did not appear to be synchronized.

Along the African coast, the Cape cormorant is a highly social species that exhibits communal gatherings and cooperative foraging. Each morning the birds depart their roosting sites in large flocks and head in apparently purposeful directions. Unlike the solitarily foraging species of African cormorants, Cape cormorants will delay their departures on foggy mornings (Siegfried et al., 1975).

The guanay shag is one of the most socially oriented foragers of all phalacrocoracids. Early each morning a few so-called scout birds reportedly fly out to sea.

When these birds drop to the water surface they are followed by veritable rivers of birds that eventually land in the same foraging places. These flocks form dense raftlike masses on the ocean surface, excitedly consuming the fleeing fish, while trailing individuals continually rise up and settle once again at the raft's forefront (Murphy, 1936).

The little black cormorant also forages in a highly social manner on shoaling fish. When a shoal is encountered the leading birds in a flock wheel around and settle on the water, with the remaining flock members landing so as to encircle the school of fish (Serventy, 1939). There is no evidence that "scouts" are used in this species (and perhaps no reason to believe that any altruistic scouting behavior is present in the guanay for that matter), but Serventy suggested that social fishing is a much more efficient method than is individualized foraging. Serventy also suggested that facultative flock-foraging, such as occurs in the European shag and double-crested cormorant, probably represents a behavioral "first step" toward the highly social pelagic foraging strategy of the little black cormorant.

Cormorants and shags typically hunt in an efficient and sometimes seemingly logical fashion. Thus, European shags may dive repeatedly in the same place where fishing is favorable, but they also often forage in a generally zigzag path, finally turning and traversing the same area back to the starting point. Such a course may extend well beyond a kilometer, with many dives en route. Among ten series of foraging dives observed by Lumsden and Haddow (1946), the number of dives per series ranged from 7 to 29 and averaged 15.

Foraging Techniques of Darters

Darters usually hunt solitarily in rather shallow, calm water, remaining under water for up to about a minute or so as they methodically stalk their prey. Smaller prey items are apparently sometimes stabbed using only the upper mandible, whereas larger prey is regularly impaled by both tips of the very slightly opened beak. This probably makes it easier for the bird to retain hold of its prey, because of the mandible's and maxilla's finely serrated edges. Earlier ideas that small prey may be captured by biting rather than stabbing have apparently now been discredited (Cramp and Simmons, 1977). Fish are by far the commonest prey, and they are usually impaled along the lower half of the body, suggesting that they were probably attacked from below. Small prey may be swallowed under water as the bird continues its swimming. Commonly a small prey item is brought to the surface, where it is flicked off onto the water and quickly retrieved for swallowing. Or it may be adroitly thrown in the air, caught head-first, and then swallowed. Large fish are normally taken to shore or a perching site to be subdued and swallowed. Very large fish may require as much as a half-hour or more to subdue before finally being swallowed. If a fish should become stuck in the bird's throat, the darter may have to go back into the water to moisten it, apparently thus making the prey easier to swallow (Harriott, 1970). Some insects (mostly aquatic beetles), crustaceans, and other aquatic animals such as frogs and turtles are occasionally eaten; some of these small prey items are more likely to be bitten than stabbed.

Foraging Depths, Durations, and Periodicities

A moderate amount of data has accrued on diving durations and diving depths among foraging cormorants and darters (table 12). Data on foraging depths are

TABLE 12   Representative Cormorant, Shag, and Darter Diving Statistics

Species	Measurement	Authority
Underwater speed (meters/second)		
Great cormorant	1.5	Junor, 1969
European shag	1.7–1.9	Wanless, Burger, and Harris, 1991
Long-tailed cormorant	1.34	Hustler, 1992
African darter	0.73	Hustler, 1992
Diving depth (meters)		
Crowned cormorant (maximum)	11	Wanless, Burger, and Harris, 1991
Bank cormorant		
Maximum	28	Cooper, 1981
Maximum	70	Wanless, Burger, and Harris, 1991
Double-crested cormorant		
Maximum	7.9	Ross, 1977
Mean	4.7	Ross, 1977
Great cormorant		
Maximum	19.8	Ross, 1977
Mean	10.7	Ross, 1977
Guanay shag (maximum)	12	Jordán, 1967
Imperial shag (maximum)	92	Wanless, Burger, and Harris, 1991
European shag		
Maximum	39.6	Barrett and Furness, 1990
Mean	28.1	Barrett and Furness, 1990
Maximum (of 39)	43	Wanless, Burger, and Harris, 1991
Mean (of 26)	26	Wanless, Burger, and Harris, 1991
Dive duration (seconds)		
Long-tailed cormorant		
Mean (in shallow water)	9	Whitfield and Blaber, 1979
Mean (in water 3 m. deep)	14	Whitfield and Blaber, 1979
Crowned cormorant		
Mean (142 dives)	23.5	Williams and Cooper, 1983
Maximum	58.5	Williams and Cooper, 1983
Pygmy cormorant		
Mean (38 dives)	5.6	Straka, 1990
Maximum	21	Straka, 1990
Little pied cormorant		
Mean (depth 1–2 m.)	13	Stonehouse, 1967
Mean (depth 2–3 m.)	16	Stonehouse, 1967
Mean (depth 3–4 m.)	22	Stonehouse, 1967
Mean (depth under 1 m.)	6.8	Trayler et al., 1989
Mean (depth 1–2 m.)	12.5	Trayler et al., 1989
Bank cormorant		
Mean (157 dives)	44.9	Cooper, 1985b
Maximum	63.8	Cooper, 1985b
Black-faced cormorant		
Mean (? dives)	35	Lindgren, 1956
Maximum	45	Lindgren, 1956

TABLE 12	(Continued)	
Species	Measurement	Authority
Pied cormorant		
Mean (depth 1–2 m.)	11	Stonehouse, 1967
Mean (depth 2–3 m.)	19	Stonehouse, 1967
Mean (depth 5–7 m.)	38	Stonehouse, 1967
Mean (depth over 8 m.)	64	Stonehouse, 1967
Mean (depth 1–2 m.)	17.3	Trayler et al., 1989
Mean (depth over 2 m.)	24.8	Trayler et al., 1989
Little black cormorant		
Mean (depth 1–2 m.)	13.4	Trayler et al., 1989
Mean (depth over 2 m.)	19.3	Trayler et al., 1989
Double-crested cormorant (maximum)	70	Lewis, 1929
Great cormorant		
Mean (135 dives)	21	Stonehouse, 1967
Maximum (ca. 6,000 dives)	71	Dewar, 1924
Imperial shag		
Mean (85 dives)	40.2	Cooper, 1985c
Maximum	312	Croxall et al., 1991
New Zealand king shag		
Mean (22 dives)	46.5	Nelson, 1972
Rock shag		
Mean (63 dives)	28.3	Wanless and Harris, 1991
Pelagic shag		
Mean (65 dives)	31	van Tets, 1959
Maximum	70	van Tets, 1959
European shag		
Mean (155 dives)	40	Lumsden and Haddow, 1946
Maximum	100	Lumsden and Haddow, 1946
Spotted shag		
Mean (31 dives)	30	Stonehouse, 1967
Anhinga (range)	40–60	Harriott, 1970
Australian darter (range)	30–60	Vestjens, 1975

generally much less precise than those for dive durations, since estimated depths are often based on water depths rather than known diving depths, the assumption being that the birds have traveled all the way to the substrate. In cases where the food is observed to consist of crustaceans or other bottom-dwelling (benthic) organisms, this is of course a reasonable assumption. In any case, it is apparent that most dives of cormorants are of no great depth, and in most cases are of less than a minute in duration. Larger species appear to be generally capable of both longer and deeper dives. Darters almost always forage in quite shallow waters, and so diving depths are of little general interest for that group.

Cooper (1985b) observed foraging bouts of breeding bank cormorants to last an average of 68 minutes for males and 84 minutes for females. This represents a statistically significant sexual difference, and apparently is associated with the females' lighter average body weights. Their smaller body weights may prevent females from making deeper foraging dives, or perhaps place upper limits on their potential prey size, thus reducing their overall efficiency. Foraging bouts during the non-breeding season were of generally shorter duration for both sexes, averaging 41 minutes in one study, possibly reflecting lower energy needs during that period. However, local prey densities certainly must greatly affect foraging duration times, and it is difficult to generalize much on these.

Overall, bank cormorants were found by Cooper to spend about 4 hours per day foraging. This represents a similar length of time to that reported by Tindle (1984) for Galapagos cormorants, which were observed to catch prey at an average rate of one item per 10–12 minutes of foraging time. The long-tailed cormorant, great cormorant, and eastern white pelican were all found to forage actively for periods of about 3–4 hours, or from 19 to 26 percent of the available daylight period (Whitfield and Blaber, 1979). Although overall mean figures for eastern white and pink-backed pelicans were not provided by Din and Eltringham (1974b), their diagrams indicate that throughout the day about 30–35 percent of the birds were actively foraging over a 13-hour period, with marked hourly variations present, suggesting a similar average daily foraging period of about 4–4.5 hours per bird.

Foraging activity by cormorants varies considerably in intensity throughout the day. For example, in the long-tailed cormorant foraging levels are very high from dawn to about 8:00 A.M. This is followed by lower morning foraging levels, almost no foraging from noon to 2:00 P.M., and finally another secondary period of foraging from 2:00 to 6:00 P.M. (Bowmaker, 1963). Similarly, the eastern white and pink-backed pelicans were found to forage strongly from dawn to midday. Desultory afternoon foraging occurred until about 5:00 P.M., when it again increased until dusk (Din and Eltringham, 1974b). Foraging times in the long-tailed cormorant, great cormorant, and eastern white pelican were reported by Whitfield and Blaber (1979) all to have early morning peaks followed by gradual declines, which in the eastern white pelican but not the other two species was followed by a secondary late afternoon peak.

At the end of a foraging period cormorants and shags often briefly dip the head under water several times, scooping water over the back in a bathing-like motion. This in turn is usually followed by a period of preening and wing flapping. The wing flapping probably assists in removing excess water from the plumage, which might seriously affect flight efficiency (Cooper, 1985b).

Human Exploitation of Cormorant Foraging Abilities

In some parts of both China and Japan the use of cormorants for human fishing is a traditional activity that has gone on for more than two thousand years; the earliest known record, from China, dates back to 317 B.C. (Egremont and Rothschild, 1979). In Japan the practice developed later, probably becoming established by the end of the sixth century A.D. (Gudger, 1926, 1929). In contrast to Japan, where fishing cormorants (including both the great cormorant and the Japanese cormorant) are now only semidomesticated and their degree of domestication in the past is uncertain, the Chinese fully domesticated their birds, which were exclusively great cormorants (Laufer, 1931). The techniques of fishing are also quite different in the two countries. In Japan the birds, which are caught from wild stock, are worked in teams of about twelve birds that are individually harnessed. The master lowers these birds into the water individually, manipulating the lines with one hand while holding them with the other. In Japan but not China the fishing is often done at night, the scene illuminated with a lamp (a brazier or cresset) placed at the prow of the boat, the light possibly also serving to attract fish to the surface. Daytime as well as nighttime fishing is common in China and, instead of fishing nonselectively, a salmonid called the *ayu* is usually sought out. In China, the eggs laid by the domesticated cormorants are hatched by hens and reared by hand on pellets of raw fish or other meat and on morsels of tofu (bean curd). After they are grown and their wings have been clipped, they are trained to respond to their master's voice and whistled commands starting at about four months of age. A neck ring of various materials is normally used, but its function is not so much for preventing the swallowing of fish as for providing a convenient means of grasping and holding the bird and for attaching a cord that may be tied to boat or raft perches. The fisherman uses a long bamboo pole, which functions both as a means of propelling the boat and also to control and direct the birds. This is done by beating the pole on the water to signal the birds to dive, and the pole is also used to recover swimming birds by allowing them to jump on it and be lifted into the boat (Laufer, 1931). In some cases a parent boat with 40–100 cormorants aboard may carry up to six small rafts, each of which is then released and subsequently manned by a boy. These rafts are organized crescentlike around the large boat, with 3–5 birds distributed per raft. Each cormorant recognizes and returns to its own raft with any captured fish, and may either disgorge its fish directly into a container or may be manually relieved of its prey. Small fish pass through the neck ring and are swallowed by the bird, but the neck ring may be removed when the bird's work is finished so it can then catch and eat larger fish as a reward.

In interesting observations made in China during 1975 by Pamela Egremont (Egremont and Rothschild, 1979), she observed a single fisherman wading chin-deep in the Li-Kiang River of Kweilin district, carrying a cormorant on his shoulder. He wore a large hat that threw a shadow on the water and perhaps helped the cormorant sight its prey. Other individual fishermen carried one or two birds on their arms, and yet others on bamboo hoops. More often several small boats worked together at dusk, using lights on the prows as typical in Japan, and with the birds on leashes. After each bird had caught 7 fish the knots holding its neckband were loosened and it was allowed to fish for itself, the eighth fish thus being the cormorant's. Once each bird had caught its seven fish it refused to fish anymore until its neckband was loosened, suggesting that these birds are able to count to at least seven!

Fishing in this traditional way is still done on the Li-Kiang downstream from Guilin, according to Hatt (1990). He stated that a cormorant fisherman can readily earn more than five times as much as a university professor (about $12 a week), and that even fishing with single cormorants can produce an income four times greater than this amount. The market value of a trained cormorant is in the range of $130–250. Individual cormorants may live up to 20 years, although a bird's most productive period is between five and ten years of age, before its eyesight begins to fail. Fishing sessions last about six hours, and when a fish is caught that is too large for a single bird to capture other cormorants will rush to get a grip on it until it can be retrieved by their master. In this way fish as heavy as about 7 kilograms can reportedly be captured, although the largest fish that can be swallowed by a single bird is about a half a kilogram.

Fishing is still done in Japan at Arakawa and Sagmigwawa in the Kanto district using great cormorants, and on the Nagara-gawa and Ohi-gawa at Kyoto using Japanese cormorants (Brazil, 1991). One of the few accurate and artistic representations of cormorant fishing in Japan is a rare woodcut by Eisen (1790–1848) showing this activity on the Nagara River. It is reproduced here in monochrome (figure 21).

Figure 21. Woodblock print by Keisai Eisen of cormorant fishing on the Nagara River, ca. 1840. Plate 55 from "Sixty-nine stations of the Kiso Kaido," by E. Hiroshige and K. Eisen.

Foods and Foraging Differences among Sympatric Species

Many cases of geographic sympatry involving three or occasionally even four species of cormorants and shags are known—for example the southeastern coast of Australia, coastal New Zealand, and the coast of Peru all represent areas of such multiple sympatry. Few of these areas have been studied with the purpose of determining the degree of foraging competition that may be occurring among these species, and it remains for future studies to analyze these interesting situations. However, a number of studies on the foods and foraging ecology of two sympatric species have been undertaken, of which several will be chosen here for discussion. One of these involves the foraging ecology of three species of cormorants in Sri Lanka.

On Lake Parakrama Samudra of Sri Lanka, the great, Indian, and Javanese cormorants are all resident. Of these, the Javanese cormorant has the most diverse diet, eating not only fish but also insect larvae and larger crustaceans. The progressively larger Indian and great cormorants have increasingly more restricted diets, although cichlids form the major dietary component of all three species (table 13). The three cormorants also take fish of differing average sizes and quantities. The Javanese cormorant takes fish averaging 30–70 mm in length and consumes an average of 8 fish per meal. The Indian cormorant takes fish averaging 60–120 mm in length and consumes an average of 2.4 fishes per meal. The great cormorant specializes on fish of about 130 mm in length and usually takes only a single fish per meal (Winkler, 1983). The great cormorants tend mostly to hunt solitarily, whereas the Indian cormorants forage socially. Adult Javanese cormorants defend individual

TABLE 13 Foraging Ecology of Sympatric Javanese, Indian, and Great Cormorants

Trait	Javanese	Indian	Great
Foraging sociality	Solitary	Social	Semisocial
Foraging territories	Present	Absent	Absent
Percent of diet from cichlid fish	ca. 50%	ca. 67%	ca. 67%
Adult body mass (g)	ca. 425	ca. 700	ca. 2,000
Favored prey length (mm)	30–70	60–120	ca. 130
Average prey per meal	8 fish	2.4 fish	1 fish
Foraging locations	Flooded plants	Vegetation edges	Open water
Foraging depths	Shallow	Intermediate	Deep
Mean dive duration (sec.)	12.4	12.9	29.8
Mean rest duration (sec.)	5.4	3.6	8.5
Dive/rest ratio	2.5	3.4	3.7

NOTE: Derived from data of Winkler (1983), except for body mass figures.

foraging territories, although immatures sometimes form feeding flocks. Diving periods of the great cormorant, which hunts in open water, average twice as long (29.8 seconds) as those of the other two species, both of which forage in shallower waters. The Indian cormorant typically forages along the edges of macrophyte stands, whereas the Javanese cormorant often forages in flooded vegetation along the edges of the lake.

The most widely distributed of all species of pelecaniform birds included within this book is the great cormorant. Although relatively little has been written of its foods in North America (summarized by Clapp et al., 1982), important dietary and foraging ecology studies have been undertaken in Britain (Rae, 1969), Europe (Madsen, Madsen, and Spärck, 1950; also summarized in Cramp and Simmons, 1977), Africa (Whitfield and Blaber, 1979), and Australia and New Zealand (summarized in Marchant and Higgins, 1990). Throughout its broad range the great cormorant apparently specializes on bottom-dwelling fish, although their taxonomic diversity is very great. In general, the birds seem to favor shallow-water marine, brackish-water, and sometimes fresh-water fishes that are at least 15 centimeters long and average about 50–100 grams, although fish weighing as little as 10 grams may be taken at times (Madsen, Madsen, and Spärck, 1950).

Over most of its European range, the great cormorant is sympatric with the European shag, which is considerably smaller (by about 20–33 percent in adult body mass). Although they are both coastal nesters, the cormorant is more prone to nest on broad, flat cliff ledges and the flattened tops of stacks, whereas the shag favors steep cliffs, where it nests on narrow cliff ledges, caves, holes, and hollows. Where they do both nest together, the cormorant is limited to the wide upper ledges and the flat ground just above the cliff edge, whereas the shag nests on the narrow lower ledges. The shag concentrates largely on marine and estuarine midwater fish rather than bottom-dwelling species, and unlike the cormorant is prone to do much of its fishing at sea rather than in harbors or estuaries (Lack, 1945).

As a result of these ecological differences, the composition of their prey differs quite markedly, in terms both of relative prey weight and of species composition of prey, judging from the results of two British studies as summarized in table 14. Additionally, in one study (Pearson, 1968), the average individual prey weights were substantially different for the two species. Bottom-dwelling fish and crustaceans,

TABLE 14   Foods of Sympatric Great Cormorant and European Shag

Factor	Great Cormorant	European Shag
Percent of birds having prey remains[1]		
Sand-eel *Ammodytes* (Ammodytidae)	—	51
Sprat *Clupea* (Clupeidae)	4	11
Dragonet *Callionymus* (Callionymidae)	11	10
Wrasse *Ctenolabrus* (Labridae)	17	13
Wrasse *Labrus* (Labridae)	15	6
Prawns (Palaemonidae)	15	5
Shrimp (Cragonidae)	33	3
Flatfish (Pleuronectidae)	52	3
Percent of individual prey represented[1]		
Small clupeoids (sprats etc.)	1	49
Sand-eel (Ammodytidae)	—	33
Wrasse (Labridae)	5	7
Gobies (Gobiidae)	17	4
Flatfish (Pleuronectidae)	26	1
Other fish taxa	17	4
Prawns and shrimp	33	2
Percent of total prey mass represented[2]		
Bottom-dwelling fish		
Gadidae	19	30
Pholidae	2	8
Trachinidae	1	—
Zoarcidae	9	3
Cottidae	10	3
Midwater marine fish		
Ammodytidae (also sand-bottom)	1	44
Salmonidae	3	4
Fresh-water fish		
Anguillidae	13	—
Bird's mean adult body mass (kg)	ca. 2.0–2.5	ca. 1.8–2.0
Mean prey mass (g)[2]	ca. 40	ca. 25
Modal prey mass (g)[2]	—	4–8

[1] After Steven (1933). Data from 27 great cormorants and 188 shags.
[2] After Pearson (1968). Data from 349 shag and 346 cormorant prey items collected at nests, plus stomach contents of 3 shags and 28 cormorants. Items present only in trace amounts are excluded.

which show up conspicuously in the prey list of the great cormorant, are clearly of secondary importance for the shag. However, midwater fish of the sand-eel family Ammodytidae (which also burrow in sand as adults) and small free-swimming fish of the herring family Clupeidae are of special importance to the shag.

Along the Pacific coast of North America two cormorant species and two shag species occur, which collectively breed all the way from the southern tip of Baja California to the tip of the Alaska peninsula and beyond to the Aleutians. Although the most southerly distributed of these species (Brandt's cormorant) is not sympatric with the northernmost (the red-faced shag), each of the four species is locally sympatric with at least two other species, and the pelagic shag is locally sympatric with all three of the others. Few studies have been undertaken to investigate all of these potentially competitive foraging and dietary interactions (Ainley and Boekelheide, 1990), but a summary of known foods for the four species in their areas of potential sympatry may prove instructive (table 15).

Among the two cormorants, the Brandt's is less prone to use pelagic or midwater fish as major prey items, but rather exploits benthic and nonbenthic fish almost equally as major and secondary food sources. It also seemingly consumes few if any crustaceans, although the remains of crabs and shrimp have been found in a few specimens (Palmer, 1962). The double-crested cormorant uses nonbenthic fish families more than twice as often as benthic fish for major or secondary prey, but does utilize decapod crustaceans fairly often as major or secondary prey. Hunting by Brandt's cormorants is usually done socially over the open sea, whereas double-crested cormorants are prone to feed on muddy bays or estuaries. The latter forage in water of only moderate depth, either solitarily or, at times, in large flocks (van Tets, 1959). Both species of Pacific coast shags are prone to forage solitarily in rocky coastal bays, and their nesting seasons (and thus their temporal needs for nestling foods) strongly overlap. Food intake data for the red-faced shag is much more limited than for the pelagic, but both species seemingly are quite dependent upon bottom-dwelling fish and crustaceans, with nonbenthic fish perhaps of only secondary significance. A detailed analysis of food and foraging adaptations of pelagic and red-faced shags in an area of local sympatry is certainly needed, as is a comparative study of their breeding ecologies.

In addition to their food differences, these four species also have somewhat differing nesting preferences, which tends to spread them out in local situations. Generally, the two species of cormorants are more prone to nest on wider and more generally sloping substrates, whereas the two shags tend to nest on steeper cliff sites. In areas of Alaska where double-crested cormorants, red-faced shags, and pelagic shags all nest together, the double-crested prefers nesting on wide platforms at the tops of rock columns, usually solitarily, whereas the red-faced and pelagic shags both were usually found nesting on narrower ledges, usually in close proximity to others of their own species. Among the two shags, the slightly smaller pelagic shag favors somewhat more inaccessible nest sites, such as small caves (Bartonek et al., 1977).

The foods of nesting double-crested cormorants and pelagic shags have been studied by Robertson (1974) in an area of local sympatry in British Columbia (table 16). He found that both species are opportunistic foragers, with the majority of their prey being taken in the littoral-benthic zone. Double-crested cormorants, but not pelagic shags, also occasionally forage socially with gull flocks over deeper waters, apparently then taking shoaling fish such as herrings. Both species typically forage in shallow waters, the pelagic shag evidently preferring rocky-bottom sites near its breeding colonies. In four of five fish taxa studied, the double-crested cormorant took larger prey items than did the pelagic shag. Additionally, its peak nesting period is separated by nearly a month from that of the pelagic shag, which would tend to reduce possible food competition during this critical time.

A similar situation occurs along coastal southwestern Africa, where the bank cormorant and Cape shag occur in sympatry. There, the Cape shag feeds mostly on pelagic shoaling fish; together with the inshore shoaling sand-eels, these comprise more than 80 percent (by mass) of its diet (table 17). The bank cormorant makes almost no use of the pelagic fish population, and instead feeds primarily in the littoral zone, especially among kelp beds. Invertebrates and fish from this zone comprise over 80 percent of its diet. Only in inshore waters having sandy bottoms

TABLE 15   Foods and Foraging Ecology of Four Cormorant and Shag Species in Western North America

	Cormorants		Shags	
Trait	D.-crested (6 studies)	Brandt's (6 studies)	Pelagic (10 studies)	Red-faced (2 studies)
Foods used				
Nonbenthic fish				
Clupeidae (11)	M-3;I-1	M-2;I-1	M-4	—
Embiotocidae (7)	M-2;S-1	S-3;I-1	—	—
Ammodytidae[1] (7)	M-1	M-1	M-3	M-1;S-1
Engraulidae (6)	I-3	M-1;S-1	S-1	—
Salmonidae (5)	I-1	S-1;I-1	M-1;S-1	—
Hexagrammidae (5)	—	I-3	M-1	M-1
Gasterosteidae (2)	M-1;I-1	—	—	—
Argentidae (1)	M-1	—	—	—
All nonbenthic fish:				
Major prey (23)	8	4	9	2
Secondary prey (9)	1	5	2	1
Incidental prey (12)	6	6	—	—
Littoral-benthic fish				
Cottidae (17)	I-3	S-2;I-1	M-8;I-1	M-2
Pleuronectidae (10)	M-1;I-2	M-1;S-1;I-2	M-2	M-1
Pholidae (6)	M-1	—	M-5	—
Gadidae (6)	M-1	M-1	M-2	S-2
Scorpionidae (4)	—	M-1;S-1;I-1	M-1	—
Batrachoididae (3)	I-2	I-1	—	—
Bothidae (3)	I-1	M-1;I-1	—	—
Gobiidae (3)	I-2	—	M-1	—
Stichaeidae (3)	S-1	—	M-1;I-1	—
Agonidae (1)	—	—	M-1	—
Ophidiidae (1)	—	S-1	—	—

are there any evident foraging overlaps between these two species (Williams and Burger, 1978).

Over a large portion of interior Africa the great cormorant is sympatric with the long-tailed cormorant, especially in southern and eastern Africa. These two species differ greatly in size, and studies in Natal by Whitfield and Blaber (1979) indicate that they take foods of significantly differing average mass (table 18). Thus, the long-tailed cormorant caught small fish in shallow waters within 100 meters of shore, whereas the great cormorant took larger fish in deeper water and farther from shore. Both species tended to feed through the day, with an early morning peak and a gradual decline through the day. Although essentially a solitary forager, the long-tailed cormorant sometimes was associated with pelicans, feeding on fishes disturbed by them. Both pink-backed and eastern white pelicans occurred in the area, but only the latter bred there. Its foods were similar taxonomically to those of the cormorants, although having a wide range of sizes, with smaller size classes of fish predominating. Each species' foods and foraging ecology were strongly variable seasonally, according to their reproductive cycles. All three species had early morning (6:00–8:00 A.M.) peak foraging periods, and all spent roughly equal percentages (19–26 percent) of the daytime hours foraging.

	Cormorants		Shags	
Trait	D.-crested (6 studies)	Brandt's (6 studies)	Pelagic (10 studies)	Red-faced (2 studies)
Pomacentridae (1)	—	S-1	—	—
All littoral-benthic fish:				
Major prey (31)	3	4	21	3
Secondary prey (9)	1	6	—	2
Incidental prey (18)	10	6	2	—
Crustaceans				
Decapods (13)	M-1;S-1;I-1	—	M-8	M-2
Amphipods (3)	S-1	—	I-1	S-1
Isopods (2)	S-1	—	I-1	—
All crustaceans:				
Major prey (11)	1	—	8	2
Secondary prey (4)	3	—	—	1
Incidental prey (3)	1	—	2	—
Other traits				
Adult body mass (kg)	ca. 2.1	ca. 2.3	ca. 1.9	ca. 2.0
Foraging sociality	Flexible	Flexible	Asocial	Asocial
Favored foraging habitats	Muddy bays	Open water	Rocky bays	Rocky bays
Favored prey	Schooling fish	Flexible	Solitary	Solitary?
Feeding levels	Middle to upper	Flexible	Substrate	Substrate?
Favored nesting sites (slope)	Gradual	Gradual	Steep	Steep
Nesting season	Jan.–June	Feb.–July	May–July	May–June

NOTES: Families arranged in descending numerical sequence of studies reporting group as prey. For each bird, numbers indicate total reports of use of prey groups, divided by prey level categories (M = major prey for this bird, S = secondary prey, I = incidental). Parenthetical numbers following prey families indicate total numbers of such reports for all species in family. Adapted from tabular summary by Ainley and Sanger (1979) plus additional data on red-faced shags by Hunt, Eppley, Burgeson, and Squibb (1981); a few incidental prey taxa were excluded from the former's summary. Ainley, Anderson, and Kelly (1981) provide additional comparisons for the first three species of birds.
1 Also utilizes sand-bottom littoral habitats as adults.

The long-tailed cormorant is also widely sympatric with the African darter, and the available evidence (table 19) suggests that foraging competition may be much stronger between these two distantly related species than between the long-tailed and the great cormorant (Birkhead, 1978). Based on studies at Lake Kariba, Zimbabwe, it appears that both species fed in littoral areas of this reservoir at depths of about two meters, and over 70 percent of their prey by mass as well as 90 percent by frequency of items ingested consisted of cichlid fish. The darter did tend to take a larger variety of prey species; 86 percent of the cormorants examined had eaten a single fish species, while 31 percent of the darters had fed on a single species and nearly half had fed on three or more species. Birkhead suggested that the absence of evidence for definite foraging segregation in the two species might have resulted from a superabundance of suitable prey, both species evidently foraging on prey that could be taken with minimal effort rather than selecting their prey on the basis of body shape or other apparent criteria.

The little black and little pied cormorants are broadly sympatric in interior Australia, and their foods and foraging ecologies have been studied in two widely sepa-

TABLE 16   Foods and Foraging Ecology of Sympatric Double-crested Cormorant and Pelagic Shag

Factor	Double-crested Cormorant (n = 547)		Pelagic Shag (n = 103)	
	Prey incidence (percent of total for bird)	Prey mass	Prey incidence (percent of total for bird)	Prey mass
Littoral-benthic prey				
Gunnels *Apodichthys* and *Pholis*	46.6	52.6	39.8	48.2
Sand-eel *Ammodytes*	20.5	4.6	31.1	18.9
Prickleback *Lumpenus*	11.5	10.2	3.9	7.3
Sculpin *Leptocottus*	'2.7	5.9	2.9	13.2
Shrimp	—	—	19.4	6.8
Surfperch *Embiotoca* and *Cymatogaster*	16.8	24.0	—	—
Stickleback *Gasterosteus*	0.4	0.1	—	—
Clingfish *Gobisox*	—	—	2.9	5.6
Midwater shoaling prey				
Herring *Clupea*	1.3	2.7	—	—
Salmon *Onchorhynchus*	0.2	0.9	—	—
Anchovy *Engraulis*	0.2	0.1	—	—
Favored feeding depths	Shallows		Shallows	
Favored feeding substrates	Non-rocky		Rocky	
Mean prey mass (g)	12.7		5.5	
Mean adult bird mass (kg)	ca. 2.1		ca. 1.9	
Peak egg-laying period	mid-May		early June	

NOTES: Data of Robertson (1974). Percentages are of relative abundance and relative total mass of prey items regurgitated by chicks.

TABLE 17   Foods of Sympatric Bank Cormorant and Cape Shag

Food	Bank Cormorant (percent total weight of 73 stomachs)	Cape Shag (percent total weight of 204 stomachs)
Pelagic shoaling fish		
Maasbanker *Trachurus*	—	20.4
Anchovy *Engraulis*	0.2	14.2
Pilchard *Sardinops*	—	11.8
Other taxa	0.8	11.5
Inshore sand-bottom fish		
Sand-eel *Ammodytes*	5.4	22.8
Other taxa	6.5	6.9
Littoral kelp fish		
Klipvis (Clinidae)	32.0	2.3
Blennie (Blennidae)	19.1	1.1
Other taxa	9.5	3.4
Unidentified fish	—	5.2
Invertebrates	21.0	3.5
Primary prey	littoral, kelp bed fish	pelagic shoaling fish

NOTES: Data of Rand (1960), as reorganized by Williams and Burger (1978).

TABLE 18   Foods of Sympatric Long-tailed Cormorant and Great Cormorant

	Long-tailed Cormorant (n = 21)	Great Cormorant (n = 155)
	Incidence of prey items (percent of birds)	
Tilapia *Sarotherodon*	52	13
Sole *Solea*	42	—
Bream *Acanthopagrus*	24	19
Thornfish *Terapon*	9	3
Mini-kob *Johnius*	9	17
Mullet (Mugilidae)	5	22
Grunter *Pomadasys*	5	3
Stumpnose *Rhabdosargus*	5	29
Glassnose *Thryssa*	—	26
Other fish taxa	5	8
Unidentified materials	14	15
Individual prey mass range (grams)	1–15	1–214
Modal individual prey mass (grams)	3–4	10–20
Foraging distance from shore (meters)	1–100	10–200
Mean diving duration (seconds)	9	14
Peak foraging period	6–8 A.M.	6–8 A.M.
Mean foraging duration (% of daylight)	26	19
Breeding season duration	December–April	March–June

NOTES: Data of Whitfield and Blaber (1979). Based on analysis of regurgitated pellets. Eastern white pelican foods were also studied, but these data are not included here.

rated areas (Miller, 1979; Dostine and Morton, 1988; summarized in table 20). In New South Wales, the little black cormorant was found to forage mainly (69 percent of total prey mass) on introduced fish that were captured by birds fishing socially in deeper waters. However, the little pied cormorant fed mostly (60 percent of prey) on native crustaceans that were captured by fishing individually on shallow parts of lakes, and in farm ponds and billabongs (oxbows). The little black cormorant evidently fed cooperatively to help capture faster and more elusive prey species, with the birds advancing in a single line directly, driving fish through beds of vegetation toward others that were waiting ahead. When not enough birds were present to form a raft, or when crayfish were exceptionally abundant, the birds also foraged individually. In conjunction with its smaller size and shorter and less strongly hooked bill, the little pied cormorant took smaller prey than the little black cormorant. The little pied is evidently unable to make dives of such long duration as the little black. Very similar results were found in northern Australia by Dostine and Morton (1988), although their sample sizes were considerably smaller and seasonal sampling was restricted. These constraints may help account for the substantial differences in taxonomic distribution of prey and average prey size that were documented in this area as compared with the New South Wales study. They further noted that the little pied cormorant is evidently able to exploit smaller water bodies than other Australian cormorant species because of its short takeoff abilities that are associated with a specialized pectoral girdle structure.

Although the eastern white and Dalmatian pelicans at least historically were

TABLE 19 Foods of Sympatric Long-tailed Cormorant and African Darter

Factor	Long-tailed Cormorant (50 stomachs)		African Darter (21 stomachs)	
	Prey incidence	Prey mass	Prey incidence	Prey mass
	(percent of total for bird)		(percent of total for bird)	
Cichlidae (several genera)	75.9	91.1	74	89.7
Mormyridae (several genera)	13.6	3.2	25.1	5.6
Schilbeidae (*Eutropius*)	3.6	0.8	6.3	3.6
Characidae (*Alestes*)	0.8	1.6	2.9	0.8
Other fish taxa	6.0	3.2	—	—
Total fish species present per stomach (percent of stomachs examined)				
One species	86		31	
Two species	12		19	
Three species	2		37	
Four species	—		12	
Mean foraging depth (m)	2–2.3		ca. 2	
Mean prey length (cm)	7.0		8.0	
Mean individual prey mass (g)	8.0		9.8	
Mean number of ingested prey present	2.7		5.5	
Mean total ingested prey mass (g)	21.6		53.9	
Mean adult body mass (g)	ca. 540		ca. 1,500	
Mean total prey mass/body mass ratio	4.0%		3.6%	

NOTES: Data of Birkhead (1978). Reported incidences of darter prey inexplicably total 108%.

widely sympatric in eastern Europe, and locally still coexist in a few areas such as Romania, no good information is available on their possible foraging competition. However, the eastern white and pink-backed pelicans are also widely sympatric in eastern Africa, and a good deal of information is available on their foods and relative ecological relationships in Ruwenzori National Park, Uganda (Din and Eltringham, 1974b). There on Lake Edward and Lake George the eastern white pelican is migratory, whereas the pink-backed pelican is resident. The daily foraging patterns for the two species were found to be nearly identical, with early morning and late afternoon peaks and a midday loafing period. In both species the commonest fish prey were various cichlid species of *Tilapia* and *Haplochromis*, as well as cichlid fry (table 21). *Tilapia* and adult *Haplochromis* were eaten more frequently by the larger eastern white pelican, whereas the pink-backed pelican more frequently consumed fish fry. A higher proportion of larger *Tilapia* was also consumed by the eastern white pelican, although there was little difference in the average size of the *Haplochromis* consumed. In both species, but especially in the pink-backed pelican, the males tended to take larger prey than the females. Thus, male pink-backed pelicans tended to eat large *Tilapia*, and females ate the smaller *Haplochromis* and even smaller fish fry. This difference is at least in part a result of foraging differences, since whereas the eastern white pelicans tended to forage socially in relatively deep water far from shore, the pink-backed pelicans foraged individually in shallow waters

TABLE 20 Foods of Sympatric Little Black and Little Pied Cormorants

Factor	Little Black	Little Pied
Relative total mass of prey (%)	(n = 625)	(n = 527)[1]
Fish	73.6	38.3
Decapod crustaceans	24.8	60.1
Insects and mollusks	1.6	1.6
Hylid frogs and their larvae	—	0.1
Relative incidence of prey (%)	(n = 11)	(n = 10)[2]
Fish	99.0	54.2
Insects and other invertebrates	1.7	19.0
Crayfish (*Cherax*)	—	15.6
Hylid frogs	—	11.0
Usual foraging location	Larger lakes	Small waters
Feeding technique	Cooperative	Solitary
Mean adult body mass (g)[2]	865	780
Usual diving depth[2]	Often >2 m	Mostly <2 m
Modal length of prey (mm)[3]	20–25	15–20
Primary breeding season		
Northern Australia	December–May	February–August
Southern Australia	September–February	September–May

[1] Data of Miller (1979), from New South Wales. Sample size represents number of stomachs examined.
[2] Data of Trayler, Brothers, and Potter (1989).
[3] Data of Dostine and Morton (1988), from Northern Territory. Sample size represents number of stomachs examined.

near shore, where fish fry and the smaller *Tilapia* were more common. The individual foraging technique of the pink-backed pelican had a higher average success rate (46 percent observed catching success as compared to 20 percent for the eastern white), but the former also spent far more time searching for prey between successive catching attempts (36.5 vs. 6 minutes on average). Thus, the searching advantages of social hunting are evidently counterbalanced by the considerably lower individual catching success rates of participating birds. Since the daily feeding patterns of the two species—as indicated by the percentage of birds observed participating in foraging during hourly intervals throughout the day—were nearly identical (the pink-backed pelican perhaps averaging very slightly less), these two counteracting effects must largely balance out over the long run.

Sex-Related Intraspecific Foraging Differences

In most of the species of pelecaniform birds considered in this book, sex differences in adult body mass and linear adult measurements are relatively slight, averaging about 5–10 percent for *Anhinga*, 5–20 percent for *Phalacrocorax* and *Leucocarbo*, and 10–20 percent for *Pelecanus*. Given the general relationship between body mass and foraging behaviors that seems to exist at least in the cormorants and shags (heavier birds being able to dive deeper and for longer periods than lighter ones), it may not be profitable to search very hard for sexual differences in foods and foraging behav-

TABLE 21   Foods of Sympatric Eastern White and Pink-backed Pelicans

Factor	Eastern White Pelican		Pink-backed Pelican	
	Percent of birds with prey taxa present			
	Males (45)	Females (20)	Males (11)	Females (61)
Tilapia	100	85	100	23
Haplochromis	36	35	9	100
Fish fry	4	30	0	61
Mean total prey mass per bird (grams)				
Tilapia	503		292.7	
Haplochromis	67.2		82.5	
Fish fry	22.5		65.8	
Foraging sociality	Social		Nonsocial	
Mean foraging group size	8.5 (354 groups)		—	
Foraging location	Deeper waters		Near shore	
Mean foraging success rate	20% (n = 430)		46% (n = 396)	
Mean individual prey mass (grams)	10.3		0.7	
Mean total prey mass (grams)	592.9		441	
Mean adult body mass (kilograms)	11.3		5.4	
Total prey mass/adult body mass	5.2%		8.2%	
Estimated daily consumption (grams)	1,201		776	
Daily consumption/adult body mass	10.6%		14.4%	

NOTES: Data of Din and Eltringham (1974b). Based on stomach contents, but excluding birds with empty stomachs and minor prey taxa.

ior except perhaps among the largest species, in which sex-related size differences are generally more evident.

Selander (1966) has pointed out that the bill lengths in male American white pelicans average about 16 percent longer than those of females, whereas in the North American brown pelican the males' bills are only 7–9 percent longer, suggesting to him that sex-related foraging differences might exist in the white pelican that are unlikely to be present in the brown pelican. Similarly large sex-related differences in bill length also are typical of the eastern white pelican (20 percent), Australian pelican (ca. 20 percent), pink-backed pelican (15 percent), and spot-billed pelican (ca. 15 percent). The few available bill length and other linear measurements for the Dalmatian pelican suggest that only an approximate 5–10 percent sexual difference may exist in this species, in spite of the fact that it is the largest of all pelicans.

Surprisingly little information is available on the possibility that sexual differences in foods taken or foraging methods used might exist among these birds as a possible means of reducing intraspecific food competition. As just noted, in a Uganda study the pink-backed pelican and to a lesser degree the eastern white pelican exhibited significant sexual differences in average prey size, with the smaller females consistently taking somewhat smaller-sized prey than did males. All 45 males of the eastern white pelican with prey remains present in their digestive tracts contained the larger *Tilapia* species, whereas these fish were present in only 85 percent of the 20 females that contained prey. More impressively, all of the 11 male pink-backed pelicans had *Tilapia* remains present in their digestive tracts, but this fish taxon was represented in only 14 (23 percent) of the 61 females. All 61 females had remains representing the smaller *Haplochromis* species as well as unidentified fish fry, but only one (9 percent) of the males had eaten any *Haplochromis*, and none had eaten any fish fry. These rather remarkable sex differences suggest that males and females had utilized significantly different foraging areas, with males probably foraging in deeper waters supporting larger prey fish, whereas females probably foraged closer to shore where smaller fish are more prevalent. Since the eastern white pelican is more prone to forage socially, such sex differences are less likely to be present in that species.

With respect to the bank cormorant, in which breeding males average about 17 percent heavier than females, there are significant sex-related differences in lengths of foraging bouts (those of females averaging longer) and in the number of foraging bouts per day (males averaging more), as mentioned earlier (Cooper, 1985b). It is thus possible that the two sexes were foraging at different depths and perhaps on different prey, although evidence on this point is lacking. In the flightless Galapagos cormorant, adult males of which average about 15 percent heavier than females, the two sexes were observed to be foraging in the same locations. However, males dived to greater average depths and remained submerged for longer average durations than did females (Tindle, 1984).

Age-Related Intraspecific Foraging Differences

Although information on foraging success in cormorants is subject to interpretation problems caused by underwater swallowing of prey, there is some evidence of age-related hunting efficiency variations in cormorants, if not differences in foraging methods or foods taken. Studying the olivaceous cormorant, Morrison, Slack, and Shanley (1978) found that the apparent foraging success of adult birds was significantly higher than that of first-year birds still in immature plumage. This conclusion was based on the frequency with which birds emerged from dives with fish in the bill (averaging 9.9 and 12.1 percent of all dives for immature birds in two study areas, as compared with 17.7 and 18.5 percent for adult-plumaged birds in the same areas). Additionally, adults had a higher rate of catching success per minute (averaging higher in both areas, but significantly so only in one), and immatures spent a greater proportion of the daytime hours foraging than did adults. Diving abilities, as estimated by dive durations and durations of pauses between dives, were apparently similar in the two age groups, which suggests that the age-related foraging differences were the result of inferior fish-catching abilities among immatures rather than inferior diving abilities. Evidently the younger birds were thus forced to spend more time foraging to compensate for their lower prey capture rates.

There is good reason to believe that in at least some pelican species, such as the brown pelican, foraging efficiencies gradually improve with age and experience, as was first suggested by Orians (1969). Schnell, Woods, and Ploger (1983) observed that adults captured prey at a significantly higher overall rate than did young birds (83.9 percent of 905 prey capture attempts, vs. 74.7 percent of 1,544 attempts), and apparently also foraged for longer periods during daytime hours, although statistics were not obtained on this point. In his study of relative foraging success of juvenile and adult brown pelicans, Brandt (1984) found that both age groups fed on the same prey base, but with greatly differing efficiencies. Adults either must have been more skilled in catching prey than were juveniles or were consistently able to select more susceptible prey. Coblentz (1985) observed that young birds spent less time in the air before beginning a dive than did adults, and seemingly were either less patient than adults or less able to evaluate their relative chances for achieving success.

Brandt (1984) observed that juvenile brown pelicans were influenced by the presence of foraging adults when selecting their own feeding locations, and vice versa. However, whereas the presence of adults foraging in an area had a net positive influence on juvenile foraging efficiency, the presence of feeding juveniles resulted in a slightly decreased adult efficiency. Not surprisingly, adults tended to avoid foraging in an area that was being most heavily used by juveniles, suggesting that limited age-based foraging segregation may indeed be present in this species.

CHAPTER 5

Social Behavior

The social behavior of pelecaniform birds has received a good deal of attention from ethologists, of which perhaps the two most important contributions are those of Schreiber (1977), on the egocentric and social behavior of the brown pelican, and van Tets (1965), a more general survey of social behavior in the entire order Pelecaniformes. That of Schreiber is more useful for providing a convenient descriptive or functional classification of pelecaniform social activities, whereas van Tets has attempted to organize these signals on the basis of their probable evolutionary (nonritualized) motor pattern origins, regardless of their apparent present-day functional roles in communication. My own preference is to classify avian social behaviors into three broadly functional, albeit interconnected, groupings: agonistic (behaviors dominated by attack or escape tendencies), cooperative (reciprocally beneficial as well as seemingly altruistic behaviors), and epigamic (sexual and parental behaviors).

Agonistic Behaviors

Threat and attack behavior. In all the groups considered here, the bill provides the primary method of attack and threat. In pelicans, where it is unusually long and provided with a hooklike tip, it is an especially effective weapon. In the brown pelican it is opened slightly at the tip and is rapidly thrust forward toward the opponent, as the mandibles are snapped together with a loud popping noise (Schreiber, 1977), and similar behavior occurs in the American white pelican (Schaller, 1964). During fights the two birds may grab at one another's bills (see figure 104). Lower intensities of pelican threat behavior consist of bill pointing toward the opponent, in either a closed-bill threat-pointing or an open-bill threat-gaping display (figure 22). Vestjens (1977a) recognized three intensities of threat in the Australian pelican, including low-threat "pointing" with the bill closed, medium-threat "gaping" with the bill open, and strong-threat "thrusting," with the bill widely open and the lower mandible bowed (see figure 102). In the American white pelican about 95 percent of all agonistic blows are directed toward the "horn" on the opponent's beak, sug-

Figure 22. Threat behavior of pelicans, including threat-pointing by the spot-billed pelican (left, after a photo in Gee, 1975), and threat-gaping by the Dalmatian pelican (right, after a sketch by van Tets, 1965).

gesting that this structure may function as a target that orients the opponent's bill toward an area where it will do the least amount of damage (Knopf, 1976a).

Aggressive postures of cormorants are similarly easy to recognize. Actual fighting involves grabbing at one another with their bills, sometimes locking beaks, and occasionally drawing blood. This often occurs when the birds are fighting over nest sites. During less intense threatening behavior, the body is held close to the ground, the wings are partly spread and also held close to the ground, and the head and bill are oriented toward the opponent. Depending upon the species, the bill may be opened, exposing the sometimes colorful gape, or the bill may be closed but the throat skin may be stretched and exposed. Additionally, the head and bill may be shaken, moved up and down, or some combination of these actions, which are often supplemented with vocalizations. Such displays may be performed both intra- and interspecifically, the latter for example toward crows, ravens, or gulls (van Tets, 1959).

Fighting in darters consists of grabbing an opponent's bill, or stabbing at an intruder's head and neck. There are at least three levels of threat display as well. During mild threat, the bird simply points its bill at the intruder, and at slightly higher levels may also gape and sometimes hiss. At medium levels of threat there is a "chase-threat," during which the bird moves toward the intruder with open bill and raised wings, calling as it goes. In "snapping threat" the bird snaps its bill toward the neck and head of an intruder for several seconds, but without actually touching it (Vestjens, 1975).

Ritualized aggressive displays. Besides these rather obvious forms of aggressive behavior, one additional putative agonistic display is the postlanding display of cormorants and anhingas. This is a distinctive posture assumed immediately after landing, typically with the anterior body raised and the head and neck briefly held in a characteristic way. This display is probably of composite or mosaic, but at least partially agonistic, origin. The posture is apparently a combination of normal bodily adjustments related to the recovery of balance following the shock of landing,

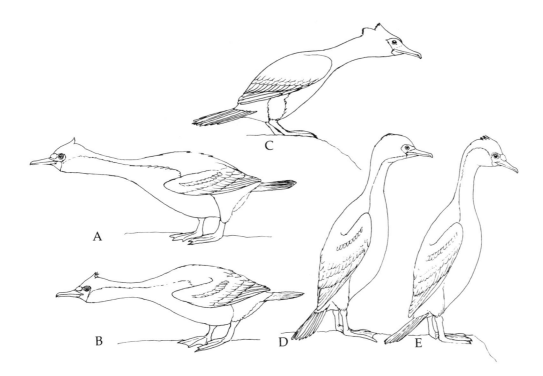

plus postural preparation for possible attack-escape behavior. The latter function may be particularly significant for individuals that have just landed in a crowded roost or nesting colony. The posture may additionally serve to provide species recognition, individual recognition, to draw the attention of actual or potential mates, and perhaps to help habituate neighboring pairs of nesting birds to one another (van Tets, 1965). In various cliff-nesting shags the postlanding posture is rather variable (figure 23), and within a species it may exhibit some individual variation depending upon the characteristics of the landing substrate (Rasmussen, 1989). The postlanding display is also performed by cormorants following a hop, rather than an actual flight, and hopping may be thought of as a reduced and symbolic flight. Hopping occurs in a variety of social contexts, such as during perching site contests, courtship, nest relief, and the gathering of nesting materials. Postlanding and associated posthopping displays have not been observed among pelicans (van Tets, 1965).

Conspicuous alarm behavior among these groups is rather surprisingly poorly developed, in view of their generally high degree of coloniality. In general, alarm calls appear to be nearly wholly lacking among them, although the little pied cormorant does utter a call in response to aerial predators (Mathews and Fordham, 1986). Otherwise, alarm may simply be indicated by an increasing postural readiness to take flight, or by the performance of various apparent "displacement" activities (see figure 36).

Figure 23. Variation in postlanding displays of shags, including horizontal postures in the Antarctic (A) and Chilean (B) races of the imperial shag, diagonal posture in the red-faced shag (C), and erect postures in the Bounty Island shag (D) and the Chilean race of the imperial shag (E). After sketches in van Tets (1959) and Rasmussen (1989).

Cooperative Behavior

Cooperative social behavior in these birds is rather limited. Besides the social and seemingly cooperative fishing behavior of such species as the white pelicans,

Brandt's cormorant, little black cormorant, and guanay shag, there are less clear-cut examples of social foraging that may simply represent aggregations of birds at favorable foraging sites. Social foraging was discussed in the previous chapter, and thus details need not be repeated here. Interspecific relationships are more complex. Brandt's cormorants at times are guided to schools of fish by observing glaucous-winged gulls (*Larus glaucescens*) hovering above fish forced to the surface by common murres (*Uria aalge*) (van Tets, 1959), and double-crested cormorants may be similarly attracted to areas used by foraging terns (Lewis, 1929). However, gulls may also harass the cormorants as soon as they emerge at the surface holding fish in the beak, forcing them to drop their prey.

One obvious potential advantage of coloniality in intraspecific foraging may also be related to food finding. Knopf (1976a, 1976b) suggested that inexperienced American white pelicans often join flocks of more experienced individuals, which then lead the less experienced birds to food sources. When a bird is relieved at its nest, it will fly directly to the rather distant feeding grounds, where it may either join in a foraging flock or independently select a new foraging area. Joining a feeding flock is more likely to be productive than selecting a new one, as evidenced by the fact that birds rarely choose to forage on their own.

Social formation flying, well developed in pelicans and most if not all cormorants, has been mentioned in chapter 3 and its mutual energy-conserving benefits noted. It has been suggested that aerial courtship might occur in the anhinga, or that some other social significance to social soaring in this species might exist, but there seems to be no recent evidence to support this idea (Allen, 1961).

Social roosting is common in most if not all other pelecaniform birds. It is probably a result of chance aggregations developing in ecologically suitable roosting sites combined with the benefits of such an assemblage for flock vigilance. Alarm calls are evidently completely lacking in all these species; evidently collective awareness of danger is transmitted by visual signals involving postural changes associated with possible imminent escape flight. Ritualized pretakeoff alert and crouching postures (the look-crouch-leap sequence of van Tets, 1965) are sometimes fairly well developed in cormorants and darters, but apparently are wholly lacking in pelicans. This difference may simply be size-related, the large and slow-moving pelicans both being generally less vulnerable to most predators and also requiring a good deal more time and space for their takeoffs.

Social nesting in these birds might well be hypothesized as a mutually beneficial activity, to the extent that such groups provide a more effective alarm and defense mechanism than would be available to solitarily nesting pairs. Additionally, the collective sexual and social activities of the group may help to stimulate and synchronize nesting (the so-called Darling effect), thus helping the population as a whole by compressing the overall nesting activity within an ecologically optimal time frame. But to my knowledge there is no good evidence to support such ideas among these birds. Thus, Knopf (1979) found no evidence for the Darling effect among American white pelicans, based on relative hatching synchronization of larger versus smaller colonies. He also found that mean productivity per clutch was comparable between colonies of differing sizes and located in different habitats. The general evidence leads me to believe that colony size and colony development depend almost wholly on the richness of the foraging resource and the number of suitable nesting sites. Chapter 7 provides some information on colony size variations among North American pelecaniform species, and these data do not obviously support the existence of minimal or optimal colony sizes for any of these species.

A related possibility is that mixed-species colonial nesting may offer some advantages. Darters often nest among colonies of cormorants, herons, ibises, and other colonial ciconiiform birds (Bowen et al., 1962; Burger, Miller, and Hahn, 1978), and it is possible that benefits of increased predator awareness might accrue to one or more of these species under such mixed-nesting conditions. However, I am not aware of any studies that have yet addressed this point.

Fledgling young of many species of colonially nesting pelecaniform birds, especially pelicans, often form aggregated "pods" or creches. It is probable that participating in such pods may be individually beneficial to the participants. Knopf (1976a, 1976b) reported that young American white pelicans are vulnerable to attack by still-nesting adults, and the chicks' survival is dependent in part on a synchronous breakdown of adult territorial behavior. By joining a group of similar-sized young the fledgling pelicans are less likely to intrude on potentially dangerous nesting birds that are still holding territories. They may also possibly be somewhat less vulnerable to predators under such conditions, although I am not aware of any evidence to that effect.

I am likewise not aware of any evidence that altruistic behavior of any kind is directed toward individuals other than direct offspring among these groups of birds.

Epigamic Behavior

As defined here, epigamic behavior includes various activities that might most conveniently be divided for discussion purposes into prefertilization behavior, nest- and egg-centered behavior, and parental phases of the overall reproductive cycle. Prefertilization behaviors would include male territorial advertisement behavior (which in these species is all nest or nest-site associated), plus early stages of pair-forming behavior. Copulation attempts and successful copulatory behavior typically begin during this pair-forming phase and continue through the egg-laying period. The second phase would include activities such as nest building and nest maintenance, nest defense, nest relief, egg laying, egg tending, and incubation. The final parental phase of epigamic behavior would include chick brooding, feeding of the young, and related brood-rearing activities.

The earlier, more socially interactive, generally taxon-specific, and more obviously highly ritualized phases of the reproductive cycle will primarily be discussed here; the later, more pair-restricted and nest-oriented phases of breeding behavior involving nest building, egg laying, incubation, and brood rearing are deferred until the next chapter.

Male Advertisement and Pair-Forming Behavior

Based on his own and earlier observations of cormorant and shag behavior, van Tets (1959) provided a typical "full courtship sequence," which he said was essentially the same for all three of the species that he had studied (Brandt's and double-crested cormorants and pelagic shag). First, the male approaches a potential nest site with nesting material, which he then places on the site. He threatens and returns the threats of any nearby territorial birds, and begins to perform his nest site advertisement display (which van Tets initially called "wing-flipping" but later "wing-waving," a more descriptive and more generally suitable designation). These male site advertisement displays tend to be quite elaborate and highly

Figure 24. Comparison of male nest site advertising displays (left) and pair-bonding (mate recognition) displays (right) in the pelagic shag (A), Brandt's cormorant (B), and double-crested cormorant (C). After sketches in van Tets (1959).

species-specific (figures 24 and 25), especially when they make use of the bird's often equally conspicuous and distinctive gape, gular pouch, forehead, eye ring, and iris coloration. In many shag species the male site advertisement display involves a backward head tossing and calling but not wing waving, and is called "gargling." Some other variations are also known to exist among cormorants and shags. In any case, the displays cease as soon as a mate or potential mate arrives, which is typically marked by her elaborate postlanding display and several hops toward the nest. The male performs a recognition display toward the female, who in turn inspects both him and his nest site. During this critical period the birds may move their heads alternately past one another, or various other pair-bonding displays may be performed that seem to emphasize the species-specific attributes of the head region.

Figure 25. Advertising displays of shags and cormorants, including gargling of the imperial shag (above), and wing waving of the great cormorant (below). After photos by Frank S. Todd.

Once paired, the mates jointly threaten other nearby nesting birds, and may sit together in the nest with their necks crossed at the base. Eventually the male leaves the nest by hopping or flying away to gather more nesting material. This process is repeated many times, with the female performing her recognition display each time the male arrives and then taking the material from him to incorporate it into the nest. Their roles may also be reversed when the male is on the nest and accepts nesting material from the returning female. The male also typically presents nesting material to the female both before and after copulation. Nest site advertisement and copulation both cease after there are eggs in the nest.

Copulation in cormorants and shags takes place on or near the nest and is evidently limited to paired birds. In the European shag, mountings without successful copulations have been observed as early as 40 days before the first egg was laid, and complete copulations as early as 20 days before the first egg. This would suggest that copulations may play some role in pair bonding, at least in that species. In the great cormorant, European shag, guanay shag, and Cape shag, reversed copulations sometimes occur, with the female on top of the male (Kortlandt, 1940; Vogt, 1942; Snow, 1963; Berry, 1976). Indeed, reversed mounting may be fairly widespread taxonomically in the Phalacrocoracidae and perhaps serves to assist in pair bonding, whereas true mounting may indicate that pair bonding has already been completed (Berry, 1976). As the male mounts the female, he grips her neck or the back of her head with his bill, depresses his tail, but does not wave or raise his wings, at least in the cormorant and shag species so far observed. During treading the female may insert her bill into the nest material, presumably to keep her neck and head steady, and holds her tail slightly sideways, rhythmically opening and closing the cloacal aperture. Copulations cease soon after the last egg is laid.

Judging from the account by Allen (1961) for the anhinga, and that of Vestjens (1975) for the Australian darter, pair bonding in the darters takes a similar form to that of cormorants and shags. Males begin by seeking out a suitable nesting site, which may be an old nest or a new site. After collecting enough twigs to make a preliminary nest, or even before the nest site is selected, the males begin site advertisement displays of wing waving and snap-bowing (see figures 88, 89, and 92). Females select their mates by visiting those areas occupied by displaying males, sometimes returning several times to visit the same males before finally apparently selecting one. When a female Australian darter has selected a male, she hops closer to him. On reaching the display site or nest she performs a "darting" display toward him with opened bill and begins to call. Males in turn respond by calling and continuing to perform wing waving and snap-bowing, plus feather-ruffling and bill-pointing postures. These are followed by mutual bill-rubbing and neck-rubbing displays. The pair-bonding process is apparently very similar in the anhinga, with neck rubbing, bill rubbing, and pointing being similar in both species. Unilateral allopreening of the mate (in the darter) or mutual preening by the pair (in the anhinga) has been reported in both species. Although mutual calling has not been specifically described during the early pair-forming phases of the anhinga, the "kink-throating" display of this species is evidently an important part of the interactions of paired birds (van Tets, 1965), and Owre (1972) emphasized that both sexes call during later mate-greeting and nest relief ceremonies, so calling very probably also occurs during the pair-bonding process.

Copulation may begin soon after the female darter initially enters the male's nest or nesting site, and she initiates this by crouching and lowering her neck. The male hops on her back with his wings partly open and usually grasps her bill with his, simultaneously pulling her head up and back. In most of the 23 observed cases, the male Australian darter thus held the female's bill and head back during copulation; in a few he held a green twig in his bill (Vestjens, 1975; and in Cramp and Simmons, 1977). Both sexes partially cock and spread their wings and tail during copulation, and in the Australian darter the tail may also be opened and closed by both sexes. Twig presentation by the male to the female just prior to copulation has been observed in the anhinga (Harriott, 1970). Reversed mounting has not yet been described in darters. Copulation is very common in the early stages of pair formation, but gradually diminishes as the nest is completed. After the first copulation, the female as well as the male begins to gather nesting material, but once the nest has been established at least one of the birds always remains at the site. This is usually the female, who adds material to the nest as it is brought in by the male.

Pair formation in most species of pelicans is still very inadequately described. It is clearly a subtle process, and may be obscured further by simple retention of mates of the previous year. Grummt (1984) mentioned a pair of captive eastern white pelicans that had remained mated since 1963, and another that had bred together regularly since 1969. At least in brown pelicans pair formation takes a rather similar form to that of cormorants and darters (Schreiber, 1977). The adult male selects and occupies a potential nest in the colony and from this site begins to perform his advertisement display, which is head swaying. Males remain on their site almost continuously without feeding, leaving it only for brief flights, until a mate is obtained or the site is abandoned. Nearby branches are needed as part of the nesting territory, for future resting, preening, and sleeping by the nonincubating (or "out") bird, and this perch as well as the nest itself is defended.

Mate selection in pelicans is evidently accomplished by the female, who selects the male (and/or the nest). After a female lands and is initially allowed by the male to remain on the perch, she intrudes on the nest itself. Males must be aggressive enough to prevent other males from usurping the site, but not so aggressive as to chase away the almost identical-appearing females. Interactions between the potential pelican pair involves a variety of displays (swaying, bowing, upright, and head turning in the brown pelican) through which the aggressiveness of the male diminishes and the assertiveness of the female increases. Early stages of courtship in brown pelicans are marked by nest building, which typically involves a "nest material presentation" display to the female (figure 26), which is always performed following a return by the male to the nest with materials. The female accepts the material with a greeting display (head swaying in brown pelicans) and adds it to the nest. This nest presentation material is evidently an important pair-bonding activity, rather than necessarily contributing significantly to the nest structure itself.

In the Australian pelican and at least some of the other "white pelicans" no clear territoriality or nest site choice is evident before pair bonding. Instead, males follow females in small groups, engaging in "courtship walks," "courtship swims," and "courtship flights." In the process of these activities the most dominant (or perhaps most favored) male takes up the optimum position, which is immediately behind the leading female. Similar mobile courtship groups have also been observed in American white pelicans, eastern white pelicans, and perhaps also pink-backed pelicans (Vestjens, 1977a). However, the tree-nesting pink-backed pelican is behaviorally much like the brown pelican in its male site advertisement behavior. This especially includes a loud beak clapping and associated backward head tossing (Burke and Brown, 1970; Din and Eltringham, 1974b), also sometimes called gargling, which greatly increases in intensity when a female lands nearby.

Figure 26. Nest building by a female Dalmatian pelican (right), as her mate brings nest material while bill-raising. After photos in Grummt (1984).

As in cormorants, copulation in pelicans occurs only at the actual or prospective nest site. No special premounting displays have been described in any of the pelican species so far studied, although a generalized "mating-challenge" behavior has been mentioned by Klös (1968) for the eastern white, Dalmatian, pink-backed, and spot-billed pelicans. In all these species the behavior is very similar, and it does not differ between the two sexes. According to Grummt (1984) this mating-challenge is very similar to the movements used during nest construction. Mounting is achieved by the male grabbing the female's neck, her head, or even her bill, and then climbing on her back. The female huddles down, spreads her wings, and raises her spread tail.

In brown pelicans, mounting attempts by the male sometimes begin as soon as the female has been admitted to the nest and before any nesting materials have been gathered. Mounting also continues through the nest-building period but rarely occurs after the laying of the first egg. In the brown pelican the male mounts from behind and waves or flaps his wings while mounted. He simultaneously grasps the female's neck and rubs his cloacal area on the female's back until she turns her tail to one side and allows access to her cloaca. The wing waving probably helps the male maintain his balance and also may add downward thrust, whereas the rubbing activity may help synchronize the copulatory behavior of the two sexes. There appear to be only very minor differences in copulatory behavior among the other pelican species. The male may either flap his wings for balance or lower them over the female, also probably to help steady himself (figure 27). In the Australian pelican, which nests on the ground, the copulation site becomes the nest site, and after one or more copulations both sexes begin scooping out a nest scrape with their mandibles (Vestjens, 1977a).

Schreiber (1977) never observed reversed mounting in brown pelicans and seemingly doubted that it normally ever occurs in that species or even in other pelicans, even though van Tets (1965) suggested that it may be typical of all pelecaniform birds.

Mate Recognition, Pair Maintenance, and Nest Relief Behavior

In all the groups considered in this book, breeding territories and associated territorial advertisement defense are almost entirely limited to an area immediately surrounding the nest. Nests composed of twigs and branches are actually constructed only by darters, some shrub- or tree-nesting cormorants, and a few tree-nesting pelicans. Even these arboreally nesting species are more prone to use preexisting nests of their own or other species, if such are already available, than to construct their own. Most shags construct nests of soft vegetation such as marine algae and other "seaweeds" that may be gathered from shoreline edges, stolen from other nests, or occasionally obtained by subsurface marine diving. Many marine cormorants and shags that live along arid coastlines have nests that primarily represent gradual buildups of guano, to which algae and other soft vegetation are added and become imbedded, eventually drying to a cementlike hardness. Nest building in the European shag has two behavioral components. One is a nest-quivering movement (also used in ritualized form during display), a lateral movement of the head

Figure 27. Copulatory behavior of pelicans, including the Dalmatian pelican (A, B), pink-backed pelican (C), and eastern white pelican (D). After photos in Grummt (1984).

and beak while material is inserted into the nest, and the second is a cup-shaping movement done as the sitting bird draws its bill back toward itself (Snow, 1963).

In many if not all of the species detailed in this book, both sexes are involved to some degree in the gathering of nesting materials, even though the quantities used for the nest may range greatly, and the male usually does most of the gathering. However, the female takes the primary responsibility for incorporating these materials in the nest. Thus, in the Australian pelican, which may nest either on the ground or in low bushes, the female typically gathers all the material available in the area immediately around the nest that can be reached without actually leaving the nest, whereas the male may obtain materials from more than a kilometer away. When the male returns with material in his bill he performs a greeting display to his mate, and the material is then added to the nest.

The nest or nest site is clearly of great importance in pair bonding and pair bond maintenance in all the pelecaniform groups. The behavior of the sitting or "in" bird differs markedly from that of the standing or "out" bird, regardless of sex (Kortlandt, 1959); thus there is "positional diethism" in these species. As a result, most or all of the social displays associated with the nest site (greeting, nest relief, etc.) may be performed by either bird, depending upon its position relative to the nest rather than its sex (van Tets, 1965).

Nest relief behavior is present in all pelecaniform species, since both sexes must participate in incubation and brooding to varying degrees. Such interactions are usually initiated by the in (incubating) bird but occasionally by the out (approaching) bird, at least in brown pelicans. For example, among nearly 200 observed nest site encounters of the brown pelican, the in bird most often initiated the interaction with head-swaying (41 percent), bowing (30 percent), or head-turning (26 percent) displays. The out bird often responded to such head swaying with similar head swaying (36 percent) or with an upright display (45 percent). It most often responded to bowing with head swaying (58 percent), and to head turning with similar head turning (57 percent). These seemingly rather flexible signals and responses suggest that a variety of message elements are innate in both partners. These elements perhaps represent a broad continuum of tendencies ranging from aggression or attack to submission or escape, as well as possibly reflecting tendencies to remain for association and interaction at the nest site (Schreiber, 1977).

In cormorants, postlanding displays represent the usual means by which a returning bird greets its mate at the nest site. Thus, in the European shag this display (the "landing gape" of Snow, 1963; see figure 81) is performed by birds of either sex when approaching their own nest. A territorial male may even perform this display before it has a mate, and whether or not any other birds are nearby. Even after the young have left the nest, a bird may perform the landing gape toward its mate on the sea rocks, or toward its own young. During nest relief in European shags the out bird also usually performs a "sitting gape" display when it takes possession of the nest, which occurs as soon as the in bird stops performing it. "Throat clicking" (now more generally called "kink-throating") is also used in situations where a male is inviting his mate to approach, or as a greeting by a bird returning to its mate on the nest. Frequently the bird returns while holding a piece of nesting material in its bill. When the returning bird presents such nesting materials to its mate, the mate accepts them and performs a nest-quivering display, a ritualized movement that is related to functional nest-building behavior, as noted earlier (Snow, 1963).

In the Australian darter (and presumably other darters as well), nest relief behavior occurs from the laying of the first egg throughout the incubation period and continues during the brooding of small chicks. It consists of a minor variant of the usual mate-greeting behavior performed between pair members earlier in the season (see figure 92). When a bird arrives to relieve its mate, it utters several "kah" notes before alighting. The in bird responds with similar calls, while the arriving bird hops from branch to branch toward the nest, now uttering clicking (kink-throating) calls. When its partner arrives at the nest, the in bird bends its neck into a sharp S-shape, with the bill along the foreneck and the hindneck against the back. The wings are lifted slightly and the tail is diagonally raised. The newly arrived bird may also adopt this "pointing" posture. After ruffling its feathers, the sitting bird stands up and is quickly replaced. Some variations have also been seen. Thus, snap-bowing may additionally be performed (mainly by males). Wing waving (a major male site advertisement display) is also sometimes performed by male darters during nest relief ceremonies. Nest relief behavior changes somewhat during the incubation period, when males cease performing the snap-bow and wing waving (Vestjens, 1975). Nest relief by the anhinga is much less well described but apparently is rather similar to that of the Australian darter (Burger, Miller, and Hahn, 1978).

Comparative Display Functions

The functions of social communication in pelecaniform birds, like those of other strongly social birds, must necessarily be highly diverse. Among these are such biologically important functions as facilitating species identification (for avoidance of hybridization), sex identification (for avoidance of same-sex pairings), announcement of internal state (for advertisement of breeding condition and pairing status), self-advertisement (for establishment, advertisement, and defense of a nesting site), recognition of mate and/or family (for efficient pair and family interactions), and coordination of group activities (for maximally benefiting from group membership).

Species identification and its associated potential for facilitating reproductive isolation is generally not a problem for the birds under consideration here. In all the cases where cormorant and shag sympatry exists, the associated sympatric species differ appreciably in facial appearance as well as bill and foot coloration, and there are no known hybrids or interspecific matings among cormorants and shags (Pierotti, 1987). Although some sympatry exists among the white pelicans (eastern white with pink-backed in Africa, and with Dalmatian in Eurasia), no wild pelican hybrids are yet known. However, in captivity hybrids have been produced between the brown and American white pelicans, the pink-backed and Dalmatian pelicans, the eastern white and Dalmatian pelicans, and probably between the eastern white and pink-backed pelicans (Grummt, 1989), all of which suggests that a potential for pelican hybridization in the wild may be present in areas of breeding sympatry. No sympatry exists among the darters.

Sexual recognition among adult individuals is quite simple in the darters, where sexual dichromatism is unusually well developed. Among pelicans a substantial amount of sexual dimorphism in overall body size and especially in relative bill length also exists in most species, making visual sex discrimination fairly easy, even for humans. The cormorants and shags exhibit the least degree of sexual dimorphism and dichromatism among these three pelecaniform groups, and both relative overall size and behavioral differences between the sexes are probably important in cormorants and shags for providing such discrimination.

Advertisement of internal reproductive state and pairing status is facilitated in all three groups primarily by changes of coloration and structure in adult soft parts, including seasonal enlargements or engorgements of specific facial areas such as papillae, caruncles, eye rings, forehead knobs, and the like, as well as associated changes in the coloration of facial and gular skin, bills, eyes, and feet. It is these "signaling devices" that tend to be conspicuously exposed and variously flaunted during male site advertisement displays. Both their behavioral use and their structural development are probably controlled by seasonal variations in gonadal steroid levels. The low level of sexual dimorphism in these structures is no doubt related to the high incidence of monogamy in all species, and to the important role of the female in helping with the defense of the nesting site as soon as pair bonding has occurred.

Signals announcing the establishment and maintenance of a nesting site are closely related to the previous internal-state advertising function. In all three groups of birds the acquisition of a nesting site is a sine qua non of successful breeding. Competition for nesting sites is usually so intense that only those males with relatively high testosterone levels and associated levels of aggressive defense of nesting territories are likely to succeed in establishing desirable nest sites.

Mate and family recognition signals must persist for longer periods than those associated with establishment and defense of nesting territories. Often, however, the two are fairly closely related—mate-to-mate interactions apparently reflect lower levels of agonistic interaction than do male site announcement signals, but nonetheless are apparently often derived from the same or similar tendencies (Schreiber, 1977). This makes a hard and fast distinction between male advertisement signals and pair interaction signals impossible to attain. Schreiber (1977) attempted a "message analysis" of various brown pelican displays. He judged that as many as six (out of eight possible) different message elements might be incorporated into a single display such as bowing, although the relative message content strengths varied considerably among the six. Generally, mate interaction signals tend to be reciprocally stimulated, and they are often performed in the same or similar manners in both sexes, either simultaneously or sequentially. Differing levels of display intensity perhaps represent significant variables in transmitting specific message contents among these signals.

Signals influencing the coordination of group activities are of course unlikely to be influenced by age, sex, season, or internal state if they are to be effective in their function. Pretakeoff, in-flight, and general alarm signals must be unequivocally interpretable if they are to be effective.

With some of these ideas and cautions in mind, a summary (table 22) of the taxonomic distribution of many of the primary displays of cormorants, darters, and pelicans is presented. It will be necessary for the reader to refer to the individual species accounts to understand and visualize many of the display names, and some fairly widespread but confusing displays are excluded from the summary. It should further be noted that this is a highly tentative summary, which is likely to be modified in the future as additional information and understanding of pelecaniform social signals are developed.

TABLE 22 Taxonomic Distribution of Major Cormorant, Darter, and
Pelican Displays

Cormorants and Shags	Darters	Pelicans
Male advertisement (mainly nest site) displays		
Wing waving	Wing waving	
Long-tailed c. (silent?)	Both species	
Brandt's c. (silent)		
Black-faced c. (silent)		
Double-crested c. (vocal)		
Neotropic c. (vocal)		
Pied c. (vocal)		
Little black c. (vocal)		
Great c. (silent)		
Imperial s. (rudimentary)		
Rock s. (silent)		
Pelagic s. (silent)		
Red-faced s. (silent)		
Spotted s. (silent)		
Pitt Is. s. (silent)		
Gargling (or "throw-back")		Bill clapping (or "gargling")
Cape s. (vocal)		Pink-backed p.
Imperial s. (vocal)		Spot-billed p.
New Zealand shags[1]		
European s. (silent)		
Wing crouching (vocal)		
Little pied c.		
Swing-pointing (silent)		Head swaying/wagging
Spotted s.		Eastern white p.
Pitt Is. s.		Pink-backed p.
		Spot-billed p.
		Brown p.
		Pouch swinging
		Australian p.
Bowing	Snap bowing	
Little pied c. (vocal)	Anhinga	
Brandt's c. (silent)		
Rock s. (vocal)		
European s. (silent)		
Spotted s. (silent)		
Pitt Is. s. (silent)		
	Twig grasping	Bill open (silent)
	Both species	Pink-backed p.
Aquatic dance (bisexual)		
Galapagos c.		
Individual recognition and pair-bonding displays (usually bisexual)		
Kink-throating	Kink-throating	Pouch flapping/rippling
Most species[2]	Anhinga	Eastern white p.
	Darter?	Australian p.

(*continued*)

TABLE 22   (*Continued*)

Cormorants and Shags	Darters	Pelicans
Gaping (bisexual)		
Many species[3]		
Pointing (bisexual)	Pointing (males)	Upright[4]
Brandt's c.	Both species	Brown p.
Double-crested c.		Head up[4]
Neotropic c.		Eastern white p.
Great c.		American white p.
Pied c.		Bill raising[4]
Little black c.		Eastern white p.
Spotted s.		Pink-backed p.
Pitt Is. s.		Dalmatian p.
Sky-upright (bisexual)		Australian p.
Spotted s.		American white p.
Pitt Is. s.		
	Darting	
	Darter (females)	
		Courtship walk/flight
		Eastern white p.
		Australian p.
		American white p.
Gargling (bisexual)		
Black-faced c. (vocal)		
Pied c. (vocal)		
Little black c. (vocal)		
Galapagos c. (silent)		
Great c. (vocal)		
Black-faced c. (silent)		
Mutual neck swaying		Bowing[5]
Great c. ("pointing")		Eastern white p.
		Pink-backed p.
		Spot-billed p.
		Australian p.
		American white p.
		Brown p.
Mutual neck twining	Mutual neck rubbing	
Long-tailed c.	Both species	
Pied c.		
Imperial s.		
Allopreening	Allopreening	
Long-tailed c.	Anhinga	
Great c.		
Pied c.		
Rock s.		
European s.		
Red-legged s.		
Mutual billing	Mutual billing	
Long-tailed c.	Both species	
Pied c.		
Imperial s.		
Head lowering (bisexual)		Mutual head bobbing
Pied c.		Pink-backed p.

TABLE 22 (Continued)		
Cormorants and Shags	Darters	Pelicans

Imperial s.		
New Zealand shags[1]		
Beg-waggle (bisexual)		
Pied c.		
Mutual head wagging		Head turning
Imperial s.		Spot-billed p.
Rock s.		Brown p.
Feather presentation	Greeting call	Prelanding call
Cape s. (bisexual)	Both species	American white p.
Agonistic displays (usually bisexual)		
Gaping threat	Gaping threat	Gaping threat
All species?	Anhinga	Pink-backed p.
		Dalmatian p.
		Australian p.
	Snapping threat	
	Darter	Pointing
		Pink-backed p.
		Spot-billed p.
Nest site displays (often mate recognition signals)		
Material presentation	Material presentation	Material presentation
Most species (males)	Both species (males)	Most species (males)
Nest worrying	Nest worrying	Nest demarcation
Most or all species	Both species?	Pink-backed p.
Bowing	Snap-bowing	
Galapagos c.	Both species	
European s.		

NOTE: Excluding preflight/hop and postlanding/hop displays, and displays of uncertain significance and/or restricted taxonomic occurrence. Displays of different taxa having the same or similar names (e.g., gargling, pointing, head wagging, and bowing) are not necessarily homologous, but similar displays are placed in juxtaposition.

[1] Includes king shag and Auckland, Bounty, Campbell, Chatham, and Stewart island shags.

[2] Includes Brandt's, Galapagos, black-faced, Neotropic, double-crested, pied, little black, and great cormorants, plus New Zealand shags (see footnote 1) and imperial, red-faced, pelagic, European, red-legged, spotted, and Pitt Island shags. Probably also pygmy, Javanese, and little pied cormorants. "Throat clicking" of the rock shag is also probably homologous.

[3] Includes Galapagos, black-faced, great, pied, and Neotropic cormorants, plus the New Zealand shags (see footnote 1) and imperial, pelagic, red-faced, European, and spotted shags.

[4] All these are regarded as variants of the "upright" display by Schreiber (1977).

[5] Terminology as recommended by Schreiber (1977), and including wave-bowing, reach-bowing, and crouch-bowing.

Phylogenetic Origins of Pelecaniform Displays

Regardless of their possible present-day functions, social displays presumably evolved from various nondisplay behaviors that may have become considerably altered (or "ritualized") both in form and function. Van Tets (1965) largely organized his survey of pelecaniform behavior around this concept. He believed that the social displays of these birds may all have been derived from four major sources, in-

TABLE 23   Possible Evolutionary Derivations of Cormorant, Darter, and Pelican Displays

Probable Origins	Derived Activities and Ritualized Signals		

Preflight movements

Prehop/preflight (CD)
Hop (CD)   —(flight intention)—   Throwback/gargling (C)
                                          Wing crouching (CD)
                                          Wing waving (CD)
                                          Swing-pointing (C)

?
|
Pointing (CD)
|
?

Threat

Darting (C)
Bill raising (P)
Pouch swinging (P)   —(agonistic gaping)—   Gape threat (CDP)
Pouch expansion (P)   Gaping (C)
                                               Forward gaping (C)
                                               Sitting gape (C)
                                               Head lowering (C)

?   ?
| |
Gape-bowing (C)   Snap-bowing (D)
| |
?   ?

Nest site

Nest worrying (C)
Twig grasping (D)   — (nest building) —   Bowing (CP)
Nest demarcation (P)   Wave-bowing (P)
                          | Reach-bowing (P)
                          ?
                          |
Nest material presentation (CDP)
|
?
|

Food begging

Prelanding call (P)   — (recognition) —   Kink-throating (CD)
Postlanding posture   Greeting call (C)
(CD)   Beg-waggle (C)

NOTES: Adapted with modifications from van Tets (1965); presumed original functions or intermediate stages shown parenthetically. Displays with uncertain or possibly mixed origins indicated by queries. Taxonomic distribution indicated as C = Cormorants and shags, D = Darters, P = Pelicans.

cluding locomotory (pretakeoff) behavior, fighting and related threat behavior, nest-building behavior, and juvenile food-begging behavior. Many of his (or anyone's) ideas on display origins must necessarily be considered as highly speculative, but nevertheless are of some theoretical interest, especially inasmuch as they may offer clues for the interpretation of present-day display functions. Table 23 provides a highly tentative classification of social signals in these groups, based largely on van Tets's (1965) classification and ideas, but with some personal modifications.

CHAPTER 6

Reproductive Biology

The reproductive cycles of these three groups of birds are fairly comparable in their broader outlines. All the species are seasonally monogamous; in all, both sexes share more or less equally in incubation and brood rearing. Brood patches are lacking in all species, and the eggs are instead heated directly from the upper or lower surfaces of the webbed feet, the efficiency of which probably also places upper limits on potential clutch sizes. In all species the chicks are hatched in a helpless (altricial) and featherless (psilopaedic) condition, and the young remain in or near the nest for a prolonged period while they are fed by regurgitation and are wholly dependent upon their parents. The young mature only gradually, and have associated immature or subadult plumages persisting for up to three years. They are all variably colonial when they become breeders, with nest sites frequently used year after year. However, the incidence of nest site fidelity and mate retention is still undocumented in most species. The clutch size is invariably fairly small, probably largely a reflection of limitations on incubation efficiency and the high food-provisioning requirements during the long fledging period of the young. Thus, in raising a pair of chicks the adult pair must essentially double their food-gathering work relative to that required of nonbreeding birds, at least during the later chick-rearing stages (Dunn, 1975a), to say nothing of the additional energy costs involved in making sometimes long foraging flights to and from the nest. Incubation usually begins with the laying of the first egg, resulting in asynchronous hatching. The young are fed on partially digested and regurgitated food, usually fish, by their parents, who learn to recognize them individually and will not feed chicks other than their own. Initially the young are fed semifluid foods dribbled from the bill tip in most species, but older chicks directly remove the food from their parent's throat or gular pouch. In at least some species water may also be delivered to the young. In apparently all of the ground-nesting species of pelicans, "pods" or "creches" of aggregated but still-dependent young often develop, and to a much more limited degree aggregations of unfledged cormorants sometimes also develop. Since these groups are not tended by any adults, it is perhaps better to refer to them as pods than as creches, to avoid any implication that they represent organized and adult-guarded "nurseries."

Within this framework of overall similarities, significant differences of reproductive strategy exist among the larger groups and even between closely related species. These differences are of special interest here, for they offer insights into the varying evolutionary histories and ecological settings of modern-day cormorants, darters, and pelicans. Boekelheide et al. (1990) judged that cormorants differ from typical seabirds in that they have (1) relatively large and variable clutch sizes, (2) low energy investment in egg production, based on their relatively small egg size, (3) nesting success rates that are largely driven by hatching success, (4) extremely altricial chicks, and (5) marked differences in within-brood chick size as a result of asynchronous hatching. However, except for their generally smaller clutch sizes, pelicans are similar to cormorants in most of these reproductive traits, and darters probably correspond in all of them.

The present discussion can conveniently be subdivided into sequential component parts of the total nesting cycle, including nest site selection, nest-building, egg-laying, incubation, pipping and hatching, brooding and early chick-rearing, and finally later chick-rearing and prefledging phases.

Nest Site Selection

Nest sites in these groups of birds fall into three general categories. The simplest and generally most widely available types are substrate nests on level ground, often islands, as are used by most of the pelicans and some of the coastally nesting shags and cormorants. Some species typically use elevated nest sites in tall shrubs or trees; frequently these are previously used nests of ciconiiform birds or other large, colonially nesting birds. Good nest sites of this type are generally less easily found than suitable substrate sites, and thus their ownership is more likely to be contested. These sites are used by darters, tree-nesting pelicans, and many species of cormorants. Finally, cliff ledge nests, ideally those least accessible to predators but with excellent visibility, are typically used by shags. Such sites are perhaps the most variable in quantity and quality, and thus highly favorable nesting locations on cliff ledges are likely to be among the most contested of all nesting sites.

Depending on the rarity of such nesting sites, searches for nest sites or actual nest-building activities by males may begin fairly early in the nesting season. In the brown pelican, males typically select potential nest sites in coastal mangrove thickets, which must include not only a suitable nest site (or the remains of an old nest) but also a nearby sturdy perching branch. Males apparently arrive at their nest sites unmated, but Schreiber (1977) suspected that from the rapidity with which bonds are sometimes formed there may be some pair bond retentions from previous years. Some males engage in site defense and advertisement for less than a day before successfully attracting a female, whereas others may spend as long as three weeks before establishing a pair bond.

In the European shag, older males normally return to the same nest site they used during the previous year; the new nests built each year are those constructed by young birds. New sites where no young are reared are often abandoned the following year, but those sites that are successful are usually reused the following year. Additionally, older male shags tend to return to the colonies earlier in the breeding season, and typically build the best-constructed nests on the best nesting sites. A very small percentage (about 3–5 percent) of the males may simultaneously pair with two females, but males are prone to mate with their mates of the previous season, especially if that breeding effort was successful (Cramp and Simmons, 1977; Potts, Coulson, and Deans, 1980).

In a 12-year study of the Brandt's cormorant, Boekelheide and Ainley (1989) determined that there was a generally low incidence of nest site fidelity by females (56 percent in birds to 6 years of age, 21 percent in older females), which together with poor synchrony in the arrival times of mates resulted in low mate retention rates. Males were generally more prone than females to use the same nest site in subsequent years, especially in the case of older age classes. All age groups of females were statistically more successful than males of comparable age groups in terms of obtaining mates, producing clutches, and successfully fledging chicks, probably in part because of a tendency of males to pair with females younger than themselves. Older breeders laid their first clutches earlier in the breeding season than did younger birds, and thus had more time for renesting when their first clutches were lost.

Nests of the double-crested cormorant are sometimes destroyed by the elements between nesting seasons, or may be torn up during the breeding season by birds in search of materials for their own nests. When the nests do survive, they are normally used year after year, although they may eventually become abandoned because of the weakening of the supporting tree. When used for several years they gradually increase in size and weight, as new materials are added annually. It has been suggested that ground substrate sites may be the ancestral site type for this species, but arboreal nests provide greater safety and thus may be preferentially used when they are available (Lewis, 1929). Some nest sites in Maine were found to be used for at least four consecutive years, although it is not known whether the same birds occupied them. Persistent nests were not only chosen first by returning birds, but also seemed to produce the highest rate of chick survival (Mendall, 1936).

Old tree nests in good condition were found to be the preferred nesting sites for double-crested cormorants in a Utah study, with higher sites preferred over lower. Often new nests were built only when all the old nests had been occupied. Limited information suggests that the first birds to return to the nesting area were the more mature ones, which presumably had their choice of the better preconstructed nest sites. The earlier arrivals tended to choose the higher and presumably safer sites, although rather surprisingly the lower nest sites were found to have a better overall hatching success (Mitchell, 1977). Obviously, however, final fledging success rather than initial hatching success would provide a better measure of the relative overall value of the nest location.

In a similar way, persistent nests were those chosen by the first-arriving males of double-crested cormorants and pelagic shags in a British Columbia site (Siegel-Causey and Hunt, 1986). As might be expected on the basis of relative expected site defense tendencies, turnovers of nesting sites were less frequent among the cliff-nesting pelagic shag than among the double-crested cormorant, which has more generalized nest site requirements and thus is less likely to strongly contest a specific nesting site. Generally, however, cormorant and shag nest sites may change ownership several times before they are finally adopted and defended by a breeding pair on a continuous basis. Deserted nests of even large size may be demolished overnight by other cormorants stealing nesting materials (van Tets, 1959).

In a Wisconsin study, artificial nesting structures were provided for double-crested cormorants in order to supplement natural nests that had been made by the cormorants and great blue herons (*Ardea herodias*) in a mixed colony. These artificial nest sites were quickly adopted by the cormorants, and production of young on the artificial sites was generally greater than on natural nest sites, probably because of their greater stability and resistance to deterioration (Meier, 1981).

Nest sites of the Australian darter are consistently located in live or dead trees, and additionally the nest trees are always surrounded by water over 0.3 meters deep. If the water level drops, the birds leave their original nest sites and move to areas of deeper water. The nesting trees also usually have a base or branches that allow the nestling birds to climb up from the water, since dropping out of the nest is a common defensive strategy of unfledged birds when they are threatened. Nests are built in forks away from the main trunk and are usually elevated about 3.5 meters above water (Vestjens, 1975). In Mexico, anhinga nests were found to average about 2.5 meters above water, and were usually placed at the junction of the tree's trunk and its branches. All of 40 nests were found to have an exposed site nearby that was used for perching and was defended by the nonincubating member of the pair (Burger, Miller, and Hahn, 1978).

Nest site selection by pelicans is still only poorly known and opinions about it are divided. It has been suggested that the choice may be made by the male (van Tets, 1965), by the female (Schaller, 1964; Brown and Urban, 1969), or by both sexes (Bauer and Glutz, 1966). At least in the brown pelican and perhaps in other tree-nesting species, the choice is apparently made by the male through his selection of an advertisement site, which is essentially a potential nest site plus an adjacent perching site. In ground-nesting pelicans the specific site requirements are certainly far less critical than in tree-nesting species. Probably few pelicans regularly nest in exactly the same site each year, and no good information seems to be yet available as to relative nest site fidelity or the incidence of mate retention among wild pelicans. Din (1979) observed promiscuous mating by male pink-backed pelicans with females of nearby pairs during the nest-building phase, but did not comment on its possible biological importance, other than to note that it is otherwise evidently very rare or absent among pelecaniform birds.

Among other pelecaniform groups, successive-year nest site fidelity is fairly well developed in the red-tailed tropicbird (*Phaethon rubricauda*), especially when the pair bond remains intact the following year. The incidence of mate retention is strongly correlated with the pair's breeding success during the prior year (Fleet, 1974). On the other hand, although white booby (*Sula dactylatra*) pairs that remain mated have a statistically higher probability of breeding success the following year, this improved prospect does not seem to predispose such pairs toward retaining their previous mates (Nelson, 1978).

Nest Construction

Nests of cormorants are constructed by both sexes, although after the foundation has been completed the male's role is often restricted to bringing materials to the female, who then incorporates them into the nest. Even in a single species exceptions to this pattern may occur, and perhaps occasionally males may participate in the actual construction as much as females. It may take a double-crested cormorant pair about four days to construct a nest from the beginning, although an old nest can be refurbished in about two days. The new materials that are brought in are added more or less haphazardly, with little apparent attempt to weave the materials together until the nest is ready to be lined. Newly constructed nests are rather shallow and flimsy, and better-constructed nests are usually the result of more than a single year's efforts. Additional material is added during the entire breeding season, although nest-building activities diminish after the young have hatched (Mendall, 1936).

Among pelicans it is also the male who brings nesting material to the female, who then adds it to the nest (Grummt, 1984). Occasionally the female may also bring materials to the nest site as well. In the eastern white pelican this nest-building process may require only 2–3 days (Dementiev and Gladkov, 1951). The somewhat larger nests of the Dalmatian pelican may require up to about 8 days to complete (Bauer and Glutz, 1966). In tree-nesting populations of the brown pelican, nest building usually requires 7–10 days, with an observed minimum of 4 days. The male begins gathering nesting material as soon as a female occupies his display site, and much of the material is gathered from the immediate area around the nest. However, males may also fly in with mouthfuls of material from some distance away. Males continue to bring in such materials through the incubation and nestling periods, but to a reduced degree. Observations on more than 400 individual brown pelicans indicate that only the male gathers nest materials (Schreiber, 1977). A similar nest-building pattern exists in the spot-billed pelican, which typically completes its nest in 6–10 days (Lamba, 1963). However, in the ground-nesting population of the brown pelican on the coast of Peru, only a shallow cavity is scratched out, and varying amounts of feathers, guano, pebbles, or other readily available materials are added to the nest (Coker, 1919; Vogt, 1942).

Nest building by the anhinga apparently begins as soon as pair formation has occurred, sometimes even within 20 minutes of the first copulation. Although a nest may be completed in a single day, in one study construction always required at least three days. In this study the females evidently stayed at their nest sites continuously during the entire nest-building period, so all the gathering of materials must have been done by the males (Allen, 1961). In the Australian darter the male constructs the nest foundation, but the female adds material that she collects near the nest or that is brought in by the male. The typical Australian darter nest contains about 150 sticks, often with a lining of tree leaves and leafy twigs. A small amount of nest material is added during incubation and brooding. During a three-year study, nine Australian darter nests (out of an apparent total sample of 178) were found to be used for two successive breeding seasons, and three were used for all three, with new materials being added to the nest each season (Vestjens, 1975).

Egg Laying

Egg laying among these groups of birds is evidently not a great physiological drain, for not only are the eggs relatively small in comparison to the mass of the adult female, but also clutches tend to be small, making the total associated physiological stress on the female during egg laying relatively low (table 24). Relative egg mass is of course inversely related to overall adult female mass; smaller species of birds necessarily invest relatively more energy into each egg than larger species. Nevertheless, among the species considered in this book the entire range of egg weights relative to adult female weights runs only from about 2.2 percent for the largest species of pelicans to about 4 percent for the smallest species of cormorants. Similarly, estimated average overall clutch weight to adult female weight ranges

TABLE 24   Relationship of Egg and Modal Clutch Mass to Average Adult Female Mass in Cormorants, Darters, and Pelicans

Species	Female mass (g)	Egg mass (g)	Modal clutch	Egg as % of female	Clutch as % of female
Cormorants					
Long-tailed	500	21	4	4.2	16.8
Crowned	725	24	3	3.3	9.9
Pygmy	600	23	4?	3.8	15.2
Javanese	425	20	4	4.7	18.8
Little pied	725	27	4	3.7	14.9
Brandt's	1,925	51	4	2.6	10.6
Galapagos	2,700	69	3	2.6	7.7
Bank	1,800	50	2	2.8	5.7
Black-faced	1,400	44	3	3.1	9.4
Neotropic	1,250	40	3	3.2	9.6
Double-crested	1,860	50	4	2.7	10.7
Pied	1,700	45	3	2.6	7.9
Little black	800	32	4	4.0	16.0
Great					
sinensis	1,900	53	3	2.8	8.4
lucidus	1,780	54	3	3.0	9.0
novaehollandiae	2,000	50	4	2.5	10.0
Shags					
Cape	1,100	38	3	3.4	10.2
Guanay	2,700	60	3	2.2	6.6
Imperial					
georgianus	2,470	55	3	2.2	6.7
melanogenis	2,000	53	3	2.7	8.0
bransfieldensis	2,575	59	3	2.3	6.9
purpurascens	2,700	56	3	2.1	6.2
New Zealand king	2,500	62	2	2.5	5.0
Rock	1,450	49	3	3.4	10.1
Pelagic	1,700	44	3	2.6	7.7
Red-faced	1,850	46	3	2.5	7.4
Red-legged	1,300	51	3	3.9	11.7
European	1,600	49	3	3.1	9.2
Spotted	1,200	40	3	3.3	10.0
Darters					
American anhinga	1,200	35	4	2.9	11.6
African darter	1,450	37	4	2.5	10.2
Pelicans					
Eastern white	7,600	185	2	2.4	4.9
Pink-backed	4,900	120	2	2.4	4.9
Spot-billed	4,650	115	3	2.5	7.4
Dalmatian	8,700	189	2	2.2	4.3
Australian	5,900	173	2	2.9	5.9
American white	5,500	150	2	2.7	5.5
Brown					
occidentalis	2,800	103	3	3.7	11.0
thagus	5,500	142	3	2.6	7.7

NOTE: In part adapted from Cooper (1987), but with many additions and modifications.

from about 4.3 percent in the largest pelicans to about 17 percent in the smallest cormorants. Considering that some birds producing precocial young lay single eggs that may represent 10–15 percent of their total body weight, this would not appear to be a very significant quantity in terms of pelecaniform energy budgets.

Rather few observations of egg laying are available, but at least in the European shag it appears that eggs are often laid at night or early in the morning (Snow, 1960). The majority of double-crested cormorant eggs are apparently deposited between an hour after sunrise and 9:00 A.M., although egg laying occasionally also occurs in the forenoon or even afternoon (Mendall, 1936). Early morning egg laying is apparently typical of the pink-backed pelican (Din, 1979). So long as the nest is continuously tended, as is typical of these birds, there are probably no special ecological reasons (such as predation avoidance) for restricting egg laying to a particular time of the day.

The egg-laying rate in cormorants and shags is somewhat variable, but laying often occurs at two- or three-day intervals (Cramp and Simmons, 1977). Eggs are most frequently deposited every other day in the European shag (Snow, 1960), but reportedly daily in the double-crested cormorant (Mendall, 1936). In the anhinga, days are reportedly sometimes "skipped" during the egg-laying period (Palmer, 1962). In the Australian darter the first egg is usually laid two or three days after pair formation has been completed, and the remaining eggs are deposited at two- or three-day intervals (Vestjens, 1975).

Similarly, in pelicans the eggs are usually laid at intervals of two or three days (Palmer, 1962; Cramp and Simmons, 1977; Vestjens, 1977a). At least among captive birds the eggs typically are laid at two- or three-day intervals, as has been documented for the eastern white, American white, Dalmatian, pink-backed, spot-billed, and brown pelicans (Grummt, 1984). A probable daily egg-laying rate has been suggested for the eastern white pelican (Brown and Urban, 1969), but Grummt observed only two-day (27 cases) or three-day (20 cases) intervals among captive birds. It has also been suggested that the brown pelican may have a daily egg-laying rate, but an interval of two or more days is typical of wild *thagus* in Peru (Coker, 1919), and captive birds of both *occidentalis* and *thagus* lay eggs at 2–3-day intervals (Grummt, 1984).

Representative clutch sizes are shown in table 24, and others can be found in the individual species accounts. In all groups the clutch sizes are rather small, usually ranging from two to five eggs, with two-egg clutches typical only of the larger pelicans and some cormorants. Clearly, in these groups the upper limits on clutch size are likely to be set by the physical limitations for adults in effectively incubating their clutches or in providing food for the chicks, rather than by any physiological stresses associated with egg laying for females.

Probabilities of renesting following complete egg or chick loss, or producing a second brood after rearing the first, are largely or entirely controlled by the length of the breeding season. There is no evidence of double-brooding among double-crested cormorants (Mendall, 1936), although renesting following clutch loss is frequent. Of 33 failed double-crested cormorant nests on Mandarte Island, no renesting efforts occurred at 4 nest sites, and from 1 to 8 replacement eggs were laid at the others as follows: 1 at 3 sites, 2 at 6, 3 at 5, 4 at 5, 5 at 2, 6 at 6, 7 at 1, and 8 at 1. Likewise, among 28 pelagic shag nests that were lost during the egg stage on Mandarte Island, no renesting attempts were made at 10 nest sites, a single replacement egg was laid at 13 sites, 2 were laid at 4 sites, and 3 at one site (van Tets, 1959). The maximum number of eggs known to be laid by a female during a single breeding season was 11 for the double-crested cormorant and 7 for the pelagic shag.

Among cormorants, a double breeding season during spring and autumn has been reported for the pied cormorant on Stewart Island, with a larger number of nests being active in spring than in autumn. It is not known whether any birds breed more than once per year (Lalas, 1979). Similarly, in coastal areas of Western Australia the pied cormorant apparently exhibits a double breeding season during autumn and spring, with autumn the favored breeding period (Marchant and Higgins, 1990). It has been suggested but apparently not proven that the great cormorant might raise two broods per year in Japan (Brazil, 1991).

In the African darter two distinct nesting peaks in a single year were reported from Ghana (Bowen et al., 1962). The first occurred during June and the second between September and November, which periods correspond to the region's bimodal equatorial rainfall regime. However, it is not clear from this study whether the second nesting cycle represented actual second broods, renesting efforts by failed breeders, or even independent nesting efforts by different population components. The indicated three- to five-month period between cycles would probably allow a pair just enough time for hatching and bringing to fledging the first brood before starting a second nest. In northern areas of Australia, darter eggs have similarly been reported from February to June, and again in November, suggesting rather erratic and irregular breeding, probably as influenced by water and food availability (Marchant and Higgins, 1990). A similarly long five- to six-month nesting period has also been reported for Oriental darters in northern India (Ali and Ripley, 1983), although Baker (1929) stated that in that area the darters breed only during the late rains, which occur between July and September. In Mexico, nesting by anhingas is related to the summer rainy season (Burger, Miller, and Hahn, 1978). In Costa Rica the nesting season is from May (when the rains begin) to February (the dry winter season), peaking from September to November. October and November are typically relatively rainy months in Costa Rica (Stiles and Skutch, 1989). Thus, there is ample evidence for rainy-season breeding by anhingas and darters, but no clear indication of possible double-brooding.

At least in the eastern white pelican, renesting is typical if the eggs are lost within 10 days of laying (Cramp and Simmons, 1977), and some renesting also occurs in Dalmatian pelicans (Crivelli, 1987). The incidence of renesting following nest failure by wild brown pelicans in Florida varied from none to as high as 26 percent over an eight-year period (Schreiber, 1979), and in four cases occurred even after the chicks had successfully hatched but subsequently died. In captivity, renesting by pelicans following clutch loss is fairly frequent, and this is probably also true under natural conditions. Grummt (1984) reported that up to three renesting attempts were made by captive eastern white, American white, Dalmatian, and brown pelicans, at intervals of from 6 to 47 days following clutch loss. In the pink-backed pelican a maximum of five renesting efforts were made, at intervals ranging from 7 to 23 days following clutch loss. Grummt observed only a single and unsuccessful attempt by a pair to hatch a second brood during a single breeding season, which involved the eastern white pelican.

Incubation

The onset of incubation is seemingly rather variable in these groups. In the double-crested cormorant, for example, it sometimes begins with the laying of the first egg, or it may begin only after the laying of some subsequent egg, including even the last one (Mendall, 1936). In most species, however, incubation apparently normally begins with the laying of the first egg of the clutch. This, of course, results in asynchronous hatching of the young, depending on the spread of days over which additional eggs are laid after incubation has begun. In the American white pelican the average hatching interval for two-egg clutches is 2.5 days, which corresponds to their normal egg-laying interval and which results in a biologically significant difference in the two chicks' probabilities of subsequent survival (Cash and Evans, 1986).

In all three pelecaniform groups considered here, as well as in the sulids (but not the tropicbirds or frigatebirds), incubation is achieved in a unique manner. Rather than using a brood patch of bare abdominal skin, the heat of the foot webs is transmitted directly to the eggs. In all the pelicans so far studied, this is normally done by placing the feet directly above the eggs (figure 28). In the larger pelicans (all surface-nesting species, often with shallow nest scrapes) the limited incubation efficiency of this trait may be a significant factor in restricting the size of the clutch to two eggs, but in the smaller forms (mostly tree-nesting species, having a generally deeper nest cup) the birds seem to be able to incubate a larger number of eggs in this manner (Grummt, 1984). Correspondingly, the species of pelicans that often lay three eggs (spot-billed and brown) are tree nesters.

In contrast, among cormorants and shags, the eggs are situated between the upper foot surfaces and the breast feathers during incubation. When settling, the bird slowly inserts its feet beneath the eggs, and at the same time raises its body feathers (Snow, 1963). According to some accounts (e.g., Coomber, 1990), in the darters the eggs are likewise incubated on the upper surfaces of the feet. However, to my knowledge this has not been specifically reported in the original literature, and should be verified.

Of related interest, it has been observed that in tropicbirds incubation is not achieved by using directly transmitted heat from the relatively small feet, but instead the single egg is "tucked among the breast feathers" (Fleet, 1974). The tropicbirds are also anomalous among pelecaniform birds in that the chick is down-covered (ptilopaedic) at hatching. This situation is especially curious in view of the fact that all three *Phaethon* species breed in relatively tropical areas, where thermoregulation of chicks should not pose a serious problem. Furthermore, although fully down-covered, the chick is nevertheless continuously brooded for about a week (Fleet, 1974). It is also not surprising that the frigatebirds do not incubate their eggs with their feet, considering that the webbing is so greatly reduced.

It is typical among the species of the three groups under consideration here (and apparently also the other pelecaniform groups) that the eggs are more or less continuously tended from the time incubation begins until hatching. Incubation is also shared more or less equally by the two sexes in these species. Incubation rhythms vary greatly between and even within species. In the European shag the female typically incubates through the night and until about 9:30 A.M. The male may then incubate until about 1:00 P.M., the female in turn until about 4:30 P.M., and the male again typically until dark (Snow, 1963).

An adult European shag will regularly try to retrieve eggs that have been pushed or fallen out of the nest cup, by placing the closed beak beyond the eggs and then drawing the head back toward the nest (Snow, 1963). Similar egg-retrieval behavior occurs in other cormorants and in pelicans, perhaps especially among the

Figure 28. Egg-turning behavior (A–C) of the eastern white pelican. Note the position of the egg under the foot webs (A). After photos in Grummt (1984).

ground-nesting pelican species having only shallow nest scrapes. On the other hand pelicans may throw pebbles, eggshells, and other debris out of the nest cup, holding such items in the tip of the bill and flicking them out with a quick jerk of the head (Schaller, 1964). Periodically during the incubation period the sitting bird rises and turns or readjusts the eggs with the tip of the bill (figure 28). Such egg turning typically occurs several times per day in pelicans (Schaller, 1964; Grummt, 1984). Until pipping occurs, the amount of egg turning is apparently random and the resultant final rotational position of the egg is variable, but once the egg begins pipping the enlarging hole made by the chick is always kept facing upward (Snow, 1963).

During warm weather, incubating cormorants may stand and shade the eggs, and wet hay and algae may be added to the nest lining, apparently to help cool the eggs. Incubating birds also often perform gular fluttering during warm weather, presumably to keep themselves cool. They may sleep or doze for short intervals on the nest during the day, and sometimes stretch themselves or flap their wings, apparently for exercise. Defecation by sitting birds is done by backing up somewhat over the nest rim before eliminating wastes (van Tets, 1959).

Both sexes of the double-crested cormorant incubate for roughly equal percentages of the total incubation period, with the female perhaps incubating slightly more during the earlier part of the period, while the male is still to some extent participating in social display activities. In that species the birds typically relieve one another at intervals of about one to three hours, and the nonincubating bird sometimes stands waiting at the side or edge of the nest while its mate incubates (Mendall, 1936). In the European shag this behavior is common early in the incubation period, when the relieving bird apparently desires to take over incubation before its mate is willing to relinquish the nest. At times the relieving bird will try to push

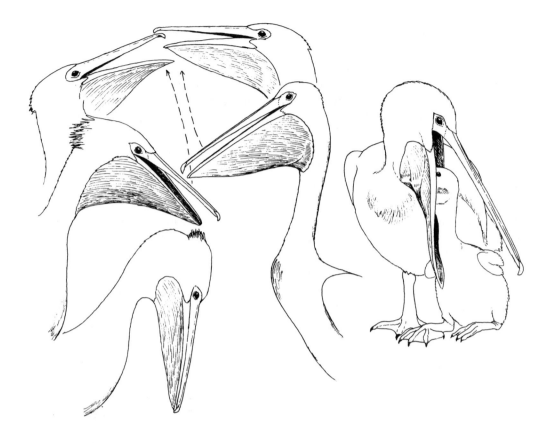

its head under its mate, and make the motion of rolling an egg toward its own body (Snow, 1963).

In one study of the anhinga, the sexes evidently incubated approximately equally, with males more frequently incubating between dusk and dawn (Burger, Miller, and Hahn, 1978). In the Australian darter the incubation duration for single birds ranged from two to six hours, with nest relief usually occurring in early morning, early afternoon, and early evening hours (Vestjens, 1977a).

Male Australian pelicans were usually observed to incubate in the morning and females in the afternoon, with incubation periods ranging from two to ten hours in duration (Vestjens, 1977a). Among pink-backed pelicans, each member of the pair reportedly incubated for nearly 24 hours at a time before it was relieved, which usually occurred during afternoon hours. The nest relief ceremony consists of the incoming parent perching on a nearby perch and bobbing its head vertically while uttering croaking sounds. Its partner reciprocates with similar behavior (Din, 1979).

Comparable nest relief ceremonies occur in other pelican species as well. Thus, in the American white pelican it consists of the head-up and bowing displays (figure 29). In that species, Schaller (1964) found the nest relief ceremony to last an average of about eight minutes and to occur at average intervals of about 22.5 hours, but with great individual variation. Nest relief during the incubation and brooding period is marked by the same kinds of mate recognition displays that are typical earlier in the nesting season. However, these are performed for shorter durations and with lowered intensities as the breeding season progresses, especially after the chicks hatch and grow older.

Figure 29. Mutual head-up and bill raising (upper left) plus the bowing display (lower left) of the American white pelican (partly after sketches in Schaller, 1964); also feeding an older chick (right, after a photo by Alan Carey).

Pipping and Hatching

In these birds the pipping process, during which the hatching chick gradually chips away an opening in the eggshell with its egg tooth until it is able to escape from the egg, is often a fairly long one. Completion of the process by the double-crested cormorant required about eight hours in one observed case (Mendall, 1936). In the European shag pipping typically requires at least 24 hours from its onset to hatching. In one instance the incubating male frequently stood up and put his bill into the nest, touching or moving the eggs. At the end of the hatching period he removed the larger part of the eggshell and then the smaller part and placed them at the edge of the nest (Snow, 1963). Unlike in many species of birds having altricial young, the eggshells are not transported far away from the nest by the parents as an apparent antipredation mechanism, nor do the newly hatched chicks produce cohesive fecal sacs to be carried away from the nesting site by the adults.

Pipping in pelicans generally requires from 24 to 36 hours, and at least in captivity an adult eastern white pelican has been seen actively helping the hatching process using the tip of her bill (Grummt, 1984). In the pink-backed pelican it has been reported that 20–24 hours are needed for pipping to be completed. During the hatching and immediate posthatching period the chick is highly vulnerable to drying and overheating, and must be constantly shaded from the sun by the brooding parent (Din, 1979).

Among pelicans, which consistently incubate their eggs underneath their foot webbing, an important change in behavior occurs at hatching. Following the onset of vocalizations from the first egg to begin pipping, the incubating adult removes its feet from on top of the eggs and shifts the eggs to the upper surface of its foot webbing (Evans, 1988). This locational change presumably not only helps to prevent crushing the eggs, but may also provide the hatching chicks with better breathing opportunities. It has been recently found that at the time of pipping of its first egg the American white pelican tends to neglect incubation of the remaining egg. This causes its temperature to fall significantly, and perhaps reduces its chances for successful hatching (Evans, 1990b). Since cormorants (and probably also darters) incubate their eggs on the upper surfaces of their feet from the outset, this shift in egg position at the time of hatching isn't required.

It has been suggested for various species of altricial birds that adaptive brood reduction is perhaps facilitated by asynchronous hatching, so that the last-hatched chick is smaller and weaker than its older sibling or siblings, and so under stressful rearing conditions is less likely to survive (Lack, 1947; Magrath, 1990). Although hatching success was not influenced by clutch size among 60 experimentally manipulated American white pelican nests having adjusted clutch sizes of from 1 to 3 eggs, the second-hatched chick survived to pod-forming stage in only 20 percent of the successful nests, and additionally the highest percent of broods having at least one survivor to this stage came from 2-egg clutches (Cash and Evans, 1986). In the American white pelican it also appears that the probability of both chicks of a brood surviving declines as their hatching interval increases (Knopf, 1980). These results support the idea that, at least in this species, the second egg indeed may function as a kind of relatively low-cost insurance against the possible loss of the first-laid egg or older chick. Hatching asynchrony may then help to prevent the loss of both young as a result of food competition and possible starvation should both eggs hatch successfully and the chicks be able to compete equally. Data on other pelicans are less complete, but in at least three other species (great white, pink-backed, and Australian) sibling aggression may serve to facilitate obligate or facultative brood reduction (Drummond, 1987).

In an informative study of the crowned cormorant, all of the chicks that died within 20 days after hatching were the last-hatched chicks of their broods (Williams and Cooper, 1983). Hatching success was 40 percent for first-laid eggs, 66.7 percent for second-laid eggs, 16.7 percent for third-laid eggs, and 6.7 percent for fourth-laid eggs. Three factors evidently accounted for subsequent differential chick mortality, including egg size (first-laid eggs are largest), hatching asynchrony, and preferential feeding by the parents of the most strongly begging chick. A review of possible brood reduction mechanisms in the Phalacrocoracidae led Drummond (1987) to conclude that nonaggressive feeding competition among asynchronously hatched chicks is the usual mechanism found in cormorants and shags, although in at least two species overt sibling aggression related to feeding competition has been reported. Both species of Anhingidae probably also employ facultative brood reduction, whether as a result of differential sibling dominance or of direct aggression.

Although it is intuitively apparent that hatching asynchrony might function adaptively as an effective brood reduction mechanism, Amundsen and Stokland have recently (1988) concluded that the brood reduction hypothesis does not provide an adequate explanation for hatching asynchrony in the European shag. Magrath (1990) has also concluded that no single hypothesis as to the possible adaptive significance of hatching asynchrony for altricial birds in general yet fully explains the available data. Other hypotheses (such as maximizing the energetic efficiency of reproduction or producing the most efficient timing of reproductive events) remain to be fully explored, as well as the possibility that hatching asynchrony is actually nonadaptive.

Brooding and Early Chick Rearing

In nearly all pelecaniform birds the young are hatched in a highly altricial condition, being blind, usually featherless, and essentially helpless, and are reared in the nest over much or all of their fledging periods. In cormorants the external nares are still open at hatching, the egg tooth is well developed, and the chick is apparently blind. The bulging eyes have the eyelids fixed and variably closed over the eyeball. The birds initially can barely lift their heads, and can only utter faint peeping calls (Lewis, 1929). Newly hatched pelicans are very comparable to cormorants in appearance and motor abilities (Grummt, 1984).

In cormorants, the newly hatched chick is carefully brooded and normally supported on the feet of its parent during the first week of posthatching life. At about four days of age the egg tooth drops off the tip of the mandible, and the sense of vision may also become functional at about the same time (Lewis, 1929). The chick begs for food by waving its head while making a squeaky begging call, with the bill closed. The parent responds by placing the upper half of its bill above the chick's head, with the lower mandible held horizontally along the chick's head. The chick then consumes a milky fluid of shredded fish from the trough formed by the gular pouch and the anterior portion of the lower mandible (van Tets, 1959). Begging for water is done by head waving with the wide-open bill directed upward. As soon as the attending parent is relieved, it flies to water and fills its gullet, quickly returns

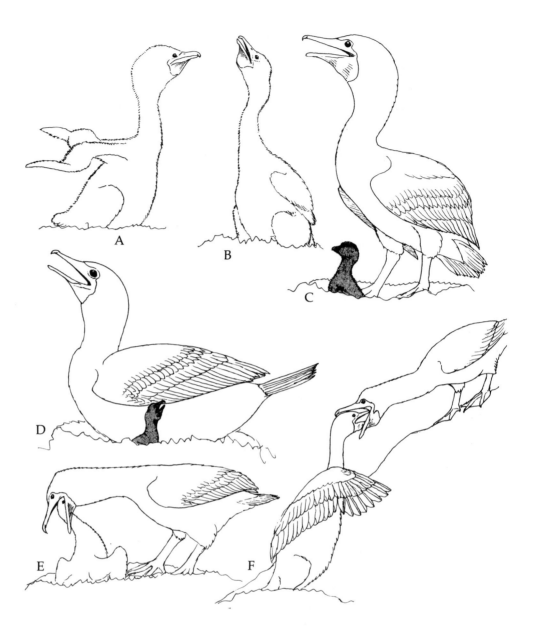

Figure 30. Parent-chick behavior in the double-crested cormorant, including wing flapping by a chick (A), food begging by a chick (B), adult shading a chick from the sun (C), adult brooding a small chick (D), adult feeding a young chick (E), and feeding an older chick (F). After photos in Mendall (1936).

to the nest, and pours water into the chicks' open mouths, and sometimes also into the mouth of its sitting mate. This may be repeated several times (van Tets, 1959, 1965).

As the cormorant chick grows somewhat older it reaches directly into its parent's mouth for food. After the first week the chicks start to perform the same comfort movements as their parents, including defecating over the nest rim. They also spend an increasing amount of time exercising, such as wing flapping, which begins at about two weeks of age (figure 30A). Adults spend a good deal of time shading their young from direct sunlight during warm and sunny days (figure 30C).

In both cormorants and darters, food begging is characterized by a forward and downward movement of the hyoid apparatus, which gives the throat an angular appearance, much like that assumed by the adults during their kink-throating displays (van Tets, 1965). Food begging in nestling pelicans is characterized by excited head waving and wing flapping, with the bill closed. Mandible spreading is

sometimes also performed by nestling birds, perhaps as an aggressive signal or a kind of begging appeal (figure 33F).

In the Australian darter, chicks under a week old are brooded constantly, being shaded during hot weather and covered by one of the adults during nighttime hours. During a period of hot weather one adult was observed to leave the nest, swim for a time, and then return to the nest and shake water from its feathers over the chicks. When very young, the chicks utter begging sounds and move their heads with great difficulty. This stimulates the adult to stand and bend its neck so that the upper mandible is oriented diagonally, its tip often resting on the nest. A fluidlike food then is regurgitated and drips along the inside of the upper mandible toward its tip, where it is taken by the chick (figure 31). Unlike in food begging, the chick holds its bill open when it is begging for water. The adult then flies to the water, dips its head several times, and returns to squirt water directly into the open bills of the young (Vestjens, 1975).

Brood reduction associated with sibling rivalry has been observed in American white pelicans (Johnson and Sloan, 1978; Cash and Evans, 1986), and the question of siblicide as a potential brood reduction mechanism in pelicans has been discussed by Cooper (1980). He stated that brood reduction as a result of fatal sibling aggression has been reported for the eastern and American white pelicans and the pink-backed and Australian pelicans, and reduction by starvation of the younger sibling in spot-billed and pink-backed pelicans. However, Crivelli (1987) failed to find evidence for siblicide or other brood reduction mechanisms in the Dalmatian pelican. He found that most nests having two eggs successfully fledged both young. He did, however, observe that most three-egg clutches failed, presumably because of inefficient parental incubation of such large clutches. This has also been reported for the American white pelican (Knopf, 1976b).

During the first two weeks after hatching, pink-backed pelican chicks are closely guarded and usually are brooded under the parent's wings, which probably not only keeps them warm at night but also may shade them from the daytime sun.

Figure 31. Food-begging posture of Australian darter chick (left), and regurgitation-feeding of a small chick by a female (right). After sketches in Vestjens (1975).

Figure 32. Parent-chick be-havior in the brown pelican, including a parent adjusting the position of its newly hatched chick with its bill (left), and a week-old chick being brooded on its parent's foot webs and swallowing a large fish (right). Adapted from photos by D. Guravich in Brown (1983).

If direct sunlight reaches the chicks the adult may lower its primaries to improve the degree of shading, but apparently does not stretch its wings laterally (Din, 1979). In this species the young chicks are fed up to 30 times per day by direct re-gurgitation on the nest platform. During regurgitation, the tip of the opened man-dible is rested against the nest floor, the pouch is extended while rapid lateral vibrations of the neck are performed, and the regurgitated food, typically small fish, flows out onto the nest floor. The young birds pick up these materials from the floor and swallow them individually (compare figure 32). By the time the young are two weeks old they are able to feed directly from their parent's pouch (Din, 1979). Similar direct pouch feeding occurs in the older young of other pelican species (fig-ure 29). Water is also delivered to the young in the parent's pouch.

In the brown pelican, the chicks are initially fed within a few hours of hatch-ing. During the first week to ten days the adult regurgitates foods about once an hour into the nest cup, which the chick then picks up and swallows (Schreiber, 1977). When very young, the young are sometimes gently moved in the nest by the adult using the tip of its bill, in a manner similar to the manipulation of eggs (figure 32). In the American white pelican, small young and eggs were thus shifted about on an average of three times a day (Schaller, 1964). The chicks only begin to beg di-rectly from their parents at about ten days of age, when they start to take materials by reaching into the parent's pouch (Schreiber, 1977).

In the Australian pelican, feeding of newly hatched young apparently takes a slightly different form (Vestjens, 1977a). Adults were observed to rest the tip of their bill on the ground in a nearly vertical position and regurgitate a liquid food, which flows down the inside of the upper mandible. The bill is slightly open, and the chick takes its food from inside the bill, near its tip (figure 33A). By the time they are two weeks old the chicks utter a lower begging call while moving the head

Figure 33. Parent-chick behavior in the Australian pelican (A–E) and brown pelican (F), including a very young chick drinking from its parent's maxilla (A), a two-week-old chick begging food (B) and feeding from its parent's pouch (C), an older chick pecking at its parent's bill to stimulate feeding (D), and a still older chick feeding from its parent's throat (E) (after sketches in Vestjens, 1977a). Also shown (F) is gaping with mandible spreading by a brown pelican chick (after a photo by D. Guravich in Brown, 1983).

up and down, with the bill in contact with the parent's (figure 33B). The adult then regurgitates, and the chick inserts its head into the pouch to take its food directly from the gullet (figure 33C).

Later Chick Rearing and Fledging

Usually by the time the chicks of cormorants, darters, and pelicans are a week or two old, they begin to acquire their first coat of down. As they do so, they also begin to develop their own thermoregulatory abilities. Development of thermoregulatory abilities and associated behavior has been studied in young American white pelicans (Bartholomew, Dawson, and O'Neill, 1953; Bartholomew and Dawson, 1954). To a lesser degree the development of thermoregulatory acquisition in young cormorants and shags has also been investigated (Dunn, 1976; Berry, 1976). In both groups it is a very gradual process, requiring several weeks for completion. In the brown pelican, naked chicks do not perform gular fluttering and apparently have little if any thermoregulatory abilities. Somewhat older chicks have a covering of white down, which together with gular fluttering and their extensive air sacs facilitates thermoregulation. American white pelicans of similar age also use shivering as a thermoregulatory mechanism, but brown pelicans apparently do not (Bartholomew and Dawson, 1954). In the pink-backed pelican, chicks were first observed gular-fluttering during the third week of posthatching life, when the parents began to dissociate themselves from their chicks. In that species brooding was terminated by the end of the third week, but some parental feeding continued on until fledging, or at least through the twelfth week (Din, 1979).

Generally, featherless chicks of cormorants are unable to maintain body temperatures when cold, but can thermoregulate using gular fluttering when hot. Perhaps the typically blackish skin and usually dark natal down of nestling cormorants is significant in absorbing heat from the sun by very young individuals. The Socotra shag is exceptional in having white down, but it also breeds in areas having extremely hot daytime temperatures. In nestlings of the double-crested cormorant the gular-fluttering cooling mechanism is better developed than in pelagic shag chicks, presumably in correlation with the species' warmer breeding climate (Lasiewski and Snyder, 1969). Effective internal temperature regulation is attained by double-crested cormorant nestlings in the natural environment at about two weeks of age, when downy feathering is well established, and parental brooding ceases at about that time (Dunn, 1976). After feathering develops, nestling cormorants start to regulate their body temperatures in much the same way as adults, except that wing spreading during very high temperatures is not performed by nestlings (Berry, 1976). Temperature regulation mechanisms of nestling darters are still unstudied, although gular fluttering is performed, as are all other adult comfort activities (Vestjens, 1975). At least in some species, such as the great, Japanese, and long-tailed cormorants, adults may regurgitate water over the backs of their chicks, presumably to help cool them.

When the young of American white pelicans, eastern white pelicans, Australian pelicans, and probably other ground-nesting species of pelicans are starting to become down-covered and to thermoregulate effectively, they begin to leave their nests and form pods. Even in the tree-nesting pink-backed pelican the young birds may try to collect in a single nest, forming small pods. In the eastern white pelican these pods begin to form when the chicks are 20–25 days old, and the chicks of this species are unique among pelicans in having black rather than white down. During the heat of the day, when the chicks gular-flutter quietly in tight groups, the black down color would seemingly be disadvantageous. The nearly uniformly black skin color of newly hatched pelicans is likewise hard to explain. However, it has been suggested that black coloration might reduce the metabolic costs of staying warm especially at dawn and dusk, especially in hot climates with large daily temperature variations (Serventy, 1971). It has also been suggested that pod formation may avoid internal temperature extremes, either of heat or of cold (Brown and Urban, 1969). In addition to any thermoregulatory advantages of joining pods, the pod also provides some protection from predators in the absence of parents (Evans, 1984b).

In the American white pelican this pod-forming process also begins at about

three weeks of age, and in one case by the time the chicks were 50 days old all of them in one colony had joined a single large pod (Schaller, 1964). In the Australian pelican the smaller chicks in pods return to their nests when one of their parents returns to the nest. Medium-sized chicks are fed in or at the edge of the pod, and there is mutual recognition between parents and chicks. Larger youngsters leave the pod and move to their parents when they land, often more than 40 meters from the group. Then feeding usually occurs in shallow water, and by that age the birds do not attempt to beg food from adults other than their parents (Vestjens, 1977a).

In at least the pelican species so far studied (Australian, American white, eastern white, pink-backed), parents will consistently feed only their own chicks. Chicks may beg to be fed by other adults, but are typically avoided or even pecked. However, feeding of another pair's chick was observed once in the pink-backed pelican, apparently in response to its violent convulsive behavior (Burke and Brown, 1970). These strange convulsive movements occur in the young of several pelican species, and it has been suggested that they may be exaggerated begging displays (Schaller, 1964). However, Vestjens (1977a) stated that such convulsions occur only after feeding, and might be triggered by some physical stimulus, such as having encountered breathing difficulties while in the parent's pouch. Drummond (1987) has recently argued that this strange behavior probably indeed serves as a display, possibly reflecting parent-offspring conflict tendencies.

Like pelicans, cormorants only very rarely feed chicks other than their own. Mendall (1936) observed only a single case of an adult double-crested cormorant momentarily feeding a strange chick that had entered the nest and was simul-

Figure 34. Growth and early plumage development of the brown pelican, showing chick at hatching (A), 3 weeks (B), 6 weeks (C), 9 weeks (D), and 12 weeks (E). Not drawn to exact scale; partly after photos by D. Guravich in Brown (1983).

TABLE 25   Reproductive and Social Traits of Cormorants, Darters, and Pelicans

Trait	Cormorants	Darters	Pelicans
Colonial breeding	Present in all groups		
Territorial defense	Limited to nest site in all groups		
Pair-bonding pattern	Seasonally monogamous in all groups		
Pair bond tenacity	Apparently slight in all groups		
Sex plumage dichromatism	Lacking	Moderate	Lacking
Sex softpart dichromatism	Slight or none	Present	Slight or none
Female : male mass ratio	ca. 80–95%	ca. 90–95%	ca. 80–90%
Years to initial breeding	2–4 (rarely 5)	2–3?	3–4 (rarely 2)
Prenuptial molt	Limited (head and upperpart) molt in both sexes		
Prenuptial skin changes	Softpart changes (color and texture) in both sexes		
Male wing-waving display	In many species	In both species	Absent
Pretakeoff display	In both sexes	In both sexes	Absent
Postlanding display	In both sexes	In both sexes	Absent
Kink-throating display	In both sexes	In both sexes	Absent
Mate recognition display	Mutual ceremonies present in all groups		
Allopreening of mate	In some species	In both species	Absent
Courtship vocalizations	Few or none	Several	Usually none
Alarm vocalizations	Absent in nearly all species		
Courtship feeding	Absent in all groups		
Nest site tenacity	Sometimes high	Unreported	Often absent
Nest material gathering	Mostly or entirely by male in all groups		
Nest building	Mainly by female in all groups		
Copulation site	On nest or potential nest site in all groups		
Reversed mounting	In some species	Unreported	Unreported
Bush or tree nesting	In some species	Typical	In small species
Usual clutch size	3–4 eggs	4 eggs	2–3 eggs
Eggshell texture	Chalky in all groups		
Egg color	Blue to green	Blue to green	Whitish
Egg mass : female mass	ca. 2–4%	ca. 2.5%	ca. 2–3%
Clutch mass : female mass	ca. 5–20%	ca. 10–12%	ca. 4–11%
Laying interval	2–3 days	2–3 days	2–4 days
Incubation roles	By both sexes in all groups		
Incubation onset	Usually with first egg in all groups		
Incubation method	Under foot webs	Under foot webs?	On foot webs
Incubation period	24–31 days	21–30 days	28–34 days
Brooding roles	Both sexes brood and feed young in all groups		
Chick food begging	With bill closed in all groups		
Chick water begging	Bill opened	Bill opened	Unreported
Initial chick feeding	Usually from bill tip of adults		
Older chick feeding	Directly from adult's throat in all groups		
Creche ("pod") forming by young	Uncommon	Unreported	Common
Fledging period	35–70 days	50–60 days	70–100 days
Postfledging independence	Shortly after fledging in all groups		

taneously food-begging along with two of her own young. A few minutes later the chick was driven out of the nest. When chicks wander off from their nests their parents sometimes go in search of them and try to drive them back, or the parents may simply go to the nest and wait for their young to return. In at least some cormorants the older and more mobile chicks may gather at communal perching areas,

TABLE 26   Selected Productivity Estimates of Cormorants, Darters, and Pelicans

Species	Total nests[1]	Total eggs	Average clutch	Chicks hatched (%)	Young fledged (%)[2]	Source
Cormorants						
Long-tailed c.						
Ghana	59	216	3.66	— (80%)	63/80 (78%)	Bowen et al., 1962
Natal	68	246	3.6	207 (84%)	149 (61%)	Olver, 1984
Crowned c.						
Cape Province	40	112	2.8	54 (48%)	—	Williams & Cooper, 1983
Brandt's c.						
age of female:						
2–3 yr.	28	—	2.5	— (41%)	— (31%)	Boekelheide & Ainley, 1989
4–5 yr.	22	—	2.9	— (52%)	— (69%)	
6–7 yr.	32	—	3.4	— (62%)	— (79%)	
8–10 yr.	17	—	3.3	— (65%)	— (81%)	
all ages:						
early nests	—	292	—	— (59%)	— (78%)	Ainley & Boekelheide, 1990
mid nests	—	293	—	— (66%)	— (79%)	
late nests	—	216	—	— (58%)	— (72%)	
Neotropic c.						
Texas	55	158	2.87	91 (57%)	52 (57%)	Morrison et al., 1979
Double-crested c.						
Mandarte Is.	66	273	4.13	165 (60%)	157 (95%)	Drent et al., 1964
Mandarte Is.	150	455	3.03	365 (80%)	283 (77%)	van der Veen, 1973
Utah	76	295	3.88	160 (54%)	—	Mitchell, 1977
Alaska	21	—	3.17	— (49%)	— (93%)	DeGange & Sanger, 1986
Quebec	195	841	4.3	476 (56%)	426 (89%)	Pilon et al., 1983
Pied c.						
Victoria	256	—	3.32	221/511 (43%)	134 (61%)	Norman, 1974
Great c.						
Natal	60	186	3.05	139 (75%)	96 (69%)	Olver & Kuyper, 1978
Quebec	112	497	4.4	344 (69.2%)	ca. 225 (65%)	Pilon et al., 1983
Shags						
Imperial s.						
Crozet Is.	20	58	2.9	34/52 (65%)	20 (59%)	Derenne et al., 1976
Marion Is.	41	—	2.6	— (53.6%)	4/18 (22%)	Williams & Burger, 1979
Macquarie Is.	58	159	2.74	119 (75%)	86 (72%)	Brothers, 1985
European s.						
England	447	1,353	3.07	632/893 (71%)	549 (86%)	Snow, 1960
Pelagic s.						
Ugaiushak Is.	78	260	3.33	166 (64%)	150 (92%)	Nysewander, 1986
Chiniak Bay	46	134	2.91	75 (55%)	44 (59%)	Nysewander, 1986
Barren Is.	124	401	3.23	180 (45%)	145 (80%)	Nysewander, 1986
Mandarte Is.	37	141	3.8	70 (50%)	77/101 (76%)	Drent et al., 1964
Alaska	179	—	3.08	— (54%)	— (75%)	DeGange & Sanger, 1986
Farallon Is.	264	891	3.37	— (48%)	— (61%)	Ainley & Boekelheide, 1990
Red-faced s.						
Pribilof Is.	41	—	2.8	— (61%)	— (50%)	Hunt et al., 1978
Alaska	264	—	2.6	— (36%)	— (86%)	DeGange & Sanger, 1986

(continued)

TABLE 26   (*Continued*)

Species	Total nests[1]	Total eggs	Average clutch	Chicks hatched (%)	Young fledged (%)[2]	Source
Darters						
Anhinga						
Arkansas	29	101	3.5	—	27	Meanley, 1954
Mexico	21	77	3.7	48 (81%)	—	Burger et al., 1978
African darter						
1st brood	26	88	3.4	— (89%)	72/89 (81%)	Bowen et al., 1962
2nd brood	19	71	3.8	— (58%)	13/58 (22%)	Bowen et al., 1962
Pelicans						
Pink-backed p.						
Kenya	—	—	—	39/41 (95%)	23/42 (55%)	Burke & Brown, 1970
Uganda	155	307	1.98	—	16/39 (41%)	Din & Eltringham, 1974a
Australian p.						
N.S.W.	67	130	1.94	104/130 (80%)	76 (73%)	Vestjens, 1977a
American white p.						
S. Dakota	20	39	1.95	20/22 (91%)	13/28 (46%)	McCrow, 1974
Brown p.						
Florida	328	860	2.62	610 (71%)	318 (52%)	Schreiber, 1979

[1] Nests lacking eggs are excluded from calculations. Some of these data represent combined results of two or more breeding seasons, and thus obscure any year-to-year variations.

[2] Represents percentage of hatched young, not of total eggs.

where they continue to be fed by their parents (van Tets, 1959). Unfledged darters may also gather on lower tree branches with nestlings of other pairs (Vestjens, 1975).

Fledging periods are of course generally size-related, being as short as about 35 days in some smaller cormorants and up to 12 weeks for pelicans. During that period the young birds first acquire two successive coats of down. The first of these coats (protoptiles) is no sooner grown than it is supplemented by a second and more luxurious generation of down that is produced by additional feather follicles. The second coat of down (mesoptiles) in turn is supplemented and soon hidden by the bird's juvenal plumage, which is apparently produced by the same feather follicles that generated the first down coat. The juvenal plumage is mostly grown at the time of fledging, with only a few areas of down still visible (figure 34).

By way of general summary, table 25 provides a comparison of some of the major features of the reproductive biologies of cormorants, darters, and pelicans as described in this and the previous chapter. Additionally, table 26 provides a summary of some representative estimates of average clutch sizes and relative hatching and rearing success in a variety of species.

CHAPTER 7

Population Dynamics and Conservation Biology

Ever since the pioneering work by David Lack (1968) on the evolutionary adaptiveness of avian life histories and breeding biology, the seabirds have been characterized as a distinctive group of species that in general possess long life spans, a similarly long period of sexual immaturity, and relatively low reproductive rates, typically involving the rearing of a single chick. Lack related these attributes to the general unpredictability of the ocean's resources, especially for those species that must travel considerable distances between their nesting grounds and their feeding areas when they are rearing young. Later, Ashmole (1963, 1971) suggested that competition for food among breeding adults could account for the evolution of a small clutch size and also regulate population size through density-dependent variations in reproductive success. Dunn (1979) argued that the small clutch sizes and slow growth rates of seabirds may be the result of long-term adaptive reductions in annual reproductive effort (which may tend to favor increased average longevities), rather than reflecting the proximate or short-term effects of immediate food shortages. Thus, in Dunn's view, typical seabird species have become adaptively "geared" to exhibit slow population turnover rates, and are unlikely to be able to rebound quickly from environmental disasters.

Ricklefs (1990) has recently reviewed Lack's and these other more recent ideas on seabird life histories. He concluded that although Lack's views were fundamentally correct, they have oversimplified the situation with regard to seabirds, and fail to provide testable explanations for the current data base of field observations. For example, competition for local food supplies near nesting colonies during the breeding season may be a limiting factor in setting reproductive limits for some species, whereas others may be limited by available nest sites, or even by density-dependent factors that operate outside the breeding season. As a result, new and more comprehensive hypotheses, and better research techniques, are needed for studying the environmental factors controlling seabird populations and influencing the evolution of their life history strategies.

Life History Strategies

To a greater extent than is true of most landbirds, it seems that sea-oriented birds, such as at least some of the species here, are exposed to and presumably adapted to population oscillations associated with periodic variations in climate, ocean current patterns, and relative food supplies. Thus, in areas such as the Pacific coast of South America, where the bird populations are dependent upon upwellings of the nutrient- and food-rich Humboldt current, there are infrequent major changes in ocean current patterns that deflect these upwellings away from the coast. These events, known as El Niño–Southern Oscillations, produce food base reductions resulting in periods of reduced avian productivity and often severe population declines. "ENSO events" may cause nest desertion, regional nonbreeding, or starvation and associated adult and young mortality.

During years of such major abnormal oceanographic conditions there are sometimes disastrous effects on the populations of three major coastally nesting seabird species, the brown pelican, the guanay cormorant, and the Peruvian booby (*Sula variegata*). All of these species depend directly on the anchoveta *Engraulis ringens* for their primary food resource. At average intervals of five years, relatively mild El Niño conditions produce an average adult mortality of 17 percent in these avian populations, representing a reduction that is probably not much higher than the normal annual mortality rates in these species. However, at intervals averaging twelve years severe El Niño conditions produce an average adult mortality of 47 percent (Duffy, 1980a). In 1983, the El Niño in the Pacific Ocean, and related effects elsewhere in the world, caused some of the most environmentally severe effects in a century. In Peru these changes produced an estimated mortality among the three primary guano species of about 85 percent, one of the highest such rates ever recorded (Duffy et al., 1988).

Apparently in association with their unpredictable conditions, the Humboldt current seabirds appear to have become somewhat adapted to unstable environments by adopting reproductive strategies that facilitate rapid population increases under favorable conditions, which range from 8 to 18 percent annually in protected nesting areas having favorable breeding conditions (Duffy, 1980a). Among birds in general, these adaptations typically include relatively large clutches, rapid growth rates, early sexual maturities, high rates of population increase, and relatively short life spans associated with high adult mortality rates. Thus, the Peruvian booby has an average clutch size of three eggs, as compared with the one-egg or two-egg clutches typical of the other booby species (Nelson, 1978). However, it should be noted that average clutch sizes in the Chilean brown pelican and the guanay shag are apparently no larger than those of their near relatives, and little if any comparative information exists on rates of sexual maturity and mortality in these South American species.

In a comparable manner, the Brandt's cormorant of the southern Californian coastline exhibits a number of life history attributes that adapt it to surviving in a relatively variable year-to-year environment. Thus, these birds begin breeding at a relatively early age, at least under favorable conditions, but in unfavorable years breeding may be delayed. Females also exhibit low site tenacity and mate fidelity, which allows for adaptive flexibility, and in poor years the birds may lay smaller clutches, abandon breeding efforts, or not attempt to breed at all, all of which may help insure better survival until the following breeding opportunity (Boekelheide and Ainley, 1989). A somewhat similar array of attributes was reported by Harris (1979) with respect to the Galapagos cormorant, which also breeds in an annually relatively variable environment that is subject to ENSO influences.

In a reduced degree, the population biologies of seabirds nesting in the Gulf of Alaska show some similarities to those of species nesting along the California and

Peruvian coasts. There too, food availability seems to have a very large influence on reproductive success, especially among surface-feeding seabirds but to some degree also among coastal divers such as cormorants and shags. In the Gulf of Alaska, two general adaptations seem to have evolved in the locally breeding seabirds to help cope with temporally unpredictable food resources, namely multi-egg clutch sizes and egg or chick neglect (DeGange and Sanger, in Hood and Zimmerman, 1986). Similarly, in the Southern California Bight the relative availability of northern anchovies (*Engraulis modax*) was found to be the most important variable affecting fledging success in brown pelicans, especially when measured on a local basis (Anderson, Gress, and Mais, 1982).

Normally, however, cormorants, darters, and pelicans are much more like typical seabirds than like more terrestrially adapted waterfowl such as geese in that they typically exhibit relatively conservative (k-based) reproduction strategies. In general, the life history strategies of a variety of seabirds suggest that most of these species are adapted to low rates of population turnover, and are unable to recover quickly from sudden increases in mortality (Dunn, 1979). These strategies seem to be associated with keeping the population at or near the environment's carrying capacity and avoiding overreproducing to the point that density-dependent types of mortality become a serious problem. These adaptations of course are the opposite of those of the seabirds of the Humboldt current, and include relatively small clutches, slow growth rates, deferred sexual maturities, rather low rates of population increase, and relatively long life spans associated with low adult mortality rates.

Over the long run, a species is likely to roughly balance its postfledging (immature and adult) mortality rates with its annual productivity rate, as reflected by the percentage of newly fledged birds "recruited" into the population each year. Typical nesting productivity estimates (at least in terms of hatching and fledging success) for a variety of species were summarized in the last chapter. However, these data are not easily converted into population productivity (annual recruitment) estimates, inasmuch as immature and nonbreeding components of the population are excluded from such figures. A much more useful (and more simply acquired) statistic for estimating annual productivity rates would consist of estimated percentages of juvenile birds in the overall postbreeding populations. Unfortunately, although these figures are easily obtained from hunter-kill data for species such as waterfowl, cranes, and gallinaceous birds that are legally "harvested," very few if any comparable population recruitment data seem to have been gathered for the species under consideration here. It is possible that die-offs resulting from oil kills or other seemingly nonselective mortality factors, although possibly biased in some ways, might provide a source of such information for coastal species.

Annual Mortality Rates

An alternate method of understanding and interpreting population dynamics in these species may be obtained by calculating annual adult mortality (or the reciprocal annual survival) rates. Such data are certainly much harder to obtain than estimates of the percentage of juveniles in a population. They are thus available for only a few species that have been banded in relatively high numbers over a long time period, resulting in an adequate sample of later band recoveries or sightings for estimating intervening mortality rates.

Adult mortality rates have been fairly confidently estimated for only a very few species of cormorants and pelicans by using band recovery data. Schreiber and Mock (1988) concluded that in spite of 60 years of banding, a complete life table cannot yet be calculated for the brown pelican, regardless of some efforts in this direction. These authors, like Henny (1972) before them, estimated a remarkably high first-year mortality rate of about 70 percent for this species. They furthermore judged that the effective reproductive life span (after initially attaining maturity at three years) for most adult brown pelicans may only be 4–7 years, thus implying that an annual adult mortality rate of 15 percent must occur. Since breeding brown pelicans typically produce about one fledged young per pair per year, it is apparent that those birds surviving to adulthood are unlikely to contribute more than four fledged young each to the overall population during their lifetimes unless they survive for at least 8 more years. It is clear from these data that mortality rates in brown pelicans must decline sharply after their first year, probably in conjunction with their improving foraging efficiencies. Indeed, assuming a 70 percent first-year mortality rate, and 15 percent mortalities yearly for the next two years, only about 22 percent of the original fledged cohort would still be alive by the end of their third year. This means that each of these birds would have to contribute about five fledged offspring during their lifetimes in order to keep the population stable, and thus must survive an average of another ten years in order to generate enough offspring at the rate of one fledged bird per pair per year. Clearly, either adult mortality rates must be well below 15 percent per year, or first-year mortality must be substantially below the estimated 70 percent rate. However, a first-year mortality of 70 percent has also been reported for the Atlantic gannet (*Sula bassana*), which forages in essentially the same highly specialized manner as the brown pelican, and similarly high first-year mortalities have been observed in some other seabird species (Nelson, 1979).

A life table for the American white pelican was constructed by Strait and Sloan (1974), based on band recoveries from more than 850 birds hatched at Chase Lake National Wildlife Refuge in North Dakota. They estimated a 41 percent mortality rate between fledging and the end of the first year of life, a 16 percent mortality for second-year birds, and a 21.3 percent annual mortality thereafter, at least through the thirteenth year. On the basis of these figures, and assuming initial breeding at three years, they calculated that in order to maintain a stable population an average of 1.08 young would have to be fledged per breeding pair each year, resulting in an annual recruitment rate of fledged young into the population of 42 percent. Since this calculated required productivity is considerably more than their observed productivity (somewhat less than 0.62 young per nest during one year of observation), they judged that their adult mortality estimates may have been artificially inflated as a result of band loss, especially among older age groups. Seemingly, adult mortality rates should be no higher than second-year mortality rates, or perhaps in the range of 15 percent annually, which as suggested may be the approximate situation with the brown pelican.

From the data provided by Strait and Sloan, and incorporating statistical adjustments to compensate for estimated band losses, Ryder (1981) recalculated a modified annual adult mortality rate of about 10 percent for the North Dakota population of American white pelicans. Ryder also estimated a first-year mortality rate of 33 percent for the Colorado population of American white pelicans, a second-year mortality of 17 percent, and a very high adult mortality of about 28 percent annually for older age classes. As Crivelli (1987) suggested, pelican populations suffering such high adult mortality rates cannot be maintained for long, and he calculated that a stable population of the Dalmatian pelican could be expected under conditions of an annual adult mortality rate of no more than about 18 percent and an annual breeding success of 1–1.05 young fledged per nest.

Great cormorant adult mortality rates were estimated in the Netherlands by Kortlandt (1942) at 9–14 percent for females at least four years old and 7–12 percent for males at least three years old. First-year female mortality rates were estimated at 36 percent, second-year rates at 22 percent, and third-year at 16 percent. Young males had similar mortality rates to those of young females. These rates occurred in a population that was expanding at a rate of about 10 percent per year. In a Scottish colony subjected to substantial loss by shooting, the first-year mortality rate was estimated at 70 percent, with subsequent yearly mortality rates ranging from 28 to 46 percent (Stuart, 1948). In a South African study, Skead (1980) reported a mean annual mortality rate of 55.4 percent for all birds banded as nestlings, but with most deaths (73 percent) occurring within a year of banding.

By far the best information on mortality rates in any species considered here comes from work on the European shag (Potts, 1969; Potts, Coulson, and Deans, 1980). Potts (1969) provided estimated first-year mortality rates for shags from ten areas, which ranged from 39 to 74 percent, averaging 61 percent. For birds on his Farne Island study area (where the population was increasing at an annual rate of about 11 percent), the first-year mortality rate was estimated as 41 percent, and annual mortality after the first year averaged 16 percent. Among birds that were at least three years old and of breeding age, the mean annual mortality rate for males was 15 percent, and for females 20 percent. Mortality rates in various multiyear adult age classes up to the oldest analyzed (10–15 years) did not differ appreciably from these overall averages, although birds older than 9 years may have survived less well in a few stressful years. Additionally, survival averaged somewhat higher in those birds having a higher level of prior-season breeding success, suggesting that individuals that are poor breeders also tend to be less likely to survive outside the breeding season.

In a more recent analysis of the Farne Island shag data (Potts, Coulson, and Deans, 1980), the mean overall adult annual mortality was recalculated at 17 percent, and in this more recent analysis breeding females were judged to have an annual survival rate averaging only 1.3 percent lower than that of males. However, overall mortality rates were much higher during years of "red tides" and associated massive shellfish poisoning of seabirds. After the first year, age apparently does not appreciably influence mortality rates in European shags, with the possible exception of the very old age classes.

Cobley (1989) estimated survival rates for imperial shags on the South Orkney Islands using 18 years of data on return of marked birds to their breeding sites. Based on the period 1984–1986, the mean annual survival rate was estimated as 89.9 percent (mortality rate 10.1 percent), which is the highest survival rate known to me for any species of this family. Using data obtained from 1979 to 1987, a somewhat lower long-term survival rate (77.7 percent) was estimated, with females possibly having a slightly lower average rate than males, although not showing a statistically significant difference.

Return rates of banded Brandt's cormorants on the Farallon Islands, California, varied from year to year over a twelve-year period, but among nearly 3,000 birds banded as chicks only 17 percent returned as potentially breeding adults, at average ages of 2.7 (females) to 2.9 years (males). Males actually first bred at an average age of 4.2 years, and females at 3.5 years. Males were found to breed subsequently for periods ranging from 1 to 8 years, averaging 2.4 years, and females were found to breed for periods of from 1 to 7 years, averaging 2.2 years. After they had reached nine years of age, males exhibited a marked drop in return rates, and females showed a similar marked decline at seven years of age. Very few birds (nearly all of which were males) lived beyond ten years. However, older age classes of both sexes exhibited higher overall rates of reproductive success than did younger birds, with a slight decline in fledging success apparent only in the oldest age classes of both sexes (Boekelheide and Ainley, 1989).

In his study of the imperial shag, Shaw (1985a, 1986) reported that at Signy Island initial breeding does not occur on average among males until they are five years old, and among females until they are 5.4 years, but with considerable individual variation. Birds as old as twelve years were still active breeders, with those at least ten years old comprising 20 percent of the breeding male sample (177 birds) in one year, and 24 percent of the breeding female sample (127 birds) in the same year. These old females showed only a slight decrease in average clutch size and average egg size as compared with middle-aged breeders. This remarkably high percentage of old individuals in the breeding population suggests that a very low annual mortality rate must occur among adults, although such estimates were not provided.

Van der Veen (1973) estimated mortality rates for double-crested cormorants on Mandarte Island, British Columbia, based on subsequent-year sightings of birds marked as nestlings. He thereby estimated a first-year mortality rate of 51.9 percent, a second-year mortality rate of 26.2 percent, and a subsequent annual mortality rate of 15.1 percent. This would mean that about 12 percent of the nestlings should survive to adulthood and potential initial breeding at nearly three years of age, or averaging slightly less than the estimates of preadult mortality just presented for the Brandt's cormorant.

Harris (1979) estimated that about 57 percent of the juvenile Galapagos cormorants living long enough to leave their nests and reach the sea survive until the end of their first year, and that the annual survival rate for immatures is 85.7 percent. Initial breeding occurs at about 30 months, so approximately 43 percent of the fledgling juveniles should survive long enough to attempt breeding at least once. Adult males had an estimated survival rate of 82.4 percent and adult females 91.4 percent.

Mortality rate data summarized for ten species of northern seabirds by Dunn (1979) indicated a range of annual adult mortality rates of 4 to 25 percent, with most species falling between 10 and 20 percent. These percentages are similar to those reported for the European shag, great cormorant, and double-crested cormorant, and suggested for the brown and American white pelicans. A larger sample of annual adult mortality rates in seabirds provided by Nelson (1979:166) shows a similar range. Associated ages of first breeding ranged from two to seven years in Dunn's summary, and most frequently was from three to four years. So far as is now known, the species included in this book require from two to four years to begin breeding, and thus seem to be fairly typical seabirds in this regard. Clutch sizes in the species mentioned by Dunn ranged from one to four eggs, and most commonly consisted of single-egg clutches. Except for the absence of any species regularly laying single-egg clutches, the three groups included in this book's coverage fall within these same general ranges.

Given the obvious limitations on available mortality rate data, which are essentially limited to six species of cormorants and two of pelicans, it is hard to be confident about overall life history trends in the groups considered here. Seemingly, however, there is a very high rate of first-year mortality following fledging, especially in species with high-risk foraging behaviors such as brown pelicans (and gannets). This early high mortality is followed by a rapid decline in mortality rates for both sexes, and a relatively long period of additional life expectancy (often ten or more years) once reproductive maturity has been attained. During the nesting cycle most losses among cormorants, darters, and pelicans occur at the egg stage rather than among nestlings, and persistent renesting after clutch loss appears to be a rather typical compensating mechanism for dealing with early nest failures. Brood reduction strategies such as "siblicide" or differential and age-related chick survival mechanisms have apparently evolved in some species to help ensure the survival of at least one chick. There also appears to be a tendency for experienced and successful breeders to survive better than unsuccessful breeders, and for experienced birds to preempt and utilize the better nesting sites. Breeding with the mate of the prior year, and at the same nesting site, appears to be positively related to prior breeding success, and relatively old age classes furthermore appear to survive just as well as younger ones. All of these traits tend to suggest that a key to successful long-term survival in these birds is the maintenance of a considerable proportion of older and reproductively experienced birds in the breeding flock, whereas the younger age classes are substantially less reproductively valuable and thus are less likely to contribute to the next generation.

If there is a conservation lesson to be extracted from these trends, it is that nonselective mortality factors—such as oil spills, red tides, and pesticide poisoning—can have surprisingly long-lasting detrimental effects on a seabird population. This is a result of the indiscriminant elimination of the older, reproductively more reliable and thus more valuable breeders as well as the younger nonbreeding and less efficiently breeding population components. Even though it may take but a few years for a local population to again start to regenerate breeding birds following such a disaster, it may be 10 or even 15 years before the population structure has regained its normal and most efficiently reproducing characteristics.

Regional and Continental Population Estimates

In contrast to many gamebird species, in which populations are monitored on a yearly basis and for which a great deal of population trend data are available, there is relatively little information on the population status of most of these species. Luckily, none of the species included in this book is currently considered endangered, although the populations of some of the insular shags (on Pitt, Bounty, and Chatham islands for example) are inherently very small and must be very susceptible to extinction, just as the Pallas' cormorant was driven to rapid extinction over a century ago.

Rare, Threatened, and Endangered Taxa

Of the world's species of cormorants, the Galapagos cormorant is probably the rarest and potentially the most threatened, with a recent known population of about 1,000 birds (Rosenberg and Harcourt, 1987). It was the only species of cormorant or pelican listed as "rare" in a recent (1988) listing of threatened animals produced by the International Union for the Conservation of Nature and Natural Resources (IUCN), although the New Zealand king cormorant and pygmy cormorant were classified as "insufficiently known." If the New Zealand king cormorant and each of its island derivatives are considered separate species, they too are candidates for "endangered" or "rare" status. The king cormorant is now considered endangered by New Zealand authorities and probably has an overall population of no more than 1,000 pairs. Similar population sizes are estimated for the Auckland Island, Bounty Island, Campbell Island, Chatham Island, and Pitt Island shags (Robertson and Bell, 1984; Marchant and Higgins, 1990). The Auckland Island, Campbell Island, Chatham Island, and Stewart Island shags are classified as "rare" endemics. The same is true for the Pitt Island shag, an insular derivative of the endemic spotted shag (Bell, 1986). The two races of the spotted shag are also listed as New Zealand endemics, but are not regarded as rare.

TABLE 27 Estimated Cormorant and Shag Breeding Populations, Western Europe and the North Atlantic

Region	Great Cormorant	European Shag	Pygmy Cormorant
Greenland	750–1,500	—	—
Iceland	3,500	6,600	—
Faeroe Islands	1–10	5,000–10,000	—
Britain	7,000	38,500	—
Ireland	4,700	8,800	—
Norway	21,000	ca. 33,000	—
Sweden	3,400	—	—
Lithuania	260	—	—
Poland	1,475	—	—
Germany	1,375	—	—
Denmark	14,100	—	—
Netherlands	13,600	—	—
Belgium	>100	—	—
France	1,100	3,900	—
Spain	1–10	—	—
Czechoslovakia	520	—	—
Hungary	600	—	—
Austria	>50	—	—
Italy	200	1,190	—
Romania	4,000	—	ca. 12,000
Bulgaria	600	—	—
Yugoslavia	—	1,000	300+
Albania	few	—	ca. 2,000
Greece	180	1,000	ca. 550
Turkey	900	—	200+
Total (pairs)	ca. 80,000	ca. 100,000	15,000+

NOTES: Estimates for the British Isles (1985–1987) are from Lloyd, Tasker, and Partridge (1991). The same source was used for figures from the Faeroe Islands, Sweden, Norway (great cormorant only), Denmark, Netherlands, Belgium, France (great cormorant only), Spain, Czechoslovakia, Austria, Italy, Greece, and Turkey. Other great cormorant estimates in Europe (for early 1980s) are mostly from Hansen (1984), but Lithuania's, for 1991, are from Dr. Prana Mierauskas (personal communication). Icelandic estimates (for 1975) are from Gardarsson (1979), and Greenland's (for 1983) are from P. Evans (1984). France's shag figures (for 1985) are from Debout (1987), and the Norwegian shag estimate (for 1970–1974) is from Brun (1979). Figures for the pygmy cormorant in Albania and Romania are from Collar and Andrew (1988).

Among noninsular cormorants, the rarest is perhaps the pygmy cormorant, recently listed as "threatened" by Collar and Andrew (1988). Its populations are still only poorly documented (table 27), especially for Romania, which is probably its greatest remaining stronghold outside the former USSR.

The only pelicans that are believed to be in current danger are the spot-billed and Dalmatian pelicans, both of which were recently listed as "threatened" by Collar and Andrew (1988). They believed that Sri Lanka may support about 900 pairs of spot-billed pelicans in 23 colonies, and India fewer than 400 pairs in four colonies. There is no information on the species' status in Burma and China.

The Dalmatian pelican was classified as "vulnerable" by the International Council for Bird Protection in the late 1970s (King, 1981) and more recently was described as "world-endangered" by Crivelli (1987). The population of this largest of all pelicans has declined very greatly during the present century, and is now quite precarious (table 28). Its population in the mid-1980s may have been between 514 and 1,368 pairs at 19 known recent breeding sites, most of which were in the USSR (Crivelli, 1987). Ecological changes in the heart of its USSR breeding range associated with river diversions for large-scale irrigation projects, with consequent associated wetland losses, do not bode well for this species.

North American and European Pelecaniform Populations

Other than for these extremely rare species, quantitative data on regional and national populations of cormorants, darters, and pelicans are generally available for relatively few areas. Available population information on the cormorants, shags, and pelicans of the western Palearctic was summarized by Cramp and Simmons (1977) for species of that region, and some of this information is tabulated here (tables 27 and 28), in somewhat expanded and updated form. Some of this is obviously outdated now, given the fact that cormorant and shag populations seem capable of increasing at rates of about 5–12 percent per year under favorable

TABLE 28   Estimated Eastern White and Dalmatian Pelican Breeding Populations, Europe and Asia

Region	Eastern White	Dalmatian
Yugoslavia	—	10–20 (1)
Romania	3,000–3,500 (1)	36–115 (2)
Albania	—	70–100? (1)
Bulgaria	—	70–90 (1)
Greece	40–150 (1)	124–210 (2)
Turkey	500–1,500 (1)	70–115 (5)
Iran	235–550 (3)	5–10 (1)
Iraq	?	?
India/Pakistan	?	—
USSR	3,070–4,300 (16–18)	1,500–2,000 (7–8)
Mongolia	?	40–50? (1)
China	?	?
Total	6,845–10,000 (22–24)	1,925–2,710 (21–22)

NOTES: Data from Crivelli, Catsadorakis, et al. (1991). Numbers indicate breeding pairs, with numbers of known breeding grounds in parentheses. Total figures for eastern white pelicans have been corrected from originals provided by authors.

conditions. However, the numbers do at least provide a baseline for future comparisons, and a guide to areas badly in need of new surveys.

A more concerted effort has been made by federal agencies in North America during the 1970s and 1980s to survey colonially breeding birds in the United States and Canada. A major attempt to summarize the data for eastern Canada has been provided by Brown et al. (1975), but no comparable summary exists for western Canada. Much of the relevant colony size and location information for the United States south of Canada has recently been summarized by Spendelow and Patton (1988). This source, together with the earlier Alaska summary (Sowls, Hatch, and Lensink, 1978) and other individual state or regional summaries provides a useful basis for deriving continental distribution patterns.

One subject of general ecological interest with regard to these species concerns average colony sizes, and the related question of whether there are species-typical predispositions in colony size for any species. Because of the large numbers of U.S. surveys from all parts of their ranges, and associated colony size data (mostly from Spendelow and Patton, 1988), it is possible to tabulate size-frequency distribution patterns for breeding colonies of the seven species of pelecaniform birds breeding in the United States south of Canada (table 29). These data suggest that the pelagic shag and anhinga are the least gregarious of the seven species, showing distribution patterns resembling Poisson curves and suggesting that aggregations, rather than congregations, typify breeding assemblages of these two species. The data are more equivocal for Brandt's and double-crested cormorants; either these species are somewhat more social than the pelagic shag and anhinga, or their site requirements for nesting are sufficiently broad as to allow relatively large breeding aggregations to form where the food base permits. Data for the Neotropic cormorant and the brown pelican are too limited to try to assess their relative coloniality, but the American white pelican would appear to be the most highly colonial of all seven species, with about as many U.S. and Canadian colonies having more than 1,000 birds present as those having fewer than 1,000 birds. This is somewhat surprising, in view of the fact that it is the largest of all the species and thus has the greatest food requirements. Clearly, very large pelican colonies can only develop where foraging opportunities are unusually good, and there must be a significant advantage to participating in colonial nesting for these birds rather than forming small colonies or nesting asocially.

Of the North American pelecaniform birds, among the smallest populations is

TABLE 29   Size Frequency Distributions of Pelecaniform Breeding Colonies
in North America

	Colony size (total birds)							
	1–50	51–100	101–200	201–500	501–1,000	1,001–2,000	2,001–5,000	5,001–10,000	Over 10,000
Brandt's c.	41	17	24	30	11	9	5	—	1
Neotropic c.	1	4	1	3	3	1	1	—	—
Double-crested c.	63	30	44	51	32	7	—	—	—
Pelagic shag	237	70	41	29	3	1	—	—	—
Anhinga	44	11	4	1	2	—	—	—	—
Brown pelican	7	6	3	9	8	1	3	—	—
Am. white pelican	6	3	5	11	5	9	12	5	1

NOTES: Based on regional U.S. breeding surveys from the 1970s, excluding Alaska (Spendelow and Patton, 1988), except for the American white pelican, which is based on 1979–1981 Canadian and U.S. surveys (Sidle, Koonz, and Roney, 1985). Underlining indicates species' median colony size category.

that of the great cormorant, which is limited to the maritime provinces of eastern Canada. There its highest populations are attained along the fish-rich areas of the Nova Scotia shelf, the Gulf of Maine, and the Bay of Fundy. Double-crested cormorants are also very common in this same region, but are also surprisingly common in the interior fresh-water lakes of Manitoba and Saskatchewan, especially the former province (table 30).

Double-crested cormorants are also increasingly common breeders along the Atlantic coast of the United States, particularly along the Maine coast, with a secondary center of abundance along coastal Florida, not only on the Atlantic side but also extending north on the Gulf coast almost to the Florida panhandle. However, they are absent as breeders from the Gulf coast of Louisiana and Texas, where they are replaced by the Neotropic cormorant. From the Carolinas south to Florida the double-crested cormorant is supplemented by the brown pelican (now slowly expanding its breeding range northward) and the anhinga, which seems to reach a peak of abundance in Louisiana but is virtually absent as a breeding species in Texas. According to available information, it is the rarest North American breeding species of pelecaniform bird (tables 31, 34).

Along the Pacific coast of the United States the Brandt's cormorant is easily the commonest of the three breeding species of cormorants and shags, with the double-crested the least common, suggesting that perhaps it suffers from competition with the Brandt's (table 31). The double-crested becomes relatively more common in British Columbia and Alaska, where the Brandt's cormorant is lacking, but not nearly so common as the pelagic shag, which is highly adapted to nesting along glacially cut fjords and similar cliff-lined coastal areas (table 32). As one proceeds northwest along the southern coast of Alaska and the Aleutian Islands the pelagic shag is in turn progressively replaced by the red-faced shag.

TABLE 30   Estimated Cormorant Breeding Populations, Atlantic Maritime and Interior Canada

Region	Double-crested Cormorant	Great Cormorant
Maritime provinces[1]		
E. Nfld. and Labrador	258/8	72/2
Gulf of St. Lawrence	11,661/29	1,754/18
Scotian Shelf, Gulf of Maine, and Bay of Fundy	37,997/41	3,547/17
Total coastal birds	49,916	5,373
Total colonies	78	37
Ave. birds/colony	640	145
Canadian interior[2]		
Ontario, Great Lakes	2,350	—
Manitoba	45,362	—
Saskatchewan	19,754	—
Alberta	3,146	—
Total interior birds	70,612	—
Grand total	120,528	5,373

[1] Data of Nettleship (1977), apparently mostly from early 1970s surveys. First figure indicates total breeding birds; second figure indicates total number of surveyed colonies.
[2] Data of Vermeer and Rankin (1984), based on surveys from 1976 to 1982, and originally reported as numbers of nests or breeding pairs, but here converted (doubled) to show total breeding birds.

TABLE 31   Estimated Breeding Pelecaniform Populations, Contiguous U.S. Coasts and Great Lakes Shores of U.S. and Canada

Region	Double-crested Cormorant	Neotropic Cormorant	Anhinga	Brown Pelican
Atlantic coast and Florida				
Maine	30,666/103	—	—	—
New Hampshire	<400/1	—	—	—
Massachusetts	9,914/14	—	—	—
Rhode Island	774/2	—	—	—
Connecticut	86/2	—	—	—
New York	986/3	—	—	—
Virginia	—	—	—	—
North Carolina	—	—	—	270/1
South Carolina	—	—	304/8	2,977/2
Georgia	—	—	169/9	—
Florida	18,090/56	—	1,364/25	11,576/28
Gulf coast				
Louisiana	—	6,872/7	2,582/17	48/1
Texas	—	1,860/7	40/3	106/3
Great Lakes				
Superior	3,242/11	—	—	—
Michigan	6,862/15	—	—	—
Huron	9,024/29	—	—	—
Erie	1,264/4	—	—	—
Ontario	6,922/7	—	—	—
Total birds	ca. 88,000	8,732	4,459	14,987
Ave. birds/colony	ca. 350	622	72	428

Region	Double-crested Cormorant	Brandt's Cormorant	Pelagic shag	
Pacific coast				
Washington	3,146/20	542/2	6,312/64	—
Oregon	1,716/14	15,932/16	6,494/143	—
California	1,850/16	64,194/75	15,684/174	4,488/2
Total birds	6,712	80,668	28,490	4,488
Ave. birds/colony	134	585	75	2,244

NOTES: Data mostly of Spendelow and Patton (1988), from regional censuses made 1976–1982. First figure of table indicates total observed breeding birds, second indicates total number of breeding colonies located. Great Lakes data from Bloekpoel and Scharf (1991), from 1987. Counts for New Hampshire, Massachusetts, Rhode Island, Connecticut, and New York are for 1984 (Hatch, 1984). Nestings have also recently occurred in New Jersey, Maryland, Virginia, and the Carolinas.

The American white pelican occupies a widespread breeding range, currently or recently breeding in 11 states and 5 provinces. In spite of various opinions to the contrary, the American white pelican has been thriving in recent years, and its population at present is probably as high as at any time in this century (table 33). This is presumably a result of reduced "hard" pesticide use as well as long-neglected breeding grounds protection. Only in rather recent times has an official acceptance of the relatively nondetrimental effects of white pelicans on sport fisheries been achieved, ending the pelican's traditional severe persecution, at times by federal

TABLE 32　Estimated Cormorant and Shag Breeding Populations, Canadian Pacific Maritime and Alaska

Region	Cormorants		Shags	
	Brandt's	Double-crested	Pelagic	Red-faced
British Columbia[1]				
Georgia Strait and southeast Vancouver Is.	—	4,064/15	4,644	—
Western Vancouver Is.	78	—	2,316	—
Queen Charlotte Is. and northern mainland coast	—	—	476	—
Queen Charlotte Strait and Scott Islands	112	—	1,554	—
Total breeding birds (B.C.)	190	4,064/15	9,000/85	—
Alaska[2]				
West coast and Bering Sea islands	—	—	6,218/65	7,700/5
Norton Bay and northern Alaska Peninsula	—	1,696/11	15,262/22	3,311/11
Aleutian Islands	—	100/2	4,019/21	20,724/33
Southern coast	11/1	2,842/67	14,285/160	19,878/130
Southeastern coast	—	100/2	1,104/17	—
Total breeding birds (Alaska)	11	4,738	40,888	51,613
Total colonies	1	82	285	179
Ave. birds/colony	11	57	143	288
Est. total population	ca. 100	7,000	90,000	130,000

[1] Figures for British Columbia are from Campbell et al. (1990) and Rodway (1991), for the late 1980s. Double-crested cormorants have been increasing, but numbers of Brandt's cormorants and of pelagic shags have been declining recently.
[2] Data of Sowls, Hatch, and Lensink (1978). First figure indicates total observed birds, second indicates total number of colonies found during 1970s surveys. Estimated total populations reflect adjustments for incomplete counts.

and state agencies, including even their systematic egg destruction in Yellowstone National Park.

By way of final summary, table 34 presents a listing of collective albeit highly tentative population estimates for nearly all the pelecaniform species that breed on the mainland of North America. It excludes only the northern gannet, which as of the early 1970s was represented by about 33,000 pairs breeding in the Gulf of St. Lawrence and along coastal Newfoundland (Brown et al., 1975). To these figures the West Indian breeding populations of the brown pelican might also be added; these have recently been documented by Halewyn and Norton (1984). However, the breeding populations of all the other West Indian pelecaniform species are still unsurveyed.

Contemporary Conservation Issues

In North America our conservation agencies helplessly witnessed the postwar population crash of the brown pelican (along with those of many other predatory spe-

TABLE 33   Estimated Total North American White Pelican Breeding Populations

Region	1963–64[1]	1967–69[2]	1971–72[1]	1979–81[3]
United States				
California	2,035/1	—	5,115/1	4,642/2
Colorado	155/1	—	375/1	1,000/1
Minnesota	0/0	—	440/3	2,022/2
Montana	10,107/3	—	5,500/3	5,584/2
Nevada	6,500/1	—	5,900/1	5,760/1
North Dakota	8,000/1	—	9,000/1	12,414/3
Oregon	0/0	—	500/1	1,320/2
South Dakota	1,825/2	—	2,075/2	4,940/3
Texas	1,750/1	—	475/1	300/1
Utah	3,750/1	—	4,750/1	6,046/1
Wyoming	600/1	—	500/1	570/1
Subtotal (U.S.)	34,722/12	—	34,630/16	44,598/19
Ave. birds/colony	2,893	—	2,164	2,347
Canada				
Alberta	—	ca. 440/4	—	1,096/7
British Columbia	—	ca. 170/1	—	240/1
Manitoba	—	13,600/15	—	28,022/18
Ontario	—	880/2	—	4,280/1
Saskatchewan	—	13,116/9	—	30,854/9
Subtotal (Canada)	—	28,206/31	—	64,492/36
Ave. birds/colony	—	910	—	1,791
Total (U.S. and Canada)	62,928/43[4]			109,090/55
Ave. birds/colony	1,463			1,984

NOTE: First figure indicates estimated total breeding birds, second figure indicates total known active colonies.
[1] Data from Sloan (1982); figures for indicated time periods are based on two-year averages.
[2] Data from Vermeer (1970a); population totals are based on twice the number of reported nests.
[3] Data from Sidle, Koonz, and Roney (1985). U.S. figures are for 1980 and 1981 surveys; Canadian figures are from 1979 and 1980 surveys.
[4] Represents composite of U.S. figures for 1963–1964 and Canadian figures for 1967–1969.

cies, such as the osprey *Pandion haliaetus* and peregrine falcon *Falco peregrinus*), and it required more than two decades of research, political action, and public understanding to begin to turn around this depressing condition. We are now entering an environmental age in which very difficult ecologic-economic choices must be made, such as deciding whether the future of spotted owls (*Strix occidentalis*) and the ecologically related biota that is associated with and dependent upon the old-growth forests of western North America are inherently worth more than the present-day commercial timber value of the forests themselves.

Similar choices may have to be made for some of the species considered here. Most are of no measurable direct economic value, although the guano birds of Peru have traditionally been so important to that country's economy that the guanay shag has been called the "billion-dollar bird" (Johnson, 1965). Coker (1919) judged that a flock of 500,000 guanay shags could produce about 5,700 tons of guano a year, or one long ton of guano per 28 nests. Guano in those preinflationary days had a commercial value of $40.00 per ton, making each breeding pair of guanay shags worth an estimated $1.43 per year in terms of their guano production. At the

TABLE 34 Estimated Total North American Breeding Pelecaniform Populations

Region	Alaska	Canada	Contiguous U.S.	Total
Brandt's cormorant	<100	190	80,668	81,000[1]
Neotropic cormorant	—	—	8,732	8,700
Double-crested cormorant	7,000	125,000	ca. 94,700	ca.
Great cormorant	—	5,373	—	220,000[2]
Pelagic shag	90,000	9,000	28,492	5,400
Red-faced shag	130,000	—	—	127,000
Anhinga	—	—	4,459	130,000
Brown pelican	—	—	19,475	4,500
American white pelican	—	64,492	44,598	19,500[3]
				109,000

NOTE: Based on data presented in four previous tables.

[1] Up to 1,000 pairs breed on the Gulf of California islands (Anderson, 1983), but the Pacific coast of Mexico supports some "tens of thousands" of additional pairs (Everett and Anderson, 1991).

[2] Exclusive of most of the interior United States, which supports several thousands of pairs. The Gulf of California islands support a few tens of thousands of pairs (Anderson, 1983), and western Mexico probably also supports an additional but apparently small population (Williams, 1978).

[3] About 35,000 pairs also nest on Gulf of California islands, and additionally considerable numbers nest along the Baja California Pacific coast, including large colonies at Santa Margarita, San Benitos, and Los Coronados (Everett and Anderson, 1991).

peak of the guano harvesting, about half a million tons of guano were annually removed from the South American deposits. Dwindling supplies of guano ultimately resulted in reduced economic importance of this industry to Peru, but through improved management of the breeding colonies and restrictions on yearly guano extraction, a significant agricultural and industrial value of guano to Peru and South Africa has continued right up to the present time.

It now appears that the brown pelican is making a significant recovery in Louisiana, where it has been designated as the state bird but was until recently extirpated as a breeding bird. There had been several pelican die-offs during the late 1950s and early 1960s, when pesticides such as DDT were being used in the lower Mississippi valley, and by 1961 there were no breeding pelicans to be found anywhere along the Louisiana coast. In 1968 the first of a series of releases of juvenile birds from Florida was made, which continued yearly through 1976. The first attempted nesting by these young birds occurred in 1971, although it wasn't until 1972 that any fledged offspring were produced. After a period of apparent success, there was again a serious die-off in 1975. At that time the pelican population suddenly plummeted about 20 percent, and it was later found that some of the carcasses contained at least eight chlorinated hydrocarbon pesticides in their brain tissues. However, starting in 1978, six years after the outlawing of nearly all chlorinated hydrocarbon pesticides for agricultural use, and the recognition and management of the brown pelican as a nationally endangered species, nesting success finally began to improve. By the early 1980s two nesting colonies had become firmly established in Louisiana (Brown, 1983), and by 1990 nearly 2,200 adults were breeding in six colonies (Martin and Lester, 1990).

In the Channel Islands of southern California and the Coronado Islands off the west coast of Baja California a similar story can be told. Perhaps starting earlier, but first documented in 1968, brown pelican populations in coastal California began a decline in numbers that over the next two decades reduced the northern populations of this species by about 90 percent. In 1969 the first indication of nesting failures by brown pelicans owing to the crushing of thin-shelled eggs was found on Anacapa Island. During that same spring a similar situation was detected on the Coronado Islands, and not a single chick was known to have fledged there that year. Only three to five young were fledged the following year, and between 30 and 40 during 1971. After some minor fluctuation in 1972 and 1973, the production of young shot up to an amazing 1,200 birds in 1974, only two years after the use of DDT had been federally prohibited in the United States. In spite of this apparent great success, the eggshells of these Pacific coast birds were still abnormally thin, and many eggs failed to hatch in 1974 (Jehl, 1973; Anderson et al., 1975). Given the long lives of seabirds generally, it is likely that a decade or more was needed to achieve a DDT-free population of pelicans. Since the mid-1970s the yearly production of pelicans on the Coronado Islands has not been nearly as high as in 1974, and it is likely that food supplies or some other density-dependent factor has begun to control the growth of the population.

The future of at least two seriously threatened Eurasian species (the Dalmatian pelican and the pygmy cormorant) seems to be closely related to the fate of their major breeding grounds in the southern regions of the former USSR, especially those around the Aral Sea and its associated rivers, the Syr Darya and Amu Darya. These breeding areas are quickly disappearing, along with the fish populations that primarily sustained the local economy, under the impact of massive river diversion irrigation projects. Thus the Aral Sea, which was once larger in area than Lake Michigan, is rapidly drying up because of governmentally financed irrigation programs along the Syr Darya and Amu Darya rivers that were begun in 1954, primarily to develop a regional cotton industry. The Aral Sea's associated fishery, which once supported some 60,000 jobs as well as very large populations of fish-eating birds such as pelicans and cormorants, has been completely destroyed as a result. Additionally, the use of persistent agricultural pesticides in the region has been blamed for unusually high human cancer rates in the region, and increased salination of the desertlike soil has caused great environmental damage to the soil and its associated biota, and now gravely threatens the future of the cotton industry. Furthermore, the blowing dusts generated around the drying shoreline have produced unusually high levels of human respiratory diseases and have caused greatly increased infant mortality rates. It is questionable whether the market value of the cotton and other crops produced from irrigation is as great as that of the fish population that has been destroyed by these water diversion activities, to say nothing of the vast associated ecological destruction and human misery brought about by these changes (Ellis, 1990).

The point of this brief review is to emphasize that the ecological effects of environmental alterations, whether ill-conceived governmental drainage schemes, introduction of inadequately tested agricultural pesticides, or possibly even inadvertent atmospheric changes in carbon dioxide levels resulting from worldwide burning of organic materials, are usually far-reaching and often impossible to predict accurately. Activities producing apparent economic benefits accruing to individual, regional, or national interests may be greatly outweighed by serious damage to the natural world and human society as a whole, and in ways we cannot even begin to understand at the time that such choices are made or actions are taken. The status, reproductive success, and incidence of pollution-induced developmental malformities of bird species such as pelicans and cormorants may provide one of the simplest and most sensitive ecological barometers available to us

(Boudewijn et al., 1989; Myres, 1991). Like the canaries carried into deep shafts by miners to warn them of dangerous gas levels, the relative health of these environmentally sensitive birds may perhaps give us our first knowledge of the dangers we are facing by failing to pay adequate attention to the potentially disastrous ecological results of our own usually shortsighted behavior.

PART TWO

SPECIES ACCOUNTS

Cormorants and Shags (Phalacrocoracidae)

Wing-waving display by male double-crested cormorant.
After a photo by the author.

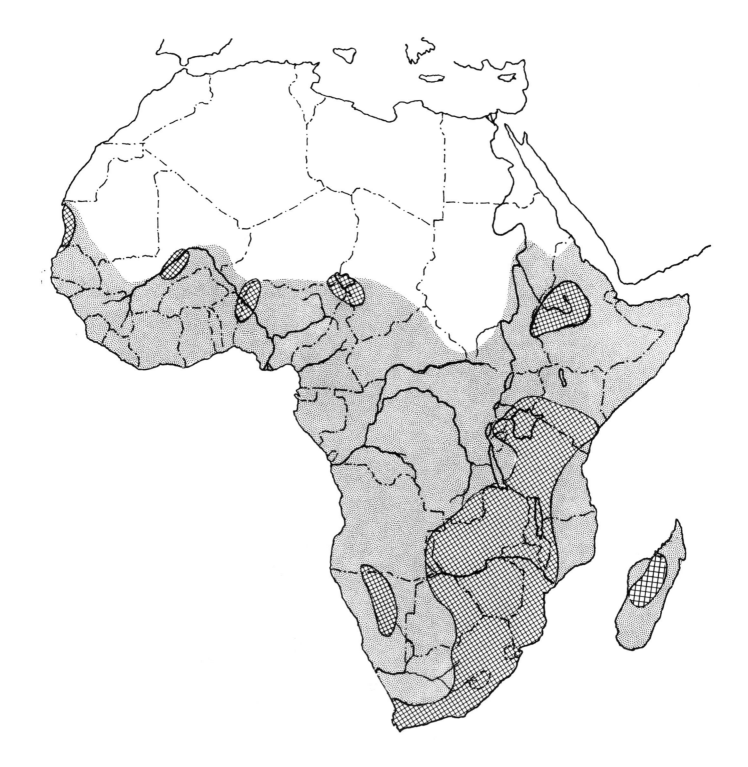

Figure 35. Distribution of the long-tailed cormorant, showing the breeding ranges of its races *africanus* (small cross-
hatching) and *pictilis* (large cross-hatching), plus the species'
additional nonbreeding range (stippled).

Other Vernacular Names

Reed cormorant; cormoran à longue queue, cormoran africain (French); Reidkormoran, Gelbschnabel-Zwergscharbe (German)

Distribution

Generally resident through the interior wetlands of Africa south of the Sahara, from Mauritania and Senegal east locally to Sudan, Ethiopia, and western Somalia, and south to the Cape, but exclusive of the coastal areas of Namibia and southwestern South Africa (which are occupied by *coronatus*, here considered a full species). Also resident throughout Madagascar. Vagrant on offshore islands, including Zanzibar, Mafia, and Pemba. (See figure 35.)

Subspecies

P. a. africanus. Resident in interior Africa as described.

P. a. pictilis Bangs 1918. Resident in interior Madagascar; possibly warrants specific separation.

Description

Prebreeding adult. Plumage generally shining black, with a dull greenish gloss; upper back and wing coverts gray to silvery white, broadly tipped with black (forming quarter-moon-like spots); scapulars brownish gray, and marked similarly. Feathers of the forehead and anterior crown white, the shaft tips black and bristlelike, forming a short forehead crest ca. 23 mm long; a superciliary tuft of white filoplumes is briefly present. Remiges and rectrices (12) black, the latter graduated in length and relatively more flexible than in *coronatus*. Iris bright crimson; eyelids pinkish; facial skin evidently highly variable, from yellow (typical, at least early in breeding season) to orange-yellow or (less typically) reddish or even bluish; bill chrome-yellow, with the culmen, tip, and outer part of mandible dusky brown, and somewhat mottled with black below; gular skin yellow; legs and toes black.
Postbreeding adult. Lacking crest and white superciliary plumes, and the plumage generally more brownish dorsally. Almost indistinguishable from immatures; the head, breast, and upperparts are all somewhat brownish, the throat is grayish brown, and grayish mottling may be present on the white belly. According to Cramp and Simmons (1977) and Harrison (1983), the upperpart feathers develop buffy feather edges in postbreeding adults. However, Crawford et al. (1982) mentioned only white fringes on the upper wing

coverts. Iris apparently as intensely red as in breeding birds, but the facial skin and gular skin only medium yellow, and the bill mostly brown, with a blackish culmen.
Immature. Very similar to postbreeding adult; the crown and neck brown, darkest above; feathers of upper back, scapulars, and wing coverts tipped with darker brown and narrowly margined with brownish white; flanks dark brown; chin and throat white; base of neck and chest brownish white; breast and belly white. The juvenal plumage is replaced through a complete molt by the immature plumage at about one year. A few months later a molt producing the definitive plumage is begun. The period to attainment of reproductive maturity is disputed but the claim that four years may be required is unsubstantiated. It is instead probable that the first adult plumage is attained at about a year of age or shortly thereafter (Bowmaker, 1963; Crawford et al., 1982).
Juvenile. Crown and hindneck dark brown; palest on cheeks and sides of neck; upperparts generally brownish black, margined with brownish white and lacking black blotches on scapulars and wing coverts; chin and throat grayish white; foreneck, chest, and upper breast brownish white; rest of breast and belly dirty white to light brown; sides, flanks, and under tail coverts black; remiges and rectrices all pointed and margined with brownish white, the rectrices with broad pale tips. Iris dark brown, later becoming light brown (also erroneously reported as orange-brown or red); bill flesh-yellow with black tip; legs and feet black.
Nestling. Initially with naked pinkish to gray skin, a pale yellow head, red throat, with a black line from nostrils across eye to ear opening, and a second black line from below the eye to the base of the hyoid. Gradually covered with jet-black down, with the crown remaining bare and white, and the gular pouch and cheeks bare and red. Iris pale blue; bare skin on head yellow, gular skin initially reddish, gradually becoming blood-red at base; bill, legs, and feet black, the toes with brown webs.

Measurements (in millimeters, of *africanus; pictilis* averages slightly larger and has appreciably longer wings)

Wing, males 205–224 (ave. of 10, 215), females 196–221 (ave. of 9, 209); tail, males 147–174 (ave. of 10, 158.6), females 143–160 (ave. of 8, 152.9); exposed culmen, males 28–31 (ave. of 13, 30.4), females 27–? (ave. of 9, 29.0); tarsus, males 36–41 (ave. of 14, 38.6), females 34–40 (ave. of 9, 37.9) (Crawford et al., 1982). Eggs ca. 44 × 29.

Weights (of *africanus,* in grams)

Adult males, ave. of 40, 568.5, adult females, ave. of 10, 513.0 (Birkhead, 1978). Sample of 66 (sex and age composition not stated), 420–650, ave. 505 (Bowmaker, 1963). Average adult weight (sample size not stated) 530 (Olver, 1984). Males 710–880 (ave. of 6, 791.7); ave. of 10 females, 513 (Crawford et al., 1982). Males 505–635 (ave. of 12, 544), females 435–600 (ave. of 7, 546) (Alletson, 1985). One female 615 (U.S. National Museum specimen). Calculated egg weight 20.4; ave. of 58 eggs, 20.9 (Olver, 1984).

Identification

In the hand. The combination of a yellow bill with a culmen length of less than 35 mm, blackish underparts, a red iris and yellow to reddish facial skin color, and a tail length averaging four times greater than that of the tarsus identifies this species. Additional distinctions from *coronatus,* beyond *africanus*'s significantly longer tail but shorter tarsal measurements, include its smaller body mass, a shorter forehead crest (ca. 23 vs. 32 mm), a variably feathered rather than featherless interramal area under the mandible, and a slightly longer maxillary unguis (bill nail) (Crawford et al., 1982).

In the field. In coastal areas of southwestern Africa, this small black-bodied and yellow-billed cormorant is likely to be confused only with the very similar crowned cormorant, a marine species that has a somewhat more distinctive crest in breeding adults, a more orange or reddish bill, and whose juveniles are not completely white below. Adult crowned cormorants also appear rather grayish brown dorsally, with small black spots, whereas adult long-tailed cormorants appear to be silvery gray above, with larger black spots that produce a generally scaly appearance. In breeding plumage, long-tailed cormorants are usually slightly mottled on the underparts rather than entirely black, and in immature and nonbreeding plumage the abdomen, breast, and throat are entirely white, rather than having a blackish abdomen, dark brown breast, and paler brown throat. The other African cormorant widespread in the interior is the much larger great cormorant, which always has white on the throat and underparts. In Madagascar the long-tailed cormorant occurs almost entirely in fresh-water habitats, where it is the only small cormorant present.

Ecology and General Biology

Breeding and nonbreeding habitats. This species is almost exclusively associated with fresh-water habitats, although in some areas where the crowned cormorant is absent the long-tailed extends to coastal islands, where it occurs on rocky outcrops or flats (Crawford et al., 1982). It ranges interiorly from rivers and creeks to swamps and lakes, and in the case of lakes is mostly limited to those with shallow shoreline

edges that are often well vegetated, where roosting and foraging opportunities exist. In the area of the Bangweulu swamps, northern Zambia, the birds inhabit shallow permanent wetlands having a dense surface growth of water lilies (*Nymphaea*), reeds (*Eleocharis*), and submerged vegetation, especially *Ceratophyllum* and *Utricularia.* Deep channels also often connect larger lakes and lagoons, and the margins of such channels support a thick zone of sedges (*Cyperus*) and ferns (*Dryopteris*), with occasional clumps of *Phragmites.* This thick vegetation zone is used for roosting, while the deeper waters provide favored fishing areas. Downstream on this same river system, the water enters Lake Mweru in an area of dense thickets of large trees interspersed with swampy lagoons and large stands of *Cyperus.* The birds probably nest in these tree thickets and forage in the nearby waters (Bowmaker, 1963).

Breeding is typically done in colonies of quite small sizes, sometimes as few as two pairs, and very often among groups of nesting herons, storks, ibises, darters, or other cormorant species. The nests of long-tailed cormorants are typically scattered throughout such colonies, rather than in groups, although they may be somewhat closer to water than are those of the other species (Brown, Urban, and Newman, 1982).

Movements and migrations. Although some fairly substantial movements occur in connection with changing water levels and water availability, these are still only poorly documented (Urban et al., 1982).

Competition and predation. Probably the crowned cormorant, which is slightly larger in size, is a serious competitor. The two species exhibit mutually exclusive, parapatric distributions that support this view (Crawford et al., 1982). On Lake Kariba, Zimbabwe, there appeared to be no obviously ecological isolation between the foraging niches of the long-tailed cormorant and the African darter (Birkhead, 1978). There is little specific information on significant predators of this species, although Cott (1961) reported that it is regularly eaten by the Nile crocodile.

Foods and Foraging Behavior

Foods consumed. Several studies have been undertaken on the foods of this species in southeastern and southern Africa (Bowmaker, 1963; Birkhead, 1978; Whitfield and Blaber, 1979; Alletson, 1985). These differ in their reports of specific items consumed, but are in overall agreement on general foraging behavior and broad prey categories. The birds prefer slow-moving, relatively small fish that can be captured in shallow water up to about 2–2.5 meters deep and within about 100 meters of shore.

In the Bangweulu swamp area, some 53 species of fish are known to occur, but the cormorant was observed to forage on only 16 of these species, and 31 percent (by number) to 41 percent (by weight) of the prey found in 66 birds consisted of elephantfishes (Mormyridae) (Bowmaker, 1963). This group of fishes, like most of the others taken (characids, schilbeids, clariids, machokiids, and anabantids), are long and tapering in shape, rather than short and deep-bodied like most cichlids (which were taken in small numbers). The prey length range was 2–20 centimeters, and the average weight of all fish taken was 20 grams. The estimated average daily intake per individual bird was estimated at 71 grams, or 14 percent of body weight. A similar estimate of daily intake of 16 percent of body weight was made by Junor (1972).

On Lake Kariba, the long-tailed cormorant fed mostly on cichlids (over 70 percent of intake by weight and 66 percent by number of prey items in 50 birds), but these fish, too, were mostly small (2.3–19 centimeters long, averaging 7.0) and light (0.4–70.1 grams, averaging 8.0). The substantially higher rate of deep-bodied fish found in samples here was attributed to the fact that many of the cichlids in Lake Kariba tend to be species that are not so easily encountered as those that were exploited by the birds. Thus, body shape may not be such an important aspect of prey selection as general prey availability (Birkhead, 1978).

At Lake St. Lucia, Natal, Mozambique tilapia (*Sarotherodon mossambicus*, Cichlidae), blackhand sole (*Solea bleekeri*, Soleidae), and river bream (*Acanthopagrus berda*) were, in descending order, the three most frequent prey species found in 21 samples. These prey ranged in mass from about 1 to 15 grams, with a modal peak of 3–4 grams (Whitfield and Blaber, 1979).

In a sample of 23 stomachs from Natal, fish were present in most of the stomachs, including *Barbus* (Cyprinidae) in 6, unknown fish in 5, and frogs in 10, plus a minor amount of snails and Odonata larvae, comprising a collective mean prey mass of 13 grams (Alletson, 1985). A large sample of foods from 99 birds analyzed by Cott (1961) from Uganda lakes consisted mainly of cichlids, especially *Haplochromis* species, but included a total of 12 genera and averaged 3.3 prey items per stomach.

Other minor prey types that have been documented include frogs, aquatic insects, crustaceans, and small birds (Urban et al., 1982).

Foraging behavior. This species is a typical diurnal forager, roosting until shortly after sunrise, then heading out singly or in small groups to favored foraging areas. Foraging is done nonsocially during the daylight hours, and foraging peaks seem to occur early in the morning and late in the afternoon. Most foraging on Lake Kariba is done within 100 meters of shore, and in water about 2 meters deep. The birds return to their roosts any time from two hours to a half-hour before sunset (Birkhead, 1978).

In Natal, cormorants on Lake St. Lucia usually foraged in sheltered waters within 100 meters of the shore, and in water up to 2 meters deep. The highest incidence of foraging was between 6:00 and 8:00 A.M., with a slight increase again toward evening. In Bowmaker's (1963) study in Zambia, it was found that the feeding incidence was very high from dawn to about 8:00 A.M., with a secondary peak in mid-morning and almost no feeding during midday. Another bout of foraging occurred between 2:00 and 6:00 P.M. Fishes captured were of the slowly moving or lurking types, and typically the bird returned to the surface to swallow each fish it captured.

Social Behavior

Age of maturity and mating system. No good evidence as to the age of initial breeding exists for this species, but adult plumage is apparently attained at about one year (Crawford et al., 1982). It is likely that the birds can breed at two years of age, if not before. It is not known if the monogamous pair bond is retained more than a single year or even possibly over two successive breeding seasons within a single year (Cramp and Simmons, 1977).

Social displays and vocalizations. This topic is surprisingly little studied, in spite of the species' broad distribution and relative abundance. Nesting birds are known to hiss, and young birds produce cackling sounds while begging. No utterances have been specifically associated with social displays by adults. Mate-seeking behavior (presumably male advertising) reportedly consists of arching the neck, pointing the bill forward and slightly upward, and raising the wings jerkily about three times every two seconds, which description seems to represent typical cormorant wing-waving advertisement display (Cramp and Simmons, 1977). Olver (1984) stated that the male throws his head backward and forward and flaps his wings in unison. When a female landed near the displaying male he put his head against his back, bobbed his head up and down a few times while the feathers on the head and neck were erected, and flapped his wings in unison while holding them slightly away from the body.

Copulation occurs on the selected nest site, and in Olver's observations was usually preceded by the male's arrival and a mutual greeting with bills gaping and gular pouches distended. The pair then pecked each other's head gently for a few minutes with crests raised and tails fanned and raised, followed by individual grooming and preening. After copulation, both birds dipped their heads and began preening. Active nest building was initiated after copulation had occurred and the male went off to search for nesting materials.

Paired birds have been observed performing mutual neck rubbing, bill touching, and mutual preening, as well as neck intertwining and stick offering. Changeovers at the nest may also include offering nesting materials to the mate. Stick offering may likewise follow copulation, which occurs on the nest, as may bill rubbing and self-preening (Cramp and Simmons, 1977).

When disturbed, swimming long-tailed cormorants

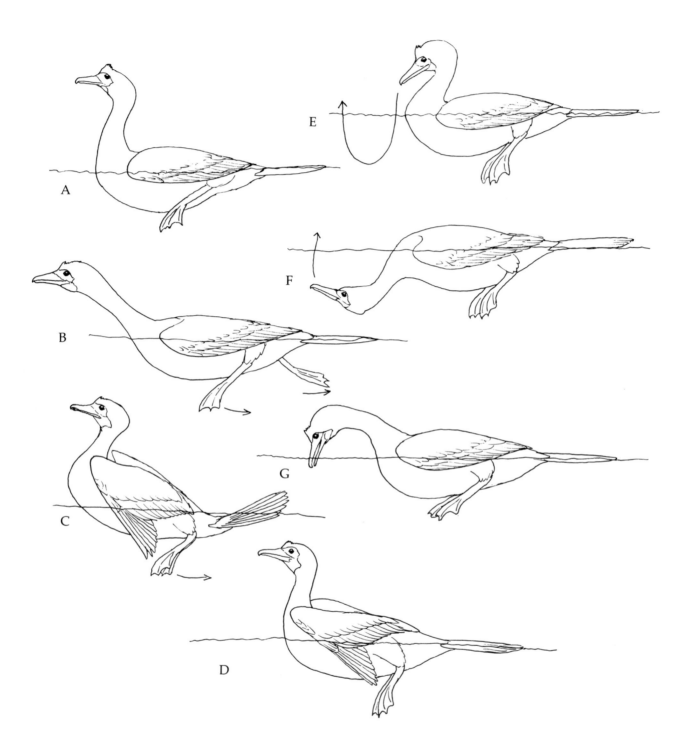

Figure 36. Fear and escape behavior of the long-tailed cormorant, including alert posture (A), swimming escape (B), flying
escape (C), flight intention posture (D), bill dipping ("displacement diving") (E, F), and displacement "drinking" (G).
After sketches in Bowmaker (1963).

perform a variety of activities that Bowmaker (1963) has described and illustrated (figure 36). These consist of a preliminary alert posture, followed by a swimming escape or half-hearted flying attempts. If unable to escape in this manner, the bird performs flying-intention movements, or begins "displacement diving." Such diving consists of a sharp and repeated dipping movement of the head and neck under the water, followed by a resumption of the alert posture. An alternative apparent displacement response is "drinking," in which only the bill is dipped into the water, followed by a return to the first phase of the diving posture.

Reproductive Biology

Breeding season.   Breeding seasons are greatly prolonged in this species. Even in southern Africa breeding occurs virtually throughout the year, although with a definite spring and summer peak, which is associated with rainfall periods. In areas with definite rainy seasons the nesting is often associated with the first heavy rains, but sometimes it occurs later in the rainy season or may even begin at the start of the dry season in recently inundated areas (Brown, Urban, and Newman, 1982).

Nest sites and nest building.   Nest sites are quite diverse, with ground sites sometimes used, as well as clumps of herbaceous vegetation, reed beds, partly submerged trees, or trees well away from water. In Olver's (1984) Natal study area the birds nested entirely in wattle trees. After copulating on the nest site, the male searched for nesting materials and the female built the nest, mostly of grasses and twigs. Nest construction was rapid, and within a week the nest could accommodate eggs. The nest was maintained throughout the incubation and to a lesser degree during the brooding period by the addition of more materials.

Egg laying and incubation.   Eggs are typically laid at 24-hour intervals, although occasionally they are laid on alternate days or a day or two may be skipped, so that a four-egg clutch may take five days to lay. Olver (1984) reported an average clutch of 3.6 eggs for 68 nests. A more general sample from various areas throughout Africa is of 3.09 eggs for 435 nests, with regional means ranging from 2.3 to 3.8 eggs (Brown, Urban, and Newman, 1982).

Incubation begins with the first-laid egg and is performed by both sexes. Eggs usually hatch in the sequence in which they were laid, at about 24-hour intervals, and after an incubation period of 23–24 days (Olver, 1984), or occasionally 25 days (Brown, Urban, and Newman, 1982). The average weight of the chicks at hatching was reported by Olver as 14.9 grams (32 chicks), as compared with mean egg weights of 20.9 grams (58 eggs).

Brooding and rearing of young.   Pinkish at hatching, the skin turns mostly black by four days of age, and the eyes are fully open by that time. At 28 days after hatching six chicks in Olver's study reached a maximum nestling weight of 466 grams, or somewhat more than the eventual fledging weight of 452 grams (two chicks at four weeks). Both parents fed their young and also regurgitated water into their mouths or over their backs, presumably to cool them. Birds that fell from their nests when younger than two weeks invariably died, but by three weeks of age they were able to climb back to their nests following disturbance.

Breeding success.   The best available estimates of productivity are those of Olver (1984), who reported on a total of 68 breeding efforts over two breeding seasons. Of 246 total eggs, 207 (84 percent) hatched, 149 (61 percent) were reared, and a collective average of 2.2 young were reared per nest. The largest average number of young per nest were hatched from three nests with 6-egg clutches (4.7 chicks). The mean number of young reared from 5-egg and 6-egg clutches was less than for the modal 4-egg clutches. The latter hatched an average of 3.6 chicks and reared an average of 2.8 young, or 70 percent of all the eggs laid. Rearing success was also lower in nests having only 2 or 3 eggs present than it was for 4-egg clutches. It would thus seem that the modal clutch size is also the most reproductively efficient clutch size in this species.

Population Status

This species is widely distributed in Africa, and although no continental population estimates are available it is clearly not in any present difficulties.

Evolutionary Relationships

Crawford et al. (1982) have effectively proven that this species and the crowned cormorant are closely related, parapatric forms, which are adapted to fresh-water and marine habitats, respectively. Given this situation, it is not hard to imagine a speciation pattern that would account for their present-day distributions and ecological adaptations.

Figure 37. Distribution of the crowned cormorant, showing the locations of known breeding colonies (inset), plus its total breeding and nonbreeding range (stippled). Small dots indicate colonies (or groups of colonies) of more than 100 birds; the larger open circle indicates a colony of 400 birds. Unmarked colonies are of fewer than 100 birds. After Crawford et al. (1982).

Other Vernacular Names

Long-tailed cormorant (when considered a subspecies of *africanus*); cormoran couronné (French); Wahlbergscharbe (German)

Distribution

Resident of Africa, along rocky coastlines of Namibia and South Africa from Swakopmund to Cape Agulhas. Reportedly wanders north to central Angola (Benguela), but Crawford et al. (1982) regard the occurrence of this species anywhere in Angola as unproven. (See figure 37.)

Subspecies

None recognized here, although this form has previously often been considered a subspecies of *africanus*.

Description

Prebreeding adult.   Very similar to *africanus*, but lacking or nearly lacking the white filoplumes behind eyes, the crest longer (ca. 32 mm), and the scapulars and wing coverts with relatively narrower black tips (forming new-moon-like, crescent-shaped spots); more orange-colored on the face and bill. Iris red; facial skin red; bill reddish orange to orange-yellow, with black spots and culmen ridge and yellow gape; gular skin orange-yellow; legs and feet black.
Postbreeding adult.   Lacking the crest (contrary to Brown, Urban, and Newman, 1982); generally very similar to the immature plumage (Crawford et al., 1982).
Immature.   Chin pale gray, the throat and upper breast grayish brown; lower breast dark brown with lighter flecks; abdomen blackish, dorsal feathers dark brown to blackish, the mantle feathers with paler fringes, rectrices black. Iris deep red, bill blackish brown, becoming yellow-horn on sides and ventrally; legs and feet black.
Juvenile.   Browner than corresponding stage of *africanus*, especially on the underparts, which are distinctly mottled with brown rather than dingy white. Chin gray (white in *africanus*), breast dark brown (pale grayish brown in *africanus*), abdomen dark brown (whitish in *africanus*). Iris pale bluish gray in younger birds; bill blackish brown to yellow-horn.
Nestling.   Naked, the skin initially dark pink to red, turning dull black a day after hatching. Becoming covered with black down by the seventh day except for a light yellow or orange crown, with a black stripe from the eye to the occiput. Iris pale gray; inflatable red cheek patch; bill black, acquiring a yellow base by the 14th day; gular skin reddish laterally, speckled with black and yellow underneath; legs and feet black (Berry, 1974; Crawford et al., 1982). Not separable from *africanus* at this stage.

Measurements (in millimeters)

Wing, males 206–220 (ave. of 10, 213.9), females 203–213 (ave. of 6, 207); tail, males 123–141 (ave. of 7, 131.7), females 136–142 (ave. of 3, 138.3); exposed culmen, males 28–31 (ave. of 10, 29.6), ave. of 8 females 28.4; tarsus, males 42–52 (ave. of 11, 46.6), females 41–49 (ave. of 8, 45.1) (Crawford et al., 1982). Eggs ca. 47 × 31.

Weights (in grams)

Four males 475–775 (ave. 675), 5 females 700–775 (ave. 730) (U.S. National Museum). Six males 710–880 (ave. 797.7), 5 females 670–780 (ave. 728) (Crawford et al., 1982). Average of 5 males 756, 1 female 679 (Rand, 1960). Calculated egg weight 24.9.

Identification

In the hand.   The combination of an orange bill with an adult culmen length under 35 mm, a red iris and facial skin color, and a tail length averaging only three times greater than the tarsal length identifies this species. It is readily distinguished from *africanus* by its shorter, stiffer, and less graduated tail, its longer tarsus, its greater mass, its longer mandibular nail, and its featherless skin between the mandibular rami (Crawford et al., 1982).
In the field.   In its very limited coastal range, this species is likely to be seen in the same areas as the Cape cormorant, which has a black bill, green rather than red eyes, and black feathering in place of the yellow facial skin of the crowned cormorant. The bank cormorant of the same area is considerably larger, lacks yellow on the face, and usually has a white rump patch.

Ecology and General Biology

Breeding and nonbreeding habitats.   This is an essentially coastal species that is confined to cold-water African coastlines washed by the Benguela current. It has never been recorded more than 10 kilometers offshore, and only a single nonmarine sighting is known, when nine birds were seen resting some 100 meters from the sea in a sewage works. The species is currently known from only 15 breeding localities in Namibia and 22 breeding localities in South Africa, ranging from Bird Rock in the north to Aasfontein in the south (Crawford et al., 1982).

Movements and migrations. There is evidently little movement away from the breeding areas; the northernmost accepted record is only 19 kilometers north of Bird Rock. Recoveries of seven birds banded as chicks showed a mean movement of only 96 kilometers, and a maximum movement of 277 kilometers (Crawford et al., 1982).

Competition and predation. Besides its habitat-limited contacts with the smaller long-tailed cormorant, this species breeds in areas supporting Cape and bank cormorants, as well as other larger seabirds including gannets and penguins. Perhaps its typically small colony size reflects an inability to cope effectively with some of these larger species, but by nesting among them it might gain some protection from predation by kelp gulls *(Larus dominicanus),* according to Crawford et al. (1982).

Foods and Foraging Behavior

Foods consumed. These birds forage off rocky shorelines, frequently among beds of kelp, but do not forage off sandy beaches. They primarily consume fish (97 percent of prey items found in 7 stomachs), which predominantly consist of bottom-dwelling forms such as klipfishes (Clinidae), pipefishes *(Syngnathus,* Syngnathidae), and some nonfish items such as shrimp, amphipods, and octopi. The mean weight of the individual pipefishes was found to be 0.97 grams, and the longest prey was a pipefish with a caudal length of 159 millimeters (Williams and Cooper, 1983). The mean number of prey items present per bird was 10.3 in this study, and the mean weight of total prey items was 21 grams in another small sample (Rand, 1960).

Foraging behavior. The birds forage close inshore, often among breaking waves, and sometimes feed in tidal pools during periods of high tides. The average dive duration for 142 dives was only 23.5 seconds, with an average observed interdive interval of 8.1 seconds (Williams and Cooper, 1983).

Social Behavior

Age of maturity and mating system. No good evidence exists on these topics, but adult plumage may be attained by about a year of age (Crawford et al., 1982), and it is unlikely that breeding is delayed beyond the second year of life.

Social displays and vocalizations. There is no information on the vocalizations of this species, and also no information on its social behavior, which presumably is generally similar to that of the long-tailed cormorant.

Reproductive Biology

Breeding season. Breeding in this species occurs throughout the year, but with a seasonal bias toward late spring and summer. Crawford et al. (1982) tabulated 1,718 nesting records for the species and found a peak number (37 percent) during December, with 62 percent of the total occurring in the 3-month period from November through January. The lowest number of records occurred in April, followed by July.

Nest sites and nest building. Nest sites are diverse in this species, ranging from ground or bush sites to those located in small trees, under guano platforms, or under kelp wracks on beaches. Ground sites include rocky cliffs, ledges, stacks, boulders, gullies, caves, and the tops of stone walls. Frequently the birds nest in small groups, commonly of less than 50 nests. They often breed among colonies of various gulls, or among colonies of other seabirds or sea mammals, and their raised nest sites may help protect the nests from being overrun by larger animals.

On Walvis Bay guano platform, the nests are built among the diagonal wooden secondary struts and beams below the main platform. They are arranged singly or in groups, and are located at a height of 2–2.5 meters above the natural rock base of the platform. They are built of sticks and dried seaweeds, with scraps of other materials woven into the structures. The nest locations are apparently chosen to provide lighted conditions but also protection from the prevailing winds, and the cups are elevated about a meter above high-tide levels during ordinary spring tides (Berry, 1974). The sites are clearly used year after year, although nothing has yet been reported on nest-building rates or nest site fidelity.

Egg laying and incubation. In one study, eggs were laid at an average interval of 2.2 days (61 cases), and the clutch ranged from 1 to 5 eggs. Among a total of 1,652 clutches, 14.8 percent were single-egg clutches, 39.2 percent had two eggs, 44.6 percent had three, 1.3 percent had four, and 0.1 percent had five present. Some of the single-egg and two-egg clutches were probably incomplete. The first-laid eggs were generally slightly heavier than later ones, which became progressively lighter (ranging from 24.3 grams to 22.5 grams in four-egg clutches). The mean laying to hatching interval was 23.0 days for all eggs, but 22.4 days for the last-laid eggs among those from two-egg or three-egg clutches, since effective incubation apparently does not begin prior to the laying of the second egg (Williams and Cooper, 1983).

Brooding and rearing of young. The average hatching weight was reported as 16.8 grams by Williams and Cooper (1983). The young hatched from eggs laid later in the sequence average slightly less than those from first-laid eggs. The chicks are fed within 24 hours of hatching, and by ten days begin to move out of their nests temporarily when disturbed. From 22 days on they might leave the nest permanently and form a creche in the vicinity of the colony, where they continue to be fed by their parents. Maximum weight is reached at about 30 days, and one chick could fly at 35 days, although the primaries are not fully grown and the body is still largely down-covered at that age. Chicks are fed for at least the first 30 days, and weights of chicks reared singly did not increase any faster than those in two-chick broods.

Breeding success.   Of 112 eggs in 40 nests, 54 chicks (48.2 percent) hatched. The highest hatching rate was for second-laid eggs (66.7 percent), followed by first-laid (40 percent), third-laid (16.7 percent), and fourth-laid (6.7 percent). Most of the chick mortality occurred during the first six days after hatching, and all of the young dying during the first 20 days were the last-hatched chicks of the clutch. Of 23 chicks, at least 30.4 percent survived a minimum of 20 days, but overall chick mortality rates prior to fledging were not determined by Williams and Cooper (1983).

Population Status

In the most recent and complete survey of this species' population, using data from 1977 to 1981, 15 Namibian colonies supported a total of 977 nest sites, and 22 South African colonies supported 1,688 nest sites. Seven of these colonies supported more than 150 breeding pairs, of which the largest was on Possession Island, Namibia, with 280 nests. Assuming that about half the species' population consists of breeding adults, the world population as of about 1980 might be about 7,000 individuals. There is no evidence of recent reductions in numbers, and although the birds are vulnerable to human disturbance during the nesting season and also to oiling, their scattered colonies help to reduce these generally localized threats (Crawford et al., 1982).

Evolutionary Relationships

As noted earlier, this species is very closely related to *africanus*, and presumably speciated from it in southern Africa during a period of prolonged geographic-ecological separation.

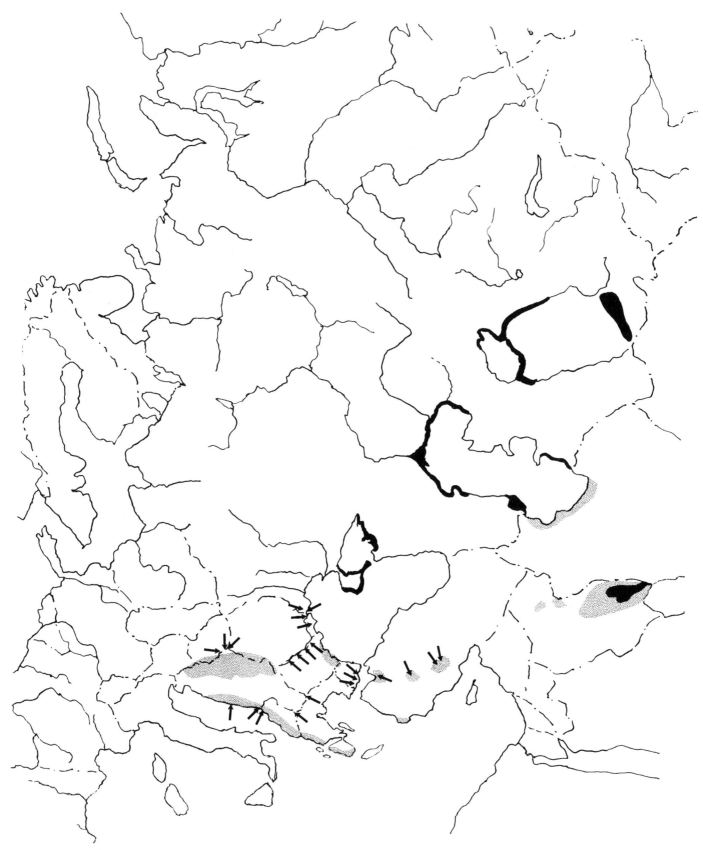

Figure 38. Distribution of the pygmy cormorant, showing its overall breeding (inked and arrows) and wintering ranges (stippled). The breeding locations indicated in the Aral Sea area of the former USSR are now probably abandoned because of recent ecological degradation there.

Other Vernacular Names

Cormoran pygmée (French); Zwergscharbe (German)

Distribution

Breeds or until recently has bred in Romania (mainly in the Danube delta), Albania (Lake Shkodra), Greece (Lake Kerkini), Yugoslavia (Montenegro, southern Macedonia), Turkey (very rare and local), southeastern Iraq (Euphrates marshes), Iran (Caspian coast), and the adjacent former USSR, mostly along the Azerbaijanian coast of the Caspian Sea, and east locally in Kazakhstan to the Aral Sea and its associated river valleys (Syr Darya, Amu Darya) in Uzbekistan (these areas around the Aral Sea are now greatly degraded ecologically). Formerly much more widespread; now threatened both in Europe and the former USSR, with the European population mostly centered in the Danube delta (now also degraded) and the former USSR population mostly confined to Azerbaijan (Collar and Andrew, 1988). Winters mostly in the Balkans, western Turkey, Iraq, and Iran, often not far from the breeding areas. The former USSR population may at least partly winter along the Iranian coast of the Caspian Sea; some wintering probably also occurs in the Tigris and Euphrates valleys of southeastern Iraq. (See figure 38.)

Subspecies

None recognized here, although the Javanese cormorant has at times been considered conspecific with *pygmaeus*.

Description

Prebreeding adult. Forehead (which is slightly crested), lores, and feathers around eyes black; rest of head varying seasonally, via partial molt, from blackish (just before breeding) to deep reddish brown (during the breeding season), becoming paler on the occiput and upper neck; lower neck and rest of plumage shining black, with a slight greenish gloss, especially ventrally; scapulars and wing coverts dark gray, with black feather margins; head, neck, back, rump, and entire underparts with scattered white plumes, these especially abundant on the head before onset of breeding; remiges and rectrices (12) black. Iris dark brown; eye ring and gular skin black, bill black; legs and feet blackish gray.
Postbreeding adult. Chin and a variable area around throat and eyes white; forehead, lores, area around eyes and rest of head, neck, and chest reddish brown; feathers of upper back and upper wing coverts glossy black, narrowly edged with

whitish brown. Bare skin around eye and at corner of mouth black tinged with pink; bill blackish brown, darkest on culmen, reddish yellow with darker spots along cutting edge, legs and feet blackish.
Immature. The juvenal plumage is apparently followed by one much like that of the postbreeding adult, but with the juvenal rectrices and remiges retained. However, this sequence remains uncertain, and it is possible that the definitive breeding plumage is directly attained following the juvenal plumage. The age of initial breeding is unknown (Cramp and Simmons, 1977).
Juvenile. Head and neck reddish brown, shading to white on chin and around throat, and to lighter brown on chest and foreneck; back and rump mostly black, each feather with a narrow sandy margin; wing coverts and scapulars gray, lacking metallic gloss, margined with black and fringed with sandy; underparts dirty white, mottled with brown becoming darker on the flanks and under tail coverts. Iris brown; bill yellowish; legs and feet brown to brownish black.
Nestling. With black skin at hatching, but soon becoming covered with dark brown down. Bill and outer side of tarsus blue; rest of tarsus and bare skin on head flesh-colored.

Measurements (in millimeters)

Wing, males 195–217 (ave. of 11, 206), females 193–208 (ave. of 7, 201); tail, males 137–145 (ave. of 6, 142), females 139–147 (ave. of 5, 141); culmen, males 29–33 (ave. of 6, 30.5), females 27–31 (ave. of 5, 29.2); tarsus, males 37–40 (ave. of 6, 38), females 36–39 (ave. of 5, 37.8) (Cramp and Simmons, 1977). Eggs ca. 47 × 30.

Weights (in grams)

Males 650, 710, 870 (ave. 743), females 564, 640, 640 (ave. 615) (Cramp and Simmons, 1977). Calculated egg weight 23.3.

Identification

In the hand. The combination of an adult culmen length of less than 40 mm, a brown to blackish brown head, a dark brown iris, and a brown to blackish facial skin color identifies this species.
In the field. Within its range, this is the only small (cootsized), short-billed cormorant, about half the size of the generally more common great cormorant. Adults have distinctly brownish heads, especially during breeding, and short black bills. In flight, the relatively long tail is evident. Juveniles have white underparts, and older immatures retain

whitish throats, forenecks, and upper breasts, but have dark upperparts like adults.

Ecology and General Biology

Breeding and nonbreeding habitats. This species is closely associated with dense stands of reeds and herbage-lined shores of fresh-water and occasionally (during nonbreeding periods) brackish and marine environments. It is a warm-climate species limited to lowland habitats. It is mostly found on still-water habitats or at most on slowly flowing waters, including oxbows, river backwaters, flooded fields, swamps, and rice paddies, which provide fishing opportunities in shallow depths. The birds are never far from heavily vegetated areas such as those with trees, shrubs, or dense emergent vegetation, which provide roosting and nesting sites, often in company with herons and other large wading birds.

Movements and migrations. Present-day populations are largely sedentary, although some migration as well as eruptive movements or erratic wanderings also occur. There is a general movement southward during winter, perhaps especially among the more northerly Soviet populations, and during mild winters in the USSR many birds remain at or near their breeding areas. Some fall nomadic movements occur in various directions (Dementiev and Gladkov, 1951).

In the Balkans, breeding birds winter either inland or along the coasts of the Adriatic, Aegean, and Mediterranean seas. Breeders in the Tigris and Euphrates valleys of Iraq are believed to be sedentary, although there is a substantial movement of birds into the Iranian Caspian region during winter (Cramp and Simmons, 1977), presumably representing birds from the north Caspian coastal colonies.

Competition and predation. No specific information. This species overlaps with the great cormorant, but the two species forage on very different-sized prey in different habitats. The birds are probably small enough to be preyed upon by the larger raptors, which may be one reason they seek dense vegetation for roosting and nesting.

Foods and Foraging Behavior

Foods consumed. This is a primarily fish-eating species, taking prey up to about 15 centimeters in length and only occasionally resorting to other kinds of prey such as crustaceans, small mammals, and leeches. Few studies are available, but the fish taken are known to include rudd (*Scardinius*), pike (*Esox*), and roach (*Rutilus*) (Dementiev and Gladkov, 1951). In the only quantitative study so far available, Andone et al. (1969) reported finding 15 species of prey fish in 130 birds from the Danube delta, with the average collective weight of the fish 15 grams, and the maximum 71 grams. Species represented in greatest number and in diminishing frequency included perch (*Perca*) at 18.8 percent, as well as roach (14.8 percent), carp (10.8 percent), loach (*Cobitis*) (9.7 percent), and pike (5.6 percent).

Foraging behavior. These birds typically fly from roosting areas twice a day to forage, and capture their prey by diving in water up to about 2.4 meters deep and for durations of up to 42 seconds. Foraging is usually done individually; less often pairs or groups forage together (Cramp and Simmons, 1977).

Social Behavior

Age of maturity and mating system. No specific information is available on these points. It is likely that an adultlike plumage is attained about a year after hatching, and that initial breeding occurs within two years.

Social displays and vocalizations. Vocalizations are little studied, but during the breeding season repeated grunting calls and higher-pitched quacking notes of unknown significance are uttered. Similarly, the displays and other social behavior associated with breeding are still unstudied. It is possible that pair bonding may occur on wintering areas, since Straka (1990) observed birds performing pairing behavior on the Danube River of Austria.

Reproductive Biology

Breeding season. This species is a spring breeder, nesting in southern Europe and the former USSR from about the end of April or early May to late June or early July.

Nest sites and nest building. Nests are in colonies, often with other colonial birds (great cormorant, spoonbills, herons, ibises, etc.), and commonly are in fairly dense vegetation, including trees, shrubs, or reed beds. Small floating islands of dead vegetation overgrown with reeds are especially favored. Tree nests are placed among medium-high crowns, while in reed beds they are often 1–1.5 meters above water. Nests are constructed of branches and reeds, with deep cups, so that incubating birds are scarcely visible. Nests are sometimes used for several years, although there is no information on nest longevity or possible nest site fidelity (Dementiev and Gladkov, 1951).

Egg laying and incubation. The clutch size is reportedly 4–6 eggs, with extremes of 3–7; the egg-laying rate is unreported (Dementiev and Gladkov, 1951). As usual, incubation begins with the first egg, and hatching is asynchronous, after an incubation period of 27–30 days (Cramp and Simmons, 1977).

Brooding and rearing of young. Both parents tend the young. These are initially fed semidigested small fish, but by late in the brooding period they consume fish of about 10–12 centimeters (Dementiev and Gladkov, 1951). The estimated fledging period is about 70 days (Cramp and Simmons, 1977).

Breeding success. No information is available.

Population Status

Collar and Andrew (1988) listed this species as "threatened," with recent known breeding only in Albania, Yugoslavia, Bulgaria, Romania, Greece, Turkey, Iraq, Iran, and the former USSR. The Caspian Sea population may consist of 3,200–6,600 pairs, and that associated with the Aral Sea is now probably entirely extirpated, considering the great ecological destruction there. Otherwise, the largest colonies are probably those on the Danube delta, with 12,000 estimated pairs, and Lake Shkodra, Albania, with about 2,000 pairs. A tabular estimate of the species' overall breeding population was presented earlier (table 27). In their recent (1988) listing of threatened animals, the IUCN listed the status of this species as "insufficiently known."

Evolutionary Relationships

Certainly this species' closest relative is the Javanese cormorant, and it is indeed questionable whether the two should be considered specifically distinct. However, Siegel-Causey (1988) found *niger* to share one osteological character with *melanoleucos* that is not found in *pygmaeus*. It seems possible that they should be regarded as separate species. Zoogeographically, *pygmaeus* falls between the two African microcormorants and the two Indo-Malaysian and Australian microcormorants, and a hypothetical speciation pattern involving these taxa is not difficult to construct.

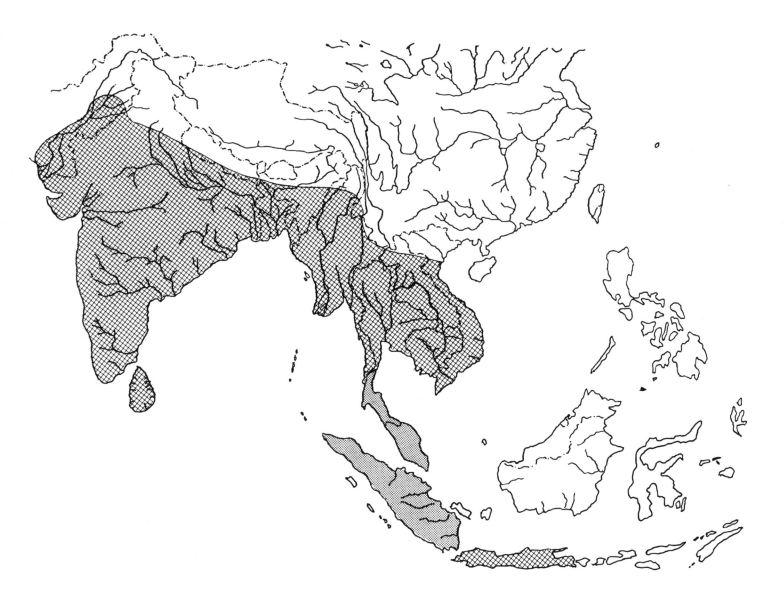

Figure 39. Distribution of the Javanese cormorant, showing its residential range (cross-hatched) and nonbreeding or vagrant range (stippled).

Other Vernacular Names

Javan cormorant, little cormorant, pygmy cormorant (when considered conspecific with *pygmaeus*); cormoran de Vieillot (French); Mohrenscharbe, Mohrenzwergscharbe (German)

Distribution

Resident in Sri Lanka (Ceylon), and from eastern Pakistan, India, and southern Nepal east through Bangladesh, Burma (Myanmar), and Thailand to southwestern China (western Yunnan, possibly also southern Guangxi and southern Guangdong) and Vietnam. No proven breeding from the Malay Peninsula, where rare; status in Laos and Cambodia (Kampuchea) unknown. Also a common breeding resident on Java, but only a nonbreeding visitor to Sumatra. At least formerly probably resident on Borneo (no modern records). (See figure 39.)

Subspecies

None recognized here, although this form has at times been regarded as a subspecies of *pygmaeus* (Dorst and Mougin, 1979).

Description

Prebreeding adult. Generally glossy black, with a slight greenish tinge; the feathers of upper back with glossy black shafts; scapulars and wing coverts silvery gray to dark ashy gray, each feather pointed and bordered with black; a line of scattered white plumes from the front of the eye back along the sides of the head; top of head and hindneck with scattered white filoplumes, the feathers of the occiput and hindneck elongated and manelike; rectrices (12) black. Iris green; eye ring and gular skin livid purple to purplish black; bill blackish brown to brownish yellow, becoming purplish basally; legs and feet black, tinged with purple.
Postbreeding adult. Nonbreeding birds are reportedly "virtually inseparable" from those of the pygmy cormorant (Roberts, 1991). Chin and throat silvery gray, the white nuptial plumes and filoplumes of the head and neck lacking, and the manelike feathers on the nape and hindneck less evident. Eye ring black; gular skin probably grayish pink (also variously described as yellow or black); legs and feet black.
Immature. Undescribed in detail, but evidently very much like the pygmy cormorant, judging from a few museum specimens.

Juvenile. Head, neck, and underparts dark brown, darkest on the flanks and back of the neck; chin and throat whitish; lower back, rump, and upper tail coverts brownish black with a slight gloss; scapulars and wing coverts dark ashy gray, very narrowly fringed with pale brownish. First-winter birds are silvery gray on their underparts, and their necks are dull rusty brown (Roberts, 1991).
Nestling. Initially naked, but within a week nearly covered with dingy black down, with the head still bald and shiny livid red, and the neck also still naked (Ali and Ripley, 1983). Even after the sooty brown down has fully grown, the livid red area on the top of the head remains (Roberts, 1991).

Measurements (in millimeters)

Wing, males 190–200 (ave. of 4, 196), females 185–200 (ave. of 4, 194); tail, males 130–139 (ave. of 4, 134.5), females 117–130 (ave. of 4, 126); exposed culmen, males 28–32 (ave. of 4, 29.7), females 28–30 (ave. of 4, 29.5) (American Museum of Natural History specimens). Eggs ca. 45 × 29.

Weights (in grams)

Sex composition and sample size not specified, range 360–525 (ave. 427) (Baker, 1929). Winkler (1983) gave an average adult weight of 475, without specifying sample size. Calculated egg weight 20.9.

Identification

In the hand. The combination of an adult culmen length of less than 35 mm and blackish underpart and head color, including the facial skin, identifies this species.
In the field. This species does not come into geographic contact with the pygmy cormorant, a very similar but more westerly species (rarely reaching Pakistan) that has brown eyes in adults and a generally more brownish head color. By comparison, the Javanese cormorant has green eyes and is uniformly dark-colored on both head and body. The Indian cormorant is sympatric and is only slightly larger, but has a more distinct blackish "scaly" pattern on the upperparts, and furthermore breeding adults of that species also have a contrasting narrow white stripe behind the eye. In the Greater Sundas the Javanese cormorant could easily be mistaken for the little black cormorant, which has also been reported from Java, but which has a longer and considerably more slender bill.

Ecology and General Biology

Breeding and nonbreeding habitats.   This species occurs throughout the Indian subcontinent wherever swamps, lakes, reservoirs, irrigation canals, tanks, or small pools or ponds occur, and also utilizes slow-moving rivers. It is apparently primarily a fresh-water species, although it also may be found feeding in estuaries (Ali and Ripley, 1983). On Sri Lanka the species occurs widely on Parakrama Samudra reservoir, near Polonnaruwa, at least along its shallower shoreline areas, where the birds form large communal roosts (Winkler, 1983).

Movements and migrations.   This is evidently a basically sedentary species, but may show some local movements associated with monsoon rainfall patterns and resultant changing water levels. In Pakistan the birds roost communally in reed beds along major wetland habitats during winter but disperse into rice fields during the late monsoon period (Roberts, 1991).

Competition and predation.   Winkler's (1983) study in Sri Lanka indicated that this species is well separated ecologically from the other two cormorants breeding there (great and Indian cormorants), as to both the size of food it selects and its foraging habitats, although all three species feed predominantly on cichlid fishes. The only predator that has been specifically mentioned is the house crow *(Corvus splendens)*, which is reportedly a serious egg predator of heronries as well (Ali and Ripley, 1983).

Foods and Foraging Behavior

Foods consumed.   Winkler (1983) reported that on Parakrama Samudra reservoir in Sri Lanka little cormorants prey on fish that are 30–70 millimeters in length, with cichlids (mostly *Entroplus* and *Tilapia,* at a frequency ratio of 2:1) representing about half the diet, and another 40 percent represented by juveniles of *Puntius.* About 300 grams of fish may be consumed per individual each day in the opinion of Mukherjee (1969), but Winkler provided a more realistic estimate of 96 grams per day, representing about 20 percent of the average adult weight. He also judged that the average meal consisted of 8 fishes. Tadpoles, frogs, and crustaceans have also been reported as foods in India (Ali and Ripley, 1983).

Foraging behavior.   These birds forage individually and maintain foraging territories, based on observations by Winkler (1983). However, immature birds may form foraging flocks, which may help to overcome the aggressiveness of the adults. This species sometimes also associates with the socially foraging Indian cormorant, and is quickly attracted to the very large feeding flocks of these birds. Winkler noted that they typically dive in flooded vegetation along shorelines, with mean diving times of only 12.4 seconds, and mean resting intervals of 5.4 seconds. According to Roberts

(1991), these birds frequently forage in flocks when pursuing schools of fish, but during the late monsoon they disperse into rice fields and may feed in very small pools or "borrow-pits," then often feeding on frogs or tadpoles.

Social Behavior

Age of maturity and mating system.   No specific information is available on these points.

Social displays and vocalizations.   Roberts (1991) noted that this species is much more vocal than other cormorants, and that the noises coming from a winter roost of 4,000 birds sound like the roaring that emanates from a sports stadium. The birds produce an "incessant variety of deep-toned grunting and groaning" calls, which are guttural and include various low-pitched sounds such as "gargling," "aah-aahing," and "kok-kok-koking" notes. Both sexes build and defend the nest, and courtship or associated display consists of ritualized appeasement movements of the head and neck, which are extended downward and forward in a snakelike series of movements. The head and neck are occasionally brought back over the back during intense excitement, and at such times the occipital crest is raised and the gular region is expanded (Roberts, 1991).

Reproductive Biology

Breeding season.   The breeding season is mainly from July to September in northern India and adjacent Pakistan, and from November to February in southern India. Breeding in Sri Lanka occurs from December to May (Ali and Ripley, 1983). In southern Pakistan (Indus Valley), incomplete nests or nests with fresh eggs have been found as early as May, and large young seen in July, but probably most nesting begins in July and August, after sites have been vacated by various ardeids *(Ardeola, Bubulcus,* and *Egretta).*

Nest sites and nest building.   Nests are often built in clumps of bamboo or trees around village ponds, with half-submerged trees being favored locations. Sometimes colonies are found in reed beds. There the birds build their nests about 1.3 meters above water on masses of broken-down elephant grass, which otherwise grows to about 3 meters high and completely screens the nests. The nests are quite small, averaging only about 30 centimeters across and up to almost a meter in depth. Nests are reused in successive years, and the birds may sometimes also use old nests of egrets or crows, which may be nesting in the same area. Most colonies are small, of no more than about a half-dozen pairs, but at times may have 50 or 60 nests (Baker, 1929, 1935). In the Indus valley, flooded *Acacia* trees, mangroves, bushes *(Salvadora),* and reeds *(Phragmites)* are all used as nest sites in various locations.

Egg laying and incubation.   The usual clutch size is from 3 to 5 eggs, but the average clutch size and incubation period are still unreported. Doubtless incubation and brooding behavior is much like that of related species, but is still undescribed.

Brooding and rearing of young. Roberts (1991) noted that the young birds solicit feeding by waving their wings and tickling the gular pouch or base of their parents' bills.

Breeding success. Hancock (1984) reported that 1,735 nests at Bharatpur, India, held 408 nestlings during a September survey. Since their ages were not specified, nor were the number of eggs possibly also present, it is impossible to judge the significance of this statistic.

Population Status

This relatively inconspicuous species can survive close to humans on small ponds and rivers of the Indian subcontinent. Winkler (1983) observed a peak population of 1,850 individuals on a single reservoir (Parakrama Samudra) in east-central Sri Lanka, as compared with 102 great cormorants and 13,700 Indian cormorants. This reservoir appears to be about 30–40 square kilometers in area (this information was not provided by Winkler), so the maximum population density must have been around 50 Javanese cormorants per square kilometer.

Evolutionary Relationships

This is apparently a very close relative of *pygmaeus* based on its overall appearance, and it is sometimes considered conspecific with this form, but Siegel-Causey (1988) found that it is also apparently anatomically very close to *melanoleucos*. Its present-day distribution would suggest that it might well have evolved in southeastern Asia, after separating from earlier *pygmaeus* stock farther to the west or northwest, or from pre-*melanoleucos* stock to the southeast.

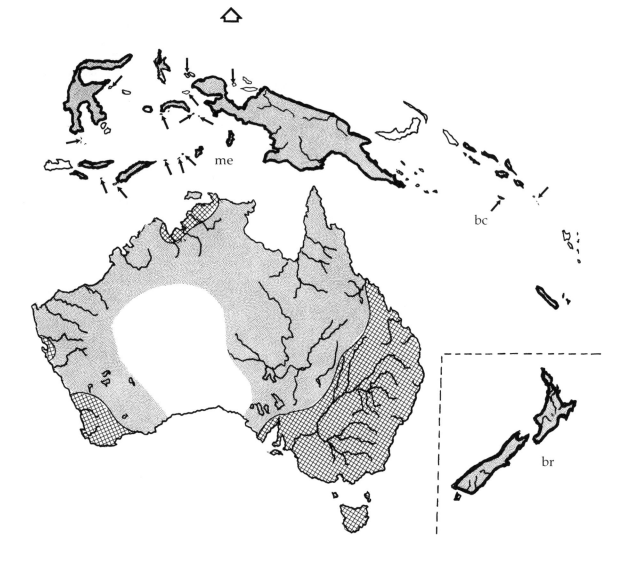

Figure 40. Distribution of the little pied cormorant, showing
the residential ranges of its races *melanoleucos* (me), *brevicauda*
(bc), and *brevirostris* (br). Denser range cross-hatched, sparser
or less certain range limits inked and/or stippled, small island populations shown by arrows. A disjunct population of
melanoleucos occurs on the Palau (Belau) Islands, beyond the
map's northern limits (open arrow).

Other Vernacular Names

Frilled shag, little black and white cormorant, little black and white shag, little cormorant, little river shag, little shag (New Zealand), white-throated shag (New Zealand); cormoran pie (French); australische Zwergscharbe, Kräuselscharbe (German)

Distribution

Resident on fresh waters and estuaries throughout New Zealand, most of Australia, New Caledonia, the Solomons, Santa Cruz, Palau, New Guinea, Moluccas, Celebes (Sulawesi), and the Lesser Sundas; vagrants rarely reach eastern Java. (See figure 40.)

Subspecies

P. m. melanoleucos. Resident in the Lesser Sundas (west to Bali as vagrants), Celebes, Moluccas, Aru Islands, western Papuan islands (Waigeo, Salawati, Misool), New Guinea, Numfoor, Palau (Belau) Islands (Caroline group), Solomon Islands (excepting Rennell Island), Santa Cruz Islands, New Caledonia, Australia (excepting the dry interior), and Tasmania. The more westerly population extending from Malaysia to northern Australia has at times been racially recognized as *melvillensis.*

P. m. brevicauda Mayr 1931. Endemic to Rennell Island (Solomon Islands).

P. m. brevirostris Gould 1837. Resident coastally and interiorly throughout New Zealand, including Stewart Island. Breeding on Campbell Island was reported in the late 1960s (Kinsky, 1969); current status there unknown. Frequently seen on Lord Howe Island; vagrants have also reached Snares and Auckland islands. Possibly should be regarded as a separate species, based on distinctive behavior and morphology (Marchant and Higgins, 1990).

Description

Prebreeding adult. Pied morph (the typical plumage type, except in New Zealand, where the melanistic morph is generally more common): Crown, nape, hindneck, and upperparts glossy black, with a dull greenish tinge. Rest of plumage white, except for the vent area and under tail coverts, which are sooty black; feathers at base of culmen white, forming a narrow stripe that passes back above the eye; wing coverts and scapulars shining grayish black, margined with black; feathers of the forehead forming a short black crest, the white feathers at the sides of the head and neck lengthened, forming a short frill along the sides of neck; scattered white filoplumes on the top of the head and neck. Remiges and rectrices (12) black. Iris dark brown, with a very narrow blue eye ring; skin of lores dark brownish gray, yellowish brown, or greenish yellow (becoming brighter at onset of breeding); gape and palate bright blue; bill yellow (becoming orange at onset of breeding), with a blackish brown culmen and more olive-colored below; gular skin yellow to orange-buff; legs and feet grayish black.

Melanistic morph (limited to New Zealand): Entire plumage glossy black, with a slight greenish tinge on upperparts and sides of body; the sides of the head, chin, throat, and foreneck all pure white below a line from nostril to the eye; a distinct black forehead crest, and scattered white plumes on the occiput and neck. Softparts as in typical morph. Intermediate variants occur, including those with white extending down to include the upper breast, and others with the abdomen mottled black and white or entirely black, mating between morphs apparently being nonassortative (Dowding and Taylor, 1987).

Postbreeding adult. Shorter forehead feathers and lacking the white frills on sides of head, otherwise similar to breeding plumage; the softpart colors less bright, the loral skin becoming dark grayish black, and the bill yellow with a darker culmen.

Immature. The black crown feathers extending down to the eye and the base of the culmen; feathers of the crown and hindneck margined with pale brown, and the upper back, wing coverts, and scapulars margined with brownish white; underparts white in Australia, highly variable in darkness in New Zealand; the darker underpart feathers (in melanistic morphs) yellowish brown toward their tips. Facial skin more blackish than in adults; bill brownish black, with a yellow to reddish base. Adult plumage is reportedly attained late in the first year of life, when the bill becomes distinctly yellower. Immatures of the pied morph have distinctive black thighs in addition to the black crown and forehead reaching down to the level of the eyes (Serventy, Serventy, and Warham, 1971).

Juvenile. Mostly brownish black above, the feathers margined with brown or brownish white; underparts probably varying from entirely black (in the melanistic morph and intermediate individuals) to white (in the pied morph). Iris grayish brown; facial skin dark brown; maxilla dark brown, mandible dull yellow; gular skin dull yellow.

Nestling. Hatched naked, with reddish to blackish brown skin, and a red throat patch. Covered with black down later, except for a bald pink, orange, or bluish crown (but not dark purplish gray, as in little black cormorant), and a pink (later white) area around the base of the bill. In nominate *melanoleucos* but not *brevirostris* a white spot is present on the upper side of the otherwise black neck (Marchant and Higgins, 1990). Iris blackish brown; bill, legs, and feet dark gray to black.

Measurements (in millimeters)

Australian *melanoleucos:* wing, males 220–240 (ave. of 6, 233), females 212–240 (ave. of 6, 227); tail, males 141–156 (ave. of 6, 150), females 142–157 (ave. of 6, 149); culmen, males 28.9–32.3 (ave. of 6, 30.8), females 28.9–33 (ave. of 6, 30.3) (Serventy, Serventy, and Warham, 1971). New Zealand *brevirostris:* wing, males 221–246 (ave. of 13, 232), females 214–239 (ave. of 28, 225); tail, males 131–164 (ave. of 13, 150), females 133–155 (ave. of 28, 145); culmen, males 26–33 (ave. of 13, 30), females 27–33 (ave. of 28, 30) (Marchant and Higgins, 1990). Eggs ca. 48 × 32.

Weights (in grams)

Males of Australian *melanoleucos* 691–963 (ave. of 28, 822), females 567–864 (ave. of 78, 730). The heaviest average weights were attained just prior to breeding, during June and July, and the lowest averages occurred in December and January (Serventy, 1939). In a sample of 313 males and 214 females obtained over a three-year period, the monthly mean weights of males ranged from 720 to 920, and females from 630 to 760; the greatest average weights were associated with periods of gonadal growth (Miller, 1980). The average weight of 21 birds (sexes and ages unspecified) from marine habitats in Australia was 683, that of 26 birds from fresh-water sites was 697 (Thompson and Morley, 1966). Of New Zealand *brevirostris,* males 715–877 (ave. of 6, 796), females 413–704 (ave. of 5, 586) (Marchant and Higgins, 1990). Six adult and subadult males (subspecies combined) 680–920 (ave. 799), 10 adult and subadult females 560–790 (ave. 659) (U.S. National Museum and Museum of Vertebrate Zoology specimens). Calculated egg weight 27.1; average of 14 eggs, 23; of 3 additional eggs, 36.3 (Marchant and Higgins, 1990).

Identification

In the hand.   The combination of an adult culmen length of less than 35 mm and white underparts identifies this species. *In the field.*   The very small size, short bill, and bicolored condition (the normally white underparts sometimes stained with rusty) helps to identify this species. Unlike in the larger pied and black-faced cormorants, the thighs are white, not black, the eyes of adults are brown (not green, as in all the other Australian cormorants), there is no bright yellow spot in front of the eye, and the bill is more yellowish below and toward the tip. Immatures do have blackish thighs, but are also blackish around the eyes; in New Zealand the common

melanistic morph is almost entirely dark except for a white face and throat, the white sometimes extending down to the upper breast.

Ecology and General Biology

Breeding and nonbreeding habitats.   A very wide variety of aquatic habitats are used by this species, including both fresh-water wetlands and coastal waters. These range in size from very small wetland ponds, pools, billabongs (oxbows), and rivers to large reservoirs, lakes, coastal lagoons, estuaries, bays, and harbors. The birds also occasionally utilize mangrove swamps, salt pans, salt marshes, and densely vegetated swamps, but seem to prefer fairly open fresh-water lakes, rivers, wooded billabongs, and permanent or seasonal swamps. Water areas larger than 100 hectares (250 acres) are evidently preferred over smaller wetlands. Typically they nest in waters having high levels of organic matter and diverse invertebrate populations, but occasionally they also nest on offshore islands (Marchant and Higgins, 1990). *Movements and migrations.*   Like many Australian species, this one is dispersive rather than regularly migratory, and the other island populations are presumably fairly sedentary. Changes in local populations are apparently sometimes but not always correlated with water levels or rainfall (Marchant and Higgins, 1990). Banding results of birds marked as nestlings indicate an average movement of 125 kilometers at two months after banding, 180 kilometers at three months, and 300 kilometers at six months. Some birds may begin to return to their natal colony after about ten months. Some unusually long-distance dispersals have been documented, including one bird that moved some 2,900 kilometers to New Guinea (Llewellyn, 1983). *Competition and predation.*   Several studies have been done on the comparative foraging ecology and foods of the little black and little pied cormorants in Australia (e.g., McKeown, 1944; McNally, 1957; Vestjens, 1977b; Miller, 1979; Dostine and Morton, 1988), as described in chapter 4. These indicate that major ecological differences exist in foraging habitats and behavioral foraging adaptations of these two similar-sized species. No specific information exists on significant predators, but crows and whistling kites *(Haliastur sphenurus)* are believed to take eggs (Marchant and Higgins, 1990).

Foods and Foraging Behavior

Foods consumed.   A substantial number of studies on the foods of this species have been undertaken, as summarized in Marchant and Higgins (1990). Among three studies that analyzed food intake by percentage of total wet weight, fish comprised 38.3–55 percent (unweighted average 47 percent) of total food intake, and crustaceans 45–61.1 percent (unweighted average 51 percent) of the total. Among eight studies that analyzed foods by proportionate numbers of total prey items, fish comprised from 19.2 to 89.6 percent of the total items (unweighted average 45.7 percent), and crustaceans from 8.7 to 80.8 percent (unweighted average 28.6 percent). These crustacean consumption levels are notably high with respect to the other Australian cormorants, and appear to be higher among birds that had been foraging in fresh-water environments than those feeding in the sea. Among the crustaceans, shrimps (*Alphaeus, Palaemon, Palaemontes*), prawns (*Metapenaus*), crayfish or yabby (*Cherax, Paranephrops*), and crabs (*Amarinus*) are commonly consumed. The fish prey included a wide variety of taxa, generally ranging in length from about 4 to 18 centimeters and usually averaging less than 1.0 grams in weight. Additionally, frogs, insects, squids, and mollusks are consumed in smaller quantities. The average total prey weight per individual in a sample of 71 birds was 24.3 grams (Trayler, Brothers, and Potter, 1989).

The largest available sample (of 527 stomachs) is that of Miller (1979), who observed seasonal changes in prey selection due to temporal changes in relative prey availability. Foods fed to nestlings were similar to those eaten by adults, although young were fed distinctly smaller yabbies and also generally fewer of these than were eaten by adults. However, atyid shrimp were eaten by young in relatively larger numbers than by adults, at least during one of the two breeding seasons studied.

Foraging behavior. As compared with the little black cormorant, the little pied cormorant forages in relatively shallow areas and hunts individually rather than cooperatively. It also hunts selectively in areas where yabby and shrimp are most abundant, and makes dives of fairly short duration as compared with other Australian cormorants (Miller, 1979; Stonehouse, 1967).

Social Behavior

Age of maturity and mating system. The age of initial breeding is unknown, but adult plumage is attained within a year of hatching, so breeding probably occurs before the end of the second year. The mating system is assumed to be one of sustained monogamy (Marchant and Higgins, 1990).
Social displays and vocalizations. Male advertising behavior is performed on potential nest sites, and two displays are then performed, each independently of the other. The New Zealand population's displays were described by Mathews and Fordham (1986), and the Australian form's displays have been recently summarized by Marchant and Higgins (1990). Apart from minor postural differences, the male advertisement displays of the two populations appear to be essentially the same. These consist of wing crouching (Marchant and Higgins)—also known in New Zealand as the squat-thrust (Mathews and Fordham)—and bowing (Marchant and Higgins)—also known in New Zealand as gape bowing (Mathews and Fordham). In wing crouching by Australian birds, the bird begins by standing

rather erect with its tail slightly cocked and its folded wings somewhat lifted posteriorly (figure 41A). The bird then briefly drops to a squatting posture for about a second (figure 41B), and quickly returns to the starting point, while holding the bill closed and the body feathers ruffled. This sequence is done repeatedly. In squat-thrusting by New Zealand birds the starting posture is similar, but in the squatting phase the head is held vertically upward (figure 41C), and the male utters a bisyllabic call on the upward return movement. This is performed only once or twice, at irregular intervals. When bowing, birds of both populations begin in an upright position (figure 41D), and then swing the head downward and forward, with the bill open, until (in Australian birds) the head is almost upside-down, while uttering a guttural cooing call (figure 41E). In New Zealand birds the neck is stretched forward and downward. With the bill directed forward, a monosyllabic call is uttered at the end of the downstroke (figure 41F). In both populations the bowing display may be repeated at short intervals, or it may be alternated with wing crouching (squat-thrusting). Both displays are associated with early stages of pair formation.

Mate recognition displays, at least in the Australian race, consist of mutual head swaying with the crest erect and the bill open (figure 41G), while uttering a repetitive mate recognition *uk* call. During chick feeding soft repetitive cooing sounds are uttered that may represent kink-throating, and during the prehop display a harsher repetitive cooing call is uttered (Marchant and Higgins, 1990).

As in other cormorants, aggression in this species is marked by bill pointing toward the opponent, and appeasement is indicated oppositely by directing the bill away from the other individual. Low-intensity threat involves simple bill pointing, medium-intensity threat is accompanied by a thrusting of the head forward and backward in the median plane, and high-intensity threat additionally involves crest raising, partial tail elevation, and slight wing raising. The bill is also opened during each forward thrust of the head; pecking and grabbing of the opponent with the bill may occur during actual fighting (Mathews and Fordham, 1986).

Vocalizations of the species are still only poorly studied, but include a guttural cooing *oo-oo* or *oo-oo-oo* uttered by the male during his advertisement display, a similar harsh cooing as a preflight or prehopping signal, and a repetitive *uk-uk-uk* when a male arrives to greet his mate on the nest or to feed the chicks. The chicks utter squeaking and sucking sounds (Robertson, 1988). Additionally, alarm notes are invariably uttered by adults at the approach of an aerial predator when chicks are present in the nest. The notes, a repeated series of loud coos, cause the chicks to fall silent and huddle in the nest. This vocalization is especially notable in that such alarm calls are very rare among cormorants, which typically simply become silent when threatened (Mathews and Fordham, 1986).

Figure 41. Social behavior of the little pied cormorant, including upright phase of squat-thrust (wing crouching) (A), followed by second phase in Australian (B) and New Zealand (C) birds; upright phase of gape bowing (bowing) (D), followed by second phase in Australian (E) and New Zealand (F) birds. Also shown is nest relief posture (G). After sketches in Marchant and Higgins (1990) and Mathews and Fordham (1986).

Reproductive Biology

Breeding season.   In New Zealand breeding is distinctly seasonal, with birds near Auckland nesting during spring and summer (August to March) and most laying occurring in September and October (Taylor, 1987; Robertson, 1988). In Australia the temporal pattern is less clear. Some breeding may occur throughout the year, although there is an apparent peak in spring and summer at least in southern Australia. In northern Australia fall and winter breeding is more characteristic. Miller (1980) studied breeding cycles in New South Wales, and found that increasing day lengths stimulated breeding there, whereas regression of the gonads was initiated by low temperatures, falling water levels, and perhaps lack of social stimulation. Laying periods tended to be synchronized within colony subunits, but were often very different between colonies, suggestive of a possible social influence in nesting cycles.

Nest sites and nest building.   Nests are built in trees, bushes, or reeds, or on rocky surfaces, jetties, or mooring spikes, depending on local situations. Probably there is a preference for tree nesting over water, or at least amid concealing foliage. A sample of 79 Australian nests averaged 2.8 meters above water. Nests are usually 30–40 centimeters in diameter, with a shallow cup. The site is chosen by the male, but the female constructs the nest with materials brought by the male, as is typical of cormorants.

Egg laying and incubation.   The typical clutch in Australia consists of four eggs, with a maximum of six (rarely seven), but the egg-laying rate is still unreported (Marchant and Higgins, 1990). In New Zealand the usual clutch is also believed to be 3–4 eggs. The incubation period is still unreported.

Brooding and rearing of young.   There is no specific information on fledging periods or other details of chick rearing. Taylor (1987) described the plumages of adult and young birds, and found that mating between dark and pied plumage morphs was random. Additionally, the plumages of the young birds indicated that the dark plumage morph is incompletely dominant over the pied morph, and is controlled by a single gene.

Breeding success.   Very little information exists on breeding success. Of nests with 24 eggs, only 14 hatched, and from 8 eggs in two nests, 7 chicks hatched and 6 fledged (Marchant and Higgins, 1990). Taylor (1987) observed a total of 90 nesting attempts (including renestings). Of these, 13 percent of the pairs failed to complete their nests, 16 percent were lost as a result of storm damage, and 22 percent were deserted during incubation. This would suggest a nest failure rate of about 50 percent. In 7 percent of the 90 attempts all the chicks died in the nest, and in 35 percent only one or two young were reared to fledging. He never saw four chicks in a nest, and only rarely observed three. During two breeding seasons, 43 pairs raised an average of 1.4 young per nest. In one year a third of all nesting attempts led to at least one young being reared to fledging.

Population Status

No complete surveys for Australia exist, but this species is generally common over much of its range. The Australian bird atlas (Blakers, Davies, and Reilly, 1984) reported that 65 percent of the survey blocks had records for this species, of which 18 percent were breeding records. The New Zealand population has been estimated at between 10,000 and 50,000 birds (Robertson and Bell, 1984).

Evolutionary Relationships

This is evidently a very close relative of the Javanese cormorant (Siegel-Causey, 1988), and the two forms might easily have evolved on the Australian mainland and on southeastern Asia or the Greater Sundas, respectively, following isolation.

Other Vernacular Names

Spectacled cormorant; cormoran de Pallas (French); Brillenkormoran (German)

Distribution

Extinct; previously endemic to the Commander Islands (Bering Island).

Subspecies

None.

Description

Prebreeding adult (sexes probably alike, although females have been questionably described as lacking both the crest and the whitish eye ring or "spectacles"). Forehead naked; a double bronze-purple crest projecting from the crown and occiput, the face also bronze-purple; back of head and upper neck bronze oil-green, shading into dark bluish green on the lower neck; head and upper neck with long yellowish white filoplumes; base of neck, interscapulars, and chest dark bronze-green, shading to deep greenish blue elsewhere on the body, except for a large white patch on each flank; scapulars and wing coverts deep purple, edged with black; remiges and rectrices (12) black, the shafts of the latter pale horny white dorsally, shading distally to blackish. Iris color uncertain; lores and bare forehead skin vermillion and blue, with a ring of thick yellowish white (or entirely white) skin surrounding the eyes, forming pale "spectacles"; bill blackish, lighter toward tip; naked gular skin orange and heart-shaped; legs and feet black.

Other plumages are undescribed.

Measurements (in millimeters)

Unsexed specimens: wing 351, 356, and 359 (ave. 355.3); tail 189, 201, and 229 (ave. 206.3), exposed culmen 95, tarsus 68 and 76 (Stejneger, 1889). An additional unsexed specimen in the Helsingfors Zoological Museum, Finland: exposed culmen 74.5, wing 364, tail (strongly frayed) 169 (Palmgren, 1935). Eggs: no information.

Weights

Adults weighed ca. 5.5–6.35 kilograms (12–14 pounds) according to Stejneger (1889).

Identification

In the hand. The very large size (tail length over 180 mm, wing length over 350 mm, and culmen length over 90 mm) easily identifies this largest of all cormorant species.
In the field. Extinct.

History of the Species

This species probably became extinct in the mid-1800s, for all the known specimens date from about 1840–1850, and natives reported to the ornithologist Leonhard Stejneger in 1882 that the species had disappeared about 30 years prior to that time. However, they had been common at the time of G. W. Steller's visit to the islands in 1741 during the arctic explorations by Bering, and indeed the birds had been eaten by this group of explorers. Later, when Aleuts were imported to the Commander Islands in 1826, they regularly ate the birds, as no doubt did visiting whalers or hunters of seals (*Callorhinus ursinus*) and sea otters (*Enhydra lutis*). Additionally arctic foxes (*Alopex alopex*) were already present on the Commander Islands when Bering's expedition was wrecked there in 1741. Foxes apparently were common on the islands by the latter part of the nineteenth century, and so probably did great damage to eggs and nestlings, if not also to adults (Greenway, 1958). Volcanic action in that geothermally active region may also have contributed to the species' extinction (Stejneger, 1889).

Only six known specimens exist, making this species one of the rarest of all birds that became extinct in the nineteenth century. Two are in the museum of the Imperial Academy of Sciences in St. Petersburg, two are in the British Museum (Natural History), and single specimens are in the Ryjks Museum of Leyden, Holland, and the Zoological Museum of Helsingfors University, Finland (Palmgren, 1935). Evidently all of these were the result of gifts from the Russian governor of Bering Island in the mid-1800s.

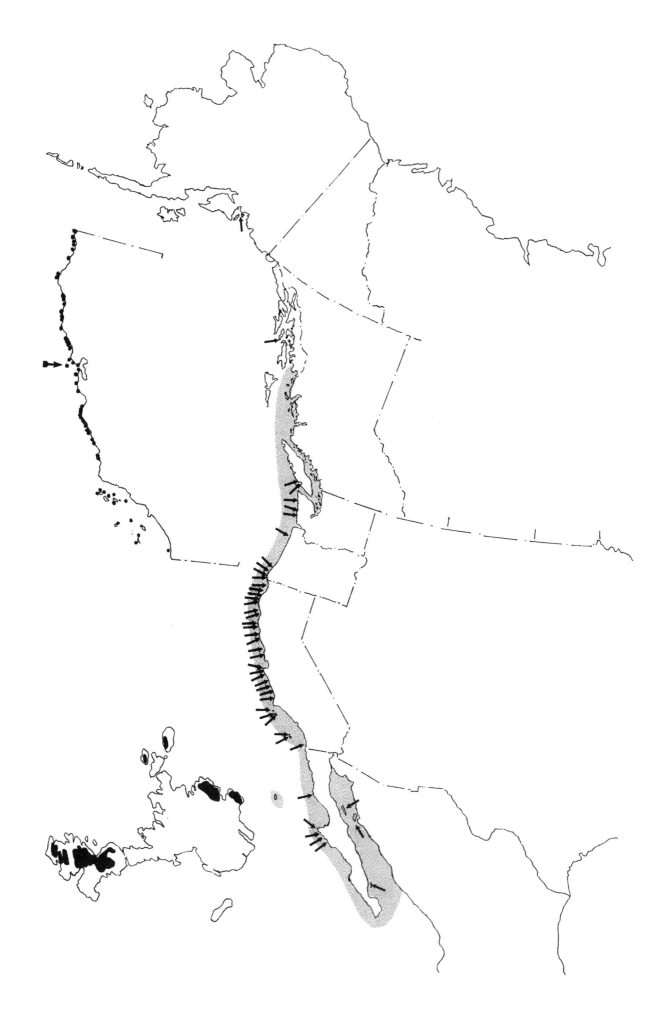

Other Vernacular Names

Brown cormorant, pencilled cormorant, Townsend's cormorant, tufted cormorant; cormoran de Brandt (French); Pinselkormoran (German); cormorán de Brandt, cormorán principal, sargento guanero (Spanish)

Distribution

Resident along the Pacific coast of North America, mainly from Vancouver Island, British Columbia, south to Baja California, including Baja's Pacific coastal islands (San Geronimo, Natividad, Asunción, and Gull Rocks, San Cristobal Bay; at least formerly on Coronados Island, and previously also on Guadalupe Island). Local on some islands in the Gulf of California (San Pedro Martir, Salsipeudes, and Roca Blanca). Also very local in southern Alaska, with colonies recently formed on Seal Rocks (Hinchinbrook Entrance, Prince William Sound) and on Hazy Island, near Coronation Island. Ranges south in winter to Cape San Lucas, Baja California; also winters in the Gulf of California to the west coast of Sonora, but mostly sedentary. (See figure 42.)

Subspecies

None.

Description

Prebreeding adult. Head and neck deep glossy purplish black, shading into very dark glossy green on the back, rump, and underparts; feathers around the naked throat forming a brownish yellow to nearly pure white border; sides of upper back, wing coverts, and scapulars dark oily green, with narrow and inconspicuous blackish margins; a tuft of long white filoplumes on each side of the neck, starting behind the ear, similar but longer ("pencillate") feathers on the

Figure 42. Distribution of the Brandt's cormorant, showing its overall residential range (stippled) and major breeding colonies (arrows). The upper inset shows the locations of California breeding colonies in greater detail, the largest of which are on the Farallon Islands (large arrow). South Farallon Island is shown in the lower inset, with breeding colony locations marked in ink (after Ainley and Lewis, 1974).

upper back and scapulars having narrow white webs; remiges and rectrices (12) black. Iris green to bright blue; facial skin and mouth lining blue to violet blue; bill dusky gray; gular skin vivid cobalt blue and heart-shaped from below; legs and feet black.

Postbreeding adult. Similar to the prebreeding adult, but the white filoplumes lacking, the feathers bordering the gular skin grayish brown, and the overall feathering of generally lower gloss; gular skin slaty.

Immature-subadult. Details of predefinitive molts and plumages still undescribed, but subadults are presumably like related forms in being piebald mixtures of brown and black, with transitional softpart colors. Some subadult birds may breed a year before their definitive adult plumage is attained, during which the white nuptial plumes are fewer than in adults (Palmer, 1962).

Juvenile. Head and neck brownish, feathers around gular skin light grayish brown; upperparts brownish black, becoming grayish to light straw-brown ventrally, the scapulars and upper wing coverts margined light brownish; a light V-shaped or Y-shaped pattern of tan to buff on the breast often extends down to the middle of the belly, and a gorget of fawn-brown surrounds the gular skin. Iris dark bluish gray or brown; facial skin brownish to violet-purple; mouth lining bluish pink; bill very dark brownish; gular skin dull grayish blue; legs and feet nearly black.

Nestling. Hatched with nearly black skin. The natal down is grayish to clove-brown, darker on the back and paler on the breast and belly, and mottled with white on the wings and underparts.

Measurements (in millimeters)

Wing, males 270–300 (ave. of 17, 290.3), females 262–293 (ave. of 9, 273.9); culmen, males 67–77 (ave. of 17, 70.9), females 63.5–69 (ave. of 9, 65.9) (Palmer, 1962). Eggs ca. 61 × 38.

Weights (in grams)

Three adult males 2,382–2,682 (ave. 2,570), 12 adult females 1,399–2,298 (ave. 1,925) (U.S. National Museum and Museum of Vertebrate Zoology). Average of 5 birds in winter (sexes and ages unspecified), 2,103 (Baltz and Morejohn, 1977); a fat female in June weighed 2,426 (Palmer, 1962); average adult weight (sample size unstated) 2,400 (Astheimer and Grau, 1990). Calculated egg weight 48.6; average weight (sample size unstated) 51 (Astheimer and Grau, 1990).

Identification

In the hand.   The combination of a generally blackish plumage and facial skin and blue gular skin that is narrowly outlined posteriorly with white to buffy feathers serves to identify this species.

In the field.   Within its rather limited coastal range, this species can be readily identified by its almost uniformly dark brownish black plumage, with white limited to a few long and wispy plumes on the sides of the head and the upper back (present only early in the breeding season), and a patch of bright blue gular skin (often hidden except during display) that is narrowly margined posteriorly with white to buffy feathers. Immatures are not quite so dark as young pelagic cormorants, and have lighter tan underparts, especially on the upper breast, where a diagnostic pale Y-shaped pattern is formed.

Ecology and General Biology

Breeding and nonbreeding habitats.   This is a coastal species that ranges from salt to brackish waters, and mainly inhabits the inshore coastal zone, especially in areas having kelp beds. It also breeds on some offshore islands. It uses offshore waters more than the smaller pelagic shag. During winter it is mostly found around sheltered inlets and similarly quiet waters (Palmer, 1962). In contrast to the pelagic cormorant, this species nests on gently sloping hillsides or islands rather than precipitous rocky cliffs or steep stacks, especially favoring the protected leeward sides of these islands (Hatler, Campbell, and Dorst, 1978).

Movements and migrations.   There is no evidence of any significant migrations or movements of this species, which at most tends to disperse somewhat from breeding areas in the fall and gathers there again in the spring. It is possible that a slight shift southward from colonies in Washington state occurs, but even this is somewhat doubtful (Palmer, 1962). In British Columbia a noticeable northward movement occurs each fall; the lowest number of records for Pacific Rim National Park, Vancouver Island, is for the month of February, which totals about seven percent of the total July records (Hatler, Campbell, and Dorst, 1978).

Competition and predation.   Baltz and Morejohn (1977) estimated foraging niche overlap for seabirds wintering off the California coast, and judged that significant food niche overlap, based on prey species consumed, occurred between the Brandt's cormorant and the common murre (*Uria aalge*), which both exhibit a diet of fishes and squid. The pelagic shag and double-crested cormorant are also potentially significant competitors with the Brandt's cormorant, but only the pelagic shag shows a substantial overlap as to prey species. In spite of this food choice overlap, the two species used different microhabitats while foraging, with the Brandt's cormorant tending to feed on bottom-dwelling prey

in areas of flat or mud (especially in northern areas) or over rocky areas (especially in southern areas), whereas the pelagic shag foraged exclusively in rock-bottom habitats, on solitary or concealed prey species (Ainley, Anderson, and Kelly, 1981). Estimates of foraging competition between the Brandt's cormorant and pelagic shag were also discussed in chapter 4.

Predators include the usual larger gulls, which prey on eggs and also on very young chicks; the western gull (*Larus occidentalis*) is perhaps one of the most serious of these predators (Bent, 1922).

Foods and Foraging Behavior

Foods consumed.   The best available summary of foods taken by Brandt's cormorants is that of Ainley, Anderson, and Kelly (1981), who summarized data from 12 geographic locations throughout the species' range, but nearly all the samples representing spring and summer foods. The most commonly and widely encountered prey types included such fish taxa as *Chromis* (Pomacentridae), *Engraulis* (Engraulidae), *Oxjulis* (Labridae), and *Sebastes* (Scopaenidae), with *Sebastes* and *Engraulis* tending to be more prevalent in the northern samples and *Chromis* in the southern ones. Roughly equal numbers of schooling and nonschooling species were represented. The majority were associated with habitat zones located at or just above the substrate, but some ranged to middepth or surface water zones.

A more recent summary of winter foods taken over a California sand and mud substrate near Monterey Bay (Talent, 1984) produced rather similar results to those just described for spring and summer. Most of the birds in this area roosted on a site that required a 55-kilometer round trip between roosting and foraging areas. However, the birds were thereby able to eat sanddabs (*Citharichthys*, Bothidae) a locally abundant food source, and additionally could avoid competition from other Brandt's cormorants and from pelagic shags that were feeding on rocky inshore zones.

Foraging behavior.   As noted above, these birds exploit the entire vertical range of the ocean from fish swimming near the water surface to almost invisible prey hiding on or just below the muddy and sandy substrates. Hubbs, Kelly, and Limbaugh (1970) noted that the cormorants leave their roosts with the first morning sunlight to fly to foraging areas, often where vast beds of giant kelp (*Macrocystis*) occur. There the flocks break up as the birds tend to forage individually in openings of the kelp bed. However, at times they will remain in a raft and follow schools of abundant fish such as anchovies or sardines, with the rear birds constantly taking flight and moving to the front of the raft as they proceed forward. Evidently shifts of foraging strategies from flock-foraging on schooling fish to individual foraging in kelp beds may be made quite rapidly and involve entire colonies of birds, suggesting that the birds are highly adept at altering their foods and feeding methods as new prey sources become available. They sometimes feed in company with California sea lions *(Zolophus californianus),* diving to considerable depths. They also exploit common murres, by foraging directly with them or feeding on fishes driven toward the surface by the murres. Perched birds also watch the behavior of gulls for clues as to the locations of nearby fish schools (van Tets, 1959).

Social Behavior

Age of maturity and mating system.   Bent (1922) believed on the basis of molt patterns and plumage changes that some birds breed initially when two years old, although the definitive nuptial plumage is not attained until the third spring. Based on banding data, Boekelheide and Ainley (1989) determined that the average age of initial breeding by 40 females was 3.5 years (range 2–7), and that of 70 males was 4.2 years (range 2–9). However, the modal age of initial breeding by all known-age females was two years, and that of all known-age males was four years. Among 34 known-age pairs, only 3 remained intact the following year, and no pair bonds persisted beyond two years. The three pairs that remained together used the same nest sites each year. Among 34 known-age pairs, the most common pairing was one in which the male was older (56 percent), followed by birds of the same age (24 percent), and ones in which the female was older (21 percent).

Social displays and vocalization.   Male advertisement display consists of the bird squatting on its nest site (the male's display site) with the tail cocked and spread, the breast almost touching the substrate, and the neck drawn back so that the nape nearly touches the back. The neck feathers are ruffled, making the white filoplumes conspicuous. In this posture the brilliant blue gular pouch is maximally exposed. Then the wings are lifted slightly and rhythmically fluttered by raising the humerus above the back (figure 43D, E), causing the primaries to oscillate rapidly. While in this position, originally called the "flutter" by Williams (1942) and wing flipping by van Tets (1959) but certainly a version of wing waving, the head may occasionally be twisted to one side. Females walk about such advertising males, peering at them in turn, which causes a sudden increase in male activity. As a female approaches a male he lowers his head into a nearly prone "lower precoitional posture" with the tail lowered and the neck slimmed, as the female stands above him jabbing at his head or nape with her bill (figure 44A), and at times even mounting the male. These two postures are reversible by sex, and are little if at all different from normal mounting by the male later on (figure 44B). After copulation a period of mutual billing often follows, as the birds grip one another's bills and rub the sides of their necks together (figure 44C–E), in a sequence called "stretch-and-ruff" by Williams (1942).

When threatening an opponent, the Brandt's cormorant repeatedly throws its head toward the opponent, with its bill closed and the throat somewhat inflated (figure 43J). When the head is nearest the opponent it is shaken, a snapping movement is made, and a growling *br-r-r, br-r-r* vocalization is produced (van Tets, 1959).

Once pair bonds have been formed, mate recognition (gaping [van Tets] or "stroke" [Williams]) displays are performed whenever a bird's mate arrives nearby, by the individual defending the nest or display site. This recognition signal consists of a forward head throw and accompanying call, seemingly little different in form from that used during actual threat (figure 43G, H), but the movements are very slow, stereotypic, and elaborate. A similar display is performed by the female just prior to copulation (van Tets, 1959). Following copulation the male often leaves briefly to gather nesting material, and returns with it in his bill (figure 44F). He then passes it to the female, who rises to receive it. The two birds briefly sway from side to side while both cling to the materials, and finally they arch their necks down to drop it on the nest in a "nest-material ceremony" (Williams, 1942).

Another important display of both sexes is the "hop," which includes a preliminary prehop (or pretakeoff) posture, a short hop, and an erect posthop (or postlanding) posture that immediately follows landing (figure 43A–C). The hop is evidently a ritualized flight and occurs in a wide variety of social situations, including courtship, nest relief, and nest material gathering (van Tets, 1959). The pretakeoff posture is an alert neck-stretched posture (figure 43F) that resembles the postlanding posture.

In addition to the peeping sounds produced by nestling birds, adults of both sexes produce low, hoarse and guttural vocalizations that function in aggressive encounters and may be described as croaks, growls, or gargles, as well as louder but similar repeated *kauk* notes that are also associated with intimidation (Williams, 1942). Compared with the pelagic shag and double-crested cormorants, it is the least vocal of the three species (van Tets, 1959).

Reproductive Biology

Breeding season.   The breeding season is rather varied through this species' range. In British Columbia nest building mainly occurs in June, with complete clutches recorded as early as June 30 but with some eggs laid as late as July, and young reported as early as July 26. Unfledged young have been seen as late as September 7 (Hatler, Campbell, and Dorst, 1978). In Washington, egg laying occurs in May and June, hatching in June and July, and fledging extends from July to early September (Speich and Wahl, 1989). In northern California, egg laying occurs in late May and June, hatching in late June and July, and fledging from late July to early September. On the Farallon Islands the season is earlier and

Figure 43. Social behavior of the Brandt's cormorant, including prehop posture (A), hopping in head-down posture (B), postlanding posture (C), male wing-waving display (D, E), lateral and front views, pretakeoff posture (F), two stages of gape-bowing (stroke) display (G, H), pointing display (I), and threat while on nest (J). After sketches in Williams (1942) and van Tets (1965).

Figure 44. Social behavior of the Brandt's cormorant, including precopulatory posture (A), copulation (B), "mild" precopulatory display (C), mutual billing (D), stretch-and-ruff display (E), and male arriving with nest material (F). After sketches in Williams (1942).

more extended, with egg laying from mid-April to early July, hatching from mid-May to early August, and fledging from mid-June to mid-September. In the Channel Islands the season is even earlier and more extended, with egg laying from late February to mid-June, hatching from late March to mid-July, and fledging from mid-May to late August (Sowls et al., 1980).

Nest sites and nest building.   Nests are typically placed near the tops of gently sloping hills, and are mostly constructed of seaweeds and other soft materials, but with some pieces of driftwood. Grasses, kelp, and materials stolen from nearby nests are all used, and the birds often dive for fresh kelp as well as using kelp that may have washed up along the shore. Virtually all the materials are gathered by the male, but both sexes help arrange them on the nest. Guano gradually accumulates as well, and materials are continually added.

Males are more prone to use the same nest site from year to year than are females; 70 percent of 110 males and only 32 percent of 28 returning females reoccupied their prior year's nest site in the study of Boekelheide and Ainley (1989), and older males (but not females) are much more likely to reoccupy their sites than are younger ones. Nearly all males at least five years old occupied nest sites, and the percentage of males that succeeded in attracting a mate steadily increased to the tenth year of life.

Egg laying and incubation.   The usual range of clutch sizes for this species is 3–5 eggs, the modal size usually being three. Of 77 California clutches, the mean clutch size was 3.05 eggs; 47 percent of the clutches were of three eggs, 27 percent were of four eggs, and 18 percent were of two eggs (Palmer, 1962). In the study by Boekelheide and Ainley (1989), clutches produced by two- and three-year-old females were smaller than those by females more than five years old. Thus, none of the former group produced four-egg clutches, but 43 percent of the clutches laid by eight- to ten-year-old females were of four eggs. The largest observed clutch in their study was of five eggs. Average clutch sizes tended to increase gradually with age, not only for females but also for males, since older males tended to mate with older females. Incubation as usual is by both sexes and lasts 28–32 days, with an average of 29.9 days (170 eggs) (Boekelheide et al., 1990).

Brooding and rearing of young.   Little specific information is available on this phase of reproduction, although it is not likely to differ much from that in similar species such as double-crested cormorants. The fledging period is of 40–42 days (Speich and Wahl, 1989). In the study of Boekelheide and Ainley (1989) it was found that younger birds of both sexes tended to lose more eggs, either accidentally or through nest abandonment, than older ones. However, in contrast to hatching success, rearing success was not related to parental age. Nevertheless, younger breeders lost more very young chicks (to 10 days old) than did older breeders, and older birds were more likely to renest and to produce

fledged young from such renesting efforts than were younger birds. Of two- and three-year-old females, 36 percent lost their first clutch and 30 percent laid replacements. Of 27 four- and five-year-old females, 27 percent lost their first clutches and 33 percent of these unsuccessful birds laid replacements. Of 20 six- to nine-year-old females, 20 percent lost their first clutches and 80 percent laid replacements. One nine-year-old female actually laid two replacement clutches in a single year. The youngest age classes bred successfully only in years of favorable food supply, whereas older birds fledged equivalent numbers of young in both good and moderately good food supply years.

Breeding success.   Breeding success of males, like their ability to attract mates, increased steadily with increasing age (Boekelheide and Ainley, 1989). Collectively, females of all age classes were more successful in pairing, producing eggs, and fledging chicks than were males, especially among the older age classes from five to nine years old. Birds typically bred for two to three seasons and fledged from two to four chicks during their lifetimes, although one male reared 20 chicks to fledging during the eight years in which he bred. One female laid 26 eggs during seven years, but fledged only 8 chicks. Two females bred throughout four- or five-year periods, and respectively fledged 10 and 12 chicks. Although females entered the breeding population sooner than males, both sexes averaged about the same number of breeding years per lifetime, with an observed maximum of eight years for males and seven for females. Of 2,876 chicks banded, 17 percent were subsequently seen as adults. Generally, females returned to breeding colonies at a slightly lower rate than males among younger and also some older age classes, but the differences were not great and were outweighed by other interannual factors.

Breeding (including both hatching and fledging) success at the Farallon Islands varies considerably between years, but in a 13-year study there were no detectable differences in hatching or fledging success among early, middle, and late-nesting birds. Second clutches following initial clutch losses were common there, and were laid in 57 percent of 108 nests where the first clutches were lost; six cases of second repeat attempts were found at failed nest sites, although the same birds may not have been involved in each of these attempts. Replacement clutches had relatively poor success (26.3 percent of the eggs producing fledged chicks, as compared with 41.1 percent for first clutches). No attempts at second broods were seen following the successful fledging of the first brood (Boekelheide et al., 1990).

Population Status

In 1982, 23 pairs of Brandt's cormorants nested at Hazy Island, off Coronation Island, Alaska, becoming the only known colony between Prince William Sound, Alaska, and British Columbia (*American Birds* 36:1007). Previously a single colony of about 100 birds was known from Seal Rocks, Hinchinbrook Entrance, Prince William Sound (Sowls, Hatch, and Lensink, 1978). British Columbian populations of Brandt's cormorants initially increased somewhat after they were first found nesting in 1965, and total nests ranged from 66 to 150 during various years through 1975 (Hatler, Campbell, and Dorst, 1978). In recent years there have been five active colonies in British Columbia, but the population has declined from about 150 pairs in 1970 to 60 in 1982 (Campbell et al., 1990). The Washington population is likewise fairly small, with only four recently used breeding sites (Speich and Wahl, 1989). However, the species comprises about 85 percent of the breeding cormorant population in Oregon (Manuwal and Campbell, 1979), and numbered about 16,000 birds in the late 1970s. A new summary of Oregon seabird colonies and breeding population estimates should be available soon (Pitman et al., in press). In California, at least 13 colonies contain more than 1,000 birds. The largest is on the Farallon Islands, where 28,000 birds nested in 1979 (Sowls et al., 1980) and the population averaged 16,049 over 1971–1986. There may be an additional 10,000–11,000 pairs present along the Pacific coast of Mexico (unpublished manuscript of R. L. DeLong and R. S. Crossin, cited in Ainley and Boekelheide, 1990).

Evolutionary Relationships

Siegel-Causey (1988) found that this species is apparently cladistically closest to the Galapagos cormorant and Pallas' cormorant. Zoogeographically it also falls between these forms, both of which show many structural modifications associated with flightlessness and doubtless also were greatly modified behaviorally in this process.

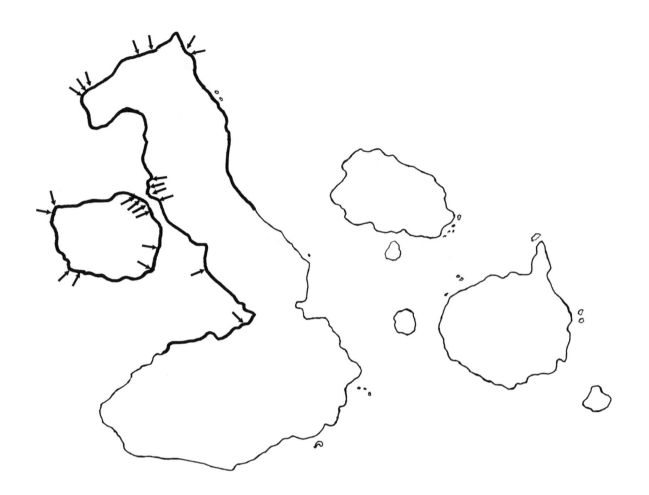

Figure 45. Distribution of the Galapagos cormorant, showing its total residential range (inked) on Narborough (Fernandina) and Albermarle (Isabella) islands, and locations of breeding colonies of ten or more nests (arrows). After Harris (1974a).

Other Vernacular Names

Harris' Galapagos cormorant; cormoran aptère (French); Stummelscharbe (German)

Distribution

Endemic to the Galapagos Islands, where rare and permanently vulnerable (Collar and Andrew, 1988), and where breeding is confined to Narborough (Fernandina) Island plus the western and northern coasts of Albemarle (Isabella) Island. Recently classified by the IUCN (1988) as "rare." (See figure 45.)

Subspecies

None.

Description

Prebreeding adult. Entire plumage soft, loosely coherent, and rather hairlike; generally blackish brown (when fresh) to seal brown or tawny (when faded) dorsally, with a faint greenish gloss on the upperparts; lighter brown ventrally; sides of head and neck sprinkled with white filoplumes; rectrices (14) blackish brown; the remiges similar, but greatly reduced in size, with the fifth primary from the outermost the longest, and some remiges usually distinctly frayed. Iris emerald-green, the pupil somewhat horizontally elongated; facial skin dusky, with parallel rows of pale dots; maxilla blackish or slaty, the tip and edges horny brown, as is the mandible; gular skin brownish purple, with whitish dots, the unfeathered area extended into a point posteriorly; legs and feet black (Murphy, 1936).
Postbreeding adult. Apparently much like the breeding adult, but perhaps with fewer or no filoplumes and less colorful softparts.
Juvenile-immature. Resembles adult, but entire plumage blacker and the remiges neater, lacking their usual frayed or ragged appearance (Harrison, 1983). Unlike in adults, the underparts are not lighter brown below; a few white filoplumes present on the neck. Iris dark gray, with a slight bluish tinge; bill dark blackish brown; legs and feet blackish brown (Snow, 1966). Sexual maturity in females may occur as early as 1.5 years, but most birds begin breeding a year later (Harris, 1979).
Nestling. At hatching covered with pinkish gray skin, and with a pale pink gular skin. By two weeks old the young are covered by a thick dark brownish black down except for their bare heads, and the gular skin gradually becomes spotted and mottled with black, eventually becoming almost entirely black by fledging (Snow, 1966). By then the iris is dark-colored, and the bill, facial skin, legs, and feet are all dark brown, scarcely different from the color of the down.

Measurements (in millimeters)

Ranges of measurements (sample sizes and means not indicated): wing, males 186–188, females 177.5–193; tail, males 154–165, females 149–165; culmen, males 65–77, females 59–76; tarsus, males 72–79, females 59–66 (Murphy, 1936). Eggs ca. 66 × 43.

Weights (in grams)

Males (and presumed males) 3,800–4,090 (ave. of 4, 3,958), females (and presumed females) 2,500–2,900 (ave. of 4, 2,715) (Snow, 1966). Calculated egg weight 67.4; ave. of 2, 69.7 (Snow, 1966).

Identification

In the hand. The rudimentary wings, which are only slightly longer than the tail, and have a reduced size and number of remiges (9 primaries, plus approximately 15 secondaries), immediately identify this distinctive species.
In the field. This is the only cormorant found on the Galapagos Islands, and occurs nowhere else.

Ecology and General Biology

Breeding and nonbreeding habitats. This species has one of the most restricted ranges of all cormorants, comparable to those of some of the New Zealand shags. It is limited to less than 400 kilometers of coastline on two islands, where cool waters of the westward-flowing Humboldt (Cromwell) current pass along their western coastlines, causing an upwelling of nutrient- and food-rich waters. Much the same also applies to the considerably smaller Galapagos penguin *(Spheniscus mendiculus)*, which has a very similar breeding range. However, the cormorant's range is even more limited, and is apparently defined by three factors, namely cold, plankton-rich waters supporting an adequate food base, shallow seas with rocky bottoms for foraging, and coastlines offering sheltered shores and easy landing places. Because of its flightless condition, an absence of terrestrial predators, as originally occurred throughout the Galapagos archipelago, is critical to its survival (Snow, 1966).

Snow (1966) has suggested that evolving a large body size enabled this species to reduce competition with the Galapagos penguin, and provided a beak that is strong enough to extract octopi and perhaps also eels from rocky crevices. Additionally, the male is considerably larger than the female, which may help to expand the foraging niche and reduce intersexual food competition. Snow further noted that the loss of flight following size increase was probably no great handicap, and that the evolution of a heavy, rather penguinlike plumage may have accelerated this process because of the added weight of the water that is thus carried by the wetted plumage.

Movements and migrations. This is a highly sedentary species; it has never been recorded more than a kilometer beyond its breeding grounds and only rarely has been seen more than 200 meters from shore. The greatest known movement was of a nonbreeder that was observed 9 kilometers away from its point of banding four years previously (Harris, 1979).

Competition and predation. The Galapagos penguin is a probable competitor of this species, as it apparently exclusively consumes small fish up to about 10 centimeters in length. However, it more probably exploits small, nonbenthic fish to a much greater degree than does the cormorant, which is known to consume eels up to about 35 centimeters in length and herrings approaching 20 centimeters in length (Murphy, 1936). The Galapagos hawk (*Buteo galapagoensis*) is a major predator on chicks (Tindle, 1984).

Foods and Foraging Behavior

Foods consumed. This cormorant evidently eats a wide variety of generally medium-sized and bottom-dwelling fish, as well as octopi up to at least 20 centimeters in diameter. Measured lengths of 27 prey fishes reported by Harris (1979) were from 4 to 34.5 centimeters, with 14 under 10 centimeters, 9 between 10 and 20 centimeters, and 4 over 20 centimeters. Fish families represented included the Serranidae, Clinidae, Pomacentridae, Blenniidae, Pomacanthidae, Scaridae, Scorpaenidae, Xenichthyidae, and Muraenidae. One adult regurgitated 8 fish representing four species, and averaging 31.5 grams in weight.

Foraging behavior. These birds mainly forage by searching for fish or other prey among seabed rocks, but also occasionally take schooling species and plankton feeders of the midwater zone (Harris, 1979). Tindle (1984) observed that adults of both sexes spent nearly equal amounts of time in daily foraging (about four hours) and caught prey at about the same rate (once every 10–12 minutes of foraging time), but that males remained submerged for longer periods and in deeper waters, probably because of their greater size, and

also were able to take larger prey than females and thus broaden the collective foraging niche, as postulated earlier by Snow (1966). Tindle suggested that optimum mate choice for this species would probably involve a large male and a small female, to reduce intersexual foraging competition, but that evidence for mate size being a factor in mate choice is still lacking.

Social Behavior

Age of maturity and mating system. Harris (1979) determined that the mean age of first breeding of six males was 30 months (range 23–38), and that of ten females was 29.5 months (range 17–50). One 18-month-old male built a nest, but no eggs were deposited in it. The mating system of this species is perhaps unique among cormorants. The birds undertake a new sequence of courtship and pair formation prior to each breeding cycle, which may occur several times per year. Thus, one male bred seven times in 24 months, and one female laid eight clutches within 36 months. Individual birds were not faithful to prior breeding sites or to prior mates. Site fidelity for the subsequent nesting cycle occurred in only 33 percent of 112 males and in only 38 percent of the 136 females studied. During a six-year period, there were only 31 cases of pairs nesting together for consecutive breeding attempts among a population of 49 males and 61 females, and only one observed instance of a pair remaining together for three successive breeding efforts. Pairs remained unchanged in only 12 percent of the 151 cases where individual prior mating histories were known, and perhaps at least some of these mate retentions were the result of random choice rather than actual mate fidelity. This idea is supported by the fact that such mate "fidelity" was not associated with previous breeding success, since there was an approximately equal probability of pairs remaining together regardless of their prior breeding success.

Social displays and vocalizations. Displays of this species were described by Snow (1966), and are in many ways different from those of other cormorant species, which presumably reflects their unique flightless condition. In contrast to other cormorants, where display begins on land and centers on a nest site, in this species display begins on the water. Only later does it shift to land, mainly at the nest site, and the pair bond apparently becomes fixed. The aquatic phase of courtship consists of the "aquatic dance" (figure 46D–F), which begins at any time from ten days to six weeks prior to egg laying (Harris, 1979). During the aquatic dance both birds swim in a half-upright position, but with only the head, neck, and upper body above water. In this posture the pair swims past or around one another, each holding its head and neck in a "snake-neck" position and slightly tilting the head each time they pass each other, exposing the throat and underside of the bill to the partner. When the birds are closest to one another they utter a

Figure 46. Social behavior of the Galapagos cormorant, including mutual snake-neck display by a pair at nest site, the male on right (A) and male behind female (B), male (at left) at nest site performing throw back display (C), with female in snake-neck posture, male leading female to shore (D), pair in "aquatic dance" (E), pair swimming in snake-neck display (F), female (at right) bowing display (G), adult performing sitting gape on nest (H), adult turning submissively away from another bird (I). After sketches and photos in Snow (1966).

growling call. The aquatic dance may be quite prolonged, lasting up to 80 minutes, with occasional dives during which the female follows the male, the two birds remaining a constant distance apart. At times the male will appear to be aggressive toward the female, causing her to dive to escape. Or he may lead her to shore, where land displays continue, especially "snake-necking." Snake-necking is used not only during pair bonding but also as a recognition signal, such as during nest relief. In this posture the body is held erect, with the head and neck feathers ruffled but the body feathers flattened, and the middle neck curved backward producing a snakelike profile (figure 46A–C). The birds, thus displaying mutually, usually face in opposite directions, or at least their necks are turned so that their heads are oriented laterally. Occasionally one of the birds may stretch its head and neck upward and flap its wings ("flutter-up") during snake-necking. A more prolonged "throw back" of the head and neck that lasts 6–7 seconds is performed only by the male (figure 46C). It is performed only infrequently, and may be homologous to other similar throw back (or "gargling") male advertising displays of other cormorants, but is evidently not as important as the aquatic dance during early pair formation behavior in this species. When the snake-necking display is performed by a single bird, or when one of the pair members is on the nest, its head and bill are pointed downward rather than horizontally. A similar posture is used in the "bow" display, when the head is lowered into a bowing position (figure 46G) and a repeated *oncha* note is produced. This is initially performed only by the male; later on both sexes perform it, either while standing or sitting. Neck lowering is more extreme when done by the male than by the female, at least when it is performed in a standing position. Another individual recognition display is the "sitting gape" (figure 46H), which is performed by the individual on the nest or nest site when approached by its mate. During this display the bill is opened, the head is moved upward, a slight lateral head shake is made, and an *aagh* call is uttered.

The threat gape of this species is similar to the sitting gape, but is directed to enemies and is more elaborately performed, with the neck fully stretched, the wings somewhat spread, and with repeated thrusting movements of the neck. The threat gape sometimes elicits a submissive posture from other birds (figure 46I), when the bill is pointed downward and away from the threatening individual.

Vocalizations include a growling call, sometimes changing to a more mooing sound, which is associated with the aquatic dance and is uttered by both sexes. The same or a similar growl that lasts up to two seconds is associated with snake-necking and may also be performed in more subdued form in the absence of snake-necking. Additionally, an *aaaha* note is produced by exhalation during the sitting gape display and especially during aggressive threat gaping, when it becomes hoarse and repetitive, with subdued growling sounds during the intervening inhalation. An *oncha* call is uttered during bowing. Nestling chicks utter a high-pitched, plaintive *wee-oo wee-oo* during food-begging, and a complaint call *wee-wee* when being handled by humans. By 20 days of age they begin to produce threat gapes, with accompanying shrill and husky *wee-aa* notes (Snow, 1966).

Reproductive Biology

Breeding season.   Breeding occurs throughout the year, but with a general peak of activity during the cold season between May and October. Such seasonality tends to reduce heat stress and also takes advantage of a peak in food availability (Harris, 1979; Trillmich et al., 1983).

Nest sites and nest building.   Nesting occurs in small scattered groups, with ten nests being about the maximum in any single area, and often only two or three present. Nests may be only a meter apart, but are usually more scattered. The nest is large and composed of seaweeds, which are gathered fresh by the male or sometimes stolen from neighboring nests. Nest building requires several weeks, perhaps at least four, and the nest is mainly constructed and shaped by the female (Snow, 1966).

Egg laying and incubation.   Egg laying occurs at several-day intervals (a three-day interval was documented in one case). Clutches usually consist of three eggs (Snow, 1966). In a sample of 109 completed clutches, there were three eggs in 76 percent of the nests, two eggs in 17 percent, one egg in 5 percent, and four eggs in 2 percent, with a mean of 2.75 eggs. Both sexes incubate, with frequent changeovers during the day. Infertility and early deaths of embryos seem to be responsible for many nest failures, but nest abandonment, nest flooding, and possible egg predation by Galapagos hawks account for other failures (Harris, 1979).

Brooding and rearing of young.   The average brood size at hatching of 91 broods was 1.7 young (range 1–3), but few last-hatched chicks in broods of three survive for long. The young are fed by regurgitation; fish up to about 15 centimeters long are offered to relatively young chicks no more than about a month old. The chicks take to water when they are about two months old, and chick losses seem to be mostly caused by starvation. Brood size at nest departure or "fledging" averaged 1.25 young. Young are fed by their parents for some time after the chicks begin swimming, and they may even continue to be fed until their parents begin a new breeding cycle (Harris, 1979). Typically, the females desert their young when they are 70–90 days old, but males continue to feed them until they are five to six months old. By this time the females are typically already breeding again, with new mates (Tindle, 1984).

Breeding success.   In Harris's (1979) study area, a total of 182 nests resulted in 92 juveniles surviving long enough to reach the sea, and in a more general survey 102 juveniles were seen in an area supporting 192 recently used nests. Both of these suggest that about 0.5 young are fledged per nesting pair.

Breeding success is apparently fairly uniform during the seasonal period when most nesting occurs, but may be lower at other times. There are also marked annual variations in productivity. In a sample of 77 juveniles that reached the sea, 74 percent were known to be alive three months later. Estimated survival of juveniles to 12 months was 56.6 percent, and annual survival of immatures was 85.7 percent. Breeding males had slightly lower (82.4 percent) estimated annual survival, and breeding females slightly higher (91.4 percent). The overall estimated annual survival rate for adults of both sexes was 87.6 percent.

Population Status

This is one of the world's rarest cormorants, and one of the few where complete censuses are possible. Harris (1974a) reported a population of 700–800 pairs in 1970–1971, all within a linear shoreline range of 363 kilometers. More recent counts from 1970 to 1986 indicate that populations remained fairly stable until the El Niño event of 1982–1983, when there was an approximate 50 percent population decline. However, by 1986 the numbers were back to earlier levels (Rosenberg et al., 1990). In addition to these unforeseeable environmental changes, the commercial crayfish fishery in the area may pose a problem for the birds if nets become used (Harris, 1974a). Feral dogs also reportedly pose a problem to the nesting birds, as might the developing tourism industry unless it is closely controlled.

Evolutionary Relationships

This is such a highly specialized form that it is difficult to suggest convincing scenarios for its evolutionary history. It is possible that both the Galapagos cormorant and the Pallas' cormorant evolved from a large marine-adapted ancestral form something like that of the Brandt's cormorant, which Siegel-Causey (1988) suggests as a probable near relative to both, based on his cladistic analysis.

Figure 47. Distribution of the bank cormorant, showing its
total residential range (stippled) and locations of breeding
colonies (inset). Unmarked arrows are of small colonies;
those with smaller dots are of 100–2,000 birds; the larger dot
indicates a colony of 2,600 birds. After Crawford et al. (1982).

Other Vernacular Names

Cormoran des bancs (French); Fischbankkormoran (German)

Distribution

Resident along the coast of southwestern Africa from Walvis Bay, Namibia, south to Cape Agulhas, South Africa, with the known breeding range extending from Hollamsbird Island, Namibia, to Quoin Rock, South Africa. (See figure 47.)

Subspecies

None.

Description

Prebreeding adult. Head, neck, and back ranging from black (when fresh), with a slight greenish bronze gloss, to dark sooty brown (when faded); a patch of long, white filoplumes present on rump (these feathers evident for only a brief period and usually lost by hatching); numerous small white filoplumes on the forehead and neck; breast and other underparts black, with a dull oil-green gloss; middle of back, wing coverts, and scapulars bronzy brown, very narrowly margined with black, and with rounded tips; remiges and rectrices (12) dark brownish black; lores feathered. Iris horizontally bicolored, orange-brown above, greenish below (the transition zone usually marked by a narrow yellow line, and the very bottom of the iris sometimes blue), surrounded by a black eye ring; mouth lining and gular skin black; bill black, with a lighter dark brown to horn-colored tip; legs and feet black. Leucistic individuals are frequent, and show varying amounts of white feathering on the sides of the head and foreneck.

Postbreeding adult. Generally browner throughout (probably from fading rather than extensive molt), and lacking white filoplumes on head, neck, and rump.

Immature-subadult. Similar to the adult, but no white rump patch, and the feathers less iridescent and more dull brownish. At least some second-year subadults have white filoplumes. Birds are probably not in full adult plumage until at least their third year, when breeding may normally begin (Cooper, 1985a). Iris green during second year, becoming bicolored by third year.

Juvenile. Completely dull blackish brown, without filoplumes. Iris dark brown, but appearing bluish in some lights.

Nestling. Sooty black, with varying amounts of white down on head, neck, leading edges of wings, and rump. Completely black at fledging. Iris dark brown (but appearing bluish gray in some lights); bill becoming black within a few days, except for white egg tooth; legs and feet black (Cooper, 1985a).

Measurements (in millimeters)

Adult and paired birds: wing, males 277–309 (ave. of 6, 292), females 262–291 (ave. of 6, 276); tail, males 113–137 (ave. of 17, 129), females 107–132 (ave. of 44, 117); culmen, males 56–64.5 (ave. of 39, 60.3), females 50–62.5 (ave. of 44, 56.9); tarsus, males 62–70.5 (ave. of 37, 66.6), females 61–66 (ave. of 40, 63.7) (Cooper, 1985a). Eggs ca. 60 × 39.

Weights (in grams)

A sample of 77 paired males ranged from 1,775 to 2,425, averaging 2,107, and a sample of 92 paired females ranged from 1,500 to 2,150, averaging 1,794 (Cooper, 1985a). Rand (1960) reported slightly lower respective averages of 1,985 (21 males) and 1,700 (14 females), and also somewhat lower maximum weights (2,183 and 1,985 for males and females respectively). Four males 1,950–2,100 (ave. 2,037); 4 females 1,700–1,800 (ave. 1,756) (U.S. National Museum specimens). Calculated egg weight 50.3; average weight (sample sizes unstated), 47 (Brown, Urban, and Newman, 1982), 50.4 (Cooper, 1987).

Identification

In the hand. The uniquely bicolored iris (brown above, greenish below), almost entirely black plumage, and feathered lores serve to identify adults of this species. Younger birds lack bicolored eyes but do have feathered lores and, unlike young Cape and Indian cormorants (both of which have overlapping measurements and also have feathered lores), are almost uniformly dark brown both above and below.

In the field. In their very limited coastal range of southwestern Africa, adults of this species are distinctive in typically appearing all black (including the gular skin, bill, legs, and feet), except for a variably large white rump patch that is evident only early in the breeding season. However, some variant birds may also show varying amounts of white on the head and neck. Younger birds generally appear more uniformly brownish and less iridescent. The slightly smaller Cape cormorant of the same general coastal region is also entirely black, but exhibits distinctive yellow to orange at the base of the bill and adjoining gular skin in both adults and immatures.

Ecology and General Biology

Breeding and nonbreeding habitats.   This is a highly sedentary species, whose range is broadly similar to that of the kelp *(Ecklonia* and *Laminaria)* beds off the coast of southwestern Africa. The birds rarely occur out of sight of land, and usually no more than 10 kilometers from shore. They evidently also do not use estuaries, coastal wetlands, or inland waters. Only 44 known breeding sites were reported in Cooper's (1981) comprehensive survey; an additional colony was reported by Williams (1987).

Movements and migrations.   Based on available banding data (22 adult recoveries and 4 recoveries of banded juveniles), some movements of significance occur. The longest movement of a juvenile was 459 kilometers, and the average of four was 153 kilometers. Most adults were recovered at the point of banding, and 86 percent of the recoveries were within 10 kilometers of this point. The average movement of adult birds recovered away from the point of banding was 37 kilometers, and the maximum was 168 kilometers (Cooper, 1981).

Competition and predation.   Although the Cape and bank cormorants overlap in range and in general feeding activities, an analysis of their foods (see table 17) indicates significant differences in their foraging ecologies, with bank cormorants feeding mainly in the littoral zone while Cape cormorants forage primarily on pelagic shoaling fishes (Williams and Burger, 1978). Evidently the kelp gull *(Larus dominicanus)* is a significant predator of eggs and chicks, and human disturbance to nesting colonies is probably likely to exacerbate this problem unless it is carefully controlled (Cooper, 1981).

Foods and Foraging Behavior

Foods consumed.   Rand (1960) analyzed the stomach contents of 73 bank cormorants obtained off Cape Province, South Africa, and these data were subsequently reorganized (Williams and Burger, 1978) into ecological-behavioral prey groups. Based on aggregate mass, 21 percent of the prey consisted of invertebrates (such as lobsters, crabs, and octopi), and the remaining 79 percent comprised marine fish. This total included only 1 percent of pelagic shoaling forms, 7 percent of benthic forms, 12 percent of sandy-bottom inshore forms, and 61 percent of kelp bed species associated with the littoral zone. This last group of prey was dominated by klipfish (Clinidae) and blennies (Blenniidae), which together comprised over half of the total food mass. In the northern parts of this species' range it feeds away from kelp beds, mostly on midwater species but also on some bottom-

dwelling forms such as crustaceans. Thus, on the Ichaboe and Mercury Islands of Namibia, which support the largest single breeding colonies of bank cormorants, this species fed almost exclusively on pelagic gobies *(Sufflogobius)* during 1978–1979. Some rock lobsters *(Jasus)* are occasionally eaten as well, but not enough to cause significant competition with the commercial fishery (Cooper, 1981, 1985b).

Foraging behavior.   Foraging is done close to the breeding locality, with maximum foraging ranges typically 8–9 kilometers away. The birds make daily flights from their roosts or nest sites, usually in small groups of up to six individuals. The birds usually forage solitarily, but loose flocks of up to 15 birds may sometimes be seen in an area. Diving is done in a nonsynchronized manner. In the southern parts of its range this species is mainly a bottom forager, feeding over rocky substrates as well as shingle or coarse sandy-bottom areas. However, to the north and away from the kelp beds the birds apparently feed mostly on midwater forms and to an apparently lesser degree on bottom-dwelling prey. When foraging on the bottom the birds swim slowly about, investigating rocky crevices for prey, occasionally entering rock lobster traps. One bird recovered from such a trap was reportedly caught at a depth of about 28 meters, but most foraging is done in waters 5–15 meters deep. In a sample of 157 dives the birds remained submerged for periods averaging 44.9 seconds, with a maximum observed dive of 63.8 seconds. These are relatively prolonged dives, considering the species' body mass. The birds sometimes surface as far as 25 meters from the point of submersion, but more often reappear within 10 meters. Females were observed to forage for longer average periods than males, while males on average made more foraging bouts per day, so that each sex averaged about four hours per day in total daily foraging time (Cooper, 1985b).

Social Behavior

Age of maturity and mating system.   According to Cooper (1985a), birds are probably not fully adult until at least their third year, and breeding does not normally occur until at least that age. No published information exists on the mating system, beyond that of obvious seasonal monogamy.

Social displays and vocalizations.   Very little has so far been written on these subjects. Nesting birds utter throaty alarm cries when disturbed, but other vocalizations are still undescribed. During courtship, males throw the head forward at first, then upward and backward until the head touches the back and the bill is pointed vertically upward. This position may be held for a minute or so, when the head and bill are then swept forward, until the bill points directly downward. In this way the white rump is alternately exposed and hidden. No other details on social display have been published (Brown, Urban, and Newman, 1982).

Reproductive Biology

Breeding season.   No information.

Nest sites and nest building.   Nest construction occurs when a male occupies a vacant site and begins to place seaweeds and similar materials on it. Materials are added throughout the breeding cycle, although most of the gathering occurs prior to egg laying. When nests are washed away by high seas, new nest construction may begin within 24 hours. After pairs are formed, the female guards the nest in the absence of the male. On his return, the male presents his newly gathered nesting materials to the female, who places them on the nest, often with the help of the male. Such nest presentation behavior may be followed by copulation, or the male may leave immediately to gather more materials. Besides diving for nest materials, he may also steal them from the nests of nearby cormorants. Apparently purposeful defecation by adults along the rim of the nest helps to hold the materials in place, and causes the gradual buildup of guano. From nest initiation to the laying of the first egg required an average of 34 days in seven nests under study at one locality, but in another nest 83 days elapsed before the first egg was laid. The complete nests are relatively large, and a great deal of time and energy is invested in their construction. It is possible that, by building a large seaweed nest, this species has become "emancipated" from a more terrestrial environment for nesting, and the species can thus breed in offshore localities where other species might not be able to (Cooper, 1986a).

Egg laying and incubation.   This species has a relatively small clutch. The laying interval averages about three days between eggs. In a sample of 252 clutches, the range was from one (15.9 percent of total) to three eggs (18.2 percent), with a modal (65.9 percent) clutch of two, and a mean clutch of 2.02 eggs. Egg size and volume decreased slightly with the order of laying, and mean egg size also increased and then decreased through the breeding season. Both sexes incubate; the mean incubation period was found to be 29.5 days for the last-laid egg. The mean hatching period (interval between initial pipping and emergence) was 1.2 days, and the mean hatching interval between successively laid eggs was 2.7 days, or not significantly different from the mean laying interval of 3.0 days. Failed clutches are sometimes replaced, but with a relatively long minimum intervening period of 23 days following clutch failure. This is very close to the minimum observed 24-day period between the start of initial nest building and the laying of the first egg. A mean renesting interval of 52 days and a maximum interval of 102 days was observed for seven replacement clutches (Cooper, 1987).

Brooding and rearing of young.   Little information exists on this phase of the reproductive cycle. Cooper (1985a) noted that the young birds attain their adult dimensions in culmen, tarsus, and tail length before leaving the nest, but have shorter wings than adults. He also commented that they can hardly fly at all at fledging, and are cared for by their parents for up to three more months.

Breeding success.   Successful nests reportedly usually have only one or two chicks, but there are no further details available (Brown, Urban, and Newman, 1982).

Population Status

In Cooper's (1981) comprehensive survey, 44 known breeding sites contained approximately 18,000 adult birds, of which 71 percent occurred on two islands (Ichaboe and Mercury) located north of kelp beds off coastal Namibia. Like all cormorants, the birds are very sensitive to disturbance during the breeding season. They are easily flushed from their nests, and their eggs and chicks are then often stolen and eaten by kelp gulls. Cooper judged that the future of the species' population will depend on adequate protection from disturbance during breeding and avoidance of conflicts with commercial fishing interests, which currently do not appear to pose a significant problem.

Evolutionary Relationships

According to the cladistic results of Siegel-Causey (1988), the nearest relative of this species is the Australian black-faced cormorant, which like it is a heavy-bodied and deep-diving marine cormorant.

Figure 48. Distribution of the black-faced cormorant, showing its total residential range (cross-hatched) and locations of
breeding colonies (arrows).

Other Vernacular Names

Black-and-white shag, black-faced shag, white-breasted cormorant; cormoran de Tasmanie (French); Tasmanien-Kormoran (German)

Distribution

Limited to the coastlines of southern Australia, from Hopetown and the Recherche Archipelago off Western Australia east locally to South Australia, western Victoria (islands off Wilson's Promontory, and Bay of Islands, near Peterborough), many Bass Strait islands (including King Island and the Furneaux Group), and coastal Tasmania. Generally sedentary, but with younger birds sometimes dispersing up to several hundred kilometers. (See figure 48.)

Subspecies

None.

Description

Prebreeding adult. Top of head (extending from crown down to middle eye-level), hindneck, back, rump, upper tail coverts, flanks, and thighs all black, glossed with dull steel-blue; sides of upper back, scapulars, and wing coverts glossed with dull oil-green, each feather with a narrow black border; sides of head, chin, throat, and underparts pure white; remiges and rectrices (12) brownish black, with some greenish gloss; hindneck with numerous white plumes and filoplumes, which are also scattered on the back and flanks. Iris dark blue-green; eye ring and facial skin purplish black, the lores dotted with tiny white feathers; bill greenish black or dark slaty black; gular skin black; legs and feet black.
Postbreeding adult. Similar to the prebreeding plumage, but lacking the larger white nuptial plumes, while retaining some white filoplumes.
Immature-subadult. Neck and upper breast brownish, becoming black on the nape and hindneck, lacking streaking on neck and sides of face. Generally similar to juvenal plumage but with more greenish black gloss on upperparts, and most underparts white as in adults. Iris dark to dull brown; facial skin pale greenish, with a blackish eye ring and loral stripe; bill fuscous, becoming lighter below; the lining of the mouth pale violet pink.
Juvenile. General plumage brown above and white below, with irregular brown patches on the underparts; a brownish wash over foreneck and upper breast. Iris brown; facial skin pale buffy brown; gular skin pink; legs and feet brown.
Nestling. The chick is naked and black when hatched, but is soon covered with down that is blackish brown above and white below, with scattered patches of white down on the upperparts. The gular skin is light yellow, and the legs and feet are gray.

Measurements (in millimeters)

Wing, males 267–290 (ave. of 12, 276), females 250–266 (ave. of 14, 259); tail, males 92–125 (ave. of 12, 107), females 91–115 (ave. of 14, 99); culmen, males 47.7–55.4 (ave. of 13, 51.4), females 43.7–53.5 (ave. of 14, 48.4). Another sample: wing, males 266–291 (ave. of 3, 278), females 259–277 (ave. of 5, 266); tail, males 92–109 (ave. of 3, 100), females 92–111 (ave. of 5, 104); culmen, males 48–55 (ave. of 3, 53), females 46–56 (ave. of 5, 51) (Serventy, Serventy, and Warham, 1971). Eggs ca. 58 × 37.

Weights (in grams)

An apparently single weight, ca. 1,330 (2.94 lb) (Serventy, Serventy, and Warham, 1971). The average weight of 30 birds (sex composition and ages unspecified) from various sites was 1,515 (Thompson and Morley, 1966). Calculated egg weight 43.8.

Identification

In the hand. The combination of a culmen length of 46–56 mm, 12 rectrices, entirely black facial skin, white underparts (except for black thighs), and a black crown color that extends downward to encompass the eye serves to identify this species.
In the field. Within its rather limited range along the coasts of southern Australia, this large bicolored species is likely to be confused only with the similar-sized pied cormorant, which has a bright yellow patch in front of the eye and below the lower mandible. The little pied cormorant is substantially smaller, has a yellowish bill, and has a white stripe extending above the eyes and reaching the front of the forehead. Juvenile black-faced cormorants are of generally similar color pattern to adults, but the upperparts which are black in adults are brown in juveniles, and the white underparts are mottled or tinged with brown, especially on the breast and throat.

Ecology and General Biology

Breeding and nonbreeding habitats. This is an almost exclusively marine and estuarine species, primarily occurring in shallow inshore waters or among reefs, although birds may sometimes forage in coastal rivers. Roosting occurs on islands, rocks, sand banks, jetties, beacons, and the like, and nesting is largely associated with rocky islands, reefs, or stacks, including cliff tops and ledges up to about 100 meters high. Sandy islands are only occasionally used for nesting (Marchant and Higgins, 1990).

Movements and migrations. This is a mostly sedentary species limited to two discrete populations along the coastlines of southwestern and southern Australia, with no proven interchange between the two populations. Banding recoveries have not indicated that any major movements occur beyond limited dispersals of young birds. There are also no apparent seasonal changes in populations in Victoria, suggesting that little or no migratory movements occur seasonally (Marchant and Higgins, 1990).

Competition and predation. This is the most marine-oriented of the Australian cormorants, which tends to remove it from competition with the other larger species such as the great cormorant and pied cormorant. Gulls reportedly take unguarded eggs, and seals sometimes cause destruction to colonies as they pass through them (Serventy, Serventy, and Warham, 1971). White-bellied sea eagles (*Haliaeetus leucogaster*) are known to take chicks (Marchant and Higgins, 1990)

Foods and Foraging Behavior

Foods consumed. The only significant study of the foods of this species is that of McNally (1957), which was based on 20 specimens from coastal waters off Victoria and included nearly 50 prey items. Of these, species of hardyheads (Atherinidae) comprised 42.6 percent of the items but occurred in only 5 percent of the specimens, and scorpionfish (*Gymnapistes*, Scorpaenidae) represented 35.2 percent of the items and occurred in half of the specimens examined. Other fish taxa that were present in smaller quantities included pipefish (*Stigmatophora*, Syngnathidae), *Platycephalus* (Platycephalidae), and dragonets (*Callionymus*, Callionymidae).

Foraging behavior. These birds forage in shallow waters, especially along reefs. They typically forage only once a day, and consume foods weighing up to about 20 percent of their own weight (Frith, 1977). They forage in depths of up to about 12 meters, and dive for durations of 20–40 seconds (Lindgren, 1956; Serventy, Serventy, and Warham, 1971), the variations in dive duration probably depending on water depths. Before going out to forage, each bird may swallow up to 16 pebbles about 10 millimeters in diameter. These serve as ballast for diving in salt water, the greater density of which makes swimming birds much more buoyant. It has been estimated that about 37.5 grams in such weight needs to be added to an average adult weight of 1.5 kilograms to compensate for the differential densities of salt water and fresh water (van Tets, 1968, 1976b). Integrated flock-foraging behavior has been observed in this species, and fish up to nearly 50 centimeters long have been noted as prey.

Social Behavior

Age of maturity and mating system. No specific information exists on these points, but presumably sustained or at least seasonal monogamy exists.

Social displays and vocalizations. Male advertising consists of wing waving (figure 49D) and gargling (figure 49C). During wing waving the tail is cocked, the head and bill tilted upward and backward, and the folded wings raised upward and outward repeatedly at a rate of about four times per second. The bill is sometimes directed toward the courted bird, but without vocalizations. During gargling the male begins in a nearly horizontal standing position, then swings his head and neck back so that the crown and nape touch his rump, while the tail is somewhat raised. This posture may be accompanied by a bisyllabic gargling note, with the first note uttered as the bill is opened and the head moves back, and the second as the head touches the rump and the bill is closed (Marchant and Higgins, 1990).

Individual recognition displays consist of gaping (figure 49A), head throwing, and kink-necking. During gaping and head throwing the bird begins with the body held horizontally and with the wings slightly drooping and the tail somewhat cocked. During gaping the bill is opened widely and pointed forward and upward, but very little head movement occurs. Males call repeatedly but females only hiss or are silent while gaping. During head throwing the head is moved forward and when it is in its most forward position the bill is closed with a sharp, mechanical snap. When a male returns to its mate kink-necking is performed, with the male calling repeatedly but the female remaining silent. Males also utter other clattering, clapping, or grunting vocalizations at various times, but females evidently only produce hissing sounds (Marchant and Higgins, 1990).

During agonistic encounters the birds gape with bulging throats; the head moves forward and back or sideways with sinuous movements. The wings may be partly spread and lowered, and the tail is fanned and vertically cocked. Threatening males utter buzzing calls, and females hiss (Marchant and Higgins, 1990).

Other displays include pretakeoff, prehop, postlanding, and posthop postures. All of these are rather similar, with the body held rather vertically, the head hunched into the shoulders, and plumage of the nape and hindneck raised. The hyoids are also slowly spread and closed, and during the pretakeoff posture (figure 49B) males may utter soft ticking sounds (Marchant and Higgins, 1990).

Figure 49. Social behavior of the black-faced cormorant and the Neotropic cormorant, including gaping (A), pretakeoff (B), gargling (C), and wing-waving (D) postures of the black-faced cormorant (after sketches in Marchant and Higgins, 1990), and wing-waving (E), pretakeoff (F), postlanding (G), pointing (H), and gaping (I) postures of Neotropic cormorant (below, after sketches in van Tets, 1965).

Reproductive Biology

Breeding season. Breeding typically occurs during late spring and summer. Thus, in most of its range incubation occurs from September until January. However, autumn and winter nesting have also been reported in Tasmania and Victoria (Serventy, Serventy, and Warham, 1971).

Nest sites and nest building. Colonies of this species are quite persistent, lasting for several years or decades. Colonies range in size from a few nests to several thousands, as for example on Dangerous Reef, English Islands, and Winceby Island, all in South Australia. The nests are constructed of seaweeds, driftwood, debris, and other available materials, on flat ledges, in clefts, or on low cliffs 2–5 meters above the high-tide level. Occasionally the nest will be placed among vegetation, up to a meter above ground level. Often the nests are closely spaced, with adjacent nests only a meter apart. The site is selected by the male, but the female constructs the nest with materials brought in by the male, and construction continues through the incubation and brooding periods (Marchant and Higgins, 1990).

Egg laying and incubation. Little information exists on clutch sizes in this species, but apparently two or three eggs represent the normal clutch, with a range of from one to five eggs. There is no information on egg-laying intervals, incubation periods, or hatching intervals. Storms are known to be a source of danger to nests, and gulls take eggs and small chicks.

Brooding and rearing of young. Evidently adults feed only their own chicks, and during food begging the young bird cocks its tail, spreads its wings, and distends its gular pouch, which is a contrasting yellowish pink to its blackish brown head. The chicks may also peck at the parent's neck to stimulate regurgitation (Serventy, Serventy, and Warham, 1971). When adults with food arrive at the colony the young that are old enough to leave their nests crowd forward to meet them. Older chicks gather in creches. At times the chicks may be fed in the water, presumably after they are somewhat older.

Breeding success. No detailed information exists on this topic. Destruction of nests by humans is apparently the greatest threat to breeding birds.

Population Status

A recent summary of known breeding colonies (Marchant and Higgins, 1990) indicates that the largest ones are located off Eyre Peninsula, which in the 1970s and 1980s probably collectively contained between 5,000 and 10,000 pairs. In the Tasmanian region the colonies are much smaller. The largest ones are in the Furneaux Group, where some colonies of several hundred birds have been reported. The colonies in Victoria and Western Australia are small, numbering under 100 pairs in each case.

Evolutionary Relationships

This species is perhaps most closely related to the bank cormorant (Siegel-Causey, 1988), and is apparently part of a larger phyletic group of rather widely distributed and generally large, heavy-bodied "marine cormorants" that are adapted to diving for prey in fairly deep marine environments.

NEOTROPIC (OLIVACEOUS) CORMORANT *PHALACROCORAX BRASILIANUS* (GMELIN) 1789[1]

Other Vernacular Names

Bigua cormorant, black cormorant, Brazilian cormorant, common cormorant, Mexican cormorant *(mexicanus)*, Neotropical cormorant, Sonora cormorant *(mexicanus)*; cormoran vigua (French); Biguascharbe (German); cormoril, covejón (Spanish)

Distribution

Breeds in southern North America from southern New Mexico, coastal Texas, and southwestern Louisiana south through Central America and virtually all of South America to Cape Horn (Tierra del Fuego); also locally resident in the West Indies (Cuba, Isle of Pines, southern Bahamas). Mostly sedentary, but with some seasonal or erratic movements at the northern end of the range, and perhaps also in Tierra del Fuego. (See figure 50.)

Subspecies

P. b. mexicanus (Brandt) 1837. Breeds from the southern United States south to Nicaragua. Also apparently locally resident in Cuba, the Isle of Pines, and the Bahamas (Great Inaqua, San Salvador, possibly also Cat Island).

P. b. brasilianus. Breeds from Costa Rica south through South America, including both coastal and fresh-water habitats, ranging altitudinally from lowland tropical zones to Andean lakes, and extending south to Tierra del Fuego, the Fuegian population sometimes being recognized as a separate race *hornensis*.

Description

Prebreeding adult. Head, neck, lower back, rump, upper tail coverts, and underparts all deep glossy black; upper back, wing coverts, and scapulars lanceolate and deep ashy, narrowly margined with black; primaries brownish black; secondaries deep ashy; rectrices (normally 12, occasionally to 14) black. Feathers of the nape elongated, forming a slight mane; lores variably feathered; gular skin slightly heart-shaped and margined with a narrow zone of white feathers terminating in a point behind and below the eye; a tuft of white feathers above the ear, a line of small white filoplumes on each side of the head above the ear, and a few scattered white filoplumes on the neck. Iris blue to green; eye ring and gular skin brownish or dusky yellow to orange (the latter color probably developing only at the peak of breeding), the

lores similar; bill brownish horn to blackish, darkest on the culmen, the basal cutting edges of the maxilla yellowish, and much of the mandible irregularly blotched with orange-yellow and black; legs and feet black.

Postbreeding adult. Similar to prebreeding plumage, but lacking the white filoplumes, and the softpart colors probably less brilliant. An adult in heavy postnuptial molt illustrated by Newell and Sutton (1982) had fully feathered lores.

Immature-subadult. Similar to the juvenal plumage, but with a white border around the gular skin, and brownish white underparts (which gradually become spotted with brown and black). The iris becomes green before the definitive plumage has been attained, which perhaps occurs at two years. Bill brown, the culmen and upper parts of maxilla darker; gular skin brown; legs and feet black.

Juvenile. Completely brown both above and below at first, with darker wings and tail, and lacking a white feathered border to the bare gular area. The dark feather tips on the underpart feathers soon abrade to reveal their brownish white bases. Iris apparently brown; bill and facial skin yellowish to buffy; gular skin yellow.

Nestling. Naked and blackish gray at hatching, but quickly acquiring a blackish down.

Measurements (in millimeters)

Of *mexicanus*: wing, males 253–287 (ave. of 7, 271.4), females 242–266 (ave. of 8, 253.4); tail, males 148–176 (ave. of 4, 159.2), females 138–160 (ave. of 8, 150.6); culmen, males 41–50 (ave. of 7, 46.6), females 43–47 (ave. of 8, 45) (Palmer, 1962). Birds from Cuba appear to average slightly smaller than Texas specimens (Watson, Olson, and Miller, 1991). Eggs ca. 54 × 34.

Of *brasilianus*: wing, males 271–305 (ave. of 28, 283.3), females 250–282 (ave. of 18, 270); tail, males 144–181 (ave. of 28, 166.6), females 139–175 (ave. of 18, 154); culmen, males 54–61 (ave. of 28, 57), females 49–58 (ave. of 18, 54) (Blake, 1977). Eggs ca. 57 × 35.5.

1. Often described as *P. olivaceus* (Humboldt) 1805, such as by Dorst and Mougin (1979), although properly called *P. brasilianus* according to Browning (1989). A change of the vernacular name to Neotropic cormorant has also been proposed and recently adopted by the American Ornithologists' Union (*Auk* 108:751), based on the fact that this species is not actually olivaceous in color, and that its range closely coincides with the Neotropical zoogeographic region.

Figure 50. Distribution of the Neotropic cormorant, showing
the residential ranges of its races *mexicanus* (hatched) and
brasilianus (cross-hatched). Arrows on the general map indicate insular populations of the West Indies; those on the inset
map indicate locations of breeding records or colonies in
Texas and Louisiana.

Weights (in grams)

Adult males (both subspecies, various locations) 1,150–1,550 (ave. of 18, 1,391); adult females 1,100–1,450 (ave. of 8, 1,256) (U.S. National Museum and Museum of Vertebrate Zoology specimens). Males of *mexicanus* (from U.S.) 1,150–1,550 (ave. of 14, 1,393), females 1,100–1,450 (ave. of 8, 1,256) (Watson, Olson, and Miller, 1991). Males of *brasilianus* (from Panama) 1,100–1,500 (ave. of 4, 1,275); one female 1,000 (Hartman, 1955); ten individuals (sexes unspecified) averaged 1,260 (standard deviation 12.6), three others averaged 1,070 (Hartman, 1961). Haverschmidt (1968) reported the range of nominate male *brasilianus* weights in Suriname as 1,113–1,400, and a female as 1,300. Three nominate males from Argentina were 1,250–2,150 (ave. 1,817), and three females all weighed 1,500 (University of Kansas museum specimens). A female from Tierra del Fuego weighed ca. 1,560 (3.44 lb), and a male ca. 1,360 (3 lb) (Humphrey et al., 1970). Calculated egg weight of *mexicanus* 34.4; of *brasilianus* 39.6.

Identification

In the hand.   The combination of a culmen length of 40–50 mm, brownish black underparts, and a yellowish to orange or brownish gular skin that is narrowly bordered with white and comes to a point below and behind the eye identifies this species.

In the field.   Among adults, this is a rather slender and relatively dark-colored cormorant. Younger birds are dark brown above, grading to very light brown or whitish below, but in all adults and at least some immatures there is a distinct whitish border to the gular skin, usually forming a distinct lateral chevron just below and behind the eye. Juveniles may not exhibit this conspicuous field mark, but the yellowish gular skin similarly comes to a point below the eye. Young birds are smaller and paler than young double-cresteds; additionally and in common with adults their tails are relatively longer and more pointed.

Ecology and General Biology

Breeding and nonbreeding habitats.   This is an ecologically tolerant species, with the broadest ecological and climatic range of any western hemisphere cormorant. It ranges from equatorial to cold-temperate (in Tierra del Fuego) climates, and from slow-moving or still-water tropical environments near sea level to mountain streams and alpine lakes at about 4,400 meters elevation. It ranges from fresh water to estuarine and inshore marine environments, but breeds primarily on coastal islands, and along inland and mostly tree-lined ponds, lakes, and reservoirs.

Movements and migrations.   There are some seasonal movements in the United States during winter, which perhaps at least in Texas partly reflect postbreeding dispersal and aggregations of birds in favored foraging areas (Oberholser, 1974). The extreme lower Rio Grande valley and adjacent Texas coastline evidently are a favored wintering area for this species.

Nestling birds banded in Argentina dispersed during the first year throughout a region roughly limited by an equilateral triangle 1,500 kilometers per side around the breeding colony. Recoveries through the eighth year were concentrated in a relatively small area within about 650 kilometers (400 miles) from the hatching site (Olrog, 1975).

Competition and predation.   Over much of its noncoastal Neotropical range this is the only species of cormorant present, but along coastlines it comes into contact with several other cormorants and shags. It often associates with double-crested cormorants and anhingas, and competes for food with both of these species in some areas. However, Morrison and Slack (1977a) found no correlation between the numbers of Neotropic and double-crested cormorants reported in Christmas count surveys. Known predators of eggs and young in Texas include raccoons *(Procyon lotor)* and boat-tailed grackles *(Quiscalus major)* (Palmer, 1962; Morrison, Shanley, and Slack, 1979)

Foods and Foraging Behavior

Foods consumed.   Over this species' very broad range there must be many variations in foods consumed, but little information exists for any single region. Coker (1919) noted that off the Peruvian coast the birds prefer bottom-dwelling fish and shallow-water fish near shore, in lengths of 6–25 centimeters. Palmer (1962) summarized the little information then available for North American populations, whose foods consisted of fresh-water fish such as top-minnows *(Gambusia)*, frogs, tadpoles, and dragonfly nymphs.

The most complete information on this species' foods is from the study of chick regurgitations by Morrison, Shanley, and Slack (1977) at Sabine Lake, Texas. Based on occurrence frequencies of more than 1,500 identified prey items, the most important prey species was the sailfin-molly *Poecilia latipinna*, which comprised 65 percent of the total prey items and 37.4 percent of total prey mass. This species and five other fish taxa, including *Cyprinodon* (Cyprinodontidae), *Fundulus* (Cyprinodontidae), *Gambusia* (Poecilidae), *Micropogon* (Sciaenidae), and *Mugil* (Mugilidae), together comprised nearly all the prey identified by both relative mass and quantity. All these taxa prefer protected inlets and ponds rather than more open waters, are very common in the area, and are tolerant of widely varying salinities and water temperatures. Mean prey lengths for these taxa ranged from 32 to 61 millimeters (extreme range of all prey items was 25–131 millimeters). The mean prey mass of the primary prey taxa, *Poecilia*, was 0.98 grams, and the mean prey mass for all prey fish taxa was 1.7 grams.

Foraging behavior.   Based on the study of Morrison,

Shanley, and Slack (1977), these birds generally prefer hunting small, abundant prey in ponds rather than larger prey species more widely dispersed in lakes. They were observed to begin foraging shortly after sunrise and fly to foraging areas about two kilometers from the breeding colony. They would begin to return to feed their young about an hour after sunrise, although most did not return for more than two hours. Evidently they gather enough food for both themselves and their young on single foraging trips, rather than making separate trips for these two purposes. From three to eight foraging flights may be made per day (Palmer, 1962). The birds terminate foraging within an hour of sunset.

Morrison, Slack, and Shanley (1978) observed that diving times of both adults and immatures averaged 6.3 seconds for 1,348 dives on a shallow (0.25–0.75 meter) pond, and 16 seconds for 773 dives on a deeper (0.75–2 meter) pond. Foraging success was higher on the shallower pond, and additionally foraging success was greater for adults than for juveniles. This difference in foraging success continued into winter; young birds increased their daily food intake by foraging twice as often as adults.

Fishing in groups has been occasionally seen in this species, although individualized foraging appears to be the typical pattern. A few observations of aerial pursuit-plunging have also been made for this species (Duffy et al., 1986; Humphrey, Rasmussen, and Lopez, 1988). In this species such feeding seems to be associated with very calm water conditions with the birds attracted to surface activity by numerous fishes, rather than specifically targeting a single fish.

Social Behavior

Age of maturity and mating system. The age of initial breeding is unreported, although Bent (1922) suggested that the adult plumage is attained in two years. Sustained or seasonal monogamy is the presumed mating system, but apparently no evidence on this point exists.

Social displays and vocalizations. Van Tets (1965) described the male's wing-waving display (figure 49E) as a simultaneous, moderately slow waving of the wings (averaging 1.7 cycles per second, and each burst lasting an average of 22 seconds), with a loud call uttered each time the wingtips were raised; the head moved in opposite sequence to the wings. The associated posture is very much like that of the double-crested cormorant, judging from his sketch.

The gaping display (figure 49I) resembles that of the double-crested cormorant in that both sexes perform it identically and the neck is stretched upward, with the head swayed slowly and the mouth wide open. The pointing display (figure 49H) is seemingly identical to that of the double-crested. Kink-throating also occurs in the Neotropic cormorant. In common with the double-crested and great cormorants the neck is not noticeably arched during the

pretakeoff or prehop display, and like the great cormorant the Neotropic cormorant performs median crest raising during both the pretakeoff (figure 49F) and the postlanding posture. In the postlanding posture the head is held high, with the neck diagonally stretched, the bill directed forward, and the neck feathers seemingly ruffled (figure 49G).

Reproductive Biology

Breeding season. The breeding season in Texas is prolonged, with egg records extending from early February to mid-October, with a peak between April and August.

Nest sites and nest building. Nests are usually situated in bushes or trees, at elevations of from 1 to 7 meters above water, but where such sites are absent the birds may nest on the ground or on bare rocks. The nest is generally constructed of small sticks (Palmer, 1962). The species also often nests within colonies of herons, egrets, or other colonial marshbirds. In a Louisiana survey most nesting occurred in heronries, with the nests in the tallest woody vegetation (Portnoy, 1981).

Egg laying and incubation. Egg laying is done at two-day intervals, with incubation starting with the second-laid egg. Although the clutch size is often reported as four eggs, Morrison, Shanley, and Slack (1979) found an average clutch of only 2.87 eggs for 66 nests in southern Texas, and a range of 1–4 eggs. Of 55 nests, 53 percent had three eggs, 27 percent had two eggs, 18 percent had four eggs, and 2 percent had a single egg present. They believed this seemingly small clutch may have reflected poor foraging conditions prior to this breeding season. The incubation period averaged 24.6 days for 15 nests, and renesting frequently occurred following the complete or even partial loss of a clutch. Such renesting occurred 1–11 days (mean 5.5) after partial clutch loss, and 2–20 days (mean 8.5) after loss of the complete clutch.

Brooding and rearing of young. In the study by Morrison, Shanley, and Slack (1979), the young hatched asynchronously over a period of several days. Although none of the four-egg clutches resulted in the fledging of all four young, these clutches produced the highest average number of young hatched per nest (2.5, as compared with 1.65 for the entire sample), and also the highest average number of young fledged per nest (1.5, as compared with 0.95 for the entire sample). Interestingly, nesting success of replacement clutches averaged higher than that of first efforts (66.7 percent vs. 44.2 percent), since most losses of the early nestings were storm-related, and later in the nesting season there was no violent weather. The fledging period was not established in this study, but young birds began swimming and diving around the nesting island by eight weeks of age, and parental feeding continued until the eleventh week. By the twelfth week the young were independent.

Breeding success. In the study by Morrison, Shanley, and

Slack (1979), losses during the egg stage (which totaled 18 percent of all eggs laid) resulted from hatching failures (39 percent of losses), falling to the ground (35 percent of losses), egg disappearance (18 percent of losses), and predation (8 percent of losses). Of 91 chicks that hatched, 52 fledged successfully, representing a prefledging chick mortality of 43 percent. Nestling losses mostly resulted from deaths in the nest (46 percent), followed by chick disappearance (33 percent) and falling to the ground (21 percent). Typically the smallest young in the brood either starved to death or was trampled to death. Fledging success was highest in one-egg (100 percent) and two-egg (71 percent) clutches, and although three-egg clutches were the most common, these nests did not produce as many successful fledglings per nest (0.9) as did either single-egg (1.0) or four-egg (1.5) clutches, but more than two-egg clutches (0.67).

Population Status

The species' historic North American status has been reviewed by Morrison and Slack (1977a), using Christmas count data. After an apparent population crash in Texas during the 1960s, the species' nesting Texas population slowly increased but with marked fluctuations in wintering numbers. The breeding populations in southwestern Louisiana showed a similar increase during the mid-1970s. In a 1976 Louisiana survey, there were 1,092 Neotropic cormorants nesting in cypress swamps, 788 nesting in brackish marshes, and 5,780 nesting in fresh-water marshes, mostly among heronries (Portnoy, 1981). Of the seven known Louisiana colonies, six were in Cameron Parish, while the remaining largest one was in Vermillion Parish, consisting of 4,000 birds (Portnoy, 1977). In 1990 the Louisiana population was estimated at 2,755 birds in 10 colonies (Martin and Lester, 1990). During 1976 there were eight known Texas colonies, nearly all located along the upper coast and collectively containing about 2,500 birds. The largest of these colonies were at Willie Slough Gully, Jefferson County (600 pairs), Atkinson Island, Chambers County (250 pairs), Sidney Island, Orange County (125 pairs), and on the Vingt'une Islands (120 pairs). However, during the next two summers the Texas breeding population declined substantially to about 350 pairs (Blacklock et al., 1979). Thus, as of that period there were only 15 known colonies in the U.S., and some were in apparent decline. Since then a few additional interior Texas nesting sites have been found, including sites in Clay, Anderson, Henderson, and Wood counties in north-central Texas (Pulich, 1988), as well as near Lake Tawakoni, Hunt County, and also at Miller's Creek Lake (*American Birds* 43:1338). In 1990 there also were second-known nesting records for Raines and Dallas counties (*American Birds* 44:1155).

Evolutionary Relationships

Siegel-Causey (1988) included this species in his genus *Hypoleucus*, along with the double-crested cormorant and several other Old World forms. He considered the Neotropic cormorant to represent the earliest phyletic divergence from this group of medium-sized cormorants.

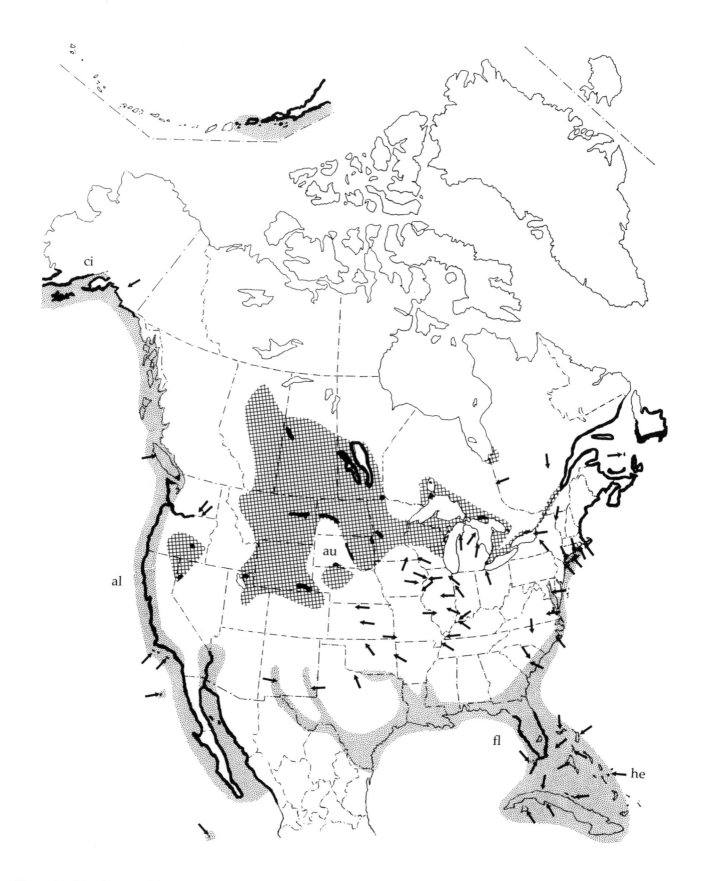

Figure 51. Distribution of the double-crested cormorant, showing its breeding range as inked (coastal residential and denser inland) or cross-hatched (general inland breeding distribution), plus its wintering range (stippled). Arrows indicate locations of insular colonies and of some extralimital records or minor breeding localities. Distributions of its races *albociliatus* (al), *auritus* (au), *cincinatus* (ci), *floridanus* (fl), and *heuretus* (he) are also indicated.

Other Vernacular Names

Farallon cormorant *(albociliatus)*, Florida cormorant *(floridanus)*, northern double-crested cormorant *(auritus)*, white-crested cormorant *(cincinatus)*, white-tufted cormorant *(cincinatus)*; cormoran à aigrettes (French); Ohrenscharbe (German); cormoril, cuervo marino (Spanish)

Distribution

Breeds in North America from the easternmost Aleutian Islands, southwestern and southern coastal Alaska, and Vancouver Island south to Baja California, the west coast of mainland Mexico, and associated islands in the Pacific Ocean and Gulf of California; in the interior from the Canadian prairie provinces and southern Ontario south locally to New Mexico, the central Great Plains, and the upper Mississippi valley; and along the Atlantic coast from coastal Quebec and Newfoundland south through New England to Massachusetts; also resident along the Florida Gulf and Atlantic coasts, north locally to coastal North Carolina. Insular residential populations occur on the Bahamas, Cuba, and the Isle of Pines. Continental populations winter variably southward to northern and central Mexico, with vagrants occasionally or rarely reaching Guatemala and Belize. (See figure 51.)

Subspecies

P. a. cincinatus (Brandt) 1837. Breeds from Unalaska Island (eastern Aleutians) east locally at least to Yakutat Peninsula. Previously assumed to breed widely in southeastern Alaska, but known Alaskan breeding sites are mostly limited to the western Gulf of Alaska and Bristol Bay, north to Nunivak Island. This race is not yet known to breed in Canada. Winters south to southern British Columbia (Vancouver Island).

P. a. albociliatus Ridgway 1884. Breeds from southwestern British Columbia (Vancouver Island and the Strait of Georgia) to southernmost Baja California, the Gulf of California, and Revillagigedo Islands; also breeds interiorly to central Washington (Columbia River valley), southeastern Oregon, central California, and the lower Colorado River valley. Also ranges along the western coast of Mexico south to Guerrero, where local offshore breeding occurs south at least to southern Sonora, but the southern breeding limits are unknown. Reportedly also breeds in western Nevada, but this Pyramid Lake population would seem to be more geographically affiliated with nominate *auritus*. The interior breeding populations are relatively migratory, wintering commonly in

southern California and the lower Colorado River valley. Coastal populations probably are more sedentary, but some winter movements away from breeding colonies occur in northern areas.

P. a. auritus (Lesson). Breeds from northern Alberta east through the prairie provinces to James Bay, southward along the Atlantic coast from Labrador and Newfoundland to Massachusetts, and south locally or occasionally to southern Idaho, Utah, New Mexico (recently), northern Texas, eastern Kansas, and the upper Mississippi valley, sporadically to as far south as northern Arkansas. Winters south to northern Mexico and the Gulf coast, with vagrants rarely reaching Cuba.

P. a. floridanus (Audubon) 1835. Breeds locally from coastal North Carolina south to the Atlantic and Gulf coasts of Florida, formerly west to coastal Texas; also probably resident in the Bahamas (northern islands), Cuba, and the Isle of Pines. The continental population winters southward along the Gulf coast, with vagrants rarely reaching Belize.

P. a. heuretus Watson, Olson, and Miller 1991. Resident on San Salvador (Watling) Island, Bahamas.

Description

Prebreeding adult. Head, neck, lower back, rump, upper tail coverts, and underparts all black, with a dull oil-greenish to bluish gloss; feathers of upper back, scapulars, and wing coverts brownish gray, widely margined with black; alula black; remiges and rectrices (12) brownish black to black. Ear-like nuptial tufts of variably white (in western populations) to entirely black (in eastern populations) plumes of varying length and density. Iris bright emerald-green, with a narrow silvery green circle around the pupil; eyelid colors apparently variable geographically or individually, from bright blue (generally), or light blue spotted with white (in *floridanus*), to yellow or orange; corner and interior of mouth bright cobalt-blue to dull blue, with greenish reflections; lores and orbital region orange; maxilla black, mottled with grayish or dull yellow along the sides; mandible yellowish to pale bluish, mottled with dusky; gular skin deep orange and rounded posteriorly, becoming more yellow-ochre basally; legs and feet black.

Postbreeding adult. Similar to the prebreeding plumage, but the ornamental tufts lacking (dropped shortly after egg laying), the bare facial skin and gular skin yellow instead of orange, and the blue color of the mouth undeveloped.

Immature-subadult. Similar to juveniles, but the throat, foreneck, and underparts mostly dull brown or whitish, and probably gradually becoming increasingly glossy black on the upperparts. The head and upperparts are usually a mixture of brown and black, and when present the nuptial crests are very short. The wing coverts are buff with brown edges (retained from the juvenal plumage) or slate-gray with black edges; alula brown. Some birds may acquire their definitive feathering within two years, a few even earlier, and many later; some two-year-old subadults have been observed to breed (Palmer, 1962). Iris greenish gray to brown; line from above eye to culmen cadmium-yellow, rest of bare facial skin clay-color, mottled with dull black; mouth lining variable, flesh to yellow or pale blue; maxilla mostly brown to brownish yellow, becoming cream-colored basally below nostril groove; corner of mouth and base of mandible cadmium-yellow, rest of mandible buffy yellow; gular skin yellow; legs and feet black.

Juvenile. Variable in color, but head mostly dark brownish gray to pale brown, shading to grayish white on chin; throat and foreneck whitish, mottled or scaled with brown; upperparts generally dark grayish brown, the darker feather margins producing a scaly appearance; underparts variably mottled with brown and whitish; remiges and rectrices brown (faded?) or black, the latter sometimes with brown tips. Iris grayish brown to brown; bare lores whitish, yellowish, or dusky; interior of mouth flesh-colored; maxilla dark brown, becoming yellowish ventrally; mandible paler; gular skin dull yellow, with black patches; legs and feet black.

Nestling. Initially naked and brownish, the skin turning black within 48 hours, but the throat area remaining mostly pink, with a trace of lavender and scattered black markings. The inside of the mouth is pink to deep flesh. The blackish eyes open in 3–5 days, and the body is mostly covered with short, black woolly down by about two weeks, when the throat skin also starts to become yellowish. Contour feathers appear soon afterward, the head and neck being the last areas to become downy, and remaining sparse until the juvenal plumage is attained at seven weeks.

Measurements (in millimeters)

Ranges, inclusive of all races: wing, males 272–349, females 260–340; culmen, males 47–63, females 42–61; tarsus, males 49–72, females 50–71; tail, males 123–165, females 120–156. There is considerable racial variation. Representative measurements of individual subspecies are as follows:

Of *albociliatus* (means of 19 males and 12 females), wing, males 311, females 297; culmen, males 57.4, females 55.2; tarsus, males 64, females 63 (Palmer, 1962).

Of *auritus* (means of 11 males and 8 females), wing, males 311, females 303; culmen, males 57, females 53; tarsus, males 61, females 60 (Palmer, 1962).

Of *cincinatus* (means of 9 males and 4 females), wing, males 331, females 334; culmen, males 59, females 58; tarsus, males 68, females 66 (Palmer, 1962).

Of *floridanus* (from Florida), wing, males 282–316 (ave. of

32, 303.1), females 275–305 (ave. of 17, 288.9); culmen, males 47–61 (ave. of 32, 56.5), females 51–60 (ave. of 19, 54.6); tail, males 130–157 (ave. of 30, 144.3), females 125–152 (ave. of 15, 135.5) (Watson, Olson, and Miller, 1991).

Of *heuretus*, wing, males 260–280 (ave. of 8, 270.6), females 259–276 (ave. of 8, 263.1); culmen, males 43.4–49 (ave. of 5, 45.8), females 43–49.5 (ave. of 5, 45.2); tail, males 123–132 (ave. of 4, 143.8), females 117–132 (ave. of 7, 121.9) (Watson, Olson, and Miller, 1991).

Eggs average ca. 60 × 38 (some minor racial variation present).

Weights (in grams)

Of *albociliatus* (New Mexico), adult males 2,200–2,750 (ave. of 16, 2,453), females 1,750–2,400 (ave. of 17, 2,056) (Watson, Olson, and Miller, 1991).

Of *auritus* (Minnesota, in May), males 1,986–2,807 (ave. of 12, 2,415), females 1,758–2,948 (ave. of 3, 2,287) (Marshall and Erickson, 1945). Adult males (Maine, in July), 2,072–2,566 (ave. of 10, 2,233), females 1,732–2,026 (ave. of 12, 1,861) (Kury, 1968).

Of *floridanus*, adult males 1,440–2,100 (ave. of 9, 1,849); adult females 1,150–2,080 (ave. of 9, 1,650) (U.S. National Museum and Museum of Vertebrate Zoology specimens). Another sample: males 1,327–2,079 (ave. of 6, 1,758), females 1,391–1,665 (ave. of 5, 1,535) (Owre, 1967). A sample of 33 males of *floridanus* averaged 1,818 (standard deviation 224), 32 females averaged 1,540 (standard deviation 215) (Hartman, 1961).

Of *heuretus*, one adult male 1,270, 3 females 1,036–1,175 (ave. 1,112) (Watson, Olson, and Miller, 1991).

Calculated egg weight 47.8; ave. of 20 *auritus*, 46.1 (Mitchell, 1977), of 13 *albociliatus*, 45.1 (Hanna, 1924), of 215 *albociliatus*, 51 (van Tets, 1959).

Identification

In the hand. The combination of a culmen length usually longer than 45 mm and a wing length greater than 260 mm, blackish underparts in adults, and orange-yellow facial skin and gular skin (the latter rounded behind and not distinctly bounded posteriorly by a line of white feathers), should identify this species.

In the field. The seemingly conspicuous and distinctive "double-crested" condition of this species is actually a very poor field mark; these feathers are fully developed only for a brief period in spring. Generally the adult birds appear to be entirely glossy black, with a bright yellow to orange throat patch and a smaller area of similarly colored skin in front of the eye. Young birds are more whitish on the anterior underparts, but nonetheless still exhibit yellowish faces and throats. In eastern Canada and during winter along the Atlantic coast of the U.S. the somewhat larger great cormorant might be confused with the double-crested, but its more limited yellow face area is usually bounded posteriorly by a distinct white band, and in full breeding plumage its flanks are also white. Young double-crested and great cormorants are quite similar, but first-year great cormorants have nearly white bellies and darker brownish breasts, rather than the reverse condition as found in juvenile double-cresteds. In Texas and elsewhere along the Gulf coast the Neotropic cormorant might also occur and provide potential confusion; as compared to the double-crested the Neotropic is somewhat smaller, it has a relatively longer tail, its gular skin is bounded posteriorly with a narrow whitish band, and its lores are variably feathered.

Ecology and General Biology

Breeding and nonbreeding habitats. Nonbreeding habitats of this species are diverse, including lakes, ponds, rivers, lagoons, coastal bays, marine islands, and open coastlines. The birds are rarely found in the open sea any distance from shore; most of the birds forage within sight of land and probably no more than about 20 kilometers from their roosting sites. Root (1988) suggested that ambient temperature strongly influences the winter distribution of double-crested cormorants, with eastern birds concentrating along the southern tip of Florida, where ocean and air temperature are mild. Areas with a minimum January temperature above freezing seem to support the highest densities of birds, which helps explain why they winter much farther north along the Pacific coast than the Atlantic coast.

Breeding habitats involve the combination of a nearby reliable food supply and suitable, secure nesting sites. These nesting sites may consist of sandy or rocky areas along islands, cliffs, reefs, or other water-lined sites, or of trees or towers standing in or near water, such as swamps, coastal woodlands, or tree-lined lakes. When rocky substrates are used, sloping areas are preferred, especially those near the highest points of islands or cliffs. As compared with other coastal-nesting species, the double-crested resembles the Brandt's cormorant in that it favors nesting sites offering an abundance of wide ledges, rocky shoulders, and fairly high sites providing excellent visibility, rather than crevices or very narrow sites on steep slopes as are favored by pelagic and red-faced shags. It is possible that ground is the preferred nesting substrate for this species, and that tree-nesting has been adopted only in those areas that are subject to disturbance by humans or terrestrial predators (Vermeer, 1973).

Movements and migrations. Depending on the severity of the winter, there is a great variation in migratory tendencies, with birds breeding in Florida essentially sedentary, those along the Pacific coast only slightly migratory, and those nesting in the interior and along the northern Atlantic coast showing the highest degree of seasonal movements. Generally on migration the birds follow coastlines and river

valleys, moving during night as well as day, and typically avoiding even visible shortcuts over land. The two primary migration routes appear to be down the Atlantic coast and through the Mississippi-Missouri valleys to the Gulf coast (Palmer, 1962). Banding results of birds in Maine indicate that the majority of them winter in Florida as expected, but a minority (15 percent) continue on to winter along the Gulf coast from Alabama as far as coastal Texas (Kury and Cadbury, 1970). The majority of birds nesting in Canada from Alberta to the Gulf of St. Lawrence probably winter between Florida and Texas, mainly concentrating in the lower Mississippi valley. The lower Mississippi delta area alone holds at least 35,000 birds (Conniff, 1991). However, little mixing occurs between birds from populations east and west of the Rocky Mountains, which evidently provide an effective migratory barrier (as also is true for American white pelicans). In general, first-year birds winter farther away from their natal colony than do older ones, and their spring migration occurs about a month later than that of older cohorts (Dolbeer, 1991).

Competition and predation. Potential foraging competition with other Pacific-coast cormorants was discussed in chapter 4, and appears to be reduced by various differences in foraging habitat preference among these species. Ecological differences and very limited geographic sympatry between the Neotropic cormorant and double-crested cormorant also reduces probable foraging competition between these species. Perhaps some limited foraging competition exists between anhingas and double-crested cormorants in areas where they both commonly occur, such as in Florida, but this is poorly documented. Owre (1967) provided some data on stomach contents of these two species in southern Florida. He suggested that different fish-catching strategies of the two may reduce any competition for foods, although both often feed on slow-swimming centrarchids.

Predation of eggs and young is probably a serious mortality factor throughout the species' range, as indicated by a variety of studies. Mitchell (1977) reviewed the evidence for avian and mammalian predation on this species. Although he found no indication that California gulls (*Larus californicus*) caused any predation in his Utah study area, this species has been implicated in egg predation elsewhere (Odin, 1957; Behle, 1958; Vermeer, 1970b). The similar-sized ring-billed gull (*Larus delawarensis*) has also been implicated as an egg predator (Ferry, 1909). The larger herring gull (*Larus argentatus*) is certainly a significant predator of both eggs and young birds (Mendall, 1936), as is the great black-backed gull (Lewis, 1929). Similarly, American crows (*Corvus brachyrhynchos*), fish crows (*Corvus ossifragus*), northwestern crows (*Corvus caurinus*), and common ravens (*Corvus corax*) are also serious predators of eggs and young (Lewis, 1929; Drent et al., 1964; Schreiber and Schreiber, 1978). Bald eagles (*Haliaeetus leucocephalus*) have also been reported as predators in Manitoba, especially during the late chick-rearing period, but human disturbance and persecution was probably more significant as a mortality factor there (Hobson, Knapton, and Lysack, 1989). Drent et al. (1964) observed no predation by bald eagles in an area of British Columbia where they are quite common.

Foods and Foraging Behavior

Foods consumed.   A great deal of information is available on this topic, most of which has been summarized by Palmer (1962) and more recently by Clapp et al. (1982). All of these studies indicate that the foods are almost entirely of fish, with very small quantities of crustaceans, amphibians, reptiles, mollusks, aquatic insects, and other aquatic invertebrates. The specific prey taxa consumed vary greatly geographically, but generally consist of slow-moving fish of both bottom-dwelling and midwater forms.

One of the few ecologically oriented studies of this species' foods is that of Campo et al. (1988), which is based on the prey found in 441 specimens obtained during winter on nine Texas reservoirs and lakes. The estimated live weight of the food contents averaged 119 grams per bird, and 29 species of fish were recorded from the samples. Prey compositions varied considerably from lake to lake and to some extent also seasonally. There were an average of 10.4 food items present per specimen, with an average weight of 12 grams per food item. Females (adult and juvenile) consumed significantly more smaller-sized items (small minnows, shad, and sunfishes) than did males; these smaller items comprised 38.4 percent by weight of all male foods as compared with 51.5 percent of all female foods. Similarly, small food items accounted for 53.6 percent of all food contents of all juveniles, as compared with 38.2 percent of all adult food items, suggesting an age-related segregation as well as an adult sexual segregation in the sizes of foods consumed. Collectively, 90 percent of the food items found in all specimens were no more than 125 millimeters in length, and 91 percent of the prey fishes weighed no more than 200 grams. The average estimated distance from the foraging area to the nearest shore ranged from 20 to 975 meters, and the average foraging water depth varied from 2 to 8 meters. Water clarity (secchi disk visibility) at foraging areas ranged from 30 to 159 centimeters. Most fishes consumed were shad, large roughfish, and small minnows of little or no interest to sport fishermen, but some other species having greater recreational values to fisherman (largemouth bass, white bass, and catfish) were also present. Assuming twice-daily foraging, the average daily consumption rate was about 240 grams, or around 10 percent of the average bird weight of 2.3 kilograms.

Based on regurgitated samples of prey fish observed by Hobson, Knapton, and Lysack (1989), mean prey length varied from 98.6 to 121.3 millimeters during the nesting and postnesting summer period, with nestling birds being fed larger fish than were eaten by the adults or newly fledged birds. Schooling, commercially nonimportant fish such as suckers *(Catostomus)*, perch *(Perca)*, and tullibee *(Coregonus)* were favored as prey over solitary fish species. Some foraging areas were located as far away as 20 kilometers from the nesting colony.

On the lower Mississippi delta, where the birds concentrate on ponds devoted to catfish aquaculture, a stomach sampling from 136 birds indicated that 65 percent of their diet consisted of catfish (Conniff, 1991).

Foraging behavior.   In contrast to the great amount of literature on the foods of this species, relatively little has been written on its foraging behavior. At least in marine waters, it appears that the birds tend to forage for midwater to bottom-dwelling fish (Owre, 1967; Ross, 1977; Ainley, Anderson, and Kelly, 1981), but there is less evidence for this with regard to fresh-water habitats. Generally the birds forage at fairly shallow depths in fresh-water lakes (see above), and it is likely that they take prey from all levels fairly uniformly. Dive durations are normally not very long, and when foraging on the coast the birds prefer areas with rocky or sandy bottoms in shoals near shore, with river mouths and shallow inlets favored. In such locations where the water is 2–7 meters deep the dives usually last 20–25 seconds, and between dives the birds sometimes swim with their heads submerged, apparently searching for prey. Foraging may be done in compact flocks, with numbers of birds continually diving and resurfacing (Lewis, 1929). Mendall (1936) reported an average dive duration of 19.3–22 seconds in water about 3 meters deep, and averages of 22.5–27.7 seconds in water about 4.5 meters deep. The maximum observed duration was 41 seconds. Nearly all the foraging observed by Mendall was in water less than 9 meters deep, but Lewis (1929) reported a single instance of a bottom-dwelling sculpin being captured in water about 22 meters deep. Muddy bays and estuaries are favored foraging sites around Mandarte Island, British Columbia, where the birds forage singly or in large flocks across narrow channels during outgoing tides, and they sometimes join foraging flocks of Brandt's cormorants that are feeding on schools of fish in open water (van Tets, 1959).

Social Behavior

Age of maturity and mating system.   The usual age of initial breeding in this species is probably three years, although successful breeding has occurred among two-year-olds (van Tets, cited in Palmer, 1962). Van der Veen (1973) observed a single female bird in first-year plumage breeding in a colony containing 320 active nest sites on Mandarte Island, British Columbia. However, he calculated that only 3.7 percent of the year-old cohort of birds probably bred, as did 17.5 percent of the two-year-olds, and 98.4 percent of the three-year-olds. Drent et al. (1964) reported mates remaining together in a single season to lay replacement clutches or even, in one case, a second clutch after a brood had been successfully raised, indicating sustained monogamy within a single breeding season. However, no good data are available on mate fidelity in successive seasons.

Social displays and vocalizations.   During the male's advertisement display (initially called "wing-flipping" by van Tets, but later the more generally used "wing-waving"), he stands in a rigid breast-down posture, with the tail strongly cocked upward beyond the vertical and the bill pointed upward (figure 52B). The wings are then raised and lowered at a rate of about 1.5–2 cycles per second, over periods of 11–12 seconds, as synchronized *ugh* sounds are uttered and the cloaca also pulsates in rhythm. After pair bonds are formed, the pair members perform their recognition gaping display whenever the mate arrives nearby. In this species the neck is stretched upward and forward, with the bill wide open and the blue mouth lining visible (figure 52D, E) while a prolonged call is uttered (van Tets, 1959). A very similar display that perhaps represents a reduced variant of gaping is "pointing" (figure 52C), which is a bisexual display in which the bird then in the nest points its head toward its mate. In this display no sound is uttered, and the head and neck are slowly waved (van Tets, 1965). Kink-throating is also performed by both sexes, under varied conditions, such as during "nest worrying" (figure 52F) or when landing near the mate (figure 52G). Following landing, a distinctive postlanding posture (figure 52A) is usually assumed for a short time.

Nest material presentation is a frequent display early in the breeding cycle, especially before and after copulation. Copulation is preceded by the female performing her recognition (gaping) display while sitting in the nest, followed by the male hopping onto her back. While copulating, the male grabs the female's neck with his bill and keeps his wings closed, except to maintain balance. No specific postcopulatory display is present, other than additional presentation of nesting materials by the male.

When threatening in a defensive manner, these birds hiss and stretch out the neck and shake the widely opened bill at the opponent, while slightly lowering or spreading the wings (van Tets, 1959). These movements may be made toward conspecifics or other species, including predators such as gulls and crows. To a greater degree than the pelagic shag, this species uses an effective nest defense behavior of energetic and aggressive responses to potential gull predation (Siegel-Causey and Hunt, 1981).

According to van Tets (1959), adult double-crested cormorants utter seven different vocalizations, in addition to the chirping (when food-begging) and hissing (in defense) by chicks. These are mostly prolonged or repetitive notes, such as a repeated *ugh* during wing waving, similar *urg* notes before landing, and an *uhr* note before feeding older chicks. A prolonged *arr-r-r-t-t-t-t-t* is uttered during individual recognition display, and a roar is produced after a hop.

Reproductive Biology

Breeding season.   Not surprisingly given the very broad geographic range of this species, its breeding season is highly variable, with the collective extremes for egg dates ranging over a ten-month period from late December until late October. There are also substantial variations in nesting onset among colonies in a single area, and among different years for the same colony. Nesting begins earliest in Florida and Baja California and is delayed seasonally as one moves northward, with egg laying beginning as late as early June in southern Alaska (Palmer, 1962; Clapp et al., 1982).

Nest sites and nest building.   The nest is constructed on the site chosen by and defended by the male, and requires an average of four days to complete (van Tets, in Palmer, 1962). Unlike the Brandt's cormorant and pelagic shag often nesting in the same vicinity (as on Mandarte Island, British Columbia), the double-crested cormorant uses sticks in its nest, inserting them into the structure diagonally using the bill. Additionally, slats, algae, feathers, eelgrass, herbs, hay, bark, and even bird carcasses may all be added, although the base consists mostly of algae, with a hay lining (van Tets, 1959). Large sticks over 15 millimeters in diameter predominate in the nest, and all the materials are gradually covered and mixed with guano, which helps hold the structure together as it hardens. Nests may be placed either on the substrate or in trees (as discussed above), but ground sites seem to be preferred when they are available and the colony is relatively safe from disturbance. When nests persist from year to year, these nests are chosen by the first males to arrive on the breeding area, and they appear to provide the greatest probability for chick survival, at least on Mandarte Island (Siegel-Causey and Hunt, 1986). Similarly, Mitchell (1977) found in Utah that old nests still in good condition were the preferred nesting sites for returning cormorants, although in his study these persistent, generally higher nest sites had a poorer average hatching success than did nests situated lower in the trees. Leger and McNeil (1987) found that the first sites to be chosen on the Madeleine Islands, Quebec, were those at the center of the colony, with features such as nest stability, nest height, and other factors apparently of little importance. DesGranges, Chapdelaine, and Dupuis (1984) found that the ecological locations of nest sites in Quebec are closely related to regional variations in the relative availabilities of different kinds of potential sites.

Egg laying and incubation.   Palmer (1962) indicated a normal clutch range of 3–7 eggs, with occasional instances of 2 or 8, or rarely even 9 eggs, although these highest numbers

Figure 52. Social behavior of the double-crested cormorant, including postlanding posture (A), male wing-waving display (B), pointing display (C), gaping while on and off nest (D, E), kink-throating while nest-worrying (F), kink-throating while landing (G), and water begging by chick (H). After sketches in van Tets (1965).

very probably represent layings of two or more females. Clutch sizes vary considerably throughout the range of this species, perhaps increasing toward the south in a somewhat clinal fashion. The mean clutch (of 21 clutches) at Ugaiushak Island, Alaska (Wehle, 1978), was only 2.7 eggs, whereas that of 21 clutches from elsewhere in the Gulf of Alaska was 3.17 (DeGange and Sanger, 1986). The mean of 76 clutches from Utah Lake, Utah, was 3.8, with two eggs in 4 percent, three in 21 percent, four in 59 percent, five in 14 percent, and six in 1 percent (Mitchell, 1977). Records of 1,022 Ontario nests indicate a range of 1–7 eggs, with a mean clutch size of 3.11 and with 40 percent of the clutches containing four eggs and 30 percent containing three (Peck and James, 1983). Mendall (1936) stated that Maine clutches range from 2 to 5 eggs (sample size not indicated), with two eggs in 8 percent, three in 40 percent, four in 50 percent, and five in 2 percent. This suggests a mean clutch of about 3.5 eggs. A sample of 171 clutches from Alberta had a mean clutch of 3.2 eggs, with four eggs occurring in 51 percent of the nests and an overall range of 1–5 eggs (Vermeer, 1969). On the Madeleine Islands the average clutch sizes over a two-year period were 3.6 and 3.2 eggs, with four eggs occurring in 41.5 percent of the nests (over two years), three eggs in 38 percent, and the observed range 1–6 eggs (Pilon, Burton, and McNeil, 1983). On Mandarte Island, British Columbia, clutches of three or four eggs were also common, and five was the maximum observed clutch size (Drent et al., 1964).

Generally eggs are laid on a daily basis (Lewis, 1929; Mendall, 1936; Behle, 1958; Mitchell, 1977), although occasionally a day may be skipped. Renesting following loss of clutches is fairly common; Mitchell (1977) stated that all of four Utah clutches that were lost early in the season were replaced, and McLeod and Bondar (1953) stated that 30–50 percent of the failed clutches were replaced in a Manitoba study. On Mandarte Island, British Columbia, replacement clutches are common. The average interval between loss of eggs and replacement was 13 days for 12 initial renesting efforts. There were two cases of second renesting efforts and one case of a third renesting effort, with a maximum of 11 eggs known to be laid in a single season by one female (Drent et al., 1964). Van Tets (1959) reported that renesting efforts were made at 29 of 33 nest sites suffering egg or clutch losses, and noted that one bird laid a total of 11 eggs. Although successful double-brooding is not known for this or any other cormorant species, Drent et al. (1964) observed that one pair actually laid a second clutch of three eggs after successfully rearing a brood of young earlier that same season. In an Ontario colony of 44 nests, there were 13 cases of renesting, and at least one second renesting effort (Peck and James, 1983).

Incubation begins with the first egg, but probably is not very effective until the laying of the second egg. The mean incubation of 40 eggs (excluding first-laid eggs) was 28 days, with an observed range of 25–33 days. The incubation period of 15 first-laid eggs averaged 29.9 days (Drent et al., 1964). Similarly, Mitchell (1977) calculated an average incubation period of 28 days for 16 Utah nests, with an observed range of 26–30 days.

Brooding and rearing of young.   From two to four days are usually required for the hatching of all the eggs in a clutch, or somewhat less than the collective time required to lay the entire clutch. Drent et al. (1964) reported an average hatching success of 60.4 percent for 546 eggs on Mandarte Island, British Columbia, with most of the losses resulting from predation (mostly by crows) or failure to hatch because of infertility or addling. Mitchell (1977) observed a similar success of 54.2 percent for 295 eggs in Utah, with cool weather during incubation, the inadvertent effects of human disturbance during the study, and predation all being possible factors in egg failures. Hatching success rates during two years of study on the Madeleine Islands, Quebec, were 74.5 percent and 71.8 percent (Pilon, Burton, and McNeil, 1983). However, success rates of the young following hatching were extremely high on Mandarte Island, with 314 of 330 (95 percent) hatched young successfully fledged, or an average of 2.4 young fledged per nest during each of three years, while in Mitchell's Utah study area 13 of 18 (72 percent) hatched young were known to survive to fledging. The young begin to leave their nests when 3–4 weeks old (averaging 29 days in Mitchell's Utah study) and often then form into small creches. Fledging occurs at 5–6 weeks, and takeoff from water is possible by seven weeks. Diving also begins at about seven weeks of age, so that independent food catching then becomes possible. Independence from the parents occurs at about nine to ten weeks (Lewis, 1929; Mendall, 1936; Palmer, 1962).

Breeding success.   Perhaps in part because of rather large clutch size and especially persistent renesting efforts, breeding success in this species appears to be fairly high as compared with other North American cormorants (Drent et al., 1964). On Mandarte Island, British Columbia, an average of 2.4 young were reared per nest in each of three years, involving a total sample of 132 nests, although the hatching success rate was relatively low. A similarly high rate of fledging success (93 percent) as compared to a rather low hatching success (49 percent) has also been reported from a rather small sample of nests (21) from the Gulf of Alaska (DeGange and Sanger, 1986). Similar rates of 2.1 and 2.4 fledged young per nest (195 nests) during two different years were reported by Pilon, Burton, and McNeil (1983) for Quebec colonies on the Madeleine Islands. Somewhat lower average rates of 1.8 young reared per nest were reported for 19 undisturbed colonies in Manitoba (Hobson, Knapton, and Lysack, 1989), and of 1.9 young fledged per nest (148 nests) in Alberta (Vermeer, 1969). In a study of cormorants on the Madeleine Islands, those chicks hatched later in the brood were no more prone to die than were those hatched earlier (Leger and McNeil, 1987), which is in marked contrast to the results in most other studies of cormorants such as Van der Veen (1973), Mitchell (1977), and Urban (1979). Robertson (1971) observed that, when food was limited, the feeding frequency of young by adults averaged higher, although individual meal sizes were smaller. Furthermore, he observed that growth rates of nestlings were not influenced by their sequence of hatching, and overall growth rates of young were not affected except among broods that were experimentally made larger than normal (more than six young). Blomme (1981) observed that renesting efforts were less successful in fledging young than were initial efforts in Ontario colonies.

Population Status

Following a long period of population decline in this species, which perhaps resulted from a combination of pesticide poisoning (Kury, 1969; Henny et al., 1989), inadequate protection from disturbance of nesting colonies, and actual purposeful destruction of nesting colonies, the population of double-crested cormorants has increased during the past decade or more almost throughout the species' range (Read, 1989). Some local populations may be stable or even declining, as a result of egging, vandalism, or even government-sponsored population control programs (as during the 1970s in Maine, and more recently on the St. Lawrence River islands in Quebec) but most are increasing significantly. Such is the case in southern New England (Hatch, 1984), where populations have shown spectacular increases of up to 26 percent annually, as well as in Michigan (Scharf and Shugart, 1981; Ludwig, 1984), Wisconsin (Matteson, 1985; Craven and Lev, 1987), Minnesota (Hirsch, 1985), Washington (Henny et al., 1989; Speich and Wahl, 1989) and California (Sowls et al.,

1980). Populations have also increased throughout nearly all of Canada (Weseloh et al., 1980; DesGranges, Chapdelaine, and Dupuis, 1984; Vermeer and Rankin, 1984; Vermeer, Morgan, and Smith, 1988; Hobson, Knapton, and Lysack, 1989; Campbell et al., 1990). There have also been recent first-time nestings in North Carolina (*American Birds* 39:900), South Carolina (Post and Post, 1988), Ohio (*American Birds* 41:1440), and New Mexico (*American Birds* 35:966), plus renewed nesting activity in Texas (Holm, Irby, and Inglis, 1978). In 1990 first-time nestings were reported for both New Jersey and Maryland (*American Birds* 44:1121, 1126), and during the same year notable inland breedings occurred in Iowa, Arkansas, Illinois, and Kansas (*American Birds* 44:1139, 1144, 1152). Wintering populations on the lower Mississippi River, where few birds wintered historically, have increased dramatically. An estimated total breeding population for the species, mostly as of 1980 or even earlier, is presented in table 34, but the absence of more recent survey data from some key areas that support significant populations (especially maritime Canada, Maine, and Florida) makes it very conservative and badly outdated. A symposium on the biology and conservation of this species sponsored by the Colonial Waterbirds Society should soon be published and provide new population data.

Evolutionary Relationships

Siegel-Causey (1988) considered this species as part of his genus *Hypoleucus*, grouping it fairly close to the Neotropic cormorant. Assuming that the latter evolved in the Neotropics and the double-crested in the Nearctic, this is a plausible affinity, although the two forms are ecologically and behaviorally isolated at present.

Other Vernacular Names

Indian shag, shag; cormoran à cou brun, cormoran indien (French); indischer Kormoran (German)

Distribution

Resident on both coastal and fresh-water habitats in Sri Lanka, and from the Indus Valley (Sind) of Pakistan eastward south of the Himalayan foothills to southern Indochina, exclusive of the Malay Peninsula. Apparently sedentary. (See figure 53.)

Subspecies

None.

Description

Prebreeding adult.   Head, neck, lower back, rump, upper tail coverts, and underparts all black, glossed with deep steel-blue; upper back, upper wing coverts, and scapulars more bronzelike, the feathers with greenish gloss and rather wide black borders; remiges and rectrices (12) black. A transient tuft or narrow line of white filoplumes on each side of the head starting behind the eye and passing above the ear, and white filoplumes also scattered on the neck. Iris greenish blue to green; eye ring and bare facial skin variously described as greenish black, purplish black, or purplish red; bill dark brownish black, the base of the mandible more reddish; gular skin purplish black, the posterior edge variably yellow; legs and feet black.

Postbreeding adult.   Differs from the prebreeding adult in lacking ornamental white head feathers; the chin and feathers around the gular pouch variably edged or mottled with white; rest of plumage generally browner, the upperparts a duller brownish gray. Facial skin yellowish, or brown with yellow specks; the gular skin also yellow, with a narrow whitish feathered posterior border.

Immature-subadult.   Underparts generally dark brown, with the bases of the feathers white; upperparts as in adults, probably with less metallic sheen. No information on immature softpart colors, but presumably the iris changes from brown to green during this period.

Juvenile.   Generally dingy white on the chin, throat, breast, and underparts; the thighs and flanks mottled with brown; the top of the head, neck, and upperparts brownish, the feathers of the upper back, wing coverts, and scapulars

margined with darker brown. Iris brown; other softpart colors uncertain.

Nestling.   Naked at hatching, but soon covered with sooty black down.

Measurements (in millimeters)

Both sexes (sample size unstated): wing, 257–276; culmen, 50–61; tail, 132–144; tarsus, ca. 47–52. Eggs ca. 51 × 33 (Baker, 1929).

Weights (in grams)

Both sexes 600–790 (ave. of 5, 706) (Ali and Ripley, 1983). Winkler (1983) indicated an average weight of 930, but did not report sex composition or sample size. Calculated egg weight 30.6.

Identification

In the hand.   The combination of a culmen length of at least 50 mm, a blackish overall plumage, the upperpart feathers with bronzy brown centers, a green iris, and the feathers of the throat not extending forward beyond the anterior margin of the eyes serves to identify this species.

In the field.   In its Indo-Malaysian range this species overlaps with the smaller but very similar Javanese cormorant, breeding adults of which lack white eye tufts and have brown rather than green eyes. The bill of the Indian cormorant is also longer and more slender than that of the Javanese. The great cormorant is substantially larger, and has varying amounts of white present behind the gular skin on the throat, cheeks, and sides of the neck.

Ecology and General Biology

Breeding and nonbreeding habitats.   This is a widespread species in India, occurring in jheels, rivers, reservoirs, mangrove swamps, tidal estuarine areas, harbors, and shallow coastlines. It occurs mostly in lowland regions, but occasionally is found on the larger rivers flowing out of the Himalayan foothills, as is the case in Sikkim. Sometimes small water areas are used, although perhaps not quite so small as those exploited by the Javanese cormorant.

Movements and migrations.   The species is mostly residential, but moves locally according to local water conditions.

Competition and predation.   Indian cormorants often

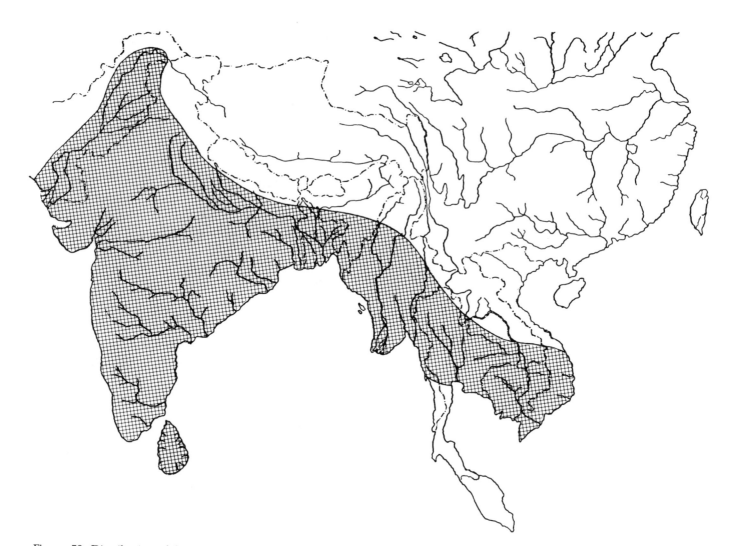

Figure 53. Distribution of the Indian cormorant, showing its probable residential range.

associate with both Javanese and great cormorants, and occupy overlapping but somewhat intermediate habitats between these two species. All three species at times forage together along the Indian coast (Baker, 1929), and the three species exploit the fish populations on lake Parakrama Samudra in Sri Lanka. There they occur in very different numbers, with the Indian cormorant the most abundant, in Winkler's (1983) observations reaching maximum numbers of 13,700 birds, or nearly 90 percent of the collective peak cormorant population. The great and Indian cormorant both foraged in shallow areas between shoreline and depths of up to 4.3 meters, but the great cormorants established foraging territories and hunted individually. Compared with the resident great cormorants, the Indian cormorant population

was nomadic, didn't form foraging territories, and formed social foraging flocks. Great cormorants took fish (mostly large *Tilapia*) averaging about 130 millimeters in length, whereas Indian cormorants consumed fish (mostly *Etroplus* and *Tilapia* in about equal proportions) between 60 and 120 millimeters in length, and Javanese cormorants took fish that were mostly *Etroplus* (Cichlidae) plus some *Tilapia* of from 30 to 70 millimeters (see table 13). Relatively little competition appears to occur between the Oriental darter and Indian cormorant on the Sundarban delta of West Bengal, where the darter consumes generally larger fish than does the Indian cormorant, and additionally a significant dietary component of the darter consists of snakes and insects (Mukherjee, 1969).

No specific information on predators is available, but probably crows (*Corvus* spp.) are significant egg predators, as is known to be the case for the Javanese cormorant.

Foods and Foraging Behavior

Foods consumed.   As noted above and in table 13, the study of Winkler (1983) provides some information on this species' foods in Sri Lanka. Indian cormorants have a more restricted diet than the smaller Javanese cormorant and more diverse than the larger great cormorant, although cichlids formed the main prey of all three species. In the Indian cormorant, cichlids comprised about two-thirds of the diet, with *Etroplus* and *Tilapia* taken in roughly equal amounts. Winkler estimated a daily consumption of 96 grams of fish, or considerably less than the 300 grams estimated by Mukherjee (1969) in West Bengal, India, which was based on an estimated (and unlikely) five foraging bouts per day, and an average stomach content mass of 60 grams in 297 stomachs. Of this mass, fish comprised 91.1 percent, tadpoles of *Rana* 6.1 percent, and mollusks 1.4 percent. A total of 18 fish taxa were found, of which 10 were fresh-water forms and 8 were brackish-water species, ranging in length from 30 to 100 millimeters. Among the sample of 125 birds collected in fresh-water habitats, a wide array of fish, tadpoles, mollusks, and crustaceans had been consumed, whereas birds collected in estuaries had consumed fish almost exclusively. Fish taxa represented in the highest numbers included (in descending frequency of occurrence) Bagriidae (*Mystus*), Cyprinidae (*Chela, Puntius, Catla*, and *Labeo*), Channidae (*Channa*), Cyprinodontidae (*Aplochaeilus, Oryzias*), Nantidae (*Nandus*), Anabantidae (*Anabas*), Mugilidae (*Mugil, Rhinomugil*), and Platycephalidae (*Platycephalus*).

Foraging behavior.   On Parakrama Samudra, Sri Lanka, this species mainly hunted in shallow water along the edges of flooded vegetation and emergent macrophytic plants. Their dives were short, averaging only 12.9 seconds (as compared to 29.8 seconds for the great cormorant and 12.4 for the Javanese cormorant). Their average meal consisted of 2.4 fishes, and typically the birds foraged cooperatively. Thus, even when only two birds were close together they synchronized their diving activities. Often they formed large feeding flocks, which sometimes attracted pelicans, herons, and terns. They also formed enormous communal roosts, so daily flights to and from the roosts were probably fairly coordinated as well. These birds always left the lake for one or other of two roosts, consistently using the same flight routes (Winkler, 1983).

Social Behavior

Age of maturity and mating system.   No information.
Social displays and vocalizations.   No information.

Reproductive Biology

Breeding season.   Baker (1929) reported breeding during the wet monsoon period from July to September, and later (1935) added that breeding may continue on into October at Bharatpur, Rajasthan. He also noted that in Sind (Pakistan) the species might have two breeding seasons, since nests were found in July and August, as well as during December and on into January in adjacent Gujarat. However, this seems more likely to represent extremes of a singly prolonged breeding period centering on the wetter seasons. Cold-weather breeding (November to February) typically occurs in southern India and also in Sri Lanka (Ali and Ripley, 1983). Recent Pakistan observations indicate that in the Indus valley (Sonmiani) nesting usually begins in July and extends to October (Roberts, 1991).

Nest sites and nest building.   Nests are often situated among heronries and among other colonial breeders, or the birds may form small colonies of up to about 50 pairs in groves and bamboos on islands or shorelines of swamps and small ponds. According to Baker (1929), large breeding colonies are not typical of the species, in spite of its highly social foraging tendencies. This may, however, not be universally true, and perhaps colony size simply reflects relative foraging opportunities nearby. Rock nesting has evidently not been reported, and instead the birds employ tree nesting. These nests range in size up to about 30 centimeters in diameter and about 10 centimeters deep, and are made principally of sticks, with some weeds and a lining of grasses or other soft vegetation. Nesting on bamboos is especially favored, as are flooded tamarisk trees or mangroves, and old nests may be refurbished if they are still usable (Baker, 1929, 1935).

Egg laying and incubation.   The typical clutch is from three to five eggs, with six-egg clutches exceptional (Baker, 1929, 1935). Incubation is by both sexes, but the incubation period is still unreported.

Brooding and rearing of young.   No specific information is available. Roberts (1991) noted that, as expected, both sexes feed their young by regurgitation.

Breeding success.   Little information is available. Hancock (1984) indicated that 3,153 nests at Bharatpur held 2,038 young of unspecified ages, suggestive of a low rate of breeding success in that year.

Population Status

This is one of the commonest and most widely distributed cormorants of the Indian subcontinent, and is unlikely to require any conservation measures in the foreseeable future.

Evolutionary Relationships

Siegel-Causey (1988) tentatively included this very poorly

Guanay shag, adults.

PHOTO BY KENNETH FINK.

Imperial shag, pair of the
race *georgianus*, with chick.

PHOTO BY FRANK S. TODD.

Imperial shag, breeding
adult of the race *georgianus*.

PHOTO BY FRANK S. TODD.

Stewart Island shag,
adults (both morphs).
PHOTO BY DON HADDEN.

Campbell Island shag,
adult. PHOTO BY FRANK S.
TODD.

Chatham Island shag,
immature.   PHOTO BY
B. G. TOTTERMAN.

Macquarie Island shag,
adult.   PHOTO BY FRANK S.
TODD.

Auckland Island shag, adult. PHOTO BY FRANK S. TODD.

King shag, adults. PHOTO BY DON HADDEN.

Rock shag, adults.

Pelagic shag, adult at nest. PHOTO BY THOMAS D. MANGELSEN.

Red-faced shag, adult at nest. PHOTO BY AUTHOR.

Spotted shag, adults.

PHOTO BY BRIAN CHUDLEIGH.

Pitt Island shag, breeding
adult. PHOTO BY BRIAN
CHUDLEIGH.

Anhinga, adult male.

Australian darter, adult
male.   PHOTO BY TOM LOWE.

Australian darter, adult
female.   PHOTO BY TOM LOWE.

African darter, adult

male. PHOTO BY AUTHOR.

Opposite. Eastern white
pelican, breeding pair.
PHOTO BY AUTHOR.

Pink-backed pelican, adults.
PHOTO BY AUTHOR.

Spot-billed pelican, adult
PHOTO BY AUTHOR.

Dalmatian pelican, adult.

PHOTO BY AUTHOR.

Australian pelican, adult
wing-stretching. PHOTO
BY AUTHOR.

American white pelican,
breeding adult. PHOTO
BY FRANK S. TODD.

Opposite. Peruvian brown pelican, nesting colony. PHOTO BY FRANK S. TODD.

American white pelican, nesting colony. PHOTO BY GARY R. LINGLE.

Peruvian brown pelican, breeding adults. PHOTO BY AUTHOR.

Galapagos brown pelican,
breeding adult.

PHOTO BY FRANK S. TODD.

California brown pelican,
nesting colony.

PHOTO BY FRANK S. TODD.

Figure 55. Social behavior of the pied cormorant, including wing-waving (A), gargling (B), pointing (C), gaping (D), pre-takeoff (E), kink-throating (F), and postlanding (G) postures. After sketches in Marchant and Higgins (1990).

Figure 56. Wing-waving advertising display of male pied cormorant (A, after a photo by Peter Slater), plus billing (B), mirror-image pointing (C), precopulatory gaping by the female with the male in beg-waggle posture (D), mounting, with the female in pointing posture (E), neck biting (F), copulation (G), and male hopping to adjacent branch, and female in pointing posture (H). After photos and sketches in Millener (1972).

tween July and September, but on Stewart Island summer and winter breeding appears to be typical, with peak activities from February to April and from August to November (Lalas, 1979). The population of pied cormorants breeding in marine habitats of Western Australia has a similar double-breeding season in autumn or winter (more typically) or spring (only at the Abrolhos Islands colony) (Serventy, Serventy, and Warham, 1971). A colony in Victoria bred from May until November, with a primary egg-laying peak in June and a secondary peak in August-September. Curiously, the highest level of breeding seems to occur when the weather is foul, but perhaps corresponds to the period of maximum prey abundance (Norman, 1974).

Nest sites and nest building.   Colonies are quite variable in size and often impermanent in duration. Frequently nests are placed among those of other cormorants, pelicans, or spoonbills. The nests in a Victoria colony were mostly constructed of *Atriplex* and other nonwoody plants, plus some feathers and sticks, and they were easily lost after high winds. Thus, 10 of 27 tree nests initially active were lost by the end of a single breeding season (Norman, 1974). Nontree nesting is common, especially in coastal and marine habitats. These nests are usually placed on the tops of bushes or artificial structures, but not directly on bare ground or rocks.

Egg laying and incubation.   Eggs are laid at two-day intervals, with nests in a single tree showing some indication of synchronization in laying. The usual clutch is of three or four eggs, with five rarely present (Millener, 1972). Lill and Fell (1990) reported an average clutch size of 3.8 eggs for 50 Australian nests. In a Victoria colony the average clutch sizes for eggs laid in successful nests early in the breeding season (before mid-August) did not show a significant difference from those laid later (3.32 for 256 clutches). Three-egg clutches comprised 37.8 percent of the total eggs laid, and four-egg clutches 54.6 percent (Norman, 1974). Incubation is performed by both adults, which exchange places at least three times a day. The incubation period averaged 31 days for the first-laid egg, 29 days for the second, 27 days for the third, and 26.5 days for the fourth (Millener, 1972).

Brooding and rearing of young.   The young are fed by both parents, in amounts ranging from about 5 to 90 grams (Norman, 1974). By the time they are 16 days old they are sitting up, and at 28 days are able to shuffle along branches. When about four weeks old the young are walking and perching about as well as adults. At that time the young birds begin to form creches on the ground, where they are fed and guarded by the parents. Fledging may occur at between 47 and 60 days, averaging 53 days. The young birds may be fed by parents for up to 80 days after fledging (Millener, 1972).

Breeding success.   Hatching and fledging success among the birds nesting in a Victoria colony were influenced by clutch size (Norman, 1974). No single-egg clutches hatched, but 28.6 percent of the eggs in 21 two-egg clutches hatched, 45 percent of those in 77 three-egg clutches hatched, and 45.3 percent of those in 58 four-egg clutches hatched. Similarly, 83.3 percent of 12 young from two-egg clutches fledged, 67.3 percent of 70 young from three-egg clutches fledged, and 51.4 percent of 134 young from four-egg clutches fledged. Collectively, the reproductive success (percentage of eggs resulting in fledged young) was 23.8 percent for two-egg clutches, 30.3 percent for three-egg clutches, and 23.3 percent for four-egg clutches, showing that the most reproductively efficient clutch size (three eggs) was also the most prevalent clutch size. However, two-egg clutches produced an average of 0.48 fledged young per nest, three-egg clutches an average of 0.91, and four-egg clutches an average of 0.93, so the added egg potential in four-egg clutches effectively compensated for the reduced rearing efficiency. In a New Zealand study (Millener, 1972), the most important single factor affecting the success of a brood was the hatching interval, with total brood size and the sex of the chicks of secondary importance.

Population Status

The New Zealand population of pied cormorants comprises less than 100,000 birds (Robertson, 1988). There are no collective population estimates for Australia, but few colonies in excess of 1,000 pairs are known (Marchant and Higgins, 1990).

Evolutionary Relationships

Siegel-Causey (1988) considered this species to be most closely related to *sulcirostris*, but suggested that *fuscicollis*, which he was unable to study, might also be part of this assemblage.

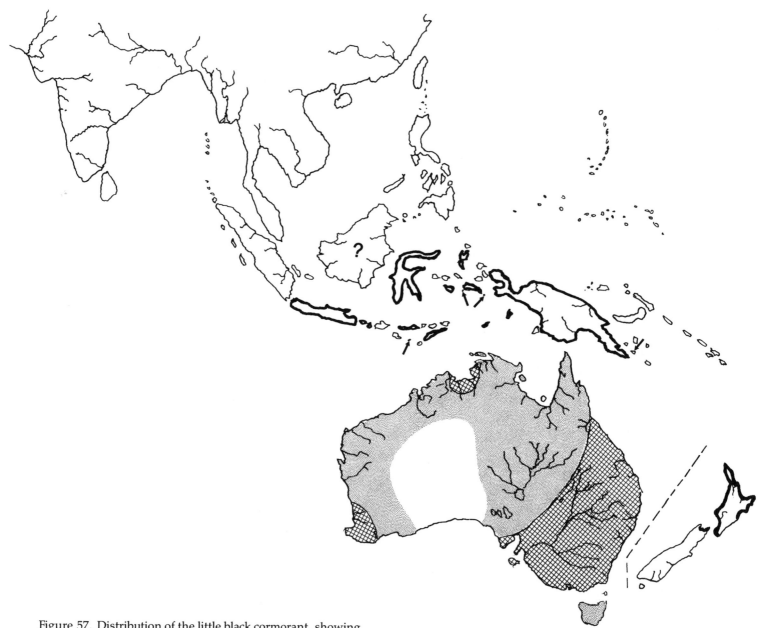

Figure 57. Distribution of the little black cormorant, showing
its breeding or residential range (inked or cross-hatched)
plus its nonbreeding or erratic range (stippled).

Other Vernacular Names

Black cormorant, little black shag; cormoran noir (French); Schwarzscharbe (German)

Distribution

Resident on inland and estuarine waters from Java east through the Moluccas to the New Guinea lowlands (including Aru Islands and Fergusson Islands); also widespread in Australia, including Tasmania, and New Zealand, where more common on the North Island but becoming increasingly common southwardly. Mostly sedentary, but with local movements probably associated with changes in water and food supplies. Nonbreeding visitor to Sumatra. Vagrants have reached Lord Howe and Norfolk islands, and have also been reported from New Caledonia. Dorst and Mougin (1979) included Borneo in the breeding range, but Smythies (1968) reported that there have been no records from Borneo since 1851, when four specimens were collected. (See figure 57.)

Subspecies

None presently recognized. The New Zealand population has sometimes been racially distinguished as *purpuragula*, and the population extending from Java to New Guinea and northern Australia as *territori*.

Description

Prebreeding adult. Head, neck, lower back, rump, upper tail coverts, and underparts brownish black, with a dull oil-green gloss; upper back, wing coverts, and scapulars ashy, each feather with a fairly wide black border; crown blackish brown, the feathers with narrow white edges, producing a grizzled appearance; a small tuft of white filoplumes may also be present behind the ear, a narrow line or cluster of white feathers on each side of the head above the eye, and scattered white filoplumes on the neck; remiges and rectrices (12) blackish. Iris deep green; skin around the eye brownish black to bluish or purplish gray; lores purplish gray to black; bill dark slaty blue-gray, with a blackish culmen, and the mandible patterned with darker tones; gular skin black; legs and feet blackish gray.

Postbreeding adult. Similar to the prebreeding adult, but lacking the white filoplumes on the head and neck, the plumage generally duller and browner, and with less colorful softparts, including a grayish black eye ring and gular skin.

Immature-subadult. The head, neck, and underparts all brownish black, and the upperparts deep brownish gray, the feathers less distinctly margined with brownish black. An adultlike plumage is apparently attained late in the first year of life.

Juvenile. Plumage generally dark silky brown, with some irregular white spots on the paler underparts. Iris brown; bill and facial skin purplish gray; legs and feet dull grayish brown.

Nestling. Initially naked, with dark skin; later covered with blackish brown down, except for a naked purplish gray crown.

Measurements (in millimeters)

Australian sample: wing, males 256–265 (ave. of 6, 260), females 234–247 (ave. of 7, 239); tail, males 126–136 (ave. of 6, 132), females 111–131 (ave. of 7, 121); culmen, males 44.8–47.6 (ave. of 6, 46.7), females 42.5–46.3 (ave. of 7, 44.4) (Serventy, Serventy, and Warham, 1971). New Zealand sample: wing, males 229–264 (ave. of 4, 251), females 230–259 (ave. of 9, 243); tail, males 121–128 (ave. of 5, 126), females 108–141 (ave. of 8, 123); culmen, males 41–53 (ave. of 5, 48), females 41–52 (ave. of 9, 46) (Marchant and Higgins, 1990). Eggs ca. 53 × 33.

Weights (in grams)

Males 794–1,162 (ave. of 27, 956), females 652–1,055 (ave. of 48, 772) (Serventy, 1939). In a sample of 313 males and 214 females collected regularly over a three-year period, the average monthly weights of males ranged from about 800 to 1,200, and females from about 750 to 950, with the highest average weights occurring during periods of rapid gonadal growth (Miller, 1980). The average weight of 20 birds (sex and age composition unstated) from fresh-water habitats was 811; a single bird obtained from a marine location weighed 1,030 (Thompson and Morley, 1966). In a sample of live birds from New South Wales, males ranged 800–1,300 (ave. of 42, 1,100), females 700–1,300 (ave. of 34, 900) (Marchant and Higgins, 1990). Calculated egg weight 31.8.

Identification

In the hand. The combination of a culmen length of 40–50 mm, a brownish black overall plumage with the upperpart feathers having ashy gray centers, and a green iris and blackish facial skin in adults serves to identify this species.

In the field. In Australia this species is the only small, all-black cormorant, and differs from the much larger great ("black") cormorant in having an entirely black bill and face, without any trace of white cheek feathering or any yellow present on the black bill or violet-black gular skin. In New Zealand, much the same applies, but juveniles of the endemic melanistic morph of the comparably sized little pied cormorant and little black cormorants both have an entirely dark plumage. However, juvenile little pied cormorants have short blackish bills that are variably reddish or yellow-orange near the base of the mandible, rather than the relatively longer, more slender, and entirely grayish bills typical of little black cormorants. In Java the much more common but very similar Javanese cormorant has a shorter and entirely yellow, rather than black or gray, bill.

Ecology and General Biology

Breeding and nonbreeding habitats.   Together with the little pied cormorant, this is one of the most widespread and common of the Australian cormorants (Serventy, 1939), occurring on shallow fresh-water ponds, semipermanent to permanent swamps, rivers, billabongs, and large lakes. It also occurs widely along the coast, on habitats including mangrove swamps, salt pans, lagoons, estuaries, brackish waters, and exposed inshore waters, and it even occasionally forages from rock platforms or along offshore islands (Serventy, Serventy, and Warham, 1971; Marchant and Higgins, 1990). It is generally more often found on Australian inland waters than on estuaries, as is also true in New Zealand, but in Tasmania (which it has only recently begun to recolonize) it is most common on estuaries. During the Australian atlas bird survey it was reported from 61 percent of all the survey blocks, which, following the little pied cormorant's 65 percent, was the second-largest proportionate geographic representation of any cormorant (Blakers, Davies, and Reilly, 1984). Based on aerial surveys in eastern Australia, 45 percent of the species' population was found on artificial impoundments, and 90 percent occurred on wetlands under 100 hectares in area (Braithwaite et al. 1985). Water areas exceeding a meter deep and large enough to allow from a few to more than a thousand birds to forage cooperatively are especially favored (Miller, 1979); deep channels of rivers may also provide such opportunities (Dostine and Morton, 1988).

Breeding habitats include areas with foraging opportunities as well as suitable nest sites. Ground nesting is unknown in this species, and trees surrounded by fairly deep water are especially favored. Often the birds nest in colonies of other cormorant species as well as among herons or other large colonially nesting birds such as spoonbills and ibises. Solitary nesting sometimes also occurs, but the social foraging tendencies of the species favor nesting coloniality.

Movements and migrations.   As compared with other Australian cormorants, this species exhibits an intermediate degree of dispersal tendencies. Of birds banded in South

Australia, 31 percent of the recoveries were well beyond the vicinity of banding. These dispersals tended to be oriented coastally, but some birds moved inland to the Murray-Darling river drainage (van Tets, Waterman, and Purchase, 1976). Based on recoveries of birds banded as nestlings, the average distances of dispersal gradually increased with time following banding, from 110 kilometers at two months, to 175 kilometers at three months, to 290 kilometers at five months (Llewellyn, 1983). It is also possible that, as has also been suggested for pied and little pied cormorants, females are more prone to wandering away from the breeding colony during the nonbreeding period than are males (Serventy, 1939; Serventy, Serventy, and Warham, 1971). The longest movement on record is that of an immature bird banded at Lake Brewster, New South Wales, and recovered more than 2,200 kilometers away in New Zealand (Anon., 1949). Additionally, coastal dispersion has been associated with recently and rapidly increasing populations in the Torres Strait region and even in New Zealand (Draffan, Garnett, and Malone, 1983; Robertson, 1988). In Australia true migration is difficult to distinguish from simple dispersal and nomadism associated with varied water conditions, but in New Zealand there may be a general movement toward coastal waters during winter (Marchant and Higgins, 1990).

Competition and predation.   Although the little pied and little black cormorants are widely sympatric, recent studies (Miller, 1979; Dostine and Morton, 1988) indicate that foraging competition between these two species is greatly reduced by differences in foraging behavior, foods taken, and habitat preference (see table 20). Most importantly, little black cormorants tend to forage cooperatively in open water, and feed primarily (ca. 70 percent numerically) on fish, whereas little pied cormorants hunt solitarily in shallow areas and margins, and forage mainly on crustaceans (ca. 60 percent) and aquatic insects. Occasionally, however, little pied cormorants will join a foraging flock of little black cormorants, and in areas where the little black cormorant is less abundant it will forage individually in shallow waters (Serventy, 1939). Significant geographic overlap with the other Australian cormorant species is mostly limited to the pied cormorant, a considerably larger species that is prone to feed on larger and heavier fish (Trayler, Brothers, and Potter, 1989). No specific significant predators have been described for the little black cormorant, but it is probable that crows (interiorly) and gulls (coastally) are important predators of eggs and possibly also young chicks. Whistling kites (*Haliastur spenurus*) have also been observed taking eggs (Marchant and Higgins, 1990).

Foods and Foraging Behavior

Foods consumed.   Several studies of the foods of this species have recently been summarized by Marchant and Higgins (1990). Among five studies that analyzed prey by relative wet weight, the fish component ranged from 73.6 to 100 percent, and crustaceans from 3.9 to 24.8 percent. Among five studies that summarized prey by number, fish comprised 91.5–100 percent, and crustaceans (mostly "yabby" crayfish) 0–3.8 percent. A favorite fish prey is common carp (*Carassius auratus*), which was present in most fresh-water samples, and comprised from 10 to 100 percent of the fish in five studies. Miller's (1979) study is the most complete yet, and involved 625 samples taken throughout the year over a four-year period. In this study, carp comprised 51.8 percent of the total wet weight of prey, followed by yabbies (*Cherax destructor*) at 21.3 percent and redfin (*Perca fluviatilis*) at 14.6 percent. Mean prey lengths for these three species varied from 6.5 to 9.4 centimeters, or slightly less than prey taken by the little pied cormorant in the case of the two fish, but not the yabbies. There were also seasonal differences apparent in mean fish prey lengths, but not in prey length of the yabbies. Somewhat similar results were obtained by Dostine and Morton (1988). There were no significant differences in prey lengths for the two cormorant species. Both concentrated on prey 15–35 millimeters in length, which in the case of the little black cormorant comprised 84.7 percent of all prey items as compared with 70.5 percent for the little pied cormorant. In the case of the fish, most of these prey items were small and relatively abundant species of the littoral zone (see also table 20).

Foraging behavior.   To a greater degree than other Australian cormorants, this species is a highly social forager. Wheeler (1946) observed that when groups of birds were "herding" schools of fish the number of cormorants involved was critical to their success; although 30 were unable to keep a school contained, a flock of 100 was easily able to do so. Thus, large companies of little black cormorants tend to forage cooperatively, often gathering in flocks of several hundred birds where schooling prey is relatively abundant. When schools of fish are seen by flying flocks, they may begin to encircle the school even before all the birds have settled on the water (Serventy, 1939). Essentially the same foraging strategy may occur in fresh-water areas (Miller, 1979). As with other cormorants, dive durations are related to water depths; Trayler, Brothers, and Potter (1989) observed that average dive durations increased from 13.4 seconds in water 1–2 meters deep to 19.3 seconds in waters more than 2 meters deep. Although hunting is certainly done visually, the birds are able to capture prey where visibility is limited to less than 10 centimeters (Barlow and Bock, 1984).

Social Behavior

Age of maturity and mating system.   The adult plumage is attained within a year of hatching, but no definite information is yet available on the age of initial breeding. The pair bond is assumed but not proven to be one of sustained monogamy, a condition that may be facilitated by the long breeding season and the possibility of breeding occurring any time during the year when food supplies and other environmental conditions permit. On the other hand, the somewhat nomadic nature of the species, and its ability to exploit an area for temporary breeding (at least in interior Australia), may make the capacity for rapid formation and dissolution of pair bonds a selective advantage.

Social displays and vocalizations.   Social displays have been little studied, but have been described by Hoogerwerf (1953) and van Tets (in Marchant and Higgins, 1990). Male advertising on the nest or potential nest site consists of wing waving (figure 58A), during which the partially folded wings are raised and lowered at the rate of once or twice per second, with the nape resting on the back, the bill tilted upward, and the tail somewhat cocked. No vocalization accompanies this display, but the violet gular pouch is bulged outward. Individual recognition displays consist of pointing and gargling. During pointing (figure 58E) the bird holds its body fairly horizontal and stretches its neck and head diagonally upward, with the tail somewhat cocked and the bill closed. This is a silent display in both sexes. Gargling (figure 58B) consists of a backward head-throw, with the neck initially extended and the bill open and directed forward and the tail lifted. As the head swings back, a hoarse *hack* note is uttered. As the head reaches the back it is rotated, with the bill now closed. A two-noted *ak-ke* call is croaked by males at this stage, but not by females. Males may perform gargling as a supplemental component to wing waving, but females use the gargling display as a greeting, or at least perform the initial open-bill phase of the display in this situation.

Other displays performed by both sexes include kink-throating (figure 58D) as a nest arrival or greeting ceremony, with males uttering a whistling *tu-tu-tu* call but females remaining silent. Later in the pair-bonding period this whistling note becomes more hoarse and eventually a croaking *krah-krah-krah*. In the pretakeoff display the bird stands very erect as in the kink-throating posture, with its head feathers flattened and its neck feathers erected to form a ruff on the nape. In this posture the throat pulses as ticking sounds are produced by the male, and perhaps also by the female. In the postlanding display (figure 58C) the head and throat feathers are flattened laterally while the crest is raised and the bill is closed and tilted downward. In the prehop posture, which resembles that of the great cormorant, a ticking sound is made. During the hopping display the male screeches loudly but the female is silent.

When threatening another bird, the bill is directed toward the opponent, with the hyoids spread and the upper neck feathers raised. Then the head is moved back and forth, with the bill partly opened and the wings partially spread. At least males call with hoarse, croaking *ake-ake-ake* notes. Nest worrying, the manipulation of nesting materials, may occur at the nest site when the bird is threatened (Marchant and Higgins, 1990).

Figure 58. Social behavior of the little black cormorant, including wing waving (A), gargling (B), postlanding (C), kink-throating (D), pointing (E). A after a photo by Brian Chudleigh; B–E after sketches in Marchant and Higgins (1990).

Reproductive Biology

Breeding season. In New Zealand, breeding occurs at any time conditions allow, but there is a peak of nesting during spring from October to November, and again in autumn from April to May (Robertson, 1988). In northern Australia summer to autumn nesting is typical, but in southern Australia spring to summer breeding is more characteristic, although favorable environmental conditions (food, water, shelter) may result in breeding at any time (Marchant and Higgins, 1990), or at least from spring through autumn (Serventy, Serventy, and Warham, 1971). Miller (1980) reported that in New South Wales the testicular cycles of males were not regulated by any single environmental factor, but the combination of food availability, water level, and temperature or daylight (photoperiod) accounted for more than 85 percent of the observed variations in testicular cycling. Reproduction occurred during wet years, but not in a drought year when there were no flooded and secluded timber sites for nesting. One 11-month breeding season ended despite favorable water levels and food supplies, probably in response to cold weather. By comparison, male little pied cormorants breeding in the same area had a more regular seasonal onset of testicular maturation, but in both species egg laying was highly synchronous within colonies, slightly staggered between colony subunits of 3–12 nests and highly varied between colonies. This high degree of intracolony synchronization, reported by both Miller and Close et al. (1982), suggests that behavioral factors such as social facilitation must also influence breeding cycles. Both species also exhibited a sudden abandonment of nests with eggs and young present at the end of each breeding season, evidently as "panic responses" to impending crashes in food supplies.

Nest sites and nest building. This is a tree-nesting species, and trees near the deeper parts of a swamp are favored. The nests may be located as much as about 15–20 meters above the water level, typically near the tops of the trees (Serventy, Serventy, and Warham, 1971). Usually breeding is colonial, with from several to more than 400 nests present in a single colony (Miller, 1980).

Egg laying and incubation. There is little information on clutch size and incubation behavior. The available evidence suggests that the most common clutch is four eggs, with three-egg and five-egg clutches also common and six eggs occasionally present (Marchant and Higgins, 1990). The incubation period is still unreported.

Brooding and rearing of young. Little information exists on the chick-rearing phase of reproduction, and nothing is known of fledging periods or other aspects of brooding behavior.

Breeding success. No information is available.

Population Status

In New Zealand this is a relatively uncommon species, although its numbers sometimes increase suddenly, apparently as a result of influxes from Australia (Robertson, 1988). It has been increasing in Tasmania since the mid-1970s, perhaps as a result of migration from the mainland. In mainland Australia it is widespread, although most colonies are fairly small and consist of fewer than 100 nests, with only a few records of considerably larger ones (Blakers, Davies, and Reilly, 1984). Mean densities of 1–2.4 birds per square kilometer have been reported for the Alligator Rivers region of Northern Territory, which are similar to densities observed for little pied cormorants in the same general area (Dostine and Morton, 1988).

Evolutionary Relationships

According to Siegel-Causey (1988), this species is a near relative to the pied cormorant, and it forms part of his proposed genus *Hypoleucus*. No other close evolutionary relationships have been proposed and none is clearly apparent, although there are some distinct behavioral similarities with the great cormorant.

Figure 59. Distribution of the great cormorant, showing its breeding or residential ranges (inked, hatched with stippling, or cross-hatched), and its wintering or nonbreeding ranges (stippled). Distributions of its races *carbo* (ca), *hanedae* (ha), *lucidus* (lu), *maroccanus* (ma), *novaehollandiae* (no), and *sinensis* (si) are also indicated.

Other Vernacular Names

Atlantic cormorant *(carbo)*, black cormorant (Australia), black shag (New Zealand), common cormorant, Chinese cormorant *(sinensis)*, European cormorant, Eurasian large cormorant *(sinensis)*, large cormorant, North Atlantic cormorant *(carbo)*, shag, southern cormorant *(sinensis)*, white-breasted cormorant *(lucidus)*, white-necked cormorant *(lucidus)*; grand cormoran (French); Kormoran (German); kawa-u (Japanese)

Distribution

Widely distributed throughout the temperate parts of the Old World, including Europe from northern Scandinavia and the British Isles eastward to the coasts of the former USSR, China, and Japan, and south to northern Africa, India, and southern China; also most of Africa south of the Sahara, much of Australia and Tasmania, and New Zealand; also breeds on Iceland, southwestern Greenland, and eastern maritime Canada (Newfoundland, Nova Scotia, and islands in the Gulf of St. Lawrence). Generally resident throughout much of the breeding range, but the more northerly populations are migratory, and vagrants sometimes stray well outside the regular range. (See figure 59.)

Subspecies

P. c. carbo (Linnaeus). Breeds in northern Europe from the Kola Peninsula and northern Scandinavia south to the British Isles; also on the Faeroes, Iceland, southwestern Greenland, and the maritime provinces of Canada (southern Newfoundland, eastern Nova Scotia, and Cape Breton, Anticosti, Madeleine, and Prince Edward islands). Winters from the breeding areas south to the Gulf coast of North America, the Canary Islands, and northwestern Africa.

P. c. sinensis (Blumenbach) 1798. Breeds in north-central Europe from Belgium and the Netherlands east to the Baltic and Black seas and the Sea of Azov; also breeds from Turkey east locally across central Asia (Kazakhstan wetlands, Lake Baikal) to the Maritime Territory of Siberia and to northeastern China (Nei Monggol Zizhiqu and Heilongjiang), and south to Pakistan, India, southeastern China, and Hainan. Winters from the breeding areas south to the north African coast, the Arabian Sea, Sri Lanka, the Malay Peninsula, Sumatra, the Sundas, and Taiwan. Apparently rare in the Philippines, where it once bred on Calayan, Luzon, and Ticao, but its current breeding status is questionable.

P. c. hanedae Kuroda 1925. Resident on Honshu Island,

Japan, in Aomori, Tokyo, Aichi, and Shiga prefectures, and on Okigurojima, between Kyushu and Shikoku. Now mostly concentrated at Unoyama, Chita Peninsula, Ilse Bay. Often considered synonymous with *sinensis*.

P. c. maroccanus Hartert 1906. Resident in coastal northwestern Africa from Morocco south to Mauritania.

P. c. lucidus (Lichtenstein) 1823. Resident on the Cape Verde Islands; also in adjoining mainland western Africa from Mauritania to Guinea-Bissau, and from Angola south to the Cape of Good Hope; also inland locally in northern Nigeria and the Lake Chad basin, and from Sudan and northern Ethiopia south generally through the Rift Valley lakes and other interior wetlands of eastern Africa to South Africa. Relatively sedentary in Africa, but with some movements of up to a few hundred kilometers. Includes *patricki* Williams. Considered an allospecies by Sibley and Monroe (1990).

P. c. novaehollandiae Stephens 1826. Resident in western, southern, and eastern Australia, Tasmania, New Zealand (all major islands), and the Chatham Islands. Strays occasionally to Lord Howe, Norfolk, Macquarie, Snares, and Campbell islands; vagrants have also reached New Guinea, Indonesia, and Christmas Island. The epithet *carboides* Gould 1838 appears to be a synonym, but was accepted by Marchant and Higgins (1990). The New Zealand population has at times been separated as *steadi* Mathews and Iredale 1913.

Description

Prebreeding adult (of *carbo*). General color black, glossed with dull purplish or bluish sheen; top of head and most of neck covered with long, white filoplumes (larger and more numerous in older birds), often hiding the shorter black plumage below; a large patch of white feathers on each flank; a well-developed crest of black feathers extending to the nape; feathers of the throat forming a wide white border behind the heart-shaped gular skin, the feathers extending medially forward almost to the unfeathered base of the mandible; upper back, scapulars, and wing coverts dull bronze-brown, each feather with a slight greenish gloss; primaries brownish black, with a slight greenish gloss; secondaries more strongly washed with greenish, and margined with blackish; rectrices (14) black. Iris emerald-green; surrounded by a narrow eye ring of variable (gray, yellow and black, or black) color; lores warty, yellow to orange, merging with a yellow to cinnamon or orange-red triangular spot directly below the eye (possibly redder in males, more yellowish in females); bill grayish horn, more dusky along culmen and increasingly yellow toward base of mandible; gular skin

227

variable, from lemon-yellow to black with yellow spots; legs and feet blackish.

Prebreeding adults of *novaehollandiae* similar to *carbo,* but the white nuptial plumes limited to a small patch on the rump and the sides of the upper neck. Orbital ring black, with light bluish purple and beadlike nodules; lores yellow to greenish black, the triangular patch of skin below eye bright orange-red; gular skin black with yellow to bright orange spots.

Prebreeding adults of *sinensis, maroccanus,* and *lucidus* less similar to *carbo,* having progressively greater amounts of white on the head, neck, and upper breast; the first two races having a black stripe extending down the cheeks and sides of the neck, separating the white feathers into two zones. In *lucidus* the white to buffy feathering is sometimes continuous from the throat to the lower breast, and includes the sides of the head and neck, but other individuals have entirely black necks and breasts; this plumage dimorphism is not accompanied by assortative mating. In breeding *lucidus* the lores become yellow (rather than blackish), and a triangular area below the eye changes from yellow to orange or (in most birds) scarlet, with a few birds retaining yellow in that area. The gular skin is olive to dark olive (Brown, Urban, and Newman, 1982).

Postbreeding adult. Similar to the prebreeding plumage, but without the white flank patches and the ornamental white filoplumes; the softpart colors also duller, the iris light green, with a greenish brown eye ring; facial skin, lores, and pouch dull yellow to olive; bill brownish black; legs and feet black.

Subadult. Sexual maturity is reached at 4–5 years, or occasionally at three (Kortlandt, 1942). Third-winter birds are similar to adults in postbreeding plumage, but are less glossy, the crown and hindneck feathers edged with brown. The underparts lack blue gloss, the belly is mottled, and the chin feathers are white, narrowly edged with brown. By their third spring and summer subadults are similar to adults in prebreeding plumage, but the upperparts are less brilliant, and the underparts not such a rich glossy black. The nuptial filoplumes and white flank patches typical of adults may be partially and temporarily acquired at this stage. (This predefinitive plumage description refers to nominate *carbo* (Cramp and Simmons, 1977), but probably is more generally applicable to the other subspecies.)

Immature. Mantle feathers and wing coverts are gradually replaced. Molt of juvenal remiges and rectrices begins during late summer in year-old birds, but primary molt cycles are complex and probably overlapping, and the tenth juvenal primary can be retained until the fourth calendar year. Second-winter birds resemble juveniles, but the crown and hindneck feathers are broader, with glossy blue tips, contrasting with dirty white on the chin and cheeks, and a mottled brown throat. Second-year birds acquire some white filoplumes on the head and neck during spring, which soon

disappear. The iris becomes green after the first year.
Juvenile. Feathers of crown and nape pale brown, with narrow bluish black tips; upperpart feathers brown, more or less tipped with glossy blue or brownish black; scapulars and upper wing coverts dull bronze, more pointed than in adults; small white filoplumes on nape and lower throat; feathers of underparts basally white, tipped with sooty black; underparts variably sooty black to white, the white sometimes extending to the under tail coverts. Iris grayish brown; bill dark brown, with a darker culmen and lighter underside; facial and gular skin greenish yellow; legs and feet black.
Nestling. Hatched naked, with dark slaty blue skin. Covered by sooty grayish brown to black down by end of first week, except for naked whitish forehead, lores, and orbital area. Iris initially bluish gray, later becoming grayish brown; naked head and throat pinkish; inside of mouth flesh-colored; bill initially pink, later becoming dark gray; legs and feet initially pale horn, gradually becoming purplish dusky, with yellowish brown webs.

Measurements (in millimeters, of nonjuveniles)

Of *carbo:* wing, males 350–363 (ave. of 6, 357), females 318–351 (ave. of 12, 339); tail, males 141–159 (ave. of 6, 154), females 135–163 (ave. of 12, 150); culmen, males 67–73 (ave. of 6, 69.6), females 59–68 (ave. of 12, 63.7) (Cramp and Simmons, 1977).

Of *sinensis:* wing, males 330–364 (ave. of 38, 347), females 311–337 (ave. of 18, 325); tail, males 145–165 (ave. of 38, 155), females 133–154 (ave. of 18, 144); culmen, males 58–67 (ave. of 34, 62.6), females 50–58 (ave. of 15, 55.7) (Cramp and Simmons, 1977).

Of *lucidus,* combined samples from coastal and interior of southern Africa: wing, males 322–353 (ave. of 18, 337.2), females 300–332 (ave. of 14, 316.6); tail, males 131–151 (ave. of 16, 139.8), females 119–146 (ave. of 10, 132.0); culmen, males 64–74 (ave. of 17, 68.6), females 60–64 (ave. of 15, 61.6) (Brooke et al., 1982).

Of New Zealand *novaehollandiae* (= *steadi):* wing, males 285–373 (ave. of 22, 353), females 331–385 (ave. of 13, 346); tail, males 141–174 (ave. of 22, 152), females 140–180 (ave. of 13, 153); culmen, males 56–73 (ave. of 22, 66), females 54–70 (ave. of 13, 60) (Marchant and Higgins, 1990).

Of Australian *novaehollandiae:* wing, males 332–355 (ave. of 11, 346), females 312–338 (ave. of 10, 325); tail, males 149–165 (ave. of 11, 153), females 135–153 (ave. of 10, 144); culmen, males 64–73 (ave. of 11, 70), females 59–72 (ave. of 10, 62) (Serventy, Serventy, and Warham, 1971). Sample of live birds from New South Wales: wing, males 320–360 (ave. of 77, 347), females 305–345 (ave. of 228, 327); tail, males 134–165 (ave. of 67, 151), females 123–159 (ave. of 209, 143); culmen, males 61–76 (ave. of 79, 69), females 54–74 (ave. of 221, 62) (Marchant and Higgins, 1990).

Eggs (some minor racial variation) ca. 64 × 41.

Weights (in grams)

Of *carbo:* adult males in spring, 3,170 and 3,600; two females in autumn, 2,127 and 3,490 (Cramp and Simmons, 1977).

Of *sinensis:* both sexes 1,800–3,000 (ave. of 55 males, 2,529; of 25 females, 2,025). Average monthly weights of males: March 2,369, April 2,650, May 2,421, September 2,570; of females: March 1,999, April 2,158; May 2,112, June 1,928, September 1,882 (Dementiev and Gladkov, 1951). Adults in spring: males 2,020–2,810 (ave. of 86, 2,423); females 1,810–2,555 (ave. of 38, 2,085); adults in June, males 1,975–2,687 (ave. of 36, 2,283), females 1,673–2,174 (ave. of 17, 1,936) (Cramp and Simmons, 1977).

Of *lucidus:* females 1,590–1,930 (ave. of 3, 1,780) (Brown, Urban, and Newman, 1982). Average of 3 males from coastal habitats, 3,090, two females were each 2,950. Seven unsexed birds from coastal habitats averaged 2,997, whereas 7 un-sexed birds from interior habitats averaged 1,780, or signifi-cantly lighter than the coastal sample (Brooke et al., 1982).

Of *novaehollandiae:* males 2,253–2,954 (ave. of 6, 2,508), females 1,545–2,110 (ave. of 5, 1,941) (Serventy, 1939). New South Wales sample: males 1,600–3,100 (ave. of 79, 2,400), fe-males 1,200–3,000 (ave. of 288, 2,000) (Marchant and Hig-gins, 1990). The average weight of 13 birds (sex and age composition unspecified) from marine habitats was 2,626; that of 16 birds from fresh-water habitats was 2,018 (Thompson and Morley, 1966).

Calculated egg weights, *carbo* 58, *sinensis* 53, *lucidus* 55 (Cramp and Simmons, 1977); ave. of 81 *lucidus* from Natal, 54 (Olver and Kuyper, 1978).

Identification

In the hand. This large and geographically variable species has a culmen length of at least 50 mm, a wing length that is usually between 320 and 350 mm, a tail (14 rectrices) that is at least 125 mm long, and a patch of generally yellowish gular skin that is margined posteriorly with a highly variable amount of white, the entire throat or neck being white in some populations. It may be distinguished from the very similar Japanese cormorant by its slightly longer wings and its relatively larger gular pouch. The area of bare gular skin extends backward well behind the posterior margin of the eye, and is margined behind with pure white feathers that extend forward medially to a point only slightly anterior to the front margin of the eye and well behind the anteriormost forehead feathers.

In the field. This is the most widespread (and the most geographically variable in appearance) of all the cormorants, and thus is potentially confused with many other large species. It is generally separable from all others by its large size, very long yellowish bill, and adjoining yellowish facial skin and throat, which are bounded posteriorly by a zone of white feathers. This area of contrasting feathering ranges from a narrow white zone (in northern European and North American birds) to the opposite extreme, in which the entire foreneck and upper breast are white (Africa south of the Sahara). Intermediate conditions include populations with white on most or all of the cheeks and throat (Australia, New Zealand), or with the throat, upper foreneck, and sides of the neck variously mottled or striped with black and white (southern Europe, central Asia, and northern Africa).

In Europe, the great cormorant and European shag have widely overlapping ranges and can easily be confused, especially in immature plumages. Alstrom (1985) has provided an extensive account (in Swedish) and numerous helpful drawings illustrating field differences in these two species. However, along the Pacific coast of China, Russia, and Japan, field separation from the very similar Japanese cormorant may often be very difficult if not impossible (see following account).

Ecology and General Biology

Breeding and nonbreeding habitats. This is the most widely distributed of all cormorant species, and occurs over the broadest range of climates, from tropical to arctic, and from sea level to 3,400 meters in elevation (Cramp and Simmons, 1977). It is present in a wide variety of interior fresh-water wetlands ranging in size from deep marshes having open water, swamps, and oxbows to lakes, reservoirs, and large rivers varying in flows from sluggish to quite rapid and even torrential. Coastally, the species occurs on a similar diversity of salt pans, mangrove swamps, deltas, estuaries, coastal la-goons, beaches, rock platforms, and shallower waters up to about 3 meters deep (Marchant and Higgins, 1990). Large, fairly open water areas are favored over shallow and rela-tively vegetated wetlands; variations in salinity and turbidity are apparently unimportant (Fjeldså, 1985). Perching sites in-clude almost any fairly secure and preferably somewhat ele-vated location, such as rocks, shingle spits, sandbanks, trees, breakwaters, seawalls, piers, floating logs, and various aban-doned or unused structures or vessels. Habitats used for breeding are likewise quite varied, and may consist of cliff ledges, rocks, stacks, islets, or stands of trees that are at var-ied distances from water. In eastern Australia an estimated 24 percent of the population was found on artificial im-poundments, and 95 percent on waters larger than 100 hec-tares (Braithwaite et al., 1985). In Africa, both coastal and interior habitats are used by two of the three resident races, but *maroccanus* is strictly coastal (Brown, Urban, and New-man, 1982). In southern Africa the coastally oriented birds sometimes breed as far as 8 kilometers from the sea. This coastal population appears to be quite discrete (being some-what heavier and longer-legged) from the interior one, al-though the two populations have not yet been distinguished racially on morphological grounds (Brooke et al., 1982). In Europe, most of the species' population occurs coastally, as is strictly the case in North America. Among coastal birds, sheltered seas are preferred over open ones for foraging, and some roosting and nesting sites may be several kilometers from the nearest water (Cramp and Simmons, 1977).

Movements and migrations.   In different parts of its range this species is variously sedentary, dispersive, or migratory. Some migration exists in birds that breed in temperate climates; thus some *sinensis* birds that breed in the former USSR are known to winter in India (Abdulali, 1976). Generally, birds from the north Caspian Sea and the Baltic are migratory, often migrating overland to the Mediterranean basin. Some of the birds from the Volga delta may winter on the south Caspian Sea or even as far south as the northern Persian Gulf. However, those from the Balkans, Black Sea, and Turkey are probably mostly dispersive. Those breeding around Iceland and northern Scandinavia disperse around their coasts, with some of the Scandinavian birds reaching the west Baltic Sea (Cramp and Simmons, 1977). British and Irish populations tend to be dispersive coastally, with a small percentage crossing the English Channel but very few crossing the North Sea (Cramp, Bourne, and Saunders, 1974).

In southern Africa there appears to be little indication of migrations rather than normal dispersals. All but two of 16 recoveries from coastal breeding sites were also coastal, the most interior recovery being 55 kilometers inland. The average distance moved was 96 kilometers, and the maximum was 570 kilometers (Brooke et al., 1982). Dispersal of fledglings from a colony in Barberspan, South Africa, was mostly southward, with a mean dispersal of 354 kilometers during the first year, and 359 kilometers for birds older than one year. The maximum recorded movement was 985 kilometers, although one bird moved 926 kilometers within four months of banding (Skead, 1980).

In Australia the species is essentially nomadic, with wide dispersal following inland breeding. Young birds tend to disperse coastally, or to follow river systems in the interiors. Among juvenile birds banded along the Murray-Darling drainage, the mean distance of displacement at two months following banding was 250 kilometers, and 440 kilometers at four months. A similar dispersal pattern was evident among birds banded in South Australia, where the average displacement after five months was 290 kilometers (Llewellyn, 1983).

In North America, birds breeding around the Gulf of St. Lawrence disperse only short distances, and most of them probably never leave the Gulf, although some may move as far as Long Island (Palmer, 1962). However, in recent years they have been reported progressively farther south in very small numbers, extending even to the Gulf coast as far west as Louisiana (Clapp et al., 1982).

Competition and predation.   Competitive interactions must vary greatly in different parts of the great cormorant's range. In Europe, the European shag is broadly sympatric with the great cormorant, and the foods and foraging areas of these two species overlap. However, as shown by Steven (1933) and Lack (1945), there are considerable differences in the foods of the two species, as well as important differences in foraging behavior and nesting habitats (see table 14). Elsewhere, food competition in eastern Asia potentially occurs with the Japanese cormorant, in eastern North America with the double-crested cormorant, in Australia with the pied and black-faced cormorants, and in Africa with Cape and bank cormorants, although no detailed information on the extent of such foraging-niche overlap exists. Egg predation by crows and gulls may well be important locally, but little specific data exists with regard to this topic. In Australia, ravens *(Corvus mellori)* and whistling kites *(Haliastur sphenurus)* take both eggs and chicks. In Nova Scotia corvids and gulls *(Larus argentatus* and *L. marinus)* normally can reach eggs only when the colony has been disturbed by humans. In Africa, eggs or young are consumed by the marabou *(Leptoptilus crumeniferus),* African fish eagle *(Haliaeetus vocifer),* black kite *(Milvus migrans),* kelp gull *(Larus dominicanus),* and fan-tailed raven *(Corvus rhipidurus)* (Brown, Urban, and Newman, 1982). The marabou may take young almost ready to fly, and African fish eagles take chicks up to three weeks old (Urban, 1979).

Foods and Foraging Behavior

Foods consumed.   There is little taxonomic uniformity in the kinds of foods consumed by this species, which primarily consist of fish throughout its broad range. The extensive data from the western Palearctic have been summarized by Cramp and Simmons (1977). British studies (e.g., Pearson, 1968; Mills, 1969) indicate that flatfish, gadoids, and shore and estuarine fish are major prey, and a small percentage of economically significant fish (clupeoids, eels, and salmonids) are consumed. At least in brackish and estuarine habitats, most of the prey are obtained from the bottom, rather than from middle or upper zones. Off the Farne Islands the cormorant consumes a wide variety of sizes of prey, from less than 0.5 to 562 grams, but averaging about 50 grams (Pearson, 1968). Similarly, studies from Denmark indicate that the major food fishes there, such as eels *(Anguilla),* viviparous blennies *(Zoarches),* and cods *(Gadus),* average about 125 grams, with the herrings *(Clupea)* about 90 grams, and secondary fishes averaging 10–75 grams. Most of these are likewise bottom dwellers, although the herrings are pelagic schooling fish that are easy prey during the spawning season when they occur near the surface and close to the coast. Studies in the Netherlands suggest that the birds consume an average of 400 grams of prey per day, with the individual fish usually ranging from 6 to about 500 grams (van Dobben, 1952).

Much less is known of this species' foods in Africa, but on Lake St. Lucia, Natal, the birds foraged in relatively deep water up to a kilometer from shore. They consumed fish that generally weighed less than 50 grams and usually 10–20 grams, although the overall range was 1–214 grams. They consumed an estimated 410 grams of prey per day (Whitfield and Blaber, 1979).

There is likewise only a scanty amount of information on the foods of the North American population, but Ross (1977) reported that, judging from more than 309 prey times obtained from a spring roost, the majority (57.8 percent) were sculpin (*Myoxocephalus*), with cod (*Gadus*) and flounder (*Pseudopleuronectes*) comprising most of the remainder. Samples from a breeding colony indicated that these same species are important during nesting, as are cunner (*Tautogolabrus*) and pollock(*Pollachius*).

Data for Australia and New Zealand are fairly extensive, and are summarized by Marchant and Higgins (1990). They include major studies from Victoria (Mack, 1941; McNally, 1957), New South Wales (McKeown, 1944), Western Australia (Serventy, 1938), and New Zealand (Falla and Stokell, 1945). In these studies fish of generally noncommercial value such as *Carrasius*, *Perca*, and *Anguilla* predominated as prey, except that McKeown's study found decapod crustaceans (*Paratya*, *Cherax*) predominating in birds from fresh-water (though not estuarine) localities. In New Zealand, trout and eels are apparently consumed more often than is the case in Australia, and similarly in Scotland both trout and eels are sometimes consumed in considerable quantities, as are flatfish and some other species of commercial fishery significance.

Foraging behavior.   In spite of the bird's fairly large body size, it generally forages in rather shallow waters. Palmer (1962) stated that the birds usually forage in water no more than about 9 meters deep, and tend to feed on fish that are associated with the substrate, which is often of sand or mud. Stonehouse (1967) stated that they are usually found foraging close inshore, in depths no greater than 2–3 meters. Occasionally the birds may fly as far as 50 kilometers to fishing areas, but they apparently avoid long overland flights, and limit them to once per day if possible (van Dobben, 1952). Foraging is usually done solitarily, although foraging flocks do at times develop; rarely such flocks will number in the thousands of individuals (Marchant and Higgins, 1990).

Social Behavior

Age of maturity and mating system.   According to Kortlandt (1942) and Palmer (1962), maturity usually occurs at 4–5 years, but breeding may occasionally occur at three. More recent estimates are that effective breeding may not occur until the birds are at least two years old, but that some pair bonding may begin in birds approaching the end of their first year. The pair bond is believed to be one of sustained monogamy, but there is no information on the incidence of "divorces" (Marchant and Higgins, 1990).

Social displays and vocalizations.   Classic descriptions of the behavior of the great cormorant were provided by Portielje (1927) and Kortlandt (1940, 1942, 1959), and have more recently been supplemented by van Tets (1965, and in Marchant and Higgins, 1990). The male's primary advertisement display is wing waving (*Flaggen* in German accounts), performed as soon as he has established a territory (figure 60H, see also figure 25). The rhythmic movement of the folded wings, oscillating upward and outward at the rate of 1–2 times per second, produces a semaphore effect as the wings alternately expose and hide the white plumes of the rump and upper thighs. At times the wings are also vibrated rapidly, momentarily exposing the more grayish primaries against the darker secondaries. During high-intensity display the tail is cocked and the head and neck may be pointed vertically upward. No vocalizations are associated with this display. When approached by a female, the male shifts from wing waving to gargling.

The major close-range courtship and individual recognition display, which occurs from the pair-bonding phase onward, is gargling (*Gurgeln* in German, *Gorgelen* in Dutch accounts, and originally called "gaping" by van Tets, 1965). This display differs both in form and vocalizations between the two sexes. In females (figure 60E) the tail is drooped and the head is pulled back only to the vertical. A soft purring call is uttered. In males the head and neck are pulled back to the back, the tail is variably cocked, and a loud double call is produced (figure 60F, G). This call begins as the head pulls back (bill closed) as a loud barking note, and becomes a purring, gargling, rattling *rooo* note as the head is rotated while resting on the back (bill opened). This gargling display corresponds functionally to the similar "gaping" display of several other cormorants, but in most of these other species (such as double-crested and Neotropic cormorants, and pelagic, red-faced, and European shags) the associated motor patterns are not sexually dimorphic (van Tets, 1965).

In contrast to gargling, pointing is similar in both sexes, and is a silent display. It is performed by the bird occupying the nest, with the bill closed but the head and neck directed diagonally upward, whenever its mate returns to the nest site. This display has also been called neck swaying (*nek-zwaaien*) by Kortlandt (1940), and the "forward" display by Palmer (1962). Similar mutual neck swaying also commonly occurs immediately after copulation. Allopreening also occurs between paired birds (Urban, 1979).

During various interactions, such as the arrival of the mate at the nest and greeting the "in" bird there, crest erection and kink-throating are commonly performed (figure 60E). Crest erection includes a general lateral flattening of the head feathers, together with a noticeable lifting of the median crown, nape, and hindneck feathers, making the head appear much larger than normal when seen in profile. This head condition is also assumed by the "out" bird during pretakeoff and postlanding postures (figure 60A–C, D).

Figure 60. Social behavior of the great cormorant, including three stages in the look-crouch-takeoff sequence (A–C), post-landing posture, with raised crest (D), male kink-throating as female performs gaping (E), two forms of the male's gargling display (F, G), male wing-waving display (H), and starting and extended-neck phases of female gaping (I, J). After sketches in van Tets (1965) except for E, which is after a photo (Spillner, 1972).

During the pretakeoff posture a purring *r-r-r-r* note is uttered, and during the postlanding and posthop posture a loud *roooo* note is produced. During kink-throating loud and repetitive sounds are produced by males, while females produce softer and more puffing notes.

Copulation may be preceded by hopping movements of the male toward the female, or sometimes the female simply assumes a receptive prone position, with the neck outstretched and the bill directed forward. Copulation lasts up to seven seconds, with the male nibbling the female's neck feathers during treading (Urban, 1979). No specific postcopulatory displays are present. Prehopping and posthopping postures are like preflight and postlanding posture, indicating that hopping is a symbolic and ritualized flight. Hopping in place may also occur. An actual "circle flight" away from and back to the nest or a nearby perch may also be performed by a pair member.

During threat or nest defense the bird on the nest will gape, spread and lower its wings, cock its tail, and sinuously move its head and neck from side to side. Nest worrying (stick manipulation) may also occur in this situation.

Reproductive Biology

Breeding season.   Breeding seasons are highly variable, with active nests concentrated during spring in the higher northern latitudes, varying from early February to September, with a peak in April or May in the western Palearctic (Cramp and Simmons, 1977; Debout, 1988), and from late May to early July in Canada (Erskine, 1972). Breeding occurs more or less throughout the year in Africa, with peaks in spring (Morocco, Cape Province), during the rainy season (Zaire, eastern Africa) or near the end of the rainy season and early in the dry season (Zimbabwe, Transvaal) (Brown, Urban, and Newman, 1982). In southern Africa the species is mostly a winter breeder, except in the southwestern Cape and along the coast, where summer or year-round breeding occurs (Brooke et al., 1982). In India and Burma the birds breed mostly during the cooler winter months from November to the end of January (Baker, 1929). In Japan eggs may be found from late January or early February onward, and two broods reputedly may be raised in a single season (Brazil, 1991), although this needs confirmation. In Australia breeding perhaps can occur at any time during the year, depending upon environmental conditions. Perhaps nesting normally occurs in cooler latitudes from spring or early summer to autumn, as in Tasmania where it occurs from September to the end of December. In northern Australia breeding is evidently concentrated during the winter from April to August, and in eastern Australia breeding is usually centered from July to the end of October during late winter and spring (Marchant and Higgins, 1990).

Nest sites and nest building.   Nests are quite large and are often substantial enough to be used for several seasons. They may be located in trees or on a rock substrate, with a variety of materials used in their construction. Fairly large sticks comprise the primary structure. Males bring materials to the female, who constructs and modifies or adds to the nest, even well into the incubation and chick-rearing phases.

In Nova Scotia this species is exclusively a ground and cliff nester, breeding on rocky islets or isolated cliffs more than 15 meters high, but on Prince Edward Island it nests in low, dense, stunted spruce (Lock and Ross, 1973). In Europe both tree nests and ground nest sites are used, and occasionally the birds nest in reed beds over water. Nests in trees up to 10 meters above ground and on cliff ledges up to 100 meters above water have been reported there. The coastally nesting population in southern Africa uses a wide array of nest sites, including ground, cliffs or rocks, trees, bushes, and reeds, as well as a great variety of human-made structures. The interiorly nesting population regularly nests in trees (Brooke et al., 1982).

Colonies containing up to 5,000 active nests and 20,000 pairs have been seen in Australia (Marchant and Higgins, 1990), but most colonies are much smaller. Sometimes nesting occurs with other cormorant species or in heronries (Lock and Ross, 1973; Cramp and Simmons, 1977; Brooke et al., 1982).

Egg laying and incubation.   Eggs are laid at intervals of 1–3 days, with two-day intervals probably typical. The usual clutch size is 3–5 eggs throughout the range. Brooke et al. (1982) reported that 332 clutches from southern Africa ranged from one to four eggs, with 41 percent being three-egg clutches. The mean clutch size of this sample was of 2.4 eggs, but some of these nests probably still had incomplete clutches. A somewhat larger sample (but with overlapping data) of 472 South African nests had a mean of 2.54 eggs (Brown, Urban, and Newman, 1982). The mean of 96 Ethiopian clutches was 2.24 eggs (Urban, 1979). A two-year sample of 60 nests in Natal had a mean clutch size of 3.05 eggs, and 40 percent of the clutches had three eggs. In Normandy, where the breeding season is quite prolonged, the mean clutch size is about three eggs, but gradually diminishes through the nesting season (Debout, 1988). North American clutches seem to average somewhat larger than these estimates. A sample of 112 nests from Quebec had a mean clutch of 4.4 eggs and a range of 2–6 eggs, with 47 percent of the clutches containing five eggs (Pilon, Burton, and McNeil, 1983). Similarly, a sample of 30 clutches from Australia averaged 4.1 eggs, with a range of 3–6 (Marchant and Higgins, 1990).

Incubation usually begins with the first egg, but occasionally later, and adults exchange incubation duties at least two or three times a day. During the first few days of incubation the parent tending the nest reportedly holds the tail at a distinct diagonal angle (Urban, 1979). The incubation period for *lucidus* is 27–28 days, with the eggs hatching 1–3 days apart, in laying sequence (Olver and Kuyper, 1978).

Another estimate for *lucidus* was of 28–29 days (Urban, 1979). Incubation estimates for *carbo* and *sinensis* are 28–31 days (Cramp and Simmons, 1977), and for *novaehollandiae* 27–31 days (Marchant and Higgins, 1990).

Brooding and rearing of young. From the time of hatching until the nestlings are 1–2 weeks old, at least one parent is always at the nest. Thereafter, parents are usually at the nest only when they are feeding the young or brooding them at night or during unfavorable weather. The young are fed at regular intervals by direct regurgitation when they are very small, with each feeding sequence lasting about 45 minutes. By about two weeks of age the chicks begin to insert their heads into the mouths of their parents. After they are three weeks old, they are usually fed only once or twice a day, usually once by each parent. In one study (Urban, 1979), feeding often occurred shortly before sunset, and the elapsed time was very short, about 4–18 seconds per feed. Water may also be directly regurgitated into the chicks' mouths, or over their backs, probably to cool them (Olver and Kuyper, 1978). Typically the most active and strongest chick is fed first, and most deaths by starvation occur in chicks under three weeks of age. When the nestling is four weeks old it may begin to hang its head over the side of the nest, and when 5–6 weeks old occasionally flies a few meters. By the time it is eight weeks of age it can fly nearly as well as adults, and at that time parental care typically ceases (van Dobben, 1952; Urban, 1979). An average fledging period of 53 days and a range of 49–56 days was estimated by Olver and Kuyper (1978).

Breeding success. An Australian sample of 19 nests and 87 eggs had a hatching success of only 41 percent, or 1.9 chicks per nest (Marchant and Higgins, 1990). In southern Africa, the average brood size in 105 nests was also 1.9 chicks (Brooke et al., 1982). In Natal, the mean brood size at fledging over a two-year period was 1.6 chicks for 60 nests. Brood size at hatching collectively averaged 2.3 young per nest for all nests, but included 1.6 young for two-egg clutches, 2.2 young for three-egg clutches, and 2.9 young for four-egg clutches. At fledging, average brood size averaged 1.6 young per nest for all nests, but included 1.2 young per nest for two-egg clutches, 1.5 young for three-egg clutches, and 2.0 young for four-egg clutches. Four-egg clutches were thus the most productive per nest, although two-egg clutches had the highest rates of hatching success (80 percent) and fledging success (63 percent) (Olver and Kuyper, 1978). Overall reproductive success (percent of eggs producing fledged young) was 63 percent for 15 two-egg clutches, 49 percent for 24 three-egg clutches, and 50 percent

for 21 four-egg clutches. In a Quebec study there was a hatching success of 69.2 percent for 112 nests, and 84 percent of the young survived for at least the first two weeks, or an average of 2.6 young per nest (Pilon, Burton, and McNeil, 1983). In Nova Scotia, 17 nests produced an average of 1.17 fledged young per nest (Lock and Ross, 1973), a rate similar to the 1.25 young estimated in the Netherlands by Kortlandt (1942).

Population Status

An attempt to summarize the recent population status of the great cormorant in western Europe is provided in table 27, and additional information for North America is presented in table 30. In Canada the species' range and status have apparently not changed in recent decades. Its numbers appear to be constrained by limited nesting habitat and human disturbance of nesting colonies (Erskine, 1972). After an earlier period of decline, the great cormorant's population in Europe has been increasing rapidly in recent years, especially in Denmark and the Netherlands (Hansen, 1984; Anon., 1985). The species' breeding range has been expanding southwardly, with several cases of nesting in France during the 1980s, but it is still absent from Belgium (where it once occurred) and Austria. In southern coastal Africa a total of 2,524 nests were located during a five-year survey, 1977–1981 (Brooke et al., 1982), but no population estimates are available elsewhere in Africa or for any parts of mainland Asia. In Japan the species has been declining for the past 150 years, and is now breeding in only five areas of Honshu, where about 11,000 birds nest (Brazil, 1991). In eastern Australia, aerial surveys covering wetlands in about 12 percent of the land area from 1983 to 1988 indicated populations of 1,745–6,949 birds (mean 3,987), suggesting a potential total Australian population in excess of 30,000 birds.

Evolutionary Relationships

According to Siegel-Causey's (1988) cladistic analysis, this species and *capillatus* are close relatives and share many structural traits, often associated with foraging in shallower waters and on midwater fish. Indeed these cormorants appear to be extremely close relatives, and one wonders what isolating mechanisms other than their well-marked ecological differences might serve to maintain their genetic identities.

JAPANESE CORMORANT *PHALACROCORAX CAPILLATUS*
(TEMMINCK AND SCHLEGEL) 1850

Other Vernacular Names

Sea cormorant, Temminck's cormorant, Ussurian cormorant; cormoran de Temminck (French); Japan-Kormoran (German); umi-u (Japanese)

Distribution

Breeds in central and northern Japan, mainly along rocky coasts and promontories along western and northern Honshu (Awashima, Sado, Hide-jima, Sanganjima), southern Hokkaido (Esanmisaki), northwestern Hokkaido (Rebun, Teuri-jima, Yagishirito), northeastern Hokkaido (Ochiishimisaki, Moyururito, Yururi-to, Daikoku-jima), off Cape Esan in southern Hokkaido, and on the southern Kuril Islands. Also breeds on Okinoshima (in the Korea Strait off northern Kyushu), and bred until 1981 on Chikusen-okino-shima, Kyushu. Breeds locally along coastal China (Gulf of Liaodong, Liaoning, south to Jiangsu), along coastal Korea, and along the southern coast of Siberia's Maritime Territory (Ussuriland north to the Amur River). Also breeds locally on Sakhalin (Cape Aniva and on Moneron Island). Winters along southern coastal Korea, coastal China south to Fujian and Yunnan, and along coastal Japan from Honshu southward through the Ryukyu Islands. Vagrants sometimes reach Taiwan. (See figure 61.)

Subspecies

None.

Description

Prebreeding adult. Head and neck partially concealed by long, white filoplumes; a large patch of white filoplumes also on each flank; a band of white feathers extends from the eye downward behind the heart-shaped gular skin, this band often thickly mottled with dark greenish black; plumage otherwise generally oil-green, shading into dark greenish blue on the head and neck; wing coverts, upper back, and scapulars more greenish bronze, these feathers narrowly margined with very dark green; remiges and rectrices (14) blackish. Iris green; naked facial skin below and behind the eye bright orange-yellow, but the lores blackish; bill yellowish horn, becoming more yellow toward the base and darker along the culmen; inside of mouth yellowish flesh; gular skin yellow; legs and feet blackish brown, with a purplish tint.

Postbreeding adult. Similar to the prebreeding plumage, but lacking the ornamental white filoplumes on the head, neck, and flanks, and the softpart colors probably less bright.
Immature-subadult. Apparently similar to juveniles, except that underparts show increasing amounts of darker feather tips on the breast and belly. Probably also with progressively more metallic sheen on the upperparts. Apparently very similar to comparable stages of *carbo*. Age at sexual maturity unreported.
Juvenile. Almost wholly dull grayish brown to dark chocolate-brown above, without metallic luster. Upperpart feathers darker near the tip, with grayish white edges. Underparts white, with brownish white tinges, and the flanks with larger brown spots. Bill dingy yellow, with a darker culmen stripe; legs and feet black. A color photo of well-grown but unfledged juveniles (Kiyosu, 1959:34) suggests that the young are generally browner (less blackish) than those of *carbo*, have more distinctly yellowish bills, and have whitish underparts that contrast markedly with their dark brown breast, neck, and upperpart coloration. Older juveniles are evidently paler overall than are juveniles of *carbo*, their underparts grading to relatively pale tones on the abdomen, lower breast, foreneck, throat, and cheeks.
Nestling. Not yet well described. The downy covering is initially all black, but the nestling later becomes white below (Yamamoto, 1967). The well-grown but still-downy young are uniform dark chocolate-brown, with blackish feet and bills, bare whitish crowns, and yellow gular skin.

Measurements (in millimeters)

Wing (flattened), males 326–337 (ave. of 6, 330), females 305–325 (ave. of 11, 315); tail, males 135–146 (ave. of 6, 139.8), females 128–144 (ave. of 8, 135.7); culmen (from forehead feathers), males 67.4–71.8 (ave. of 6, 70.1), females 59.2–72.5 (ave. of 12, 63.9); tarsus, males 67–73 (ave. of 6, 70.5), females 62–70 (ave. of 12, 65.8) (specimens in Yamashina Institute for Ornithology, courtesy T. Hiraoka). Eggs ca. 62 × 40.

Weights (in grams)

One adult male 3,325, 2 adult and 1 immature female 2,356–2,419 (ave. 2,394); 2 unsexed birds 2,542 and 2,587 (specimens in Yamashina Institute for Ornithology; courtesy T. Hiraoka). One adult female 2,860; 1 immature female 2,460 (Museum of Vertebrate Zoology specimens). Calculated egg weight 54.7.

Figure 61. Distribution of the Japanese cormorant, showing its overall Asian breeding range (inked), known breeding localities in Japan (arrows), and its overall wintering range (stippled).

Identification

In the hand. Identified by the combination of a wing length of (usually) no more than 330 mm, a tail length of (usually) no more than 140 mm, and a yellow gular skin that extends back only to a point directly below the posterior margin of the eye. The yellow gular skin is margined posteriorly by a zone of usually mottled dark and white feathers that extend

forward medially approximately to a point directly below the anteriormost feathers of the forehead. Additionally, only the facial skin below and behind the eye is bright yellow. In the great cormorant the area of exposed gular skin is more extensive, and the median throat feathers do not reach so far forward. Further, the bare skin in front of the eye is often yellowish or reddish. In breeding condition the white filoplumes on the head of the Japanese cormorant are much longer and more conspicuous. Most skeletal elements of the Japanese cormorant are distinctly longer than those of the great cormorant. The pectoral appendage bones collectively average 8 percent longer, and the pelvic appendage elements average 21 percent longer (Ono, 1980).

In the field. The only serious problem for field identification involves the nearly identical but slightly smaller great cormorant, which is essentially limited to fresh-water habitats and generally exhibits a more immaculate white margin behind the gular skin, rather than the somewhat mottled black and white band typical of the marine-oriented Japanese cormorant. The yellowish gular skin visible from the side below the lower mandible is somewhat less evident in the Japanese cormorant than in the great cormorant, and scarcely extends backward to a point below the posterior edge of the eye (forming a rather V-shaped lateral profile, similar to that of the Neotropic cormorant, rather than a relatively U-shaped profile). The Japanese cormorant also exhibits a somewhat more greenish (less bronzy brown) gloss on its upperparts. The Japanese cormorant has more conspicuous white filoplumes on the sides of the head and neck when in full breeding plumage than does the great cormorant, but in both species these ornamental feathers are fully developed for only a relatively short time in spring, making this a rather questionable criterion for practical field use. Juvenile Japanese cormorants are paler throughout, but especially on the cheeks, throat, foreneck, breast, and lower underparts, than are juvenile great cormorants, which tend to have distinctly dark breast and foreneck coloration. The Japanese cormorant rarely winters on inland waters, whereas the great cormorant is mostly limited to fresh-water habitats throughout the year.

Ecology and General Biology

Breeding and nonbreeding habitats. Nesting typically occurs on the tops of rocky coastal islands, where the cliffs often rise 20–60 meters in height and are fairly flat-topped (Yamamoto, 1967; Fujimaki, Hyakutake, and Matsuoka, 1976; Nakagawa, 1985).

Movements and migrations. Only a limited amount of information exists. The few band recoveries so far available from Japanese banding efforts (Yamashina Institute for Ornithology, 1987) suggest that only short-distance dispersals are typical.

Competition and predation. On many islands off Hokkaido this species nests in close proximity to red-faced shags, but these species use quite different nest sites, and so do not compete on that basis. Various gulls and corvids (*Corvus corone, C. macrorhynchos*) also occur on these islands, and probably represent potential egg and chick predators. The black-tailed gull (*Larus crassirostris*) and especially the large and predatory slaty-backed gull (*L. schistisagus*) often nest in close proximity to the cormorants, and thus may be

significant predators. Predation by white-tailed sea eagles (*Haliaeetus albicilla*) has also been observed (Yamamoto, 1967).

Foods and Foraging Behavior

Foods consumed. No detailed information.
Foraging behavior. No information from the wild; foraging behavior by captive birds was described in chapter 4.

Social Behavior

Age of maturity and mating system. No information, beyond the obvious typical pelecaniform condition of seasonal monogamy.
Social displays and vocalizations. No information.

Reproductive Biology

Breeding season. Nesting times for various populations of this species were summarized by Fujimaki, Hyakutake, and Matsuoka (1976). On Yururi and Moyururi islands, off eastern Hokkaido, eggs were laid in early May and hatched in early June, with some eggs reported as late as mid-July and fledged young by as early as July 21. On Teuri and Esan islands, off Hokkaido, eggs have been seen from June 11 to 19, while on Shirotsune Island (Iwate Prefecture) eggs have been seen from May 4 to June 17, small young in mid-June, and middle-sized to older young from mid-June to early July. On a colony on the Shiretoko Peninsula, northern Hokkaido, nests with incubating eggs have been reported as late as July 26 (Nakagawa, 1985).

On Karamzina Island, Peter the Great Bay, Russia, nest building has been seen in mid-May, and both fledged and large unfledged young were observed in mid-August. Likewise in Primorskiy, Maritime Territory of Siberia, eggs have been reported in early to mid-July (4–12), and chicks of small to large size in mid-July (Fujimaki, Hyakutake, and Matsuoka, 1976).

Nest sites and nest building. Nest sites on Yururi and Moyururi islands are entirely limited to flat and fairly broad cliff tops and rocky islets. Where it nests close to red-faced shags, the Japanese cormorant takes the flat areas just above the cliffs while the red-faced shags nest on the lower cliff ledges (Fujimaki, Hyakutake, and Matsuoka, 1976). Nest building takes about 10 days, and materials are collected from near the nest site. Many of the nests are scanty, but materials continue to be brought in by the male after egg laying is complete (Yamamoto, 1967).

Egg laying and incubation. Mean clutch size is still unknown for this species, but since the typical initial brood size is three young, it is likely that three eggs constitute the usual clutch. Incubation lasts an estimated 34 days and is performed by both sexes. At times the apparent male has been observed to feed his incubating mate and then remain standing nearby (Yamamoto, 1967).

Brooding and rearing of young. Shibata (1972) observed adults feeding small chicks in late June near Miyako city, Iwata Prefecture. He observed that some pairs fed their young as often as seven times during a little more than an hour, and others nine times during about three hours. Generally, foraging activities occurred about five times a day, with a high level of morning and evening activity. The chicks were brooded in shifts of 2.5–3 hours. Occasionally the adults would regurgitate water, perhaps to cool the chicks, but it usually missed them. Yamamoto (1967) also observed the parents disgorge water on their chicks, which was done twice per chick, the parents thus returning with water four times at intervals of about five minutes. He also observed that the chicks began to leave their nests at about 40 days.

Breeding success. Little information is available. Fujimaki, Hyakutake, and Matsuoka (1976) reported a minimum average brood size of 2.5 young for 71 nests. Those nests located on isolated rocks had a higher average brood size (2.8 chicks) than those located on cliff tops (2.4). Nakagawa (1985) tabulated nests in one colony containing chicks of small, medium, and adult size. Among the nests having adult-sized young (and including some apparent repeat counts), 9 contained one chick, 7 contained two chicks, and 6 contained three chicks, representing an average brood size of about 1.9 nearly fledged chicks.

Population Status

Watanuki, Kondo, and Nakagawa (1988) estimated the Hokkaido population at 1,900 breeding pairs in the 1980s, and considered it to have increased during the previous decade at a substantial annual rate of 5.1–17.9 percent. They listed known recent colonies at Shiretoko Peninsula (508 pairs in 1987), Yururi Island (68 pairs in 1987), Moyururi Island (150+ pairs in 1987), Daikoki Island (214 pairs in 1986), Cape Esan (3+ pairs in 1965), Cape Ofuyu (80+ pairs in 1984), and Teuri-jima (estimated 500 pairs in 1984). On the western coast of the Shiretoko Peninsula 20 colonies are known to exist; these have fluctuated considerably between 1979 and 1985, but with no clear upward or downward direction. From south to north they occur near Horobetu (7 colonies), Iwaobetu (7 colonies), Kamui Wakka (1 inactive colony), Takoiwa (1 colony), Itashube Watara (2 colonies), and Misaki (2 colonies) (Nakagawa, 1985). Hasegawa (1984) estimated the Hokkaido population at about 1,000 birds, plus another 100 birds located north of the Noto-Izu peninsula on the western coast of Honshu. Brazil (1991) has also very recently summarized the distribution and status of this species in Japan, noting that the three largest known breeding areas are at Yururi-to and Moyururi (over 200 nests in 1972), the Shiretoko Peninsula colonies (690 nests), and Teuri-jima (750 pairs). Nearly 16,000 breeding birds probably occur in southeastern Siberia, with about 7,000 on the Kuril Islands, 5,000 along the mainland coast of the Japan Sea, 3,000 at Peter the Great Bay, and 100–150 along the south coast of Sakhalin Island at Cape Aniva and on Moneron Island (Litvinenko and Shibaev, 1991).

Evolutionary Relationships

The closest relative of this species is certainly the great cormorant, and it is interesting that the two species seem to be parapatric in their Japanese breeding distributions.

Other Vernacular Names

Socotra cormorant; cormoran de Socotra (French); Sokotra-Kormoran (German)

Distribution

Resident or periodic resident on islands in the Persian Gulf, including Umm al Maradim (1905), Qaruh (1905), Kurayn (1979, 1980), Arabiya (1938), Zakhnuniyah (1980), and Sama-mik (1980) islands in the northwestern Gulf off the Kuwait and Saudi Arabian coast (Gallagher et al., 1984; Bundy, Conner, and Harrison, 1989). It has also bred (1972, 1976) on Sheedvar Island off southern Iran, and possibly (1921) on Farisiya Island (Gallagher et al., 1984). It sometimes breeds (1974, 1976, 1981, 1983) in large numbers on the Howar group off Qatar, and has bred on Halul (1919, 1921), Al Ashat (1970, 1972), and Shara'awh (Gallagher and Rogers, 1978; Jennings, 1981; Gallagher et al., 1984). Also breeds on several islands off the Trucial Coast of the United Arab Emirates, especially Zarka (1965, 1977, 1981), but also Furayjidat (1972) and Dalma (1975) (Gallagher et al., 1984; Richard, 1990). Other recent UAE breeding locations include Siniyal (off Umm al Quwain), Arzanah, and Qarnein (Dipper, 1991). Also probably breeds regularly on Hasikiyah (1977, 1978, 1984) in the Kuria Muria group off Oman, and perhaps on other islets of the Arabian Sea coast off South Yemen, such as Baraqa (Bailey, 1966; Gallagher and Rogers, 1980). Uncommon migrant west to the Red Sea coast, but probably does not breed on Socotra Island (Gulf of Aden), where the type specimen was obtained (Meinertzhagen, 1954; Ripley and Bond, 1966; Gallagher et al., 1984). (See figure 62.)

Subspecies

None.

Description

Prebreeding adult. Entire plumage black, with purplish gloss on forecrown; feathers of upperparts glossed deep slate-green with black feather tips, producing a marbled effect; a tuft of whitish filoplumes behind eye; neck also flecked with white filoplumes and rump with fine white streaks. Chin feathers terminating in a straight line below the base of lower mandible. Remiges and retrices (14) black. Iris green; facial skin and gular skin blackish; bill grayish black, becoming greenish at base of lower mandible; legs and feet black.

Postbreeding adult. Like the prebreeding adult, but less glossy in color, and lacking the tuft of white behind each eye and the white streaks on the rump, and with less white flecking on the neck.

Immature-subadult. Generally brownish above, the mantle and scapulars with darker spotting, and the underparts browner than in juveniles, with darker spotting on the throat and breast. It is not known when the iris becomes green, nor when the facial skin, gular skin, and legs become black. It may perhaps require three or four years to attain the definitive plumage (Gallagher and Woodcock, 1980).

Juvenile. Crown and upperparts mostly dull grayish brown, the upper wing coverts pale brown, most feathers with indistinct paler edges and darker centers. Chin, throat, and foreneck whitish, and the underparts generally dirty white, washed with speckled brown; remiges and rectrices brown. Iris gray; facial skin dull yellowish; bill dark gray or pale brown; legs and feet brownish.

Nestling. Naked at hatching; later covered with white to grayish white down; iris dark; facial skin, gular pouch, and bill flesh-colored; legs and feet ivory-white to yellow-flesh.

Measurements (in millimeters)

Wing (sample size unspecified), males 285–310, females 275–298; two adult males 288 and 296; one immature female 274; tail, one adult male 85, two immature females 83 and 84; culmen, two adult males 69 and 73, one immature female 74; tarsus, two adult males 73 and 75, two immature females 73 and 74 (Cramp and Simmons, 1977). Eggs ca. 57 × 39.

Weights

No information. Calculated egg weight 47.8 grams.

Identification

In the hand. The combination of an adult culmen of at least 69 mm, a tail of 80–85 mm with 14 rectrices, and the black facial and gular skin serves to identify this species.

In the field. This shag is likely to be encountered only in the Persian Gulf or off the northeastern coast of Africa (Gulf of Aden and Red Sea coasts), and is the only one that appears entirely black when adult, including its relatively long, slender bill and softparts. The great cormorant also winters in some of these same regions, but is considerably larger, has a relatively heavier and shorter bill, and has yellow on the face and gular skin that is bounded posteriorly by white or buffy feathers.

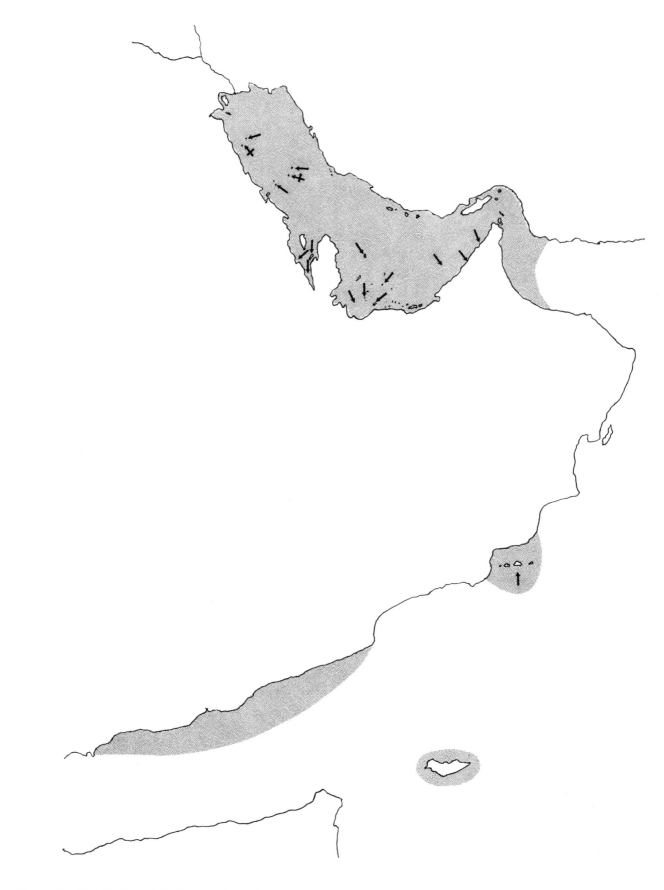

Figure 62. Distribution of the Socotra shag, showing known breeding localities (arrows), inactive breeding sites (crossed arrows), and its overall wintering range (stippled).

Ecology and General Biology

Breeding and nonbreeding habitats. Little information is available, but the birds occupy coastal cliffs and islets as roosting sites, and forage well offshore. Breeding is apparently limited to offshore islands and islets with level sand or gravel areas, or sloping hills (Gallagher and Woodcock, 1980).

Movements and migrations. There is probably some dispersal during the nonbreeding season, at least within the Persian Gulf, but separating seasonal movements from dispersal is difficult. There is no evidence yet of any mixing between the Arabian Sea and Persian Gulf populations (Gallagher et al., 1984). On the southeastern coast of Arabia the birds probably breed during the summer (July-August) monsoon, when cool and nutrient-rich waters occur inshore (Cramp and Simmons, 1977).

Competition and predation. The appreciably larger great cormorant also occurs on the Persian Gulf during winter, but the degree of ecological interaction between these species is unknown. No information on predators exists, but the birds are known to be sensitive to tick ectoparasites that might cause them to desert their nests (Gallagher et al., 1984).

Foods and Foraging Behavior

Foods consumed. No specific information; fish are believed to be the main prey (Cramp and Simmons, 1977).

Foraging behavior. When fishing, the birds are reported to remain submerged for 1–3 minutes, in water 6–10 meters deep (Meinertzhagen, 1954). These surprisingly long diving times suggest that very deep diving might also occur. Flock foraging is apparently well developed (Ticehurst and Cheesman, 1925; Gallagher and Woodcock, 1980), so probably many of the fish are of schooling type, and taken from middle to upper water levels. Bundy, Conner, and Harrison (1989) stated that the birds are usually seen as large packs flying low over the surface, with individuals reportedly "plunge-diving" into the sea at regular intervals, and then rising and circling in hurried flight to repeat the dive. Such behavior by adults is especially associated with the times that most young are being fed at the breeding colonies.

Social Behavior

Age of maturity and mating system. No information.

Social displays and vocalizations. Nothing is known of these topics. The birds are highly gregarious at all times, and colonies of up to as many as 250,000 pairs have been reported, as well as flocks of up to 25,000 birds at sea (Gallagher et al., 1984; Bundy, Conner, and Harrison, 1989).

Reproductive Biology

Breeding season. Breeding in the Persian Gulf reportedly occurs during summer and on the islands off southeastern Arabia during winter (Gallagher and Woodcock, 1980), although Meinertzhagen (1954) stated that eggs are laid on Halul Island (Persian Gulf) from the last week in January to mid-March. On the Kuria Muria islands nesting reportedly occurs from late June to October (Gallagher & Woodcock, 1980). On islands off Saudi Arabia nests with eggs have been reported in April, May, September, November, and December (Bundy, Conner, and Harrison, 1989). Available information suggests that the species breeds in most months of the year, although it may nest only during late summer off southern Arabia (Gallagher et al., 1984). Probably the breeding season is rather irregular, and presumably is keyed to local food supplies.

Nest sites and nest building. Nests are sometimes placed quite close together. Colonies usually number 50–100 pairs, but assemblages of as many as 10,000 pairs are known, and as many as 250 nests within an area of 1,000–1,500 square meters, or a density of a nest per 4–6 square meters (Ticehurst, Cox, and Cheesman, 1925; Löppenthin, 1951). The largest reported nesting colonies are from the Howar group, off Qatar, where up to 250,000 birds were seen nesting in October of 1981, but several other locations along the Trucial Coast (Furayjidat, Dalma, Zarka) have also supported thousands of nests (Gallagher et al., 1984).

Egg laying and incubation. The nests are simple scrapes on gravel or on stony ridges of low islands, or among boulders. The usual clutch is reported to be of 2–4 eggs, but Löppenthin (1951) found no clutches of three, 15 of two eggs, and most of the rest (out of a total of about 250 nests) with only a single fresh egg. So far, very little information exists on nesting biology (Gallagher et al., 1984).

Brooding and rearing of young. No specific information is available.

Breeding success. No information. The birds are said to be very shy and susceptible to disturbance by humans, aircraft, and related human activity (Gallagher et al., 1984).

Population Status

Recent information (Gallagher et al., 1984; Bundy, Conner, and Harrison, 1989) predates the Persian Gulf war, and thus is of uncertain value. The latter account mentioned flocks numbering up to 25,000 or more near the mainland from December to May, and some colonies of 10,000–25,000 nests. Gallagher et al. (1984) summarized available information on all the known breeding areas for the species, and noted that in October 1981 some 50,000–250,0000 birds were nesting in the Howar group, off Qatar, and 20,000–30,000 were nesting on Zarka (Zirkuh), off the United Arab Emirates. In December 1987 about 100,000 birds, with at least 1,000 on eggs, were seen at Siniyal, off the UAE coast near Umm al Quwain (Dipper, 1991). However, these large colonies are few in number, and many are located in areas affected by the recent Gulf war. The species has recently been classified as "near-threatened" by the ICBP (Collar and Andrew, 1988), and probably has been additionally endangered by recent oil spills and other environmental disturbance in the Persian Gulf. In the August 1991 issue of *National Geographic* (180 [2]:14–15) a map showing the extent of oil spills emanating from Kuwait, as of March 1991, indicated that several known "cormorant and tern" breeding areas had probably been directly affected by the oil, including Awhah, Kubbar, Qaruh, and Umm al Maradin off Kuwait, and to a lesser degree Harquis, Karan, Kurayn, Al Arabiyah, and Abu Ali off Saudi Arabia. Breeding sites off Bahrain (Al Manamah), those in the Gulf of Bahrain, and several in the lower Gulf between Qatar and the Trucial Coast (Halul, Zarka, Qarnein, and Arzanah) had not yet been affected.

Evolutionary Relationships

Siegel-Causey (1988) considers this species plus the Cape and guanay shags to represent a well-isolated group of "guano" or "trek" shags. All of these species are highly gregarious, flock foragers of tropical to southern geographic orientation, and mostly associated with cold-current ocean upwellings.

Other Vernacular Names

Cape shag; cormoran du Cap (French); Kapkormoran (German)

Distribution

Endemic to the coastlines of southwestern Africa, ranging during the nonbreeding season from the mouth of the Congo River south and east to Durban. Breeding colonies are restricted to the coasts of Namibia (north to Walvis Bay and Sylvia Hill) and adjacent western South Africa (south and east to southern Cape Province). (See figure 63.)

Subspecies

None.

Description

Prebreeding adult. Head, neck, lower back, rump, upper tail coverts, and entire underparts black, glossed with dull purplish blue, the head, neck, and cloacal area with scattered white filoplumes; upper back, wing coverts, and scapulars dark bronze-green, each feather margined with deep steel-blue; remiges and rectrices (14) black, with some greenish gloss; lores feathered. Iris turquoise-blue; beads on eyelids bright blue; gape skin yellow; bill black distally, the basal third bright bluish gray; gular skin coarsely surfaced and deep yellow-orange; legs and feet black.
Postbreeding adult. Differs from the prebreeding plumage in lacking the white filoplumes. Iris gray to light turquoise-blue; eyelids with pale blue margins; gular skin yellow.
Immature-subadult. Wing and scapulars brown with glossy sheen; throat and breast paler brownish, more or less glossed with oil-green, and the chin, foreneck, and upper breast paler brown. Iris bluish gray; bill yellowish to black, gular skin smooth and pale yellow (with black and/or white speckling in younger birds); legs and feet black.
Juvenile. Generally dark brown on the upperparts, with the sides of the face, throat, lower neck, and upper breast grading sharply into whitish. Iris gray; gular skin dull black, white, or speckled; legs and feet brownish.
Nestling. Hatched with black naked skin, with pink undersides and extremities. Covered with charcoal to dull black down within a week.

Measurements (in millimeters)

Both sexes, wing 245–275 (ave. of 10, 254), tail 86–100 (ave. of 10, 95), culmen 50–56 (ave. of 10, 54) (Brown, Urban, and Newman, 1982). Eggs ca. 55 × 35.

Weights (in grams)

Seven adult males 800–1,550 (ave. 1,171), 6 adult females 1,000–1,225 (ave. 1,142) (U.S. National Museum specimens). Average of 24 males, 1,330 (47 oz.), of 11 females, 1,104 (39 oz.); of immatures of both sexes, 1,160 (41 oz.) (Rand, 1960). Average of males 1,306, of females 1,155 (sample sizes unstated, but over 200 birds in total) (Berry, 1976). One male 1,306, one female 1,155 (Brown, Urban, and Newman, 1982). Calculated egg weight 37.1; average of 25, 38 (Berry, 1976).

Identification

In the hand. The combination of a culmen exceeding 49 mm, a tail of 14 rectrices and no longer than 100 mm, feathered lores, and yellow gular skin identifies this species.
In the field. Limited to the southwestern coast of Africa, this species is the only cormorant or shag of that region that is all black except for a bright yellow throat and gape area.

Ecology and General Biology

Breeding and nonbreeding habitats. This is strictly a coastal species. It ranges from the coast outward to about 70 kilometers, but is usually found within 10 kilometers. It is more often seen at sea off southern Africa than any of the other coastal cormorants, and it is perhaps the most abundant of these, with a probable population in excess of a million birds (Rand, 1960; Brown, Urban, and Newman, 1982).
Movements and migrations. During the nonbreeding season there is an extensive dispersal or migration away from the breeding localities, with the limits of the nonbreeding range extending from the mouth of the Congo River in the northwest to Durban in the east. Much of this movement is probably undirected, as flocks follow schooling fish, and additionally dispersal by immatures must also contribute. Berry (1976) listed over 30 band recoveries representing movements of more than 100 kilometers, with a maximum of 1,430 kilometers. The longest period between banding and recovery was slightly more than nine years. He also observed daily one-way movements of at least 40 kilometers by adults during the chick-feeding period.
Competition and predation. Potentially great foraging competition exists between the extensively sympatric Cape shag and the bank cormorant, but a comparison of the ecology of their major prey species (see table 17) indicates

Figure 63. Distribution of the Cape shag, showing overall
residential range (stippled) and locations of breeding colonies (arrows). Unmarked colonies have only a few birds present. Small dots indicate colonies of up to 10,000 birds; open
circles those of 10,000–100,000 birds, and large dots those of
more than 100,000 birds. After Crawford et al. (1982).

that the degree of foraging overlap is actually small. Substantial differences in the foods and foraging behaviors of the other two coastally distributed cormorants (the considerably larger great cormorant and the much smaller crowned cormorant) also exist (Rand, 1960). In another study, Cape shags were found to take considerably smaller prey (pelagic gobies *Sufflogobius*) than the slightly larger bank cormorant (Cooper, 1985b).

Studies of nest site preferences of the four major seabird species (Cape shags and bank cormorants, plus jackass penguins *Spheniscus demersus* and Cape gannets *Morus capensis*) nesting on islands off southern Africa indicate that marked habitat partitioning exists (Duffy and la Cock, 1985). The gannets and penguins are larger and can effectively displace cormorants, but minor interspecific differences exist in nest placement. Of the various interspecific combinations, Cape shags and Cape gannets had an estimated 9–21 percent overlap of nesting habitats, and a slightly lower overlap existed between Cape shags and jackass penguins. Cape shags nested mostly on very steep slopes or rock outcrops not used by gannets, and also on mainland cliffs. The penguins nested mostly under rocks or in burrows. Bank cormorants nested on large boulders along the intertidal zone. Very little overlap in nesting areas occurred between these species.

Berry (1976) reported that black-backed jackals (*Canis mesomelas*) cannot reach nesting islands and thus are a threat only along the coast, mostly to roosting birds. Other large mammalian predators such as hyenas, cheetahs, and domestic dogs may also catch a few birds along the coastline. On their relatively isolated and secure nesting platforms the most evident predators are adult great cormorants and adult as well as fledgling eastern white pelicans (which share the nesting platforms). Both of these species sometimes swallow young nestlings alive, and the pelicans additionally consume eggs. Kelp gulls (*Larus dominicanus*) also consume eggs and young birds as large as the downy stage.

Foods and Foraging Behavior

Foods consumed. The major foods consist of pelagic schooling fish. Rand (1960) reported that the foods found in 204 stomachs of birds obtained off the South African coast consisted numerically of 91 percent fish, 9 percent crustaceans, and a few cephalopods. Fish comprised 94 percent of the total prey mass. Numerically the inshore schooling sand eels (*Ammodytes*, Ammodytidae) were most important, followed by the more pelagic windtoys (*Pterosmaris*, Centrocanthidae), massbankers (*Trachurus*, Carangidae), pilchards (*Sardinops*, Clupeidae), and anchovies (*Engraulis*, Engraulidae). The mean weight of prey per stomach was 51.6 grams, and the estimated daily consumption was 140–280 grams. From the same region, Davies (1956) observed a higher incidence of pilchards and anchovies. Berry (1976) examined the food remains found in 93 birds collected in Namibia, and determined an average total

undigested prey weight of 133 grams. He also estimated a daily food intake of 133–266 grams per day. There, pilchards and secondarily anchovies comprised over 90 percent of the prey by both mass and number. Similarly, Matthews (1961) found in a sample of 210 birds from Namibia that pilchards were the most important prey, as was likewise reported in a later analysis by Matthews and Berruti (1983).

Foraging behavior. These birds often forage in flocks, whenever schooling fish are available. Flocks will swoop down on such a school and pursue it, the individual birds moving forward in a series of leapfrogging movements. Additionally, they sometimes feed solitarily in bays and harbors, sometimes even when others are hunting in flocks nearby. Foraging activity seems to peak during three periods: 10–11 A.M., 1–2 P.M., and again at 5–6 P.M. (Rand, 1960). Dive durations are still little studied, but three dives lasted an average of 24 seconds, with a mean resting interval of 7.7 seconds (Cooper, 1985b).

Social Behavior

Age of maturity and mating system. The age of initial breeding is unknown, but probably occurs by the third year (Berry, 1976). Berry (1977) reported that he found several color-marked adults nesting at almost exactly the same spot as he had banded them three years previously. Within an hour of searching, he found 4 of 25 previously marked birds in a large colony of about 2,000 nesting pairs, and all were nesting within 10 meters of where they had been caught as adults three years earlier. This high degree of fidelity would suggest that sustained monogamy exists in the species.

Social displays and vocalizations. According to Berry (1976), male advertisement display in this species consists of a "throw-back" posture (figure 64A), from a standing, squatting, or sitting position on the nest site. In this posture the neck lies along the back, the tail is held erect and fanned, the bill is opened or closed, the bright orange-yellow gular skin is exposed, and a low-pitched clucking call is produced. The vocalizing and posture may be maintained for several minutes, and are terminated with the arrival of a female. Then the head and fully extended neck are brought forward to a vertical or diagonal position in a "forward-head-and-neck-stretch" (figure 64B). This threatlike movement, which may include gaping, perhaps corresponds to the "gaping" or "pointing" displays of related species. It evidently also serves as a recognition signal, and may be performed up to 10 times in 30 seconds when a female approaches. The female response is apparently similar, performed with an arched neck while uttering a repeated *gra-gra-gra* note. Such recognition sequences may be repeated several times. After pair bonding, the voice of the male resembles that of the female. Postlanding displays resemble those of other marine shags, especially the pelagic shag, and during hopping the neck is held in a curved manner, with the bill open and pointed downward and the gular skin exposed.

Figure 64. Social behavior of the Cape shag, including male advertisement display (A), male recognition display (B), feather presentation by male during reversed mounting (C), feather presentation by female to sitting male (D), normal copulatory mounting (E), and defense of nest site (F). After photos in Berry (1976).

Copulation occurs at the nest site and involves two temporal stages. The earlier stage, reversed mounting, occurs when the female straddles a male's back, without making cloacal contact. During reversed mounting or prior to actual copulation a feather or other object may be presented by one of the partners to the other (figure 64C), at times being placed on the back of the other bird (figure 64D). True copulation involves the female assuming a prone receptive position and the male mounting her and grasping her neck feathers during treading (figure 64E).

Threat display involves gaping with an extended neck toward an intruder (figure 64F), alternating with withdrawing the head and shaking it sideways. During actual fighting, the wings and tail are spread to provide additional anchorage points and the body is held low. Fighting is done by biting with the bill, but such fights typically result in little actual injury. Most fights are between males contesting nest sites. After pair bonding, fights are replaced by threat displays, which are most intense during the incubation period and early hatching stages. Both sexes utter hissing clucks during threat, which become more croaking and finally a penetrating gaggle at high intensities.

Reproductive Biology

Breeding. Breeding is extended, with the peak depending on availability of prey, especially schools of fish such as pilchards (Berry, 1976). Similarly, breeding activity is terminated if the prey supply suddenly ceases. At that time the birds may move to another area. The usual peak breeding period is in September or October, but some breeding occurs throughout the year (Brown, Urban, and Newman, 1982). In Namibia maximum sexual activity is reached in October and maintained until February, as "waves" of newly matured breeders take up nesting sites on guano platforms (Berry, 1976).

Nest sites and nest building. On the guano platforms, roosting and nesting sites safe from land-based predators are available. Additionally, some nesting occurs on the mainland, on cliff ledges overlooking bays or in sea caves (Loutit, Boyer, and Brooke, 1986). Nest building is done by the female using materials brought by the male, often materials stolen from nearby nests. The materials, including seaweeds, sticks, stalks, and debris, are drawn into the nest with the bill and prodded down to form a cup. The distance between adjacent nests in dense colonies is about 30 centimeters, which is also the average nest diameter. Nesting densities in five plots, each of 25 square meters, averaged 3.1 nests per square meter (Berry, 1976).

Egg laying and incubation. The observed clutch range for this species is 1–5 eggs, but 2–3 is typical, and the mean of 1,626 clutches was 2.39 eggs (Brown, Urban, and Newman, 1982). In one sample among nests near the middle of the nesting colony a large percentage (65 percent) held three-egg clutches, suggesting that these areas are used by the older breeding birds. Older birds probably start nesting somewhat

sooner than younger ones and are evidently able to select and defend the best nesting sites. First-time nesters begin breeding at the colony's edges, where more than half of the nests held fewer than three eggs. Eggs are laid at intervals of 1–3 days, and most clutches are completed within a week. Incubation begins with the first egg, which hatches in about 28 days. The second hatches in about 25 days, and the third in 22–23 days (Berry, 1976, 1977).

Brooding and rearing of young. The growth of chicks falls into four general stages, including naked (to six days), downy (1–3 weeks), feathering (3–6 weeks), and fledging (7–9 weeks). The eyes are fully open at a week, which is when the first down appears on the back. Parental recognition of young occurs somewhat later, since naked chicks can successfully be experimentally exchanged in nests. The young are fed about five or six times per day, with each feeding lasting about three minutes. The older birds generally get fed first, so that the younger ones typically receive the more digested foods. At 18 days the remiges and rectrices begin to erupt, and juvenal feathers also appear on the wings, tail, and scapulars. The head remains bald, probably to facilitate feeding from the parent's gullet, and at five weeks the brood leaves the nest site. The number of foraging trips by adults, which require from a half-hour to three hours and may involve round trips of as much as 80 kilometers, may reach ten per day for adults with well-grown chicks. Maximum weight of about 1,400 grams is attained just prior to fledging. Fledging begins at the seventh week, when different broods begin to form small groups of up to 10 birds. Parental recognition of young continues, and food chases of the parent may lead to attempted flights, which are achieved at about two months following hatching. Independence from the parents occurs a few weeks later (Berry, 1976).

Breeding success. No specific information is available.

Population Status

This is one of the most abundant seabirds off the coast of southern Africa, and its breeding population probably averages more than a million birds. Nonbreeding juveniles and immatures may double this total figure. It has a high degree of population stability because of the reliable food supply. During the 1950s the minimum population was estimated at more than 1,100,000 breeding birds (Rand, 1960; Cooper et al., 1982). Most of these were breeding on Namibian platforms, such as Cape Cross and Bird Rock. In the early 1970s the Namibian breeding population was estimated at 1,053,000 birds (Berry, 1976).

Evolutionary Relationships

Siegel-Causey (1988) considered on the basis of his cladistic studies that the nearest relative to this species is the guanay shag of South America.

Peru

Trujillo

Chimbote

Lima

Other Vernacular Names

Bougainville's cormorant, guanay cormorant, Peruvian cormorant; cormorán guanay (Spanish); cormoran de Bougainville (French); Guanokormoran (German)

Distribution

Breeds along the Pacific coast of South America from Macabi and Guañape islands, Peru, south through Chinca and Lobos islands to Chile, where formerly bred south to Mocha Island, and now breeds south at least to Concón Island (near Valparaiso). Also breeds on the Atlantic coast between Puerto Deaeado and Santa Cruz, Chubut, Argentina. Nonbreeders on the Pacific coast range south in winter to Valdivia, Chile, and north to Buenaventura, Colombia. (See figure 65.)

Subspecies

None recognized.

Description

Prebreeding adult. Top of the head and crest dark oil-green, rest of the head and neck glossed with steel-blue; middle of the interscapular region, lower back, rump, upper tail coverts, and thighs glossed with dark bluish green; sides of the upper back, wing coverts, and scapulars dull bronze-green, with narrow margins of darker greenish blue; chin, throat, base of foreneck, and rest of underparts pure white; a patch of white plumes above the eye and scattered on the neck; remiges and rectrices (12) brownish black. Iris dark brown, surrounded by a white corneal ring; orbital skin olive-green, forming a distinct eye ring, below which is a crescent of dull brown skin; rest of facial skin red, becoming orange above the eye and more brownish behind it; bill horn-yellow to brownish black, becoming pinkish to bluish at the base; gular skin red; legs and feet pink to flesh, the toes and back of the tarsus brownish.

←

Figure 65. Distribution of the guanay shag, showing its major breeding range (small cross-hatching), peripheral breeding range (large cross-hatching), and nonbreeding range (stippled). Arrows indicate locations of twentieth-century breeding sites off Peru (after Murphy, 1936); the crossed arrow indicates an abandoned breeding site in central Chile.

Postbreeding adult. Like the prebreeding plumage, but lacking a crest and the white facial plumes; the head and neck brown, with a dull greenish gloss; sides of the back, wing coverts, and scapulars a more brownish bronze, with much less gloss, and the darker feather margins less conspicuous; wings and tail more brownish.
Immature-subadult. Not easily separated from the postbreeding adult, but browner, with the foreneck entirely or extensively white.
Juvenile. Resembling the postbreeding adult, but generally duller brown above, and the white underparts sullied with brown.
Nestling. After acquiring a downy cloak, an even mixture of black and white, producing a distinctive salt-and-pepper effect.

Measurements (in millimeters)

Wing, males 281–303 (ave. of 5, 296.4), females 270–287 (ave. of 4, 281); tail, males 96–104 (ave. of 5, 100), females 96.6–108.5 (ave. of 4, 103.3); culmen, males 65–78 (ave. of 5, 71.4), females 65–73 (ave. of 4, 69.1); tarsus, males 66–71 (ave. of 5, 68.8), females 66–67 (ave. of 4, 66.6) (Blake, 1977). Eggs ca. 65 × 41.

Weights (in grams)

Three males 2,478–3,222 (ave. 2,832) (U.S. National Museum specimens). Duffy (1980b) reported the average adult weight as 1,800, but without specifying the quantitative basis for this statistic. Calculated egg weight 60.3.

Identification

In the hand. The combination of white underparts, scarlet to flesh-colored feet, and a brown eye with a greenish eye ring serves to identify this species.
In the field. This is the only South American cormorant or shag with flesh-colored feet and rather dark brown to blackish upperparts. The somewhat similar rock shag has more pinkish feet, and the red-legged shag is distinctly grayish overall.

Ecology and General Biology

Breeding and nonbreeding habitats. Habitats are circumscribed by the Humboldt current, which extends about 5,000 kilometers along the coasts of Chile and Peru, roughly within limits set by Peru's northern boundary with Ecuador and the vicinity of Corral, Chile. The guanay shag moves up and down the coast following migrating schools of surface-swimming fish, especially anchovetas and young sardines. It nests on fewer than 40 small islets and islands, which are concentrated along the northern two-thirds of the Peruvian coast (Murphy, 1924, 1936).

Movements and migrations.   Normally guanay shags are confined to the area of the Humboldt current just mentioned, except during periodic incursions of a warmer counter-current from the north, or El Niños. The resultant rapid decline of aquatic food supplies causes a crash in dependent animal populations and often stimulates mass emigrations, often as far north as central Ecuador and occasionally to Panama. Similarly, many birds move southward into Chile. Outside the breeding season there may be regular migrations south to Chile too, sometimes to the vicinity of Valdivia (Johnson, 1965). It is possible that a previous emigration resulted in some birds reaching Cape Horn and entering south Atlantic waters, thereby allowing the recent colonization of the Argentine coastline.

Competition and predation.   At their limited breeding localities, the other major breeding species are the Peruvian booby (*Sula variegata*) and the brown pelican. Pelicans easily dominate the two smaller species but nest only on level surfaces, whereas the booby and guanay shag nest over a broader range of substrate gradients. The guanay and booby are similar-sized and unable to displace each other from nest sites, and so must "scramble" to occupy space on a first-come basis (Duffy, 1983a).

Important nest predators include kelp gulls (*Larus dominicanus*), but turkey vultures *Cathartes aura* and Andean condors (*Vultur gryphus*) also cause destruction of eggs. Sea lions (*Zalophus*) are said to consume the fledglings, but there is apparently little actual evidence of this (Murphy, 1936). Duffy (1983b) never saw kelp gulls or the smaller band-tailed gulls (*L. belcheri*) attack nests defended by adults, and considered all such accounts as secondhand, but noted that they did quickly consume untended eggs. Coker (1919) observed that kelp gulls can swallow a newly hatched pelican with some effort, and can tear a larger one to pieces, so they are probably of considerable danger to young shags as well.

Foods and Foraging Behavior

Foods consumed.   According to Murphy (1924, 1936), the guanay forages entirely on surface-swimming fishes, including anchovetas (*Engraulis*), sardines (*Sardinops*), and silversides (Athineridae), all of which travel in extremely large schools that are attacked en masse by great flocks of shags. Johnson (1965) stated that the guanay exploits a single species, the anchoveta. Up to 76 anchovies, all about 10–15 centimeters in length, have been found in a single bird's stomach.

Foraging behavior.   The foraging behavior of the guanay has been described by many people, including Murphy (1924, 1936). He reported that during early morning hours small "scouting parties" leave the vast roosts and fly erratically above the ocean, sometimes hovering or backpedaling when they see prey near the surface. As they begin to dive for prey they quickly attract great hordes of birds from the roosts. These build into feeding frenzies as the fish are attacked from above by the shags as well as brown pelicans and gulls, and from below by bonito (Scombridae) and sea lions. Occasionally a school of fish will be driven against the sandy beaches in their frantic efforts to escape.

Duffy (1983b) estimated that in his study area (Mazorca Island) guanay shags spent an average of less than two hours per day foraging, and noted that Vogt (1942) had postulated that foraging durations of more than six hours per day would indicate food shortages and foretell mass nest desertions.

Social Behavior

Age of maturity and mating system.   There is no information on the age of maturity. The breeding season is nearly continuous, and individual pairs commonly produce two broods in a single calendar year, suggesting that some sustained monogamy probably exists (Murphy, 1924, 1936). Murphy states that in early stages of courtship "most" of the birds in a nesting colony may be courting, and as many as five males may simultaneously court a single female, suggesting that perhaps a good deal of new pair bonding may occur during each nesting cycle.

Social displays and vocalizations.   No detailed information exists on pair-forming displays. Vogt (1942) and Murphy (1924, 1936) have described the agonistic interactions of pairs fighting over nest sites, and Duffy (1983a) discussed the agonistic behavior between shags and boobies. Murphy (1924, 1936) stated that sexual display of the guanay is much like that of the imperial shag. Two birds will stand side by side, or breast to breast, and wave their heads back and forth or caress each other's necks. Their short crests are often erected; their nape feathers are puffed out to increase their necks to twice normal size. Their cheeks and gular pouches continually tremble, and their chattering bills are opened widely. Occasionally a bird will bend its body forward and simultaneously extend the head upside down along the spine (presumably the gargling posture), and may hold this position for several seconds. Vocalizations are poorly described, but evidently include sonorous bass grunts and "screepy" calls. Coker (1919) described the call as a sort of a croak, less deep, less hoarse, and less powerful than a bullfrog's, but of that general character. Hissing, with a widely opened bill and head waving, also occurs (Murphy, 1936).

Reproductive Biology

Breeding season. According to Murphy (1924, 1936) the breeding season is nearly continuous but reaches a peak in summer during December and January. The fledging of the last families from the first breeding cycle in May or June is quickly followed by courting for the next breeding season.

Nest sites and nest building. Nest sites in this species are among the most crowded of all cormorant species, the nest densities at times reaching 2–3 nests per square meter (Vogt, 1942). Coker (1919) found the nest density in three sample plots to be 2.9, 3.25, and 3.6 nests per square meter, with the distance between the centers of adjacent nests ranging from 50 to 70 centimeters, but usually slightly under 60 centimeters. On the Chincha Islands, a single rookery covering about 60,000 square meters (15 acres) supported about 360,000 breeding adults plus a comparable or greater number of immatures, or about 750,000 birds in all. A month later the flock was at least 50 percent larger, apparently as additional birds began breeding. On the Ballesta Islands one island rookery measured about 4,600 square meters, another about 11,000 square meters, and the third was about the same size as the second. These three islands supported about 150,000 breeding birds during May of one year (Coker, 1919). On central Chincha Island more than a million nests, supporting 4–5 million birds, have been estimated (Murphy, 1936).

Duffy (1983a) described mean nest site characteristics, which included a slope of 21 degrees, a microsite slope of 12 degrees, a nest density of 3.0 per square meter, a nest area of 0.08 square meters, a nest diameter of 32 centimeters, and a nest height (downhill side) of 17 centimeters. Initially, the birds picked sites on the sloping areas, but gradually moved into less favorable sites. The middle parts of windy hillsides were preferred, probably to facilitate takeoffs, for cooling, or to facilitate "phalanx" effects in defending against aerial predators such as kelp gulls.

Egg laying and incubation. According to Murphy (1936), this species lays three eggs and rears an average of more than two young. Johnson (1965) states that three or occasionally two eggs are laid. The incubation period is evidently unknown.

Brooding and rearing of young. Little information is available on the brooding period. Murphy (1936) observed that many birds were feeding nearly full-grown young in December while others were tending new nests that he believed to be second broods. The older chicks tended to wander, and would be quickly chased back to their nest sites by neighboring parents. Food begging consisted of a "shiver and plead" activity, in which chicks try to ram their heads down the throats of the parents, sometimes two or even three at a time. Older fledglings would move down to quiet rock pools and practice diving, but would return back to the nesting colony before dark. By late afternoon the chicks were often brooded by both parents, huddled so close together that they would appear to be a single bird with two heads. The fledging period of the guanay is about ten weeks (Duffy, 1983b).

Breeding success. Apart from the general comment by Murphy (1936) that pairs typically rear at least two young, there does not seem to be much information on normal breeding success, which is perhaps hard to estimate because of the long breeding season and probable double-brooding or at least persistent renesting. Some nest abandonment at both egg and chick stages results from heavy infestations by argasid ticks (*Ornithodoros*) (Duffy, 1983b). However, in El Niño years breeding success is nil, with massive abandonment of nests and starvation of both adults and young common. Over an historic period of 80 breeding seasons, on three islands (Mazorca, Macabi, and Don Martín), desertions of more than 10 percent of the nests occurred in 32 years (40 percent). Eleven of these years were during El Niño events, but desertions also occurred in 30 percent of the remaining 69 breeding seasons, perhaps because of ectoparasites, especially ticks.

Population Status

This is a boom-or-bust species, and its total population probably is normally in the several millions, making it perhaps the most abundant of all the world's cormorants. Early estimates of as many as 10 million birds breeding at the Chincha Islands alone have been made, although these appear to be unfounded (Coker, 1919). Duffy (1983a) stated that in the 1940s the combined Peruvian population of guanay shags, Peruvian boobies, and brown pelicans was stable at about 8 million, but with better protection of breeding areas it later rose to 20 million birds, and the percentage of annual population increase doubled to 18 percent, exclusive of El Niño years. More recently the populations have fallen sharply, probably as a result of commercial overfishing. The Peruvian population was estimated at 3 million birds in 1981 (Duffy, Hays, and Plenge, 1984).

Evolutionary Relationships

Siegel-Causey (1988) concluded from cladistic evidence that the nearest relative of this species is the Cape shag. However, Dorst and Mougin (1979) placed these two forms in separate subgenera, and although van Tets (1976a) placed them in the same subgenus, he apparently did not consider them extremely close relatives. Murphy (1936) commented on the close structural similarities of the guanay shag to the blue-eyed shag group, and Devillers and Terschuren (1978) considered these forms to be very closely related, and believed that they had observed a wild hybrid between *atriceps* and *bougainvillii* in Argentina. Malacalza (1991) described a hybrid of *bougainvillii* with *albiventer* and reported it to be fertile, suggesting that a very close genetic relationship exists between them.

Other Vernacular Names

Antarctic blue-eyed shag (*bransfieldensis*), blue-eyed shag (or cormorant), crested shag, emperor shag, Falkland blue-eyed shag (*albiventer*), Georgian shag (*georgianus*), Heard shag (*nivalis*), Kerguelen shag (*verrucosus*), king shag (*albiventer*), imperial cormorant, Macquarie Island shag (*purpurascens*), Magellanic blue-eyed shag (*atriceps*), subantarctic king shag (*bransfieldensis*), South Georgian blue-eyed shag (*georgianus*), white-bellied shag (*albiventer*), white-necked shag (*albiventer*); cormoran impérial (French); Falkland-Kormoran, Weisrückenkormoran (German); cormorán imperial (Spanish)

Distribution

Circumpolar in subantarctic latitudes, breeding in coastal South America from Tierra del Fuego north to Mocha Island, Chile, and to Punta Tombo (Chubut), Argentina; disjunct populations are also resident coastally along the Antarctic Peninsula, on the islands of the Antarctic Archipelago and the Scotia arc (South Shetland, South Orkney, and South Sandwich), and on Shag Rocks, Falkland Islands, South Georgia, Prince Edward and Marion islands, Crozet Islands, Kerguelen Islands, Heard Island, and Macquarie Island. These insular populations are often variously considered specifically distinct, as summarized below. (See figure 66.)

Subspecies

L. a. atriceps King. Resident from Tierra del Fuego, western Straits of Magellan, and islands of the Beagle Channel north along coastal Chile to Mocha Island, and also along the coast of Argentina to Punta Tombo, Chubut; also breeds on lakes of Tierra del Fuego, at Lago Nahuel Huapi (Neuquén), and at Lago Vinter (Chubut), Argentina. Vagrants have been reported north to Uruguay.

L. a. albiventer (Lesson) 1831. Endemic to the Falkland Islands. Mainland populations previously referred to this race are best assigned to nominate *atriceps* (Devillers and Terschuren, 1978). Often (e.g., Blake, 1977) specifically separated from *atriceps*, and considered by Dorst and Mougin (1979) as comprising part of a superspecies with *atriceps*.

L. a. bransfieldensis (Murphy) 1936. Resident along the Antarctic Peninsula, including the Antarctic Archipelago and other nearby islands, north at least to South Shetlands and Elephant Island. Possibly also includes birds from the South Orkney and South Sandwich groups (Dorst and Mougin, 1979), but these are here considered part of *georgianus*. Considered a full species by Siegel-Causey (1988), Sibley and

Monroe (1990), and in Marchant and Higgins (1990), but regarded as a synonym of *atriceps* by Dorst and Mougin (1979).

L. a. georgianus (Lönnberg) 1906. Resident on South Georgia Island. Additionally, birds from South Sandwich Islands and the South Orkneys (Laurie, Signy) have recently been included in this form (Marchant and Higgins, 1990) but have previously been attributed to *bransfieldensis* (Murphy, 1936) or to *atriceps* (Dorst and Mougin, 1979). Those from Shag Rocks are also now assigned to this form (Dorst and Mougin, 1979), but may be phenotypically closer to South American birds (Parmelee, 1980). Considered a full species by Siegel-Causey (1988), Sibley and Monroe (1990), and in Marchant and Higgins (1990).

L. a. melanogenis (Blyth) 1860. Endemic to Prince Edward, Marion, and Crozet islands (breeding on Possession, l'Est, Pingouins, Apôtres, and Cochons islands); vagrants rarely reach the Kerguelens. Considered a full species in Marchant and Higgins (1990), and as part of *atriceps* by Sibley and Monroe (1990); not assigned by Siegel-Causey (1988).

L. (a.) verrucosus (Cabanis) 1875. Endemic to Kerguelen Islands; breeding on the main island (Grand Terre) and some small offshore islands. Sometimes accorded specific recognition (e.g., Marchant and Higgins, 1990; Sibley and Monroe, 1990), but Derenne, Mary, and Mougin (1976) observed local interbreeding with birds of *albiventer* phenotype, which makes full specific separation questionable (Watson, 1975).

L. a. nivalis (Falla) 1937. Endemic to Heard Island; not reported from outlying islands. Considered a full species in Marchant and Higgins (1990), and as part of *atriceps* by Sibley and Monroe (1990); not assigned by Siegel-Causey (1988).

L. a. purpurascens (Brandt) 1837. Endemic to Macquarie Island and nearby Bishop and Clerk Rocks. Considered a full species in Marchant and Higgins (1990), and as part of *atriceps* by Sibley and Monroe (1990); not assigned by Siegel-Causey (1988).

Description

Prebreeding adult (of nominate *atriceps*). The crown, nape, and hindneck bluish black, with a wispy recurved crest; lower cheeks, chin, and foreneck white, the line of demarcation level with the eye; feathering behind gular skin extending forward medially to a point about directly under the eye. Upperparts mostly bluish black, with a median white dorsal patch on middle back and white alar stripes on anterior margins of wings appearing at about the time of egg laying. Remiges and rectrices (12) blackish. Iris brown to pale green, eyelids ("eye ring") bright blue; nasal caruncles saffron-yellow to gamboge-yellow (less inflated, more crescent-

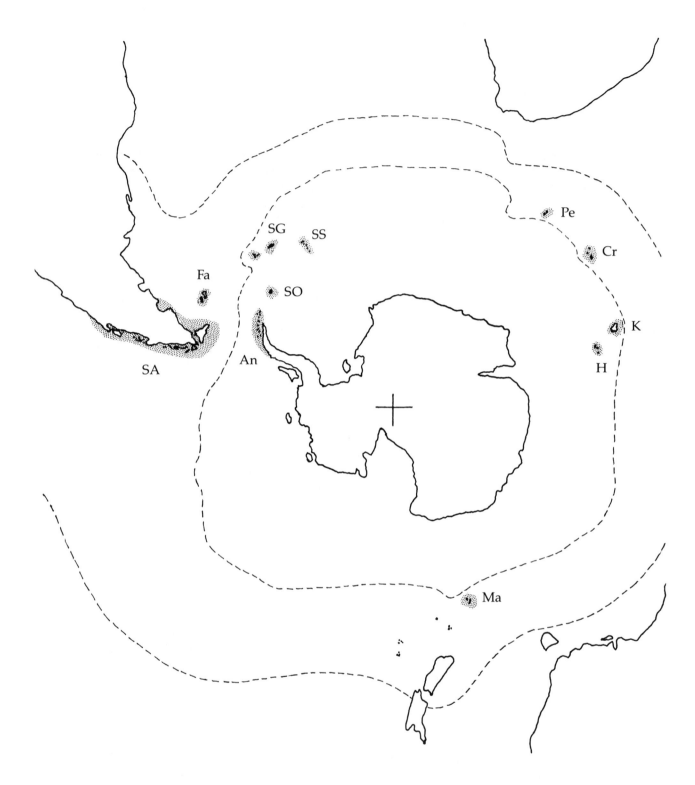

Figure 66. Distribution of the imperial shag (stippled), showing locations of its nominate South American race (SA), plus
additional populations on the Antarctic Peninsula (An), and
on Crozet (Cr), Falkland (Fa), Heard (H), Kerguelen (K), Macquarie (Ma), Marion and Prince Edward (Pe), South Georgia
(SG), South Orkney (SO), and South Sandwich (SS) islands.
The dotted lines enclose the nutrient-rich subantarctic oceanic zone between the subtropical and antarctic convergences.

shaped, and of more variegated and "colder" shades of yellow than in the insular forms); marks between the eye and angle of the gape orange; bill gray to olive or sooty, becoming horn-colored near tip of lower mandible, the inside surface of bill black; mouth lining red; lores and gular skin sooty, with fine yellowish specks; legs and feet pink to flesh-colored, the rear of tarsi and tips of toes purplish gray. (This description refers to the typical Pacific coast, or "*imperialis*," morph of *atriceps*. Populations from the Patagonian coast and from Tierra del Fuego are polymorphic, with some individuals closely approaching the *albiventer* phenotype (see below), and with many transitional phenotypes also present (Devillers and Terschuren, 1978).)

Prebreeding adults of *albiventer:* similar to *atriceps,* but the demarcation line separating black and white of head is located lower on cheeks, approximately at level of gape; a wispy white tuft of filoplumes briefly present above and behind the eye, white alar stripes (75–120 mm long) present (at least during the egg-laying period) but no white dorsal patch ever developing. Facial skin olive or brown; caruncles yellow-orange and more strongly developed than in *atriceps;* legs and feet pink, with darker webs.

Prebreeding adults of *bransfieldensis:* similar to *atriceps,* but with larger caruncles. White alar stripes conspicuous, and white patch present on back. Iris pale brown, eyelids cobalt-blue; bill olive to sooty; caruncles bright orange-yellow; gular skin sooty, with fine yellowish speckles; legs and feet flesh-colored, with an olive wash.

Prebreeding adults of *georgianus:* similar to *atriceps,* but the forehead caruncles slightly larger and deep chrome-yellow, and the line of cheek demarcation crosses the ear opening. White patches on wings and back may be prominent, reduced, or absent. Iris brown to grayish; eyelids cyanine-blue; bare skin of lores blackish brown, with deep chrome caruncles; gular skin blackish brown; legs and feet salmon, the undersides of the toes clove-brown.

Prebreeding adults of *melanogenis:* similar to *albiventer,* with the black of the cheeks extending below the level of the ear, and a wisp of white filoplumes often present above and behind the eye; white alar stripes (up to 75 mm long) present in some breeding birds; white scapular patches rare; no white present on back. Iris dark brown; eyelids blue; facial skin grayish black, with bright yellow caruncles; gular skin grayish black; legs and feet pink, with brown joints.

Prebreeding adults of *verrucosus:* similar to *albiventer,* but with breeding adults usually lacking the alar stripe and also nearly always lacking the white dorsal patch. The black on the cheeks is continued down below the ear opening in a narrow pointed band that runs between the white throat and the naked gular skin, and extends halfway toward the middle line of the throat. Although this population typically lacks white alar markings, about 20 percent of the breeding population from the east coast of Ronarch and Jeanne d'Arc Peninsula have incomplete alar stripes (Weimerkirch, Zotier, and

Jovetin, 1988). Softpart colors somewhat less bright than in *albiventer,* the eyelids tending toward dark grayish blue, iris dark brown; lores grayish black, with orange-buff to chrome-yellow caruncles; gular pouch grayish black, lined with orange-buff; legs and feet a dirty pink, heavily tinged with dark brown.

Prebreeding adults of *nivalis:* similar to *atriceps* (but closest geographically to *verrucosus*), but with a lower cheek line, and only scattered white feathers in alar region. Some white normally present in the scapulars. A distinct white dorsal patch develops during the breeding season (Devillers and Terschuren, 1978), but the scapular and alar markings may be reduced or absent (Marchant and Higgins, 1990). Iris dark brown; eyelids blue; lores grayish black with prominent orange caruncles; orange skin at base of lower mandible; gular skin grayish black, lined with orange-buff; legs and feet bright pink, with brown joints.

Prebreeding adults of *purpurascens:* similar to *albiventer,* with the black of the crown extending down the cheeks to below the level of the ear. The white alar and scapular patches are prominent in some birds, but reduced or lacking in others, and the back lacks white patches (Marchant and Higgins, 1990). Iris dark brown; eyelids grayish blue to dark black; facial skin bluish green to grayish black, with orange-buff papillae and caruncles; legs and feet pink to dull red, with darker brownish webs.

Postbreeding adult (all races). Similar to the prebreeding adult, but the crest lacking, the caruncles shrunken in size and duller in color, and the eyelids and other softpart colors generally less bright. In *atriceps* and perhaps other forms having white alar stripes and dorsal patches, these areas are at a maximum development after the crest has been molted, during the chick-raising period, and may later be partly or entirely lost. The remiges and rectrices are reportedly then also molted and the worn body plumage is replaced. By the time the body plumage has been entirely replaced and the crest has fully regrown these white markings will again usually have been lost (Murphy, 1936; Watson, 1975). However, at least in some populations (such as *bransfieldensis*) the dorsal white patch may be retained year-round and, rather than having two distinct molts per year, molting patterns may be irregular and multicyclic (Bernstein and Maxson, 1982).

Immature-subadult (all races). Year-old immatures are intermediate between the juvenal and definitive plumages, having some glossy feathers on the back, but the wings remaining brown, the head uncrested, and a few streaks or spots of grayish brown on the breast. The black feathers of adults are represented by slaty feathers that fade to brownish. A white dorsal patch may appear (at least in those races that have this marking as breeding adults) after the molt of the second summer. Some juvenal remiges may still be present in birds that are two or even three years old. Breeding may initially occur in the second through fourth or even the fifth year (Croxall, 1984; Brothers, 1985; Marchant and Higgins, 1990). Iris brown; eyelids dull lead-blue; facial skin and small caruncles purplish brown; legs and feet dark gray, with a pink tinge, or pinkish edged with gray.

Juvenile   (all races). Lacking crest and caruncles, and if present at all the alar bars are mottled pale brown rather than pure white. The feathers of the wings and lower back are edged with grayish white, and are relatively pointed. Juveniles of typical *atriceps* have the crown and hindneck black, the sides of the head and the lores black grading into brownish black on the cheeks (superficially resembling adults of *albiventer* in having dark cheeks). The chin, throat, lower half of auriculars, and ventral half of neck are white, sometimes also with a few faint darker streaks. Juveniles of *albiventer* are similar to those of *atriceps* except that the auriculars are black, and the black on the sides of the neck extends ventrally to cover all but the ventral third of the neck (Rasmussen, 1986). Juveniles of *verrucosus* sometimes have entirely dark plumages (Devillers and Terschuren, 1978). Iris brown; eye ring purplish brown to black; nasal caruncles represented by brownish papillae and mingled with feathers; bill dark gray; gular skin pale violet, black posteriorly; legs and feet gray to brown.

Nestling   (all races). Initially with a livid naked skin, which very soon turns shiny black, except for a pinkish (*georgianus, purpurascens, verrucosus*), yellow (*melanogenis*), or bluish (*atriceps*) gular area; bill slaty blue, with a more bluish gray base; legs and feet lead-colored to brownish gray. The body is covered within a week with sooty or grayish brown (in *albiventer*) to blackish (in *atriceps*) down. White down erupts on the head, throat, and belly at about the time the remiges and rectrices also begin to appear.

Measurements (in millimeters)

Nominate *atriceps:* wing, males 282–287 (ave. of 3, 284), females 258–282 (ave. of 10, 271.4); tail, males 117–131 (ave. of 3, 124), females 112–132 (ave. of 10, 121.4); culmen, males 59–64 (ave. of 3, 61.8), females 55–60 (ave. of 10, 57.8). A mixed sample of *albiventer* phenotype specimens from Argentina and of true *albiventer* from the Falkland Islands have essentially identical mean measurements as follows: wing, males 284, females 276; tail, males 125, females 121; culmen, males 61.6, females 58.1. Malacalza and Hall (1988) have suggested a method for reliably sexing *albiventer* using discriminant analysis techniques and have provided relevant measurements.

Of *bransfieldensis:* females, wing 302–330 (ave. of 7, 311); tail 162–208 (ave. of 7, 185); culmen 51–62 (ave. of 7, 56) (Murphy, 1936). Sample of 8 unsexed birds: wing 320–330 (ave. 325), tail 136–158 (ave. 146), culmen 57–62.5 (ave. 59) (Behn et al., 1955).

Of *georgianus:* wing, 36 males from Signy Island (South Orkneys) averaged 304.5, 23 females averaged 289.6; tail, 36

males averaged 137, 24 females averaged 128.6 (Shaw, cited in Marchant and Higgins, 1990). Females (South Georgia): wing 270–278 (ave. of 5, 275), tail 116–122 (ave. of 5, 118.6), culmen 44–51 (ave. of 5, 48.4) (Murphy, 1936).

Of *melanogenis:* Crozet Islands sample: wing, males 272–299 (ave. of 8, 286), females 257–270 (ave. of 8, 268); tail, males 74–120 (ave. of 9, 102), females 98–115 (ave. of 9, 107); culmen, males 56–64 (ave. of 8, 58), females 55–60 (ave. of 8, 56) (Derenne, Mary, and Mougin, 1976). Marion Island sample: wing, males 290–300 (ave. of 4, 293), females 270–279 (ave. of 3, 274); tail, males 124–137 (ave. of 4, 131), females 106–115 (ave. of 3, 112) (Marchant and Higgins, 1990).

Of *verrucosus:* wing, males 254–280 (ave. of 8, 272), females 248–281 (ave. of 11, 263); culmen, males 46–52 (ave. of 9, 50.3), females 45–52.5 (ave. of 11, 47) (Derenne, Mary, and Mougin, 1976).

Males of *nivalis:* wing 305–335 (ave. of 9, 322), tail 116–136 (ave. of 9, 129), culmen 57–67 (ave. of 9, 60) (Marchant and Higgins, 1990).

Of *purpurascens:* wing, males 301–322 (ave. of 16, 311), females 285–304 (ave. of 18, 293); tail, males 100–134 (ave. of 16, 121.4), females 104–120 (ave. of 18, 112.7); culmen, males 57.2–61.5 (ave. of 16, 59.3), females 52.1–57 (ave. of 18, 54.8) (Brothers, 1985).

Eggs (some racial variation) ca. 64 × 39.

Weights (in grams)

Of *atriceps,* 5 adult males 2,104–3,341 (ave. 2,721); 3 adult females 2,087–2,389 (ave. 2,193) (U.S. National Museum specimens). Two *albiventer* phenotype males from Tierra del Fuego, ca. 2,664 (5.875 lb.) and ca. 2,547 (5.625 lb.) (Humphrey et al., 1970).

Of *bransfieldensis,* 16 males averaged 3,022 (standard deviation 170), 21 females 2,576 (standard deviation 138) (Bernstein and Maxson, 1982). One male 2,948 (Murphy, 1936); 8 unsexed specimens 2,750–3,250, averaging 2,994 (Behn et al., 1955).

Of *georgianus,* 130 males from Signy Island averaged 2,883 (standard deviation 255.3), 101 females averaged 2,473 (standard deviation 154.5) (Shaw, 1984).

Of *melanogenis,* 8 males from Crozet Islands 1,700–2,700 (ave. 2,283), 11 females 1,500–2,250 (ave. 1,895). Five males from Possession Island 1,700–2,700 (ave. 2,450), 5 females 1,950–2,250 (ave. 2,040) (Derenne, Mary, and Mougin, 1976). Mean weight at fledging of 3 *melanogenis* was reported as 2,487 by Williams and Burger (1979), and as 2,265 for a larger sample of 21 (Derenne, Mary, and Mougin, 1976).

Of *verrucosus,* 3 males 1,840–2,240 (ave. 2,000), 3 females 1,500–1,730 (ave. 1,600) (Derenne, Mary, and Mougin, 1976). Two males 1,500 and 1,800, two females 2,000 and 2,000 (Marchant and Higgins, 1990).

Of *nivalis,* 7 males 2,800–3,300 (ave. 3,100) (Marchant and Higgins, 1990).

Of *purpurascens*, breeding adults at start of breeding season: males 2,950–3,500 (ave. of 8, 3,320), females 2,550–2,990 (ave. of 8, 2,700); at end of breeding season: males 2,650–3,200 (ave. of 16, 2,864), females 2,180–2,700 (ave. of 18, 2,434) (Brothers, 1985). Another sample, males 2,900–3,500 (ave. of 11, 3,200), females 2,200–2,900 (ave. of 12, 2,600) (Marchant and Higgins, 1990).

Calculated egg weight 53.7; ave. weight of eggs of two-egg clutches of *bransfieldensis* 51.6, of three-egg clutches 52.2 (Shaw, 1985b). Average of 3 *melanogenis* eggs from Marion Island 51, of 3 from Crozet Islands 59 (Derenne, Mary, and Mougin, 1976).

Identification

In the hand. The combination of white underparts, pinkish flesh feet, a bright blue eye ring, yellow to orange facial caruncles, and the throat feathers reaching forward to a point directly below the middle of the eye serves to identify adults of this species.

In the field. Depending on taxonomic limits, species identification in southern South America may be fairly simple, or (if *atriceps* and *albiventer* are considered separate species) quite difficult. The bicolored black-and-white plumage easily separates the species from South America's Neotropic cormorants, red-footed shags, and guanay shags. In extreme southern South America and on the Falklands the more similar rock shag also occurs, but has a black foreneck and red facial skin, and lacks forehead caruncles. The presence of pink feet and a bluish eye ring, at least in adults, separates this species as here constituted from all the other cormorant or shag species potentially occurring in the same geographic regions. These criteria would not, however, serve to distinguish it from the allopatric Campbell, Bounty, and Auckland island shags nor from the New Zealand king shag. On most of the subantarctic islands the imperial shag is the only resident shag or cormorant, although on the Falkland Islands the smaller rock shag also breeds. On Macquarie Island the nearly all-black great cormorant is a rare vagrant.

Ecology and General Biology

Breeding and nonbreeding habitats. This is a coastal species, associated with cool to cold oceanic environments. Breeding occurs mostly on cliffs or rocky islets and stacks, and roosting sites are similar but include sandy and boulder-strewn beaches.

Movements and migrations. These birds remain close to their breeding sites throughout the year, although occasionally birds (mostly immatures) will stray as far as 80 kilometers seaward. There may be some dispersion during the nonbreeding season, but no good evidence exists on this point.

Competition and predation. Over much of its subantarctic range, this is the only breeding cormorant or shag. Competition with other close relatives is probably limited to local contacts with the rock shag, red-footed shag, and Neotropic cormorant. Several penguins such as various *Pygocelis* and *Eudyptes* species breed in the same general area and may locally compete for nest sites. Additionally, the diet of the gentoo penguin (*P. papua*) may overlap with that of this shag (Conroy and Twelves, 1972; Espitalier-Noel, Adams, and Klages, 1988).

Among predators, the kelp gull (*Larus dominicanus*) and sheathbills (*Chionis*) occasionally take eggs and small chicks (Derenne, Mary, and Mougin, 1976; Bernstein and Maxson, 1982). Over much of the species' range the brown skua (*Catharacta skua lonnbergi*) is a serious pirate of food, and takes both eggs and young as well. At least in some areas predation on small nestlings by skuas ranks with starvation as a major cause of chick mortality (Brothers, 1985).

Foods and Foraging Behavior

Foods consumed. Fish, supplemented by crustaceans and additional mostly benthic-dwelling invertebrates, comprise this species' foods throughout its range. On Macquarie Island a sample of 45 stomach regurgitations (Brothers, 1985) revealed a diet entirely of benthic fish, including the nototheniid *Paranotothenia*, the harpigiferid *Harpigifer*, other unidentified fish, and some crustaceans. The mean regurgitation mass was 77 grams, and the mean fish weight was 3.1 grams. A maximum of 20 fish were present in a single sample. On Marion Island a mixture of stomach samples (representing recently swallowed prey) and regurgitation casts (representing accumulated and generally more resistant hard parts) averaged 58 grams. Fish comprised the majority of prey remains from stomach samples (on a mass basis) and regurgitation casts (on a prey frequency or percent-numbers basis), although crustaceans made up the largest component of stomach samples on a prey frequency basis (Espitalier-Noel, Adams, and Klages, 1988). In both sample types benthic *Notothenia* comprised the largest fish component, with *Paranotothenia* represented in very small amounts. The size distribution of *Notothenia* ranged from about 30 to 110 millimeters and from 0.6 to 23.8 grams; all fish consumed were juveniles. Supporting the results of earlier studies at Marion Island (Blankley, 1981; Cooper, 1985c), the imperial shag there apparently forages entirely on benthic foods, mostly fish such as nototheniids, as has also been reported from Macquarie Island (Brothers, 1985), Heard Island (Downes et al., 1959), and the South Shetland Islands (Schlatter and Moreno, 1976). An average intake of about 0.45 kilograms of fish per adult bird daily has been estimated (Brothers, 1985).

Foraging behavior. Foraging may be done either solitarily or socially, but probably solitary foraging is the more typical method. It is primarily a bottom feeder, diving in only moderately deep water, for durations of up to 88 seconds and averaging about 40 seconds, and returning to the surface within 25 meters of the point of diving (Cooper, 1985c). Cooper observed that at Marion Island the birds forage in relatively calm waters over kelp beds, and bouts last approximately an hour. One bird was seen foraging in water no more than 2 meters deep, but most diving was in deeper waters, probably to depths of at least 25 meters (Conroy and Twelves, 1972), and possibly but not certainly even to depths of 50 meters (Brothers, 1985). Although the largest number of birds Cooper observed foraging socially was five, others have reported seeing larger flocks of up to 40 birds farther from shore, and have also observed groups diving in unison (Brothers, 1985).

Social Behavior

Age of maturity and mating system.   At Signy Island and South Georgia, the minimum age of first breeding is three years, but initial breeding at 4–5 years is more typical (Croxall, 1984; Marchant and Higgins, 1990). Cobley (1989) found that breeding on the South Orkney Islands began as early as two years of age, but that most breeding recruitment occurred between three and five years. Shaw (1986) reported that initial breeding in the same area varied greatly, ranging from three to nine years, with males averaging 5.0 years and females 5.4 years. The proportion of pairs that remained mated the following season was only 22.6 percent. There was no apparent difference in reproductive success among pairs that retained and pairs that changed their mates in successive seasons. It is possible that mates are selected partly on the basis of their age (Shaw, 1985a). Among cormorants, only the Galapagos cormorant is known to have a higher average rate (88.1 percent) of partner changing between breeding cycles. Likewise, on Macquarie Island there was a frequent exchange of mates between seasons, which was not apparently influenced by prior reproductive success. The minimum age of initial breeding was two years, when adult plumage was first attained, but some birds did not breed until they were at least four years old. The commencement of breeding may depend on a bird mating with an experienced breeder that already has a nest site, which probably places inexperienced birds at a considerable disadvantage (Brothers, 1985). Mate changing between breeding cycles was also reported from the Crozet Islands (Derenne, Mary, and Mougin, 1976) and also among a small sample of birds observed on Anvers Island, off the Antarctic Peninsula, by Bernstein and Maxson (1982).

Social displays and vocalizations.   Although the imperial shag (as recognized here) is sometimes considered to comprise at least two species, Siegel-Causey (1986b) was unable to establish any distinct differences in form among displays of sympatric *albiventer* and *atriceps* on the Patagonian coast, including those of both taxonomically mixed as well as nonmixed "conspecific" pairs. Some minor differences might exist between these forms and the displays of *bransfieldensis* as described by Bernstein and Maxson (1982) (pointing and darting were not seen by the latter authors but were among the most common recognition displays observed by Siegel-Causey), but such apparent differences might not have taxonomic significance. The behavior as described here is that reported by Bernstein and Maxson as typical of *bransfieldensis*. That of *melanogenis* appears to be virtually identical (Marchant and Higgins, 1990), and a more limited description of the displays of *purpurascens* (Robertson, 1988) suggests that they are also essentially similar.

Male advertisement display at the nest or nest site consists almost entirely of gargling, with the wing-waving component virtually absent and reduced to slight movements in only a few individuals. Instead, the display consists of a throwback of the head to the back (figure 67D), with the bill open and an *aark* call sounded, which may be followed by a second note during the return head movement. The tail is raised to varying degrees, and is cocked forward in the most intense version. In the Patagonian population the head is rolled from side to side once while in the full throwback posture, but this is only occasionally performed by *bransfieldensis* (Siegel-Causey, 1986b).

Individual recognition displays between mated birds consist of gaping, head lowering, throat clicking, and possibly also allopreening. Gaping is an extended-neck threatlike posture (figure 67C), with the bill open, the tail partly cocked, and the head moved sideways back and forth. Pointing, performed by the "in" bird on the nest with an extended neck but the bill closed, was observed by Siegel-Causey but not by Bernstein and Maxson. During darting, the neck is retracted but the bill is opened and the head is moved from side to side. A similar posture to gaping and darting is used as a direct threat, when the males utter a raucous *harrr* or growling *wirrr*, and the females hiss. During head lowering ("head-wagging" of Bernstein and Maxson) the birds lower and sometime cross their extended necks, swinging them back and forth in synchrony (figure 67E), usually without vocalization. This display is especially common during courtship and nest building. Throat clicking (figure 67F) is related to kink-throating, and consists of the birds waving their heads back and forth, with the female holding her bill wide open and the male's bill only slightly open, but without also swinging the neck as during head lowering. Throat clicking typically occurs on departure from and arrival at the nest, and in association with copulation. Kink-throating also occurs (Marchant and Higgins, 1990), but was not mentioned by Bernstein and Maxson or by Siegel-Causey. Allopreening by the pair is directed toward head and neck, and often toward the eye region. Self-preening of the white alar bar on the wings also sometimes occurs in the context of social display, and may represent a ritualized signal in the view of Siegel-Causey.

Figure 67. Social behavior of the imperial shag, including postlanding posture (A), penguin-walking by female (B), male gaping (C), male gargling (D), mutual head lowering (E), and mutual throat clicking (F). After sketches in Bernstein and Maxson (1982).

Other displays include a distinctive postlanding posture (figure 67A), which is performed silently and with the gular area expanded, and "stepping" (Bernstein and Maxson) or penguin-walking (Marchant and Higgins, 1990), a possible appeasement gesture during which a bird makes a high-stepping walk through the colony, with (especially in the female but not so clearly in the male) the neck distinctly arched and the bill held down on the breast, and with the tail held down and the wings tightly folded on the back (figure 67B).

Reproductive Biology

Breeding season. In all parts of its range this species breeds in the spring, with the egg season ranging from mid-June to late January or early February. The peak egg-laying period varies locally and becomes progressively later at higher latitudes (Pemberton and Gales, 1987; Marchant and Higgins, 1990). At least in some areas, the colony remains occupied throughout the year, and in places such as the Kerguelen Islands there may be a renewed period of courtship and nest building after the young are fledged in March and April (Marchant and Higgins, 1990).

Nest sites and nest building. Nests are low cone-shaped structures, consisting mostly of soft vegetation such as grasses and algae to which debris, mud, and guano are added. The sites are often in tussocky grassland, on the edges of cliffs, or on the tops of stacks. Sometimes the nests are close enough to the high-tide line that they are washed away between successive seasons. Nest site retention for successive breeding cycles is variable, with males more prone than females to retain their nest sites. Some birds of both sexes are known to retain their nest sites for up to four years. Males often remain at their nest sites year-round, even when nest materials are absent (Brothers, 1985). Pairs that nest in the center of colonies, which on average are older birds, tend to have greater levels of social contact, poorer access to their nests, and less exposure to wind and high seas than do peripheral nesters. However, in one analysis there was no clear relationship between nest site and clutch size, egg survival rates, or numbers of chicks hatched or fledged (Shaw, 1986).

Egg laying and incubation. On Macquarie Island, the average clutch sizes over two seasons were 2.93 and 2.50 eggs, averaging 2.72 and ranging from one to three eggs. Of 58 clutches, 76 percent contained three eggs. Replacement clutches were of the same average size as original clutches (Brothers, 1985). Similarly, on Heard Island, the average clutch size of 11 clutches was 2.5 eggs, with a range of 1–4 eggs (Pemberton and Gales, 1987), and on the Crozet Islands it was 2.9 for 20 clutches, with a range of 2–5 eggs (Derenne, Mary, and Mougin, 1976). On Marion Island the mean was 2.6 eggs for 41 clutches, with a range of 1–4 eggs and with 59 percent of the nests containing three eggs (Williams and

Burger, 1979). On the Falkland Islands the average of 5 clutches was 2.8 eggs, with a range of 2–3 (Murphy, 1936). At Punta Tombo, Argentina, the two-year average clutch size was 2.45 eggs for 199 clutches, and 60 percent of the clutches had three eggs (Malacalza, 1984). Shaw (1986) found that clutch size was evidently influenced by age, at least during one of two seasons, with average clutch size increasing in females between the ages of 3 and 6–7 years, and declining at 10 to 12 years old.

Williams and Burger (1979) reported egg-laying intervals of 2.8–2.9 days on Marion Island, and an average incubation period of 28.7 days for 7 last-laid eggs. The eggs hatch in the order in which they are laid, usually at an average interval of 1.6 days, but ranging 1–4 days. Incubation is by both sexes, with nest reliefs occurring at roughly 12-hour intervals. According to Derenne, Mary, and Mougin (1976), on the Crozet Islands the average incubation period for 11 eggs was 28.8 days, with a range of 27–31 days. Shaw (1986) reported a mean incubation period of 29.3 days for 372 eggs on Signy Island, South Orkneys, and Malacalza (1984) a period of 28.7 days for six *albiventer* eggs in Argentina. At least on Prince Edward Island very early nesters may be double-brooded (Ryan and Hunter, 1985), and it is generally likely that the early nesters are the older and most experienced birds. These tend to have lower mortality rates of both eggs and chicks than do later nesters (Derenne, Mary, and Mougin, 1976). Similarly, Shaw (1986) found that eggs laid later had lower average clutch sizes, as well as a lower initial brood size and a lower number of young fledged per nest, in one or both of two breeding seasons.

Brooding and rearing of young. Chicks are fed within 24 hours of hatching, and the first-hatched chicks are substantially heavier than those hatching from the last-laid egg. They are naked for the first five days, but by 18–19 days are well covered with down and begin to thermoregulate. Primaries are the first contour feathers to appear, usually at about 16 days, and fledging at Marion Island occurred at 75–80 days (Williams and Burger, 1979). Brood reduction is common, and typically involves the last-hatched chicks. In one study (Shaw, 1985b), 78–84 percent of first- and second-hatched chicks fledged, but only 11 percent of the third-hatched. The greater the hatching interval between first- and last-laid eggs, the earlier the average age of death of the last-hatched chick. Most of these deaths occurred during the first 12 days after hatching, or well before the time of maximum food demands by the young (at 41–65 days). On average, the oldest adults laid and hatched their young more synchronously than did younger birds, and subsequently sustained their last-hatched chicks for longer periods. However, Cobley (1989) found no significant differences in post-fledging survival of young in relationship to their hatching sequence. His estimates of first-year survival rate were quite variable, from 54 to 87 percent. Later long-term annual survival rates of adults were judged to be 77.7 percent, although his year-to-year estimates of survival rates ranged 86.7–92.2 percent, the highest reported for any cormorant or shag species.

Breeding success. Apparently a variety of factors might influence breeding success. Shaw (1986) found that the number of chicks hatched per pair was significantly influenced only by clutch size. When this factor was removed, the laying date was found to influence breeding success inversely (earlier laying produced greater average numbers of fledged chicks). The most important factor influencing brood size at fledging was brood size at hatching. In general, there was a gradual increase in productivity in birds aged from three to six years (although this may have been a statistical artifact) and after 10–11 years clutch size, egg size, and chick hatching weight significantly declined.

Hatching and fledging success varies from place to place and year to year. On Marion Island, egg mortality was 38.1 percent in one year and 54.8 percent in another, with most losses caused by high seas or hatching failures (Williams and Burger, 1979). On the Crozet Islands there was an average egg mortality of 44 percent, with most losses caused by gull predation or hatching failures (Derenne, Mary, and Mougin, 1976). Chick survival to fledging in these two studies averaged 22 percent and 59 percent, with starvation the main cause of death at Marion Island and a combination of starvation and predation by skuas (*Catharacta*) or giant petrels (*Macronectes*) at the Crozets. On Signy Island, South Orkneys, the average chick survival to fledging was 44 percent, with starvation the major cause of mortality (Shaw, 1985b). At Macquarie Island the average hatching success over three seasons was 75 percent, and the survival of young about 72 percent, producing an average fledging rate of 1.0–1.9 young per nest during these three seasons, with predation by skuas and starvation the major causes of chick losses. Although three-egg clutches had a higher hatching success than did two-egg clutches, they produced fewer fledged chicks, suggesting that starvation is an important factor in chick survival (Brothers, 1985). As noted earlier, breeding success there was also somewhat influenced by prior experience (faithful breeding pairs were more successful on average than those that changed mates between seasons, and younger birds usually nested near the edges of the colony, where the nests were sometimes washed away by storms), but the annual variations in breeding success were evidently mainly the result of food availability.

Population Status

The overall population of this widely dispersed species cannot be guessed, but the sizes of some small island populations are well known. According to Pemberton and Gales (1987), the Heard Island form consists of 600–1,000 birds, with about 90 breeding pairs and widely fluctuating annual productivity. Based on information recently summarized by Marchant and Higgins (1990), the Kerguelen Islands population comprised about 6,000–7,000 pairs in the mid to late 1980s, and was apparently stable. The Crozet Islands population was at least 815 pairs in 1981–82, and that of the Prince Edward Islands (including Marion Island) about 400 pairs. The latter population is protected by a nature reserve, but the former has been subject to human disturbance. The Macquarie Island population may consist of about 760 pairs, including about 100 pairs on Clerk and Bishop islands. The populations of *bransfieldensis* include about 10,000 pairs in 56 colonies on coastal islands of the Antarctic Peninsula, plus 700 pairs in 21 colonies on the South Shetlands and 205 pairs on Elephant Island. The population of *georgianus* includes less than 4,000 pairs on South Georgia, more than 1,000 pairs on Shag Rocks, 100–1,000 pairs on the South Sandwich Islands, and 2,000 pairs on the South Orkneys. Finally, *albiventer* is very common on the Falkland Islands (Woods, 1975), but no numbers are available. There were an estimated 30,000 breeding adults breeding in Chubut province, Argentina, during the mid-1980s (Punta, 1989). The populations of imperial shags breeding in Tierra del Fuego and along the mainland Chilean coast are unknown, but must be quite substantial.

Evolutionary Relationships

The species limits of this group of birds will no doubt remain controversial, but as defined here the nearest relatives of the imperial cormorant are obviously the complex of New Zealand blue-eyed shags and the Campbell Island shag. Voisin (1973) derived the *atriceps-albiventer* group from the *carunculatus* type, believing that during evolution the group gradually moved eastward, assisted by the prevailing westerlies and ocean currents. With regard to the South American complex, Devillers and Terschuren (1978) argued that the white-cheeked *atriceps*, in Argentina and Tierra del Fuego ("*imperialis*"), is a morph of mainland *atriceps*, and further that present-day contacts between the two plumage types in Patagonia resulted from the invasion of previous *albiventer* territory by *imperialis* birds that crossed overland from the Chilean fjords via newly formed gaps in the Andean ice sheet at the end of the last glaciation. They suggested that *georgianus* is no more closely related to *albiventer* than it is to the birds of mainland South America, and instead that all were separately isolated by former climatic events. They also suggested that *bougainvillii* may be part of this same general evolutionary assemblage in South America.

Other Vernacular Names

Campbell Island cormorant; cormoran de Campbell (French); Campbellscharbe (German)

Distribution

Endemic to Campbell Island and adjacent rocks, stacks, and islets. (See figure 69.)

Subspecies

None recognized here. However, *colensoi* and *ranfurlyi*, currently regarded as full species (Siegel-Causey, 1988; Marchant and Higgins, 1990; Sibley and Monroe, 1990), are often considered as only racially distinct from *campbelli* (Dorst and Mougin, 1979).

Description

Prebreeding adult. Upperparts and most of foreneck blackish with blue sheen; upper wing coverts and scapulars purplish gray, with green sheen and narrow indistinct black borders; white alar stripes variable in development, sometimes absent; no white on scapulars or back; a well-developed forehead crest, and a number of white filoplumes forming a thin patch above the eyes and scattered over the head and neck; rectrices (12) black, with white shaft bases. Iris dark brown to grayish brown (also described as greenish gray); an indistinct purplish to grayish black eye ring; facial skin variable (brown, dirty pink, dark purple, or blue), with crimson dots in front of and below eye, but no nasal caruncles; gape edge and mouth interior orange-yellow to red (the latter probably at start of breeding); narrow zone above and below the gape line yellow (becoming orange-red at onset of breeding season); bill blackish brown, grading to yellowish toward the base; gular skin purple to red; legs and feet dull pink, with dark gray smudges at the joints and webs.
Postbreeding adult. Similar to the prebreeding plumage, but lacking crest and filoplumes; no white dorsal postbreeding patch; softpart colors paler, the bill light grayish brown at the sides.
Immature-subadult. Dark brown above and white below, patterned like the adult. Iris grayish brown; facial skin dull purple; bill light orange-brown, becoming yellow or orange at base and gape; gular skin and mouth lining dull yellow-orange; legs and feet dull orange, pink, and gray. Age of maturity unknown.
Juvenile. Similar to the immature, but more gradually grading from brown above to whitish below. Iris dark brown; bare patch around eye pinkish gray; culmen brownish black, the rest of the bill pinkish, shading to orange at gape; legs and feet flesh-colored, the soles brownish black.
Nestling. Naked at hatching, with black skin, but soon covered with gray down; the throat and lower mandible pink.

Measurements (in millimeters)

Live birds: wing, males 280 and 285, females 270–280 (ave. of 8, 272.5); tail, males 105 and 130, females 115–125 (ave. of 8, 119); culmen, males 52 and 55, females 47–52 (ave. of 8, 50.1) (Bailey and Sorensen, 1962). Museum skins: wing, males 262–287 (ave. of 7, 275), females 255–284 (ave. of 14, 268); tail, males 106–134 (ave. of 6, 123), females 107–132 (ave. of 9, 119); culmen, males 48–53 (ave. of 7, 50), females 43–52 (ave. of 8, 50.1) (Marchant and Higgins, 1990). Eggs (of suspect origin, possibly not of this species) ca. 61 × 38.

Weights (in grams)

Two adult males, 2,041 (4.5 lb.) and 2,097 (4.625 lb.); 8 adult females 1,616–1,927 (3.562–4.25 lb.), ave. 1,750 (Bailey and Sorensen, 1962). Calculated egg weight 48.6 (but see measurements caution above).

Identification

In the hand. The combination of white underparts (but a black foreneck), pinkish flesh feet, a purplish eye ring, and no facial caruncles separates this form from all but the Auckland Island shag, which often has a complete neck band, and the Bounty Island shag, which has a white foreneck.
In the field. This is the only cormorant or shag native to Campbell Island, although vagrant little pied cormorants have been reported there.

Ecology and General Biology

Breeding and nonbreeding habitats. Like the imperial shag and the *Euleucocarbo* or "New Zealand shags" (see table 22, note 2), this is a marine species, foraging out to sea as well as along shorelines, bays, and inlets, and nesting on adjacent cliffs, ledges, or sea caves (Marchant and Higgins, 1990).
Movements and migrations. Apparently sedentary, this species is unlikely to leave the vicinity of Campbell Island, although vagrant individuals (of this species or of the Bounty Island shag) have reached the Antipodes Islands, more than 800 kilometers distant (Marchant and Higgins, 1990).

Figure 68. Social behavior of the Campbell Island shag, including male gargling (A), gaping (B), mutual head lowering (C), pretakeoff posture (D), kink-throating (E), penguin-walking (F), and prehop posture (G). After sketches in Marchant and Higgins (1990).

Competition and predation.   There are no other cormorants or shags on the Campbell Islands, but various introduced or domesticated mammals (rats, cats, etc.) do occur. Probably skuas (*Catharacta*) are the most important natural predators, taking eggs and probably also young birds. Antarctic terns (*Sterna vittata*) and silver gulls (*Larus novaehollandiae*) sometimes nest near the shags and provide defensive mobbing behavior (Robertson, 1988; Marchant and Higgins, 1990).

Foods and Foraging Behavior

Foods consumed.   Almost nothing specific has been recorded, but apparently fish, crustaceans, and mollusks are consumed. Bailey and Sorenson (1962) noted that some specimens they collected had stomachs that were filled with small shells (*Cantharidus*).

Foraging behavior.   Bailey and Sorenson (1962) watched a group of 40 birds foraging on a harbor. The birds drifted with the wind, diving singly or in twos or threes, until all were submerged. They would reappear some distance apart about a minute later and regroup. Judging from the description, this evidently represented solitary rather than social foraging behavior. However, later on "vast groups" were observed fishing daily, one group numbering more than 2,000 birds, with adults and young mingling together. Simultaneous diving by large flocks that fan out over the water has also been observed. Petrels, terns, and gulls have been observed feeding with these flocks, suggesting that they may have been feeding on schooling fish rather than benthic prey. After the birds have finished foraging they rest on intertidal rocks and headlands (Robertson, 1988), but in common with the other subantarctic shags they evidently do not perform wing-spreading behavior.

Social Behavior

Age of maturity and mating system.   No specific information.

Social displays and vocalizations.   Social behavior of this species has been observed by van Tets (1980; also summarized in Robertson, 1988, and Marchant and Higgins, 1990). Male advertising consists of gargling (figure 68A), with the head thrown back on the rump, where it may be bounced or moved back beside the body, the tail held variably upward, the wings drooping without waving, and the bill open but without vocalizations. Individual recognition displays performed when a pair greets each other consist of gaping, head lowering, and nest worrying. During gaping (figure 68B), the head is held horizontally and is waved sideways as well as moved backward and forward once or twice per second, while the tail is somewhat cocked and the wings drooped. Head lowering (figure 68C) consists of the pair standing facing each other or side by side, with necks outstretched and heads lowered in parallel. In this posture their heads are silently moved up and down several times,

with the throat bulging during the downward phase. Nest worrying reportedly occurs in association with individual recognition as well as during disturbance by intruders; in this behavior the birds manipulate nest materials or dig at the nest site with their bills.

The only reported vocalization occurs during kink-throating (figure 68E). This is performed in an upright posture with lowered hyoids, and the male utters a repeated *kor* note, but the female is silent. The pretakeoff posture (figure 68D) is similarly upright, and the neck and upper abdomen pulsate silently. Likewise during the prehop posture (figure 68G) there is a silent pulsation of this same area, but the bill is directed downward. A silent hopping display is performed by both sexes. During penguin-walking (figure 68F) the neck is likewise arched and the bill position varies from the horizontal to diagonally downward.

During threat display, silent gaping movements are made, with the throat bulging and the bill widely opened. Other displays and copulatory behavior are still undescribed.

Reproductive Biology

Breeding season.   The breeding season is fairly long, with the birds probably laying from about August to December. Fully grown chicks have been seen as early as November, but eggs have been reported as late as December (Bailey and Sorensen, 1962; Marchant and Higgins, 1990), suggesting that renesting following egg loss may occur.

Nest sites and nest building.   Nests are constructed of tussock grasses, other plant materials, and available debris, either on grass tussocks or on the ground. They are colonially situated on seaward-facing cliffs, ledges, stacks, or more sheltered but generally inaccessible locations, such as in sea caves. This species sometimes nests among colonies of Antarctic terns or silver gulls.

Egg laying and incubation.   No information. Skuas evidently take some eggs.

Breeding and rearing of young.   No information.

Breeding success.   No information.

Population Status

The only available estimate of the population is one of about 2,000 nests and 8,000 total birds in 1975 (van Tets, 1980).

Evolutionary Relationships

This insular form is presumably an offshoot from an ancestor that perhaps originated in New Zealand. Voisin (1973) suggested that its nearest affinities are with *carunculatus*. He regarded it as a monotypic subgenus that he named *Nesocarbo*, thus separating it from the more typical blue-eyed shags (*verrucosus, carunculatus, albiventer,* and *atriceps*) of his proposed subgenus *Euleucocarbo*. Siegel-Causey (1988) generally agreed with this alliance, but raised these subgeneric groups to full genera.

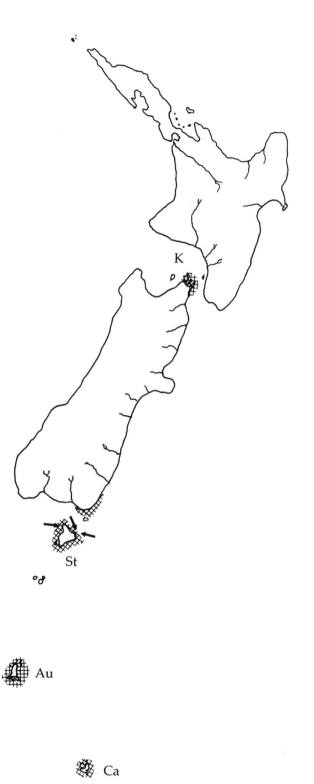
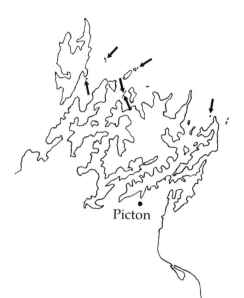

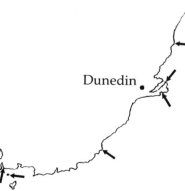

K

Picton

Ch

Bo

St

Au

Ca

Dunedin

Other Vernacular Names

Carunculated shag, Cook Strait shag, king cormorant, Marlborough Sounds shag, New Zealand king shag; cormorant carunculé (French); Warzenscharbe (German)

Distribution

Endemic in New Zealand's Marlborough Sounds area of coastal northeastern South Island, where since 1960 breeding records have been confined to five sites (Te Kuru Kuru Island, North Trio Island, Duffer's Reef, Sentinel Rock, and White Rocks). Now very rare and classified as threatened by the ICBP (Collar and Andrew, 1988), and as endangered by New Zealand authorities (Bell, 1986). According to some taxonomies (such as Peters, 1931; OSNZ, 1970; and Dorst and Mougin, 1979), additional conspecific populations are resident on Stewart Island and nearby portions of southern South Island, as well as on the Chatham Islands. These latter disjunct populations are here tentatively considered full species to conform with recent regional references (e.g., Falla, Sibson, and Turbott, 1981; Robertson, 1988; Marchant and Higgins, 1990). (See figure 69.)

Subspecies

None recognized here, but *chalconotus* and *onslowi* are often (e.g., Voisin, 1973; Dorst and Mougin, 1979) considered subspecies. Peters (1931) included *ranfurlyi, colensoi,* and *campbelli* as additional conspecific races of *carunculatus*, although these latter three forms are now more commonly grouped as a separate taxonomic cluster consisting of from one to three species.

Description

Prebreeding adult. Top of head, sides of throat, sides and back of neck black glossed with dull bluish green; interscapulars and most of scapulars and wings glossed with oil-green;

Figure 69. Distributions of the New Zealand king shag (Ki), and of the Auckland (Au), Bounty (Bo), Campbell (Ca), Chatham (Ch), and Stewart (St) Island shags. Inset maps show breeding locations of the New Zealand king shag in Marlborough Sounds, northern South Island (above), and of the Stewart Island shag, southern South Island (below), with arrows indicating breeding records.

---

lower back, rump, and upper tail coverts dark metallic bluish green, but one or two white back patches usually present (these feathers often covered by scapulars); remiges and rectrices (12) black; a white alar stripe usually but not always present on the marginal upper wing coverts; some of the outer scapulars also usually white; middle of throat and foreneck and rest of underparts pure white, the white throat feathers extending forward under the lower mandible; at onset of breeding season a black forehead crest develops temporarily, and the nasal caruncles are especially conspicuous. Iris hazel-gray; eye ring blue; facial skin blackish gray; nasal caruncles bright yellow to orange; bill pale horn-brown; gular skin grayish black; legs and feet grayish pink with brownish joints and webs.

Postbreeding adult. Similar to the prebreeding adult, but crestless, and the softparts generally duller, the facial skin very dark reddish brown to grayish red, and the yellow caruncles probably smaller and more subdued in color.

Immature-subadult. Darker but rather similar to the juvenal plumage, the upperpart feathers with a more definite greenish gloss and not so pointed, the underparts a clearer white, and the softpart colors probably generally brighter. Age of maturity unknown.

Juvenile. Upperparts brown, the feathers of the upperparts and tail with whitish or buffy margins; dull white underparts. No caruncles; the face, legs, and feet all flesh-colored; bill brownish.

Nestling. Initially with naked black skin; later mostly covered with sooty brown down. Iris greenish gray; bare facial skin black; bill mostly brownish black, becoming white or pink at base of mandible; gular skin pinkish; legs and feet brown or blackish gray.

Measurements (in millimeters)

Wing, males 305–323 (ave. of 9, 312), females 284–307 (ave. of 10, 298); tail, males 111–132 (ave. of 9, 123), females 109–129 (ave. of 9, 116); culmen, males 63–68 (ave. of 9, 66), females 62–69 (ave. of 10, 64) (Marchant and Higgins, 1990). Eggs ca. 67 × 43.

Weights (in grams)

One adult male 2,655, one female 2,500 (Marchant and Higgins, 1990). Calculated egg weight 68.4; ave. of 2, 62 (Nelson, 1972).

Identification

In the hand. The combination of white underparts, pinkish feet, a culmen length of 62–72 mm, and blackish facial skin with a blue eye ring and bright yellow caruncles serves to identify this species from all other shags except perhaps some of its closely related island vicariad populations (see four following descriptive accounts).

In the field.　This is the only New Zealand *Leucocarbo* shag with entirely dark adult facial skin. In its limited range the only cormorant or shag likely to cause confusion is the pied cormorant, which has black feet, white cheeks, and uniformly dark upperparts. Adults of the king shag have blue eye rings, white bars on the anterior wing coverts ("alar stripes"), and variably developed white markings on the scapulars that often resemble a pair of white "headlights" in flight when seen from the front. Young birds are much browner above, but the white wing and scapular markings of adults are apparently represented as pale buffy areas. The pied morph of the closely related Stewart Island shag (which is unlikely to be found within this species' range) is also very similar, but lacks reddish orange on the face, lacks white dorsal "headlights," and in breeding plumage the head appears smaller and is more distinctly crested.

Ecology and General Biology

Breeding and nonbreeding habitats.　This is a marine species with a highly restricted distribution; the waters surrounding the breeding habitats are subantarctic (mean annual temperature 12°C). The birds are associated with rocky islets, rock stacks, and pinnacles. They forage in sheltered bays and inlets near their breeding sites.

Movements and migrations.　There is no evidence of any seasonal movements, and only a few records of birds occurring outside of their general breeding grounds in the Marlborough Sounds.

Competition and predation.　No specific information. The pied cormorant also occurs in the same general range, but it is doubtful that serious competition exists. Nelson (1971) judged that the king shag has no competing species, and no apparent food limitations. Little information exists on possible egg or chick predators, but silver gulls (*Larus novaehollandiae*) are known to take eggs when nesting birds are disturbed (Marchant and Higgins, 1990).

Foods and Foraging Behavior

Foods consumed.　Foods regurgitated at nests included rhombosoleid soles (*Peltorhamphus*) and sand eels (*Gonorhynchus*, Gonorhynchidae), which are both bottom-dwelling fish (Nelson, 1971). Additionally, blue cod (*Parapercis*, Pinguipedidae) have been reported as foods at one colony (Falla, 1933).

Foraging behavior.　Nelson (1971) observed a mean dive duration of 46.5 seconds for 22 dives, and a maximum dive of 95 seconds, in water of unstated depth. Waters surrounding one of the breeding sites was 25–80 meters deep (Falla, 1933).

Pebbles are sometimes swallowed, perhaps to provide ballast for deep dives. During wing drying the birds beat their wings, rather than using wing spreading (Robertson, 1988).

Social Behavior

Age of maturity and mating system.　No specific information.

Social displays and vocalizations.　The only available information is from some relatively distant observations by G. van Tets (in Marchant and Higgins, 1990). Based on his information, it appears the species' displays are very much like the other blue-eyed shags of New Zealand, although no observations on possible vocalizations were possible from his observational distances. Male advertisement consists of gargling (figure 70A), in which the head is thrown back to the rump. No rotation occurs at that point, although the head may be bounced back against the rump, and the bill may be opened or closed during the throwing movements. Individual recognition displays include mutual head lowering and gaping. Gaping (figure 70B) is performed with the bill widely opened and the head raised. During mutual head lowering (figure 70D) the pair stands close together, lowering and raising their heads and extended necks in synchrony, with their bodies held horizontally and their tails lowered.

Other displays observed by van Tets at the nest site include an erect pretakeoff posture (figure 70E), with a few swallowing movements often made with the bill closed. The prehop posture is similar (figure 70H), but the bill is strongly declined. The postlanding posture (figure 70C) is an exaggerated landing recovery movement, with the neck outstretched and the head lowered. During penguin-walking through the colony (figure 70G) the neck is arched and the bill is inclined downward. Kink-throating is the primary display performed in the vicinity of the nest (figure 70F), and consists of hyoid lowering with a closed bill.

During aggressive interactions the bird assumes a posture similar to that of gaping, and the head is moved back and forth as well as sideways. No information on copulatory behavior exists.

Reproductive Biology

Breeding season.　The normal breeding season takes about five months, and most breeding occurs between March and December. Evidently the birds usually nest once per year, but rarely they may nest twice in a 12-month period (6 reported times in 49 colony-years). Breeding normally begins about May, but may begin 2–3 months sooner when two breeding cycles are attempted (Nelson, 1971).

Nest sites and nest building.　Nests are constructed of locally available vegetation, including grasses, cemented together with guano. They are usually placed about 1 meter (40 inches) apart, but this varies with nest density and slope.

Figure 70. Social behavior of the king shag, including male gargling (A), gaping (B), postlanding posture (C), mutual head lowering (D), pretakeoff posture (E), kink-throating (F), penguin-walking (G), and prehop posture (H). After sketches in Marchant and Higgins (1990).

Typically the nests are on rocky slopes (37–45 degrees) above the reach of wave action, and sometimes on stacks 15–20 meters high, but they may be located as close to water as 1–2 meters above sea level. The sites are sometimes protected from the wind by taupata (*Coprosma*) scrub (Nelson, 1971).

Egg laying and incubation.   Of 167 clutches (probably not all of which were complete), the range of eggs was 1–3, the mean was 1.8 eggs, and 52.7 percent of the nests contained two eggs. The incubation period is unknown, but the adults incubate in the usual cormorant fashion, between the feet and the abdomen (Nelson, 1971).

Brooding and rearing of young.   No specific information.

Breeding success.   No information. Many eggs are said to be lost by rolling away from the nest, and others are taken by silver gulls when the adults are disturbed.

Population Status

This is an extremely rare and endangered species (Robertson and Bell, 1984; Bell, 1986), with a population that ranged during the 1960s from 192 to 260 birds (Nelson, 1971). It has been protected since 1924, but has continued to suffer from illegal killing (mostly by fishermen) and human disturbance to the few nesting colonies. The small colony size might have generated undesirable genetic effects, and inadequate social stimulation for effective breeding. Its population has been estimated more recently at less than 500 individuals (Robertson, 1988). Disturbance by boats and skin divers may be a factor in the species' survival (Bell, 1986).

Evolutionary Relationships

Voisin (1973) believed that *carunculatus* (including the races *chalconotus* and *onslowi*) forms a close-knit group with *campbelli*, *colensoi*, and *ranfurlyi*, which he collectively considered as a trio of subspecies (of *campbelli*) showing varying degrees of morphological differentiation away from the condition found in *carunculatus*. Slightly more distantly related, and recognized as specifically separate forms within the subgenus *Euleucocarbo* by Voisin, are *verrucosus*, *albiventer*, and *atriceps*. I would generally agree with this suggested hierarchy of affinities, although species limits are impossible to test in this entire group of essentially allopatric populations.

Other Vernacular Names

Gray's shag, pink-footed shag; cormoran de Stewart (French); Stewartscharbe (German)

Distribution

Limited to Stewart Island, New Zealand, plus adjoining islands (including Codfish), the islands of Foveaux Strait (breeding on Centre Island), and the adjoining coastline along the southern tip of South Island (breeding locally from Bluff Harbour northeast to the Otago Peninsula). Considered threatened by the ICBP (Collar and Andrew, 1988), but classified as "rare" by New Zealand authorities (Bell, 1986). (See figure 69.)

Subspecies

None recognized here, but this population is often (e.g., Peters, 1931; Falla, Sibson, and Turbott, 1981; Voisin, 1973; Dorst and Mougin, 1979; Lalas, 1983) considered a subspecies of *carunculatus*. The two plumage morphs have at times also been considered separate subspecies.

Description

Prebreeding adult. Pied morph: Very similar to adults of *carunculatus*, but the caruncles vestigial and the head more distinctly crested. Upperparts black, with blue sheen; upper wing coverts dark brown, with green sheen and narrow black margins; white alar stripes present and a single dorsal back patch usually present; rectrices (12) black, with white bases. Underparts, including throat, foreneck, breast, belly, and under tail coverts all pure white. A black forehead crest, and a much shorter occipital crest; white filoplumes on sides of crown, and elsewhere on head and neck. Iris golden brown to dark brown; eye ring iridescent purplish blue to lavender; facial skin usually grayish (also reported as dark blue or purplish brown), with a row of small yellow, orange, or red papillae (vestigial caruncles) between culmen and eye; mouth lining, skin at base of lower mandible, and gular area red; bill grayish brown to horn-yellow; legs and feet pink, with the toes and soles dark brown.

Melanistic (or "bronze") morph: Similar to the pied morph in its softpart colors, but the plumage entirely black, the feathers of the back edged with pale glossy brass-green, and the other upperpart feathers glossed with darker and more bluish green. Intermediate examples, which are rela-

tively infrequent, may have white spotting on the lower breast and belly, or even entirely white underparts.

Postbreeding adult (both morphs). Similar to the prebreeding adult of the same morph, but lacking the crests and white filoplumes; the softpart colors less bright, the facial papillae perhaps slightly reduced.

Immature-subadult. Undescribed in detail but presumably similar to the juvenal plumage, if somewhat brighter. Immatures of the bronze morph are slightly glossy black above and below (P. Rasmussen, personal communication). In the pied morph the underparts are probably variably white, and in both morphs the softparts are probably more colorful than in juveniles. Initial breeding occurs at ca. three years (Lalas, 1983).

Juvenile. Upperparts dark brown, the pied morph individuals apparently showing indications of white alar stripes and dorsal patches; underparts dark brown (melanistic morph), white (pied morph), or mixed. Iris pale brown; eye ring gray; facial skin dark brown; gape yellow; bill light gray or sandy, with a darker culmen; legs and feet flesh-colored.

Nestling. Initially with naked black skin; later covered with brown down that is darker on the head and neck, with white down intermixed on the head and neck (P. Rasmussen, personal communication). Maxilla, face, and naked crown gray; the mandible and throat pale iridescent blue, with black patches.

Measurements (in millimeters)

Wing, males 278–310 (ave. of 10, 293), females 269–314 (ave. of 22, 287); tail, males 105–122 (ave. of 10, 113.7), females 104–122 (ave. of 21, 112); culmen, males 49–59 (ave. of 10, 54), females 48–60 (ave. of 22, 53) (Marchant and Higgins, 1990). Clinal in size, the birds from the northern end of the range (Otago Peninsula) being considerably larger than those from southern areas (Falla, Sibson, and Turbott, 1981). Eggs ca. 61 × 38.

Weights (in grams)

Males 1,797–3,875 (ave. of 6, 2,717), females 1,447–2,356 (ave. of 8, 1,813.6 (Marchant and Higgins, 1990). Calculated egg weight 48.6.

Identification

In the hand. The combination of variably dark (white to black) underparts, pinkish feet, a culmen length of 51–69 mm, and dark red facial skin with virtually no caruncle development should identify typical examples of this questionable species. It is unique in having the combination of a blue eye ring, a red gular pouch, and lacking definite caruncles.

In the field. In its limited range around Stewart Island and adjacent South Island of New Zealand this is the only cormorant or shag with pink legs. Adults also have a distinctive blue eye ring, and underparts that vary from immaculate white to sooty black. The dimorphism in immature and adult plumages may cause confusion, since mated pairs may be either of the same plumage morph or mixed, the birds not exhibiting definite assortative mating.

Ecology and General Biology

Breeding and nonbreeding habitats. This is a marine, relatively sedentary species that forages in coastal waters near its breeding grounds, which are on rocky headland cliffs and islands.

Movements and migrations. No movements of note have been reported.

Competition and predation. Some competitive contacts with spotted shags may perhaps occur during foraging, but no specific information exists. There is no information on possible egg or chick predators such as gulls.

Foods and Foraging Behavior

Foods consumed. The best available evidence on this species' foods comes from the work of Lalas (1983, and as summarized in Marchant and Higgins, 1990). Some 28,000 prey items were analyzed from regurgitated pellets at Otago Harbour. By weight, these consisted of 70 percent fish, 25 percent crustaceans (stomatopods and crabs), and 5 percent cephalopods, plus a few polychaete worms. The importance of crustaceans and cephalopods was greatest in winter, when these sources collectively comprised 65 percent of the total weight. Fish were most important during spring, when they represented 85 percent of total prey weight. Among fish, the most important taxon represented was the clinid *Tripterygion*, which comprised 35 percent of the foods by weight and 61 percent by number, with a mean length of 4 centimeters and a mean weight of 1.0 grams. Also important was the bothid *Arnoglossus*, representing 23 percent of the weight and 31 percent of the items. Samples from elsewhere gave different results, indicating that the birds took prey according to their relative availability. The average daily intake was estimated as 180 grams, and the average number of prey items was also 180.

Foraging behavior. This is mostly a benthic-foraging species, feeding at depths as great as 30 meters and as far as 15 kilometers offshore. Food is located visually and by tactile means as the birds move across the bottom, at times probing with the bill to find or flush prey. Diving durations are directly related to water depth, and durations of 4,560 dives varied from 8 to 169 seconds. Diving is done solitarily, and foraging bouts lasted from 45 minutes to two hours (Lalas, in Marchant and Higgins, 1990).

Social Behavior

Age of maturity and mating system. The age of maturity is believed to be three years. The mating system is probably one of sustained or seasonal monogamy, although specific evidence is lacking.

Social displays and vocalizations. Available information is limited to that provided by G. van Tets, as summarized in Marchant and Higgins (1990). The male's advertising display consists of gargling (figure 71A), which as in the other New Zealand shags consists of a posterior head throw, the body held upright, with or without an accompanying *borr* call. Individual recognition displays between paired birds consist of gaping and head lowering. During gaping (figure 71B) the bill is opened and the head is moved both back and forth as well as sideways. The tail is partly cocked and the body is held horizontally. During gaping the male calls with a soft, repeated *eh* note, but the female is silent. During head lowering (figure 71C) the pair stand close together, sometimes facing each other. The birds bulge out their bare red throats as their heads and extended necks are lowered, sometimes mutually.

Several other social displays occur including a kink-throating display usually performed toward its mate at a bird's arrival at the nest (figure 71D). It is performed with an erect body posture and lower hyoids. Males also produce a barking, repeated *cor* note at this time, but females are silent. The pretakeoff posture is similar but is silent, and the bill is held slightly open and the breast pulsates. During penguin-walking through the colony the neck is arched (figure 71E) and the bill is variably pointed downward. In the post-landing posture (figure 71F) the neck and extended head are lowered, and the crest is somewhat raised but the crown feathers are sleeked.

Reproductive Biology

Breeding season. Apparently breeding can occur at any time during the year, depending upon the weather and food availability (Marchant and Higgins, 1990). Nesting has been reported from September to December, and downy chicks have been seen at least as late as March (Watt, 1975).

Nest sites and nest building. Nests are placed on bare, sloping rocks, in colonies of up to several hundred nests. These are positioned close to one another but just out of the neighbor's pecking reach, with the nests in the middle of the colony more closely spaced than those near the periphery. They are constructed of vegetation and debris and held

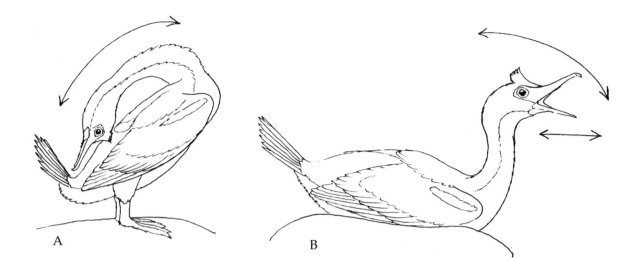

Figure 71. Social behavior of the Stewart Island shag, including male gargling (A), gaping (B), mutual head lowering (C),
kink-throating (D), penguin-walking (E), and postlanding (F)
posture. After sketches in Marchant and Higgins (1990).

together with guano, and some may form columns up to 1.5 meters high.

Egg laying and incubation.   The clutch size reportedly consists of 2–3 eggs (Robertson, 1988), but no quantitative data exist. The egg-laying interval and incubation period are also unknown, as are most details of this phase of reproduction.

Brooding and rearing of young.   No detailed information.

Breeding success.   No information.

Population Status

This species is now classified as "rare" by New Zealand authorities (Bell, 1986). Watt (1975) estimated 1,500–2,000 nesting pairs and listed 12 known breeding sites, including four from the Dunedin-Otago area, four from Stewart Island, two from Codfish Island, and one each from Centre Island and Bluff Harbour. The recent summary by Marchant and Higgins (1990) listed all of the 11 historically known colonies between 1911 and 1974. The largest of these, on Centre Island, was of at least 1,200 birds in 1955.

Evolutionary Relationships

As noted earlier, Voisin (1973) and others have considered this as a subspecies of *carunculatus*, a view to which I would subscribe. Siegel-Causey (1988) considered these as distinct species, although he did not cladistically evaluate any specimens of *carunculatus*.

Other Vernacular Names

Chatham Island cormorant; cormoran de Chatham (French); Chathamscharbe (German)

Distribution

Endemic to Chatham Islands (800 kilometers east of New Zealand's South Island), breeding locally on Chatham Island, near Pitt Island (Rabbit Island), and at Star Keys. Rare, and classified by the ICBP as threatened (Collar and Andrew, 1988). (See figure 69.)

Subspecies

None recognized here. This population is often (e.g., Peters, 1931; Dorst and Mougin, 1979) considered a race of *carunculatus*, but most recently (Marchant and Higgins, 1990) has been separated specifically.

Description

Prebreeding adult. Upperparts black, with a bluish sheen, the upper wing coverts dark grayish brown, with narrow and indistinct black margins; white alar stripes, one or two white back patches often present, and white spotting on scapulars often present; underparts including ventral neck and throat white; rectrices (12) black, the shafts with white bases; a well-developed black forehead crest. Iris brown, eye ring purplish black; facial skin dark purple to blackish gray; nasal caruncles and patch of skin at base of mandible bright orange to orange-red; bill grayish brown; gular skin brick-red; mouth lining bright red; legs and feet flesh-colored.
Postbreeding adult. Lacking the forehead crest; eye ring blue; nasal caruncles yellow; facial skin blackish; gular skin and mouth lining brick-red or orange; bill grayish brown; legs and feet pink.
Immature-subadult. Apparently mixed glossy black and slightly green-glossed brown above, and white ventrally, with white alar and scapular stripes. Iris grayish brown; eye ring pale blue; facial and gular skin brown; bill bluish gray, with a darker ridge; legs and feet pink. Age of first breeding unknown.
Juvenile. Mostly dark brown on the head, upperparts, and tail, the larger mantle feathers blackish near the tips and often edged with buffy; mostly dull white below, with or without a brown breast band. Iris grayish blue; facial skin brown; bill yellow, with a dusky culmen; gular skin yellow; legs and feet yellow to brownish yellow.

Nestling. Initially naked black; later covered with smoky brown, with scattered white down feathers. Softparts undescribed, but at fledging the iris grayish brown, bill blackish brown above, the lower mandible bluish white basally; gular skin pale bluish white; facial skin, legs, and feet brownish black (Marchant and Higgins, 1990).

Measurements (in millimeters)

Wing, males 278–292 (ave. of 5, 286), females 261–284 (ave. of 5, 271); tail, males 109–124 (ave. of 4, 116), females 99–116 (ave. of 5, 108); culmen, males 51–56 (ave. of 5, 53), females 52–55 (ave. of 4, 53) (Marchant and Higgins, 1990). Eggs ca. 61 × 38.

Weights (in grams)

Males 2,400 and (fat) 2,525; females 1,790 and (fat) 2,230 (Marchant and Higgins, 1990). Calculated egg weight 48.6.

Identification

In the hand. The combination of white underparts, pinkish feet, a culmen length of 52–56 mm, and dark purple facial skin with bright orange caruncles should serve to identify at least typical examples of this form, which is only questionably separable from *carunculatus* at the species level.
In the field. This is the only cormorant or shag native to the Chatham Islands that has pink feet and white underparts. The distinctively gray-bellied Pitt Island shag and the black-bellied great cormorant also occur there, but both lack orange facial caruncles.

Ecology and General Biology

Breeding and nonbreeding habitats. This is a sedentary species, limited to the coastlines and adjoining oceans around the Chatham Islands, including offshore islets.
Movements and migrations. No movements of significance have been reported.
Competition and predation. Limited food competition with the Pitt Island shag and the great cormorant may possibly occur. Silver gulls (*Larus novaehollandiae*) are known to take many eggs when nesting colonies are disturbed.

Foods and Foraging Behavior

Foods consumed. There is almost no information on this, but small fish about 10 centimeters (4 inches) long have been reported regurgitated by breeding birds.

Figure 72. Social behavior of the Chatham Island shag, including male gargling (A), gaping (B), head lowering (C), pretakeoff posture (D), kink-throating (E), penguin-walking (F), and prehop posture (G). After sketches in Marchant and Higgins (1990).

Foraging behavior. No detailed information. Foraging is typically done within a few kilometers of shore.

Social Behavior

Age of maturity and mating system. No information.
Social displays and vocalizations. The only available information on this comes from observations by G. van Tets (summarized in Marchant and Higgins, 1990). This form's displays are very much like those of the king shag and Stewart Island shag. Male advertising consists of gargling (figure 72A), which is like that of the king shag except that the body is held more nearly vertical, and the head-throwing movement may be rapidly repeated up to 13 times. The male may call during the display or remain silent, and the bill is variably opened. Individual recognition displays consist of gaping (figure 72B) and head lowering (figure 72C). During gaping the bill is opened and the head is simultaneously swung laterally and moved back and forth, with the male uttering a barking note and the female a soft puffing sound. Actual threat displays are similar to gaping, with the male calling but the female silent. During head lowering the pair stands close together and each bird raises and lowers its head while extending the neck.

Other social displays include kink-throating (figure 72E), in which as a greeting display the male calls repeatedly but the female is silent, with the hyoid strongly lowered in both sexes. During the erect pretakeoff posture (figure 72D) the lower and upper breast pulsates, while the bill is opened slightly. In the similar prehop posture the neck is arched and the bill is directed downward, the males making ticking sounds but the females silent. The penguin-walking posture is similar to the prehop posture and is performed as a bird walks through a nesting colony. Finally, the postlanding posture closely resembles those of the king and Stewart Island shags (see previous accounts).

Reproductive Biology

Breeding season. The egg-laying period is from September to December. At a colony at Okawa all stages from fresh eggs to fledged young were seen in December, while at another colony all but three of the approximately 50 nests still contained only eggs (Falla, 1937). This suggests that a fairly long season, with possible renesting, may occur. No other details are available.

Nest sites and nest building. Nests are placed on level or sloping rocks of headland cliffs, islets, or islands, often close to the high-tide line but sometimes 15 meters or more above sea level. They are shaped like chimney pots and constructed of grasses and other readily available vegetation, cemented with guano. The nests are regularly arranged, with the birds just out of pecking range of one another, providing "alley-ways" between the nests along which birds can make their way (Fleming, 1939).

Egg laying and incubation. No specific information. The normal clutch is believed to be of three eggs, but ranges from two to five (Falla, 1937).

Brooding and rearing of young. No information.
Breeding success. No information.

Population Status

This form is classified as "rare" by New Zealand authorities (Bell, 1986), numbering less than 5,000 birds (Robertson, 1988). No recent and complete surveys are available, but Star Keys may hold the largest single breeding population, with 530 nests in the only available survey (Robertson, 1988). Additional nests (60) were found on Rabbit Island (off Pitt Island) in the 1930s, and along the coast of Chatham Island there have been small colonies found at Cape Fournier, Okawa, Matarakau Point, and Tuparonga (Fleming, 1939; Marchant and Higgins, 1990).

Evolutionary Relationships

Voisin (1973) believed this form to represent the most typical of the blue-eyed shag group, and together with the Stewart Island shag to closely resemble the Kerguelen shag in morphology, especially in head characteristics. He considered the Stewart and Chatham Island shags to be subspecies of *carunculatus*, which seems to make logical sense. More recently they have been regarded as full species, as for example by Siegel-Causey (1988).

Other Vernacular Names

Auckland Island cormorant; cormoran de Auckland (French); Aucklandscharbe (German)

Distribution

Endemic to the Auckland Islands (500 kilometers south of New Zealand's South Island). (See figure 69.)

Subspecies

None recognized here, but this population at times has been considered either as a race of *campbelli* (Dorst and Mougin, 1979), or as its closest species-level relative (Falla, Sibson, and Turbott, 1981). It has also sometimes been considered most closely related to *carunculatus,* and either recognized as a race of that species (Peters, 1931) or maintained as a separate allospecies (Siegel-Causey, 1988; Marchant and Higgins, 1990; Sibley and Monroe, 1990).

Description

Prebreeding adult. Upperparts black, with a bluish sheen, the black of the neck often extending downward to merge and to form a continuous but usually narrow black area at the base of the neck, separating the white of the throat from that of the underparts; the upper wing coverts dark purplish gray, with a greenish sheen and indistinct black margins; one or two white back patches sometimes present, a white alar stripe also sometimes present, the scapulars more rarely exhibiting a second white stripe in some males; rectrices (12) black, with white basal shafts; a very long and bushy forehead crest present at start of breeding season. Iris dark brown; eye ring shiny mauve to violet-purple; facial skin dark purple, grayish, or reddish brown and lacking papillae, the skin at the base of the maxilla bright yellow, and at the base of the mandible red to dull orange; mouth lining orange; bill dark gray or blackish, the mandible tipped with orange or yellowish horn; gular skin bright red; legs and feet pink.
Postbreeding adult. Lacking the crest, and the softpart colors less bright.
Immature-subadult. Upperparts brown with a green gloss, the rump and thighs darker; white alar and scapular stripes apparently present. Softparts probably somewhat more colorful than in juveniles, but less colorful than in adults. Age of first breeding unknown.
Juvenile. Generally dark brown above and white below, sometimes with a dark band or spots across foreneck; the alar and scapular stripes pale sandy. Iris and bare facial skin brown; bill brownish horn, tinted with pinkish toward the tip.
Nestling. Initially naked gray or black skin; later covered with gray down; the throat and mandible pinkish.

Measurements (in millimeters)

Wing, males 255–283 (ave. of 12, 269), females 237–278 (ave. of 15, 263); tail, males 112–126 (ave. of 12, 117), females 103–126 (ave. of 15, 115); culmen, males 47–54 (ave. of 10, 51), females 45–53 (ave. of 15, 49) (Marchant and Higgins, 1990). Eggs ca. 59 × 38.

Weights

No information. Calculated egg weight 47.0 grams.

Identification

In the hand. The combination of white underparts (with a narrow white foreneck stripe), pink feet, reddish brown facial skin lacking papillae, and a mauve-colored eye ring should serve to identify typical examples of this questionably distinct species, except perhaps from the Bounty Island shag. It differs from *ranfurlyi* and *campbelli* in having varying amounts of white and dark feathering on the foreneck and a purple eye ring, contrasting with a dark purple face (Robertson and van Tets, 1982), and has more varied facial coloring prior to breeding than does *ranfurlyi* (P. Rasmussen, personal communication).
In the field. This is the only cormorant or shag found on the Auckland Islands.

Ecology and General Biology

Breeding and nonbreeding habitats. This is a sedentary species that occasionally forages well out to sea, but is essentially confined to the vicinity of the Auckland Islands.
Movements and migrations. No significant movements are likely to occur in this species.
Competition and predation. No information.

Foods and Foraging Behavior

Foods consumed. Little information, but pilchards (Clupeidae) and small crustaceans (*Munida*) have been reported as foods.
Foraging behavior. This species sometimes forages well out

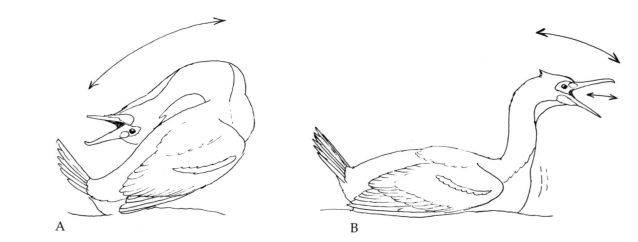

Figure 73. Social behavior of the Auckland Island shag, including male gargling (A), gaping (B), head lowering (C), kink-throating (D), penguin-walking (E), and pretakeoff posture (F). After sketches in Marchant and Higgins (1990).

to sea, but also in bays and inlets. During the breeding season females leave the nesting areas soon after dawn to forage, returning at midday; their mates then leave and return before dusk (Marchant and Higgins, 1990).

Social Behavior

Age of maturity and mating system.   No information.
Social displays and vocalizations.   The only available information on this comes from observations by G. van Tets (summarized in Marchant and Higgins, 1990). The form's behavior is much like that of the Bounty Island shag and those of the three preceding species. Male advertisement consists of gargling (figure 73A), which is performed with a rather upright body and somewhat drooping wings. The head-throwing movement may be repeated several times at an irregular but slow rate, with the male either calling loudly with a variable barking note as the head touches the rump, or displaying silently. Individual recognition displays consist of gaping (figure 73B) and head lowering (figure 73C). During gaping the bird moves its head back and forth and side to side, with the bill opened and the lower neck pulsating as the male utters loud, repeated barking notes and the female soft and puffing sounds. Actual threat display is very similar. During head lowering the pair raise and lower their heads and extended necks in unison, usually silently.

Other displays include kink-throating (figure 73D), performed with the bill closed and hyoid lowered, the male calling repeatedly with *ergh* notes and the female silent. In the postlanding and posthop postures the body is held high, the head is raised, and the neck is slightly arched as the bill is closed. The pretakeoff (figure 73F) and prehop postures are similar, but the neck is more arched, and the upper breast pulsates as the bird utters a repeated ticking note. Penguin-walking (figure 73E) is performed as in related species, with the neck arched and the bill held horizontally or tilted downward slightly.

Reproductive Biology

Breeding season.   The egg-laying season is from November to February (Robertson, 1988).

Nest sites and nest building.   Nests are constructed on the ground on grass tussocks, typically under overhanging rocks or overhead bushes or trees. This overhead cover helps protect the eggs from skuas (*Catharacta*), and when it disappears the site is likely to be abandoned. The nests are bulky, constructed mostly of available nearby vegetation and seaweeds. Nesting is colonial, the centers of the nests averaging only about 75 centimeters apart, with the same nests probably used year after year (Marchant and Higgins, 1990).
Egg laying and incubation.   The usual clutch is three eggs, laid at two- or three-day intervals. Incubation is by both sexes, the male incubating during morning hours and the female in the afternoon. The incubation period of first-laid eggs averaged about 29 days (range 28–32 days), and that of the second-laid egg was 26 days in one observed case (Marchant and Higgins, 1990).
Brooding and rearing of young.   Typically each pair is able to rear two young.
Breeding success.   Evidently skuas are a significant threat to both eggs and chicks, but no statistics on breeding success are available.

Population Status

The total population of this form is probably fewer than 5,000 birds, which mostly occur at the northern and southern ends of the Auckland Islands (Robertson, 1988). Breeding occurs on Auckland Island, where the population is less than 2,000, and also on Enderby Island and at Cape Crozier (Marchant and Higgins, 1990).

Evolutionary Relationships

This is obviously a close relative of the Bounty Island shag and the two mainland forms (Stewart Island and king shags).

BOUNTY ISLAND SHAG *LEUCOCARBO (CARUNCULATUS) RANFURLYI* (OGILVIE-GRANT) 1901

Other Vernacular Names

Bounty Island cormorant; cormoran de Bounty (French); Bountyscharbe (German)

Distribution

Endemic to the Bounty Islands (600 kilometers southeast of New Zealand's South Island). (See figure 69.)

Subspecies

None recognized here, but this population has been variously considered as a race of *campbelli* (Dorst and Mougin, 1979), a race of *carunculatus* (Peters, 1931), or a separate species (Marchant and Higgins, 1990; Sibley and Monroe, 1990). This species is probably most closely related to *carunculatus* (Siegel-Causey, 1988), or part of the *campbelli* group (Robertson and van Tets, 1982).

Description

Prebreeding adult. Upperparts generally black, with a bluish sheen; the upper wing coverts dark brown, with a green sheen and indistinct black border; white alar stripes present in some, absent in others; white scapular stripes unrecorded. White back patches absent on more than 90 percent of individuals, the remainder having poorly developed to prominent patches. Underparts, including the throat, foreneck, and undersides of body, white; rectrices (12) black, with white basal shafts; a black recurved forehead crest. Iris light brown; eye ring red-orange, purple, or pale brown (the last perhaps typical of nonbreeding or postbreeding birds); facial skin bright red (at times orange and/or purple) with black feathered spots but no caruncles present; skin at base of the maxilla orange-yellow; gape orange-yellow; bill brown to pink, with a darker culmen, a paler tip, and orange to yellow basally; gular skin scarlet, becoming orange-red toward base of bill; legs and feet pink, with gray smudges on tarsus and toes (Robertson and van Tets, 1982).
Postbreeding adult. Like the prebreeding adult but without the forehead crest, and the softpart colors less bright.
Immature-subadult. Generally brown above and white below, corresponding to the adult pattern. Sometimes with dark spots or a continuous band across the foreneck. Softparts probably brighter than in juveniles. Age of first breeding unknown.
Juvenile. Upperparts, including head and back, dark brown, the feathers with glossy blackish green tips and brownish fringes; throat white, this area extending to foreneck as elongated ellipse; lower neck dark brown; rest of underparts white, with dark brown thighs. Iris pale brown; facial skin and eye ring brown; gular skin gray; bill, legs, and feet brownish flesh.
Nestling. Undescribed, but probably closely resembling *carunculatus* and similar forms.

Measurements (in millimeters)

Wing, males 285–300 (ave. of 11, 294), females 272–287 (ave. of 10, 278); tail, males 117–134 (ave. of 11, 127), females 107–137 (ave. of 8, 116); culmen, males 56–62 (ave. of 11, 59); females 52–59 (ave. of 8, 55) (Robertson and van Tets, 1982). Eggs average 64 × 41 (Robertson and van Tets, 1982).

Weights (in kilograms)

Males 2.3–2.9 (ave. of 7, 2.5), females 2.0–2.7 (ave. of 6, 2.5) (Robertson and van Tets, 1982). Estimated egg weight 59 grams.

Identification

In the hand. The combination of white underparts (the foreneck with only a narrow white stripe), pink feet, and bright orange-red, red, or purplish facial skin, lacking papillae or caruncles but with small black spots, should serve to identify most individuals. This form differs from *campbelli* and *colensoi* in being larger and having variable amounts of yellow at the gape, a light brown iris, and orange-red to purple facial skin (Robertson and van Tets, 1982).
In the field. This is the only shag found on the Bounty Islands.

Ecology and General Biology

Breeding and nonbreeding habitats. This is a species associated with coastlines and apparently with inshore waters around the Bounty Islands.
Movements and migrations. No documented movements away from the Bounty Islands, but two vagrant birds at Antipodes Island may have represented this form.
Competition and predation. This is the only shag found on the islands. Erect-crested penguins (*Eudyptes sclateri*) are common and often nest near the shags, but on broader slopes. Skuas (*Catharacta*) and kelp gulls (*Larus dominicanus*)

Figure 74. Social behavior of the Bounty Island shag, including male gargling display (A), forward-gaping recognition display (B), pretakeoff posture (C), prehop posture (D), post-landing posture (E), kink-throating display (F), and penguin-walking (G). After sketches in Marchant and Higgins (1990).

also occur, and both probably represent serious threats to the eggs and young of shags.

Foods and Foraging Behavior

Foods consumed.   Nine stomachs analyzed by Robertson and van Tets (1982) contained remains of fish (in 8 stomachs), snail shells (8 stomachs), cephalopods (4 stomachs), isopods (4 stomachs), a hermit crab, a crab, a sea urchin, two nematodes, plus coral bits and small stones. Regurgitated food pellets contained remains of cephalopods, fish, snails, hermit crabs, sea urchins, and miscellaneous materials. This would suggest bottom foraging.

Foraging behavior.   Feeding is done around the islands and out to sea. Paired females leave to forage around dawn and return at midday, after which their mates depart and return again at dusk. Like other subantarctic shags, the birds do not use wing spreading to dry their wings after foraging. Social foraging apparently occurs; one foraging flock of more than 300 birds was seen, more than half of which were immatures.

Social Behavior

Age of maturity and mating system.   No information.

Social displays and vocalizations.   All available information on this topic is from Robertson and van Tets (1982), summarized in Marchant and Higgins (1990). Male advertisement consists of gargling (figure 74A), performed with the body in a relatively upright posture. The display is also at times performed while in a sitting position, and in either case the bill is either closed or kept widely open, the tail is partly raised, and the wings somewhat drooped. There may be a soft *hargh* note with this display.

Individual recognition displays consist of gaping (figure 74B), head lowering, and nest worrying. Gaping is performed as in other subantarctic shags, with lateral and anterior-posterior head movements and the bill widely opened. Males call softly with repeated *he* notes when gaping, but females are silent. Actual threat displays at the nest are quite similar to gaping, and may include soft *borr* notes by the male. Females are silent when threatening. Head lowering is a mate-greeting ceremony, often performed in synchrony by the pair, and during nest worrying nest materials are silently manipulated with the bill.

Other displays include kink-throating (figure 74F), which is used when approaching the nest site and when manipulating materials near the nest. Males sometimes utter soft notes when kink-throating, but females are silent. In the pretakeoff posture (figure 74C) the bird stands erect and the lower neck and breast pulsate as soft ticking notes are uttered by males, but females are silent. In the similar prehop

posture (figure 74D), the neck is more arched and the bill directed downward, as ticking sounds are produced. Circle flights may be performed away from and back to the nest. Simple hopping movements from one perch to another may also occur, or even alternations between pretakeoff and postlanding postures without actual intervening hops or flights. In the postlanding (figure 74E) and posthop posture the head is raised with the bill closed and the throat bulged. This same general attitude is assumed during penguin-walking (figure 74G) through the colony.

Reproductive Biology

Breeding season.   Egg laying occurs in October and November, with hatching occurring as early as November 17 (Robertson and van Tets, 1982).

Nest sites and nest building.   After a male has defended a display site and a female has chosen him, the female builds the nest, using materials brought in by the male. Additional materials may be brought by both sexes during the incubation period. The nest is constructed of brown seaweeds (*Marginarilla*), which are combined with mud, stones, and debris to form a cone-shaped nest up to 15 centimeters high and 35 centimeters wide. Nests are typically situated about a meter apart from center to center (Robertson, 1988).

Egg laying and incubation.   The usual clutch is of 2–3 eggs.

Brooding and rearing of young.   No information.

Breeding success.   No information.

Population Status

The total population of breeding pairs in 1978 was fewer than 1,000. Colonies were located mostly on the western group of islands (330 pairs at Lion, 132 at Ranfurly, 60 at Tunnel, 40 at Proclamation, 24 at Spider, 22 at Depot). There were three colonies in the central island group (70 pairs at Prion, 64 at Funnel, 20 at Coronet), and on the eastern group there were colonies at North Rock (142 pairs) and Molly Cap (80 pairs) (Robertson and van Tets, 1982). The species is considered "rare" by New Zealand authorities (Bell, 1986).

Evolutionary Relationships

Robertson and Bell (1984) stated that the three forms *ranfurlyi*, *campbelli*, and *colensoi* differ in some details of their social behavior, as well as in some mensural, plumage, and softpart features, and they thus regarded them as separate species rather than as subspecies of either *campbelli* or *carunculatus*. This treatment was adopted by Marchant and Higgins (1990) but is clearly open to argument, depending on how species limits might be defined.

Other Vernacular Names

Magellanic cormorant, Magellanic shag, rock cormorant; cormorán de las rocas (Spanish); cormoran magellanique (French); Felsenscharbe (German)

Distribution

Breeds along the coasts of South America from about Valdivia, Chile, and Punta Tombo, Argentina, south to Tierra del Fuego; also resident on the Falkland Islands. Moves north in winter as far as Santiago, Chile, and the Valdez Peninsula, Argentina, but vagrants have been reported as far north as Uruguay. The Falkland Islands population is presumably sedentary. (See figure 75.)

Subspecies

None.

Description

Prebreeding adult. Head and neck black, with a steel-blue gloss, but a more greenish, short and wispy median crest; upper back, scapulars, and wings dull oil-green, the feathers indistinctly margined with blackish; lower back, rump, tail coverts, flanks, and thighs black, glossed with bluish, and thickly interspersed with white filoplumes, which are also scattered over the head, neck, and upperparts, and form a distinct tuft on the ear coverts; chest and rest of underparts white; remiges and rectrices (12) black. Iris variable, from brown or red to whitish; eyelids, facial skin, and gular skin brick-red, the face flecked with yellow papillae and bordered with black; legs and feet flesh-colored.
Postbreeding adult. Lacking the forehead crest and white filoplumes, and reportedly with varying amounts of white feathering on the head and throat. However, Rasmussen (1987) observed that the nonbreeding (or "basic") plumage is almost identical with that of breeding birds (the "alternate"

Figure 75. Distribution of the rock shag, showing its residential or breeding range (cross-hatched) and its additional wintering range (stippled). The inset map shows the distribution of guano islands off southern Argentina, which mostly lie outside this species' breeding range but may be used by nonbreeders.

plumage). She concluded that adults with adventitious white feathers on the head and neck represent plumage variants rather than distinct transitional or winter plumages, such as those illustrated and so designated by Harrison (1983).
Immature-subadult. Entire head, neck, chest, and upperparts all brownish black, with some greenish gloss; belly brown; only the anterior throat white, some tiny filoplumes on the head and neck; breast and belly lighter brown, mixed here and there with white feathers. Iris brown, yellowish, or white; legs and feet blackish. The white throat may not develop until the first nuptial plumage has appeared, but more often appears before (through molt) or simultaneously with (through wear) the white belly typical of adults. The iris color gradually changes from brown through yellowish and whitish to pink and finally red with maturity. At the end of the first year there may be a complete molt of body as well as wing feathers, leading to the first breeding plumage (Murphy, 1936). However, contrary to Murphy, Rasmussen (1987) reported only a single predefinitive plumage (the juvenal), which is polymorphic with underparts ranging from pure white to nearly or completely black.
Juvenile. Head, neck, upperparts, wings, and tail dull blackish brown; the upper breast, flanks, and thighs brown; lower breast and belly white, blackish, or a mixture of blackish and white. Iris brown; legs and feet blackish.
Nestling. Initially naked black skin, but soon covered with clove-brown down; soon mixed with white down on the belly.

Measurements (in millimeters)

Wing, males 233–263 (ave. of 15, 252.2), females 236–255 (ave. of 29, 244.7); tail, males 127–155 (ave. of 15, 138.6), females 123–146 (ave. of 29, 133); culmen, males 48.5–54.5 (ave. of 15, 52.7), females 46–55 (ave. of 29, 51) (Blake, 1977). Eggs ca. 62 × 38.

Weights (in grams)

Four adult females 1,360–1,551 (ave. 1,445), one immature female 1,100 (U.S. National Museum specimens). Ten females 1,300–1,550 (ave. 1,417), 7 males 1,440–1,680 (ave. 1,553) (University of Kansas Natural History Museum specimens). Two subadult females, 1,386 and 1,472 (Humphrey et al., 1970). Calculated egg weight 49.4.

Identification

In the hand. The combination of pale pink to brown feet, a black bill, and no distinct eye ring separating the red face and red to brownish iris should identify this distinctive species. *In the field.* This is the only South American and Falkland Islands cormorant or shag having pinkish feet and a blackish bill; breeding birds also have a distinctive white ear patch.

Ecology and General Biology

Breeding and nonbreeding habitats. This species inhabits the winding coastlines and hidden channels of Chile, and its relatively rounded wings seemingly are adapted to its "sluggish," slow-flying behavior (Murphy, 1936). It has a strong preference for rocky coastlines (Humphrey et al., 1970). On the Falkland Islands it is associated with sheltered harbors and estuaries, never venturing very far offshore (Woods, 1975).

Movements and migrations. It is apparently sedentary, judging from its limited powers of mobility. However, it has wandered north in Chile to the vicinity of Santiago, and on the Atlantic side of the Andes to Uruguay.

Competition and predation. On the Falkland Islands this species and the imperial shag forage in quite different areas, the imperial foraging farther offshore. The same may be true in South America, where other species such as the Neotropic (olivaceous) cormorant and to a limited degree the red-footed shag also occur. No doubt the most serious predators are skuas (*Catharacta*), which "invariably attach themselves" to shag colonies to take eggs and hatched chicks, and which sometimes steal just-captured prey from adults (Murphy, 1936).

Foods and Foraging Behavior

Foods consumed. Fish and fish bones have been seen in collected specimens (Humphrey et al., 1970), and it has been suggested that fish such as mullet (Mulgidae) and smelt (Osmeridae) are probably major foods (Woods, 1975). Mullets up to about 20 centimeters long can be swallowed (Cawkell and Hamilton, 1961).

Foraging behavior. Rock shags begin foraging soon after daylight, when they leave their roosts in the hundreds to feed in kelp beds. They evidently feed on fish hiding in the kelp tangles, which means that solitary searches rather than social foraging techniques are primarily used. Wanless and Harris (1991) reported that the birds would dive mostly within or at the edges of beds of giant kelp within 50 meters of shore. They foraged mainly solitarily, in water 1–6 meters deep, and remained under water for an average duration of 28 seconds. Most prey were apparently small fish about 5 centimeters long, but remains of crustaceans, isopods, and polychaete worms were also found in pellets.

Social Behavior

Age of maturity and mating system. Rasmussen (1987) determined that only a single predefinitive (juvenal) plumage

exists, so it is likely that the definitive adult plumage occurs within a year of hatching. However, no information on the usual age of initial breeding is available.

Social displays and vocalizations. Observations by Siegel-Causey (1986a) provide the only available descriptions of social display. Male advertising consists of two displays, wing waving (figure 76G–K) and darting (figure 76D–E). When a female approaches a territorial male he begins wing waving, with the body held horizontal, the breast near the ground, the head laid back along the back, the closed bill pointed back beyond the vertical, and the gular pouch expanded. In this gargling-like posture the wings are irregularly lifted 2–4 times per second, in pulses lasting about a second. This display is silent. The female may respond with gaping, may gently bite or nibble the male's bill and gular pouch, or may perform hopping. During darting the male initially retracts his head with wings slightly spread, his hyoid depressed to expose the gular skin, his tail raised, and his dorsal feathers erected (figure 76D). From this posture he darts his head forward, with the bill slightly opened at the end of the movement (figure 76E); rarely a faint clicking sound may be produced. The tail is evidently lowered at the end of the display. At the end of a wing-waving sequence the male may arch his neck in a bowing posture, and utter a loud *ow* call.

Individual recognition displays observed by Siegel-Causey included "throat-clicking" and head wagging. During throat clicking one bird taps the other bird's bill and then waves its open bill horizontally in the other's face (figure 76F). During head wagging the two birds face in the same direction, with their necks erect. One bird places its neck over that of its mate, and both birds move their heads laterally away. Allopreening and nest worrying (figure 76C) were also observed among paired birds.

Other observed displays included a pretakeoff posture with depressed hyoids and the plumage usually sleeked. There is also a hopping display, with the hyoid depressed and the bill directed downward, a landing display (figure 76A) with the undersides of its feet conspicuously exhibited as the bird approaches a landing site, and a distinctive postlanding posture (figure 76B), with the neck and head held upward while a low croak is uttered. A deliberate high-stepping walk or "stepping" (= penguin-walking) display was observed when one bird walked near nests of others, with the head and neck plumage erected and the hyoid depressed.

Reproductive Biology

Breeding season. Near the northern limit of the Chilean breeding range the nesting season lasts from November to April or later (Murphy, 1936). In Tierra del Fuego and along the Beagle Channel breeding has been observed from November to January, with well-grown young already present

Figure 76. Social behavior of the rock shag, including landing display posture (A), postlanding and hopping posture (B), nest worrying after a threat display (C), initial and final phases of male darting (D, E), and final phase of mutual throat clicking (F). Sequence G–K shows a female approaching a male on a nest site below. The male begins wing waving (G), while the female performs a hop display (H), followed by nest indicating (I). Finally, the female performs gaping (J) and bill biting (K). After sketches in Siegel-Causey (1986a).

in one colony by early December (Humphrey et al., 1970). In the Falkland Islands eggs have been found between early November and mid-December, with fledged birds observed leaving their nests between mid-January and the end of February (Woods, 1975).

Nest sites and nest building.   Nests are constructed mostly of algae collected on the beaches and molded into a tight cup that is held together with guano. The materials are collected by the male during courtship, but females may also bring in small quantities until the egg-laying period. Males may present nesting material to females during the postlanding display, when both birds simultaneously place items on the nest rim (Siegel-Causey, 1986a). Nests are usually on cliff ledges at least 6 meters above the sea, but sometimes individual nests are placed on jetties or ship hulks. Colonies are normally located on cliffs of inlets, where some shelter from the wind is available, and on the Falklands they range in size to about 400 nests (Woods, 1975). On the coasts of Tierra del Fuego and western Chile the birds may nest on leeward-facing cliffs or sometimes in sea caves, back as far as 50 meters from the entrance. They only rarely nest on flat and open surfaces such as are often used by imperial shags.

Egg laying and incubation.   Clutch sizes are usually of three eggs, with a range of 2–5 (Johnson, 1965; Woods, 1975). Although the parents change places quickly during nest relief, they often lose eggs to skuas, and other eggs are sometimes accidentally broken during the departure of one of the adults (Murphy, 1936).

Brooding and rearing of young.   No specific information.

Breeding success.   No detailed information. Wanless and Harris (1991) noted that the incidence of recently fledged immatures (about two per pair) indicated a high rate of breeding success in a colony of 70 birds on the Falkland Islands.

Population Status

Johnson (1965) stated that over most of its Chilean range this species is about as common as the imperial shag. On the Falkland Islands it is less common than the imperial shag but there are more than 34 known colonies, and more than a thousand breeding pairs (Croxall, McInnes, and Prince, 1984).

Evolutionary Relationships

Siegel-Causey (1986a) reviewed the general opinions on this species' possible affinities, which has typically been associated with the "blue-eyed shags" and considered as either a relative of the imperial shag (Dorst and Mougin, 1979) or possibly a primitive member of this general taxonomic complex (Voisin, 1970). Siegel-Causey (1986a) judged that in its behavior the rock shag has greater similarities to the *Stictocarbo* group of cliff shags, including the red-legged, pelagic, and red-faced shags. His later (1988) cladistic analysis supported this general position.

Other Vernacular Names

Baird's cormorant, pelagic cormorant, resplendent cormorant (*resplendens*), shag, southern violet-green cormorant (*resplendens*), violet-green cormorant; cormoran pélagique (French); Nordpazifischer-Kormoran (German); hime-u (Japanese); pato sargento (Spanish)

Distribution

Breeds from the Chukchi Peninsula, Siberia (west to about Cape Schmidt, plus Wrangel and Herald islands in the Arctic Ocean), east to Point Hope, Alaska (including St. Lawrence and Diomede islands); south in Asia through Kamchatka, Sakhalin, the Kurils, and northern Japan (Hokkaido and northern Honshu); also breeds on the Commander and Aleutian islands; south in North America locally to the Alaska Peninsula; thence eastward and southward coastally through British Columbia (including Queen Charlotte Islands and Vancouver Island) and the Pacific coastal states to northern Baja California (Coronado Islands). Winters from the northern limits of open water south to southern Japan and the coast of China, Taiwan, and in North America casually reaching Cape San Lucas (Baja California Sur). (See figure 77.)

Subspecies

L. p. pelagicus (Pallas). Breeds along coastal northeastern Asia and on the Bering Sea and Arctic Ocean islands as described above, and along the coasts of mainland North America from Point Hope, Alaska, southward to at least the Queen Charlotte Islands, British Columbia. Birds breeding between the Queen Charlotte Islands and southern Vancouver Island (Queen's and Simon sounds, Scott Islands, and northern Vancouver Island) are of still-undetermined racial affiliation. Includes *aeolus* Swinhoe, of the Siberian mainland and Wrangel Island; reputedly significantly larger than birds from the Bering Sea region (Portenko, 1981).

L. p. resplendens (Audubon) 1838. Breeds coastally from southwestern British Columbia (north at least to Mandarte Island, off southeastern Vancouver Island; many other colonies in the Strait of Georgia probably also belong to this race) south to the western coast of Baja California (breeding irregularly on the Coronado Islands), south regularly in winter to Laguna San Ignacio and casually to Cape San Lucas.

Description

Prebreeding adult. Plumage all black except for white flank patches, the neck strongly glossed with violet-purple, and the sides of upper back and scapulars greenish and violet-bronze, changing to bright metallic green; neck, lower back, and rump ornamented with dispersed white filoplumes; a black forehead crest of recurved feathers, and a second wispy occipital crest; gular sac inconspicuous and heart-shaped. Iris yellow-green to deep sea-green; facial skin vivid ruby-red to magenta; interior of mouth red; bill horny blackish brown, becoming orange to reddish at base; gular skin covered with vermillion papillae; legs and feet black.

Postbreeding adult. Similar to the prebreeding plumage, but lacking the crests (lost shortly after egg laying), white flank patches (lost shortly after the chicks hatch), and the other scattered filoplumes. Facial skin dull brownish orange, gular skin more brownish gray, the other softpart colors probably also less brilliant.

Immature-subadult. Intermediate between the brown juvenal plumage and the glossy adult or definitive plumage, forming a piebald black and brown appearance. The facial skin darkens to red or blackish during the first winter; the iris remains brown, and the mouth lining is red. Molt into the definitive plumage probably begins at about ten months and is completed during the second year, with initial breeding probably occurring when the birds are approaching two years old (Bent, 1922; Palmer, 1962).

Juvenile. Almost uniformly dark brown above, the head gray, the neck gray and black, and the upperparts blackish somewhat glossed with dull green; the underparts only slightly paler, grayer, and more dull; rectrices, remiges, and wing coverts all black. Iris brownish; facial skin ashy-flesh, with a pink gular patch; bill, legs, and feet all blackish.

Nestling. Initially naked, with blackish gray skin; later covered with sooty to purplish gray down, especially around the neck, the thighs distinctly paler (but not white as in *urile*). A white underdown eventually develops below the dark primary down. Gular skin whitish to pinkish; this area irregularly separated from the lead-colored skin on the rest of the body. The head remains almost naked until the juvenal plumage develops; the legs and feet gradually darken and become permanently black.

Measurements (in millimeters)

Overall range for species (24 males, 16 females): wing, males 239–290, females 244–274; culmen, males 43–56, females 44–50. Averages (15 males, 6 females) for nominate *pelagicus*: wing, males 276.5, females 260.7; culmen, males 50.2, females 47. Averages (9 males, 10 females) for *resplendens*: wing, males 255.3, females 252.3; culmen, males 48.7, fe-

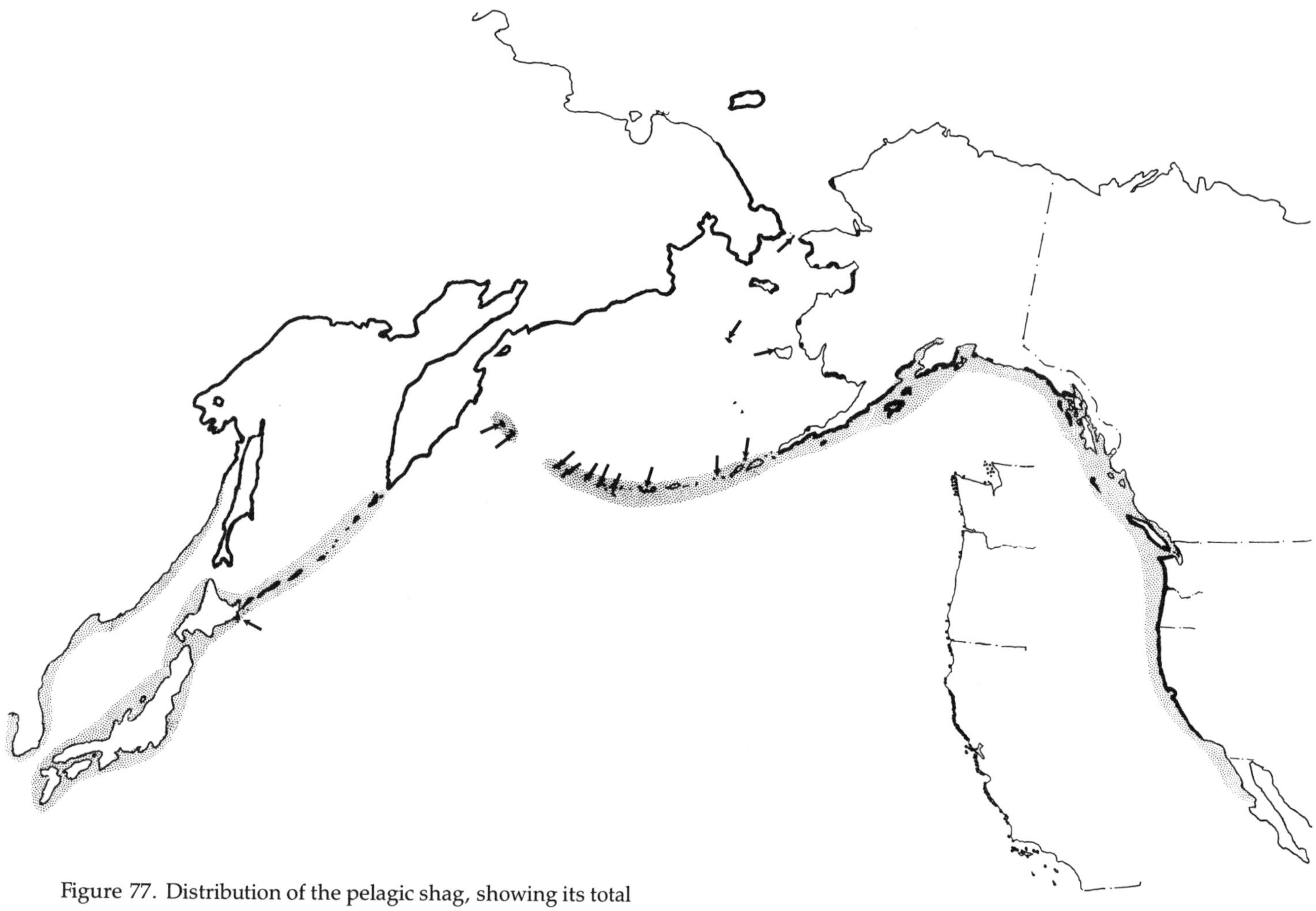

Figure 77. Distribution of the pelagic shag, showing its total breeding range (inked), locations of insular or isolated breeding colonies (arrows), and its additional wintering range (stippled). Inset map shows colony locations (dots) from Washington to California. Subspecies range limits are uncertain (see text) and are not indicated.

males 47.2 (Palmer, 1962). Tail, both sexes, ca. 150–180 (Coues, 1894). Eggs ca. 59 × 37.

Weights (in grams)

Adult males of *pelagicus* ca. 1,814–2,440 (4–5.375 lb.) (ave. of 9, 2,034), adult females ca. 1,474–2,041 (3.25–4.5 lb.) (ave. of 5, 1,702) (Palmer, 1962). Adults of both subspecies, males 1,888–2,097 (ave. of 3, 2,005), females 1,214–1,631 (ave. of 5, 1,523) (Museum of Vertebrate Zoology specimens). Three males of *pelagicus* collected during May on Wrangel Island, 2,040–2,295 (ave. 2,208); a pair obtained there in August weighed 1,930 (female) and 2,200 (male) (Portenko, 1981).

Calculated egg weight 44.6; ave. weight of 143 eggs (not necessarily unincubated) 40 (van Tets, 1959).

Identification

In the hand.   The combination of an adult culmen length of 43–56 mm, generally greenish sheen to plumage and black feet, and red facial skin, which does not extend continuously around the forehead, should serve to identify adults of this species. Young birds are sometimes quite difficult to separate from those of the red-faced shag, but have considerably slimmer bills (the maxilla 4.4–6.0 times longer than it is deep at the base, vs. 3.7–4.1 times longer than deep in the red-faced) with little if any yellow evident on the sides of the mandible. *In the field.* Throughout its northern Pacific Ocean range adults of this species are separable from those of the very similar red-faced shag in that their red facial skin does not extend continuously around the front of the forehead, and no blue skin is evident in the gular area. The bill is also darker basally than in the red-faced shag, in both adults and younger birds. In contrast to the larger and more robust Brandt's and double-crested cormorants, a conspicuous patch of white feathers is present on the flanks for about two months during the breeding season. First-year birds are uniformly dark brown above and below, and are nearly identical to those of red-faced shags, but are darker below than are young Brandt's and double-crested cormorants.

Ecology and General Biology

Breeding and nonbreeding habitats. This is a coastal species that forages in bays, inlets, and along outer coastal areas, especially in rock-bottom habitats. Around the Pribilof Islands and in coastal California they are usually found within 1–2 kilometers of shore, in waters up to 100 meters deep (Hunt et al., 1981; Ainley and Boekelheide, 1990). However, Gould, Forsell, and Lensink (1982) noted that several sightings were made in waters of the Gulf of Alaska and Bering Sea 2,000–5,000 meters deep, probably representing wandering immatures or nonbreeding adults.

Movements and migrations. Movements are most evident at the northern edges of this species' range, in response to pack ice cover. The birds arrive on the Chukchi Peninsula between mid-April and mid-May and usually leave between late September and the end of October (Portenko, 1981). The birds probably arrive at and depart from St. Lawrence Island on similar schedules, but arrival at Norton Sound and at St. Lawrence Island may sometimes not occur until the beginning of June. The birds usually arrive at the southern Bering Sea colonies of coastal Alaska in mid-April and at the more northerly ones by middle to late May. Fall departure from the Bering Sea colonies occurs in late September and early October, the birds perhaps wintering in the eastern Aleutians (Bent, 1922). Farther south the species occurs throughout the year, with little indication of seasonal population fluctuations (Hatler, Campbell, and Dorst, 1978; Ainley and Boekelheide, 1990). The more northerly race that breeds from the Queen Charlotte Islands northward reportedly visits the coast of southern British Columbia during winter (Godfrey, 1986).

Competition and predation. The pelagic shag overlaps considerably in range with the red-faced shag, and these species also seem to have similar foraging ecologies (see table 15). However, although their overall nesting distribution in the Gulf of Alaska overlaps completely, the actual breeding populations on most islands are quite different. Thus where red-faced shags are common (e.g., Semidi Islands, Ugaiu-

shak Island) pelagic shags are uncommon, and where pelagic shags are abundant (e.g., Kodiak and Middleton islands) the red-faced is uncommon or absent. It is possible that the larger red-faced shags arrive earlier and occupy nesting cliffs before pelagic shags arrive, possibly thus dominating and excluding them from the best nesting sites (Nysewander, 1986). The smaller size of the pelagic shags allows them to nest in more inaccessible sites than can red-faced shags, such as in small caves or on narrow ledges (Moe and Day, 1977). Where the two shag species nest together, the pelagic shag also usually nests on lower ledges than does the red-faced (Wehle, Hoberg, and Powers, 1977). The red-faced shag seems to be more successful in fledging young where both breed locally. Furthermore, it is possible that corvids, gulls (especially larger species), and raptors represent the most important sources of egg and chick mortality in some southern breeding areas, whereas in more northern colonies bald eagles (*Haliaeetus leucocephalus*), food, or weather may be the more important factors limiting productivity (Nysewander and Hoberg, 1978). In the Aleutian Islands the major avian predators are apparently bald eagles (which not only sometimes eat shags but also frighten the breeding birds and expose their nests to other predation), peregrines (*Falco peregrinus*), and glaucous-winged gulls (*Larus glaucescens*) (Murie, 1959). Foxes (*Alopex lagopus* and *Vulpes fulva*) and river otters (*Lutra canadensis*) have been implicated in egg or chick predation in Alaska, and the arctic fox may be a significant threat wherever it is very common. The danger from glaucous-winged gulls and northwestern crows (*Corvus caurinus*) is greatly influenced by nest location, with steeper and more centrally located sites significantly less likely to be affected by such predation (Siegel-Causey and Hunt, 1981).

Besides the red-faced shag, murres (*Uria* spp.) and kittiwakes (*Rissa* spp.) are nest site competitors of uncertain significance, but at least the kittiwakes are unlikely to be able to displace shags from their nests. The presence of the nesting black-legged kittiwake (*R. tridactyla*) may force the shags to nest in a more dispersed manner, but starting their nesting somewhat earlier than the kittiwakes may allow them to compete more effectively with the kittiwakes for nest sites (Dick, 1975). On Kodiak Island, shags that nested close to kittiwakes had a lower nesting success than others, for still uncertain reasons (Nysewander, 1986), but perhaps the shags were forced to nest in a more dispersed and less protected manner.

Foods and Foraging Behavior

Foods consumed. A general summary of this species' foods was provided earlier in table 15. Like red-faced shags, pelagic shags forage individually, primarily in the intertidal zone of rocky shoreline areas, or in the surf zone below cliffs that border deeper waters (Nysewander, 1986). Ainley, Anderson, and Kelly (1981) noted that in theirs and three other studies the proportion of prey taken by this species in rocky reef habitats was 99, 78–80, 65, and 54 percent, with flat sand or mud habitats comprising nearly all of the rest. In their study nonschooling fish comprised the majority of fish taken, and additionally the majority of fish were bottom-dwelling cryptic forms rather than from higher zones in the water column. Throughout the species' range there was little similarity in major species consumed, although large decapod crustaceans were represented in samples from all geographic regions, and in northern areas sand eels (*Ammodytes*, Ammodytidae) are often eaten in considerable quantities (Robertson, 1974; DeGange and Sanger, 1986), as are the bottom-dwelling sculpins (Cottidae, including *Myoxocephalus, Megalocottus*) (Preble, 1923; Hunt et al., 1981). In all geographic regions nonschooling fish species that occupy rocky reefs and are mostly of cryptic appearance appear to be the primary prey. Estimated dietary overlap was higher between the pelagic shag and the Brandt's cormorant than between the pelagic shag and double-crested cormorant, and in some years the diets of pelagic shags and Brandt's cormorants overlap completely (Ainley, Anderson, and Kelly, 1981; Ainley and Boekelheide, 1990). On Mandarte Island, where double-crested cormorants and pelagic shags breed together, some dietary overlap did occur in one study (Robertson, 1974), but double-crested cormorants tended to take larger prey, and the peaks of their breeding seasons (and associated food requirements) were substantially separated temporally. Foods regurgitated to the young on Mandarte Island include blennies (Xiphisteridae) and shrimps (*Pandalus*).

Foraging behavior.   According to DeGange and Sanger (1986), pelagic and red-faced shags forage in water about 30 meters deep, mainly on demersal and epibenthic organisms. This places them in the same general category of foraging ecology as pigeon guillemots (*Cepphus columba*), which are inshore foragers of the intertidal zone. The birds have been caught in fishing nets set at 20 fathoms (ca. 35 meters). Occasionally they will be attracted to schools of fish by the actions of gulls or other birds, but coordinated social foraging is evidently not typical of this species. Of 65 timed dives in the intertidal zone off Mandarte Island, the average dive duration was 31 seconds and the longest was of 70 seconds (van Tets, 1959).

Social Behavior

Age of maturity and mating system.   Pelagic shags are generally believed to acquire their first nuptial plumages and begin breeding at two years, but data from banded birds on Mandarte Island apparently indicates that the species reaches maturity at three years (van Tets, 1959).

Social displays and vocalizations.   Van Tets (1959, 1965) reported that the male advertisement display consists of wing waving (originally called "wing-flipping" by van Tets). Wing waving (figure 78F) is performed with the head and bill

directed vertically upward and the tail held level or, more usually, declined about 45 degrees. There is a rapid simultaneous wing fluttering (at the rate of about three cycles per second) in several irregular bursts of about 2–6 seconds duration, alternately exposing and hiding the white upper thigh and rump plumes, and with the head moving slowly from side to side, but without associated vocalizations.

Individual recognition displays of the pelagic shag include a gaping posture (figure 78H), in which the head is moved vertically up and down with the bill open; in males a drawn-out *arr-arr-arr* note is produced, and in females a rhythmically repeated *igh-ugh* call. Unlike in the outwardly similar defensive threat display, the wings are not spread downward, and the movements are slower and more stereotyped. The gaping movements average 1.3–2.7 per second, and have an average of 2.1–3.6 cycles per display sequence (van Tets, 1965).

During copulation the male pelagic shag holds onto the nest rim rather than the female's neck or nape, according to van Tets (1959). No specific postcopulatory display was noted, only normal preening and nest maintenance activities.

Other displays of this species include a distinctive prehop posture (figure 78A), in which the bill is opened and directed downward. During the hop the bill remains down and open, so that when the bird lands it is already in its posthop posture (figure 78B). The pretakeoff posture (figure 78C, D) is similar to the prehop, but typically the bill and head are pointed toward the takeoff direction while the feet are still oriented inwardly, so that the neck is twisted. As the bird takes off its bill remains open, which is in contrast to the takeoffs of red-faced shags (figure 78E). The usual postlanding posture (figure 78G) consists of stretching the neck and pointing the bill forward, without expanding the gular pouch.

Reproductive Biology

Breeding season.   At the southern end of their range in California, the egg-laying season occurs from mid-April (Channel Islands) or early May (Farallons and northern California) until June or early July (Sowls et al., 1980). In Washington the egg-laying period is from early May to mid-July (Speich and Wahl, 1989). At Mandarte Island, British Columbia, laying extends from mid-May until as late as early August as a result of persistent replacement laying (Drent et al., 1964). Within the Gulf of Alaska, the start of egg laying generally occurred between May 23 and June 3 for a variety of studies. At individual sites, laying spanned a period of 21–45 days, but was generally completed between June 13 and 30 except at one location (Barren Islands) where it lasted as late as July 15. Hatching ranged from June 4 to August 15, with fledging between July 21 and September 1 at five Alaska localities. The incidence of renesting evidently accounts for much of

Figure 78. Social behavior of the pelagic shag, including prehop posture (A), midhop phase (B), pretakeoff look-and-
crouch postures (C, D), leap of takeoff (E), male wing-waving
display (F), postlanding display (G), and gaping display (H).
After sketches in van Tets (1965).

the annual variations occurring in hatching and fledging dates (Nysewander, 1986). In California variations are principally related to food availability (Ainley and Boekelheide, 1990).

Nest sites and nest building.   The propensity for pelagic shags to nest on narrow, relatively inaccessible cliffs is well known. On Middleton Island, where one of the densest concentrations of pelagic shags in Alaska occurs, most nests were placed in linear formation along a narrow ledge just below the tops of the cliffs (Hatch, Pearson, and Gould, 1979). The birds also use ledges below rock overhangs, sea caves, brackets, crevices, and other similarly protected sites for nesting (Hatler, Campbell, and Dorst, 1978; Drent et al., 1964). In Barkley Sound, British Columbia, cave nesting predominates over cliff nesting, probably because cliff sites are of limited availability. As elsewhere, sites are often changed both within and between years, perhaps in response to varying levels of disturbance (Carter, Hobson, and Sealy, 1984). Defensive behavior is relatively ineffective in pelagic shags as compared with double-crested cormorants. The reproductive success of different colony locations probably depends greatly on individual habitat characteristics as they affect the birds' security against predation (Siegel-Causey and Hunt, 1981) but in California success is a function of food availability (Ainley and Boekelheide, 1990).

Egg laying and incubation.   Eggs are laid at an average interval of two days (Dick, 1975). There is no indication of any geographic cline in clutch sizes. In the northern range (Norton Sound) the average clutch size is about 3.5 eggs (Biderman et al., 1978), and somewhat farther south at Cape Pierce it is 3.1 eggs (Dick, 1975). Among four studies in the Gulf of Alaska the mean annual clutch sizes ranged from 2.17 to 3.52 (unweighted average 3.09), with annual variations of the means at three of the sites ranging from 0.26 to 1.35 eggs, and averaging 0.97 eggs, or as much as the observed regional variations. On Mandarte Island the modal clutch size was four (Drent et al., 1964). A sample of 37 nests had an average of 3.8 eggs per nest. Among 28 failed nests, no renesting was attempted at 10, one replacement egg was laid in 13 nests, two were laid in 4, and three in 1 nest. Seven eggs was the maximum known to be laid by a single bird during one breeding season (van Tets, 1959). At the Farallon Islands, the mean clutch size of 259 nests was 3.4 eggs, with the modal clutch size being four eggs (46.7 percent), and the range 1–5 eggs. Clutches laid late in the season tended to be smaller than early ones, and hatching success of late clutches also tends to be lower (Ainley and Boekelheide, 1990).

Incubation begins with the first egg. Van Tets (1959) reported that for 49 eggs (of varied position in the egg-laying sequence) the average incubation period was 31 days, with 70 percent hatching in 30–32 days and an overall range of 27–37 days. The average incubation period for 21 eggs exclusive of first-laid eggs was 30.7 days (Drent et al., 1964).

Brooding and rearing of young.   Van Tets (1959) found that weight gains of the chicks during their first three weeks, from 30–40 grams at hatching to 1,150 grams, closely resemble the pattern typical of double-crested cormorants as reported by Mendall (1936). During the first week the young mostly feed and sleep, but after the first week they begin to perform adultlike comfort movements and also begin to defecate over the nest rim. After their second week they start to exercise their wings, and after the third week may start to make short trips beyond the nest rim. From the third week onward they can swim and dive when chased into the water. After a month they start to make longer excursions, and occasionally become lost. Then they remain at the communal perching area, where they are fed by their parents. When the juvenal plumage is completed during the sixth and seventh week the birds begin to swim and bathe voluntarily. Short flights may be made during the fifth and sixth week, but some time is required for them to become skillful at flying.

Drent et al. (1964) reported that nest departure times for Mandarte Island birds ranged from 42 to 52 days for seven chicks, but in one other case a chick was still in the nest at 58 days. At the Farallon Islands the average nest departure age was 47.4 days for 101 chicks, with an observed range of 30–59 days (Boekelheide et al., 1990).

Breeding success.   At Mandarte Island, hatching success in one year was 50 percent for 141 eggs, and over a three-year period the chicks hatched per nest ranged from 1.9 to 2.6. Predation accounted for 63 percent of the losses in one year's sample of 71 egg losses, with the rest of the eggs failing to hatch. Rearing success during various years was 74–79 percent, and averaged 2.0 chicks per nest (Drent et al., 1964). On the Farallon Islands, the pelagic shag had a 13-year average hatching success of 48 percent (annual range 32–71 percent), and a collective fledging success of 61 percent (annual range 0–94 percent), producing a collective overall breeding success of 29 percent. It exhibited a higher degree of annual variation in breeding success than did the double-crested or the Brandt's cormorants, which reflected the fact that the pelagic shags were almost completely dependent for their successful breeding on the availability of juvenile rockfish (*Sebastes*), which are midwater shoaling fish when young. Generally the birds did not lay a second clutch if their first one was lost or deserted; of 80 pairs that lost their eggs before hatching only five replacement clutches were produced and only six young were fledged from these nests (Boekelheide et al., 1990).

A substantial amount of information on the breeding success of pelagic shags at seven different locations in the Gulf of Alaska has been summarized by Nysewander (1986). Hatching success at three locations, over six breeding seasons, ranged from 32 to 69 percent, with initial brood sizes ranging from 2.09 to 2.88 chicks. The fledging success varied from 44 to 93 percent, and the average numbers of chicks fledged per active nest from 0.33 to 1.86. Yearly variations were considerable; thus at one location (Chiniak

Bay) the fledged chicks per active nest averaged 0.33 in one year and 1.48 in another, and in a second location (Barren Islands) the averages for two years were 0.7 and 1.62. In one colony (at Chiniak Bay) crows were a serious egg predator one year, but during the next year gulls were a significant predator in the same area. Where red-faced and pelagic shags occurred together the red-faced shags usually but not invariably had higher overall reproductive success. In a study on the Semidi Islands (Hatch and Hatch, 1990b), hatching success was highly variable in both species but generally higher for red-faced than for pelagic shags (overall five-year average brood size at fledging 1.9 for red-faced, 1.6 for pelagic, and overall five-year average number of young fledged per active nest 1.0 for red-faced and 0.6 for pelagic). Major mortality factors for both species were egg predation by gulls and ravens and apparent starvation of young. In this area no renesting efforts were observed.

Population Status

The world population of this species cannot be judged with certainty, since the Asian population is still incompletely known. Golovkin (1984) estimated at least 47,000 pairs in the Bering Sea area, more than 2,500 pairs in the Sea of Okhotsk, and about 300 in the Chukchi Sea. Litvinenko and Shibaev (1991) estimated that 50,000–60,000 occur in the Kuril Islands, about 1,700 along the mainland coast of Siberia along the Japan Sea, and a few hundred additional birds on the Shantar Islands, on Peter the Great Bay, and on Sakhalin Island. A few also breed along northern coastal Japan, along the southeastern Hokkaido coast, but the species has been declining steadily there, with less than ten pairs present in recent years (Brazil, 1991). Sowls, Hatch, and Lensink (1978) estimated the Alaska population at about 90,000 adult birds, with the largest components (44 percent) occurring in the Aleutian Islands and along the southern Alaska coast. The Bering Sea colonies comprised most of the rest, and a few occurred along the southeastern Alaska coast (table 32). The British Columbia population is on the order of 9,000 breeding birds (table 32). Most of these (about 52 percent) are located in the Strait of Georgia, and about 26 percent are on the west coast of Vancouver Island (Campbell et al., 1990; Rodway, 1991). The Strait of Georgia population increased considerably during this century, but appears to have leveled off in the late 1980s (Vermeer, Morgan, and Smith, 1988). Populations in Washington, Oregon, and California may total about 28,000 birds (table 31). Thus, the North American population of pelagic shags probably approaches 130,000 adults, making it second only to the double-crested cormorant in relative abundance (table 34).

Evolutionary Relationships

There can be no doubt that the pelagic and red-faced shags are very close evolutionary relatives, and Siegel-Causey (1991) has recently described a third closely related species (*kenyoni*) based on contemporary skeletal materials obtained from Amchitka Island. It is smaller than the pelagic shag, but anatomically appears to be closer to the red-faced shag. No skins are yet available, and the species' validity remains to be independently verified.

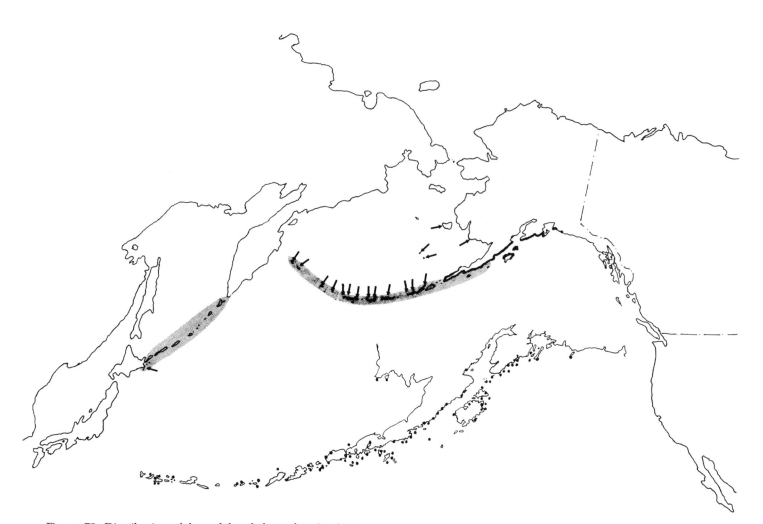

Figure 79. Distribution of the red-faced shag, showing its total breeding range (inked), locations of insular or isolated
breeding colonies (arrows), and additional wintering range
(stippled). Inset map shows colony locations (dots) in the
Gulf of Alaska and the Aleutian Islands.

RED-FACED SHAG *LEUCOCARBO URILE* (GMELIN) 1789

Other Vernacular Names

Red-faced cormorant, violet shag; urile (Russian); cormoran à face rouge (French); Aleuten-Kormoran (German)

Distribution

Breeds from the Nemuro Peninsula, Hokkaido, Japan, north and east in the Bering Sea to the Commander, Pribilof, Nunivak, and Aleutian islands, and east to the Shumagins and Kodiak Island; also along coastal mainland Alaska from the tip of the Alaska Peninsula northeast to Bristol Bay and Cape Newenham, and east along the southern coast of Alaska to Prince William Sound (where recently increasing). Generally winters on open-water areas near the breeding range, although the wintering distribution is still poorly documented, and only a single authentic record exists for British Columbia. (See figure 79.)

Subspecies

None yet recognized. Siegel-Causey (1991) has recently described a new species so far known only from four contemporary skeletons from Amchitka. He designated it as *Stictocarbo kenyoni*, or Kenyon's shag, which he considered a close relative of *urile*. It is substantially smaller in its skeletal measurements than *pelagicus*, but shares most skeletal features with *urile*. No nonskeletal specimens are known, and it remains to be seen whether this is a valid species or a well-marked subspecies of either *urile* or *pelagicus*. No colonies of red-faced cormorants are currently known to exist on Amchitka, and only a few pelagic cormorants are known to breed there (Sowls, Hatch, and Lensink, 1978).

Description

Prebreeding adult. Head deep greenish blue, becoming steel-blue on the neck, base of neck black, lower back, rump, tail coverts, and underparts dark bronze-green, with an oily gloss, sides of upper back and scapulars greenish- and violet-bronze, becoming purplish bronze, the feathers without definite dark margins. Two semierect median crests of bronze-green, the first on the crown, the second on the nape; a large patch of white filoplumes on the flanks, and the neck and rump with scattered white filoplumes; remiges and rectrices (12) blackish brown; gular skin heart-shaped from below. Iris light brown; front of the forehead, lores, and naked area around the eyes bright orange to red and somewhat engorged and carunculated; maxilla pale blue basally, contrasting with a blackish tip and culmen, the mandible also with a dark tip but grading to bright yellow at the base; interior of mouth, underside of mandible, and gular skin bright blue, the skin tinged with violet and bordered behind with a narrow border of cadmium-yellow, orange, or livid purplish red corrugations; legs and feet brownish black.

Postbreeding adult. Like the prebreeding adult, but lacking the crests, the white flank patch, and other white filoplumes; the softpart colors duller, the facial skin dull reddish, and the bill colors much paler.

Immature-subadult. The naked forehead gradually develops in older immature birds, then serving to distinguish them easily from pelagic shags, which have virtually identical immature plumages, except for the more greenish (rather than purplish) gloss dorsally.

Juvenile. Almost uniformly dark brown, with the underparts slightly paler, and the upperparts slightly glossed with purplish. Iris light brown; bill dark horny brown, becoming flesh-colored to yellowish, with a tinge of bluish toward the base; facial skin flesh-colored, the eye ring with an olive tinge; feet brownish black, the toes with lighter, dark brown webs (Stejneger, 1889).

Nestling. Initially naked, with purplish brown skin, but soon covered with a dusky brownish down, tipped with brownish gray. White down soon becomes interspersed on the underparts, and large whitish spots develop on the thighs. Gular skin whitish, contrasting with the lead-colored skin elsewhere on the body (Stejneger, 1889).

Measurements (in millimeters)

Wing, males 269–288 (ave. of 6, 277.3), females 255–296 (ave. of 9, 272.2); culmen, males 50–58 (ave. of 6, 53.8), females 50–58.5 (ave. of 9, 55.5) (Palmer, 1962). Tail, both sexes ca. 180–200 (Coues, 1894). Eggs ca. 61 × 37.

Weights (in grams)

Fifteen adult males 1,922–2,267 (ave. 2,208); 14 adult females 1,550–2,050 (ave. 1,857) (U.S. National Museum and Museum of Vertebrate Zoology specimens). Two adult males ca. 2,492 and 2,551 (5.5 and 5.625 lb.), two adult females ca. 1,644 and 1,937 (3.625 and 4.25 lb.). Three immature males ca. 2,154–2,608 (4.75–5.75 lb.), averaging ca. 2,400 (Palmer, 1962). The average adult weight (sample size and sex composition unstated) was reported as 1,900 by Hunt, Burgeson, and Sanger (1981). Calculated egg weight 46.1.

Identification

In the hand. The combination of an adult culmen length of 50–59 mm, generally glossy greenish plumage, and red facial skin that is continuous around the forehead should readily identify adults. Juvenile red-faced and pelagic shags are nearly identical in plumage, but in juvenile pelagic shags the feathering at the base of the bill forms a well-pronounced malar apex below the angle of the mouth, whereas in red-faced shags the feathers run downward below the base of the bill without forming such a conspicuous point. The two species also differ slightly in bill shape, the red-faced shag having a deeper, heavier, and more uniformly tapering maxilla that averages about 14 mm in depth proximally, rather than the pelagic shag's about 10 mm, or under four (rather than about five) times as long as it is deep at the base. According to Siegel-Causey (1991), his newly described form *kenyoni* has a distinctly narrow maxilla that in skeletal width averages 8.8 mm, as compared with 10.8 for the pelagic shag and 11.0 for the red-faced shag. Portenko (1981) has commented on the marked size difference between *pelagicus* specimens breeding on the Asian mainland and those from the Commander and Aleutian islands, which are currently considered (Dorst and Mougin, 1979) to represent a single subspecies.

In the field. This is the only cormorant or shag in its limited northern Pacific range having bright red facial skin that is continuous about the forehead. Younger birds lack this feature, and are probably sometimes impossible to separate from those of the somewhat smaller pelagic shags. The bill of the red-faced is slightly longer, thicker, more distinctly tapering, and paler (yellowish rather than brownish, at least basally) than that of the pelagic, but the visual differences between them in the field are sometimes apparently slight.

Ecology and General Biology

Breeding and nonbreeding habitats. Like the pelagic shag, this species is closely associated with rock-bottom coastlines, often feeding close to shore and probably not highly dispersive or migratory. Gould, Forsell, and Lensink (1982) had only a single observation of one bird in Gulf of Alaska waters deeper than 200 meters, but nevertheless believed that red-faced shags might be more likely to be found in offshore waters of the Bering Sea than are either pelagic shags or double-crested cormorants. Hunt et al. (1981) observed that red-faced shags around the Pribilof Islands were mostly found within 1–2 kilometers of shore, and rarely as far as 5 kilometers. They were never seen in water deeper than 100 meters.

Movements and migrations. Even in the northern parts of their range, such as the Pribilof Islands, these birds are essentially sedentary, so long as open water remains available (Hunt et al., 1981). There is no evidence of any significant seasonal movements away from breeding areas (Palmer, 1962). However, the birds are inclined to abandon local colonies from year to year, for no obvious reasons. Thus, at Chiniak Bay, Kodiak Island, the breeding populations of this species as well as the pelagic shag varied greatly from year to year over a three-year period, and at Ugaiushak and Chowiet islands, Gulf of Alaska, there was a 400 percent increase in breeding birds and active nests in a single year (Nysewander, 1986). Perhaps this low level of philopatry helps to explain the recently expanded breeding range of the species into the Prince William Sound area of southern Alaska.

Competition and predation. It seems very likely that the red-faced and pelagic shags are significant food and nest site competitors where they occur together, although their comparative diets in areas of sympatry are not yet established. The larger size of red-faced shags might allow them to dive in deeper waters or stronger surfs, and probably also is an advantage in areas where they might be competing for nest sites. On St. George Island, where pelagic shags don't breed, the primary competitors for nest sites are the northern fulmar (*Fulmarus glacialis*), black-legged kittiwake (*Rissa tridactyla*), and thick-billed murre (*Uria lomvia*). All of these species nest on rock ledges averaging 2–4 decimeters wide, whereas the red-faced shag nests on ledges 3–6 decimeters wide (averaging 4 decimeters). Although the shags cannot nest on ledges as narrow as those used by kittiwakes, the kittiwakes can exploit the wider ledges used by the shags. Observations suggested a high rate of nest site exchange involving shags and both the kittiwake and the thick-billed murre (Squibb and Hunt, 1983). On Ugaiushak Island and on Chiniak Bay (Kodiak Island) the red-faced and pelagic shags compete for similar nest sites, but in both locations the start of egg laying is earlier in the red-faced shag, suggesting that it may thereby be able to exclude the smaller pelagic shag from favored sites (Nysewander, 1986). Where red-faced and pelagic shags were found to nest in the same locations some overlap occurred, but red-faced shags tended to nest at higher levels than did pelagic shags, and they also were more prone to leave their nests unattended during disturbance than were pelagic shags (Bartonek et al., 1977).

Predators include the same array of foxes, corvids, larids, and falconiforms that were mentioned earlier as significant predators of the eggs and young of pelagic shags. However, the relative importance of specific predators probably varies greatly locally or from year to year, depending on predator access to other more readily available foods. At Ugaiushak Island the primary egg predators were judged by Hatch et al. (1978) to be glaucous-winged gulls (*Larus glaucescens*) and northern ravens (*Corvus corax*), and studies elsewhere in Alaska also tend to implicate these two species, especially the former, as serious egg predators (Bartonek et al., 1977; Hatch and Hatch, 1990b).

Foods and Foraging Behavior

Foods consumed. There is still only a rather limited amount of information on the foods of this species as compared with those of other Pacific coast cormorants and shags (see table 15). A few earlier observations from a small sample of stomachs obtained at the Pribilofs (Preble, 1923) indicated that bottom-dwelling fish, especially cottids, and shrimp comprise the typical foods of this species as well as of the pelagic shag. Hunt, Burgeson, and Sanger (1981) examined a much larger sample of stomachs and found that, by percentage of occurrence and relative volume, fish comprised the vast majority of prey taken. Of the identified prey, cottid fish made up the single greatest component, with walleye pollack (*Theragra*, Gadidae) and sand eels (*Ammodytes*, Ammodytidae) also represented in moderate quantities. Among crustaceans, both decapods (shrimps and crabs) and amphipods (mostly gammarids) were present, with decapods outnumbering amphipods in all categories of relative importance. Comparing foods of adults (from stomach samples) and chicks (from regurgitations), cottid fish were more heavily represented among chick foods, whereas adults consumed a higher proportion of invertebrates, mostly crabs (Hunt, 1976; Hunt et al., 1981).

Foraging behavior. The just-mentioned results of Hunt, Burgeson, and Sanger (1981) suggest that, like the pelagic shag, the red-faced shag is mainly a bottom or near-bottom forager, taking epibenthic and often cryptic organisms found in rocky substrates. Most of the observations indicate that the birds forage close to shore and near their breeding colonies or roosts, in relatively shallow waters. Wehle (1978) noted that the birds foraged within 3 kilometers of their nesting island throughout the breeding period.

Social Behavior

Age of maturity and mating system. Since the pelagic shag evidently breeds when three years old this is likely to be the case with the red-faced also. Considering the relatively transient nature of certain local breeding colonies and apparently generally low level of philopatry in both pelagic and red-faced shags, it is unlikely that pair bonds normally persist for more than a single breeding season in such situations.

Social displays and vocalizations. No extended descriptions of this species' displays are available, but van Tets (1965) provided a few observations. It is probable that few significant differences exist between the displays of the pelagic and red-faced shags. During the male's wing-waving display the head is held over the back, with the bill pointed upward, and the head is moved upward and downward at the same rates as the wingtips are raised and lowered, but in opposite synchrony. These head and wing movements occur at a rate (more than twice per second) resembling that of the pelagic shag, and in common with that species the white thigh patches are alternately hidden and exposed during the display.

Among the individual recognition displays of this species is gaping. Also in common with the pelagic shag, a "purring" call note is uttered by males during their gaping display each time the bill is opened, whereas females alternate between two call notes, like the ticking of a grandfather clock's pendulum. In these two species the bill is opened several times per gaping display, including once at the end of each upward movement of the head, with the head moving up and down at the rate of about twice per second (van Tets, 1965).

Additionally in common with the pelagic shag, presentation of nesting materials is performed by males of this species. Adults also perform kink-throating, a prehop posture with the neck arched, a pretakeoff posture with the body twisted, and an undescribed "gargle-threat" posture. During the postlanding display a call note is uttered that is identical in both sexes, as is also true in the pelagic shag (van Tets, 1965).

Reproductive Biology

Breeding season. On the Pribilof Islands this species is one of the earliest nesters of all the seabirds, typically starting its egg laying in early May, with a peak in mid-May (Hunt et al., 1981). On Chowiet Island (Semidi Islands) red-faced shags were highly synchronous in egg laying within seasons, but quite variable between years. The overall mean initial laying date was May 26, with a range of 13 days in annual means. Generally in the Gulf of Alaska the egg-laying period begins in mid-May or early June, with hatching from late June to mid-July onward and fledging from mid-August or early September onward (Nysewander, 1986).

Nest sites and nest building. Throughout its range this species nests on steep, relatively inaccessible slopes, using narrow ledges that average only about 4 decimeters wide (see above). On the Pribilof Islands it prefers nesting on lower sections of cliffs; nests there are rarely higher than 122 meters elevation (Hickey and Craighead, 1977). It is possible that red-faced shags use slightly broader ledges than do pelagic shags, but specific measurements of these differences are lacking (Nysewander, 1986).

Egg laying and incubation. Summarizing data from several study areas in the Gulf of Alaska, Nysewander (1986) noted that mean annual clutch sizes varied from 2.12 (32 nests) to 3.08 (49 nests) for two different years at Ugaiushak Island, and averaged 2.5 eggs for 37 nests during one season at the Semidi Islands. Of 51 nests on Ugaiushak Island, the modal clutch (37 percent) was of 4 eggs, and the mean was 3.1 (Wehle, 1978). On the Pribilof Islands the overall mean clutch size was 2.84 eggs (214 nests), with yearly and local variations from 2.62 to 3.0 eggs (Hunt et al., 1981). The incubation period is not known with certainty, but probably lasts 32–34 days (Nysewander, 1986). Hunt et al. (1981) estimated the incubation period at about 31 (range 26–37) days.

Brooding and rearing of young. Chick growth rates on St. Paul and St. George islands ranged from 48.5 to 61.8 grams per day, with the highest rates for each island occurring in different years, suggesting that the two populations were operating independently (Hunt et al., 1981). Nysewander (1986) estimated a fledging period of 49–50 days, but Hunt et al. (1981) estimated an average fledging period of about 59 (range 54–64) days.

Breeding success. Great local and annual variations in productivity appear to be typical. Hatching success on the Pribilof Islands varied from 25 to 64 percent for various localities and years, and the number of chicks fledged per incubated nest ranged from 1.2 to 1.45, with an overall average of 1.25 (Hunt et al., 1981). Summarizing data from five Gulf of Alaska study areas, Nysewander (1986) noted that the number of chicks fledged per nest built ranged from 0.0 to 1.91.

Lensink, Gould, and Sanger (1979) estimated the major decimating factors on Kodiak Island, Gulf of Alaska, to be in decreasing order of significance (1) glaucous-winged gull predation on eggs and chicks, (2) attempted predation by river otters (*Lutra canadensis*), (3) corvid and bald eagle (*Haliaeetus leucocephalus*) predation, (4) human disturbance, and (5) losses caused by storms. Additionally, colonies near kittiwakes produced fewer average fledged young per nest (1.42 vs. 2.14) than denser, less disturbed single-species colonies. In some areas American crows (*Corvus brachyrhynchos*) are a significant cause of nest failure where periodic human disturbance is also present (Nysewander and Hoberg, 1978). At Ugaiushak Island, northern ravens and glaucous-winged gulls apparently accounted for an 81 percent nest failure rate (Bartonek et al., 1977). On the Pribilof Islands, nest desertion was the most important single cause of mortality, with fox predation and hunting by native Aleuts secondary (Hunt et al., 1981). In areas where pelagic and red-faced shags breed together, it is typical for the red-faced to be more successful in producing fledglings (Nysewander and Hoberg, 1978).

Population Status

Most observers agree that this species has increased its range and numbers in recent decades in Alaska (Palmer, 1962), especially at the eastern edge of its range in the Prince William Sound area. Sowls, Hatch, and Lensink (1978) estimated a total Alaskan population of 130,000 birds in the 1970s, with a probable center of population in the Near Islands, these having an estimated total of 88,000 birds. Evidently the majority of the species' population occurs still farther west, especially along the Kamchatka Peninsula and the Kuril archipelago (Lobkov and Alexeev, 1987). On the Kurils about 20,000–30,000 birds are now known to breed, and the species also breeds on the Commander Islands and southern Kamchatka (Litvinenko and Shibaev, 1991). Golovkin (1984) estimated that at least 12,000 pairs occur in the Bering Sea region, plus unknown additional numbers in the Sea of Okhotsk and along the Sea of Japan. Hasegawa (1984) reported that about 500 birds occur along the Hokkaido coast.

Evolutionary Relationships

This is obviously a very close relative of the pelagic shag. Siegel-Causey (1991) commented on several museum specimens for which the species identifications of these two forms were apparently confused for one another. His description of a possible third extant species in this phyletic group makes their relationships even more difficult to assess.

Other Vernacular Names

Green cormorant, shag; cormoran huppé (French); Krähenscharbe (German)

Distribution

Breeds along the coast of western Iceland, the Faeroes, the British Isles, and the coastal mainland of western Europe from Russia's Kola Peninsula south to Gibraltar; also along the Mediterranean coast locally from southern Spain, Yugoslavia, and Greece to Turkey, on nearly all the larger Mediterranean islands excepting Sicily, and along the Black Sea coast to the Crimea; also locally on Africa's Mediterranean coast and more widely along the Atlantic coast of Morocco. Winters mostly at breeding areas, but with some dispersal southwardly, especially in the northern parts of the breeding range, and probably mostly by young birds. (See figure 80.)

Subspecies

L. a. aristotelis (Linnaeus). Breeds in Iceland, the Faeroes, and Great Britain, and from the Kola Peninsula south through coastal Norway; locally also in northwestern France and the Atlantic coast of Spain and Portugal.

L. a. desmarestii (Payraudeau) 1826. Resident in the Mediterranean coastal region from Spain and France east locally to Turkey, and northeast to the Crimean peninsula of the Black Sea. Also resident on most of the Mediterranean islands, including the Balearics, Corsica, Elba, Sardinia, Crete, the Aegean islands, Rhodes, and Cyprus.

L. a. riggenbachi (Hartert) 1923. Resident locally along the Atlantic coast of Morocco from the vicinity of Casablanca south to Puerto Cansado. Possibly not taxonomically separable from *desmarestii* (Vaurie, 1965).

Description

Prebreeding adult. Head and neck dark glossy green, shading into oily bronze-green on the rest of the body; crown with a median semierect, recurved crest; numerous white filoplumes among the neck feathers; upper back, wing coverts, and scapulars often purplish bronze, and narrowly margined with greenish black; remiges and rectrices (12) greenish black to black. Iris bright emerald-green, with a very narrow yellow inner ring; orbital skin in front of eyes blackish; bill gray to lead-colored, culmen black and sides of the mandible and maxilla bright yellow basally (the bill mostly yellow in *desmarestii*); inside of mouth yellow; naked gular skin black, thickly dotted with rows of yellow spots; legs and feet blackish, with paler webs (the feet brown with yellow webs in *desmarestii*).

Postbreeding adult. Like the prebreeding adult, but lacking a crest and the white filoplumes; the throat feathers immediately adjoining the gular skin white to pale grayish white. Primary molt begins in late summer, with usually two and sometimes three molt centers simultaneously active (Potts, 1971).

Subadult. Sexual maturity and first breeding occur at three or four years of age (Snow, 1960). The glossy black definitive plumage is acquired between the second and third autumn, although some brown immature feathers may persist on the underparts or wing coverts until the fourth or even fifth year. Subadults resemble adults but have some brown mottling on the head, and the upperpart feather edges are broader and less velvety black.

Immature. By their second summer the underparts and part of the back and rump are still pale and juvenile-like, contrasting with darker immature feathers elsewhere on the body. Following postjuvenal molt, the underparts are darker brown than in juveniles, the scapulars and wing coverts more rounded and less pointed; the chin is pale buff, and the throat and foreneck are dark brown, speckled with white. The juvenal primaries begin to be molted during spring of the second year; this molt is arrested the following winter, and the tenth juvenal primary may be retained in a few birds up to their fourth year (Potts, 1971). By the second summer the iris is yellow-green and the bare skin of face and gape bright yellow; the legs and feet are dark brownish black. The definitive nuptial plumage is attained by males when three years old, and by females when four (Potts, 1971).

Juvenile. Whole of upperparts and flanks brown, with faint green gloss; underparts uniform buffy brown to pale buff, palest on vent (and lightest below in *desmarestii*); remiges and rectrices dull black, edged or tipped with buff; upper wing coverts pointed and slightly glossed with green and edged with buff. Iris yellowish white; bare facial skin, gape, and base of bill pale flesh, with yellow tinge; gular skin brown; webs of toes and insides of tarsus yellow-brown to pale flesh-brown, the legs and feet otherwise brownish black.

Nestling. Naked brownish skin at hatching, but covered within a week with brown down, except for bare brownish to gray skin on throat, lores, and forehead region. Iris grayish white, bluish gray, or light brown; bill blackish, with a fleshy yellow gape; legs and feet dark brown.

Figure 80. Distribution of the European shag, showing its total breeding range (inked), locations of major insular breeding colonies (arrows), and its wintering range (stippled). The ranges of its races *aristotelis* (ar), *desmarestii* (de), and *riggenbachi* (ri) are also indicated.

Measurements (in millimeters)

Nominate *aristotelis:* wing, males 261–278 (ave. of 12, 271), females 251–269 (ave. of 18, 258); tail, adult males 119–133 (ave. of 6, 129), adult females 114–125 (ave. of 10, 119); culmen, males 51–61 (ave. of 45, 56.4), females 51–63 (ave. of 34, 56.7). Of *desmarestii:* wing, males 243–271 (ave. of 12, 258), females 240–265 (ave. of 11, 249); culmen, males 58–65 (ave. of 6, 61), females 61–65 (ave. of 5, 63) (Cramp and Simmons, 1977; Brown, Urban, and Newman, 1982). Vaurie (1965) reported average exposed culmen lengths for *aristotelis* as 59 (10 males) and 58.8 (10 females), as compared with substantially longer culmen measurements of 69.2 (7 males) and 69.4 (9 females) for *desmarestii.* His combined measurements of 5 adult females and 2 immatures of *riggenbachi* are as follows: wing 243–254 (ave. 247) and exposed culmen 59–63 (ave. 61.5). Eggs ca. 62 × 38.

Weights (in grams)

Nominate *aristotelis,* three adult males 1,760, 1,930, and 2,154 (Cramp and Simmons, 1977), averaging 1,948. Seven breeding females 1,407–1,788, averaging 1,598 (Snow, 1960). The mean weight of 26 adults of nominate *aristotelis* (sex composition not specified) was 1,785, with a standard deviation of 43.66 (Pearson, 1968). Average weight of young in 30 unmodified broods at fledging was 1,710; fledging weights of experimentally manipulated (as to hatching intervals) broods averaged 1,689–1,716 (Amundsen and Stokland, 1988). Calculated egg weight 49.4; average of 303, 49.4 (Snow, 1960).

Identification

In the hand. The combination of an adult culmen length of 51–63 mm, generally greenish black plumage and black feet, a bright yellow gape and bill base, and densely spotted black and yellow gular skin should serve to identify this species.
In the field. Within its range this is the only cormorant or shag having a generally uniformly greenish black plumage and face, with a strongly contrasting bright yellow bill base. This yellow bill base, which is reminiscent of the colorful gape flanges of many nestling passerine birds, is also visible in juvenile and even in nestling birds. European shags are considerably smaller and more slender than partially sympatric great cormorants. Under good light conditions adults appear to be more glossy greenish rather than brownish black, and also lack the distinct, broad white border behind the gular skin typical of adult great cormorants, although in postbreeding birds there is a much less definite area of whitish feathers immediately behind the gular skin. Alstrom (1985) has extensively reviewed and illustrated the field identification features of this species, especially as compared with the great cormorant.

Ecology and General Biology

Breeding and nonbreeding habitats. This species occurs in both inshore and offshore marine habitats, but rarely extends far from the coast. Like the pelagic and red-faced shags it prefers rocky coastlines adjoining fairly deep waters, ranging from subarctic to quite mild-temperate (Mediterranean) climatic zones. Fresh and brackish waters, as well as muddy and sandy-bottom habitats, are generally avoided (Cramp and Simmons, 1977).
Movements and migrations. In general, this species is sedentary to dispersive rather than migratory, at least over most of its range. In the north there are increasingly greater southward displacements during winter, with mean January displacements increasing from 100 to 600 kilometers as one proceeds northwardly along the Norwegian coast (Johansen, 1975). However, there are marked geographic variations, and age-related as well as annual variations exist in some populations. For most northern European populations the median winter movements are less than 100 kilometers; additionally, wintering populations tend to be fairly discrete. Populations of exposed coasts are more prone to dispersal, perhaps as a result of weather influences on food supplies. Although no part of the British population can be considered migratory (average winter dispersal ranges from 58 to 184 kilometers), that of northern Norway is apparently more properly considered migratory rather than dispersive. It is possible that periodic large-scale "eruptive" movements simply represent the later stages of a graded response to deteriorating local environmental conditions (Galbraith et al., 1986).

During eruptive years the rate of dispersal of first-year birds from colonies in eastern Scotland and northeastern England diminishes progressively with distance, suggesting that the proximate causes of dispersal are most intense near the point of origin. Periodic eruptions are known to occur here in addition to annual dispersal of young birds during autumn. During eruptive years the movement averaged 167 percent more than in noneruptive years, or 240 kilometers in first-year birds, as compared to about 90 kilometers otherwise. Older age groups remained within 30 kilometers of the colony (Potts, 1969).
Competition and predation. The foods and foraging behavior of the European shag and the great cormorant were compared in chapter 4 (see table 14). It is apparent that these two broadly sympatric species have a relatively low incidence of food and foraging overlap (Steven, 1933; Lack, 1945). Pearson (1968) determined a low incidence of foraging competition among shags and seven other species of seabirds breeding on the Farne Islands, although some overlap existed in the species and size ranges of captured fish. Substantial differences occurred in the distance from the colony that each species foraged, with shags foraging close to the colony. Estimates of dietary overlap among European

shags and six other seabird species were also provided by Barrett and Furness (1990). Although there were no differences in average diving depths of razorbills (*Alca torda*), Atlantic puffins (*Fratercula arctica*), and shags, these species took different foods and when a prey species was common, each predator took a different size of the prey.

Nest site competition occurs with herring gulls (*Larus argentatus*) and to some extent also with razorbills (Snow, 1963). Egg predators are known to include the usual corvids and larids such as northern ravens (*Corvus corax*), herring gulls, and great black-backed gulls (*L. marinus*) (Snow, 1960), and some or all of these egg predators doubtless also prey on young nestlings. Among 877 band recoveries of fledged birds, almost 80 percent of the causes of death were unknown, and predators were not implicated in any of the others (Potts, 1969). However, mammalian predators such as foxes (*Vulpes vulpes*) may be locally important on breeding grounds.

Foods and Foraging Behavior

Foods consumed. A comprehensive summary of foods of the European shag throughout its range has been provided by Cramp and Simmons (1977), who pointed out that mostly midwater and some bottom-dwelling fish are taken in coastal and estuarine habitats. Predominant taxa are sand eels (*Ammodytes*, Ammodytidae), herrings (Clupeidae, especially *Sprattus*), and cods (Gadidae, including *Clupea, Merlangius, Pollachius, Gadus,* and *Boreogadus*). Shore-dwelling fishes and crustaceans are secondary prey items. In the relatively rare cases when the birds forage in fresh-water habitats they have eaten such prey as sticklebacks (*Gasterosteus*), trout (*Salmo*), and pike (*Esox*). Foraging may be done once or, more commonly, twice a day (following tidal cycles), and perhaps an average daily consumption of about 13.5 percent of body weight is typical (Cramp and Simmons, 1977).

Foraging behavior. Lumsden and Haddow (1946) noted that the durations of dives bore no relation to water depth, suggesting that the birds were feeding on midwater fishes. Of 155 observed dives, the mean duration was 40 seconds, and the longest was 100 seconds. Barrett and Furness (1990) recorded a median maximum diving depth of 28.2 meters, which reflected the vertical distribution of prey species (mostly sand eels) rather than maximum diving capabilities. The deepest observed dive (of 12 dives) was 39.6 meters. This is similar to the estimated mean diving depth of 26 meters, and a maximum of 43 meters, provided by Wanless, Burger, and Harris (1991). These birds typically foraged in waters 21–40 meters deep (mean 29 meters), with a bottom of gravel, sand, or rock having a thin sediment cover, the favored habitats of sand eels, their primary prey species. They also foraged within 7 kilometers of land, had average foraging ranges of 7 kilometers from their breeding sites, and

had a maximum observed foraging range of 17 kilometers (Wanless, Harris, and Morris, 1991).

Social Behavior

Age of maturity and mating system. Males attain their full nuptial plumage at three years, and females at four years. Second-year breeding birds are primarily males. Two-year-old females may visit the breeding grounds but usually do not breed. About half of them breed for the first time when they are three years old (Potts, Coulson, and Deans, 1980). There is no evidence of pair bond retention through the winter season, and 13 of 21 marked females changed their nest site in the following year (Snow, 1963). The overall rate of mate retention in successive seasons has been estimated as 48.1 percent (Potts, 1966). Additionally, a small proportion of males may pair with two females, but such matings usually do not result in any young being produced. Males also usually keep their same nest site from year to year if they are successful but move to a new site if they are not. Mobility probably influences the rate of remating. Most of the long-term relationships are apparently the result of the tendency for older and more experienced birds to nest on progressively better sites (Potts, Coulson, and Deans, 1980).

Social displays and vocalizations. The study by Snow (1963) is still the primary source of information, although van Tets (1965) provided some additional observations. Male site advertisement ("courtship" in Snow's terminology) consists of inviting prospective mates to approach by performing the dart-gape display (figure 81E) and the throwback (figure 81F). The dart-gape consists of a series of darting thrusts of the bill toward the female, with the bill opened and the yellow gape exposed with each forward thrust. A faintly audible clicking noise is also produced. When the female looks toward him or moves in his direction, the male performs the throwback display, holding his head back toward the back with the tail cocked (in a posture comparable to and probably homologous with gargling in other shags). During the throwback the gular pouch is quivered and the beak makes slight upward jerking movements. This posture is not held for long (3–6 seconds), and if the female delays approaching, the male may again begin dart-gaping, but later again performs the throwback when the female finally approaches closely. As the female approaches the male she typically runs ("upright-run") to a position beside and behind his back as she performs throat clicking, and stretches her neck over the male's back (figure 81C). She may then preen his head and neck, and the male may perform a sitting gape or a bowing display (figure 81D, G) This display sequence may be performed away from the nest site, such as on nearby sea rocks, when the position of the nests makes it necessary. Perhaps the most important moment in pair bonding occurs when the male rises and allows the female to

Figure 81. Social behavior of the European shag, including threat gape (A), postlanding ("conciliatory gape") display (B, left), upright-aware display (B, right), throat clicking (C), sitting gape display (D), male dart-gape display (E), male throwback display (F), bowing (while sitting) (G), copulation (H), and mutual nest quivering (I). After sketches and photos in Snow (1963).

sit on the nest site. Soon after pairing, males stop courtship display, but other mutual recognition or greeting displays continue through the season.

Throat clicking is also performed as a greeting display between paired birds. The posture is quite variable, but the hyoid is always moved up and down and the gular pouch thus exposed, producing a kink-throated appearance. Male shags apparently do not recognize the sex of other birds, and perform displays toward all birds that are in the upright-aware posture (figure 81B, right) but ignore those in a resting position. This same posture is used in pretakeoff, and is also the posture assumed when a bird is hopping out of the sea or up a rock slope. It is very similar to the postlanding or "conciliatory gape" (figure 81B, left) performed by birds that have just landed near others. A "sitting gape" (figure 81D) is used by both sexes on the nest (such as during nest relief) and also during courtship. An "upright run," apparently comparable to "penguin-walking" in other shags, may be used rather than hopping when approaching the nest site on level ground. A more aggressive "threat-gape" may be used when defending the nest site from intruders, or when the bird is away from the nest and unwilling to move when disturbed (figure 81A). At high intensity the displaying bird may stand in a nearly horizontal posture, and when the neck is fully extended the bird quivers its head laterally and hisses (females) or utters an *ark* call.

Nest building is done by functional nest-quivering movements of the head and bill, but nest quivering also occurs as an aggressive or "friendly" signal. During the early stages of courtship, nest-quivering movements are frequent (figure 81I). Copulation occurs at the nest or nest site, and in some cases the female may assume the upper position ("reversed copulation"). Just before copulation the female sits with her tail cocked and nibbles at nest material. The male mounts with a hop and grasps the female's neck or nape with his bill during treading, while the female inserts her bill into the nest material a short distance (figure 81H), producing a posture much like the ritualized bowing display that is used during courtship. After copulation is completed the male hops off while performing a landing gape and associated call. At the same time the female usually performs the sitting gape, and typically alternates this display with nest-quivering movements.

Vocalizations of this species are extremely limited among adults. In addition to the throat-clicking sounds of both sexes and hissing by females, males utter a repeated *ark* in a variety of situations such as during the landing gape, in flight, or when leaving the nest. In general, it is used in all situations where aggressiveness is evoked.

Reproductive Biology

Breeding season.   The breeding season is latitudinally variable, with nesting in northern Africa occurring as early as February (Brown, Urban, and Newman, 1982). In Britain and southern Norway most of the egg records are from March to June, and on the Kola Peninsula egg laying begins in early May. The egg-laying season is long, and replacement clutches following loss are common, especially when the first clutch was not yet complete at the time of loss (Cramp and Simmons, 1977).

Nest sites and nest building.   Nests are situated on rock ledges of cliffs, which range in elevation from slightly above the high-tide line to more than 100 meters elevation. Much competition for good nest sites typically occurs. Characteristics of a good nest site include protection from high seas, relative exposure to rain, capacity to hold up to three young, and relative terrestrial access to the sea. In one area only 4 percent of the nests evaluated were optimum with regard to these aspects (Potts, Coulson, and Deans, 1980). Vulnerability to predation by red foxes or other terrestrial predators may also influence nest site quality.

Nest sites are reoccupied by older males as early as February or March in Britain, followed later in the season by progressively younger age groups, with two-year-olds arriving in May. The oldest birds on the best nest sites may begin breeding five weeks sooner than the youngest age groups. Typically experienced males keep their nest sites from year to year if they are successful in producing young, but move to others if unsuccessful. The prolonged nesting season and the correlation between nest site quality and the age of the occupying pairs apparently result from nest site competition whose outcome has a significant impact on breeding success (Potts, Coulson, and Deans, 1980).

Egg laying and incubation.   Eggs are laid at an average of three-day intervals, either at night or early in the morning. Some long egg-laying intervals of up to 20 days also occur, usually in nests destined to be unsuccessful. Among 10 nests that were still incomplete when the clutches were lost to predation, the intervals between the onset of laying of the first clutch and the start of the replacement clutch was 8–29 days, averaging 17.3 days. Replacement clutches for two nests that were lost late in incubation were begun between 21 and 22 days after the loss of the first clutch. Clutch sizes for 447 British nests ranged from one to six eggs, with a modal clutch of three and a mean of 3.07. Mean clutch size decreased slightly through the season, and also varied annually. During years of high average clutch size the fledging success was also fairly high. Adults cover the first-laid egg, but actual incubation may not begin until the second egg, or possibly even later in some cases. For second or third eggs the incubation period averages 30–31 days. First-laid eggs usually hatch in 33–35 days (Snow, 1960).

Brooding and rearing of young.   The young typically hatch at daily intervals, with a pipping period of at least 24 hours prior to actual hatching. The newly hatched chicks weigh about 30–40 grams, are brooded on the upper surfaces of the parents' feet in the same way that eggs are incubated, and are fed by both parents. The average nestling period for 35 young was 53 days, but with a range of 48–58 days. Most chick losses occur during the first 10 days, and many of the losses of older chicks apparently result from the birds falling from the nest rather than from starvation (Snow, 1960). In a test of the brood reduction hypothesis, Amundsen and Stoklund (1988) modified the hatching spread of nests, and found that the fledging success rates and fledging weights of broods hatching asynchronously were no higher than those that had been experimentally altered to provide for synchronous hatching. Last-hatched chicks from broods where the hatching was more asynchronous than normal exhibited higher mortality and lower growth rates than those from naturally spaced broods. Additionally, both relative egg size and relative parental quality (as judged by relative size of eggs laid by females) influence the rate of nestling growth, the former factor perhaps being more important early in nestling development, and the latter later on.

Breeding success.   Snow (1960) provided data indicating an overall hatching success rate of 71 percent (range of annual averages 69–73 percent) for 893 eggs studied over four successive breeding seasons. Annual fledging success rates ranged from 67 to 95 percent during the same period. Of 833 nests that were fully incubated, 76 percent of the eggs hatched. The mean number of young fledged per nest varied annually from 1.32 to 2.25. Most failures at the egg stage resulted from apparent infertility or early embryonic death, with predator or egg disappearance from unknown causes of secondary importance. Nearly half (47 percent) of the total chick losses occurred among birds up to 10 days of age, and relatively few (5 percent) occurred among chicks at least 41 days of age. Breeding success was lower in birds having new nest sites compared to older, established sites. It was also lower for pairs with clutches laid late in the breeding season, and for cliff-nesting sites as compared with noncliff sites.

The most complete study of the factors influencing breeding success in European shags is that of Potts, Coulson, and Deans (1980), which covered a period of 10 years and involved over 800 pairs. The most important variables influencing the seasonal start of laying were the ages of the partners, with experienced breeders breeding earlier and selecting the best nest sites. Exclusive of their differences in nest site choice, first-time breeders were 70 percent as successful reproductively as were established breeders. Variations in clutch size had very little influence on overall numbers of chicks hatched. Hatching success (87 percent) was mostly limited by the weather, particularly by rough seas, which greatly affected the success of poorly sited nests. Variations in the number of young fledged was mainly influenced by the quality of the nest site, and secondarily by previous breeding experience. The survival of young older than five days was not measurably affected by their parents' age or experience.

Population Status

A summary of recent shag populations in western Europe and the north Atlantic region is provided in table 27. In Britain the species has been increasing markedly in recent decades, particularly along the eastern coast (Cramp, Bourne, and Saunders, 1974). About a third of the species' population is concentrated in Norway, where at least locally it has been increasing (Godö, 1983), although in other locations it is still well below the 1930 level (Rikardsen and Strann, 1983). The Mediterranean population (*desmarestii*) is poorly documented, but that of the Chafarinas Islands off Morocco's northern coast has recently been discussed by de Juana, Varela, and Witt (1984). Nothing is apparently known of the status of *riggenbachi* on Morocco's western coast.

Evolutionary Relationships

Siegel-Causey (1988) considered this species to be part of a "basal group" of cliff shags, with its nearest geographic relatives being the pelagic and red-faced shags, and the rest of the group being southern-hemisphere in orientation.

Peru

Trujillo

Chimbote

Lima

Other Vernacular Names

Gaimard's cormorant, gray cormorant, red-footed shag, red-legged cormorant, scarlet-footed cormorant; cormoran de Gaimard (French); Rotfuss-Kormoran (German); cormorán de patas coloradas (Spanish)

Distribution

Resident along the Pacific coast of South America, from the Macabi Islands, Peru, south to Chiloé Island, Chile; also breeds between Puerto Deseado and Santa Cruz, Argentina, where probably also resident. Considered "near-threatened" by the ICBP (Collar and Andrew, 1988). (See figure 82.)

Subspecies

None recognized by Dorst and Mougin (1979). The Argentine population averages slightly smaller and paler than Pacific coast birds, and has by some authorities (e.g., Blake, 1977) been racially recognized as *cirriger* King, 1928. Rasmussen (1988) has recently supported this racial distinction on the basis of additional plumage criteria.

Description

Prebreeding adult. Head, neck, lower back, rump, and upper tail coverts mostly smoky gray; chest and rest of underparts paler; an elongate white patch on each side of the neck; sides of upper back, wing coverts, and scapulars silvery gray toward the tip and rather widely margined with brownish black; a scattered patch of white filoplumes behind the eye and down the foreneck; remiges and rectrices (14) dark gray. Iris pale green, surrounded on the dark eyelids by 16 pale blue papillae; bare lores orange-vermillion; bill horn-yellow to cadmium-yellow distally, becoming greenish brown along the culmen and grading to orange or orange-vermillion toward the base; gular skin orange-red; legs and feet coral-red.
Postbreeding adult. Similar to the prebreeding adult, but lacking the white filoplumes, and the upperparts very

Figure 82. Distribution of the red-legged shag, showing areas of denser breeding (small cross-hatching) plus peripheral breeding areas (larger cross-hatching). Arrows on the inset map indicate locations of twentieth-century breeding localities off Peru (after Murphy, 1936).

slightly darker. Softparts probably also duller (the "gray" iris color mentioned by Blake, 1977, may refer to this seasonal period, or possibly relates to immature birds).
Immature-subadult. Similar to the postbreeding adult, the white patches of the neck less clear, and generally dark brownish gray above, the wing coverts and underparts mottled with brownish white.
Juvenile. Usually paler than immatures, with a grayish brown breast, and a sprinkling of white filoplumes on the sides of the neck and the center of the throat. Juveniles from the Atlantic coast population are very pale in plumage, whereas those from the Pacific coast are highly variable, ranging from very dark throughout to those with pale gray underparts and whitish throats. Gular skin color variable, from black to orange, and leg and foot color from dusky orange to reddish black (Rasmussen, 1988).
Nestling. Initially naked; later covered with brownish drab down.

Measurements (in millimeters)

Wing, males 240–254 (ave. of 10, 248), females 232–245 (ave. of 8, 239); tail, males 92–101 (ave. of 10, 97.2), females 92–103 (ave. of 8, 97.5); culmen, males 55–62 (ave. of 10, 58.2), females 55.5–62 (ave. of 9, 58.8) (Murphy, 1936). Eggs ca. 64 × 38.

Weights (in grams)

Six males 1,375–1,550 (ave. 1,471), three females 1,400–1,500 (ave. 1,433) (University of Kansas Museum of Natural History specimens). Two unsexed and unaged specimens, 1,304 and 1,417 (Murphy, 1936). Average weight (sample size unstated) 1,300 (Duffy, 1980b). Calculated egg weight 51.0.

Identification

In the hand. The combination of bright red feet and a yellow to orange bill serves to identify this highly distinctive cormorant species.
In the field. This is the only South American cormorant having bright red feet, a bright yellow to orange bill, and a medium gray (adults) to brownish gray (immatures) plumage. The white patch down the side of the neck is longer and more posteriorly located than it is on the rock shag. In flight the silvery white upper wing coverts are highly visible on both adults and young birds, and these areas contrast strongly with the darker flight feathers and undersides of the wings.

Ecology and General Biology

Breeding and nonbreeding habitats.   This species occupies the narrow ledges of steep coastal cliffs, rock promontories, islets, and rocky caverns, where its plumage pattern (especially that of the juveniles) blends in remarkably well, so that the birds are nearly invisible against their normal backgrounds unless the red feet and white necks of the adults are seen (Coker, 1919). The species is considered to be relatively nonsocial and is usually found in pairs or only small groups, but has been observed in flocks of 20–30 individuals on occasion. The Atlantic coast population may be somewhat more social than the Pacific coast group, but it is not known whether these differences are ecological or genetic (Siegel-Causey, 1987). It occurs in deeper coastal waters but never enters fresh water (Murphy, 1936; Johnson, 1965). At times both juveniles and adults rest on sandy beaches at the mouths of rivers, but they seem to prefer the flat tops of rocks and islets. Siegel-Causey (1987) did not observe wing-spreading behavior in either adults or juveniles.

Movements and migrations.   No evidence exists for migrations or dispersals of any distance. Johnson (1965) stated that in Chile the red-legged shag is not subjected to the massive population fluctuations typical of the guanay, since it feeds on a variety of small marine fish rather than concentrating on the highly variable anchoveta. The fairly small Argentine population is also relatively sedentary, with both adults and juveniles remaining close to shore and moving no more than about 300 kilometers from the breeding colony (Jehl and Rumbull, 1976).

Competition and predation.   Murphy (1936) believed that this species has no apparent enemies other than humans, who often catch and eat the nestlings.

Foods and Foraging Behavior

Foods consumed.   Coker (1919) believed that red-legged shags captured eels (Anguillidae), and Murphy (1936) noted that the contents of four stomachs he had analyzed contained only anchovetas. No other specific information is available, but Johnson (1965) believed that a variety of prey is consumed.

Foraging behavior.   Murphy (1936) observed these birds diving in water 8–10 meters deep for food as well as nesting materials. They are normally solitary foragers, and their short wings and associated rapid wingstrokes make for laborious flying.

Social Behavior

Age of maturity and mating system.   No information, although at least seasonal monogamy prevails (Siegel-Causey, 1987).

Social displays and vocalizations.   The only detailed information on this topic comes from Siegel-Causey (1987), who studied a colony of birds representing the Argentine population. Male advertising display consists of the darting and throwback postures. When darting, the male begins with a semierect body posture and closed wings. He then draws his head back and forth (anteriorly-posteriorly) along the midline of the body, while making faint clicking notes during the forward phase. When the head is at the forwardmost position the bill is opened and the red gape exposed. During the throwback display, which is typically performed as a female approaches, the neck is stretched along the back, the bill is pointed toward the tail, and silent kink-throating movements are made. This posture is held for 3–5 seconds, with the wings usually held against the body, but at times a single wing-flipping movement is made, with the wingtips moved sharply away from the body and quickly returned.

Individual recognition and pairing displays primarily include gaping, throat clicking, allopreening, and occasionally bowing. The gaping display (figure 83E–G) is used during nest greeting and nest relief. The neck is laid on the back as in the throwback display, but the bill is slightly opened, the head is rolled quickly from side to side a few times, and a single clicking sound is produced with each roll. Siegel-Causey observed this display only in males. Throat clicking (figure 83B) is used during nest ceremonies and also occurs after copulation. The head is held horizontal, the beak is closed, and a series of clicking sounds are uttered. Kink-throating may accompany this throat clicking. Throat clicking is frequently alternated with nest-worrying movements, which are used during greeting, during other pair-related displays, and also between threat displays. Allopreening is commonly performed by paired birds, and may be initiated by either bird waving its head in front of the other's face. Both birds then begin to perform neck-twining movements (figure 83C) and nibble at each other's white neck patches (figure 83D). After about 10–15 seconds preening terminates, but may be repeated later in bouts lasting up to four minutes. Siegel-Causey only infrequently saw a bowing display similar to that of the European, pelagic, and red-faced shags, and was unable to establish a pattern for its use.

During intensive courtship, the male performs the throwback display, to which the female responds with throat clicking and hopping. Bouts of allopreening follow, and mounting is usually preceded with nest worrying by the female and throat clicking by the male. These same displays are also performed immediately after copulation. These pair-forming displays are gradually replaced with nest-building and pair-bonding displays.

The pretakeoff posture is much like that of the pelagic and European shag, in that the neck is twisted as the bird looks out toward the water while its body points toward the land (figure 83A). It then crouches and leaps while uttering a

Figure 83. Social behavior of the red-legged shag, including pretakeoff posture (A), pair throat-clicking (B), with the male on left also kink-throating, pair neck-twining (C), pair allopreening (D), and male gaping sequence (E–G), including start, head-rolling phase, and finish. After sketches in Siegel-Causey (1987).

clear, sparrowlike chirping whistle that rises and quickly falls in pitch. When landing, the birds utter a similar kink-throating call, and land in a distinctive postlanding posture with the neck feathers erected and the hyoid depressed. The birds frequently hop both after landing and prior to takeoff, the hopping serving as a pair-bonding display as well as a functional means of locomotion. When used as a display, the hop is performed with the bill closed, the hyoid depressed, and the wings slightly opened. A postlanding display follows the hop. Hopping occurs in many social contexts, including greeting, before allopreening, before and after copulation, and apparently also as a kind of "punctuation" between other displays.

During threat the bird gapes and (at high intensities) thrusts with the bill directed toward the intruder. The latter action is followed by nest indicating. In general, threat displays appear to be poorly developed as compared with related species, perhaps as a reflection of this species' more solitary nest spacing.

Reproductive Biology

Breeding season.   Breeding is very extended in this species; Murphy (1936) considered it to be absolutely continuous in Peru. In Chile, egg laying begins in October or November and continues to December or January (Johnson, 1965). In Argentina, Siegel-Causey (1987) observed courtship during January and February, although this was apparently late in the nesting season.

Nest sites and nest building.   Murphy (1936) observed adults collecting billfulls of nesting materials in water 8–10 meters deep. The nest is composed of various seaweeds, worm tubes, straw, feathers, and other readily available materials. The worm tubes are especially important in binding the looser materials together. A partial nest weighed by Coker (1919) weighed 3.6 kilograms, and the entire nest was judged to weigh about 5.5 kilograms, with the worm tubes representing about a third of the total weight and seaweeds the remainder. In some areas nests are only a few meters apart, but Murphy (1936) generally regarded it as a "hermit" species, and Coker (1919) said that nest sites are always isolated.

Egg laying and incubation.   The usual clutch size is three eggs, but four are sometimes laid (Johnson, 1965). At one Chilean locality five three-egg sets were collected (Murphy, 1936). Coker (1919) observed only two-egg and three-egg clutches. The incubation period is unreported. The nests remain fairly damp and soft as they decompose during the incubation and early brooding period, but turn dry and hard by the time the young are ready to fledge.

Brooding and rearing of young.   Coker (1919) never observed a nest with more than two chicks. The fledging period is unknown. Rasmussen (1988) commented on the fact that juveniles of the Pacific population show a high level of individual variation in gular pouch color, filoplume development, and head feather patterning, which might help facilitate parental recognition. During begging the wings are waved, shrill cries are uttered, the gular pouch is expanded by hyoid depression, and jabbing movements are made toward the parent's bill. Rasmussen noted that fledged juveniles tend to creche below the nesting cliffs where their parents can locate them for feeding.

Breeding success.   No information.

Population Status

This species is most common on the Pacific coast of South America, but no comprehensive population estimates are available. Duffy, Hays, and Plenge (1984) provided estimates for three Peruvian nesting areas. On the Atlantic coast a colony of about 200 pairs nests near the mouth of Rio Deseado, and an equal number are distributed in four other locations up the river. Additionally, a colony of about 50 pairs breeds at Cabo Blanco (20 kilometers north of Puerto Deseado), and a small colony of about 30 pairs breeds on Roca Olorosa in Bahia Oso Marino (Siegel-Causey, 1987).

Evolutionary Relationships

Siegel-Causey (1987) reviewed the evidence on this species' relationships, and concluded that behavioral evidence suggests it is most closely related to the European shag and the spotted shags of New Zealand.

Other Vernacular Names

Blue shag (*oliveri*), bravo duck (Stewart Island), crested shag, flip-flap (Canterbury), ocean shag, spotted cormorant; pare-kareka (Maori); cormoran moucheté (French); Tüpfelkormoran (German)

Distribution

Resident coastally and discontinuously along headlands and rocky shorelines of North, South, and Stewart islands of New Zealand. The disjunct population *featherstoni* on Chatham and Pitt islands is often considered conspecific (e.g., Dorst and Mougin, 1979), but this book follows recent regional treatments such as Marchant and Higgins (1990). (See figure 84.)

Subspecies

L. p. punctatus (Sparrman). Resident locally on North Island (Hauraki Gulf, Auckland's west coast, and Wellington Harbour), and much more commonly on the eastern coast of South Island, from Marlborough Sounds southward to Otago Peninsula; especially abundant at Goose Bay, Banks Peninsula, and Otago Peninsula.

L. p. oliveri (Matthews) 1930 (= *Stictocarbo steadi*, preoccupied by *Carbo c. steadi*). Resident on Stewart Island and adjacent Foveaux Strait islands (Codfish and Centre), and extending northward along the adjacent western coast of South Island, breeding from Open Bay Islands to Perpendicular Point (3 kilometers north of Punakaiki) and possibly to "the Steeples" (Steep Point?) and Westport (Kinsky, 1970). The validity of this race has recently been questioned (Lalas, 1983; Siegel-Causey, 1988).

Description

Prebreeding adult. Scattered white filoplumes on the dark parts of the head, neck, back, and vent; crown, two semierect crests on the forehead, and occiput grayish black, with some bluish gloss; hindneck black, with greenish blue gloss; sides of head, chin, throat, and foreneck sooty black, shading into pale gray on the base of the neck and rest of underparts; two wide white stripes (narrower in *oliveri*) extend back from the base of the bill, passing above the eyes and down the sides of the neck to the shoulder; upper back, scapulars, and wing coverts brownish gray, each feather tipped

with a round black spot; lower back, rump, upper tail coverts, flanks, lower half of abdomen, and under tail coverts black with greenish blue gloss; remiges dark grayish brown; rectrices (12) black. Iris hazel to dark olive; papillose eye ring greenish blue (grayish olive in *oliveri*), naked skin of lores at the bases of upper and lower mandibles opalescent blue and green (more greenish in *oliveri*), becoming closer to bright sky blue at peak of sexual activity; bill yellowish brown to dark brown, but at peak of courtship apparently becoming mostly bright pink to purplish, grading to paler pinkish at the tip and just anterior to the bluish base of the lower mandible; gular skin grayish black with narrow greenish blue wartlike lines; legs and feet bright orange-yellow (becoming more pinkish at peak of display period) with slightly darker toe joints (the toe joints and edges of webs distinctly brown in *oliveri*).

Postbreeding adult. Lacking the head crests and the white filoplumes on the head, neck, back, and rump; the clear white areas also becoming more mottled. The black areas of the head and neck are replaced by light brownish gray feathers while the young are still in the nest, so that the lateral white neck stripes are then only slightly apparent. The eye ring, facial skin, and gular skin are medium blue (seagreen in *oliveri*), the bill is brownish yellow, grading to horn-colored toward tip, and the legs and feet are pale yellowish.

Immature-subadult. Forehead slightly if at all crested; crown, hindneck, lower back, rump, upper tail coverts, flanks, and posterior underparts dark smoky brown, sometimes with a slight greenish gloss; back and scapulars smoky brown, the feathers with dark spots and marginal bands; wing coverts paler with dark tips; sides of the head, chin, throat, and anterior underparts grayish white; stripe on side of neck pale gray. Iris dark brown; eye ring probably pale green; facial skin and gular skin yellow to brownish yellow; bill yellowish pink; legs and feet yellow. Sexual maturity is apparently attained at two years (Lalas, 1983).

Juvenile. Upperparts dark gray, with a few small white filoplumes; upper wing coverts grayish brown, the feathers with narrow borders and black tips; flanks, thighs, and lower underparts brown; remaining underparts pale gray to dull fawn. Iris brown; eye ring pale green; facial skin, bill, legs, and feet brownish yellow to flesh-colored.

Nestling. Initially naked with dark gray skin, the face, legs, and feet flesh-colored. Later becoming covered with dark grayish brown down above, and white down with grayish brown spots below. Iris dark brown; naked crown, throat, and mouth lining orange-pink; gular skin purplish flesh; legs and feet gray.

Figure 84. Distribution of the spotted shag, showing the residential ranges of its races *punctatus* (small cross-hatching) and *oliveri* (small cross-hatching plus stippling), and the residential range of the Pitt Island shag (large cross-hatching). Arrows indicate some reported breeding locations, and the inset shows the locations of spotted shag colonies in the Hauraki Gulf, North Island.

Measurements (in millimeters)

Of *punctatus:* wing, males 235–264 (ave. of 17, 248), females 233–266 (ave. of 29, 244); tail, males 70–97 (ave. of 17, 87), females 78–99 (ave. of 29, 85); culmen, males 56–70 (ave. of 17, 61), females 56–61 (ave. of 29, 60). Of *oliveri:* wing, males 238–272 (ave. of 8, 251), females 231–255 (ave. of 8, 243); tail, males 79–102 (ave. of 8, 86), females 77–92 (ave. of 8, 83); culmen, males 54–64 (ave. of 8, 59), females 54–61 (ave. of 8, 57) (Marchant and Higgins, 1990). Eggs ca. 61 × 36.

Weights (in grams)

Males 850–1,670 (ave. of 14, 1,210), females 770–1,610 (ave. of 8, 1,160) (Marchant and Higgins, 1990). Average adult weight, sample size unspecified, 1,275 (Fenwick and Browne, 1975), also more questionably reported as 1,800 (Astheimer and Grau, 1990). Calculated egg weight 43.6; ave. of 12, 48.8 (Marchant and Higgins, 1990).

Identification

In the hand. The combination of a medium-gray back, the feathers spotted rather than margined with black, and a white stripe extending from the eyes down each side of the neck serves to identify this species.
In the field. This is the only New Zealand cormorant or shag with distinct black spotting on its otherwise pale grayish back and scapulars, and the only one with bright orange-yellow legs and feet.

Ecology and General Biology

Breeding and nonbreeding habitats. This is a highly marine species, although bays, inlets, and estuaries are regularly entered, perhaps especially during winter periods. The birds feed out to about 16 kilometers from the coast, but roost on stacks, cliffs, islands, and breakwaters (Marchant and Higgins, 1990).
Movements and migrations. This species is probably more dispersive than migratory, with the maximum movements of banded birds up to 500 kilometers. Thus, a fairly large winter population of about 600 birds is present near Kaikoura, although the nearest large breeding colony is 160 kilometers away. A nucleus of nonbreeders remains in the Kaikoura area during summer (Stonehouse, 1967). The breeding and immature birds may move out of their nesting areas to generally nearby coastal sites during winter, although vagrant birds may reach extreme northern portions of New Zealand (Marchant and Higgins, 1990).
Competition and predation. Compared with the little pied, pied, and great cormorants, the spotted shag forages in deeper waters farther from the coast. Additionally, the other species are fish-eating bottom foragers, whereas the spotted

shag feeds mostly on planktonic crustaceans and possibly also some small fish (Stonehouse, 1967).

The major egg predator of this species is probably the silver gull (*Larus novaehollandiae*), which effectively steals eggs when the breeding colony has been disturbed (Gale, 1984).

Foods and Foraging Behavior

Foods consumed. Evidently crustaceans and some small fish are eaten. Regurgitated materials are known to include crustaceans, anchovies (*Engraulis*, Engraulidae), gastropod mollusks (*Zethalia*), and algae (Marchant and Higgins, 1990).
Foraging behavior. Foraging is done solitarily or sometimes gregariously, in groups of 50–100 or more birds, well away from shore (2–16 kilometers from the coast), and in relatively deep water. Perhaps the birds select plankton-rich upwelling zones for their foraging. In a sample of 31 dives, the mean diving duration was 30 seconds, and the modal period was 32 seconds, in water of unstated depth (Stonehouse, 1967).

Social Behavior

Age of maturity and mating system. Birds begin to breed when two years old (Lalas, 1983). Pairs are certainly seasonally monogamous and perhaps exhibit sustained monogamy.
Social displays and vocalizations. Information on the social behavior of this species is from G. van Tets, in Marchant and Higgins (1990). Male advertisement displays consist of wing waving, swing-pointing, and bowing. Wing waving (figure 85C) is performed with the head nearly touching the back, and with the folded wings moved up and down at the rate of about four times per second, but without vocalization. Swing-pointing (figure 85B) consists of a slow, silent movement of the head and stretched neck along the vertical plane from a point near the ground back to the base of the tail, and a return movement, with the head vibrating rapidly. No vocalization is produced. During bowing (figure 85A), the neck is arched and the bill is directed downward and back toward the breast, again silently.

Individual (mate) recognition displays consist of the darting, sky-upright, gaping, and pointing postures. During darting (figure 85D) the bird alternates between a head-back posture, much like that of wing waving, and a vertically extended head and neck, at a rate of about once per second. In the sky-upright (figure 85E) the bird begins from the vertically extended neck position of darting, but raises the body so that it is standing upright, and holds the neck in a slightly S-shaped curve as its lower neck and breast pulsate at the rate of about twice a second. During pointing (figure 85F) the bird silently stretches its neck and head at a diagonal angle, and in the similar gaping display its bill is widely opened and the head is silently drawn back and forth

Figure 85. Social behavior of the spotted shag, including male bowing (A), male swing-pointing (B), male wing waving (C), darting (D), sky-upright (E), pointing (F), postlanding posture (G), pretakeoff posture (H), kink-throating (I), and prehop posture (J). After sketches in Marchant and Higgins (1990).

horizontally, from the middle of the back to the front of the neck and back again.

Other displays performed at the nest site include a pretakeoff posture (figure 85H) with the bill slightly lowered, the bird standing erect, tail cocked and the throat silently bulging or pulsating. Although no sounds have been heard in this situation, it is likely that one is produced, as is the case in the Pitt Island shag. In the similar postlanding posture (figure 85G) the bill is held horizontally and there is no throat pulsing. The prehop posture (figure 85J) differs from the pretakeoff posture in that the bill is more strongly lowered and the throat bulging is more pronounced. Ticking noises are produced in this situation in the Pitt Island shag, and perhaps also occur in this species. Kink-throating (figure 85I) is performed with the bill widely opened (except when nest materials are being carried) and a loud, repetitive call is uttered by males, whereas females are essentially silent.

During defensive threat a loud *hergh-hergh* note is uttered by males with the bill open as the head is moved back, forth, and laterally and the wings partly spread. No other adult or nestling calls have yet been described.

Reproductive Biology

Breeding season.   The breeding season varies from year to year and from site to site, depending upon food availability and local weather. Thus, in various areas egg laying has been reported in early August, from July to October, from August to March, and from November to January (Kinsky, 1970; Robertson, 1988). The general pattern would seem to be that eggs are initially laid in August or September, with egg laying at a peak in October and terminating in December, but with later secondary peaks possibly caused by re-laying (Turbott, 1956; Marchant and Higgins, 1990).

Nest sites and nest building.   Nests are placed on cliff ledges, alcoves, or niches, the rocks above often overhanging the nest site. They are constructed of grasses, seaweeds, twigs, and ice plant (*Dysphema*), which are gathered near the colony. Nests may be as close as a meter apart. The nests are well constructed but deteriorate after the chicks hatch, and may actually be dismantled by the chicks, so that they disappear a few weeks following hatching (Marchant and Higgins, 1990).

Egg laying and incubation.   The modal clutch size is of three eggs; the mean of 102 nests was 2.7, with a range of 1–4. The eggs are laid at two-day intervals, and effective incubation begins with the second egg. Nest relief occurs at least three times per day. The typical incubation period is 28–35 days, averaging 32 (Fenwick and Browne, 1975; Gale, 1984).

Brooding and rearing of young.   At hatching, the chicks weigh an average of 40 grams. They open their eyes at three days, and by two weeks are mostly covered with down except on the head and underwing. At that time they undergo a rapid weight increase, with a maximum growth rate attained at 15–17 days. By 34–38 days they have nearly attained their final fledging weight (Gale, 1984). Fledging occurs at 57–71 days, averaging 62 days (Gale), or about nine weeks (Turbott, 1956).

Breeding success.   In one study involving 256 eggs, hatching success was 72 percent, with a subsequent rearing success of 70 percent and an overall breeding success of 50.4 percent. The average brood size at fledging was 1.9–2.15 for successful nests. Nests with two-egg clutches were more successful than those with three eggs, and clutches laid early in the season (October) were more successful than later ones (Gale, 1984). The silver gull is sometimes a serious threat to eggs.

Population Status

Robertson and Bell (1984) estimated the population of the nominate race of this species to be 50,000–100,000 birds and that of *oliveri* to be 10,000–50,000. Thus the total population of the species may be 60,000–150,000, with some local declines evident, perhaps as a result of shooting, recreational boating, fishing, and some purposeful nest destruction (Marchant and Higgins, 1990).

Evolutionary Relationships

Other than the questionably distinct Pitt Island shag, this species is evidently a fairly close relative of the red-legged shag (Murphy, 1936), and is more distantly related to several cliff-nesting northern hemisphere shags including the European, pelagic, and red-faced (Siegel-Causey, 1988).

Other Vernacular Names

Chatham Island shag, double-crested cormorant, double-crested shag

Distribution

Endemic to the Chatham Islands, including Chatham (mostly on the southern coast, from Waitangi to Uwenga, and northeastern coast), Pitt, and outlying islets south of Pitt Strait (Mangere, Little Mangere, Star Keys, Pyramid Rock, and Rabbit). (See figure 84.)

Subspecies

None recognized here, but this form is often considered (e.g., Peters, 1931; Dorst and Mougin, 1979) an allopatric subspecies of *punctatus*. More recently (Siegel-Causey, 1988; Marchant and Higgins, 1990; Sibley and Monroe, 1990) it has been regarded as specifically distinct.

Description

Prebreeding adult. Resembles *punctatus*, but head, including crown and occipital crests, chin, throat, upper foreneck, entire hindneck, lower back, rump, and tail coverts, all black glossed with dark greenish blue; the distinct white eye stripe typical of *punctatus* lacking, but scattered white filoplumes present on head and neck; upper back, wing coverts, and scapulars deep brownish gray, all with an oil-green gloss, and each feather tipped with a triangular black spot; rest of underparts dark silvery gray; remiges brownish black; rectrices (12) black, with pale gray bases; iris reddish or brownish to dark hazel; facial skin purple (probably at peak of sexual activity) to grass-green, and warty; bill black, becoming light brown toward the tip, a cream-colored bar at base of lower mandible; mouth lining brownish black; gular skin black, with lines of blue-green warts, and edged with yellow; legs and feet orange (probably at peak of sexual activity) or yellowish brown, with brown at web tips.
Postbreeding adult. Like the prebreeding adult, but lacking the crests and white filoplumes, and the gular skin grass-green. Probably also with generally duller softpart colors, as in the spotted shag.
Immature-subadult. Dark brown to bluish brown dorsally, including the entire head, lighter grayish white below with a more brownish wash on the breast. The same general black-tipped plumage pattern as in the adult especially evident on the scapulars and wing coverts. Lighter and faded upper wing coverts lacking black tips may persist from the juvenal plumage. Iris dark grayish brown; facial and gular skin yellow to orange-brown; bill grayish brown, becoming orange-brown basally and with a darker culmen; legs and feet yellow, changing with age to orange.
Juvenile. Crown to hindneck dark brown, with numerous filoplumes but no crest, rest of neck brown; upperparts and wing coverts mostly dark brown with darker blackish green tips and some overall dull greenish gloss; rectrices blackish brown; remiges dark brown to blackish green; underparts generally dull brown, the thighs and under tail coverts a mixture of dark brown and glossy bluish black. Iris brown to grayish brown; bill horn-colored with darker culmen; facial skin brown; gular skin grayish yellow; legs and feet yellow and brown.
Nestling. Naked at hatching. Downy plumage still undescribed.

Measurements (in millimeters)

Wing, males 228–255 (ave. of 12, 243), females 209–243 (ave. of 9, 228); tail, males 81–97 (ave. of 13, 90), females 75–103 (ave. of 9, 90); culmen, males 48–54 (ave. of 12, 52), females 44–51 (ave. of 9, 49) (Marchant and Higgins, 1990). Eggs ca. 58 × 35.

Weights (in grams)

Two males 645 and 1,325; two females 1,078 and 1,127 (Marchant and Higgins, 1990). Calculated egg weight 39.2.

Identification

In the hand. The combination of a dark gray back, the feathers spotted rather than margined with black, and the head uniformly blackish, with no definite white stripe extending posteriorly from each eye, serves to identify this species. Overall, darker than the possibly conspecific spotted shag.
In the field. Including the nearly black great cormorant and the strongly bicolored Chatham Island shag, only three cormorants occur on the Chatham Islands, and this is the only one having distinct blackish spots on its generally grayish upperparts.

Ecology and General Biology

Breeding and nonbreeding habitats. This species is confined to the coastlines and islets around the Chatham Islands, with an unknown foraging range out to sea.

322   *Leucocarbo (punctatus) featherstoni* (BULLER) 1873

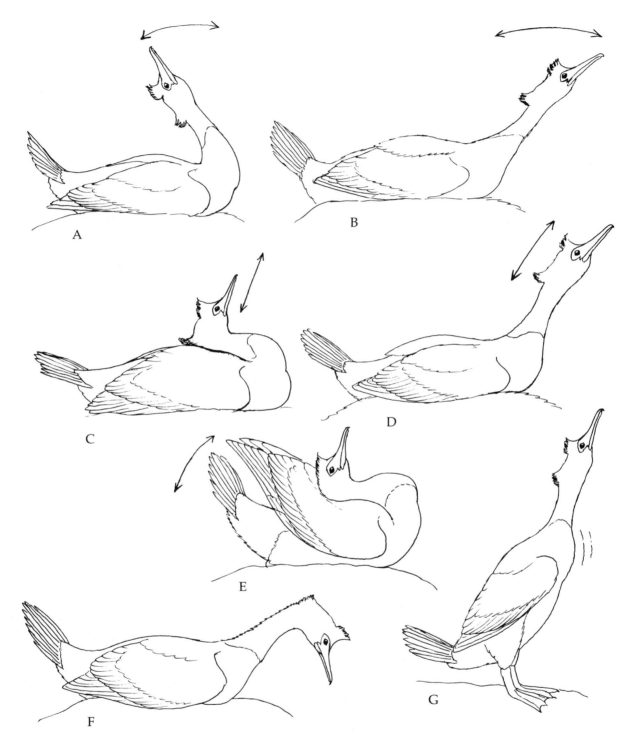

Figure 86. Social behavior of the Pitt Island shag, including male swing-pointing (A, B), darting (C, D), male wing waving (E), bowing (F), and sky-upright (G). After sketches in Marchant and Higgins (1990).

Movements and migrations.   Probably no movements occur except within the Chatham Islands group (which cover an area about 100 kilometers in diameter).
Competition and predation.   No information.

Foods and Foraging Behavior

Foods consumed.   No information.
Foraging behavior.   Much foraging is done in coastal kelp beds (Marchant and Higgins, 1990).
Competition and predation.   No information.

Social Behavior

Age of maturity and mating system.   No specific information, but at least seasonal monogamy presumably prevails.
Social displays and vocalizations.   Available observations are by G. van Tets (in Marchant and Higgins, 1990). The displays are obviously very much like those of the spotted shag. Male advertisement displays include wing waving, swing-pointing, and bowing. During wing waving (figure 86E) the rate of wing movement is about the same as in the spotted shag, but the tail raising may be more pronounced. During swing-pointing (figure 86A, B), the head and neck are swung back and forth over a narrower arc (of less than 90 degrees) than in the spotted shag. During bowing (figure 86F) the bill is not deflected back toward the breast, but remains in a vertically downward position or even stops short of the vertical.

Mate recognition displays are also similar to those of the spotted shag, although gaping has not yet been observed. Darting (figure 86C, D), pointing, and the sky-upright (figure 86G) are all performed silently; the sky-upright posture is performed with more variation in angle of the body axis than in the spotted shag, and at times may be horizontal.

During the pretakeoff (and also the identical prehop) display there is more throat bulging than in the spotted shag; males sometimes utter ticking sounds as their necks pulsate. Males also utter ticking sounds during the hop display. Females appear to be voiceless. Kink-throating is very similar or identical to that of the spotted shag, as is the postlanding posture, although the bill may be more elevated and the feathers of the hindneck more erected.

Reproductive Biology

Breeding season.   Breeding occurs between egg laying in August and fledging in December (Fleming, 1939).
Nest sites and nest building.   Apparently the breeding biology of this species is much like that of the spotted shag. Nests are located on the ledges of cliffs as in spotted shags, and are constructed of grasses, ice plant, and other vegetation. Some old nests persist through the nonbreeding season and may be refurbished, with females using materials brought in by the males.
Egg laying and incubation.   The modal clutch size is probably three, but no detailed information exists on this point.
Brooding and rearing of young.   No information.
Breeding success.   No information.

Population Status

This species was estimated by Robertson and Bell (1984) to number less than 1,000 birds, and has been classified as a "rare" species (Bell, 1986). No specific threats to its survival have been identified.

Evolutionary Relationships

As mentioned above, this form is often considered only a subspecies of *punctatus*, and is certainly its nearest relative.

Darters (Anhingidae)

Preening by male African darter. After a photo by the author.

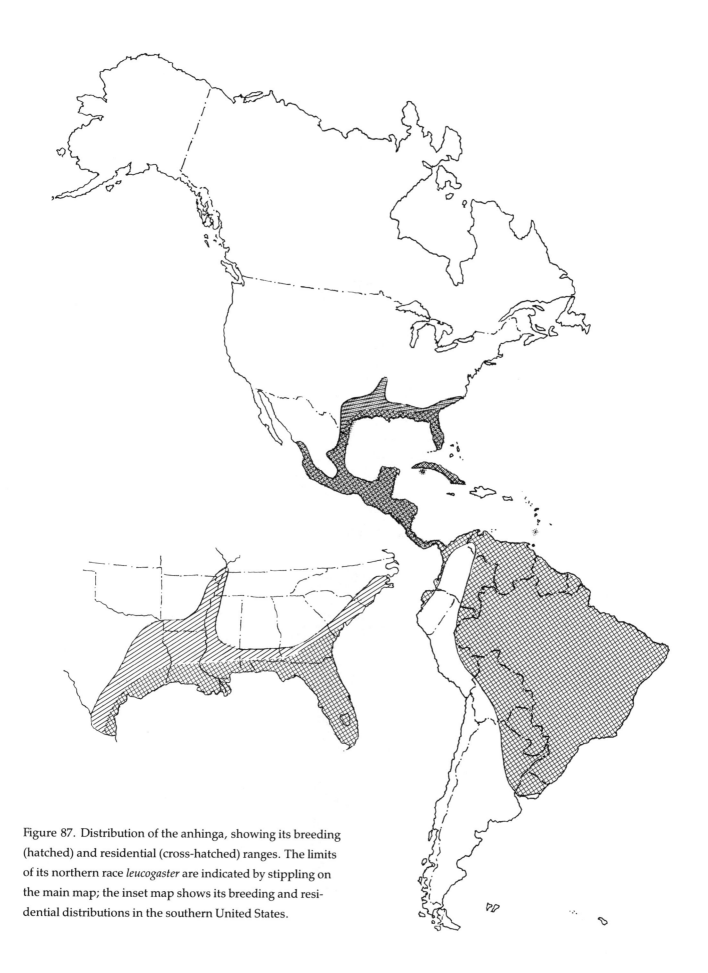

Figure 87. Distribution of the anhinga, showing its breeding (hatched) and residential (cross-hatched) ranges. The limits of its northern race *leucogaster* are indicated by stippling on the main map; the inset map shows its breeding and residential distributions in the southern United States.

Other Vernacular Names

American anhinga, American darter, black darter, black-bellied darter (*anhinga*), darter, Florida anhinga (*leucogaster*), North American darter (*leucogaster*), snake bird, South American darter (*anhinga*), water turkey, white-bellied darter (*leucogaster*); anhinga noir (French); Amerika-Schlangenhalsvogel (German); acoyotl, huizote (Spanish)

Distribution

Breeds in fresh-water and brackish wetlands of North America from coastal North Carolina, the lower Mississippi valley (north to Arkansas and western Tennessee), and (rarely) eastern Oklahoma south to Florida, Louisiana, and eastern Texas; thence through Mexico and Central America to Colombia and most of the lowlands of South America east of the Andes to the vicinity of Buenos Aires, Argentina; also resident on Cuba, Isle of Pines, Grenada, Trinidad, and Tobago. (See figure 87.)

Subspecies

A. a. leucogaster (Vieillot) 1816. Breeds from southeastern United States south to Panama; also resident on Cuba, Isle of Pines, and Grenada. In winter the Mississippi valley population moves southward toward the Gulf coast of Texas, and the Atlantic coast population to South Carolina and northern Florida. The residential population in western Mexico, Guatemala, and El Salvador has at times been dubiously separated as a distinct race *minima* (Wetmore, 1981). Birds from Panama and Colombia intergrade with the nominate race.

A. a. anhinga (Linnaeus). Resident on Trinidad and Tobago, and throughout most of tropical and subtropical South America from Colombia south to the Rio de la Plata, Argentina. The southernmost populations may be somewhat migratory.

Description

Prebreeding male.   Head, neck, middle of upper back, rump, upper tail coverts, and underparts black, glossed with oil-green; the feathers along the upper half of the hindneck form a mane, on each side of which and along the middle of the head are lines of elongated brownish white filoplumes (held for only a short period). Scapulars acutely elongated; these feathers, most wing coverts, and the longest proximal secondaries all black with ornamental white central stripes. The other remiges black; the alular feathers also black and unusually long (about 30 percent of the wing length); greater secondary coverts mostly silvery white, the basal half of the inner web black; outer webs of the longest remixlike wing coverts (termed scapulars by Owre, 1967, and "tertials" by Cramp and Simmons, 1977) and the middle pair of rectrices corrugated with about 30 equally spaced transverse corrugations or flutings; all rectrices (14) black, becoming more brownish distally and tipped with brownish white. Iris bright carmine; eye ring, lores, and adjacent facial skin variable, from yellow or greenish yellow (early in the season) to bluish green and finally vivid emerald or turquoise (at peak of courtship); maxilla dusky olive basally and along the culmen, the sides and tip more yellow to orange or reddish; mandible brighter yellow, especially basally (the entire bill surface becoming more orange to reddish at start of courtship); interior of mouth jet-black; gular skin changing from yellow or pink (early in the season) to jet-black (at peak of courtship); legs and feet dusky olive anteriorly, yellow on the webs and posteriorly.

Prebreeding female.   Crown and back of neck brown, the feathers fringed with whitish or rufous, producing a mottled appearance; sides of head, throat, and underside of neck and chest pale whitish buff, becoming richer on the chest; head and sides of neck with scattered bands of longer dirty white feathers; upper back black, each feather margined with brown and with a white center; rest of upperparts much like those of the male; a narrow band of chestnut divides the chest from the black breast and underparts. Transverse feather ribbing present on the middle rectrices and longest wing coverts as in the male. Iris paler than in male, varying from pale red to yellow or dark reddish brown; eye ring, lores, and adjoining facial skin bright bluish as in breeding males (at least during the peak courtship period); bill generally less colorful than in male, the maxilla more uniformly brownish and the mandible more muted yellow distally to orange-yellow basally (but sometimes—presumably also during courtship—almost entirely bright yellow to orange, with a contrasting bright blue zone at the base); gular skin dull orange (early in the season) to deep black (at peak of courtship); legs and feet dull orange-brown.

Postbreeding adult   (both sexes). Similar to the prebreeding plumage, but lacking the filoplumes (in both sexes) and the manelike feathers (in the male); the pale terminal tail band largely worn away. Flutings on the rectrices less apparent. Softpart colors more muted, the eye ring and adjacent lores dull greenish black to dusky brown or yellow, the bill generally darker, with a dusky ridge and tip, the gular skin dusky olive (in males) to yellowish (in females), and the legs and feet mostly dusky olive, with paler webs.

327

Immature-subadult. The definitive plumage and sexual maturity are apparently attained in two years (Bent, 1922; Palmer, 1962); in the Old World species of darter a probable three-year period to maturity has been suggested. Predefinitive plumages still poorly known; the sexes apparently become differentiated during the second fall of life. By 12–14 months the wings and scapulars show more whitish than do those of juveniles; by the second winter the central rectrices of both sexes may show some transverse ribbing. Gular skin yellow, edged with fuscous; a dull reddish orange iris in immature males.

Juvenile. Sexes nearly alike; head, neck, and upper breast cinnamon-buff, becoming darker brownish on the other underparts; the back feathers dusky, bordered with lighter brownish; the wings and tail mostly dusky, with some diffuse silvery gray markings, bordered with brownish, on the wing coverts, scapulars, and perhaps the upper back. Compared with adult females, the upperparts of juveniles are browner, the white stripes down the middle of the feathers are rudimentary, the remiges are margined with whitish, the transverse ribbing of the innermost secondaries and central rectrices is lacking or barely apparent, the dark chestnut band at the base of the chest is lacking, and the rest of the underparts are pale brownish white.

Nestling. Naked at hatching, with buffy yellow skin, a pale pink head, yellowish legs and feet similar in color to the body skin, the bill and iris blackish, and the gular pouch orange. Within a day or two uniformly covered with pale buffy tan down, but with a grayish neck. At about 10 days the buffy down changes to white on the sides, rump, and belly, and at 2–3 weeks the back is a mixture of white and yellow down (Harriott, 1970).

Measurements (in millimeters)

Inclusive ranges for both races (58 males, 44 females): wing, males 316–347, females 312–361; culmen (from base), males 74–98.8, females 74–91.5. Means for *leucogaster* (44 males, 28 females), wing, males 330, females 327; culmen, males 81.8, females 77.8; for nominate *anhinga* (14 males, 16 females), wing, males 341, females 335; culmen, males 91.8, females 86.3 (Blake, 1977). Eggs ca. 52 × 35.

Weights (in grams)

Average of 6 males of *leucogaster* from Florida 1,279, of 6 females 1,257 (Hartman, 1955); 26 unsexed *leucogaster* from Florida averaged 1,235 (standard deviation 54.8) (Hartman, 1961). Nine males from Florida 1,120–1,389 (ave. 1,245), 7 females 1,057–1,420 (ave. 1,174) (Owre, 1967). A male of nominate *anhinga* from Suriname 1,250; one female 1,115 (Haverschmidt, 1968). Calculated egg weight 35.2.

Identification

In the hand. Distinguished from the Old World forms of *Anhinga* by the pale tips of the rectrices, which are whitish (males) to buffy-colored (females), although in some specimens these pale tips may be nearly worn off. The pale tip is also broader in *anhinga* than in *leucogaster*.

In the field. Easily distinguished from cormorants by the long, turkeylike tail, the narrow, permanently kinked neck, and the tapering, sharply pointed bill. The snakelike swimming mode, with only the head and neck above water, is unique to darters. Flight is relatively slow, done with a series of rapid wingstrokes alternated with periods of gliding. Hawklike soaring in thermals is common.

Ecology and General Biology

Breeding and nonbreeding habitats. Clear and quiet or slowly moving fresh-water cypress swamps and sawgrass-edged sloughs and marshes are this species' favored habitats in the United States, with some additional use of mangrove-edged brackish or salt-water tidal lagoons, bays, and estuaries. All favored habitats have areas of open, nonturbid water for foraging (Palmer, 1962). In a nesting survey of Louisiana, Mississippi, and Alabama, Portnoy (1977) reported that 89.7 percent were found on fresh-water sites, 9.3 percent on brackish sites, and none on saline sites. By habitat type, 93 percent of the breeding birds were located in cypress swamps and 7 percent in fresh-water marshes, with none in brackish or salt marshes or on coastal beaches.

Movements and migrations. Movements outside the United States are unstudied. In the southeastern United States the northernmost limits for this species depend upon two physical factors rather than the simple presence of open water, namely the ambient temperature and the availability of adequate solar insolation. Anhingas extend north of a line representing the 10°C isotherm only in areas (the Carolina coasts, northwestern Louisiana and southwestern Arkansas) that receive a substantial amount of sunshine during December (Hennemann, 1985). Birds nesting north of this zone migrate south varying distances during colder months. Some birds banded in Mississippi have subsequently been recovered in Veracruz, Tabasco, and Campeche (Palmer, 1962).

Competition and predation. Owre (1967) concluded that although the anhinga and double-crested cormorant in Florida often both fish larger bodies of fresh water, their different fish-catching behaviors may reduce any competition for the food supply. There, the cormorant often forages in marine habitats, but the anhinga forages on fresh-water fishes that are generally not fast-moving or thick-bodied. Specific predators have not been identified, but probably some birds are caught by alligators.

Foods and Foraging Behavior

Foods consumed. No extensive studies on foods have been performed, but Palmer's (1962) summary indicates a diet of a wide array of roughfish in addition to some reptiles, amphibians, and invertebrates (crustaceans, leeches, insects). Fishes eaten included catfish (Ameiuridae), pickerel (*Esox,* Esocidae), suckers (*Catostomus,* Catostomidae), mullet (*Mugil,* Mugilidae), mojarrita (*Eucinostomus,* Gerreidae), sunfish (*Lepomis,* Centrarchidae), gizzard shad (*Dorosoma,* Clupeidae), and bream (Centrarchidae). Owre (1967) examined the stomachs of 14 anhingas from southern Florida and found a variety of generally slow-moving, midwater, and generally narrow-bodied species. Four fish families were represented, the Cyprinodontidae (*Lucania, Fundulus, Jordanella,* and perhaps *Floridichthys*), Poeciliidae (*Gambusia, Heterandria,* and *Molliensia*), Centrarchidae (*Chaenobryttus* and *Lepomis*), and Percidae (*Etheostoma*). In descending frequency of occurrence were 37 mosquitofish (*Gambusia*) from 25 to 50 mm, 35 mollies (*Molliensia*), to 66 mm, 12 sunfish (*Lepomis*), 10 warmouth (*Chaenobryttus*), the largest 132 mm long and 45 mm deep, and 6 killifish (*Lucania*). The largest fish was a 55.7 gram warmouth, and the largest number of prey in any single stomach was 37. The stomach contents weighed 105.3 grams in one specimen.

Foraging behavior. According to Owre (1967), the anhinga is not a bottom feeder but tends to concentrate on slow-swimming centrarchids. A stalking approach is typical rather than a direct chase. When swimming it holds its neck back in an S-shaped configuration, ready to strike, and is completely submerged when hunting prey (Harriott, 1970).

Social Behavior

Age of maturity and mating system. The age of maturity is still uncertain but unlikely to be more than two years. The length of the pair bond is also unknown, but Meanley (1954) judged that some birds may have been paired before they arrived on the nesting grounds. Owre (1967) observed that some courtship activity begins before birds disperse to breeding areas. Harriott (1970) believed that anhingas "probably do not choose a life mate," and Burger, Miller, and Hahn (1978) observed attempted rape behavior.

Social displays and vocalizations. A complete inventory of displays is not available for detailed comparison with the Old World species. The descriptions of Meanley (1954), A. Meyerriecks (in Palmer, 1962), and Allen (1961) are the only accounts of note, as supplemented by comments by Owre (1967) and van Tets (1965).

Male advertising consists of wing waving, snap-bowing, and twig grasping ("forward snap" in Palmer). Territorial males watch alertly ("peering around") for other birds, and when one is seen they begin an elaborate wing waving (figure 88D). Wing waving ("wing-flapping" of Meanley)

initially begins as simultaneous movements of the folded wings, but soon changes to alternate movements of the two wings, at the rate of about two cycles per second. The bird's body may begin to sway from side to side. The head, median crest, and neck feathers are erected, but the tail is variably lowered (van Tets, 1965). In the snap-bowing display (figure 88E, F), the tail is erected over the back while the bird crouches horizontally and erects its head and neck feathers (figure 89D). It then suddenly raises its head, the bill first points vertically, the head is drawn backward in a "reverse bow," and finally it is extended forward and the bill is directed downward (figure 88F). At this point the tail is spread and inclined forward of the vertical. In this posture the bird lowers its head below foot level and peers slowly from side to side, with the tail cocked and the wings waved alternately, thus swaying the body. This posture may be held for up to a minute or more before the normal posture is resumed. At the peak of snap-bowing a guttural sound may be uttered. Snap-bowing and wing waving are most strongly performed when a female is nearby, but may also be performed in the absence of females. During the twig-shaking display ("forward-snap" display of Allen) a nearby twig is suddenly grabbed and shaken, sometimes with slight accompanying wing extension or wing waving, and then released. Or the bird may simply snap its mandibles together after darting the head forward. All of these displays are more frequent when a female lands nearby, with the snap-bowing performed at the rate of about once a minute, twig shaking 2–3 times a minute, and wing waving 4–5 times a minute (Palmer, 1962).

Twig shaking is also used as a bisexual greeting by paired birds, with the "in" bird grabbing a nearby twig and shaking it vigorously with a sideways movement of the head, the wings somewhat spread and the tail cocked (figure 89B). Other bisexual or mutual displays that may relate to pair bonding include pointing while sitting on the nest (figures 88G and 89A), bill rubbing (figure 89E), mutual preening, mutual neck waving with extended necks ("stiff-necked" posture of Allen) (figure 89C), unison bowing, and mock-feeding of the female by the male (figure 89F). Copulation occurs after the female has stepped onto the nest and begun to respond to the male's displays with similar gestures. According to Harriott (1970), twig presentation by the male immediately precedes copulation. Twig presentation together with neck extension and bill crossing may occur just prior to copulation (Palmer, 1962), and feather ruffling, wing waving, and bowing (Allen, 1961) may also precede copulation. During treading, the male grasps the bill of the female and pulls her head upward and backward. Copulation lasts about five seconds, and afterward both birds resume the same postures that preceded copulation. Copulation and associated behaviors are normally rare after the fourth day following initial mating (Allen, 1961; Harriott, 1970), although Burger, Miller, and Hahn (1978) observed

Figure 88. Social behavior of the anhinga, including takeoff sequence (A–C), male wing waving (D), snap-bowing (E, F), pointing (G), and kink-throating on nest (H). After sketches in van Tets (1965).

Figure 89. Social behavior of the anhinga, including pointing display by male on nest (A), male twig shaking as female watches (B), male stiff-necked display (C), mane erection by male (D), bill rubbing by pair (E), and male mock-feeding female (F). Mostly after sketches in Allen (1961).

copulations and attempted rapes up to 15 days following the start of incubation.

Defensive threat consists of gaping toward the intruder with the wings slightly spread, and with occasional bill-snapping movements. The pretakeoff postures (figure 88A–C) consist of partial wing spreading and bill pointing in the direction of takeoff. The postlanding posture is apparently quite similar but has not been described in detail. Kink-throating (figure 88H) is also present (van Tets, 1965), but is not very conspicuous since the gular pouch is small. The rapid throat-vibrating movements observed by Allen may represent kink-throating, as may the "chittering" calls during greeting and nest exchange ceremonies heard by Owre (1967).

Reproductive Biology

Breeding season.   In Florida and perhaps elsewhere along the Gulf coast the breeding season may be continuous, although there is a peak during late winter and spring (Palmer, 1962). Egg records for Florida range from February 15 to June 16, with a peak between March 16 and April 29. A small sample of egg records (8) from Louisiana and Texas are from April 14 to June 2. Burger, Miller, and Hahn (1978) noted that on the west coast of Mexico egg laying occurred during the rainy season from July 8 to 28, with a peak in mid-July, just after a prolonged rainy period.

Nest sites and nest building.   Nests are typically placed in open areas at the top of trees. In western Mexico, 41 percent of 40 pairs nested solitarily, 34 percent in trees with other species (herons or cormorants), and 25 percent in trees with only other anhingas. The average nest height was 2.45 meters above water, and 80 percent of 32 nests were placed at the junction of the tree trunk and branches. All of the nests had exposed perch sites nearby (Burger, Miller, and Hahn, 1978). Harriott (1970) observed that nests were usually placed in upright three-forked limbs, about 1.5–6 meters above water. She also noted that old nests may be remodeled, and that two anhinga nests may be placed less than a meter apart.

Nests may sometimes be completed in a single day (Meanley, 1954), but probably more often nest building continues for at least three days following pairing (Allen, 1961), or even 9–12 days (Harriott, 1970). Some additional materials may be brought in during the incubation and early brooding stages (Harriott, 1970). The female evidently remains at the nest constantly during the first few days after pairing and perhaps is fed by the male (Allen, 1961). Harriott observed that when the female left the nest site the male sat on it.

Egg laying and incubation.   Eggs are laid at a roughly daily rate, although sometimes a day is skipped. The mean clutch size of 16 nests in Mexico was 3.89, with a range of 2–5 eggs (Burger, Miller, and Hahn, 1978), and for 29 nests in Arkan-

sas it was 3.8, with a range of 2–5 and a modal size of four (Palmer, 1962). Ten Mississippi nests had an average clutch size of 3.6 eggs (White, Fleming, and Ensor, 1988). The eggs are incubated continuously, with both sexes incubating about equal amounts (females 45 percent, males 55 percent in 14 nests studied). Males averaged slightly longer average incubation bouts (2.67 hours vs. 1.56 hour), although at times a bird would incubate for an entire eight-hour period. Nest exchanges were most frequent in early morning and late afternoon, although few occurred before 6 A.M., during midday, or after 5 P.M. During nest relief the approaching bird always vocalized and waved its head from side to side with outstretched neck and the bill pointing downward toward the mate. The sitting bird did the same, with the bill pointing upward. The pair would intertwine their necks and vocalize before the sitting bird left the nest. Males arrived at the nest with nesting material 75 percent of the time but females did only 20 percent of the time, although females brought in more materials during the brooding phase than did males (Burger, Miller, and Hahn, 1978). The incubation period is probably 25–28 days (Palmer, 1962) or 26–29 days, with a mean of 27.8 days for the first-laid eggs in 14 nests (Burger, Miller, and Hahn, 1978). Harriott (1970) first saw young in a nest 28 days after it was completed and 40 days after it had been started, and noted that the chicks hatched one or two days apart.

Brooding and rearing of young.   The pair spend equal amounts of time in brooding the newly hatched young, with continuous brooding for the first 10–12 days. Thereafter the length of the brooding periods decrease, and after 10–16 days the chicks may be left alone while adults are foraging. Both sexes feed the young, with males feeding somewhat more often than females in one study (Burger, Miller, and Hahn, 1978), while in another (Harriott, 1970) the male turned the care of the young over to the female when the chicks were a month old.

At 10 days the birds can take a few steps. Within six weeks they can fly 100–150 feet, but come back to roost near the nest. At seven weeks they can swim, dive, and fly 200 yards. They are independent at eight weeks (Harriott, 1970).

Breeding success.   Of 77 eggs laid in 21 nests, there was a 19 percent loss of eggs, as a result of nest desertion (7 eggs) or loss of individual eggs (8 eggs). Among 36 eggs in 9 nests that survived to hatching, 35 hatched, and 42 of another group of 44 chicks were known to have survived for periods ranging up to 16 days after hatching. The two chicks that died were the last-hatched chicks in four-egg clutches. The average size for 14 broods of apparently varied ages was 3.0 young (Burger, Miller, and Hahn, 1978). Among six nests in Florida, one was abandoned shortly after hatching had occurred and the other five produced 17 young. Of a group of 19 hatched young, 14 survived long enough to fledge and leave the nesting area. Some young that fall out of nests in southern Florida are eaten by alligators (*Alligator*) (Harriott,

1970). Among 10 nests from Mississippi, 9 hatched eggs successfully, 74 percent of the eggs hatched, and there was a significant negative correlation between hatching success and pesticide (DDE) contamination levels. Significant eggshell thinning was also evident in this population (White, Fleming, and Ensor, 1988).

Population Status

The United States population of breeding anhingas has been estimated as about 4,500 birds (table 31), nearly all of which occur in Louisiana and Florida. A recent (1990) estimate for Louisiana was 245 breeding adults in 17 colonies (Martin and Lester, 1990).

Evolutionary Relationships

The problem of judging the number of species of Anhingidae has been discussed in chapter 1. Under the taxonomy adopted here it can only be stated that the nearest living relative of the anhinga is the darter, without further definition of potential intrageneric relationships.

Figure 90. Distribution of the darters, including the breeding (cross-hatched) and nonbreeding (stippled) ranges of the African darter, the residential range of the Oriental darter (light vertical hatching), and the breeding (heavy diagonal hatching, with denser populations cross-hatched) and nonbreeding or erratic (stippled) ranges of the Australian darter.

Other Vernacular Names

African darter (*rufa*), Australian darter (*novaehollandiae*), diver, eastern darter, Indian darter (*melanogaster*), needle-beak shag (Australia), Oriental darter (*melanogaster*), shag, snakebird; oiseau-serpent, anhinga roux (French); Altwelt-Schlangenhalsvogel (German)

Distribution

Widely distributed residentially in tropical to subtropical fresh-water or brackish habitats of the Old World, including most of sub-Saharan Africa, Madagascar, southeastern Iraq, most of the Indian subcontinent north to the Nepalese lowlands, and east through Burma to Vietnam; also resident on Sri Lanka (Ceylon), Java, Borneo, Sulawesi (Celebes), the Moluccas, the Philippines, New Guinea, and Australia. (See figure 90.)

Subspecies (these forms are often regarded as three separate species)

A. m. rufa (Daudin) 1802: African darter. Resident in sub-Saharan Africa, from the Sahel zone of Senegal, Niger, Chad, Sudan, and Ethiopia south to the Cape of Good Hope. Also resident in Madagascar and at least until recently in southeastern Iraq (lakes Antioch and Huleh, and lower Tigris-Euphrates valley). The Madagascan and Iraqi populations have at times been racially recognized as *vulsini* and *chantrei*, respectively.

A. m. melanogaster Pennant: Oriental darter. Resident in Pakistan, India, Nepal, Burma, Thailand, Cambodia, and Vietnam; formerly also in the Malay Peninsula and southern Turkey. Insular residential populations exist on Sri Lanka, Java, Borneo, Sulawesi, Sumbawa (one record), Buru (one record), Seram, Babar, and the Philippines (Luzon, Mindoro, Palawan, Negros, Mindanao). Nonbreeding visitor to Sumatra; rare or absent on Palau Islands.

A. m. novaehollandiae Gould 1847: Australian darter. Resident in Australia, excepting the dry interior and Tasmania. Also resident in lowland New Guinea, including Fergusson Island; the New Guinea population at times has been racially distinguished as *papua*. Vagrants have reached the Lesser Sundas and the southern Moluccas. Considered part of *rufa* by Dorst and Mougin (1979), whereas Vaurie (1965) considered it to be the most distinctive form in the Old World complex, all of which he regarded as separate species.

Description

Prebreeding male. Top of head and back of neck brown to blackish brown; throat and foreneck rufous to cinnamon-brown, darker basally; a white band begins below the eye and extends down each side of the neck; a narrow line of feathers bordering the facial skin as well as the forehead and throat white; base of neck, upper back, lower back, rump, upper tail coverts, and all remaining underparts black, with an oil-green gloss; median and lesser wing coverts and scapulars black, with ornamental brownish to whitish (in *novaehollandiae* and *melanogaster*) to rufous (in *rufa*) narrow shaft streaks or broader central stripes; the scapulars noticeably acute and variously elongated (least in *novaehollandiae*, most in *melanogaster*); outer webs of the greater secondary coverts dark reddish brown (in *rufa*), very pale brown (in *novaehollandiae*), or silvery white (in *melanogaster*), sometimes narrowly margined with black; alula black and unusually well developed, the remiges and rectrices (12) also black; outer webs of the central pair of rectrices with numerous (over 30) equally spaced transverse and wavelike corrugations or flutings; the longest secondary-like wing coverts (described as tertials by Cramp and Simmons, 1977; as scapulars by Owre, 1967; and as subscapulars by Marchant and Higgins, 1990) similarly corrugated and with pale shaft streaks (reduced fluting and shaft streaking may also occur on some adjoining feathers). Iris color evidently highly variable seasonally and/or geographically, typically patterned (at least in *rufa*) with a dull orange-buff interior ring, followed by a middle ring of marbled brown and buff, which is finally bounded by an outer ring of orange-buff; reported in *rufa* as yellow interiorly and brown peripherally, and as entirely salmon-pink or red; described as white interiorly and yellow peripherally in *melanogaster*, and variously as brown, yellow, or orange in *novaehollandiae*. Eye ring and facial skin also variable seasonally and/or geographically, ranging from green (*rufa*) to brownish gray (*melanogaster*) or yellow (*novaehollandiae*). Gular skin yellow (apparently becoming greenish black during courtship, at least in *novaehollandiae*); maxilla basally olive or brown, more yellowish toward tip; mandible dull yellow (the maxilla and tip of the mandible becoming light green during courtship, at least in *novaehollandiae*). Legs and feet varying seasonally and/or geographically, and variously described as ranging from gray or brown (in *rufa*) to yellowish flesh or pink (in *novaehollandiae*).

Prebreeding female. Sexual dimorphism present in all forms, but most pronounced in *novaehollandiae*. Generally differs from the male in having the top of the head and middle of the neck reddish brown, not black. The brown zone bordered on each side of the head and upper half of the neck by a whitish band, and the black foreneck and chest bordered on each side by a rufous band that is continued to the shoulder. Wing and tail as in the male, including the transverse feather ribbing, but the streaks on the scapulars and wing coverts averaging whiter. Underparts whitish in *novaehollandiae*, blackish in other two races. Iris yellow (*novaehollandiae*), or buff, latticed with brown (*melanogaster*); naked skin at base of bill and gular area orange-yellow; bill olive-colored to yellow as in male (and also becoming greenish during courtship, at least in *novaehollandiae*); legs and feet pale yellow to brownish yellow.

Postbreeding adult (both sexes). Similar to the prebreeding plumage, but the head, neck, and upper mantle browner, the whitish neck streak not bordered with black ventrally and sometimes separated from the dark hindneck by a pinkish buff area. The softpart colors are also certainly quite variable seasonally or geographically, but these differences are still only very poorly documented.

Immature-subadult. The juvenal plumage is apparently carried through the first year. The definitive plumage may require three years to attain, but breeding has been reported among birds still in immature plumage. Transitional plumages are still poorly known. Year-old birds are similar to the adult female, but the neck is much lighter and a pale brownish white, becoming white down the middle of the foreneck; the feather edgings and streaks on the upperparts are more yellowish white, and the long, pointed scapulars are not apparent or are poorly developed. The remiges and rectrices are pointed and narrowly margined with pale whitish brown, and the transverse ribbing on the innermost scapulars and middle rectrices is only slightly apparent. Softpart colors of immatures still inadequately described.

Juvenile (of *rufa*, the other races not greatly different). Sexes nearly alike: crown and hindneck buffy gray; sides of head and neck pale buff, usually (or always) lacking a white streak; upperparts brown to brownish black, the feathers with buffy edges; underparts mostly pale buff (more brownish in other races), the flanks and thighs dark brown; rectrices black, the central pair not transversely ribbed; remiges as in adults, but the upper wing coverts strongly edged with pale brown. Iris brown outwardly, a gray or yellowish gray middle zone, and a narrow white or yellow inner ring; naked skin around eye green; bill grayish green; gular skin pale yellow, pale pink, or orange; legs and feet gray to brownish. Softparts of juvenile *novaehollandiae* (termed "immature" by Vestjens, 1975): iris and naked skin around eyes pale yellow or orange; maxilla black or brown; mandible grayish brown, yellow, or fleshy; gular skin fleshy yellow or yellow-orange; legs and feet pink, light brown, or dark brown (Marchant and Higgins, 1990).

Nestling. Hatched with naked brownish to blackish skin, but covered within a few days by white to buffy or brownish

down. Downy chicks of *melanogaster* are entirely white (Ali and Ripley, 1983). Those of *rufa* are mostly white, with upperparts buff (males) to pale buff (females), but at times may be entirely brown (Cramp and Simmons, 1977). In *novaehollandiae* the down is pale buff below and darker brown dorsally; the upper neck may be light or dark brown, with or without a white stripe on the side of the head and upper neck (Vestjens, 1975). Iris dark gray or bluish gray; bill pale horn; gular skin yellowish; legs and feet ivory-white to flesh-colored.

Measurements (in millimeters)

Of *rufa*: wing, males 328–364 (ave. of 8, 349), females 331–360 (ave. of 7, 344); tail, males 229–253 (ave. of 8, 238), females 233–248 (ave. of 4, 239); culmen, males 75–89 (ave. of 12, 81), females 71–78 (ave. of 6, 76) (Brown, Urban, and Newman, 1982). Of *melanogaster* (both sexes, sample size unstated): wing 331–357; tail 202–240; culmen 74–90; tarsus 42–47 (Ali and Ripley, 1983). Of *novaehollandiae*: wing, males 329–373 (ave. of 11, 351), females 304–375 (ave. of 26, 344); tail, males 183–240 (ave. of 46, 215), females 177–238 (ave. of 25, 215); culmen, males 61–81 (ave. of 45, 74), females 54–85 (ave. of 26, 73) (Marchant and Higgins, 1990). Eggs, *rufa* ca. 55 × 35, *melanogaster* ca. 53 × 34, *novaehollandiae* ca. 59 × 37.

Weights (in grams)

Adults of *rufa*, ave. of 11 males 1,485.5, ave. of 10 females 1,530.3 (Birkhead, 1978). Adults of *rufa*, males 948–1,815 (ave. of 7, 1,292), 2 females 1,358 and 1,530 (ave. 1,444); 5 immatures 1,055–1,224 (ave. 1,178) (Brown, Urban, and Newman, 1982). Another sample of *rufa*, 10 males 1,206–1,711 (ave. 1,436), 9 females 1,055–1,660 (ave. 1,357) (Royal Ontario Museum specimens). Another sample of *rufa*, 4 males 1,100–1,600 (ave. 1,375), 6 females 1,150–1,400 (ave. 1,298) (Alletson, 1985). Two adult males of *rufa* 1,058 and 1,815; one immature male 1,100 (Cramp and Simmons, 1977). One female of *rufa* 1,525 (U.S. National Museum specimen). Four unsexed nominate *melanogaster* 1,160–1,500, ave. 1,340 (Ali and Ripley, 1983). Adults of *novaehollandiae*, males 1,450–2,100 (ave. of 9, 1,759), females 1,300–2,077 (ave. of 9, 1,790); another sample of 16 males 1,200–2,100 (ave. 1,600), of 18 females 900–2,600 (ave. 1,700) (Marchant and Higgins, 1990). One *novaehollandiae* male 1,950, one female 1,810 (Museum of Vertebrate Zoology specimens). Calculated egg weight 35.8; average of *rufa* (sample size not indicated), 37 (Brown, Urban, and Newman, 1982); average of 17 *novaehollandiae*, 44 (Marchant and Higgins, 1990).

Identification

In the hand. Distinguished from the anhinga by the entirely black tail. However, immature birds have buffy edgings to their wing coverts, and their rectrices are also tipped with buffy. Diagnostic variations in the Old World forms are summarized in table 6.

In the field.   Easily distinguished from cormorants by the long tail and the long, snakelike head and neck, with a sharply pointed bill. When swimming, often only the head and neck are visible above water. Formation flying is unreported. In flight, darters fly slowly and with apparent ease, often soaring vulturelike in thermals. Unlike cormorants, they exhibit extremely long tails and also show a more distinct kink in the neck while in flight.

Ecology and General Biology

Breeding and nonbreeding habitats.   Darters occur widely in interior fresh-water wetlands and also in coastal or alkaline waters, where the combination of nonturbid, open water (but not very deep) and trees or other natural projections exist for wing drying. Slow-moving rivers, oxbows (billabongs in Australia), lakes, reservoirs, swamps, estuaries, and other wetlands are all used, with a probable preference for fairly large and open waters at least half a meter deep. Wetlands surrounded by emergent vegetation or with aquatic vegetation may be used if open areas are available for foraging (Vestjens, 1977b; Marchant and Higgins, 1990). Salinity variations are unimportant, and fluctuating water transparencies are also tolerated (Fjeldså, 1985). Narrow, steep-banked, seasonally drained, and floating-leaf or excessively weed-fringed areas are generally avoided. During Australian aerial surveys nearly 90 percent of the darter population was found on wetlands larger than 100 hectares (Braithwaite et al., 1985).

Movements and migrations.   Only local movements occur in Africa and in Iraq (Cramp and Simmons, 1977; Brown, Urban, and Newman, 1982). Australian movements are only poorly documented, but dispersions occur among young and nonbreeding birds, sometimes exceeding 2,000 kilometers. One juvenile was recovered 120 kilometers from its natal area when it was only about 67 days old (Vestjens, 1975). Winter or dry-season movements also occur locally, as in Queensland, but in Victoria there is no evidence of seasonal movements (Marchant and Higgins, 1990). In India the birds are resident, but with local movements associated with varying water conditions (Ali and Ripley, 1983).

Competition and predation.   In Africa, significant foraging competition apparently exists between the darter and the long-tailed cormorant, though there are foraging differences between the two as discussed in chapter 4 and summarized in table 19 (Birkhead, 1978). Presumably similar competition with other cormorants might occur in India and Australia, but this remains undocumented. Predators in Africa are known to include crocodiles (*Crocodilis*) (Cott, 1961), and the gymnogene (*Polyboroides typus*) is an egg predator (Marshall, 1972). In Australia, ravens (*Corvus coronoides*) are known to

take eggs, and marsh harriers (*Circus aeruginosus*) sometimes attack immature birds. In northern India the house crow (*Corvus splendens*) takes eggs, and the Pallas' eagle (*Haliaeetus leucoryphus*) is a serious threat to nestlings (Ali and Ripley, 1983).

Foods and Foraging Behavior

Foods consumed.   In Birkhead's (1978) study on Lake Kariba, Zimbabwe, cichlid fish constituted the primary prey, particularly *Haplochromis*, *Pseudocrenilabrus*, and *Tilapia*. The mean prey length was 8 centimeters (range 2.2–16.5), and the mean individual prey mass was 9.8 grams (range 0.5–73.1). Fish were selected that could be easily captured in fairly shallow waters; specific body shapes were apparently not selected. There are probably considerable regional variations in prey taken, since Cott (1961) found few *Tilapia* and no *Pseudocrenilabrus* in a sample of 50 stomachs from Uganda, but a very large number of *Haplochromis* were present. Little information exists on the Oriental darter's foods, but Mukherjee (1969) reported that 19 stomachs from West Bengal contained mainly fish (81.2 percent mass) of 50–150 millimeters in length, with 8.4 percent insects and 7.4 percent snakes, plus some tadpoles and crustaceans. The average prey mass per stomach was 43 grams. This is similar to the average total prey mass (65 grams) reported by Alletson (1985) for 10 African darters from Natal, in which *Barbus* was present in six, as well as some other unidentified fish and frogs. Studies in Australia (Serventy, 1939; McNally, 1957; Vestjens, 1975) have indicated a variety of prey, with a predominance of introduced fish such as perch (*Perca*) and goldfish (*Carassius*). Vestjens found 19 fish prey to average 130 millimeters in length (range 90–198). A recent study by Dostine and Morton (1989) indicated that in Northern Territory the Australian darter tends to feed more on smaller and native rather than introduced prey fish. Prey found in the stomachs of 14 darters included nine species of fish representing seven families, with plotosid catfish making up 60 percent of the prey by dry weight. Prey varied from 27 to 161 millimeters in length; the larger prey were mostly plotosid catfish having a tapering attenuate body form. Generally the birds had eaten slower benthic fish, but occasionally captured more agile midwater species.

Foraging behavior.   Foraging is usually done solitarily, in smooth water of moderate depth. Up to 12 birds have been seen foraging in mixed-age and mixed-sex groups during autumn, sometimes only a few meters apart. Prey is caught in the usual darter way by stabbing it with a slightly opened bill with one or both mandibles. Typically the prey fish have two stab wounds on the ventral side, 5–25 millimeters apart, although small fish may be stabbed with only the upper mandible and small turtles may be speared through the shell. Water insects are apparently picked up and eaten whole. One bird was observed to remain submerged for periods of

Figure 91. Wing spreading and feather erection by a male African darter. After a photo by Geoffrey Allan. Also shown (upper left) is a mostly submerged anhinga (after a photo in Coomber, 1990).

up to a minute while foraging (Vestjens, 1975). When swimming, often only the birds' head and neck are above the water. Or they may pause in this partially submerged position, with the tail somewhat spread and the wings also spread (figure 91, above), possibly to attract fish to the shaded water. A prolonged period of wing drying typically follows each bout of foraging (figure 91, below). The human exploitation of tamed Oriental darters for fishing, in a manner similar to cormorant use in China and Japan, has been observed in Assam (Stoner, 1948).

Social Behavior

Age of maturity and mating system.   It has been suggested that breeding can occur at one year, while the birds are still in immature plumage, but this needs confirmation. The breeding condition may be one of sustained monogamy, as two broods have been observed in a single season in Africa (Bowen et al., 1962). Some pairs have nested in the same nests for two successive years in Australia (W. Vestjens, cited by Cramp and Simmons, 1977).

Social displays and vocalizations. The most complete descriptions of social displays are those of the Australian darter by Vestjens (1975), summarized and somewhat supplemented in Cramp and Simmons (1977) and Marchant and Higgins (1990). It is not known whether significant differences occur among the African and Indian populations, but considering the display similarities between the darter and the anhinga (which seem to differ mostly in their vocalizations), this would appear unlikely. However, Roberts (1991) noted that birds of the Indian population, which have very long scapulars, raise them in an apparent aggressive display early in the breeding season (see drawing on page 1 above). The African birds have much shorter scapulars and such a display has not been observed there. In the Indian population, the commonest vocalization is a series of repeated *kek* notes lasting about 2.5 seconds and accelerating toward the end (Roberts, 1991). This probably corresponds to the "clicking" notes of the Australian darter, which also speed up toward the end and last up to four seconds. These notes are uttered by both sexes, often as part of the greeting ceremony at the nest. Other kaws, hissings, and rattling sounds are also produced, but their functions remain little understood (Marchant and Higgins, 1990).

Male advertising consists of wing waving and twig grasping; unlike in anhingas, the snap-bowing display occurs only during pair formation. The wing-waving display is much like that of anhingas, and may be performed on the nest site (figure 92D) or on a nearby branch, the neck typically held in a more S-shaped profile when the display is performed on a branch (figure 92E). In either case the tail is cocked upward and the wings are waved alternately, the speed of the waving increasing as females are attracted. During twig grasping (figure 92J) a twig near the nest is grasped and shaken. Both of these displays are performed almost exclusively by males, and nearly cease after egg laying.

Several pair-forming displays are performed by males when a female approaches. When a female is approaching a displaying male she performs darting (figure 92B), with horizontal back-and-forth head movements, the bill opened or closed, while she calls softly. Males respond with calls and pointing (figure 92H, I), with the head moved slowly sideways or directed vertically upward without moving, and with the tail only slightly raised. The female then stands beside the male, and both may perform neck rubbing (figure 92A). The male then may perform snap-bowing (figure 92C), which involves raising the tail, raising and vibrating the folded wings, and making a snapping movement with the bill. The female may perform the same display at this stage of pair formation. After displaying to the female the male may remain on the nest, hop to a nearby branch, or perform a short circle flight away from and back to the nest.

Mate recognition displays include pointing, the snap-bow (which terminates after egg laying), gaping, and wing lifting, all of which are performed at or very near the nest site. Gaping (figure 92F) consists of the female shaking her head vertically and horizontally with the bill open; while the male nibbles her bill he may insert his inside hers (as in mock feeding by anhingas). This display has only been observed prior to copulation. The wing-lifting (Marchant and Higgins) or greeting (Vestjens) display (figure 92G) consists of the "out" bird calling in a ratchet-like call (kink-throating?) for up to four seconds as it approaches the nest. The "in" bird on the nest bends its neck into a sharp S-shape and lifts both wings simultaneously 2–8 times, at the same time cocking the tail diagonally. Sometimes a snap-bow display follows the greeting, and *kah* notes are uttered. Unlike in anhingas, allopreening has not been observed, but mutual nibbling of the mate's bill occurs. Copulation is preceded by the female crouching in the nest and lowering her head and neck. As with anhingas, the male typically grabs the female's bill during copulation, or occasionally may hold onto a twig or simply place his head alongside the female's. Copulation lasts 4–9 seconds, and frequently occurs at the nest site immediately following pair formation.

Reproductive Biology

Breeding season. Breeding seasons are generally greatly variable and quite extended throughout this species' broad range. In Africa breeding may occur year-round (as in northern Tanzania, Uganda, and western Kenya) or seasonally, but in most areas the period of heaviest rain is avoided, and nesting occurs either at the end of the rainy season or during the dry season. Peak periods may occur in February–March (Zimbabwe, late rainy period), in March (Ethiopia, early rainy period), May–September (northern Tanzania, western Kenya), or August–January (Uganda, avoiding the wettest months) (Brown, Urban, and Newman, 1982). Two separate annual breeding cycles, reportedly involving double-brooding, have been reported from Ghana (Bowen et al., 1962). Similar bimodal patterns (but not double-brooding) have been reported from southeastern Australia (Vestjens, 1975). More broadly in Australia the species appears to be an erratic and irregular nester, perhaps timing its nesting locally to the water conditions and relative availability of food and shelter (Marchant and Higgins, 1990). In northern India and Pakistan, breeding occurs from June or July to December, and in southern India from November to February. In Sri Lanka nesting occurs from January to March (Ali and Ripley, 1983).

Nest sites and nest building. Darters often nest colonially with various species of herons, egrets, and cormorants; when this is the case they tend to choose relatively high sites around the upper periphery of the trees (Bowen et al., 1962). In Australia they build their nests in trees standing in water more than 0.3 meters deep, usually located in forks away from the main trunk, and averaging (178 nests) 3.5 meters

Figure 92. Social behavior of the Australian darter, including mutual neck rubbing (A), female darting (B), female snap-bowing (C), male wing waving while standing on nest or branch (D, E), gaping by female on nest (F), greeting ceremony (G), pointing by male on nest (H, I), and twig grasping by male (J). After sketches in Vestjens (1975).

above water (range 0.6–5.7 meters). Nesting may be solitary or colonial, with nests occasionally as close as 0.3 meters from species such as yellow-billed spoonbills (*Platalea flavipes*), and as many as five darter nests may occur in a single tree. Colonies of 8–10 pairs at times occur within an area of less than 100 square meters (Vestjens, 1975).

Before mating has occurred, the male gathers material (mostly twigs) for the nest foundation. After pairing, the female brings in additional materials, and materials are added during the incubation and brooding periods. A lining of leaves is common, and although some nests are relatively flimsy others may weigh nearly 1,000 grams. When nests are used for subsequent seasons more materials are added; a small percentage may be used for three successive seasons (Vestjens, 1975).

Egg laying and incubation. Eggs are laid at intervals of 1–3 days, starting only a few days after pairs are formed. In an Australian study the first egg was laid 2–3 days after pair bonding and the remaining ones at intervals of 1–3 days, for an average clutch size of 4.0 and a range of 2–6 eggs (Vestjens, 1975). The same range of clutch sizes has been observed in Africa, with mean clutch sizes ranging from 2.95 to 3.82 eggs. A grand mean clutch size for 906 African clutches was 3.23 (Brown, Urban, and Newman, 1982). In India the usual clutch is 3–4 eggs, more often the latter (Baker, 1929).

Incubation begins with the first egg, and individual incubation bouts last 2–6 hours, with nest reliefs usually occurring in early morning, near midday, and again in the evening. No feeding of the mate occurs during incubation. Incubation periods in an Australian study averaged 28 days, with a range of 26–30; successively laid eggs hatched in sequence, at intervals of up to 3 days (Vestjens, 1975). African records suggest a similar incubation period of 21–28 days (Brown, Urban, and Newman, 1982).

Brooding and rearing of young. The young are hatched naked, but within two days their bodies are down-covered, with considerable individual variation in down color. They are fed 6–9 times a day for the first few days, but this is reduced to only twice a day at two weeks, and once a day at five weeks. Water may also be provided by regurgitation. The brooding adult feeds the chicks for the first week after hatching, and thereafter both adults feed them, with the

older and stronger chicks being favored. Flight feathers and rectrices begin to appear at about a week, and by 20 days the chicks are sitting on branches near the nest for short periods. By four weeks they have well-developed wing feathers and exercise their wings. By then they can hop from branch to branch and can swim for short distances. When about 40 days old, and sometimes earlier, they begin to drop off the nest when disturbed, and may remain submerged for a short time. After 50 days they are able to fly short distances, and they probably begin to disperse before they are two months old (Vestjens, 1975). Similarly, fledging in three captive African darters occurred at 58 days (Junor, 1972).

Breeding success. In Ghana, 89 percent of the eggs in 15 nests hatched, and 72 percent of the chicks survived to fledging during the first round of breeding, resulting in an overall breeding success of 64 percent. In the second breeding cycle, 58 percent of the eggs in 13 nests hatched, and 40 percent of the chicks survived to fledging, producing an overall breeding success of 23 percent (Bowen et al., 1962). In an Australian study (Vestjens, 1975) there was a high rate of egg loss due to human disturbance (31 percent of 122 nests were affected), with Australian ravens taking the eggs following disturbance. Of 64 nests that successfully hatched chicks, the average brood size at fledging was 3.0 young. Brood losses occurred as a result of falling accidents, drowning in fish nets, and shooting. Predation of chicks by Australian raptors is apparently not a significant factor in breeding success. One report exists of an immature being attacked by a marsh harrier.

Population Status

There are no population figures for the major populations of this species, which is generally common to locally abundant over much of its range. Its status in peripheral Palearctic populations (Iraq) is questionable.

Evolutionary Relationships

The possible relationships between darters and cormorants, and the still highly uncertain species limits of the darters, were discussed in chapter 1.

Dalmatian pelican in prebreeding plumage.

Figure 93. Distribution of the eastern white pelican, including its general breeding range (inked) or locations of recent breeding colonies (arrows), and its additional nonbreeding or wintering range (stippled). Probable inactive colonies indicated by crossed arrows.

Other Vernacular Names

African white pelican (*roseus*), European white pelican (*onocrotalus*), roseate pelican, rose-colored pelican, rosy pelican, white pelican; pélican blanc (French); Rosapelikan (German)

Distribution

Breeds widely but locally in sub-Saharan Africa, from coastal Mauritania (Ariel and Kianone islands) and the Senegal delta eastwardly sporadically across the Sahel zone (the Lake Chad basin) to the Ethiopian highlands (Lake Shala); thence southward through the Rift Valley lake region of eastern Africa to Natal (St. Lucia Bay) and the Cape of Good Hope (Dassen Island); very local elsewhere in southwestern Africa, including the Etosha Pan and Walvis Bay of Namibia and Lake Ngami in Botswana. Breeds very locally in Greece (Lake Mikri Prespa), and along the western and northern coast of the Black Sea, from Romania's Danube delta east to the Sea of Azov, coastal Ukraine; also in Kazakhstan, from the Volga and Ural river deltas and the Aral Sea east to Lake Balkhash and the smaller lakes in the Turgai region of eastern Kazakhstan. Also probably breeds locally in Iran (lakes Uromiyeh, Parishan, and Bakhtagan) and also may still breed locally in Anatolian Turkey (Hotamis and Eregli marshes) and on Lake Van near the Iranian border. Has bred historically in the northwestern Persian Gulf (Kuwait/Iraq), and during the late 1950s bred in the Rann of Kutch in Gujarat. Perhaps still breeds in the Pakistan-Gujarat border region, but now known with certainty only as a migrant. Possibly also breeds locally or occasionally in wintering areas of southern Vietnam (no recent information), also perhaps in lakes of western China (northwestern Xinjiang Zizhiqu).

Mainly residential around breeding areas in Africa, but with some irregular movements probably associated with changes in food or water availability. Southern European and Turkish birds migrate through the Gulf of Suez and the northern Red Sea to winter in the southern Nile valley, and local wintering probably occurs elsewhere along Africa's Mediterranean coast. Wintering also reportedly occurs in west-central China and scattered northern areas of the Indian subcontinent (Pakistan, northern India, Nepal, and Burma) and in southern Vietnam, these birds presumably coming from the Kazakhstan breeding population. (See figure 93.)

Subspecies

None recognized here; the African population has often been racially separated as *roseus*—an epithet that has in the past also been confusingly applied to both the Dalmatian and spot-billed pelicans—but the taxonomic validity of racially separating the African population has been recently discounted (Brown, Urban, and Newman, 1982). African birds do, however, average slightly larger than those from elsewhere in the species' range (see measurements below).

Description

Prebreeding adult. The entire body plumage white, variably tinged rosy pink cosmetically (with secretions of the uropygial gland); an ochreous yellow breast patch of stiff, lanceolate feathers; primaries, their dorsal coverts, and the alula feathers black with white shafts, the secondaries (30–35) ranging from blackish distally to more ashy proximally, at least on the outer webs; undersurfaces of remiges mostly black; dorsal and ventral wing coverts and axillaries white; rectrices (22–24) white. An occipital crest (often longer in females), a distinctly swollen bare forehead knob (pinkish yellow in males, intense orange in females), and the yellow breast patch are maximally present only during the courtship period. Variable degrees of brown staining on the breast, and to varying degrees on the neck, throat, and abdomen, may also be present, at least in Africa. Iris deep hazel-red to crimson; bare skin of forehead and around eyes pale pinkish yellow in males, purplish pink and intense orange in females; lateral surfaces of bill dull grayish blue basally (the blue more extensive on the mandible, extending in a tapering manner out to about half its length, as compared to about one-fourth the length on the maxilla), the rest of the sides of the maxilla pale orange-yellow, with streaks of light red radiating from the reddish edges; the dorsal midrib dark grayish blue basally and tapering to a point near the bright red nail; terminal half of mandible (beyond the tapered blue area) mostly pale grayish yellow, the upper edge a dusky red; pouch bright orange-yellow; legs and feet orange or pinkish to straw-yellow (tinged with crimson during courtship), the webs grayish yellow.

Postbreeding adult. Crest short or lacking, the yellow breast patch absent, the forehead knob less swollen, the facial skin less colorful and pale flesh-pink, the bill uniformly pink, with a light red nail, the pouch medium yellow, and the legs and feet lacking reddish tints. The bluish bill color and crest may persist through incubation and part-way into the brooding period, but the forehead knob begins to diminish almost as soon as the first egg is laid.

Subadult. The transition to the mature plumage and sexual maturity occurs four years after hatching, at least in captivity (Grummt, 1984). It largely consists of the brownish or grayish juvenal feathers of the body and wing coverts being progressively replaced with white ones. The feet, bill, and pouch also become increasingly yellow as maturity approaches. Din (1979) recognized a third predefinitive plumage category ("juvenile III") that perhaps represents third-year immatures. Individuals in this category were characterized as having a mottled brown-and-white rather than uniformly brownish upper wing surface, and by being mostly or entirely yellow on the bill, pouch, and legs.

Immature. Head, neck, and back initially pale gray as in juveniles, the longer scapulars dark gray, remiges duller and more uniformly black than in adults; upper wing coverts brownish; underparts mostly white, excepting the smaller under wing coverts, which initially are mottled with grayish brown; rectrices grayish. Din (1979) distinguished a second predefinitive plumage stage ("juvenile II")—possibly but not specifically representing second-year birds—that includes individuals having dark brown upper wing surfaces, legs and bills with mixed black and yellow tones, and yellow pouches.

Juvenile. Crest very short, of soft, loose feathers; a line of similar feathers down the hindneck; head and neck brownish to grayish white, darker on the hindneck, sometimes heavily stained with rusty; underparts (unless stained with rusty brown) mostly white, the undersides of the wings with white axillaries and greater secondary coverts, contrasting with dark gray to brown undersurfaces of the flight feathers and smaller under wing coverts; upperparts mostly cinnamon-brownish, with lighter feather edges; rectrices gray; primaries and their upper coverts black; outer secondaries ash-brown, scapulars and inner secondaries dark brown; remaining upper wing coverts cinnamon-brown to ash-brown, with lighter edges. Iris grayish brown; bill grayish black, pouch black; legs and feet black. Din (1979) defined his "juvenile I" category as including those individuals having dark brown wings and being entirely black on the bill, pouch, and legs.

Nestling. Hatched with naked pink skin, which turns black after a few days. A covering of dense brownish black down then develops (this being the only pelican species not having white down), which gradually becomes paler. Iris lead-gray; bill, legs, and feet initially pink like skin, later becoming dark slate-gray, and virtually the same color as the natal down.

Measurements (in millimeters)

General range of species: wing, males 665–772 (ave. of 24, 684), females 586–650 (ave. of 17, 620); tail, males 155–188 (ave. of 6, 176); females 138–178 (ave. of 7, 162); culmen, males 347–471 (ave. of 9, 409), females 289–400 (ave. of 14, 328) (Cramp and Simmons, 1977). African population: wing, males 650–735 (ave. of 11, 702); tail, males 150–210 (ave. of 11, 181); culmen, males 370–455 (ave. of 40, 418), females 275–345 (ave. of 22, 314) (Din, 1979). Eggs ca. 93 × 60.

Weights (in kilograms)

African population: males 9–15 (ave. of 52, 11.45, standard deviation 1.34), females 5.4–9 (ave. of 22, 7.59, standard deviation 1.02) (Din, 1979). Range of 5 females 6.3–7.6 (ave. 6.94), of 3 males "0.9" (probable misprint for 9.0)–10.4 (Schreiber, 1985). Range of 3 wild males, various populations, 11–12.1; of 12 captive males (including 8 juveniles) 8–13.8; of 13 captive females (including 10 juveniles) 6.5–8.9. The average of 4 captive and 3 wild nonjuvenile males was 10.6; that of 1 wild and 3 captive nonjuvenile females was 7.8. The average of 8 captive juvenile males was 10.9, and of 10 captive juvenile females was 7.7 (Grummt, 1984). One male 7.0, one female 7.35 (U.S. National Museum specimens). Calculated egg weight 184.8 grams; mean of 178, 188 (Berry, Stark, and van Vuuren, 1973).

Identification

In the hand. The presence of feathers on the forehead coming to an acute point serves to separate this species from all other pelicans.

In the field. This is the only Old World white pelican that exhibits extensive black on the dorsal as well as ventral sides of most secondaries, as well as on all the primaries, which color contrasts strongly during flight with an otherwise pure white adult plumage. Where this species occurs sympatrically with pink-backed pelicans in Africa the eastern white pelican can be easily recognized by its considerably larger size, its contrasting black flight feathers, and its immaculate white rather than grayish- to brownish-tinted general plumage coloration. In Europe and Asia, the sympatric and slightly larger (but much rarer) Dalmatian pelican is much more silvery gray on the undersides of the flight feathers (apparent only in flight), is generally grayish to black on the bill and feet, is more grayish white dorsally, and has much paler eyes and facial skin. Juveniles of the eastern white pelican are considerably darker brown dorsally than are young Dalmatian pelicans, and furthermore would normally be in company with the much more easily recognized adults of their own species.

Ecology and General Biology

Breeding and nonbreeding habitats. This species is mostly associated with relatively large but often shallow lakes and broader rivers or river deltas, at times extending to alkaline or brackish wetlands or saline lagoons, in a variety of climatic zones ranging from desert or tropical to cool-temperate. Water conditions must support a large supply of medium-sized fish. For breeding, secure nearby to quite distant (up to 10 kilometers) land areas or islands must be suitable for nesting, such as flat soil, sand, gravel, or even rocky substrates. The vegetation of nesting areas can range from emergent wetland plants such as reed beds or even woody plants to vegetation-free ground. Heavy woody vegetation is probably avoided, as perching is never done.

Nonbreeding habitats differ little from those used for breeding, since areas that may be used for nesting during the breeding season may serve for roosting outside of it. Areas that regularly develop atmospheric thermals suitable for sustained soaring are probably favored for use whenever possible. Din (1979) reported that an area of Lake Amin's coastline having several rivers, plus tributaries and flood plains plus two large lagoons, was used extensively by nonbreeding birds, as was an area with a large and small bay plus a river delta, but a straight and hilly section of coastline was avoided. Generally, favored loafing grounds are flat and open areas lacking in cover that might conceal approaching predators, whereas steep, heavily vegetated areas are avoided (Din and Eltringham, 1974b).

Movements and migrations. The European and Black Sea breeding populations are certainly migratory, with some birds moving south to Egypt or beyond, the Red Sea, and the Araqi marshes bordering the northern Persian Gulf, these birds presumably representing the more western breeding populations. Wintering also occurs across the northern parts of the Indian subcontinent, from Pakistan to northern Burma, these latter birds perhaps originating from Kazakhstan colonies (Cramp and Simmons, 1977). In recent years few birds have wintered in Egypt, but they are fairly common spring (March–May) and very common autumn (September–November) migrants (Goodman and Meininger, 1989), so they presumably must winter farther south in the upper reaches of the Nile watershed, perhaps with resident African pelicans. Crivelli, Leshem et al. (1991) have recently summarized known migration routes of the population breeding in the Palearctic, and indicate African wintering as probable, most likely in the Sudanese Sudd. Large numbers of birds are known to cross Israel each autumn, with a remarkable maximum estimate of about 77,000 birds reported in 1988 and 1989, but their winter destination still remains to be established.

In Africa, resident birds sometimes undertake long movements from lake to lake at various times of the year, for reasons not fully understood but presumably related to varied food supplies or breeding activities (Brown, Urban, and Newman, 1982). Additionally, there is a general dispersal of young birds from breeding colonies as in other species. Thus, juveniles have been found to disperse from a large colony at Lake Shala, central Ethiopia, over a broad area of about 720,000 square kilometers, with some individuals following the Rift Valley south about 1,000 kilometers into Kenya (Urban and Jefford, 1977).

Competition and predation. The best study on ecological contacts with other pelicans is that of Din and Eltringham (1974b) on the eastern white and pink-backed pelicans, which was discussed in chapter 4 (see table 21). This study showed that substantial ecological separation exists between these two species in Uganda. Relatively little contact evidently now occurs between the eastern white and Dalmatian pelicans in the Black Sea area and Kazakhstan, and possible competitive interactions between them are still unreported, although both species are known to concentrate on slow-moving roughfish.

Egg predators are known to include Egyptian vultures (*Neophron percnopterus*), black kites (*Milvus migrans*), fan-tailed ravens (*Corvus rhipidurus*), and sacred ibis (*Threskiornis aethiopicus*). Of these, only the vulture is very important and can break open the eggs (by throwing them on rocks), but the others will scavenge exposed contents. In southern Africa the kelp gull (*Larus dominicanus*) can be an effective egg predator following colony disturbances (Schreiber, 1985). Marabou storks (*Leptoptilos crumeniferus*), African fish eagles (*Haliaeetus vocifer*), and Egyptian vultures sometimes take young birds, but these sources of mortality are thought to be generally insignificant in their overall population impact. In some areas jackals, hyenas, and even lions might pose a threat to unfledged young (Berry, Stark, and van Vuuren, 1973), and perhaps a few adults are occasionally taken by crocodiles and even sharks (Feely, 1962).

Foods and Foraging Behavior

Foods consumed. Several studies of this species' foods have been undertaken in Africa. Thus, in South Africa Whitfield and Blaber (1979) examined the contents of 61 stomach regurgitations from a breeding colony, and found that 86 percent of the fish regurgitated were under 100 millimeters long; overall the fish ranged from 0.1 to 2,818 grams, with a peak in the under-100-gram category. Most of the fish represented had been obtained in a river system 100 kilometers to the north of the colony, and those obtained in the largest number included the Mozambique tilapia (*Sarotherodon*, Cichlidae), barb (*Barbus*, Cyprinidae), and southern mouthbrooder (*Pseudocrenilabrus*, Cichlidae). At the highly alkaline Lake Natron, Tanzania, pelicans have been observed to feed on the introduced and small but extremely abundant cichlid *Tilapia grahami*, which normally lives in hot springs around the lake edges. Cichlids such as *Tilapia* are also abundant at other less alkaline Rift Valley lakes (Turkana, Nakuru, Rukwa, Shala), where they supply a reliable and perennial supply of fish for pelicans (Brown and Urban, 1969). Besides these several cichlids, the sharp-toothed catfish *Clarias* (Clariidae) has also been reported as a food of white pelicans from various African localities in spite of its well-developed pectoral spines (Whitfield and Blaber, 1979). White pelicans in the Ruwenzori National Park of Uganda evidently concentrate on cichlids (*Tilapia, Haplochromis*) as well as some cichlid fry. *Tilapia* up to 700 grams are eaten and *Clarias* up to as much as 1,200 grams. Fish that are laterally compressed and not protected by spines such as *Tilapia*, *Haplochromis*, and *Barbus* are evidently easily and quickly swallowed, but prey such as *Clarias* as well as frogs (*Bufo regularis*) are swallowed only reluctantly (Din, 1979). Fish taken from the stomachs of unfledged chicks in a colony on the Etosha Pan, Namibia, ranged in length from 10 to 29 centimeters, and generally included forms (such as *Tilapia*, *Shilbe*, and *Clarias*) that were relatively abundant in nearby river systems (Berry, Stark, and van Vuuren, 1973).

Foraging behavior.   In contrast to the pink-backed pelican, the eastern white forages socially as well as solitarily. Din and Eltringham (1974b) observed foraging flocks up to a maximum of 129 birds, but averaging (354 flocks) 8.5 birds per flock. Such flocks often swim in organized groups of one to four rows of birds, which collectively remain in a rather confined area, moving slowly through the water and periodically breaking their formation to capture fish. When fish are very abundant this coordinated system breaks down and the birds begin to forage individually, although they remain within a loose cluster. The birds swim either parallel to shore or at right angles to it. They frequently reverse their direction when moving at right angles to shore, but their swimming tempo typically increases as they swim toward shore, suggesting that they may be driving fish into shallower waters. When swimming parallel to shore they reverse directions less frequently and stay in deeper waters, evidently catching surface-dwelling fish by simply surrounding them. When making half-circle turns to retrace their paths, there is a simple about-face of the flock, so that the leading birds now become the trailing ones, and vice versa. During the searching phase (figure 94A) the birds swim alertly, with necks stretched and bills pointed slightly downward. In the trapping phase (figure 94B) the pelicans in the front row gently tap the water with their bills, the birds forming a semicircle or a V-formation. In the catching phase (figure 94C) they thrust their bills and heads into the water, as their wings open slightly and the feet are pushed backward and upward. The bill is then slowly raised sideways so that water can drain out. Finally, in the swallowing phase (figure 94D) the bill is raised, the prey swallowed, and the formation is reestablished (Din and Eltringham, 1974b).

Fishing activity tends to be concentrated during the early morning and again during the late afternoon and early evening, with a midday resting period. It is likely that 900–1,200 grams of feed are consumed per day, representing 10–10.6 percent of average adult weight (Brown and Urban, 1969; Berry, Stark, and van Vuuren, 1973; Din and Eltringham, 1974b). Daily time spent foraging is certainly affected by the distance between nesting or roosting and foraging sites. In Africa daily foraging round trips of 100 kilometers (Berry, Stark and van Vuuren) or 200 kilometers

(Whitfield and Blaber, 1979) sometimes occur. In the Lake Mikri Prespa area of Greece some birds fly round trips of more than 300 kilometers for their daily foraging. Early in the breeding season these latter birds flew to Lake Kastoria (66 kilometers round-trip) to forage, but later in the season flew as far as Lake Kerkini and the Axios River delta (354 kilometers round-trip) (Pyrovetsi, 1989). When long foraging trips are needed the adults may not return to their nest sites until midday to feed their chicks (Whitfield and Blaber, 1979).

Social Behavior

Age of maturity and mating system.   It is generally believed that wild eastern white pelicans breed initially at 3–4 years (Cramp and Simmons, 1977; Brown, Urban, and Newman, 1982). Data from birds in captivity would suggest a four-year period to sexual maturity and attainment of definitive adult plumage (Grummt, 1984). At least in captivity, where little or no mate choice might occur, sustained monogamy prevails (Grummt, 1984), but comparable data do not exist for wild birds.

Social displays and vocalizations.   The most complete study of this species' displays is that of Brown and Urban (1969), but observations have also been made by Feely (1962) and Schreiber (1985). Brown and Urban recognized four different display activities associated with pair formation, which in approximate diminishing frequency of observation were "group display," "setting to partners," "the strutting walk," and "head-up and bow."

Group display consists of from a few to 200 or more birds, all or almost all in breeding condition, with enlarged forehead knobs (figure 95A). These groups are evidently all initially composed of males, which gradually attract females. The birds gather on the shore of the breeding island, milling about and sometimes suddenly and simultaneously thrusting their beaks toward the center of the assemblage in a group-point (Schreiber). Schreiber noted that during the group-point the bill is opened and the birds appear to be grabbing at one another. Much preening occurs during general group display, and rapid gular fluttering occurs virtually the entire time the birds are in group-point. Males participating in such groups often raise the bill vertically in a "head-up" (Brown and Urban), "vertical-bill" (Feely), or "erect" (Schreiber) display (figure 95F). This display, which also occurs after disturbance or after landing near other birds, is evidently indicative of appeasement (Feely). It is highly variable in the degree of bill raising, and has differing degrees of pouch inflation and an associated pouch-flapping movement that begins at the neck and proceeds outwardly. Gular distention and pouch flapping are evidently attained by a different muscular mechanism than is kink-throating in cormorants and darters, and Schreiber believed that it communicates indecisive intentions of association, seeking, and interaction. In high-intensity display the pouch is greatly

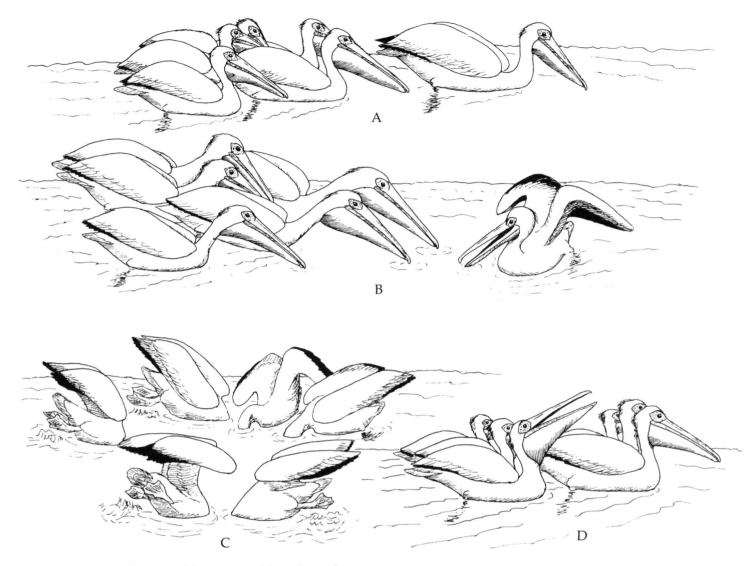

Figure 94. Social foraging of the eastern white pelican, showing searching phase (A), trapping phase (B), catching phase (C), and swallowing phase (D) of the feeding cycle. After sketches in Din and Eltringham (1974b).

distended and an *aar* or "mooing" sound is uttered, perhaps as air is forced out of the chest as the body is stretched upward. Lateral head turning also occurs as a display that apparently indicates tendencies for association, interaction, and indecision, with the bill moving faster and more nearly horizontal in more intense versions. Finally, the bow display (figure 95E) is sometimes performed after an upright display. The bow is infrequent in courtship groups and seems to indicate a tendency to remain in place rather than to move. This display is more typically performed by the "in" bird of a pair at the nest site (see below).

From these larger courting groups smaller assemblages of 1–3 potential pairs fly out to the water and alight. There the competing males perform the head-up display toward one another, utter "moo" calls, and sometimes grasp one another's bills. This head-up display and associated moo call when performed by the male alone are evidently an aggressive signal, but in common with the bow display the same posture also occurs during nest relief toward the mate, in this case by the "out" bird. Potential pairs sometimes leave the courting flocks and walk sedately about in an upright posture, heads raised, bills inclined upward, and wings

Figure 95. Social behavior of the eastern white pelican, including forehead enlargement of prebreeding adult (A), sideways shoveling by male gathering nest materials (B), male carrying nest materials (C), strutting walk, the female leading (D), and head-up (E) and bowing (F) displays. After sketches in Brown and Urban (1969).

sometimes partly opened, the male following the female. This strutting walk (figure 95D) may well be initiated by a female that is ready to pair, but is not immediately or usually followed by copulation.

Copulation usually occurs on the nesting area, and lacks specific precopulatory displays, although the pair usually leaves the group display area and moves to the nesting colony location. They then squat or stand together, and both birds may make nest-scraping movements with the bill. Copulation then follows, with the male grasping the female's neck with his bill and flapping his wings to maintain balance (see figure 27). There is evidently no special postcopulatory display, although Schreiber said that an indistinct post-mounting display sometimes occurs. The male leaves the female at the nest site while he departs to gather nesting materials.

The nest relief and general mate greeting display consists of the head-up and bow postures. The relieving or "out" bird approaches the nest with the bill distinctly raised, sometimes almost to the vertical, as in the aggressive head-up display. The "in" bird rises and slowly backs off the nest, sometimes also with the bill up, but sometimes with the bill lowered toward the feet in a bow display. There are no preflight or postlanding displays in pelicans. Adult vocalizations other than the "mooing" consist of deep nasal aggressive grunting or growling notes, and low, repeated grunting notes made by adults calling to their young to be fed or when leading them about. High-pitched wailing or yelping calls are uttered by nestlings, especially younger ones (Brown and Urban, 1969).

Reproductive Biology

Breeding season.   In Africa the breeding season is highly variable, with breeding sometimes occurring year-round, sometimes during the rainy season, and often during the dry season. The presence of a suitably secure nesting site may be the most important factor regulating breeding there (Brown, Urban, and Newman, 1982). However, in South Africa the timing of breeding may be correlated with the temporal food supply, and in one locality breeding occurred during three major waves in spring and summer, coinciding with seasonal periods of suitable foraging habitat and readily available fish prey (Guillet and Crowe, 1983). In the Balkans breeding is distinctly seasonal, with eggs found from mid-April to late June, and young present from mid-May to mid-September (Cramp and Simmons, 1977). In the Volga delta egg laying begins in April, and during late April or early May on the Syr Darya delta (Dementiev and Gladkov, 1951).

Nest sites and nest building.   Nests are usually grouped into colonies, with densities of about a nest per square meter (Ali and Ripley, 1983), or even 1.55 per square meter (Brown and Urban, 1969). Under conditions of extreme crowding as little as 48 centimeters may separate the centers of adjacent nests,

but the average internest distance in one large colony was about 77 centimeters. Materials are accumulated by carrying or throwing. Males may also bring materials such as green vegetation or rubbish from some distance, carrying them within the bulging pouch (figure 95C) and disgorging them in front of the female. The female then pulls the material toward her and organizes it below her at the nest site. Nests may be located on almost any flat surface. If no vegetation is present no real nest may be made, the birds simply shoveling and scraping materials with the bill (figure 95B) until a hollow is made large enough to contain the eggs (Brown and Urban 1969). Where the nest is located in a reed bed or similar site, it may be a substantial accumulation of vegetation, or may even be partly constructed of available feathers (Ali and Ripley, 1983). Berry, Stark, and van Vuuren (1973) observed that in one year a colony of about 1,500 pairs attempted to nest on a sandy islet, but was forced to desert because of human disturbance. They then moved about 130 kilometers away and attempted to nest on a small island, which was disrupted by hyenas. They finally nested 10 kilometers away from the second site among a colony of lesser flamingos (*Phoeniconaias minor*), placing their own nests at random between those of the flamingos on the hard clay.

Egg laying and incubation.   Successive eggs in a clutch are possibly laid daily in wild birds (Brown and Urban, 1969), but two- or three-day egg-laying intervals are typical of captives (Grummt, 1984). The range of clutch sizes in a large Ethiopian colony was 1–5, with the single-egg clutches probably mostly incomplete and the five-egg clutches probably the work of two females. The mean clutch size for 577 Ethiopian nests was 1.74 eggs, but by eliminating nesting groups with large proportions of incomplete clutches the adjusted mean was 1.88 (Brown and Urban, 1969). Other samples from elsewhere in Africa had similar means of 1.89–1.91 (Brown, Urban, and Newman, 1982), although recent samples from South Africa have averaged somewhat smaller (Cooper, 1980). Among a sample of 98 first renests in Namibia, 78 of the nests held two eggs, 19 were single-egg clutches, and there was one clutch of three (Berry, Stark, and van Vuuren, 1973).

Incubation is begun with the laying of the first egg, with both sexes participating about equally. Nest relief occurs rather infrequently, probably only after incubation bouts of 24–72 hours. Whichever member of the pair is incubating in late evening continues through the night, and even during the day only a few nest relief ceremonies may be observed in a colony of several hundred pairs. However, neither sex feeds the other at the nest. The incubation period has been indirectly estimated at about 38 days for wild birds (Brown and Urban, 1969), and more precisely as 29–31 days for captive ones (Grummt, 1984), which also agrees with an estimate of 29–30 days for wild birds by Dementiev and Gladkov (1951). In captivity 1–2 renestings have been documented after durations of 10–47 days following the loss or removal of the first clutch, and one second brood attempt has also been reported (Grummt, 1984).

Brooding and rearing of young. Hatching is asynchronous, and requires about 24–36 hours. The young are initially brooded continuously on the parent's spread feet for the first 2–3 days, with the parent holding its body slightly raised and its wings slightly opened. The chick is fed fluid food while the parent holds its bill tip upside down, the inner surface of the bright red nail apparently serving as a kind of feeding bowl. Both parents brood the young about equally. Near the end of the first two weeks a black downy coat begins to develop, and by 14 days the chick may be sheltered from the sun to keep it cool as much as it is brooded. By then it is starting to eat solid foods as well as fluid regurgitations, and may begin to squat below or beside its parent. Sometimes young from nearby nests will collect under a single brooding adult, providing the initial basis for pod formation. The young begin to leave the nest and form pods at 20–25 days. They are now given fish 15–18 centimeters long or even larger. They are fed less often and torpid or lethargic young are often dragged out of the pods by their parents for feeding once they have been located. At 28–42 days the young begin to acquire contour feathers, and may form into pods of 100 or more chicks. By that age they can recognize their own parents and run to them to be fed. When 42–56 days old they are almost fully feathered, and the large pods begin to break up. The young are by then about three-fourths adult size, and violent struggles may develop when they are being fed. At 56–70 days the birds are free-swimming and approaching fledging. They then begin to perform group fishing and practice short flights. After the chicks can fly, at 65–70 days, their parents appear to lose interest in them, and the young no longer solicit food. Widespread dispersal of the young birds follows fledging (Brown and Urban, 1969).

Breeding success. In a large Ethiopian colony, the brood size at hatching was about 1.5 young per nest, as compared with an initial clutch size of about 1.88 eggs. During the first 10 days of the nestling period there was a loss equal to about 20 percent of the total eggs laid, and by the end of the first month about 40 percent. The breeding success at fledging was estimated as about 0.8–0.9 young per pair, or about 50 percent of the total eggs laid (Brown and Urban, 1969). In Namibia, the fledging success of 5,000 hatched young was estimated at 40 percent, with insufficient food a major cause of death, as well as disturbance caused by attempted rescue and transport of chicks to a new area when the original area dried up (Berry, Stark, and van Vuuren, 1973). At Lake Mikri Prespa, Greece, the four-year mean clutch size was 1.93 eggs, the mean hatching success was 41.4 percent, and the mean number of chicks raised per breeding attempt was 0.64. The six-year hatching success of the Dalmatian pelican was significantly higher (65.3 percent), as was the mean number

of chicks raised per breeding attempt (1.03) (Crivelli, Catsadorakis, et al., 1991).

Population Status

The total breeding population of Africa is perhaps 50,000–75,000 pairs, with one or more fairly regular colonies known from Mauritania (Ariel and Kianone islands), Senegal (Senegal delta), Nigeria (Wase Rock), Chad (Ab Toyour), Ethiopia (Lake Shala), Kenya (Lake Elmenteita), Tanzania (Lake Rukwa), Namibia (Etosha Pan, Walvis Bay), and South Africa (St. Lucia Bay, Lake Dassen) (Brown, Urban, and Newman, 1982). Breeding has also occurred in Zambia (Mweru Marsh), Botswana (Lake Ngami), and Mali (Lake Chilwa). The largest recent African colony, with 20,000–40,000 pairs, is at Lake Rukwa, Tanzania, and the Lake Shala colony in Ethiopia sometimes supports 6,000–12,000 pairs.

In Europe the known population has been generally believed to be much smaller (Crivelli and Schreiber, 1984), with drainage and persecution reducing the breeding range to only a few active colonies recently estimated to number only about 1,500 pairs (Cramp and Simmons, 1977; Rüdiger, 1984). The Kazakhstan population (centered on the Aral Sea and secondarily in the Turgai area) is now apparently seriously endangered (Romanov, 1987). Indeed, nesting colonies associated with the Aral Sea wetlands and those of Lake Lop in northwestern China have completely disappeared in recent years because of divergence of waters flowing into these lakes for irrigation purposes (Crivelli, Catsadorakis, et al., 1991).

Crivelli, Leshem, et al. (1991) and Crivelli, Catsadorakis, et al. (1991) have provided a current summary of this species' status throughout the Palearctic, and their numerical estimates for breeding pairs are summarized in table 28. They judged that this population (exclusive of any additional birds in China) might total close to 10,000 breeding pairs (and a total population of 70,000–80,000 birds including nonbreeders), with the largest numbers in the former USSR (3,070–4,300 pairs) and Romania (3,000–3,500 pairs), both of which have seen recent increases in populations. However, in Greece the population is declining, and in Turkey the situation is uncertain but apparently bad with no proven current breeding there. There is also no certain current breeding in Iraq, but in Iran breeding has been reported in three areas.

In 1960 several hundred pairs of eastern white pelicans were found breeding in the Great Rann of Kutch (Ali and Ripley, 1983), but the species now appears to be only a migrant in Pakistan (Roberts, 1991). It has been suggested that breeding may occur on the border area between Pakistan and India (Sind and Gujarat provinces), but this is still unproven (Crivelli, Leshem, et al., 1991).

Evolutionary Relationships

Schreiber (1985) was not able to establish this species' relationships based on its behavior, because of the lack of adequate comparative data, but noted that it seemingly diverged quite strongly from the brown pelican in its displays. DNA-DNA hybridization data provided by Sibley and Ahlquist (1985) suggest that this species is the most isolated of the white pelican assemblage, although the spot-billed and Dalmatian pelicans were not included in the species sampled. Grummt (1989) reported seeing two age classes of immature zoo-bred hybrids between the eastern white and Dalmatian pelican at the Shanghai zoo; it would be of interest to learn their relative fertility.

Figure 96. Distribution of the pink-backed pelican, including its overall residential range (stippled) and the locations of recent breeding colonies (arrows).

Other Vernacular Names

Pélican à dos rosé, pélican gris, pélican roussâtre (French); Rotrückenpelikan, Rötelpelikan (German)

Distribution

Breeds widely but locally in lakes and wetlands of sub-Saharan Africa, from Senegal and Gambia east across the Sahel zone to the Gulf of Aden, and thence south through the Rift Valley of eastern Zaire, Uganda, and Kenya to Malawi and South Africa (where currently classified as threatened). Local breeding was reported from western Madagascar (Antsalova area) from 1958 to 1960 (Milon, Petter, and Randriansola, 1973), but no known breeding has occurred since then (Landrand, 1990). Breeding has also occurred on the Red Sea coast of Saudi Arabia (near Kunfuda and Al Lith) (Jennings, Fryer, and Stagg, 1982) and in Yemen (Jennings, 1987). Generally resident, but subject to some local movements in connection with seasonal water availability, and vagrants occasionally reach southern Egypt. (See figure 96.)

Subspecies

None.

Description

Prebreeding adult. Generally mottled, pale gray and white, the head tufted with long and pointed grayish crest feathers, the hindneck, mantle, scapulars, and upper tail coverts also pale gray, the larger upperpart feathers usually with brown to blackish shafts or shaft streaks and somewhat more brownish centers; face, throat, and underparts somewhat whiter; a patch of slightly yellowish and stiff, lanceolate feathers on the breast; the back and rump usually cosmetically tinted with pinkish, and the underparts also variously washed with pink; primaries and their dorsal coverts mostly blackish gray, the secondaries more extensively grayish, edged with silvery gray; remaining upper wing coverts pale gray, the greater coverts with brown shaft streaks and mostly hidden under the long and black-shafted median wing coverts; undersurfaces of remiges pale gray, with white shafts; under wing coverts and axillaries white, often with pinkish tints; rectrices (20) grayish white, with blackish shafts. Iris apparently blackish brown or reddish brown (but see variations noted below for postbreeding adults); eyelids deep yellow (males) to dark orange (females); the remaining facial skin pale grayish flesh, with a small pink patch above the eye (paler in male), a smaller pale yellow patch below it, and an irregular large black patch in front of the eye; bill yellow, with a brighter yellow to reddish nail, the pouch deeper yellow, pigmented with deep red internally during the peak of the display period, and striped exteriorly with numerous closely spaced and vertically oriented brownish black or yellowish brown lines; legs and feet apricot, becoming bright crimson during display.

Postbreeding adult. Like the prebreeding adult, but the plumage lacking in pink tones, the crest shorter or absent (regressing by the third week of incubation), and the general plumage color more grayish, the upperparts perhaps somewhat more sullied with brown. The deep red color of the inside of the pouch disappears shortly after courtship is over, and the softpart colors of the face, pouch, bill, and feet all fade during incubation. Iris color apparently highly variable (variously reported as black, brown, red, and yellow-brown); orbital and facial skin gray, somewhat smudged or mottled with black, especially in front of the eye; bill rather uniformly gray, pale yellow, or pinkish, with an orange to pink nail; pouch pale yellow to flesh-colored, crossed with numerous vertically oriented narrow sulfur-yellow to reddish brown lines; legs and feet grayish yellow (becoming yellow to dull orange when in transition to breeding condition).

Immature-subadult. Later predefinitive plumages are apparently not strongly differentiated from the juvenal plumage, and evidently gradually merge with the definitive plumage condition. Din (1979) recognized a "juvenile II" plumage stage in which he included birds having mottled brown (and white) upper wing coverts (rather than uniformly brown, as in his "juvenile I" category), and with pale yellow (rather than simply "pale") pouches. Din distinguished only two distinct "juvenile"—apparently thereby meaning predefinitive—plumage stages in this species, as compared with three in the eastern white pelican. This difference might suggest that the definitive plumage and sexual maturity are normally reached a year sooner (at three years) in the pink-backed than in the considerably larger eastern white pelican, which would correspond to Grummt's (1984) conclusions concerning ages of sexual maturity in pelicans relative to their adult body size.

Juvenile. Generally browner than the adult, and the feathers lacking pink tints; head and neck gray, with a brownish cast and the crown somewhat tufted; the back, rump, and underparts pale gray to whitish (whiter than in adults); scapulars and wing coverts brown, edged with whitish, median upper wing coverts not elongated nor covering the greater coverts; primaries blackish brown; secondaries dark gray to brownish, with paler edges; rectrices pale brown to grayish brown. Iris yellow-brown; facial skin and bill dull gray to grayish pink; pouch pale yellow-green to grayish pink; legs and feet grayish pink to creamy or yellowish white.

Nestling.   Initially naked, with fleshy pink skin; later covered with whitish down, which becomes increasingly grayer.

Measurements (in millimeters)

Wing, males 595–615 (ave. of 5, 605), females 545–580 (ave. of 6, 560); tail, males 160–185 (ave. of 5, 172), females 140–180 (ave. of 7, 166); culmen, males 335–375 (ave. of 19, 357), females 230–335 (ave. of 68, 305) (Din, 1979). Eggs ca. 82 × 55.

Weights (in kilograms)

Males 4.5–7 (ave. of 19, 5.97, standard deviation 0.78), females 3.9–6.2 (ave. of 64, 4.92, standard deviation 0.63) (Din, 1979). One captive male, 5.5 and 6.1 (two weights of same bird), one female 4.5 (Grummt, 1984). A highly questionable and undocumented maximum weight of ca. 10.0 (22.4 lb.) was included by Fisher and Peterson (1964) in a list of the heaviest known flying birds. This weight is more than 40 percent greater than the maximum of 83 wild birds weighed by Din, and if valid perhaps relates to a captive specimen. Calculated egg weight 137 grams; average (sample size not indicated) 119.8 (Brown, Urban, and Newman, 1982).

Identification

In the hand.   The combination of silvery grayish rectrices, wings with mostly black primaries but generally grayish inner secondaries and upper wing coverts (when seen from above), and a smudgy black area of skin directly in front of the eye (in adults) serves to identify this species of pelican. Its small measurements separate it from all the other predominantly white pelicans except for the spot-billed, which has a whitish rather than dark iris and varying amounts of dark spotting on the bill and pouch.

In the field.   In Africa this species can be distinguished from the eastern white pelican by the pink-back's substantially smaller size, its generally more grayish overall plumage tones, and its less extensive black on the flight feathers, which appear rather uniformly silvery gray rather than almost entirely black when seen from below. As compared with the eastern white pelican it also has a fairly uniformly yellowish bill (without contrasting bluish gray "racing stripes" on the sides), no forehead knob, and pale grayish (not bright yellow to orange) facial skin, with a blackish smudge in front of each eye. The cosmetic pink plumage

color is variably present in adults only during the breeding season, and may not be very evident even then.

Ecology and General Biology

Breeding and nonbreeding habitats.   Like the eastern white pelican this is an extremely adaptable species, occurring on virtually any wetland that supports an adequate food supply, ranging from fresh-water to alkaline or saline sites, and from small, seasonal ponds to larger, slow-moving rivers and lakes or reservoirs. Unlike the eastern white pelican it needs trees for nesting and prefers them for nocturnal roosting. In further contrast to that species its more solitary foraging behavior and smaller size allow it to exploit habitats with more limited fish resources. In a study at Ruwenzori National Park, Uganda, both species tended to loaf in the same habitats, mostly rivers and bays with flat and open sandy areas nearby that were free of human disturbance and predators, but flock sizes averaged smaller (22 vs. 37) for the pink-backed pelican. Diurnal densities and distribution differences between the two species were not usually apparent, but nocturnal roosting of the eastern white occurred on the water, while the pink-backed would fly to trees to roost (Din, 1979).

Movements and migrations.   No clear-cut migrations are known to exist, but in western Africa there is some population movement north during the wet season, with a return south in the dry season (Brown, Urban, and Newman, 1982). Probably some local movements occur as a result of juvenile dispersal as well, but this remains undocumented (Din, 1979).

Competition and predation.   Competition between this species and the eastern white pelican was discussed in chapter 4 (see table 21). Din (1979) found little evidence of predation, although he believed that hyenas (*Crocuta crocuta*) or leopards (*Panthera pardus*) may occasionally take pelicans that are roosting on the shore. Pelican chicks that fall from the nest are sometimes eaten by pythons (*Python*), and other potential ground predators include lions (*Panthera leo*) and hyenas. Possibly monitor lizards (*Varanus niloticus*) take some eggs or chicks from tree nests, but parental protection is apparently strong enough to ward off most raptors (Din and Eltringham, 1974a).

Foods and Foraging Behavior

Foods consumed.   The foraging ecology of this species has been well studied in the Ruwenzori National Park of Uganda (Din, 1979; Din and Eltringham, 1974b). Based on the stomach contents of 72 pink-backed pelicans, cichlid fish (*Tilapia* and *Haplochromis*) and fish fry are the species' foods in that area, with the males concentrating on larger fish and the females largely living on fish fry. The largest individual fish found in a stomach was a *Barbus* cyprinid weighing 470 grams, although the usual prey range was 80–290 grams. Fish remains regurgitated by nestling birds were likewise mostly of *Tilapia* (44 percent) and *Haplochromis* (28 percent), and their sizes ranged from 19 to 500 grams. It was indirectly estimated that each adult consumed an average of about 776 grams of food per day, or 14.4 percent of the adult body weight.

Foraging behavior. Although the pink-backed pelican normally forages solitarily, Din (1979) observed groups of as many as 30 or more birds feeding together at times. The stages of searching, trapping, catching, and swallowing prey are basically like those described for the eastern white pelican, but are performed individually rather than collectively. Din observed a generally higher individual success rate (46 percent vs. 20 percent) for trapping attempts in this species as compared with the eastern white pelican. Fish-trapping efforts in the pink-backed pelican averaged 2.2 per minute, with the more successful efforts occurring fairly close to shore. Both species had an early morning foraging period that lasted until about noon, followed by a long afternoon loafing period and a second evening foraging session that ended about a half-hour before sunset.

Social Behavior

Age of maturity and mating system. Grummt (1984) believed that the age of maturity and assumption of the definitive plumage occurs at three years in this species, based on information from other similar-sized pelicans in captivity. Din (1979) observed that the birds were highly promiscuous during nest building, with males observed copulating with the mates of neighboring males. There is no information on mate retention rates between successive breeding seasons, but it is quite possible that new pair bonds are formed annually (Brown, Urban, and Newman, 1982).

Social displays and vocalizations. Displays of this species have been described by Burke and Brown (1970), Din and Eltringham (1974a), Din (1979), and Grummt (1984). The account by Din and Eltringham is perhaps most usefully organized into courtship displays, pair recognition displays, and copulatory behavior.

Male advertising occurs on actual nests or potential nest sites in tree tops, and consists of bill clapping (also called beak clapping and gargling), head wagging, the bill-open (also called mouth-open) display, and bowing. During the bill-clapping/gargling display (figure 97C) the head is thrown back to the back, the bill is opened, the lower mandible spread, and the mandibles clapped together two or three times. The wings are also variably raised or opened and thrashed or waved several times. The gular pouch is strongly stretched, with the carmine-colored inside surface visible, and a soft *cho-cho* may be uttered. The mandibles may be

clapped together at a rate of 25–35 times per minute, the latter rate typical if a female appears. Lateral head wagging with the head on the shoulders, the bill closed, and the wings slightly raised is also performed, usually when another pelican (presumably a female) is sitting nearby. These movements are similar to those of food begging by nestlings. In the bill-open display (figure 97A), the lower mandible is spread and the gular pouch expanded. In this position the pelican may point his bill toward another, thrash his wings slightly, and apparently expose the inside of his pouch. This display is evidently different from the threatlike bill pointing with a closed or only slightly opened bill that is performed toward intruding birds (including other species) that fly nearby (figure 97D). Finally, bowing (figure 97B) resembles bowing in the eastern white pelican, and is similarly rare. During bowing the bill is closed but the pouch is greatly distended, and the bird directs the display toward other pelicans.

Possible individual recognition displays include head bobbing, and perhaps also bill raising and nest demarcation. The mate is greeted with a vertical head-bobbing movement and guttural calls, which are reciprocated by the other bird. A rapid bill raising, performed when other pelicans flew over the nest, probably corresponds to the pointing display mentioned above. Nest demarcation behavior consists of touching the edges of the nest with the bill while holding the wings half opened. This may well correspond with nest-worrying behavior in cormorants, and disappears soon after the nest is completed (Din and Eltringham, 1974a). Head throwing/gargling is performed by females as well as males, but the female's performance is less energetic, with no wing spreading but slight wing lifting, and the bill opened or closed as she utters a soft *cho-cho* note. Female head throwing perhaps serves as a pair maintenance display, and may serve as an additional sex identification signal.

Copulation occurs on the nest and begins soon after pairs are formed. Prior to copulation the male is usually found on the resting branch near the nest. Copulation is evidently not preceded by any specific behavior, except possibly by general preening behavior, but treading is accompanied by male wing waving as both sexes orient their bills downward (figure 27C). Following copulation the male flaps his wings, wags his tail, stretches his pouch over his neck, and stretches his neck with the bill pointed upward (Din and Eltringham, 1974a), all of which are apparent comfort activities.

Reproductive Biology

Breeding season. The breeding season is highly variable, but in general tends to occur late in the rainy season, with the young fledging during the dry season. There is no clear correlation between the breeding season and relative availability

Figure 97. Social behavior of the pink-backed pelican, including threat-gaping ("bill-open") (A), bowing (B), gargling
("beak-clapping") (C), and threat-pointing ("bill-pointing")
(D) displays. After sketches in Din and Eltringham (1974a)
and in Burke and Brown (1970).

of foods. In South Africa breeding occurs during the summer rains (December–January). In Nigeria and West Africa breeding begins at the end of the rains (September–November), likewise in western Kenya and Uganda (August–November), and similarly in eastern Kenya and Tanzania (May–June) (Brown, Urban, and Newman, 1982). In the Ruwenzori Park of Uganda the overall breeding season is from mid-July to early March, with nest building starting in July, during the dry season, and eggs laid in August. Most juveniles start leaving the area during the second rainy period in November, and all birds are gone by March (Din, 1979). In a Kenya colony (Burke and Brown, 1970) nest building began in August, when the heaviest rains had eased, most eggs were laid in October and November, the first young fledged in January, and all young had fledged by the end of March.

Nest sites and nest building. Nests are usually located in trees, but occasionally are placed in low bushes, reed beds, or rarely even on the ground. In Din's (1979) study, nearly 98 percent of the nests he found were in the tops of *Euphorbia dawei* trees more than 12 meters tall, and within a narrow forest of these trees. Lower portions of the same trees were also used for nesting by marabou storks (*Leptotilus crumeniferus*). Nests may be situated at elevations of 10–50 meters above ground (Brown, Urban, and Newman, 1982), and in contrast to the eastern white pelican nesting sites seem to be highly traditional, with the use of certain localities possibly going back as far as two centuries (Burke and Brown, 1970). In one Kenya colony, 250 nests were located in three fig trees. Only live trees were used, surviving nests from the previous year are rebuilt, and nests that have been abandoned or failed may be taken over, repaired, and used again in the same season by another pair.

Nests are often surprisingly small platforms that sometimes become intermingled with those of adjoining pairs; the distance between adjoining nests is often so small that the bodies of neighboring incubating birds may actually touch one another. Nests are constructed of dead as well as leafy twigs, and nest building continues through the breeding season, but at a reduced rate after eggs are laid. Materials are gathered only by the male, from nearby trees, shrubs, or old nests that have fallen to the ground, but the female does the nest construction. She accepts the stick from the male, places it on the nest, and presses it down with her feet. The nest is typically built in an umbrella of branches that provide firm support and also relative inaccessibility to ground predators. The nest-building period for a single pair lasts about 6–8 days and is interspersed with repeated copulations. A "resting branch" is always located near the nest, and provides access during nest relief as well as a place from which adults can easily feed older young. During early nest-building stages "circle-flying" is commonly performed: the partner that has been relieved at the nest flies around in a short circle and then returns to the same resting branch (Din, 1979).

Egg laying and incubation. Eggs are perhaps rarely laid on successive days, but more probably are laid every other day, with an average interval of 2.2 days (range 40–60 hours), and starting 3–4 days after the nest has been completed. The mean clutch size for 155 nests was 1.98 eggs, with 82.5 percent of the nests having two eggs and the rest either one (9.8 percent) or three (7.7 percent). The incubation period was observed to be a uniform 30 days for 7 eggs in four clutches, with a pipping period of 20–24 hours. Nest relief was accompanied by mutual head bobbing and typically occurred between noon and 3:00 P.M., with each parent spending 24 hours on the nest per sitting (Din and Eltringham, 1974a).

Brooding and rearing of young. Chicks are hatched in the same sequence as the eggs are laid in each nest, in an overall period of 2–5 days. In each of three nesting seasons, involving a total of 174 broods, the average brood size at hatching was 1.9 chicks, with 64.9 percent of the nests having two chicks. There was a higher hatching success in nests having a single egg than in those with two or three eggs. Additionally the smaller and younger chicks are often attacked by their older siblings, and these younger chicks sometimes fall from the nest in their efforts to escape. The greatest period of chick mortality is evidently thus not during the first week after hatching but rather later on, when competition for food is evidently severe and danger of falling from the nest the greatest. Brooding is intensive during the first two weeks after hatching (Din and Eltringham, 1974a; Din, 1979).

By the age of 10–12 days the chicks no longer need to be brooded continuously, their primaries have begun to emerge, and they have some brown body feathers. At that age the parents often stand beside their chicks, shading them rather than brooding them. The wings are well developed and dark brown, and a short crest becomes evident by 35 days, but the body is still largely down-covered and white at that time. Once the young are partly feathered both adults may leave the nest simultaneously, returning between midmorning and noon to feed their chicks. Fish fed to the young range in length up to about 20 centimeters, and two feedings are often given from a single parental load of fish. By the time the young are 40 days old they can readily recognize their own parents arriving with food, and perhaps can do so even at a younger age. At the age of 70–75 days the young birds begin practice flights, which are gradually extended in length. They are still fed by their parents during this time, sometimes up to hundreds of meters from the nest (Burke and Brown, 1970). Down feathers are completely lost by the tenth week, and the young then exceed average adult weight by 13 percent. They are fully fledged at 12 weeks (Din and Eltringham, 1974a).

Breeding success. In the study by Burke and Brown (1970), the average brood size at hatching was 1.95 in 20 nests, and these 20 nests produced 20 fledged young, or 1.0 fledged young per pair. Most mortality occurred between 11 and 30 days of age, often as a result of reduced parental attention at this time and when the chick was exposed to strong sunlight and rain. During the first 60 days there was an overall mortality of 54 percent among 42 chicks. It was estimated that an entire colony of 540 breeding adults produced 150 flying young, or 0.55 young per pair. Counting 275 nonbreeding birds, the overall recruitment rate for the year was about 18 percent.

In Din's (1979) sample he observed that 16 young survived to fledge from an initial cohort of 39 hatched chicks in 20 nests, a 41 percent fledging success rate. More broadly, about 350 juveniles were produced from approximately 500 nests, or 0.7 fledged young per pair. In his study most of the chick mortality occurred at 3–7 weeks following hatching, apparently mostly as a result of falling from the nest, and with few if any losses to predators.

Population Status

The total population of this species is unknown, but it is variably common to locally abundant over much of Africa, although it is considered threatened in South Africa. Known breeding colonies tend to be fairly small (up to 500 pairs), and include sites in Nigeria (Sokoto), Kenya (Turkana and Naivasha lakes; Rakewa, south Nyanza District; Tana River and Lamu District), Uganda (Kamulikwesi, Kasazu, Rwenshama, Nakitoma, Nakakono, Pallisa, Ruimi, and Kabelega and Ruwenzori National Parks), and Zaire (Parc National Albert and Lufira Plains, Katanga) (Din, 1979). Small nesting colonies of about 40 breeding pairs were reported in 1980 and 1981 on the Red Sea coast of Saudi Arabia (Jennings, Fryer, and Stagg, 1982), but the current status of that population is unknown.

Evolutionary Relationships

Sibley and Ahlquist (1985) indicated that DNA-DNA hybridization data suggested a close relationship between this species and the American white pelican, although there is little other information to support this suggested affinity. Brown, Urban, and Newman (1982) suggested that the spot-billed pelican is a likely near relative, and as indicated in chapter 1 these two species seem to share a considerable number of attributes.

Other Vernacular Names

Gray pelican, Philippine pelican, spotted-billed pelican; pélican à bec tacheté (French); Fleckschnabelpelikan (German)

Distribution

Currently resident in Sri Lanka and southeastern India; perhaps also still breeds in Burma (Myanmar), where it was once extremely common. Previously also reported from Sumatra, Java, and the Philippines (at least Luzon and Mindanao). Now classified as threatened by the ICBP (Collar and Andrew, 1988), and probably mostly or entirely confined as a breeding species to Sri Lanka (where apparently still fairly widespread) and southeastern India (where now quite rare and local in Karnataka and Andhra Pradesh) (Crivelli and Schreiber, 1984). Possibly still breeds in Assam; rare in Nepal, and not yet proven to breed there; also reported, without proven recent breeding, from Pakistan, Thailand, Cambodia (Kampuchea), Laos, and Vietnam. Reliable Chinese records from the breeding season ("summer visitors") seem to be limited to the lower Changjiang River, Fujian (Fukien); winter records in China are mostly from southeastern Yunnan, Guangxi (Kwangsi), and Guangdong (Kwangtung) (Cheng, 1987). Reports from elsewhere in China, especially from north of the Yangtze River (Schauensee, 1984), probably are the result of taxonomic confusion of records of *philippensis* with those of the Dalmatian pelican. (See figure 98.)

Subspecies

None recognized here, although this form and the Dalmatian pelican were judged as conspecific (and "very similar in all characteristics") by Delacour and Mayr (1945), in spite of the fact that none of their primary external measurements overlap. These writers thus confusingly classified the spot-billed pelican as *P. r. roseus*, and the Dalmatian pelican as *P. r. crispus*. The epithet *roseus* has subsequently been regarded as a synonym of *onocrotalus* (Chapin and Amadon, 1952); thus when the spot-billed and Dalmatian pelicans have more recently been treated as conspecific they have been respectively designated as *P. p. philippensis* and *P. p. crispus* (Dorst and Mougin, 1979). These two taxa have also recently been treated as allospecies (Sibley and Monroe, 1990).

Description

Prebreeding adult. General color grayish dorsally to white ventrally; forehead, crown, a fairly long brownish gray crest, cheeks, and neck covered with dense, curly white feathers, their black bases more or less visible; hindneck covered with soft grayish brown feathers, forming a mane; upper back, scapulars, and wing coverts silvery gray, the feathers with black shaft streaks and tinged with cream color, especially on the lesser wing coverts; alula, primaries, and primary coverts brownish black, with the upper surfaces of the shafts dark; scapulars and secondaries grayish brown, shading into paler brownish gray on the proximal secondaries; lower back, rump, flanks, under tail coverts, axillaries, and under wing coverts pinkish vinaceous; rest of underparts usually dull white to pale grayish, sometimes lightly tinged with pinkish, the under wing coverts and axillaries also pinkish white, the undersides of the remiges medium brown; rectrices (22) ashy to silvery brown, grading to white, and paler toward their tips. Iris dull white to pale yellow, clouded with brown, and surrounded with a narrow scarlet sclerotic membrane; eye ring and most facial skin orange-yellow, the skin in front of the eye livid purplish; bill pinkish yellow, the terminal portions of both halves grading to orange-yellow; the sides of the maxilla and mandible with large bluish black spots or smeared with bluish black; nail orange-yellow; pouch dull purple, blotched with bluish black; legs and feet very dark brown to blackish.

Postbreeding adult. Similar to the prebreeding adult, with a somewhat shorter crest, and generally somewhat browner on the head, nape, back, scapulars, and wings coverts. Facial skin purplish gray; other softparts probably less colorful. At least in some (possibly younger) birds the legs and feet are grayish rather than the more typical brown.

Subadult (third year). The molt into adult plumage begins by about 30 months and is nearly completed by autumn, except that the wing coverts are not completely white, with some brown feathers persisting. The iris becomes paler brown, the pouch becomes as colorful as in adults, the dark blotches extending to the face, and those on the bill become firm and well defined (Ogilvie-Grant, 1898).

Immature (second year). By about 12 months the head and neck are covered by soft, downy feathers, with white tips and blackish bases, and the crest and mane are fully developed; the scapulars are wood-brown, with paler edges. The greater wing coverts are darker brown with lighter edges, and the tertial coverts grayish brown, edged with pale fulvous; the wing coverts are relatively narrow and sharply pointed. The primaries, their upper coverts, and rectrices are dark brown, the rectrices with whitish bases; the secondaries are lighter brown, tinged with ashy; the back, rump, upper tail coverts, and flanks are white, and the upperpart feathers are mostly white with brownish tips (Ogilvie-Grant, 1898).

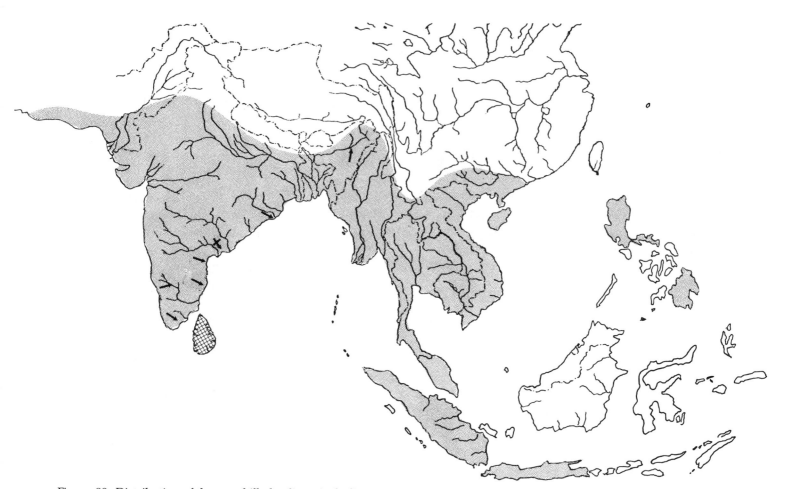

Figure 98. Distribution of the spot-billed pelican, including its probable overall historic range (stippled), its more recently known breeding range (cross-hatched), locations of recently active breeding colonies (arrows), and the location of an abandoned but historically important colony at Kolleru, Andhra Pradesh (crossed arrow).

Juvenile. The brownish juvenal plumage is retained for about a year, the brown color gradually becoming more uniform as the rufous feather edges become more worn and less evident. The spots on the bill are not apparent until the sixth month, and are still indistinct at 12 months. Toward the end of the first year a livid purplish spot appears in front of each eye and soon is clearly defined. The iris is brown, the nail and terminal edges of the bill are yellow, and the legs and toes are pale flesh-colored (Ogilvie-Grant, 1898).
Nestling. Initially naked, with light-flesh skin, but soon covered with white down; iris dark brown; bill pale plumbeous, with a pale bluish white pouch and a blackish nail; legs and feet dirty white, with black claws.

Measurements (in millimeters)

Sample sizes and ages unspecified: wing, males 530–607, females 525–550; tail, males 168–198; culmen, males 324–355, females 285–308 (Baker, 1929). Two males: wing 585 and 605; tail 170 and 190; culmen 335. One female: wing 560; tail 180; culmen 290 (Grummt, 1984). Eggs ca. 80 × 51.

Weights (in kilograms)

One unsexed immature 5 (Ali and Ripley, 1983). Two captive males 5.1 and 5.7; one female 4.65 (Grummt, 1984). Calculated egg weight 114.8 grams; average of 2, 109.5 (Grummt, 1984).

Identification

In the hand.   The combination of a bill and pouch that are spotted or blotched with black, and primaries that are black-tipped but secondaries that are mostly grayish, serves to identify this species.

In the field.   Anywhere in its range (or outside of it) this species can be recognized by its black-spotted mandible and pouch. Its grayish brown upperparts and dark brown to grayish black legs and feet further distinguish it from the eastern white pelican, and in flight both its upper and lower wing surfaces show less contrast between the remiges and their coverts than is true of the eastern white pelican. It is not only much smaller and generally more grayish throughout than the Dalmatian pelican, but also lacks that species' dark grayish bill and bright orange (breeding-season) pouch. Immatures of the two species are much more similar (and both are much lighter brown above than are juvenile great white pelicans), but by a year of age the spot-billed has at least some dark bill or pouch spotting evident.

Ecology and General Biology

Breeding and nonbreeding habitats.   Like other pelicans, this species is broadly tolerant of a variety of wetland habitats, with an adequate fish supply probably being the primary criterion, using swamps, lakes, rivers, and reservoirs of all types and sizes. Roosting and nesting is done in tall trees, with nesting preferably in trees that are branchless for the first 15 or more meters above the ground, and sometimes in trees with smooth branchless trunks of about 30 meters (Baker, 1929, 1935).

Movements and migrations.   No specific information, but probably the usual dispersal of juveniles occurs. At least in some breeding areas the birds arrive in flocks on their nesting grounds prior to breeding, and depart again at the end of the breeding season (Neelakantan, 1949; Lamba, 1963; Nagulu and Rao, 1983), so some limited migrations evidently occur.

Competition and predation.   Egg predators are known to include crows (*Corvus* spp.), and young chicks that fall from their nests are quickly eaten by crows, Brahminy kites (*Haliastur indus*), or jackals. However, the nests are well protected by the adults, and crows or kites are likely to obtain eggs only when the adults have been disturbed by humans (Lamba, 1963).

Foods and Foraging Behavior

Foods consumed.   Little specific information exists on prey species. The birds are said to prefer fish weighing up to 225 grams, but at times will take larger ones too, as well as frogs, lizards, and harmless snakes (Baker, 1929).

Foraging behavior.   Gee (1975) stated that these birds sometimes perform communal foraging, forming a line or semicircle and driving fish into shallow waters. Flocks of breeding birds have also been observed (Neelakantan, 1949) to leave each morning after about 8 A.M. for feeding, generally in groups of about 50–60 birds, suggesting that social rather than solitary foraging may be common. Nagulu (undated) observed that both solitary and communal fishing techniques are used, and identified some of the items found in regurgitated foods.

Social Behavior

Age of maturity and mating system.   No specific information exists, but these are probably similar to those of the pink-backed pelican.

Social displays and vocalizations.   Pairing reportedly occurs about a week after arrival on the breeding ground, and includes a variety of social signals such as bowing, head swaying, bill clapping, and head turning. Details of these displays are unavailable to the writer but have been described by Nagulu (undated), and would appear to be much like those of the pink-backed pelican. The bill-clapping display is associated with crouching and throwing the head back (Gee, 1975), as in the pink-backed pelican's advertisement display. Hissing and sighing sounds are uttered and associated bill-jabbing movements are made when another bird lands too close to a nest (Lamba, 1963).

Individual recognition and threat displays are also performed, but their details are unavailable. Neelakantan (1949) noted that the greeting ceremony of the mate at the nest consists of neck stretching and uttering a series of groans. When adults are "excited" (Gee, 1960) they extend their pouches with closed bills in what appears to be a pointing display (see figure 22). Nesting birds also utter various moaning, grunting, and high-pitched yip-yapping sounds (Gee, 1975), the last-named sounds perhaps actually being the so-called screeches of angry or frightened birds (Baker, 1929). Copulation occurs at the nest site, and the peak frequency of such matings is during the nest construction phase of breeding. The initial mating may occur a few hours after the initial contacts between the sexes (Nagulu, undated).

Reproductive Biology

Breeding season.   The breeding season in Sri Lanka extends from December to March or April, but over much of southern India it is mostly from October to March, and egg records from Burma are from October to December, with a peak in November (Baker, 1935; Ali and Ripley, 1983). In Tamil Nadu breeding at the now-abandoned colony at Vedanthangal occurred from October to March (Gee, 1975), and at the similarly abandoned colony at Kollair, Andhra Pradesh, breeding occurred from October to May, with egg laying from October 30 to November 22 and chicks appearing as early as November 29 (Lamba, 1963).

Nest sites and nest building. Nests are apparently always placed in trees, often at considerable height. The nests are often located 30 meters above ground, in very tall trees that are bare of branches for much of their height. The nests are placed near the trunk, on nearly horizontal branches, occasionally as many as 15 to a tree (Baker 1929, 1935). At Kollair Lake rain trees (*Pithecolobium*?) are reportedly the most favored sites, but nests are also placed in coconut (*Cocos*), palmyra (*Barringtonia*), and mango (*Mangifera*) trees. In coconut trees they are placed at the bases of the lower, nearly horizontal fronds, and nests are often placed all around the stem in a continuous ring (Neelakantan, 1949). Lamba (1963) stated that large branching trees of almost any kind are used, with vertical forks as well as horizontal ones used, as long as they are more than about 4.5 meters above ground. Gee (1960) found the birds nesting in palmyra and babool (*Acacia*) trees, sometimes fairly close to the ground and with up to about 12–15 nests in a single tree.

Nest building begins with sticks brought in by the male to the female, who places them under her feet and waits for the male to bring more. Up to six trips per hour may be made by the male, who gathers materials from under the trees or wrenches green twigs off them, returning with them in the bill. Later, fine straw and water weeds are brought to line the nest (Lamba, 1963). Nest building is mostly done during early morning hours, and apparently within 5–7 days after a nest is started the first egg is deposited (Nagulu, undated). When completed, the nest is roughly circular, about 0.3 meters thick, and about 0.5 meters in diameter (Neelakantan, 1949).

Egg laying and incubation. The clutch size of this species is rather consistently of three eggs, which are laid at intervals of 36–48 hours. If all the eggs of a clutch are removed or destroyed, a second clutch is begun in 6–8 days, but if one or two eggs are lost from a full clutch these are not replaced. Incubation begins with the first egg, and is perhaps mostly done by the female, who is a close sitter and seemingly very reluctant to leave the nest, even after being pushed off by the male. In 8 of 10 cases the incubation period was found to be 30 days for the first-laid egg; in the others it was 29 and 31 days. The pipping period requires about 24 hours (Lamba, 1963).

Brooding and rearing of young. The young hatch at intervals of 24–48 hours and are initially naked, but within 3–4 days begin to become covered with snow-white down. They are fed on fluid foods that are poured down their throats by both parents for the first week. Among nests with three young it is common for one of the chicks to fall from the nest before it is two weeks of age, and be quickly consumed by

predators or scavengers. However, after two to three weeks the nestlings are often able to defend themselves, and gather around the bases of the nesting trees, living on food scraps that fall from the nests above (Lamba, 1963). By 62 days the wing and tail feathers are fully formed, although some growth of the bill and wing may continue until about 90 days (Nagulu, undated), so fledging perhaps occurs at between 60 and 90 days.

Breeding success. Fertility and hatching rates are apparently high in this species. Lamba (1963) found that 102 young fledged from 50 nests that had initially held 150 eggs, representing a breeding success of 68 percent, and an average of 2.0 fledged young per nesting pair. Neelakantan (1949) estimated that 400 nests contained roughly 1,200 chicks, representing a remarkably high hatching success of 3.0 unfledged young per nest.

Population Status

This is probably the most threatened of all the pelicans, and is apparently now limited to a few colonies in India and a larger number in Sri Lanka. At most there are 2,000 birds in India and 3,600 in Sri Lanka (*Wingspan* 2:20, 1991). The Sri Lanka population may be fairly stable and includes about 900 pairs in 23 colonies (Hoffman, 1984; Collar and Andrew, 1988). The Indian population is now known to include only a few active colonies as of 1981–82. They are Nelapattu, near Pulicat Lake, Nellore District, in extreme southeastern Andhra Pradesh (the largest, but no numbers available); Telineelapuram, near Tekkali, in Srikakulam District of Andhra Pradesh (65 nests in 1981); Kundakolam (no breeding in 1981) and Moondraidapu, in southern Tirunelveli District of Tamil Nadu (two nesting trees; no breeding in 1981); and Kokkare Bellur and Bannelli, in Mandya District of Kanataka (about 12 pairs in 3 trees; no breeding in 1981) (Nagulu and Rao, 1983). In 1984–85 and 1985–86 they also bred at Vedanthangal Water Bird Sanctuary, Chingleput District, Tamil Nadu, with 65 birds present the first year and about 100 present the second (Paulraj and Gunasekaran, 1988). Spot-billed pelicans have been occasionally seen in Sumatra, and perhaps breed locally there (Danielson and Skov, 1985; Silvius, 1986).

Evolutionary Relationships

Although little information on this species exists, it would certainly appear to be a much closer relative to the pink-backed than is the Dalmatian, the species usually closely associated with the pink-backed. Thus, Elliot (1869) associated the pink-backed and spot-billed pelicans taxonomically. He actually included *philippensis* within *rufescens*, saying that "the differences that are claimed as sufficient to separate them are very slight." Later, Ogilvie-Grant (1898) regarded them as separate species but listed them sequentially.

Other Vernacular Names

Curly-headed pelican; pélican frisé (French); Krauskopfpelikan (German)

Distribution

Breeds (or has until recently bred) very locally in southeastern Europe (Yugoslavia, Albania, Greece, Romania, Bulgaria), and locally in Turkey, western Iran (perhaps), and from the western coast and Volga delta of the Caspian Sea, around the Aral Sea and Syr Darya valley, and eastward locally across Kazakhstan to Lake Zaysan, probably also to northwestern China, where breeding at least formerly occurred on Lop Nor in Sinkiang (Xinjiang Zizhiqu), and to western Mongolia, where recently found nesting on Har Us Lake. Now classified as threatened by the ICBP (Collar and Andrew, 1988); among EEC countries only Greece still supports breeding colonies (on Lake Mikri Prespa and on the Amvrakikos Gulf).

Winters from the Balkans (mainly lakes Kerkinitis and Vistonis, in Greece) and coastal Turkey (previously south to the Nile valley) southeastward through the northern Persian Gulf coast, the western coast of Iran, coastal Pakistan, northeastern India, and southeastern China. Vagrants have been recorded from Korea, Japan, and Taiwan. (See figure 99.)

Subspecies

None recognized here, but the spot-billed and Dalmatian pelicans have since 1945 sometimes been considered conspecific. As a result, some ornithological literature confusingly refers to the Dalmatian pelican as either a race of *P. roseus* (Delacour and Mayr, 1945; Cheng, 1955) or, more recently, of *P. philippensis* (Dorst and Mougin, 1979). Although the epithet *roseus* thus has at times been applied both to the spot-billed pelican and the Dalmatian pelican, it is now considered invalid, and regarded as a synonym of *P. onocrotalus* (Chapin and Amadon, 1952).

Description

Prebreeding adult. Plumage generally silvery white; the crown covered with long, loose plumage, forming a thick, slightly curly and shaggy crest (slightly shorter in females), and a patch of golden yellow or reddish golden lanceolate feathers on the upper breast; the dorsal neck feathers lengthened to form a permanent mane; primaries and primary coverts brownish black; secondaries mostly ashy gray, grading to white toward their bases and on the inner webs; mantle feathers, most wing coverts, and scapulars with contrasting black shafts; rectrices (22–24) white, some with black shafts; undersurface of flight feathers pale gray, the primaries with darker tips. Iris varying from pale straw-yellow to whitish, surrounded by a narrow sclerotic membrane of livid purple; facial skin varying from yellow to orange or even livid purple; bill generally grading from gray or grayish pink basally to orange-yellow distally, the dorsal ridge of the maxilla horn-gray, the sides of the bill grading distally to more yellowish red, the nail being bright orange; pouch usually deep yellow (more amber-colored in females), but becoming orange-vermillion to blood-red at peak of sexual display; legs and feet usually dark gray, becoming dull pinkish gray at peak of display.

Postbreeding adult. The crest is molting when incubation is under way; by then the birds have rather uniformly dark grayish bills and only moderately bright orange-yellow pouches. After breeding the crest is gradually lost, the yellow chest patch is reduced, and the softpart colors become generally less vivid. The bill becomes a more uniformly dingy gray, with a somewhat brighter yellowish tip and nail, the pouch changes from orange to rather pale yellow, and the facial skin fades to pale ivory. The iris remains ivory-white, surrounded by a narrow scarlet sclerotic ring.

Immature-subadult. Transitional stages to the definitive plumage are still only poorly described. The mantle, smaller upper wing coverts, and tail are a variable mixture of grayish brown and white feathers (third-year subadults probably being generally whiter dorsally than second-year individuals, which are likely still to retain at least most of their juvenal brown wing coverts). The larger wing coverts are white, faintly mottled with gray; retained juvenal primaries are browner and duller than in adults. Facial skin leaden purplish, bill varying from yellow to gray or purplish gray, becoming more grayish dorsally and basally and more yellow toward the tip; the pouch is yellow to grayish yellow; the legs and feet gray. Sexual maturity occurs at four years, at least in captivity (Grummt, 1984).

Juvenile. Back and scapulars mottled grayish brown; lower back and rump white; underparts dirty white; primaries and their dorsal coverts brownish black; upper wing coverts and secondaries pale sandy brown; rectrices with white inner and brown outer webs; crest and mane only slightly developed. Iris pearl-gray; bill yellow-gray; gular pouch grayish yellow; legs and feet gray.

Nestling. Initially naked but soon covered with pure white down, though retaining an orange-pinkish naked patch on the forecrown. Iris initially pale gray, later becoming reddish

Figure 99. Distribution of the Dalmatian pelican, including its major recent breeding range (inked), additional known recent breeding localities (arrows), historic breeding records (crossed arrows), and probable current wintering range (stippled). The wintering importance of eastern China and northeastern India is uncertain.

gray; facial skin initially blue, later pale gray, bill and pouch initially pink, later becoming dark gray; legs and feet initially pink-flesh, probably gray later.

Measurements (in millimeters)

Overall range of available measurements for wild birds (sample size uncertain, but greater than 26 males and greater than 18 females, including some juveniles): wing, males 680–800, females 630–720; tail, males 200–250, females 190–235; culmen, males 365–450, females 330–440 (Grummt, 1984). Range for 10 males and 8 females: wing, males 700–770, females 660–700; culmen, males 390–450, females 360–400 (Bauer and Glutz, 1966). Averages of 15 apparently unsexed adults: wing 745, tail 230, culmen 420; of 15 adult females: wing 725, tail 235, culmen 390 (Korodi Gál, 1964). Averages of 11 juvenile males: wing 706, culmen 405; of 9 juvenile females: wing 653, culmen 352 (Grummt, 1984). Eggs ca. 95 × 60.

Weights (in kilograms)

Overall range of available adult weights, including wild and captive birds: males 9.5–12.0 (ave. of 6, 10.4); females 7.25–10.0 (ave. of 4, 8.7). Overall range of wild and captive juveniles: males 7.25–10.8 (ave. of 15, 9.2), females 7.5–11.5 (ave. of 13, 8.4) (Grummt, 1984). This is one of the heaviest of all pelicans; maximum weights of up to 13 kilograms have been reported (Dementiev and Gladkov, 1951). Calculated egg weight 188.7 grams.

Identification

In the hand. The combination of white rectrices, wings having black-tipped primaries but mostly grayish secondaries, and a mostly grayish bill with a uniformly orange (when breeding) to yellow (nonbreeding) pouch is sufficient to identify this species. Both adults and juveniles can readily be separated from the great white pelican by the fact that the line of feathers where the forehead meets the bill form a concave border rather than a convex curve or coming to a point. *In the field.* Adults are relatively easy to identify by their generally crested head, dark grayish legs and bill, and orange to yellow pouch. When in flight overhead they lack the contrasting black flight feathers (including most secondaries) of eastern white pelicans, and instead the flight feathers appear rather gray to silvery gray from below, much like those of spot-billed pelicans. Juveniles can perhaps be distinguished from eastern whites by their lighter brown upperparts and lighter-colored secondaries. Field distinction from spot-billed pelicans (which are very unlikely to occur in the same area) would be more difficult, but spot-billed pelicans are substantially smaller and lack the curly-headed appearance of the Dalmatians.

Ecology and General Biology

Breeding and nonbreeding habitats. Foraging and general nonbreeding habitats used by this species are essentially like those of the eastern white pelican, including not only a variety of fresh-water sites but also inshore coastal localities. The birds also breed in a wide variety of wetlands, including slow-moving rivers, deltas, marshes, lakes, and estuaries, with the primary considerations being a reliable source of nearby (or sometimes relatively distant) food, and freedom from human disturbance and large predators. Unlike the eastern white pelican's, this species' nests are apparently always located in and constructed of vegetation, especially reed beds or similar emergent vegetation.

Movements and migrations. Dalmatian pelicans evidently tend to disperse and wander more than actually migrate. However, birds often move to coastal areas during winter, and few if any overwinter in the former USSR, except perhaps in extreme southern areas. The birds arrive on their breeding areas in that area about mid-March, and begin to depart in mid-October, with some stragglers remaining until freeze-up (Dementiev and Gladkov, 1951). Coastal China may also support some wintering birds, which are from uncertain breeding areas but presumably originate in China or Mongolia.

In Europe, seven major wintering areas are known, all in Greece and Turkey, most of which are on coastal deltas. Additionally the Nile delta was previously an important wintering area (Crivelli, 1987). Of the birds hatched at Lake Mikri Prespa, most apparently winter or preferentially stop over at Lake Kerkinitis located to the east in northern Greece or at Porto Lago and Lake Vistonis on the Aegean coast in eastern Greece. Likewise most of the birds bred at Lake Srebena, Bulgaria, disperse to Porto Lago and probably continue east to wintering areas in Turkey. The birds from Lake Skadar, Yugoslavia, probably move to Albania and remain there through their period of immaturity. Wintering in Greece also occurs on the Amvrakikos Gulf, so probably few of the birds reared there move out to more easterly wintering areas. The Menderes delta of Turkey is the species' most important wintering site in that country (128 birds in 1986), and apparently supports at least some birds coming from breeding sites such as Lake Mikri Prespa. The Goksu delta has also supported birds at least until 1986, but other traditional areas were used little if at all in 1986 (Crivelli, 1987).

Elsewhere in its western Palearctic and Middle Eastern range, wintering occurs along the Iranian coast, in the Tigris-Euphrates delta, along the southeastern Caspian coast, and along the Karakum canal of Turkmenistan (Crivelli, 1987). The lower Tigris-Euphrates valley marshes are perhaps still an important wintering area, this region presumably receiving birds from breeding areas around the Black and perhaps also the Caspian seas. The birds breeding elsewhere in Kazakhstan, such as around the Aral Sea, probably funnel into the riverine and coastal habitats of the Indian subcontinent from Baluchistan in Pakistan to Bengal and Bangladesh (Cramp and Simmons, 1977).

Competition and predation. This is the largest of all pelicans, and its size plus its tendency to nest in aquatic habitats may reduce the levels of egg and chick predation, but magpies (*Pica pica*), hooded crows (*Corvus corone*), and various gulls are all known egg predators that readily exploit disturbances to nesting colonies. In contrast to the American white pelican's, this species' nests are well-constructed cups, reducing accidental egg losses, and the birds are additionally relatively reluctant to leave their nests when minor disturbances occur. Thus, little or no evidence of egg predation has been found on the Greek nesting colonies (Crivelli, 1987), and purposeful or unintentional human disturbance or destruction of birds, eggs, or nesting habitats is probably by far the largest factor in the birds' survival.

Foods and Foraging Behavior

Foods consumed. Crivelli (1987) observed major breeding-season food differences among birds breeding in the two Greek breeding colonies at the Amvrakikos Gulf and Lake Mikri Prespa, based on analysis of regurgitates. Among a total of 40 regurgitate samples from the Amvrakikos Gulf taken over two breeding seasons, eels (*Anguilla*, Anguillidae) were the main food consumed (occurring in 94–96 percent of regurgitates), and the remaining foods were other marine fish (*Gobius, Blennius, Crangon, Atherina*) plus some vegetative materials. Food loads ranged from 27 to 576 grams, averaging about 200 grams. The length range of the eels was 14–51 centimeters, and that of other prey fish 7–17 centimeters. At Lake Mikri Prespa the main food eaten during all three years of study was bleak (*Alburnus*, Cyprinidae), with roach (*Rutilus*, Cyprinidae) of secondary importance. Food loads there averaged somewhat higher, about 300 grams (range 49–1,284 grams), and individual regurgitates represented 8–15 percent of chick weights. For both the bleak and roach prey length was highly variable, with smaller and more abundant size categories generally prevailing, but with an apparent overrepresentation of larger bleaks in the regurgitates relative to their abundance in the population, perhaps because the pelicans prefer to forage in deeper waters, where the larger prey individuals are more prevalent. Apparently roach are taken only during the early part of the season (until mid-May); thereafter bleak is the only species consumed. On Lake Skadar, Yugoslavia, the contents of 234 regurgitates were comprised nearly half (49 percent) of rudd (*Scardinus*, Cyprinidae), with the rest mostly of roach (21 percent), eels (20 percent), and bleak (9 percent) (Crivelli and Vizi, 1981).

In Bulgaria, pelicans breeding on Lake Srebena consumed mostly carp (*Carassius*, Cyprinidae) and tench (*Tinca*, Cyprinidae), plus smaller amounts of roach, rudd, and other fish (Bauer and Glutz, 1966). In Romania, the Dalmatian pelican consumes a wide variety of fresh-water fish taxa (*Albernoides, Aspius, Blicca, Carassius, Cyprinus, Esox, Scardinus*), and 12 stomachs analyzed had an average of 1,269 grams of food present, or somewhat more than 10 percent of the total body mass (Korodi Gál, 1964). Dementiev and Gladkov (1951), Korodi Gál (1964), and Crivelli (1987) all estimated an average daily pelican food intake of 1–1.2 kilograms, or the equivalent of a single full stomach's contents or 3–4 regurgitates in the case of nearly fledged young.

Foraging behavior. These pelicans forage primarily during morning and late afternoon hours, preferably close to breeding or roosting areas. They forage singly or in rather small groups of 2–5 birds, mostly in fairly deep water (6–8 meters). They catch fish in the same bill-thrusting manner as shown earlier for American white pelicans (see figure 19), but also often forage in mutualistic association with great cormorants in deep water. Typically the great cormorant dives first; the pelican, still airborne, quickly propels itself forward for 3–5 wingbeats, then drops back to the water again after 10–20 meters. At that point the cormorants are coming back to the surface, with the fish they are chasing also driven close to the surface, where the pelican can readily capture them. Evidently the cormorants also benefit, as it is they that join the pelicans rather than the reverse, perhaps because of the ability of the pelicans to locate a fruitful fishing area (Crivelli and Vizi, 1981).

Social Behavior

Age of maturity and mating system. Crivelli (1987) believed (without direct evidence) that sexual maturity was attained at three years, with a minority of the birds probably breeding at that age, and that all birds probably breed by five years of age. Based on initial breedings of three known-age captives (two males, one female), Grummt (1984) believed that the Dalmatian pelican regularly breeds at four years, so perhaps four years can be used as a general estimate of initial breeding. There does not appear to be any evidence on mate retention rates between successive breeding seasons.

Social displays and vocalizations. A detailed description of sexual displays is still not available. The male courtship/pair-forming display evidently consists of standing laterally to the female and performing a bowing display, with the carpal joints of the wings drooping but the wingtips elevated and the tail spread; both the rectrices and remiges are vigorously vibrated. Additionally the bill is snapped shut, the gular pouch is expanded maximally, while hissing and spitting sounds are uttered. The female does not respond obviously to this. The male initially defends a small area around the courting couple, but later restricts such defense to the nest site, which is apparently chosen by the female. At the nest site the birds copulate frequently, up to ten times a day (Bauer and Glutz, 1966; Cramp and Simmons, 1977). Copulation occurs on the nest site, accompanied by vigorous wing beating by the male as he maintains balance while grasping the female's nape or neck (see figure 27) (Grummt, 1984). Generally 8–10 days are needed from the time of initial occupation of a breeding unit to the start of egg laying, which represents the time needed to complete courtship, mating, and nest building (Crivelli, 1987).

Individual recognition displays include bill raising, which is performed when a pair member approaches the nest, as when a male is bringing nesting material (see figure 26). This may be a low-intensity version of the bowing display, and perhaps has a threat component as well. Bill clattering may also be used by both adults and juveniles during antagonistic behavior. More specific or intense threat is indicated by an approach while gaping widely; courting males regularly drive off other males or even intruding immatures (see figure 22).

Reproductive Biology

Breeding season.   In the Balkans and Turkey the egg-laying period begins in March, and maximum numbers of eggs are found from mid-April to early June. Hatching begins in April and is over by mid-July, with unfledged young present until September (Cramp and Simmons, 1977). At Lake Mikri Prespa in Greece the overall range of nest initiation dates varied from 33 to 49 days during three years (mostly peaking in late March or early April), whereas at the Amvrakikos Gulf it varied from 18 to 25 days during two years. Some probable renesting initiations (or possibly initial nestings by first-time breeders) occurred beyond these time spreads, namely after the first of May. The timing of breeding activity was strongly associated with the time of arrival of birds on their breeding grounds. There was little indication of highly synchronized breeding within the colony as a whole. However, within the colony smaller breeding units ranging from 2 to 30 (but usually 6–10) nests existed, and synchronized laying occurred within these smaller units. The overall breeding season at Lake Mikri Prespa (March–August) apparently averages about a month later than at the Amvrakikos Gulf, where it extends from February to July (Crivelli, 1987). On the Syr Darya River egg laying begins at the end of April and continues until mid-May, whereas on the Volga it begins about April 20 and continues until late May (Dementiev and Gladkov, 1951). The breeding season in Mongolia is still little known, but appears to be relatively late and roughly extends from May to August (Crivelli, 1987).

Nest sites and nest building.   On Lake Mikri Prespa most nests were located on islands or on trampled reed beds, the island nests sometimes being situated in close association with colonies of breeding eastern white pelicans and great cormorants. Of 11 separate breeding units, four were located on islands, and the other seven were situated among trampled reeds. The largest island supported from 31 to 54

nests during four successive years, and the three smaller islands supported 0–14, 0–13, and 7–24 nests during those years. None of the reed bed units were in use during all four years, but when in use these variously held from 5 to 35 nests. Evidently the birds remain faithful to particular breeding grounds from year to year, but not to specific breeding units (Crivelli, 1987). This would tend to reduce the probability of mate renewal in successive years.

Nests are built relatively rapidly, by the male gathering and carrying materials to the nest site in his bill. He may make 25–40 trips a day, and the female may complete construction of the nest in 3–5 days. The nest is a large and untidy pile of herbaceous materials, twigs, water plants, and reeds, variously held together with droppings. At times it may be as large as 1.5 meters in diameter and its top 1–1.5 meters above water level (Dementiev and Gladkov, 1951). *Egg laying and incubation.*   Eggs are laid at intervals of two, or more commonly three, days (Grummt, 1984). The clutch size ranges from one to three eggs, but Crivelli (1987) reported that in various years and in two different breeding locations the average clutch size ranged from 1.6 to 1.89 eggs. The mean clutch size was found to diminish as the laying date was delayed, although the effect was rather slight. These later and slightly smaller clutches may represent renesting or young birds laying for the first time. Renesting was not found to occur in breeding units of smaller sizes (under about 10 birds), perhaps because of inadequate social stimulation. In captivity, from one to three renesting efforts have been documented, at intervals of 11–30 days after loss of the first clutch (Grummt, 1984).

The eggs are incubated for periods of 31–34 days (Grummt, 1984), averaging 31.4 days, and generally hatch 24–28 hours apart, rarely up to 72 hours apart (Crivelli, 1987). Both sexes incubate, but the female does most of it. The usual lengths of individual incubation bouts is uncertain, but the male is said to sit on the nest only during morning and evening hours when the female is off foraging (Dementiev and Gladkov, 1951).

Brooding and rearing of young.   Crivelli (1987) noted that most clutches of three eggs failed, perhaps because the parents were unable to incubate that many eggs properly. At hatching, the chicks average 110 grams, but incredibly by the second day they may weigh as much as 200 grams, and by six days 480 grams! At 20 days they average 3,500 grams, at 30 days 6,930 grams, and at 60 days 9,200 grams. Their downy cover first appears at five days, and they are well covered by down at nine days, with some down persisting on the back until about two months of age. Young birds are able to swallow fish weighing 800–1,200 grams, or a full day's food requirement. The fledging period of these large birds is among the longest of any pelican species, about 85 days, and the young are not independent until they are 100–105 days old (Dementiev and Gladkov, 1951). Crivelli (1987) reported a 84–91 day fledging period.

Breeding success. Crivelli (1987) reported hatching success rates of 66.9–69.1 percent during three years of study at Lake Mikri Prespa, and 35.5–58 percent at Amvrakikos Gulf during two years. Potential causes of egg losses included nest abandonment, egg infertility, eggs rolling out of the nest, egg crushing, and predation. No direct evidence of predation was found, and only a few cases of egg crushing. Most losses resulted from eggs rolling out of the nest, with progressively lower losses due to infertility and nest abandonment. Eggs laid early in the season had a higher hatching success rate than those laid later, perhaps as a result of reduced social stimulation and a higher rate of nest abandonment in the later period. Crivelli found that, in contrast to most other pelicans, brood reduction does not seem to occur in this species. In one year the successfully hatched 2-egg clutches produced 1.79 fledged young per nest (89.5 percent rearing success in 23 nests), and in another year 1.92 fledged young (96 percent rearing success in 62 nests), whereas the clutches hatching only a single chick produced 0.87 fledged young per nest in both years (87 percent rearing success). No cases of "siblicide" were seen, and only one instance of sibling aggression. Additionally, he found that the mortality rate of the second-hatched chick of a brood of two was statistically no higher than that of the first-hatched chick, based on the recoveries of dead web-tagged chicks. Overall productivity (number of young fledged per active nest) was not correlated with colony size or the relative synchronization of laying within breeding units. However, it was higher at Lake Mikri Prespa (0.99–1.2 in three years) than at Amvrakikos Gulf (0.58–0.89 in two years). This difference might relate to differences in the quality of the breeding habitats (lagoons are less sheltered from waves than are reed beds and nests are thus more vulnerable to their destructive effects), or to the quality of the foraging habitat (foraging may be more difficult at Amvrakikos Gulf during the breeding season). Additionally, infertile eggs were more common at Amvrakikos Gulf, and pesticide contamination may pose a problem there. However, DDE levels sufficient to affect eggshell thickness have been recently reported from Lake Mikri Prespa (Crivelli et al., 1989). The difference in breeding success may also be partly related to food supplies, as the ease of capturing eels diminishes during the breeding season, whereas at Mikri Prespa high water levels in June create large areas of shallow waters that are rich in spawning fish.

Population Status

Rüdiger (1984) estimated that only about 100 pairs of Dalmatian pelicans might still exist in Europe, mostly in the Danube delta. At about the same time Kolosov (1983) judged that 1,500–2,000 pairs existed in the USSR. Crivelli, Catsadorakis, et al. (1991) recently reviewed the world status of this species and concluded that 21–22 known breeding grounds exist, with a collective population of about 1,900–2,710 pairs. Countries with two or more probable remaining breeding grounds are the former USSR (7–8 sites, 1,500–2,000 pairs), Turkey (5 sites, 70–115 pairs), Romania (2 sites, 36–115 pairs), and Greece (2 sites, 125–210 pairs). The remaining countries, mostly with only single known breeding grounds, are Albania (70–100 pairs), Bulgaria (70–90 pairs), China (no estimate available), Iran (5–10 pairs), Iraq (no estimate available), Mongolia (40–50 pairs), and Yugoslavia (10–20 pairs). The birds are protected in reserves or parks in seven areas (Lake Srebena, Bulgaria; Lake Mikri Prespa, Greece; Danube delta, Romania; Lake Manyas, Turkey; Volga delta, Kazakhstan; Lake Skadar, Yugoslavia; and Karavastas lagoons, Albania).

Evolutionary Relationships

The continuing controversy about the specific status of this form was discussed under "Subspecies" and earlier in chapter 1. Additional biochemical or behavioral evidence as to its relationships is badly needed.

Other Vernacular Names

Australasian pelican, spectacled pelican; pélican à lunettes (French); australischer Pelikan (German)

Distribution

Resident in Australia, including Tasmania, where widespread in fresh-water lakes, rivers, shallow wetlands, and especially around coastal estuaries, inlets, and islands, wherever surface-dwelling fish are abundant. Nonmigratory, but subject to periodic food-related dispersals. A regular vagrant or periodic migrant to southern New Guinea; vagrants have also reached New Zealand and other islands as far away as Sulawesi (Celebes). (See figure 100.)

Subspecies

None recognized by Dorst and Mougin (1979); the western population has at times been very questionably separated as *westralis*.

Description

Prebreeding adult. A fairly long, erect white crest on the nape and hindneck; the feathers of the chest pale straw-yellow. Otherwise mostly pure white, except for the remiges, alula, primary coverts, greater secondary coverts, more proximal upper wing coverts, scapulars, sides of rump, anterior upper tail coverts, and rectrices (22), all of which are black; undersides of flight feathers also black, the rest of the underwing surface usually entirely white. Iris dark brown, bounded by an eye ring of pale indigo-blue; orbital skin sulphur-yellow (becoming yellow-orange during peak of courtship); maxilla and mandible mostly pinkish to pale blue, with slate-blue edges, a pink culmen, and a yellowish to yellow-orange nail; gular pouch basally pink, the anterior two-thirds of the pouch becoming scarlet during the peak of courtship, with a red (bright blue during courtship) stripe running parallel to the bill from the base to the center of the pouch, and also extending vertically along the base of the pouch; legs pale slate grayish, the feet and webbing more bluish gray.

Postbreeding adult. Like the breeding adult, but with a grayish nape crest, and the ornamental pale yellow feathers of the chest are replaced by white feathers. Iris brown; naked skin around eye pale yellow, the blue eye ring inconspicuous; bill mostly pinkish to pale blue, with a yellow nail; gular pouch pale pinkish yellow or orange-yellow, the dark blue stripe changing to red during incubation and fading after breeding; legs and feet slate-blue to pale bluish pink.

Immature-subadult. Plumage as in postbreeding adult, but the crest and lengthened neck feathers are smoky brown, tipped with white, and the black upperparts of the adults are partially represented by more brownish feathers that are probably remnants of the juvenal plumage. The ornamental white upper wing coverts are shorter than in adults. Bill and gular pouch pink, legs and feet gray. The period of time to sexual maturity is still uncertain, but in the other white pelicans of comparable size it apparently is normally four years. The full courtship colors initially appeared as early as four years after hatching in one captive bird, but had still not yet appeared in others after six years (Vestjens, 1977a).

Juvenile. The black plumage areas of the adults are represented by brown, the upper wing coverts are all relatively short and rounded, and the head is white, gray, or brown. The naked eye ring is pale yellow, with or without a blue tinge, the bill and pouch are flesh-yellow, and the legs and feet are brownish gray.

Nestling. Hatched with naked orange-pink skin; but within a week covered with grayish white down, the head and neck down varying from white to gray or brown. Iris gray to dark brown; naked skin around eye flesh-colored to dark brown; bill varying from flesh-colored to gray, mottled, or black.

Measurements (in millimeters)

Wing, males 560–690 (ave. of 132, 637.8), females 541–605 (ave. of 25, 581.2); tail, males 154–226 (ave. of 6, 181.8), females 147–182 (ave. of 4, 165.7); culmen (live birds), males 410–495 (ave. of 260, 453.3), females 355–408 (ave. of 34, 382); culmen lengths of skins from 6 males averaged 459.2, and from 5 females 407.4 (Marchant and Higgins, 1990). Eggs ca. 90 × 59.

Weights (in kilograms)

Marchant and Higgins (1990) give an overall weight range of 4–6.8, listing two males as 5.4 and 5.82, and a female (stomach removed) as 3.3. One adult female, 5.9 (Museum of Vertebrate Zoology specimen). According to Frith (1969), this species may attain a weight of ca. 7.7 (17 pounds). Calculated egg weight 172.9 grams; average of 17, 168 (Marchant and Higgins, 1990).

Identification

In the hand. This is the only species of pelican having the eyes totally encircled by feathers rather than with bare lores,

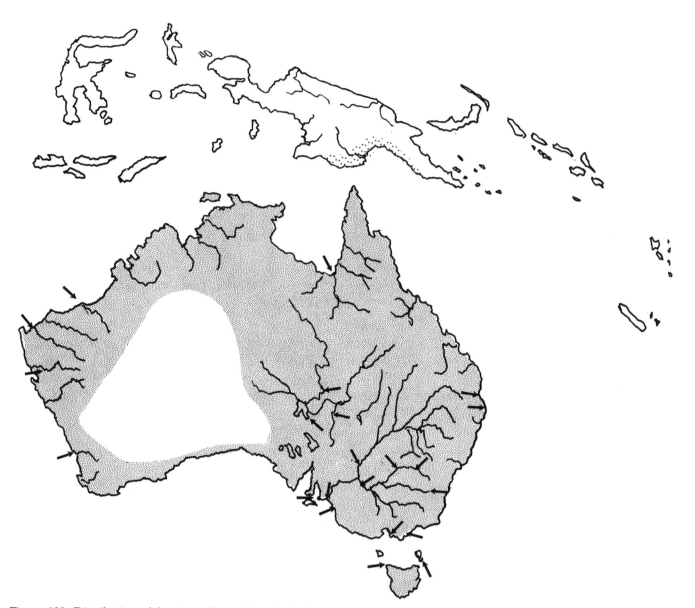

Figure 100. Distribution of the Australian pelican, including its usual residential range (darker stippling), its periodic or erratic range (lighter stippling), and recent breeding sites (arrows).

and the only white pelican having a black tail and extensive areas of black on both the scapulars and upper wing coverts. *In the field.* This is the only species of pelican native to Australia, and the only large Australian water bird with a white body but a black tail and mostly black wings.

Ecology and General Biology

Breeding and nonbreeding habitats. Like many pelicans, this species needs an adequate and reliable food supply in

the form of fish, and a suitable breeding area (with bare ground or low, patchy vegetation for nesting) that remains undisturbed for at least three months in order to breed successfully (Vestjens, 1977a). A variety of aquatic habitats in Australia provide those basic needs, including coastal islets, islands, and shorelines, inlets and salt marsh estuaries, and permanent or ephemeral lakes, salt pans, swamps, and rivers of interior regions. Outside of the breeding season the birds may frequent a broader array of wetlands, including ornamental waters in parks, marine areas near wharves and boats, and almost any other habitats supporting fish. Generally, the birds seem to prefer using relatively vegetation-free larger lakes, reservoirs, rivers, and billabongs, but areas fringing emergent vegetation or other shoreline vegetation may be used if suitable loafing sites exist. Reefs, rock platforms, and other similar sites are also used for loafing. Available loafing areas such as sandy beaches or areas of short shoreline vegetation are also sought out. The birds tend to forage in deeper pools and channels where there is room for cooperative feeding but where it is also possible to concentrate fish effectively. Levels of salinity are evidently unimportant to the pelicans, at least up to the point where fish are unable to tolerate them. However, if salinity increases to the point where the fish population dies or if falling waters allow predators to gain access to breeding areas, significant pelican mortality may occur (Marchant and Higgins, 1990).

Movements and migrations. This species is nonmigratory but dispersive, with movements associated with relative water availability during wet and dry seasons within Australia, and occasional long-distance movements that at times take single birds or entire flocks well beyond Australia (Marchant and Higgins, 1990).

Competition and predation. Probably some competition from cormorants and various herons or egrets occurs, but it has not been studied. Predators of chicks include Australian ravens (*Corvus coronoides*), and disturbance or destruction by dogs, cattle, and humans also sometimes occurs.

Foods and Foraging Behavior

Foods consumed. Little detailed information on foods exists, but fish eaten by adults or reportedly fed to young include mostly economically unimportant species such as carp (*Cyprinus*, Cyprinidae), perch (*Perca*, Percidae), goldfish (*Carassius*, Cyprinidae), *Leiopotherapon* (Tereponidae), gudgeon (*Gobio*), and whitebait (*Galaxias*). Additionally, tadpoles, various reptiles including small tortoises, crayfish (*Cherax*), shrimp (*Macrobrachium*), insects, and diverse other prey have been reported. These include rather unexpected items such as ducklings, young and adult silver gulls (*Larus novaehollandiae*), gray teal (*Anas gibberifrons*), and even some mammals, probably including small dogs (Marchant and Higgins, 1990). Vestjens (1977a) observed that the fish fed to young birds included items 60–247 millimeters in length and 17–320 grams in weight. One single regurgitation contained seven goldfish weighing 870 grams.

Foraging behavior. Foraging may occur throughout the day, or even during dark nights as well as moonlit nights. Feeding may be done individually, by the usual bill-thrusting technique of all white pelicans, or at times by simply scooping prey from shallow waters or near the surface while swimming or half-flying (figure 20). Occasionally this species has also been seen performing a kind of aerial surface-plunging from a meter or two above water, which is a rather surprising type of feeding for a pelican of such large size and is apparently unreported for any other pelican species except for the brown. Surface foraging is often performed cooperatively, in flocks reportedly sometimes as large as 1,900 individuals. As with the other cooperatively foraging species, fish are driven into shallows or confined areas by the birds swimming in loose lines, where they can be readily captured (Marchant and Higgins, 1990).

Social Behavior

Age of maturity and mating system. The age of maturity is not known but is probably three or four years. Seasonal monogamy exists, but there is no information on mate fidelity or nest site tenacity. The high incidence of courtship observed by Vestjens (1977a) about a month before breeding suggests that pair bonds last only a single season and must be renewed before the next breeding season.

Social displays and vocalizations. Unlike in the tree-nesting pelicans, nest-based territories are not used for male advertisement, but instead the reproductively active gather in groups near or at the general nesting area, performing a variety of displays while walking, swimming, or flying. These mobile displays include courtship walks, courtship swims, and courtship flights, which all involve a nuclear group of a female and two or more males; but several such groups may form larger aggregations that vary greatly in size. During courtship walks (figure 102E), males perform a strutting walk (figure 101I) with the head raised, the wings slightly raised, and the bill resting on the neck. A similar posture is assumed by males during courtship swims (figure 102D). Evidently birds of both sexes perform pouch rippling, but in a sexually dimorphic manner (figure 101H). This consists of a series of muscular waves moving anteriorly down the pouch, as the mandible is slightly opened and closed rapidly (about 3 times per second) producing a rattling sound in males but not in females. It probably corresponds to pouch flapping in eastern white pelicans. Pouch swinging (figure 101G) consists of lateral and pendulous head-swinging movements (1–2 per second) with the bill open and the lower mandible spread and the neck held straight and vertical. Typically at the start of a courtship walk a dominant male, followed in turn by several other males, would follow the leading female closely in strutting posture, performing pouch rippling and pouch swinging. Males additionally perform a series of progressively stronger aggressive displays toward one another. These include low-intensity threat-pointing, medium-intensity gaping, and high-intensity thrusting (figure 102A–C). Pouch rippling and pouch swinging as well as aggressive thrusting displays are also performed by males during courtship swims, but only during courtship walks do males perform "throwing and catching," during which they pick up items with the bill, toss them in the air, and catch them again. Courtship flights

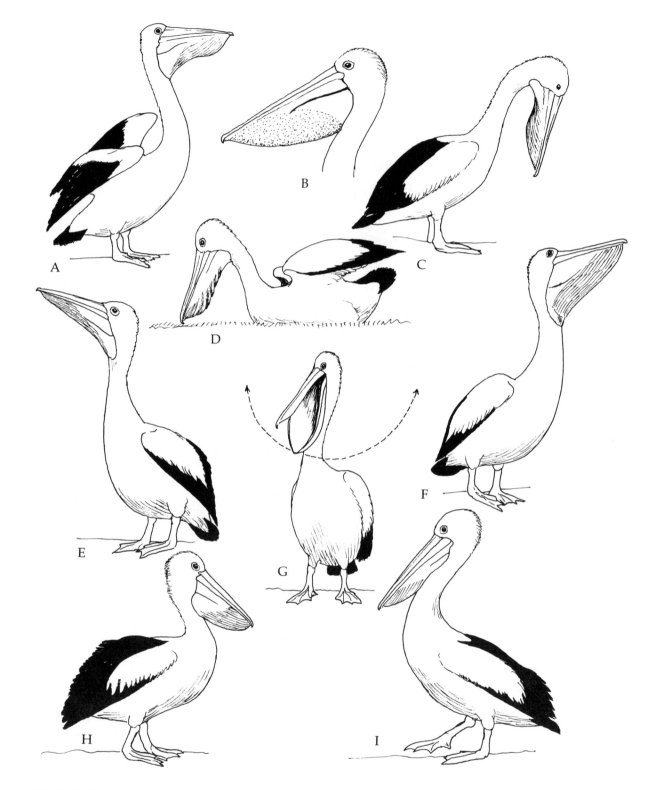

Figure 101. Social behavior of the Australian pelican, including alert posture (A), pouch pattern during courtship (B), bowing display (C), crouch-bowing (D), bill raising (E), head-up display (F), pouch swinging (G), pouch rippling (H), and strutting display (I). After sketches in Vestjens (1977a).

Figure 102. Social behavior of the Australian pelican, including threat-pointing (A), threat-gaping (B), aggressive thrusting (C), courtship swimming (D), and courtship-walking group (female in lead) (E). After sketches in Vestjens (1977a).

consist of generally circular flights by a pair around the nesting area, lasting up to eight minutes, and with the male closely behind the female. Upon landing the pair struts up to the nesting area and establishes a nest site (Vestjens, 1977a). There is a progressive reduction in the number of participating birds in the courtship walk, courtship swim, courtship flight sequence, as mates are chosen.

Individual recognition or greeting displays include the head-up, bowing, and the crouch-bow. The head-up (figure 101F) is performed when approaching the mate on the nest or the nest site. Bowing (figure 101C) is evidently performed in similar situations, but consists of a lowering rather than raising of the bill. The crouch-bow (figure 101D) consists of touching the ground with the breast and bill as the tail and folded wings are raised and the pouch is folded and sagging. The crouch-bow may be performed by males before copulation as the female sits on the nest. This display may be followed by the head-up and bowing, and finally by stepping on the back of the sitting female. After copulation the male may stand beside the female, who starts picking up nesting materials or scooping out a scrape. Males begin to collect nesting materials with their pouch after the second or third copulation (Vestjens, 1977a).

Adult vocalizations are quite limited, but include hoarse repetitive *orrrh* or *thuh* notes during the head-up, bill-raising, pouch-swinging, pointing, gaping, and thrusting displays, as well as during fighting. Other repetitive *uh* notes are uttered during greeting, and repeated soft *oh* sounds are produced at the nest when preening, turning eggs, or touching nestlings with the bill.

Reproductive Biology

Breeding season. Information on the breeding season suggests that it is mainly affected by the water conditions (flooding, drought, rainfall, water levels), and probably is little if at all influenced by the actual season of the year. However, most nest records seem to fall between March and December, albeit with great seasonal variation.

Nest sites and nest building. Colonies are often situated on islands, spits, or along the shorelines of generally sheltered waters. Colony locations are not strongly traditional, and areas may be abandoned for a time only to be recolonized later. Nests are placed on bare, level ground or in low vegetation, or even occasionally on bushes growing in water. The nests are often so close to water that they can be readily flooded if the water levels rise. Nests are often simple shallow depressions or hollows in the ground, with a variety of materials added later to line the site. When materials are plentiful, the nests tend to be large, but where they must be carried in the nests are often quite rudimentary. When the nests are located on bushes more materials are used, and the shrubs are trampled down to provide a flat platform. Both sexes collect materials, but the female gathers material only

from the actual site, whereas the male may bring in material from at least a kilometer away. Typically the male drops the material in front of the female who adds it to the nest, but sometimes the female takes the material from the male's bill, or rarely the male may add it to the nest himself. Nest materials continue to be added through incubation and the brooding period (Vestjens, 1977a; Marchant and Higgins, 1990).

Nests are often very closely spaced; in Vestjens's (1977a) colony nest centers averaged less than a meter apart, and occasionally touched one another. Nest building does not require much time; in that colony the first egg was laid only 2–3 days after a site was selected.

Egg laying and incubation. Eggs are laid at 2–4 day intervals, with a two-day interval probably typical. The usual clutch is of two eggs, but extremes of 1–4 have been reported. Incubation is performed by both sexes alternately, with males usually incubating in morning and females in the afternoon, over periods of 2–13 hours. Reliefs often occurred early in the morning, around noon, and again in the evening. No apparent changeovers occur at night. The incubation period is 32–35 days under natural conditions; one egg hatched under a hen in 32 days (Vestjens, 1977a).

Brooding and rearing of young. The chicks are hatched naked, but within a week are covered with short grayish white down. Very young chicks are fed from inside the parent's upper mandible near the tip (figure 33A). By then they may move out from under the brooding parent for short periods, but usually remain under its breast. At two weeks they may stand inside their parent's pouch to obtain food (figure 33C). At that time they are fed about three times a day, as compared with up to eight times for very young chicks. By the time they are 25 days old the chicks may be left alone at the nest for some time during the day. At this time they begin to leave the nest and form creches of up to 30 chicks, either inside or at the edge of the nesting area. The young remain in these creches until they are able to fly, and the creches move about to some degree. At two months of age the young are performing all the usual comfort activities seen in adults. As the chicks get older they leave the creche for periods to wade or swim, but return to it to rest and be fed. By the time they are three months old they are making their first efforts at flying, but are still being fed by their parents (Vestjens, 1977a).

Breeding success. In Vestjens's (1977a) study area eggs were laid in 144 nests, but only 42 nests (29 percent), containing 73 eggs, were still intact after walking displays (which often resulted in fights or egg losses) had ceased. Of these 73 eggs, 68 hatched (93 percent). Of 68 hatched eggs from ground nests, 49 chicks reached the creche stage, and 38 (56 percent) survived to flight. Of 104 chicks that hatched from nests on bushes, 86 reached the creche stage and 76 (73 percent) fledged. Egg mortality as well as chick mortality was lower on bush nests than on ground nests, as the nests on bushes were evidently less affected by disruption associated with courting groups. Most egg losses were the result of disturbance during these courtship walk displays, and most losses of chicks resulted from starvation of the second-hatched young.

Population Status

No information on population size exists, but this species is widespread and relatively common over much of Australia. Historically, colonies as large as 100,000 nests have been reported, and colonies with thousands of nests have been seen in South Australia as recently as the 1980s (Marchant and Higgins, 1990).

Evolutionary Relationships

Data from DNA-DNA hybridization by Sibley and Ahlquist (1985) suggest that this species may be the most isolated of the white pelican group, and it is also unique in its pattern of facial feathering. Additional information is obviously needed before any convincing phylogeny of the pelicans can be produced.

Nests (1980s)

• 1–100 ○ 100–500 ● 500–1000 ▽ 1000–1500 ▼ 1500–2000
◇ 2000–2500 ◆ 2500–3500 □ 3500–4500 ■ 4500–5000

Other Vernacular Names

Rough-billed pelican, white pelican; pélican à bec rouge, pélican blanc d'Amérique (French); Nashornpelikan (German); pelicano blanco (Spanish)

Distribution

Breeds in interior North America from northeastern British Columbia, Alberta, Saskatchewan, Manitoba, and southwestern Ontario south locally (through Oregon, Idaho, Montana, Wyoming, and North Dakota) to northern California, western Nevada, northern Utah, northeastern Colorado, southern South Dakota, and western Minnesota; also a frequent local breeding resident in central coastal Texas and adjoining coastal Tamaulipas, and breeds sporadically in Durango, Mexico. Has also bred occasionally in central to southern California, and formerly bred on Salton Sea. Winters interiorly and especially coastally from central California east through Texas and the Gulf states to Florida, and south throughout Baja California and along both coasts and the interior of northern Mexico, very rarely straying south to Guatemala, Costa Rica, Nicaragua, and Panama. Summer vagrants have also reached Alaska, Victoria Island, Hudson Bay, New Brunswick, and Nova Scotia. (See figure 103.)

Subspecies

None.

Description

Prebreeding adult. A variably shaped and elevated horny knob (about 50 mm high and at least as long) near the middle of the culmen; a thick yellowish crest of narrow feathers covering the occiput and nape, and a patch of feathers on the chest and lesser wing coverts lanceolate and also variably pale lemon-yellow (these traits all fully developed in adults during late spring and early summer only). The primaries,

---

Figure 103. Distribution of the American white pelican, including locations of active breeding colonies (arrows), abandoned or inactive colonies (crossed arrows), and its overall wintering range (stippled). Insets show locations of colonies in Alberta and Saskatchewan (lower left) and the Manitoba lake region (upper right).

their dorsal coverts, the alula, and the majority (ca. 18 of 33) of the secondaries all black; the more proximal secondaries increasingly margined on both webs with white, so that the inner secondaries are mostly to entirely white. Remainder of plumage pure white, including the rectrices (24). Iris dark brownish red; eyelids dull red; orbital skin red; naked facial skin orange and wrinkled; bill mostly orange to salmon, but paler yellow on the culmen, the nail and cutting edges of maxilla more reddish, and the mandible grading to deep red toward base; pouch yellow, grading to whitish in front and to deep orange or red basally; legs and feet orange-red, becoming bright red at peak of breeding.

Postbreeding and nonbreeding adult. Lacking the horny knob on the culmen, and the yellowish feathers on the chest and upper wing coverts. The horny knob is shed and the faded white to yellowish crest feathers are lost early in the nesting season. These nape feathers are replaced by shorter, gray feathers during the incubation and brooding season, which persist throughout the following period of sexual inactivity (Knopf, 1975). Iris bluish gray to brownish; bare facial skin, bill, and gular pouch bright yellow; legs and feet pale yellowish green to yellow. Bright yellow areas around the eyes and fleshy protuberances on the face persist through the breeding season but then are gradually lost.

Subadult (third year). The definitive plumage is present, including the yellow feathers of the breast and lesser wing coverts, and the bill knob is fully developed seasonally. The occipital crest may be white or very pale buff, with the middle of the occiput more or less brownish. At least in captivity, sexual maturity occurs at four years of age (Grummt, 1984).

Immature (second winter and spring). Similar to first-year birds, but the upper secondary coverts mostly white, with some brown, and with a mixture of white and dark gray feathers on the head and nape. A small bill knob, about half normal size, may develop seasonally in males but perhaps not in females at this age, judging from two captive birds. The specialized golden yellow lesser wing coverts, crest, and chest feathers are lacking. Lores bluish yellow, and lacking fleshy protuberances; pouch less brightly colored than in adults (Lingle, 1977).

Juvenile-immature transition (first winter and spring). Most of the dusky feathers of the juvenal plumage are lost by spring, and the birds are mostly white, with no ornamental head plumes or bill knob. A spring head molt occurs in first- and second-year immatures, during which short white (rather than gray, as in nesting adults) crest feathers emerge. The lesser and median secondary coverts are still mostly brown and juvenile-like, but with some white feathers present. Molt of the rectrices and remiges is essentially continuous and gradual in immature birds, with three molt cycles of the rectrices and two of the remiges apparently occurring during the first 30 months of life (Lingle, 1977). Iris brown; bill mostly vinaceous buff, but the culmen pinkish to orange-buff, and the nail dull orange; gular sac dull yellow; legs and feet yellow.

Juvenile. Plumage mostly dusky brownish, with a streaked dark crown; occipital feathers very short; primaries and secondaries slate-colored; all but the innermost secondaries fuscous; lesser wing coverts drab or light brown, with white edges and tips. Iris hazel to dark brown; bill, pouch, and facial skin gray; legs and feet dull yellow.

Nestling. Hatched naked, the skin bright flesh-colored. Covered with white down within a week of hatching; iris lead-gray, facial skin and bill blackish gray; pouch grayish pink; legs and feet pale yellow to pinkish.

Measurements (in millimeters)

Wing, males 575–630 (ave. of 9, 608.2), females 525–603 (ave. of 10, 558.5); tail, males 153–167 (ave. of 9, 159.7), females 135–166 (ave. of 10, 144.8); culmen, males 320–365 (ave. of 9, 342.3), females 265–320 (ave. of 10, 287.6) (Palmer, 1962). The mean culmen length of 26 adult males in another sample was 338.1, and that of 21 adult females was 299.4, with males typically distinguishable (95 percent probability) in having culmen lengths of at least 344.6, and females likewise separable as those with adult culmen lengths of no more than 284.1 (Lingle, 1977). Eggs ca. 87 × 56.

Weights (in kilograms)

Two males 3.51 and 5.0, two females 4.5 and ca. 3.63 (8 lb.) (Royal Ontario Museum specimens). Two males 6.818 and 8.0 (University of Kansas Natural History Museum specimens). One adult male ca. 7.15 (15.75 lb.) (Museum of Vertebrate Zoology specimen). One adult female ca. 5.9 (13 lb.) (U.S. National Museum specimen). Other single specimens, male ca. 6 (13.23 lb.), female ca. 5.32 (11.75 lb.) (Palmer, 1962). Grummt (1984) listed two captive males as weighing 7.2 and (ave. of two weights) 7.68, and two captive females as (averages of two weights each) 5.15 and 5.32. Marshall and Erickson (1945) reported two males as 5.98 and 4.384. Audubon (1840–44) reported that a male weighed ca. 7.9 (17.5 lb.). One immature male 5.117; 11 immature females 4.213–8.0 (ave. 5.474) (U.S. National Museum specimens). Averages of the preceding data are: 12 males, 6.228 (range 3.5–8.0), 17 females 5.296 (range 3.62–8.0). Range, sample size, and sexes unstated, ca. 4.36–4.77 (9.6–10.5 lb.) (Roberts, 1936). A few adult weights well in excess of 8 kg have been alleged but have apparently not been adequately documented, up to a maximum of about 13.6 (Behle, 1958; Palmer, 1962). Calculated egg weight 150.6 grams; ave. of 26, 154.2 (Evans, 1969).

Identification

In the hand. The combination of white rectrices, wings with black primaries and most of the secondaries also black, and the feather boundary of the forehead forming a concave line serves to identify this species.

In the field. This is the only species of white pelican in North America. In flight it shows the same general plumage pattern as do snow geese and whooping cranes (all white except for black wingtips), but pelicans have much slower, more ponderous wingbeats than do either of these, and also a long and conspicuous yellow bill and pouch. The birds often fly in loose formation, and while soaring among thermals frequently wheel about in large circles, acting much like soaring cranes.

Ecology and General Biology

Breeding and nonbreeding habitats. Diverse aquatic habitats are used by American white pelicans, ranging from slow-moving rivers to lakes, permanent or semipermanent marshes, and reservoirs among fresh-water sites, as well as coastal bays, estuaries, and, to a more limited degree, inshore marine habitats, but the birds rarely venture very far from shore. Breeding habitats typically consist of flat or nearly flat islands with little or no vegetation present, but rarely the birds may also use dry islands of tules (*Scirpus*) in large marshes (Bent, 1922), or even peninsulas of floating vegetation or shrub hummocks along shorelines (Knopf, 1974). Bare and relatively flat island, peninsula, or shoreline sites, often of sand or gravel, are used for loafing outside the breeding season. Smith, Steinbach, and Pampush (1984) noted that 68 percent of all loafing they observed occurred on islands, and most of the rest took place on peninsulas of some kind. Areas with fairly shallow open water (not much deeper than they can reach with their bill from the surface) are preferred for foraging in fresh-water sites, but the birds often forage along vegetated shorelines. Like other communal foragers, these birds often cooperatively drive their prey to shallow water where the fish can be more readily captured. Thus the pelicans would be prone to forage near shorelines under such circumstances, but might be more likely to use deeper waters when foraging individually.

Movements and migrations. Nearly all of the breeding colonies of American white pelicans are migratory, with the Texas coastal site the only significant exception. Important wintering areas in the eastern United States include the Gulf coast of Florida (especially Tampa Bay) and the Everglades area of southern Florida, and the Gulf coast from Louisiana west to the Mexican line, particularly southern Texas (especially Galveston Bay). Generally wintering occurs along coastline areas where the minimum January ambient temperature is above 40° F, with highest densities where the minimum January temperature is above 45° F and the average minimum winter temperature is above 50° F (Root, 1988). Wintering also occurs along the Caribbean coast (and also the Pacific coast) of Mexico a substantial distance south, but quantitative surveys for these regions are not available. Major sources of wintering birds along coastal Texas and Louisiana include the large Chase Lake, North Dakota, flock (Strait and Sloan, 1974) and several of the Saskatchewan colonies (Houston, 1972). Banded birds from the Chase Lake flock were recovered from as far away as El Salvador and Nicaragua, but most of those recovered from Mexico were obtained in Tamaulipas and Veracruz. A few birds from Saskatchewan were recovered on the Pacific coast of Mexico and El Salvador.

By comparison, birds breeding on the Molly Islands, Yellowstone National Park, primarily winter in southern California and along the Pacific coast of Mexico, although there is also some movement to the Gulf coast (Diem and Condon, 1967). Likewise, British Columbia birds from the Stum Lake colony migrate south to California and probably continue on to western Mexico (Vermeer, 1977), as also do birds from Nevada and Utah (Behle, 1958). The continental divide would thus seem to be a general dividing line between birds primarily wintering on the Pacific coast and those using the Gulf coast. In addition to these definite migration routes, considerable dispersal of young birds also occurs. Thus, young birds raised in Utah tend to fly northward into Idaho before eventually moving southward for the winter.

Competition and predation.   Probably relatively little competition occurs between the brown pelican and this species, considering their very differing foraging behaviors and generally nonoverlapping distributions. However, double-crested cormorants and American white pelicans often nest in mixed colonies, and probably overlap to some degree in foods taken, albeit by very different means. In an area of common occurrence at Pyramid Lake (Anaho Island National Wildlife Refuge), Nevada, Knopf and Kennedy (1981) found that the lengths of tui chubs (*Gila bicolor*, Cyprinidae) obtained as regurgitates from chicks differed significantly, with those from double-crested cormorants substantially larger. Apparently the pelicans took the smaller and readily available fish near the surface, whereas the cormorants obtained generally larger prey by diving. Additionally, all of the fish obtained from the cormorants were of this species, but chubs represented only 39.5 percent (by weight) of the 344 fish obtained from pelican chicks. Instead carp (*Cyprinus carpio*, Cyprinidae) represented 54 percent of the total pelican food by weight, which was obtained by flying to outlying wetlands that were evidently beyond the foraging range of the cormorants.

Significant mortality to eggs and newly hatched chicks is sometimes caused by California gulls (*Larus californicus*) (Schaller, 1964; Smith, Steinbach, and Pampush, 1984). Probably other gull species as well as large corvids and mammalian predators may have locally important effects,

especially where human disturbance is frequent. However, in a survey of mortality factors at 12 breeding colonies or concentration areas, gull predation was listed as a significant factor at only one (Bowdoin National Wildlife Refuge, Montana), and mammalian predation at two, whereas human disturbance was listed at four and shooting at five sites. Predation by coyotes (*Canis latrans*) is a significant factor influencing productivity at Stum Lake, British Columbia (Dunbar 1984).

Foods and Foraging Behavior

Foods consumed.   A very large amount of qualitative information has accumulated on the foods of this species, much of which was summarized by Palmer (1962). Palmer concluded that the foods were almost entirely comprised of "rough fish of little market value," especially carp, chub (*Siphalteles*, Cyprinidae), and suckers (*Catostomus* and *Chamistes*, Catostomidae). The only exception to these was at Yellowstone Lake, where nearly all the diet is of trout and no other prey fish are available. More recently Lingle (1977) reviewed the food prey from six locations, representing five areas of the breeding range (Nevada, North Dakota, Utah, Wyoming, and Canada) and a wintering area (Salton Sea, California). Of these, carp was listed as a food in four areas, suckers in three areas, chubs and cyprinid minnows (*Siphalteles*, *Leuciscus*, and *Gila*) in three areas, and cutthroat trout (*Salmo clarkii*, Salmonidae) in two areas. In his own study area (Chase Lake, North Dakota) adult and larval tiger salamanders (*Ambystoma tigrinum*) were the most important foods given to chicks during two seasons, comprising a majority by estimated total volume (60–64 percent) during both seasons. The other prey consisted of fish, of which black bullheads (*Ictalurus melas*, Ictaluridae) were the most important single species by volume (13.5–13.6 percent) in both years. He estimated that adults averaged 0.6 kilograms of food intake per day, as compared with 1.4 kilograms per day for chicks.

In a study of 245 fish regurgitated by juvenile birds at Clear Lake, Klamath Basin, California (Smith, Steinbach, and Pampush, 1984), 71 percent of the prey items and 80 percent of the total prey mass were represented by largemouth bass (*Micropterus salmoides*, Centrarchidae), with bluegill (*Lepomis macrochirus*, Centrarchidae) making up most of the remainder. The average individual weight was 35 grams for all prey fish. The bass ranged from 4 to 24 centimeters long, with a modal peak at 5 centimeters and a mean weight of 25 grams. The *Lepomis* prey ranged from 4 to 15 centimeters long, with a modal peak at 5 centimeters and a mean weight of 55 grams. However, although chubs were rarely caught by pelicans in the 1983 studies (a year of unusually high water levels) they were the most abundant fish in this immediate area, judging from gill net samples. Evidently there were no shallow areas of concentrated chub spawning that might attract the pelicans. In 1982, however, both at Clear Lake and Lower

Klamath Lake the most common prey fish regurgitated by pelicans were chubs, and in that year birds in the Clear Lake colony evidently foraged mostly within the Klamath Basin. The two major prey species in 1983 were scarcely encountered in Klamath Basin gill net samples, and were evidently obtained by foraging flights elsewhere in the region. In the Harney Basin to the north in Oregon, regurgitation of carp by pelicans was frequently observed, and there carp accounted for 86 percent of the fish sampled in gill nets.

Foraging behavior.   As in most pelicans, this species' foraging tends to be concentrated during early morning and late afternoon or evening hours (Palmer, 1962). Smith, Steinbach, and Pampush (1984) estimated that 75 percent of the pelicans in their area were feeding during morning hours (8–11 A.M.), as compared with 61 percent later in the day (11 A.M.–7 P.M.). A disproportionately high amount of foraging occurred at the mouths of tributaries, and foraging was also concentrated along shorelines, and along canals, ditches, and ponds. In deeper water foraging sometimes occurred far from shore, often by single birds or small groups. Lakes with a combination of high turbidity, rocky shoreline bottoms, and considerable depth received little use.

Relatively long foraging flights have been documented by many observers for this species. Behle (1958) reported one-way foraging flights of up to 160 kilometers at Great Salt Lake, and Low, Kay, and Rasmussen (1950) estimated round trips of up to 240 kilometers. Knopf and Kennedy (1980) reported foraging at sites up to 100 kilometers from the Nevada breeding area. Johnson (1976) estimated round-trip flights of 96–611 kilometers for birds at Chase Lake, North Dakota, based on recoveries of fish tags. Apparent foraging flights between Harney and Warner basins, a one-way distance of 147 kilometers, have been observed, as have foraging flights of 40 kilometers that required an elevation gain of 600 meters (Smith, Steinbach, and Pampush, 1984).

Social Behavior

Age of maturity and mating system.   This species is generally believed to breed in the wild at three years of age (Lingle, 1977), but hard evidence is seemingly lacking. Courtship and copulations have been observed among two-year-olds, and a two-year-old has also been observed feeding a nestling (Miller, 1977). Two females hatched in the wild but raised in captivity bred for the first time at four years (Grummt, 1984). There is no evidence of mate renewal in subsequent years among wild birds. Nest locations and indeed colony locations are quite flexible in this species, which greatly reduces the probabilities of two birds remaining together in successive breeding seasons.

Social displays and vocalizations.   The only available detailed studies of this species' social behavior are those of Schaller (1964) and Knopf (1979). In Schaller's study area courting parties of 4–20 birds formed before nesting began and milled about the nesting island. Four displays were performed by these birds. The first was a head-up posture (see figure 29), with the bill raised above the horizontal, the neck stretched, and the colorful pouch extended or inflated and made more conspicuous by lateral head-turning movements. Up to five birds would respond to this display by assuming similar attitudes toward one another, suggesting a possible hostile basis for this signal. However, the head-up is also performed between pair members during nest relief, before and after copulation, and as a greeting ceremony when two birds meet another. The bow (figure 104B, C) is performed in conjunction with slow lateral head waving, and Schaller believed that it may function as an appeasement gesture. This display, called reach-bowing by van Tets (1965), is somewhat sexually dimorphic, with the female bowing lower than the male. Occasionally a male and female would break away from larger courting groups and perform a "strutting walk," with the male closely following the female and both birds walking with the neck arched backward, the occipital crest feathers pointing upward, and the bill titled downward and resting on the chest. Occasionally apparent males performed the strutting walk alone.

Knopf (1979) noted that when a new bird entered a courtship group it was jabbed at and received jabs from other birds. When jabbed at, a female would perform a bow, to which the nearest male would respond by moving alongside, expanding his pouch, extending his neck over her head, and moving his head back and forth, displaying his pouch while simultaneously grunting. This elicited jabbing from other birds, and both the male and female would then jab back. The male would then typically follow the female and respond to her bowing as before. If he did not keep up with her, a new male would respond to her bowing display. Sometimes a pair would leave a larger courtship group and walk about in a strutting walk, which would at times be joined by others, creating a new courting party.

The last display observed by Schaller was a courtship flight involving as many as 14 birds, which would circle the rookery in a compact flock. After landing they resumed performing the head-up and bow displays. Besides their presumed role in pair bonding, it is possible that prenesting flights of adult birds over their nesting colonies may also serve to attract other pelicans to active colonies, and thereby facilitate synchronous breeding aggregations (Evans and Cash, 1985). Knopf (1979) stated that courting flights involved a female, her associated male, and any other bachelor males. During such flights the male would remain close to the female and frequently expand his pouch (figure 104D). Knopf occasionally saw birds perform raptorlike stoops from such flights, but judged that they were probably not essential components of courtship. Bachelor males would usually abandon the courtship flight during the flight or shortly after returning to the ground. It is possible that a

Figure 104. Social behavior of the American white pelican, including gaping threat (A), reach-bowing by male (B), reach-bowing by female (C), and pouch expansion in flight (D), as compared with normal pouch appearance (E). Mostly after sketches in van Tets (1965).

"rumbling" call is uttered by birds prior to landing, but prelanding calls are generally lacking in pelicans, and this needs to be confirmed.

Aggressive displays consist of a graded array of postures and movements, ranging from a slight head jerking in the direction of the other bird, to pointing the bill at the offender with a raised head and nonextended pouch, to bill-clapping, single jabbing, and bill-snapping movements, and finally to direct jabs at the head of the other individual (Schaller, 1964).

Paired birds strut-walk rapidly, with the male sometimes jabbing at the back of the female's head, making her walk even faster. Strutting terminates with the female bowing, and bowing by females also occurs when the pair is close to a dense aggregation of pelicans. Nest relief consists of the head-up and bow display (see figure 29), which are performed by both birds in no definite sequence, and frequently with accompanying *ho-ho-ho* notes. This display may begin when the birds are as far as about 6 meters from one another. Nest relief ceremonies in one study lasted an average of 8.4 minutes, but with great variation and occasional substantial prolongation because the relieved bird refused to leave the nest (Schaller, 1964).

Copulation behavior begins during the courtship phase, and thus is not limited to the nest site. On eight occasions Schaller saw females in courtship parties assume receptive positions. On five occasions this elicited no response, but twice a male tried to climb on the female's back, and once he grabbed the female's neck. During actual copulation the male holds the female's neck or bill with his bill, beats his wings, and both sexes utter loud grunts. Only two of six observed copulation attempts appeared to be completed.

Reproductive Biology

Breeding season.   The breeding season is quite varied over this species' broad breeding range. Along the Gulf coast of Texas eggs have been reported from as early as May 3 to July 14 (Oberholser, 1974). In Utah laying usually occurs in May and June (Behle, 1958), but Knopf (1979) estimated that in 1973 and 1974 most egg laying occurred in late April and early May, with only a few nests initiated as late as the end of June.

Nest sites and nest building.   The newly paired male and female remain at their chosen nest site or in the vicinity of the nesting colony for 3–5 days after their initial defense of the nest site. Choosing a site evidently involves the pair defending their chosen position from repeated jabbings by established birds already on nests or flocks of birds that have not yet begun nests. After 30–60 minutes of repeated jabbings and bowings, the rate of jabbing declines and a site is apparently attained. Once a site has been successfully defended, mounting of the female by the male might occur. However, paired birds may continue to join the general precolony flock for about seven days. Such flocks are occasionally located near nesting groups, resulting in peripheral nest additions to the colony (Knopf, 1979).

The nest is usually a simple scrape made by constructing a low mound in sandy areas, with a central depression. The bird typically sits on the site and hauls in material with the bill from all directions. Both sexes build in this manner, and occasionally eggs are simply laid on the ground without any mound construction. Materials are added to the nest as long as it is in use (Schaller, 1964).

Egg laying and incubation.   Eggs are laid at an average rate of one per two or, less commonly, three days (Grummt, 1984). The usual clutch is certainly of two eggs, and Dunbar (1984) reported a mean clutch size of 1.94 eggs for those years during which little colony disturbance occurred. However, a considerable number of eggs tend to roll out of the nests and are lost, or may be stolen by egg predators, resulting in a lower mean clutch size. Thus, Schaller (1964) reported a mean clutch of 1.67 eggs for 212 nests, with 141 of the nests containing two eggs. The number of clutches containing either a single egg or more than two eggs gradually increases through the incubation period, as eggs roll from nests. These extra eggs are sometimes retrieved by nearby nesting birds that are already incubating two eggs, thereby increasing their clutches to three or sometimes even to as many as five eggs (Knopf, 1979). However, since the birds incubate their eggs by placing one under each foot, incubation of three eggs becomes almost impossible, and all of 22 nests with three or more eggs that were observed by Knopf during two breeding seasons had complete nest failures as a result of addled eggs.

Incubation begins with the first egg, so that the chicks hatch asynchronously, at average intervals of 2.5 days (Cash and Evans, 1986). The average incubation period of 13 eggs has been reported as 31.5 days (Knopf, 1976b). Nest relief occurs usually between midmorning and midafternoon, approximately once every two days, and in nine cases documented successive reliefs averaged 54 hours apart (Schaller, 1964).

Brooding and rearing of young.   During the first day after hatching the chicks are naked and barely able to raise their heads. Small young are fed four times a day, but the feeding frequency declines as the chicks grow larger. By six days they are peering out from beneath the parent and are squab-sized. At ten days the chick is able to sit up on its tarsi, and at 16–17 days it is preening, wing-stretching, and able to crawl a short distance. At 20 days it begins to walk, and may start to sleep with the bill tucked in along the back. By this age brooding becomes intermittent during the daylight hours, and at three weeks the young begin to form pods of 2–6 birds. These pods gradually increase in size until all the young of the colony are part of a single large pod by about 50 days of age. Recognition between adults and young is mutual and is probably based primarily if not exclusively on visual clues. Primaries begin to erupt after about four weeks, and adultlike swimming begins at about eight weeks, when the young are two-thirds adult size. Fledging occurs at between 62 and 71 days (Schaller, 1964).

Brood reduction mechanisms evidently exist in this species, so that in most cases only a single chick survives. Among marked broods, the second-hatched chick survived in only 20 percent of the successful nests studied by Cash and Evans (1986). They found that in manipulated clutch sizes (1–3 eggs) the hatching success did not vary with clutch size, but that two-egg clutches had the largest number of young per brood (0.7 young) surviving to about 18 days, and also yielded the highest percentage of broods successfully raised to creche stage (88.2 percent). The second-hatched chick thus contributes significantly to the reproductive success of the parents, supporting the idea that the second egg provides a kind of "insurance" against early loss of the first egg or chick. Selective feeding by the parents of the stronger and more dominant chick probably maximizes the probability of their raising the more viable youngster.

Breeding success. Knopf (1976b, 1979) reported that, of the total eggs laid each season in his Utah study area, there was an approximate 70 percent mortality of eggs or chicks. This mortality included a 29 percent loss from chicks dying from starvation or harassment, a 25 percent loss due to nest abandonment, a 9 percent loss due to eggs rolling from nests, and 6–7 percent loss from miscellaneous causes. The mean productivity per clutch (collectively averaging 0.85 fledged young per nest in 1,323 nests) was comparable between colonies of differing sizes and in different nesting habitats, but the incidence of egg and chick mortality increased as the breeding season progressed. Chicks that were lost usually died during their first three weeks after hatching. Furthermore, during both years of study, one of the two chicks died as a nestling in 90 percent of the nests where both chicks successfully hatched. Similarly, Johnson and Sloan (1978) noted that in more than 9 percent of the nests they observed, the smaller nestling died as a result of physical abuse by the older chick.

Sloan (1973) summarized breeding success data from six major nesting colonies during 1971 and 1972, and reported annual fledging rates of 0.45–1.22 young per nest. The lower fledging rates (0.45–0.83 young per nest at the time of leaving the nest) appeared to be associated with the two smaller colonies (Sand Lake, South Dakota, and South Bird Island, Texas) having less than 600 adults, whereas the four larger colonies (with 1,750–6,000 adults) had fledging rates of 0.86–1.22 young per nest. Later, Johnson and Sloan (1978) summarized productivity figures for nine North American pelican colonies, and reported productivity (young "fledged" per nest) rates of 0.39–1.23 young per nest. Again, lower productivity rates seemed to be associated with smaller colonies or small nest samples (0.21–0.45 young for colonies up to 300 nests, vs. 0.99–1.23 young for colonies or samples of at least 900 nests). However, the authors noted that high productivity rates seem to be associated with quick visual estimates, whereas actual counts of nests and young result in smaller production statistics. They determined that the actual productivity of a sample of 21 nests at Chase Lake, North Dakota, in 1974 was 0.21 young per nest, but the overall estimated productivity at Chase Lake that year (3,082 nests) was about 0.39 young per nest. During 1973 and 1974 nest abandonment was a serious problem at Chase Lake, with annual nest losses estimated at 31 percent and 75 percent. Even higher estimated nest losses occurred at other North Dakota colonies, which were believed possibly related to relative food availability. There is so far little or no evidence that significant renesting occurs in this species following clutch loss, and nest abandonment rates tend to increase later in the nesting season (Schaller, 1964; Knopf, 1979). In Knopf's study area about a quarter of the nests were abandoned each season (22 percent in 1973, 29 percent in 1974), and annual differences in nest abandonment rates were the primary factor influencing annual productivity rate differences. On Stum Lake, British Columbia, predation by coyotes (*Canis latrans*) as well as human disturbance during nesting have had major effects on annual productivity (Dunbar, 1984).

Population Status

Recent population estimates for this species in the United States and Canada have been summarized in chapter 7 (see table 33). Additionally, about 10 pairs sporadically breed at Laguna de Santiguillo, Durango, Mexico, and another colony of 100–500 birds sometimes breeds in the Laguna Madre de Tamaulipas, Tamaulipas, Mexico (Chapman, 1988). Better population data exist for this species than for almost any other North American pelecaniform bird, because of the limited number of breeding colonies and the relative ease with which the birds can be counted. Although some colonies have disappeared or been diminished in recent years, others have been reestablished or newly established, as in Wyoming (Findholt and Diem, 1988) and in the Malheur basin of Oregon (Paullin, Ivey, and Littlefield, 1988). About 1,500 pairs nested at Malheur National Wildlife Refuge in 1988, only three years after the birds recolonized that refuge (Littlefield, 1990). Breeding now also occurs at Minidoka National Wildlife Refuge, Idaho, where 90 young were fledged in 1990. First-time nestings also occurred on Canyon Ferry Reservoir, Montana, and Antero Reservoir, Colorado, in 1990 (*American Birds* 44:1159, 1161). There have been great fluctuations in productivity at Anaho Island (Pyramid Lake), Nevada, in recent years (*American Birds* 41:1467; 42:1321; 43:1346). Fluctuating levels of Great Salt Lake, Utah, have impacted the colony nesting on Gunnison Island, mainly by reducing populations of saline-sensitive fish prey. That colony reached a peak population of 16,000 breeding adults in 1988 (as compared to an average of about 3,000–6,000 during the past 50–75 years), with an estimated 8,536 nests and 5,890 fledged young. Since then the breeding population has dropped some (5,802 nests in 1990, and 4,003 young fledged) (Don Paul, personal communication). During the 1970s as few as 129 pairs were present along the Texas coast (Texas Colonial Waterbird Society, 1982), but generally the breeding population there has varied from 200 to 500 nests from 1907 to the late 1980s (Chapman, 1988). However, the general trend of populations in North America has been distinctly upward since the era of inadequate colony protection and hard pesticides ended in the early 1970s.

Evolutionary Relationships

Sibley and Ahlquist (1985) judged from DNA-DNA hybridization data that this species and the pink-backed pelican are close relatives, although no confirmatory data supporting that point exists to my knowledge. In most aspects of their biology the American white and eastern white pelicans appear to be very similar, although additional data are needed before that position can be readily supported.

Other Vernacular Names

Eastern brown pelican (*carolinensis*), California brown pelican (*californicus*), Chilean pelican (*thagus*), Molina's pelican (*thagus*), Peruvian pelican (*thagus*), West Indian brown pelican (*carolinensis*); pélican brun (French); brauner Pelikan, Meerpelikan (German); alcatraz, pelecano moreno (Spanish)

Distribution

Resident in North America, breeding locally on the Atlantic coast from Maryland south to Florida, thence west along the Gulf coast to Texas, and along the Pacific coast of southern California south through Baja California; also locally along the Pacific and Caribbean coasts of Mexico and Central America to South America, where breeding occurs along the Caribbean coast from Colombia east to the southern Lesser Antilles, and (when *thagus* is considered conspecific) south along the Pacific coast to near Valparaiso, Chile. Also resident throughout most of the West Indies, including the Greater and Lesser Antilles, and on the Galapagos Islands. (See figure 105.)

Subspecies

P. o. occidentalis Linnaeus. Breeds widely in the West Indies, including Cuba (possibly also the Isle of Pines), the southern Bahamas (Great Inagua, Caicos), Jamaica, Hispaniola, Puerto Rico, the northern Lesser Antilles (St. Thomas and St. Croix east to Barbuda), the Colombian coastal Caribbean islands, and the islands off Venezuela (from Aruba and Los Roques east locally to Isla Margarita, Trinidad, and Tobago).

P. o. carolinensis Gmelin 1789. Previously bred coastally from North Carolina to Texas; now breeds locally in Maryland and Virginia, and very extensively in Florida; also breeds locally in Louisiana (where successfully reintroduced after extirpation), and in central coastal Texas; previously also resident in the northern Bahamas. Also breeds locally off northeastern Yucatan and Belize, and ranges southward through coastal Honduras (Bay of Fonseca) and Costa Rica (Guayabo and Bolaños) to Panama, where local breeding occurs off the Pacific coast (Coiba, Taboga, and Pearl Islands). Vagrants wander north to New England, and casually occur inland to the Great Lakes and Great Plains states.

P. o. californicus Ridgway 1884. Breeds off southern California (now limited to Anacapa Island), and on islands off Baja California and in the Gulf of California (south to Isabella and the Tres Marias Islands); also possibly breeds locally along the coast of Sonora and Sinaloa. Vagrants have occurred north to British Columbia and Idaho.

P. o. murphyi Wetmore 1945. Resident along the Pacific coast of northwestern South America, breeding on islands from northern Colombia (Octavia Rocks, Bahia de Málaga, Gorgonilla Island), and southward through southern Ecuador (Los Ríos, Guayas, and El Oro provinces) to Talara, Peru.

P. o. urinator Wetmore 1945. Endemic to the Galapagos Islands, where resident on all the central islands as well as on Hood (Española) and Bindloe (Marchena) islands.

P. (o.) thagus Molina 1782. Breeds on offshore islands along the Pacific coast of South America from Peru south to central Chile (Concon Island near Valparaiso); nonbreeders casually ranging to Chiloé Island and rarely beyond. Usually treated as a race of *occidentalis* (Wetmore, 1945; Blake, 1977; Dorst and Mougin, 1979), but considered by some to be an allospecies, based on its larger size, streaked underparts, distinctive facial skin and bill colors, and well-developed crest (Sibley and Monroe, 1990; Frank S. Todd, personal communication).

Description

Prebreeding adult. Crown, anterior occipital crest, sides of head, and lateral neck feathers bordering the gular pouch white; most or all of the head and anterior crest tinted with deep golden yellow; a V-shaped or diamond-shaped patch of bright golden yellow plumes also present at the base of the foreneck in most races; posterior occipital crest (longest in *thagus*), nape, rest of hindneck, and lower foreneck dark velvety brown, the feathers of the nape forming a short mane; upperparts otherwise pale ashy or silvery gray, the feathers of the back, rump, lesser and median wing coverts, and scapulars mostly elongated and edged with blackish brown, producing a striped silvery and brown appearance; primaries black; secondaries (27–33) and rectrices (usually 22, extremes 19–24) mostly ashy; rest of underparts smoky brown; the sides of the breast and flanks with narrow whitish shaft streaks (the shaft streaks extending to the abdomen in *thagus*). Softpart colors highly variable geographically and also with age and season (see color plates in Forbes, 1914, and in Schreiber et al., 1989). Iris straw-white to light sky-blue (but reportedly yellow in females and grayish in males of *thagus*); eye ring pink (in North America) to carmine (in *thagus*); facial skin in front of eyes individually or seasonally variable and variously lavender-blue, purple, or blackish (the upper lores and fleshy base of bill black and strongly carunculated in *thagus*, especially males); bill color highly variable, the maxilla typically pearl-gray to grayish green basally (but bright yellowish orange in *thagus*), variously grading into or spotted irregularly with brighter yellow, orange, or carmine

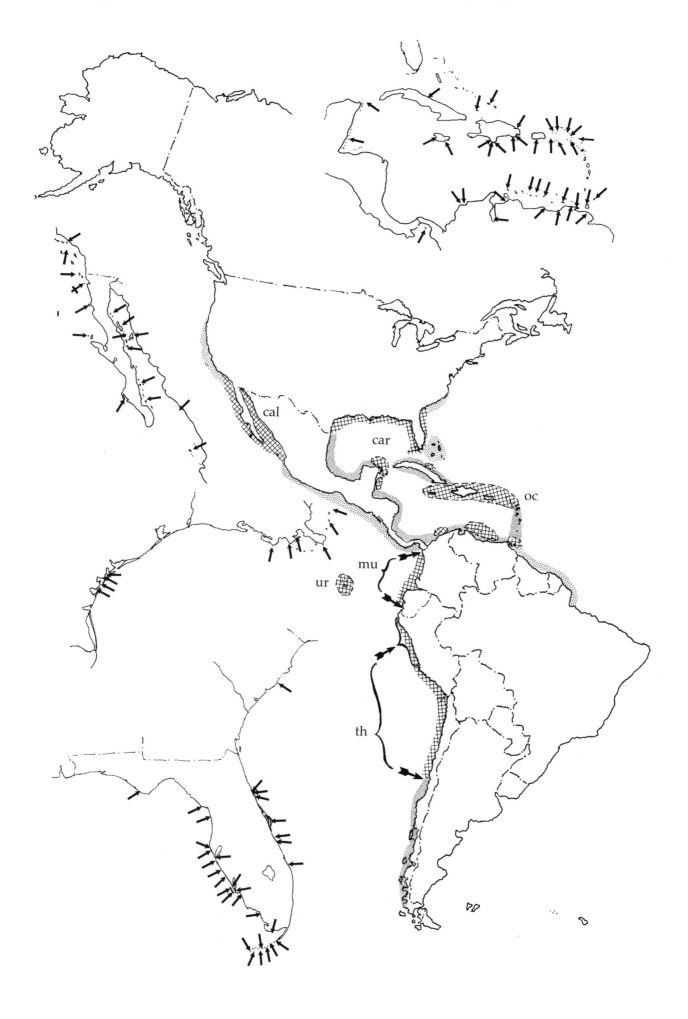

(these colors generally brighter in Pacific coast populations, and in all populations brightest during courtship); dorsal tip of maxilla and sides of mandible usually gray to blackish blue with yellow to red spotting or mottling (but the mandible entirely orange-yellow to red in *thagus*); nail bright buffy yellow; pouch color also highly variable, ranging from uniformly metallic greenish black, olive-brown, or blackish (in *carolinensis* and *occidentalis*) to bluish black, striped or patterned ventrally with bright poppy-red (in *californicus*), or blackish gray with numerous lavender-blue stripes parallel to the bill (in *thagus*); legs and feet black (in most races) to lavender-gray (in *thagus*).

Postbreeding adult. Similar to the prebreeding adult, but the softpart colors less intense, and the sides and back of the neck pure white to creamy white, the hindneck and crest gradually (through molt) becoming darker brown and with increasing tones of yellow evident on the face and crown toward the end of the postbreeding period. The silver-striped upperparts and wing coverts become faded and frayed after breeding so as to produce a more uniform dorsal appearance. The underparts are mostly black, but many of the newly molted feathers are tipped and striped with white or pale gray. The long golden forehead and crown feathers are lost soon after egg laying, and are replaced initially by white and later (in a supplemental molt during the nestling period) by a salt-and-pepper mixture of dark and white feathers. The generally faded patch of golden breast feathers is held through the fall, when it is replaced. In postbreeding North American birds the iris gradually changes from dark gray or brown (late summer) to light blue (in winter), the pinkish eye ring and adjoining darker facial skin become uniformly dull bluish black or dark green, and the legs and feet fade to dark gray. The bill becomes mottled gray basally, grading to dull orange toward the tip (and developing a yellow spot on the proximal mandible during the nestling phase, at least in some populations), and the blackish pouch becomes dark grayish green (but in western North America the red portion of the pouch dulls to yellowish gray). Brooding adults of *thagus* apparently have changes in the head and neck plumage fairly comparable to those of North America, but

Figure 105. Distribution of the brown pelican, including its breeding (cross hatching) and nonbreeding or wintering (stippling) ranges. Distributions of its races *californicus* (cal), *carolinensis* (car), *murphyi* (mu), *occidentalis* (oc), *thagus* (th), and *urinator* (ur) are indicated. Small arrows in inset maps represent locations of breeding colonies; crossed arrow indicates an abandoned colony. The larger arrows delimit approximate breeding ranges of Neotropic subspecies; the southern nesting limit of *thagus* is uncertain.

these plumage and associated softpart color changes are still unstudied in detail (Schreiber et al., 1989). Furthermore, plumage sequences and softpart colors of *murphyi* and *urinator* are still completely undescribed, but are unlikely to differ much from those of other South American populations.

Subadult (2–3 years). With increasing age the top of the head and the feathers surrounding the pouch become mostly white, the underparts become progressively mixed with grayish brown feathers, and the dorsal feathering becomes increasingly streaked with silvery gray. Two-year-old birds resemble adults, but may still have varying amounts of white mottling on the dark underparts, and have generally darker and duller upperparts, the crown and hindneck feathers still entirely brown or heavily mottled with brown. The definitive plumage probably is reached after the bird is about 36 months of age, although sexual maturity and breeding may sometimes occur before the definitive plumage is attained, especially in females. During the second to third year the bill becomes increasingly pale yellow and finally turns orange, the iris color lightens, the eye ring becomes pale blue and then pinkish, and the pouch may become increasingly tinted with reddish (at least in *californicus*) (Schreiber et al., 1989). At least in captivity, initial breeding and the definitive plumage occur at three years of age (Grummt, 1984).

Immature (1–2 years). Year-old birds are entirely brown on the head and neck, retaining most or all of the juvenal plumage, and have white underparts, sometimes with scattered brownish feathers, and may have a scattering of striped silvery gray feathers dorsally. Molt of the juvenal remiges begins at 12–14 months; by 18 months most primaries are new and the rectrices are probably already being replaced for a second time, the tail feathers apparently being in more or less continuous molt between 8 and 16 months (Schreiber et al., 1989).

Juvenile (first year). Head and neck medium brown to pale brown around the auriculars, the upperparts generally dull grayish brown, each brown feather with paler edges and tipped or edged with rufous to pale buff, but lacking any white streaking; remiges and rectrices more brownish than in adults; underparts from the breast backward dull white, including the under wing coverts, but with a grayish brown wash on the flanks. The feathers of the flanks, wing coverts, and most upperparts relatively wide and rounded, rather than narrow and pointed as in adults. Iris yellowish brown to dark brown; orbital skin dusky bluish; bill gray to grayish blue, edged or tinged with grayish yellow and with a darker tip (more orange, with a greenish base and dorsal ridge in *thagus*); pouch dull grayish blue (orange-yellow in *thagus*); legs and feet dull lead-colored.

Nestling. Naked and dull pink or grayish in color until 3–5 days; the skin turning dull gray, purplish, and finally blackish by 9 days, and a coat of white down developing by about the tenth day. Contour feathers first appear at 30 days, and some down persists until about 70 days. Iris dark brownish black; facial skin and bare crown gray; bill and pouch pale gray initially, later becoming black; legs and feet grayish white to yellowish.

Measurements (in millimeters)

There are marked, possibly clinal geographic size variations, with *occidentalis* averaging the smallest and *thagus* the largest. Total overall extremes of measurements for the species (104 males, 87 females): wing, males 461–625, females 448–606; tail, males 114–177, females 114–174; culmen, males 255–425, females 251–390 (Wetmore, 1945). Average measurements of all races, arranged in an approximate increasing size gradient, are as follows:

occidentalis (16 males, 14 females): wing, males 478, females 462; tail, males 126, females 124; culmen, males 288, females 261.

murphyi (11 males, 8 females): wing, males 513, females 485; tail, males 135, females 139; culmen, males 328, females 293.

carolinensis (28 males, 23 females): wing, males 526, females 501; tail, males 136, females 136; culmen, males 319, females 294.

californicus (34 males, 23 females): wing, males 551, females 519; tail, males 154, females 151; culmen, males 347, females 312.

urinator (9 males, 5 females): wing, males 561, females 527; tail, males 140, females 137; culmen, males 361, females 329.

thagus (6 males, 14 females): wing, males 606, females 576; tail, males 152, females 146; culmen, males 397, females 354.

Eggs, of *thagus* ca. 82 × 56; of northern races ca. 75 × 50.

Weights (in kilograms)

Florida *carolinensis*, adult males 2.38–4.04 (ave. of 13, 3.29), immature males 1.95–4.24 (ave. of 12, 2.628), adult females 1.83–3.99 (ave. of 13, 2.824), immature females 1.4–3.8 (ave. of 16, 2.316) (Schreiber et al., 1989). Averages of *carolinensis* from Florida, 53 males, 3.636; 42 females, 3.148 (Hartman, 1955). Males (number unspecified) of *occidentalis* from Suriname, 2.16–3.0 (Haverschmidt, 1968). Adults and subadults of *californicus*, males 2.806–9.75 (ave. of 5, 5.044), females 2.721–4.623 (ave. of 5, 3.769) (Museum of Vertebrate Zoology specimens). Captive females of *thagus*, 4.7, 4.9, and (ave. of two weights) 5.5 (Grummt, 1984); a wild female 3.316 (U.S. National Museum specimens). Male weights of *thagus* are not available, but perhaps exceed the maximum weight reported above for *californicus*, which was of a "very fat" specimen. Calculated egg weights (in grams), of *thagus* 141.9, of other races 103; average of 9 *thagus*, 133.6 (Grummt, 1984), of 21 *californicus*, 110.3 (Hanna, 1924).

Identification

In the hand.   The generally overall grayish brown to brownish black plumage, including the rectrices and all the flight feathers, and the large blackish pouch that extends about halfway down the neck, readily identify this distinctive species of pelican.

In the field.   This is the only pelican with a predominantly brownish plumage and a mostly black pouch, and the only species of pelican regularly occurring south of Guatemala. It is limited to coastal habitats, and is the only pelican that regularly plunge-dives for food. The birds frequently fly in loose linear formation low over the surf, often only a few feet above the crests of the waves, with leisurely wingbeats averaging about 2–2.5 per second, and with airspeeds averaging 25–30 miles per hour.

Ecology and General Biology

Breeding and nonbreeding habitats.   Breeding is preferentially done on islands, often fairly close to high tide line. Although trees and shrubs are preferentially used in eastern North American populations, where such elevated sites are not available ground nesting may commonly occur. In the Gulf of California the birds nest on steep, rocky slopes, with the nests usually located on the middle to upper parts of the slopes rather than close to the shoreline.

Sandbars exposed to the Gulf of Mexico were the most important nonnesting habitat identified by Schreiber and Schreiber (1982) in Florida, and were used for loafing and roosting throughout the year. There is often a gradual progression of islands from loafing areas to roosting and loafing areas throughout the year, and finally to nest colony islands. In some locations the birds used the nest colony islands throughout the year, but many roosting-loafing sites do not become nest colonies. The former remain important for resting, sleeping, and performing maintenance activities, and sandbars are especially important for newly fledged juveniles unable to land in trees. Since brown pelicans evidently cannot remain on water indefinitely without becoming waterlogged, dry roosting sites are essential. Foraging habitats could not be specifically localized or identified by Schreiber and Schreiber, but are generally known to occur in shallow estuarine and inshore waters mostly within 10 kilometers of the coast, and rarely as far as about 50 kilometers offshore.

Movements and migrations.   Over most of this species' range it is probably nonmigratory, but some seasonal migratory movements do occur at the northernmost edge of its range in the southeastern United States. Schreiber (1976b) documented movements of color-marked nestlings in Florida and South Carolina. There was a general southward dispersal following fledging, with a good deal of wandering evident. At least during their first year of life the birds hatched on the eastern coast of Florida and South Carolina generally moved south along Florida's eastern coast and the upper Keys. Those hatched in Tampa Bay moved south along the Gulf coast and into the lower Keys and as far as the Dry Tortugas. Thus the Atlantic and Gulf coast populations remained essentially distinct during their first year.

Schreiber and Mock (1988) confirmed this general migration pattern using band recovery data, noting that birds from Carolina colonies were mostly found wintering in eastern Florida (40 percent), with some in western Florida (18 percent) plus the Florida Keys (8 percent) and a few (2 percent) reaching Cuba. Pelicans banded in Florida tend to be year-round residents, with little movement from one coast to the other, but a significant percentage (22 percent) of Atlantic coast birds were recovered in Cuba. Carolina-banded birds typically move more than 500 kilometers from their natal site in their first and second years, but those from Florida generally do not disperse more than 250 kilometers from their natal sites. Adults in Florida may move 450–575 kilometers away from the colony during the nonbreeding season.

An earlier report by Mason (1945), also based on recoveries of banded birds, indicated that some of the South Carolina and eastern Florida birds may continue on to Cuba, whereas birds banded in the St. Petersburg area were mostly recovered near the point of banding. One bird banded in Louisiana was also recovered in Cuba, and another as far southwest as Campeche, Mexico. Most birds banded in California were recovered within 500 kilometers of the banding point, but one was recovered about 2,200 kilometers away in Colima, Mexico. Substantial dispersal or migration also occurs along the Peruvian coast, and one bird banded there was recovered in Chile, more than 3,800 kilometers away. *Competition and predation.* In South America, known predators of eggs and young include kelp gulls (*Larus dominicanus*), band-tailed gulls (*L. belcheri*), and turkey vultures (*Cathartes aura*) (Murphy, 1936). Schreiber and Risebrough (1972) observed egg predation by fish crows (*Corvus ossifragus*) after pelicans had been disturbed from their nests in Florida. Northern ravens (*Corvus corax*) and western gulls (*Larus occidentalis*) may be minor egg predators in western Mexico (Keith, 1978).

Foods and Foraging Behavior

Foods consumed. Most of the early literature on the foods of this species in North America was summarized by Palmer (1962), who judged that most of the prey fishes were not economically significant for humans. Only 27 individual fish out of 3,428 examined in Florida waters represented human food fishes. In many colonies from South Carolina to Texas menhaden (*Brevoortia*, Clupeidae) provides 90–95 percent of all food, with a variety of other taxa such as *Archosargus* (Sparidae), *Diplodus* (Sparidae), *Gambusia* (Poeciliidae), *Mugil* (Mugilidae), *Orthopristes* (Pomadasidae), and *Opisthonema*

(Clupeidae) represented in small quantities. Other than fish, a few crustaceans (prawns) were also represented in the foods.

Fogarty, Nesbitt, and Gilbert (1981) found a lower proportion (21 percent) of menhaden in regurgitates of nesting brown pelicans in Florida than intimated in Palmer's summary, and judged that it was not so important as previously imagined. A total of 30 additional species of fish were represented in these authors' regurgitate samples, with threadfin (*Polydactylus*, Polynemidae), mullet (*Mugil*), pinfish (*Lagodon*, Sparidae), and sea trout (*Cynoscion*, Otolithidae) present in substantial number.

On the California coast, northern anchovies (*Engraulis mordax*) are by far the most important food for both adult and young brown pelicans, though they additionally forage on other schooling fish, especially sardines (*Sardinops*, Clupeidae) and mackerels (*Scomber*, Scombridae) (Anderson and Anderson, 1976; Anderson and Gress, 1982). Thus, as in South Carolina, where the diet is almost exclusively menhaden, and in Peru, where according to Murphy (1936) it is the Peruvian "anchoveta" (*E. ringens*), in California the brown pelican is heavily dependent on a single food source, and in all these localities its populations may fluctuate with variations in this food supply.

In the Netherlands Antilles the brown pelican forages on small schooling fish such as anchovies, sardines (*Sardinella*, Clupeidae), and dwarf herring (*Jenkinsia*, Dussumieriidae), as well as some larger marine fish such as masbangu (*Selar*, Carangidae) and horse-eye jacks (*Caranx*, Carangidae). It has also been observed feeding on *Tilapia* in fresh-water sewage ponds (Voous, 1983). In the Puerto Rican region the species' foods are dominated by dwarf herring, anchovies (*Anchoa*, Engraulidae), and menhaden (*Harengula*, Clupeidae), with *Tilapia* also being consumed in estuaries and closed impoundments (Collazo, 1986). Murphy (1936) noted that one Peruvian bird had two needlefish (*Tylosurus*, Beloniidae) in its stomach, and Coker (1919) saw an adult Peruvian regurgitate a mullet more than 30 centimeters in length. *Foraging behavior.* An account of the unique plunge-foraging behavior of the brown pelican was provided in chapter 4. In addition to plunge-diving, the brown pelican has occasionally been observed surface-feeding in the manner of and in company with American white pelicans (Dinsmore, 1974).

Foraging is normally done mostly during early morning and late afternoon hours, in the manner of most pelicans, or on a rising tide (Palmer, 1962). Most foraging is done in shallow estuaries, but birds rarely have been observed foraging as far as 60 kilometers from shore (Schreiber, 1978).

Social Behavior

Age of maturity and mating system. Blus and Keahey (1978) found a two-year-old pelican incubating an egg, but believed

Figure 106. Social behavior of the brown pelican, including sequential stages of head-swaying display (A), bowing display (B), head-turning display (C), male carrying nest materials (D), upright display in flight and while standing (E, F), and fighting (G). After sketches in Schreiber (1977).

that initial breeding might occur anywhere between one and four years of age. They estimated that about 1 percent of the birds breeding in a South Carolina colony were in immature plumage, although these birds had a lower breeding success (lower average clutch size, lower percent of successful nests, and lower number of young produced per nest) than did birds in adult plumage, which can be attained as early as three years. Williams and Joanen (1974) observed breeding by three-year-old birds (in advanced subadult plumage) that had been moved from Florida to Louisiana as nestlings, but judged that the age of initial breeding may be earlier in newly forming colonies than in established ones. Among two reestablished breeding sites in Louisiana, successful breeding began at one site (North Island) when the birds were approaching two years old (21 months), and at the other (Queen Bess/Camp Island) when they were three (McNease et al., 1984). It is possible that in stable populations initial breeding may not occur until the birds are 4–7 years old (Anderson and Anderson, 1976).

Social displays and vocalizations.   Schreiber (1977) described the social displays of this species in detail, although in terms of pair-forming and pair-bonding behavior he did not clearly distinguish between male advertisement displays and individual recognition signals. Excepting those behaviors associated primarily with aggressive interactions, he listed the species' major displays as including head swaying, bowing, head turning, upright, and nest material presentation. The first four of these, in various intensities and combinations, are used between potential pairs after a female intrudes on a male's nest site, which is the means by which pair bonding begins. Only two of these (bowing and upright) have associated vocalizations, which are the only known vocalizations of adult brown pelicans.

Head swaying is performed by unpaired males at the potential nest site and also later on, during pair interactions at the nest. It consists (figure 106A) of a generally lateral movement of the head and bill, so that the tip of the bill produces an arc in the form of a horizontal figure-8 with the neck variously extended or withdrawn, and with the bill open and the lower mandible spread. The display is performed by unpaired males toward other adults of both sexes, but stops when a female begins to intrude on the nest site. Head turning (figure 106C) is similar to head swaying, but the bill and head are moved in a more distinctly horizontal arc, and the bill is closed, with the gular pouch flaccid. The display varies greatly in intensity; at high intensity the wings are partly opened, but they are only slightly drooped at low intensity. Head turning is performed by both sexes, while either standing or sitting, and most frequently occurs between members of a pair at the nest.

Bowing (figure 106B) consists of pointing the bill downward and slightly backward, while standing with the wings folded but variously raised. The wingtips are jerked rhythmically at about one-second intervals, with each jerk

accompanied by a low and hoarse *hraa* note. Bowing is used by both sexes and occurs only on the nest site. Paired birds never bow simultaneously, but rarely two or more males on nearby perches may bow simultaneously. The upright consists of wing spreading while lifting the bill and stretching the tightened gular pouch. The bill is sometimes closed but usually slightly opened, and is usually held in line with the body. The display is normally performed in a standing posture (figure 105F) but is also performed in flight (figure 106E). The aerial version of the upright is held for a shorter period (less than one second, vs. up to three seconds for the standing version). The upright is the only display that is performed in flight, as well as the only one sometimes performed away from the nesting colony. At high intensities it is accompanied by the same call that occurs during bowing.

All four of these displays are used by members of a pair during nest relief ceremonies as apparent recognition signs, but at quite different frequencies and with differences in performance by the "in" and "out" bird (see chapter 5). Nest material presentation also occurs at the nest site between paired birds, and additionally plays a role in pair bond formation and in nest building. This display is performed only by males, and appears to be a modification of the upright display (figure 106D). The male always performs this display when he arrives at the nest with nest materials. He presents the material he is carrying to the female while facing her or from over her side or back. The female typically performs head swaying and then takes the material from the male to deposit in the nest. If the female does not respond to his display, he may simply drop the material, often on the female's back. Aggressive behaviors are the same in both sexes and range from simple threatening movements of the bill to overt jabs and bill grabbing (figure 106G). Such behavior is common during early stages of pair bonding.

Copulation (figure 107A–E) occurs only at the nest site, and usually before any nest materials have been gathered. It continues through the nest-building period, but only rarely occurs after the laying of the first egg. The total duration of copulatory behavior was observed by Schreiber to range from 3 to 10 days prior to egg laying for 13 nests, with an average of 7.1 mountings per day prior to egg laying. Female behavior prior to copulation is quite variable, and may include any of the just-described pair-bonding displays, as well as general egocentric behavior such as preening (figure 107A) or sunning. Head turning was the activity among males that most often directly preceded mounting. Immediately prior to mounting the male grabs the female's neck and holds it throughout the entire duration of treading. He additionally waves his wings, rubs his cloaca on the female's back, and erects the feathers surrounding his uropygial gland (figure 107F). The entire duration of mounting and copulation lasts 7–14 seconds. The post-mounting display invariably consists of the male holding the bill open while the head is retracted (figure 107E).

Figure 107. Copulation sequence in the brown pelican, including male approaching (A), male mounting female (B), treading (with wing waving) (C, D), and postcopulatory postures (E). Also shown are the male's erected tail coverts during treading (F). After sketches in Schreiber (1977).

Reproductive Biology

Breeding season.   The chronology of breeding of the eastern race of the brown pelican, including nesting records from Texas to North Carolina, was summarized by Schreiber (1980b). Nesting by southern populations (10–20° N latitude) is prolonged and irregular, usually starting in late fall and lasting through June. Nesting by intermediate populations (20–30° N latitude) is more seasonal, and occurs during winter and spring, with some irregularity. Nesting by the northernmost populations (30–35° N latitude) occurs during spring and summer. Freezing temperatures may control the timing of nesting in southwestern Florida (Tarpon Key), and additionally selection against nesting during the hurricane season may have been an ultimate factor in setting nesting chronologies for the subspecies as a whole, as much of its range occurs within a broad hurricane belt. The species is limited to areas where 5–7 months of frost-free temperatures occur, and it is possible that it has an annual endogenous breeding periodicity of about 8.5–10 months that is expressed wherever seasonal cold weather does not interfere with it (Schreiber, 1980b).

On Aruba Island, Netherlands Antilles, nesting activity by *occidentalis* over nine seasons ranged from May through September, with year-to-year variations (Voous, 1983). On Taboga Island, in the Bay of Panama, nesting may be timed to coincide with periods of oceanic upwelling (Montgomery and Martinez, 1984). The Peruvian race of the brown pelican breeds throughout the year, but less prolifically during the winter months of May to September, and with a peak of pairing activity in October (Murphy, 1936).

On the Pacific coast of North America breeding of the California race of brown pelicans occurs during spring, with a peak in egg laying around March or April. Egg laying on Isla San Lorenzo, Gulf of California, occurred during three years of study from late February to early May, with a peak in late March and early April, but with some variation among colonies and from year to year (Keith, 1978).

Nest sites and nest building.   Nest sites vary from simple ground scrapes (as in Peru and western Mexico), where little or no building is required, to rather elaborately constructed nests in shrubs or trees. Probably elevated sites are used whenever they are available, inasmuch as they provide a degree of protection from terrestrial predators as well as from flooding. Along the Florida coast most nesting occurs in groves of mangroves (*Avicenna* or *Rhizopora*), with other species of trees used less frequently and only a few nests placed directly on the ground. Along the less well vegetated Louisiana and Florida coasts, ground nesting or nesting in shrubs is much more frequent.

Nest building in Florida's Tarpon Key colony involves males pulling and tearing materials from mangroves, as well as gathering some loose sticks and grasses. Gathering of materials begins soon after a female is allowed to intrude on the nest site, and most materials are gathered from the nesting island. Such gathering defoliates large areas, and may limit an island's ability to support a pelican colony indefinitely. Males continue to gather materials throughout the incubation and nestling stages, but to a greatly reduced degree, and this behavior may be more important for pair bond maintenance than actual nest maintenance. Most nests require 7–10 days to construct, with an observed minimum of four days (Schreiber, 1977). On coastal Peru, where the nests are scrapes about 25 centimeters in diameter, the density of nests may be as high as two per square meter of land surface, with the length of the birds' necks and bills evidently determining the spacing (Coker, 1919).

Egg laying and incubation.   A minimum of two days elapse between the laying of successive eggs, and often three-day intervals occur (Coker, 1919; Grummt, 1984). Schreiber (1977) stated that 24–64 hours separate deposition of eggs, with most eggs laid early in the morning hours. In Schreiber's Florida study area the first egg was usually deposited 1–3 days after the completion of the nest, although intervals as long as three weeks were observed. Clutch sizes are typically of 2–3 eggs in the Atlantic race. In eight years, the average clutch size at Tarpon Key ranged annually from 2.5 to 2.8 eggs, with an overall mean of 2.62 (328 nests). The modal clutch size for 328 nests was of three eggs (68 percent). This is somewhat lower than historic clutches from museum collections (mean 2.95), and also slightly lower than the estimate of 2.85 for 89 nests from South Carolina in 1975 (Blus and Keahey, 1978). A very similar mean clutch of 2.88 eggs (305 nests) was found for three years of study at Isla San Lorenzo Norte, Gulf of California, with annual means of 2.83–2.95 (Keith, 1978).

It is possible that the clutch of the Peruvian race averages slightly less than that of North American birds, but few comparative data are available. Coker (1919) observed a range of 1–8 eggs in 209 nests. The mean clutch size was 2.41 eggs, with 40 percent of the nests containing three eggs, and 35 percent holding two eggs. The two eight-egg clutches he found might have represented the work of two or more females, but all the embryos in one of these clutches were found to be at the same stage of development.

Incubation begins with the first egg, and at least in the case of the eastern race lasts 30 days (Schreiber, 1977, 1979). Grummt (1984) reported 30- and 31-day incubation periods for brown pelicans of unspecified race. Both parents share incubation, with the nonincubating bird often sitting on the perch near the nest, sleeping, loafing, or preening.

Schreiber (1979) estimated the rate of relaying following nest failure to vary from 0 to 26 percent during various years. Clutch sizes in renesting efforts averaged very slightly higher (2.5 vs. 2.4) than clutch sizes in original nests, and an average of 1.2 young per nest fledged in replacement nests, which was not a significant difference from the estimated success of original nests.

Brooding and rearing of young. The young weigh 45–80 grams at hatching. They are initially fed within a few hours after hatching, by the adult regurgitating well-digested fish onto the floor of the nest, where it is picked up by the chick. Feeding initially occurs at the rate of about once per hour. Down begins to cover the chicks at 7–10 days and is fully grown at 2–3 weeks. As the downy covering develops, parental brooding is reduced. At about 10 days the chicks begin to beg directly from their parents and take their food directly from the parent's pouch. Scapular feathers first appear at about 30 days. One or both parents continue to guard the young until they are 4–6 weeks old, after which they no longer spend the night on the nest. Maximum weight is attained at 45–60 days, after which about 16 percent of the weight is lost before fledging. The first flights are made when the young are 11–12 weeks (range 71–88 days) of age (Schreiber, 1976a, 1977).

Survival of the young varies with number of siblings. The fledging success is highest in nests with a single chick (19 chicks fledged in 19 nests) and for the first-hatched chick of a multi-chick nest (31 young fledged in 31 nests). In two-chick nests, 13 of 21 second-hatched chicks fledged, and in three-chick nests only 1 of 16 third-hatched chicks fledged (Schreiber, 1976a).

Breeding success. A great deal of information is available on the reproductive success of brown pelicans in eastern North America, which was summarized by Schreiber (1979). He documented both seasonal and annual fluctuations in reproductive success. In his study area, birds nesting at the peak of laying were most successful, not only producing larger average clutches (2.5–2.6 for early and middle portions of the breeding season vs. 2.2 for late nesters) but also most successfully rearing fledglings (1.1 young fledged per nest for midseason nests, vs. 0.8 for early and 0.6 for late nests). Hatching success was highest (84 percent) for early nests, and lowest (43 percent) for late nests. Contrariwise, the percentage of hatched eggs that produced fledged young was highest (64 percent) for late nests, and lowest (39 percent) for early nests, which tended to make midseason nesting efforts the most productive.

Schreiber (1979) also documented annual variations in reproductive success, as have many other investigators such as Keith (1978) and Blus and Keahey (1978). The latter authors observed a relationship between productivity and age, with immature-plumaged birds nesting later than adults, having a lower average clutch size (2.16 vs. 2.85), a lower percentage of successful nests, a lower percentage of successfully hatched eggs, and a lower average number of young produced per active nest (0.11 vs. 0.89). Schreiber (1979) reported annual variations in productivity ranging from 0.33 to 1.7 young fledged per nest, with an overall eight-year mean of 0.93 young per nest (376 nests). The overall reproductive success was highest for three-egg clutches (1.14 fledged young per nest), less in two-egg clutches (0.7 fledged

young per nest), and lowest in one-egg clutches (0.28 fledged young per nest). Additionally, three-egg clutches had the highest hatching success (74 percent, vs. 61 percent for two-egg clutches and 28 percent for one-egg clutches), whereas one-egg clutches had the highest rearing success (100 percent). This high hatching success rate for three-egg clutches seemingly separates the brown pelican from the American white pelican and the Dalmatian pelican, in which hatching success rates for three-egg clutches are distinctly lower than for two-egg clutches. It would seem that since both hatching success and overall reproductive success are highest in three-egg clutches of brown pelicans, selection in this species might favor the production of three-egg clutches, whereas in at least some of the white pelicans it seems to favor two-egg clutches.

Productivity estimates for brown pelicans have been made for various other regions, such as South Carolina (Blus and Keahey, 1978), Anacapa Island, California, and Los Coronados islands, Mexico (Anderson and Anderson, 1976), and the Gulf of California (Keith, 1978), but variables such as degree of human disturbance and of pesticide effects on reproductive success make comparisons difficult if not impossible. In particular there is a strong correlation between the intensity of human disturbance during the breeding season and reproductive success rates (Anderson, 1988; Anderson and Keith, 1980). Additionally, starvation of young and flooding of nests are often locally important sources of mortality for eggs or young (Schreiber, 1978). At least in some areas tick (*Ornithodoros*) infestations may also cause large-scale nest desertion (King et al., 1977).

Population Status

The population status of brown pelicans in North America has been discussed in chapter 7 (see table 31). Additionally there may be about 2,300 individuals of *P. o. occidentalis* in the Puerto Rican Bank region (Collazo, 1986), representing a considerable part of the entire Caribbean population, which is perhaps generally declining except for the Virgin Islands population (Halewyn and Norton, 1984). The Peruvian population consisted of about 800,000 birds in 1981 (Duffy, Hays, and Plenge, 1984). The North American populations of this species underwent serious declines during the hard pesticide era (Laycock, 1974; Simmons, 1974; Keith, 1983). This decline occurred on the Pacific coast (Keith, Woods, and Hunt, 1970) as well as on the Gulf and Atlantic coasts (King, Flickinger, and Hildebrand, 1977; Brown, 1983). However, recovery plans were initiated on the west coast (Gress and Anderson, 1982), and restocking of the extirpated Louisiana population began in 1968 (Nesbitt et al., 1978; McNease et al., 1984). It now appears that the Gulf coast population is increasing, although pesticide residues (DDE and DDT) are still fairly high in some areas, such as coastal Texas (King et al., 1985). During 1989 brown pelicans nested in five locations along the

Texas coast (*American Birds* 43:1338). They also nested for the second successive year on coastal Virginia, and for the third year on the Maryland coast (*American Birds* 43:1300). During that same year there were 12,000 nesting pairs in 34 colonies in Florida (*American Birds* 43:1307). By 1990 there were 2,196 breeding adults at six colonies in Louisiana (Martin and Lester, 1990), and the Virginia colony (Fish Island) had 97 nests (*American Birds* 44:1121).

Evolutionary Relationships

Sibley and Ahlquist (1985) judged from DNA-DNA hybridization evidence that this is the most isolated of the pelicans, which is in agreement with a variety of other lines of anatomical evidence. They placed the temporal separation of this form from the other pelicans at about 15 million years ago, although more recently (1990) these authors have been more cautious about assigning definite divergence dates based on their DNA hybridization data.

APPENDIX 1

Keys for Species Identification

KEY TO SPECIES OF ADULT CORMORANTS AND SHAGS (PHALACROCORACIDAE)

A. Exposed culmen (from forehead feathering to tip of nail) <40 mm; adult weight usually <900 g
  B. Cheeks and foreneck white ... Little pied cormorant
  BB. Entire underparts including throat black
    C. Iris not red, facial skin brown to blackish
      D. Head and neck brownish; iris brown .... Pygmy cormorant
      DD. Head and neck blackish, iris green .... Javanese cormorant
    CC. Iris red, facial and gular skin red to yellow
      D. Ratio of tail to tarsus 4:1; scapulars with broad (quarter-moon) black tips; facial skin yellowish; crest small .... Long-tailed cormorant
      DD. Ratio of tail to tarsus 3.5:1; scapulars with narrow (crescent-moon) black tips; facial skin reddish; forehead crest well developed .... Crowned cormorant
AA. Culmen >40 mm; adult weight usually >900 g
  B. Tail of 14 rectrices
    C. Legs coral-red, underparts pale gray .... Red-legged shag
    CC. Legs blackish, underparts black or mostly black
      D. Nine rudimentary primaries; flightless .... Galapagos cormorant
      DD. Ten functional primaries; capable of flight
        E. Tail <120 mm, throat feathers black
          F. Black facial skin; culmen >60 mm .... Socotra shag
          FF. Yellow facial skin; culmen <57 mm .... Cape shag

        EE. Tail >130 mm, cheek and throat feathers white or mottled black and white
          F. Gular skin extends backward only to a point directly below the eyes; wing:tarsus ratio <4.8; wing to 330 mm .... Japanese cormorant
          FF. Gular skin extends backward to well behind the rear margin of the eyes; wing:tarsus ratio >4.8; wing usually >330 mm .... Great cormorant
  BB. Tail of 12 rectrices
    C. Underparts immaculate white in adults
      D. Legs and feet brown to black, iris green
        E. Facial skin orange-yellow; no feathering directly below base of gape .... Pied cormorant
        EE. Facial skin blackish; feathers of cheek extend forward to terminate in front of base of gape. Black-faced cormorant
      DD. Legs and feet red to pink, iris brown to reddish
        E. Feet coral to scarlet; red facial skin lacks caruncles; eye ring green or lacking
          F. Bill black; no eye ring; ear coverts white .... Rock shag
          FF. Bill yellowish, eye ring green; little or no white on sides of head .... Guanay shag
        EE. Feet pinkish; facial skin often with colorful caruncles or papillae; eye ring often blue
          F. Throat feathers extend forward to no more than about midpoint of the eye .... Imperial shag (key to subspecies .... follows)
            G. Black on cheeks terminates below mandible in a sharp point; feet distinctly brownish; 1.7–2 kg; Kerguelen Islands ..... *verrucosus*

GG. Black on cheeks terminates at or above gape; feet more pink, less brown; >2 kg

    H. Ear coverts white or partly white; white spots on scapulars and anterior wing coverts

        I. Wing length >300 mm

            J. Heard Island .... *nivalis*

            JJ. Antarctic Peninsula and South Shetlands .... *bransfieldensis*

        II. Wing length <300 mm

            J. South American coast .... *atriceps*

            JJ. South Georgia Island .... *georgianus*

    HH. Ear coverts black; often no white on scapulars or anterior wing coverts

        I. Falkland Islands .... *albiventer*

        II. Crozet Islands .... *melanogenis*

        III. Macquarie Island .... *purpurascens*

FF. Throat feathers extend forward to a point beyond the anterior margin of the eye

    G. Foreneck white; face with orange-red caruncles; eye ring bright blue

        H. Face bluish gray, culmen >62 mm, crest almost absent .... King shag

    HH. Face purplish to reddish; culmen usually <60 mm (but max. 69 mm), forehead crest more evident

        I. Face and gular skin more purplish, caruncles larger .... Chatham Island shag

        II. Face and gular skin more orange-red, caruncles smaller .... Stewart Island shag (pied morph)

GG. Foreneck black, or the white foreneck area very reduced; no facial papillae or caruncles; eye ring not bright blue

    H. Foreneck entirely black; face purple with orange near bill .... Campbell Island shag

    HH. Foreneck usually with white median streak; face more reddish

        I. Face purple to red; culmen usually <50 mm (but max. 56 mm) .... Auckland Island shag

        II. Face scarlet with black spots; culmen usually >55 mm (but min. 53 mm) ... Bounty Island shag

CC. Underparts dark gray to black in adults (often light gray or brownish in immature or nonbreeding birds)

D. Plumage mostly bluish gray below, the upperparts with triangular blackish spots

    E. With a broad white eyebrow stripe .... Spotted shag

    EE. No white eyebrow stripe .... Pitt Island shag

DD. Underparts black to greenish black, the upperpart feathers usually edged with blackish

    E. Wing >290 mm .... Pallas' cormorant (extinct)

    EE. Wing <280 mm

        F. Legs pinkish; a bright blue eye ring present .... Stewart Island shag (melanistic morph)

        FF. Legs black; no blue eye ring evident

            G. Facial skin bright carmine to dull red

                H. Forehead bare; iris brown .... Red-faced shag

                HH. Forehead feathered; iris green .... Pelagic shag

            GG. Facial skin not bright carmine or dull red

                H. Dorsal feathers with purplish green sheen and inconspicuous darker edges

                    I. Bill all black; gular pouch blue . Brandt's cormorant

                    II. Bill yellow basally; gular pouch black .... European shag

                HH. Dorsal feathers brownish, with black edges

                    I. Iris bicolored brown and green ... Bank cormorant

                    II. Iris entirely green

                      J. Tail length >50% of wing length

                        K. Culmen 40–50 mm .... Neotropic (olivaceous) cormorant

                        KK. Culmen 50–60 mm .... Indian cormorant

                    JJ. Tail length 40–50% of wing length

                      K. Culmen >50 mm; gular skin orange .... Double-crested cormorant

                      KK. Culmen <50 mm; gular skin grayish .... Little black cormorant

---

KEY TO SPECIES AND SUBSPECIES OF ADULT DARTERS (ANHINGIDAE)

A. Tail pale-tipped; the breast either black (males) or buffy (females) .... Anhinga

AA. Tail blackish to tip in adults .... Darter
    B. Ornamental scapulars no more than 10 cm long; adult females with white underparts .... Australian darter
BB. Longest ornamental scapulars 15–20 cm; adult females with blackish underparts
    C. Outer webs of ornamental secondary coverts and scapulars silvery white; neck more silvery gray ....Oriental darter
CC. Outer webs of secondary coverts and scapulars reddish brown; neck more rufous .... African darter

---

KEY TO SPECIES OF ADULT PELICANS (PELECANIDAE)

A. Body mostly dark brown; pouch blackish, extending halfway down the neck .... Brown pelican
AA. Body white to grayish; pouch not blackish nor extending halfway down the neck ("white pelicans")
    B. Bare eye ring enclosed by feathers; the tail and most dorsal wing coverts black .... Australian pelican
BB. Lores entirely naked; the tail and most dorsal wing coverts white or grayish white
    C. Primaries and inner vanes of most secondaries black
    D. Forehead feathers ending in a line or concave curve; facial skin orange-yellow .... American white pelican
DD. Forehead feathers ending in a point or convex curve; facial skin pink to red .... Eastern (great) white pelican
CC. Primaries dusky, grading to grayish white secondaries
    D. Wing >625 mm; crest long and shaggy; bill blackish; legs dark gray .... Dalmatian pelican
DD. Wing <625 mm; crest straighter; bill mostly flesh-colored
    E. Pouch with blackish spots; no black smudge in front of eye; legs brown .... Spot-billed pelican
EE. Pouch with parallel reddish stripes; skin of lores smudged black; legs pinkish .... Pink-backed pelican

Glossary of Scientific and Vernacular Names

Anhinga: A South American (Tupi-Guarani) word meaning "snake bird." Perhaps also related to the Portuguese *anguina*, meaning "snakelike." The earlier generic name *Plotus* is Greek, meaning a "skilled swimmer" or "sailor." The vernacular name "darter" describes its darting or stabbing behavior.

> *melanogaster:* from the Greek *melas*, "black," and *gaster*, "stomach."
>> *movaehollandiae:* "of New Holland," the original official name (until 1849) for colonial Australia.
>> *rufa:* Latin, "reddish."

Leucocarbo: Greek *leukos*, "white," and Latin *carbo*, "coal." The vernacular name "shag" refers to the shaggy head of breeding adults.

> *aristotelis:* named by C. Linnaeus in honor of the Greek philosopher and naturalist Aristotle (384–322 B.C.).
>> *desmarestii:* after Anselme-Gaétan Desmarest, French naturalist in the early 1800s.
>> *riggenbachi:* after F. W. Riggenbach (1864–1944), who collected the first specimens.
> *atriceps:* Latin *atrum*, "black," and *caput*, "head." This form is sometimes separated as the type species of the genus *Notocarbo*, meaning "black-backed."
>> *albiventer:* from the Latin *albus*, "white," and *venter*, "underside."
>> *bransfieldensis:* "of Bransfield Strait," and honoring Lieutenant Edward Bransfield, who first surveyed the South Shetland Islands region in 1820 for Great Britain.
>> *georgianus:* "of South Georgia Island."
>> *melanogenis:* from the Greek *melas*, "black," and *genys*, "the cheeks."
>> *nivalis:* Latin, "snowy."
>> *purpurascens:* Latin, "purplish or dark red."
>> *verrucosus:* Latin, "full of warts."

bougainvillii: in honor of H. Y. P. Bougainville (ca. 1781–1846), French naval officer and naturalist. The vernacular name "guanay shag" is related to guano, derived from the Kechuan *huana*, "dung."
carunculatus: Latin, "carunculated." This form is sometimes separated as the type species of the genus *Euleucocarbo*, the prefix meaning "true" or "authentic."
campbellii: "of Campbell Island." This form is sometimes placed in the monotypic genus *Nesocarbo*, meaning a "black islander."
capensis: Latin, "of the Cape of Good Hope."
chalconotus: from the Greek *chalkos*, "copper," and *notos*, "back."
colensoi: in honor of Rev. William Colenso (1811–1899), New Zealand missionary, botanist, and ethnologist.
featherstoni: in honor of Dr. I. E. Featherston (1813–1876), Superintendent of the Province of Wellington.
gaimardi: in honor of the French biologist Joseph P. Gaimard, naturalist on the explorations of the oceanic vessels *Astrolabe* and *Uranie*.
> *cirriger:* Latin, "bearing curls."
magellanicus: Latin, "of the Strait of Magellan," named for its discoverer, F. Magellan (ca. 1480–1521).
nigrogularis: from the Latin *niger*, "black," and *gula*, "throat." The vernacular name refers to Socotra Island, the type locality (but an unproven breeding location).
onslowi: in honor of Sir W. Hillier, 4th Earl of Onslow (1853–1911), Governor of New Zealand from 1888 to 1892.
pelagicus: Latin, "marine or pelagic."
> *resplendens:* Latin, "resplendent."
punctatus: Latin, "spotted." This form is sometimes separated as the type species of the genus *Stictocarbo*, meaning "dappled or spotted with black."

oliveri: in honor of W. R. B. Oliver, authority on New Zealand birds who first named this form *steadi,* for E. F. Stead (1881–1949), who collected the first specimens.

ranfurlyi: in honor of Earl V. J. Ranfurly (1856–1933), Governor of New Zealand from 1897 to 1904, who organized the specimen collections that resulted in the discovery of this form.

urile: from the Russian vernacular name for this species, probably referring to the Kuril Islands (where it is now very rare).

> *kenyoni:* in honor of Karl W. Kenyon, who collected the first specimens.

Pelecanus: Latinized from the Greek *pelikon,* "pelican." The related Greek word *pelikys* means "axe" (perhaps in reference to the long, sharp-nailed bill), or "woodcutter"—the "pelican" referred to by the Athenian poet Aristophanes apparently was a woodpecker. *Alcatraz,* a Spanish and Portuguese word for pelican, is derived from the Arabic *al-quadus,* "water carrier," and may also be related to the Greek *kados,* "water pot."

> *erythrorhynchos:* from the Greek *erythros,* "red," and *rhynchos,* "beak." This form is the type species of the subgenus *Cyrtopelicanus,* meaning "arched pelican," perhaps referring to the somewhat archlike bill horn typical of breeding adults.
>
> *conspicillatus:* Latin, "spectacled."
>
> *crispus:* Latin, "curled" or "uneven," in reference to the neck and head feathers. The vernacular name "Dalmatian pelican" refers to Dalmatia, Yugoslavia.
>
> *occidentalis:* Latin, "western." This form has at times been separated as a monotypic subgenus *Leptopelicanus,* meaning "slender pelican"; the species is relatively long-winged and light-bodied.
>
>> *californicus:* "of California."
>>
>> *carolinensis:* "of Carolina."
>>
>> *murphyi:* in honor of Robert C. Murphy (1887–1973), American authority on oceanic birds.
>>
>> *thagus:* a derivation of "il Thage," the name used in describing this form by Giovanni I. Molina, Italian authority on Chilean birds.
>>
>> *urinator:* Latin, "diver."
>
> *onocrotalus:* Latin, a kind of pelican. Literally, "ass castanet," a seemingly senseless combination, unless it refers to the braying calls of adults.
>
> *philippensis:* "of the Philippines."
>
> *rufescens:* Latin, "reddening."

Phalacrocorax: Greek, *phalakro,* "bald," and *korax,* "raven." The vernacular name "cormorant" is directly from the French *cormoran,* and originally from the Latin *corvus,* "crow," and *marinus,* "of the sea."

> *africanus:* "of Africa." The vernacular name "reed cormorant" refers to its tendency to roost in reed beds.
>
>> *pictilis:* Latin, "embroidered."

auritus: Latin, "eared."

> *albociliatus:* from the Latin *albus,* "white," and *ciliatus,* "having cilia" (hairlike feathers).
>
> *cincinatus:* Latin, "having curly hair" (in reference to the nuptial plumes).
>
> *floridanus:* "of Florida."
>
> *heuretus:* Latinized Greek, "discovered" (referring to this form's recent discovery and the fact that Columbus may have made his New World landfall on San Salvador Island).

brasilianus: "of Brazil."

> *mexicanus:* "of Mexico."
>
> *olivaceus:* Latin, "olive-colored."
>
> *vigua:* presumably related to the vernacular name "bigua cormorant," which is derived from *mbigua,* a Brazilian name for this species that supposedly imitates its grunting call.

capillatus: Latin, "hairy" (in reference to the filoplumes). This species' alternative name *filamentosis* has similar meaning. It is often called Temminck's cormorant, after its describer, C. J. Temminck (1775–1858), of the Leiden Museum, Holland.

carbo: Latin, "coal."

> *hanedae:* "from Hanada," Japan, the type locality.
>
> *lucidus:* Latin, "shining."
>
> *maroccanus:* "of Morocco."
>
> *novaehollandiae:* "of New Holland," the original official name for colonial Australia.
>
> *sinensis:* "of China."

coronatus: Latin, "crowned."

fuscescens: Latin, "blackish brown."

fuscicollis: Latin *fuscus,* "dusky," and *collum,* "neck."

harrisi: in honor of C. M. Harris, chief naturalist of the Galapagos Islands during the 1890s. This form is sometimes considered the type species of the genus *Nannopterum,* meaning "small-winged."

melanoleucos: Greek *melas,* "black," and *leukos,* "white."

> *brevicauda:* Latin *brevis,* "short," and *cauda,* "tail."
>
> *brevirostris:* Latin *brevis,* "short," and *rostrum,* "bill."
>
> *melvillensis:* "of Cape Melville."

neglectus: Latin, "neglected."

niger: Latin, "black."

pencillatus: Latin, "penciled" or "brushy," in reference to the elongated nuptial plumes. The vernacular name "Brandt's cormorant" refers to Johann F. Brandt (1802–1879), head of the Zoological Museum at St. Petersburg, who described the species. This form has been separated as the type species of the genus *Compsohalieus,* meaning "elegant seabird."

perspicillatus: quasi-Latin, "wearing spectacles." The vernacular name "Pallas' cormorant" refers to Peter S. Pallas, Russian biologist and zoogeographer of Siberia, who described the species.

pygmaeus: Latin, "pygmy-like." This form has been separated as the type species of the genus *Microcarbo,* meaning "small and carbon-colored."

sulcirostris: from the Latin *sulcus,* "furrow or groove," and *rostrum,* "bill."

    purpuragula: Latin, "purple-throated."

    territori: Latin, "of Northern Territory."

varius: Latin, "variable." This form has been separated as the type species of the genus *Hypoleucus.*

    hypoleucos: from the Greek *hypo,* "below," and *leukos,* "white."

Figure 108. Breeding adults (left) and juveniles (right) of the great cormorant's nominate Atlantic race *carbo* (A) and its African race *lucidus* (B), as compared with those of the Japanese cormorant (C).

Head Profile Identification Drawings

A

B

C

0 Cm. 5

0 In. 2

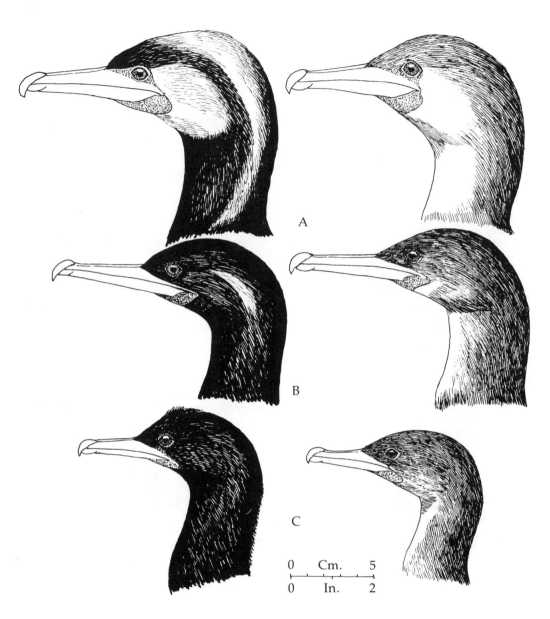

A

B

C

0   Cm.   5
0   In.   2

Figure 109. Asian cormorants, including breeding adults (left) and juveniles (right) of the great cormorant's Asian race *sinensis* (A), Indian cormorant (B), and Javanese cormorant (C).

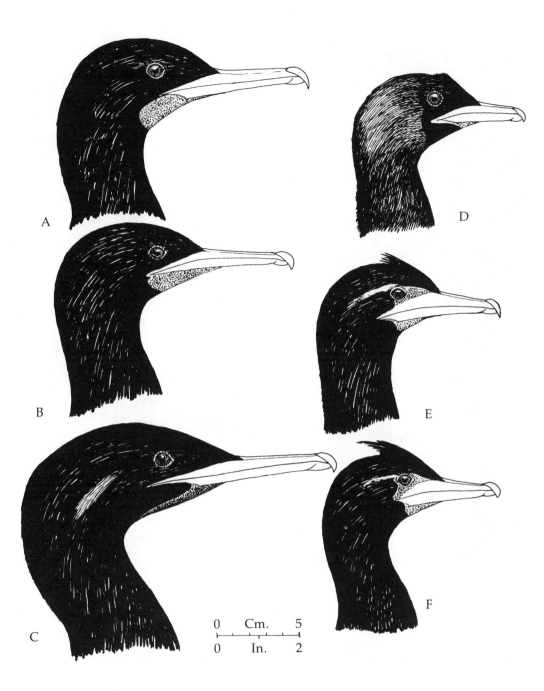

0   Cm.   5
0   In.   2

Figure 110. African cormorants and shags, including breeding adults of the bank cormorant (A), Cape shag (B), Socotra shag (C), pygmy cormorant (D), long-tailed cormorant (E), and crowned cormorant (F).

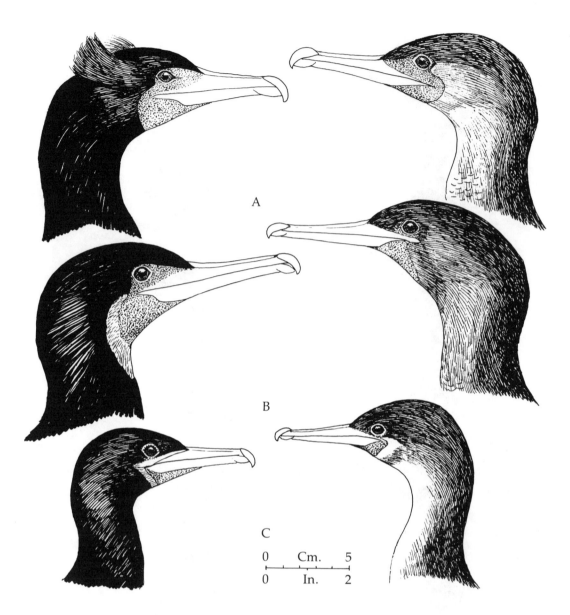

Figure 111. North American cormorants, including breeding adults (left) and juveniles (right) of the double-crested cormorant (A), Brandt's cormorant (B), and Neotropic cormorant (C).

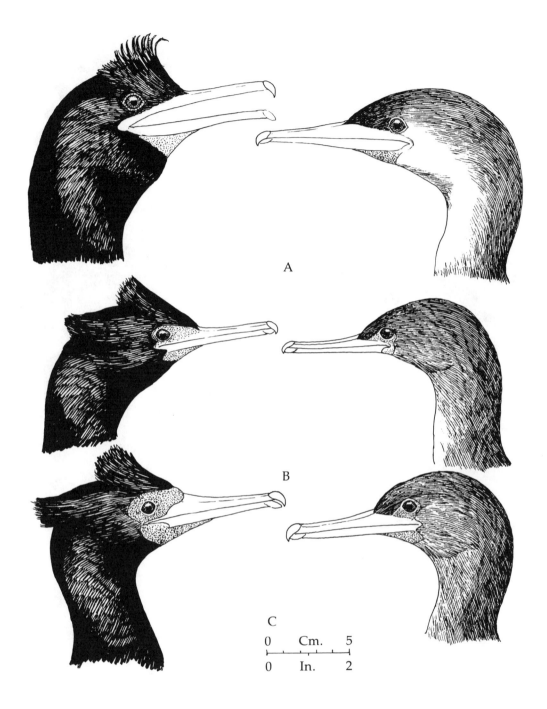

Figure 112. Northern hemisphere shags, including breeding adults (left) and juveniles (right) of the European shag (A), pelagic shag (B), and red-faced shag (C).

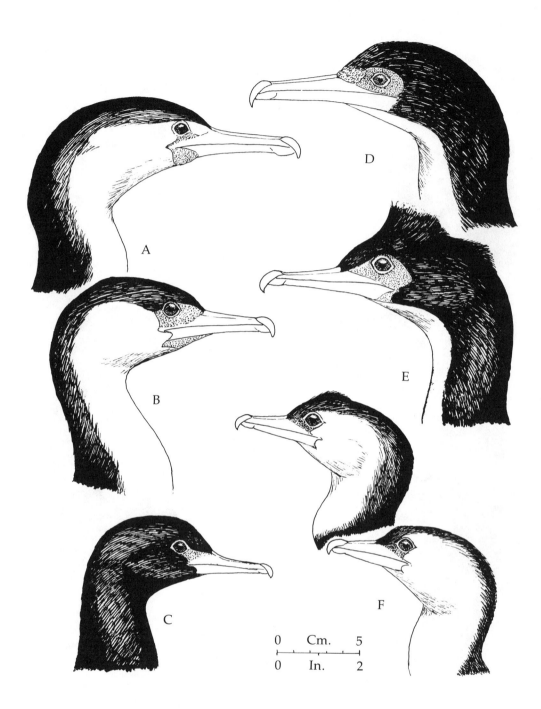

Figure 113. Australian and New Zealand cormorants and shags, including breeding adults of the black-faced cormorant (A), pied cormorant (B), little black cormorant (C), king shag (D), Stewart Island shag (pied morph) (E), and little pied cormorant (melanistic and pied morphs) (F).

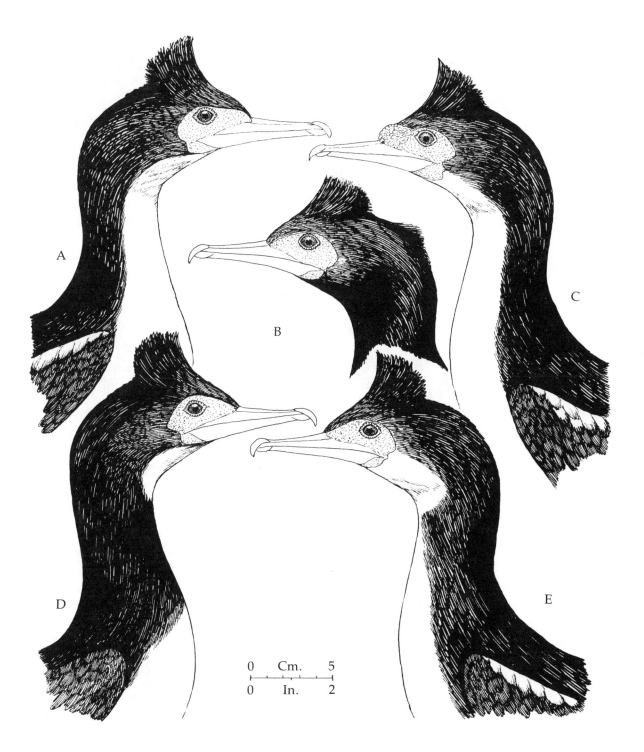

Figure 114. Insular New Zealand shags, including breeding adults of the Bounty (A), Stewart (melanistic morph) (B), Chatham (C), Campbell (D), and Auckland (E) Island shags.

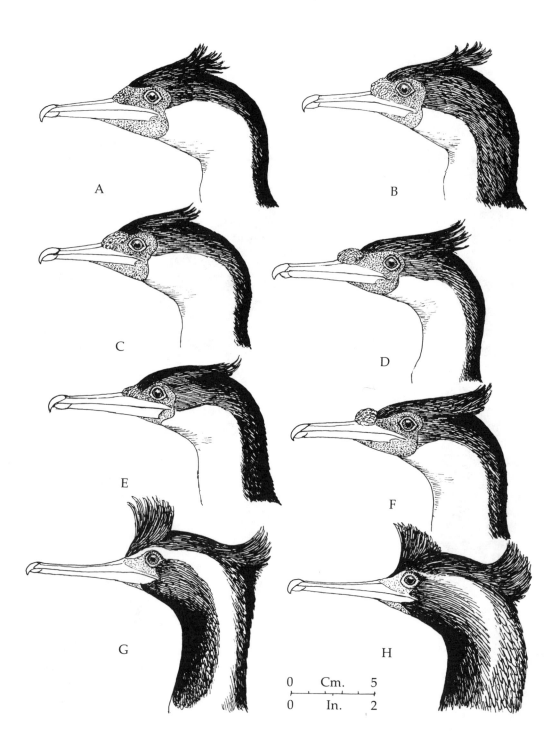

Figure 115. Subantarctic shags, including breeding adults of the imperial shag's nominate South American race (A) plus its additional races on the Falkland (B), South Georgia (C), Marion and Prince Edward (D), Macquarie (E), and Kerguelen (F) islands. The spotted (G) and Pitt Island (H) shags are also shown.

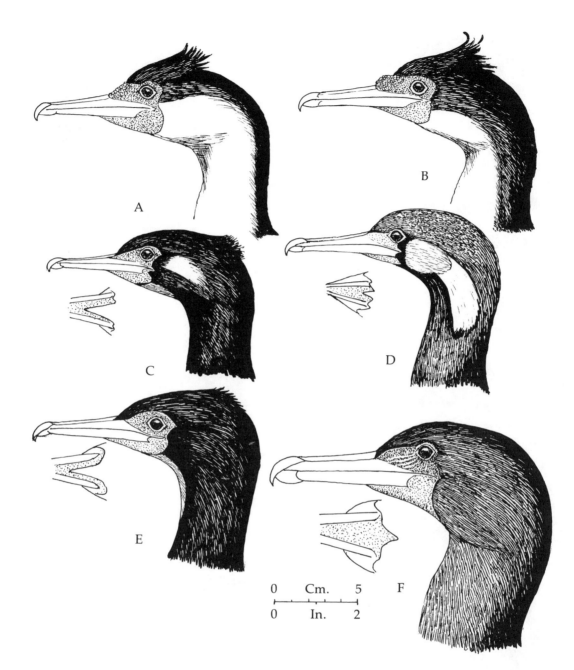

Figure 116. South American cormorants and shags, including breeding adults of the imperial shag's *atriceps* (A) and *albiventer* (B) morphs, plus adults of the rock shag (C), redlegged shag (D), guanay shag (E), and Galapagos cormorant (F). Insets show gular skin outlines from below. In part after Murphy (1936).

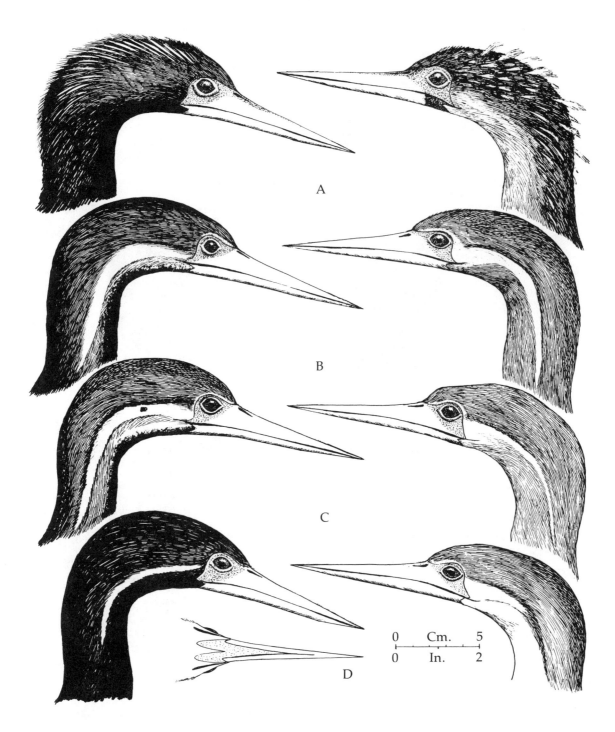

Figure 117. Breeding males (right) and females (left) of the anhinga (A) and the African (B), Oriental (C), and Australian (D) darters.

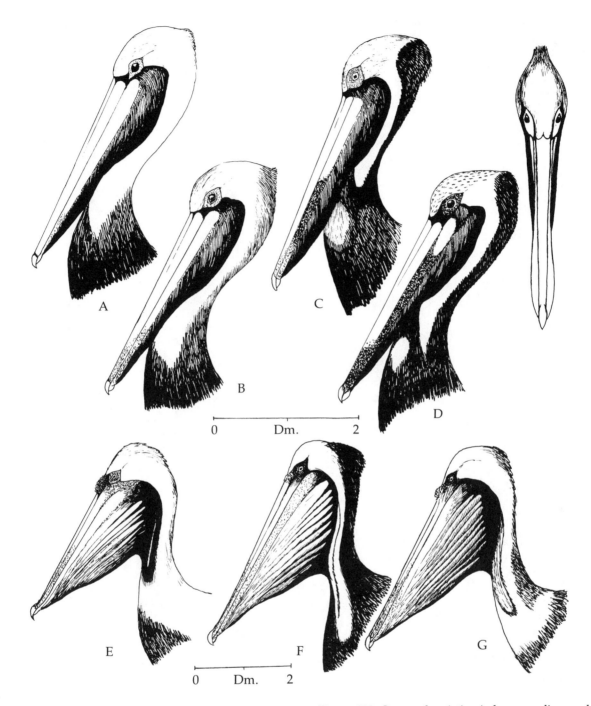

Figure 118. Seasonal variation in brown pelicans, showing *carolinensis* in postbreeding plumage (January) (A), transition to prebreeding plumage (March) (B), prebreeding plumage (courtship aspect, April) (C), and postbreeding plumage (incubation aspect, June) (D). Also shown are adults of *thagus* in probable postbreeding plumage (October) (E), probable prebreeding plumage (January) (F), and during incubation (G). Adapted from Schreiber et al. (1989) and Forbes (1914).

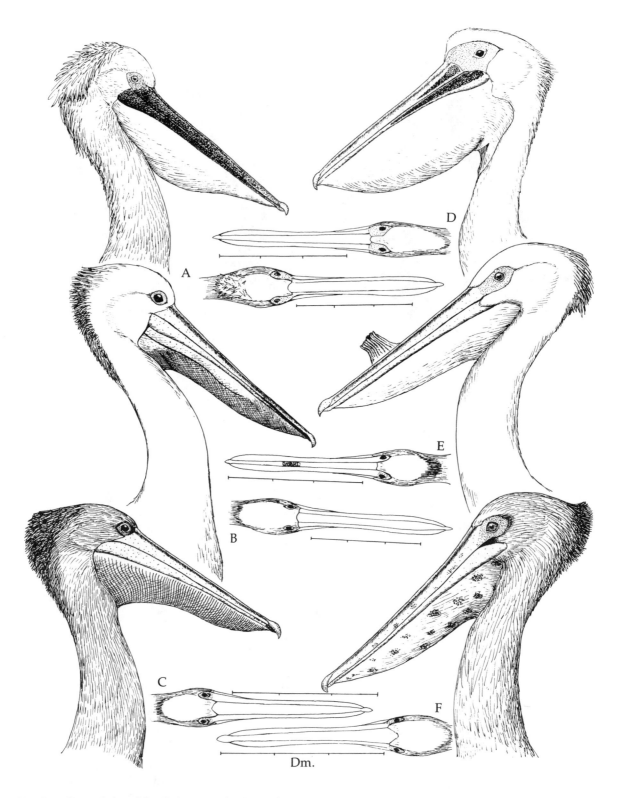

Figure 119. Breeding adults of the Dalmatian (A), Australian (B), pink-backed (C), eastern white (D), American white (E), and spot-billed (F) pelicans. Smaller sketches show head and bill outlines from above. Scales are adjusted for uniform visual comparisons.

Literature

Abdulali, H. 1976. The occurrence of Russian-ringed large cormorants (*Phalacrocorax carbo sinensis* Shaw) in India. *J. Bombay Nat. Hist. Soc.* 73:212–13.

Ainley, D. G., D. W. Anderson, and P. R. Kelly. 1981. Feeding ecology of marine cormorants in southwestern North America. *Condor* 83:120–31.

Ainley, D. G., and R. J. Boekelheide (eds.). 1990. *Seabirds of the Farallon Islands: Ecology, structure and dynamics in an upwelling-system community.* Stanford Univ. Press, Palo Alto.

Ainley, D. G., and T. J. Lewis. 1974. The history of Farallon Islands marine bird populations, 1854–1972. *Condor* 76:432–46.

Ainley, D. G., and G. A. Sanger. 1979. Trophic relationships of seabirds in the northeastern Pacific Ocean and Bering Sea. Pp. 95–122, in: J. C. Bartonek and D. N. Nettleship (eds.), *Conservation of marine birds of northern North America.* U.S. Dept. of Int., Fish and Wildl. Serv., Wildl. Res. Rept. 11:1–319.

Ali, S., and S. D. Ripley. 1983. *Handbook of the birds of India and Pakistan.* Compact ed. Oxford Univ. Press, Oxford.

Allen, T. T. 1961. Notes on the breeding behavior of the anhinga. *Wilson Bull.* 73:115–25.

Alletson, D. J. 1985. Observations on some piscivorous birds in a trout fishing area of Natal. *Lammergeyer* 35:41–46.

Alstrom, P. 1985. [Identification of cormorant, *Phalacrocorax carbo*, and shag, *Ph. aristotelis*]. *Vår Fågelvårld* 44:325–50. (Swedish, English summary.)

Amundsen, T., and J. N. Stokland. 1988. Adaptive significance of asynchronous hatching in the shag: a test of the brood reduction hypothesis. *J. An. Ecol.* 57:329–44.

Amundsen, T., and J. N. Stokland. 1990. Egg size and parental quality influence nestling growth in the shag. *Auk* 107:410–13.

Anderson, D. W. 1988. Dose-response relationship between human disturbance and brown pelican breeding success. *Wildl. Soc. Bull.* 16:339–45.

Anderson, D. W., and I. T. Anderson. 1976. Distribution and status of brown pelicans in the California Current. *Am. Birds* 30:3–12.

Anderson, D. W., and F. Gress. 1982. Brown pelicans and the anchovy fishery off southern California. Pp. 128–35, in: D. N. Nettleship, G. A. Sanger, and P. F. Springer (eds.), *Marine birds: their feeding ecology and commercial fisheries relationships.* Proceedings of the Pacific Seabirds Group Symposium, Seattle, Wash., 6–8 January 1982.

Anderson, D. W., and F. Gress. 1983. Status of a northern population of California brown pelicans. *Condor* 85:79–88.

Anderson, D. W., F. Gress, and K. F. Mais. 1982. Brown pelicans: influence of food supply on reproduction. *Oikos* 39:23–31.

Anderson, D. W., and J. J. Hickey. 1970. Oological data on egg and breeding characteristics of brown pelicans. *Wilson Bull.* 82:14–28.

Anderson, D. W., J. R. Jehl, Jr., R. W. Risebrough, L. A. Woods, Jr., L. R. Deweese, and W. G. Edgecomb. 1975. Brown pelicans: improved reproduction off the southern California coast. *Science* 190:806–8.

Anderson, D. W., and J. O. Keith. 1980. The human influence on seabird nesting success: conservation implication. *Biol. Cons.* 18:65–80.

Andone, G., H. Almasan, D. Rudu, L. Andone, E. Chirac, and G. Sclarletescu. 1969. Cercetare asupra pasarilor ichiof age din delta Dunarii. *Inst. Cercet. Pisc. Studi si Cercetari* (Romania) 27:133–83. (Not seen.)

Anonymous. 1949. Recovery round-up: little black cormorant. *Aust. Bird Bander* 14:55.

Anonymous (ed.). 1985. Cormorants in northern Europe. Proc. of meeting at Falsterbe, Sweden, Sept. 26–27, 1985. Natl. Swedish Environ. Protect. Board, Rept. 3211.

Ashmole, N. P. 1963. The regulation of numbers of tropical oceanic birds. *Ibis* 103b:458–73.

Ashmole, N. P. 1971. Sea bird biology and the marine environment. Pp. 223–86, in: D. S. Farner and J. R. King (eds.), *Avian biology,* vol. 1. Academic Press, N.Y.

Astheimer, L. B., and C. R. Grau. 1990. A comparison of yolk growth rates in seabird eggs. *Ibis* 132:380–94.

Audubon, J. J. 1840–44. *The birds of America.* Chavalier, Philadelphia.

Bailey, A. M., and J. H. Sorensen. 1962. *Subantarctic Campbell Island.* Denver Museum of Nat. Hist., Denver.

Bailey, R. 1966. The sea-birds of the southeast coast of Arabia. *Ibis* 108:224–64.

Baird, P. A., and P. J. Gould (eds.). 1985. The breeding biology and feeding ecology of marine birds in the Gulf of Alaska. Outer Cont. Shelf. Environ. Assess. Progr., Final Repts. of Princ. Invest. 45:121–504.

Baird, P. A., and R. A. Moe. 1978. The breeding biology and feeding ecology of marine birds in the Sitkelidak Strait area, Kodiak Island, 1977. Pp. 313–524, in: Ann. Rept. Princip. Invest., Environ. Assess. of Alaskan Cont. Shelf, NOAA, Boulder, Colo., vol. 3 (Birds).

Baker, E. C. S. 1929. *The fauna of British India, including Ceylon and Burma. Birds,* vol. 6. Taylor & Francis, London.

Baker, E.C.S. 1935. *The nidification of birds of the Indian Empire.* Vol. 4. Taylor & Francis, London.

Baltz, D. M., and G. V. Morejohn. 1977. Food habitats and niche overlap of seabirds wintering on Monterey Bay, California. *Auk* 94:526–43.

Barlow, C. G., and K. Bock. 1984. Predation on fish in farm dams by cormorants, *Phalacrocorax* spp. *Aust. Wildl. Res.* 11:559–66.

Barrett, R. T., and R. W. Furness. 1990. The prey and diving depths of seabirds on Honoy, north Norway, after a decrease in the Barents Sea capelin stocks. *Ornis. Scand.* 21:179–86.

Bartholomew, G. A., Jr. 1942. The fishing activities of double-crested cormorants on San Francisco Bay. *Condor* 44:13–21.

Bartholomew, G. A., Jr., and W. R. Dawson. 1954. Temperature regulation in young pelicans, herons and gulls. *Ecology* 35:466–72.

Bartholomew, G. A., Jr., W. R. Dawson, and E. J. O'Neill. 1953. A field study of temperature regulation in young white pelicans, *Pelecanus erythrorhynchos. Ecology* 34:554–60.

Bartholomew, G. A., Jr., R. C. Lasiewski, and E. C. Crawford, Jr. 1968. Patterns of panting and gular flutter in cormorants, pelicans, owls and doves. *Condor* 70:31–34.

Bartonek, J., C. Lensink, P. Gould, R. Gill, and G. Sanger (eds.). 1977. Population dynamics and trophic relationships of marine birds in the Gulf of Alaska and southern Bering Sea. Pp. 1–757, in: Ann. Repts. of Princ. Invest., Environ. Assess. of Alaskan Cont. Shelf, NOAA, Boulder, Colo., vol. 4 (Birds).

Bauer, K. M., and Glutz von Blotzheim, Urs. N. (eds.). 1966. *Handbuch der Vögel Mitteleuropas.* Vol. 1. Akademische Verlags., Frankfurt.

Becker, J. J. 1986. Reidentification of *"Phalacrocorax" subvolans* Brodkorb as the earliest record of Anhingidae. *Auk* 103:804–8.

Beddard, F. E. 1892. Notes on the anatomy of the Indian darter (*Plotus melanogaster*). *Proc. Zool. Soc. London, 1892,* pp. 291–96.

Behle, W. H. 1958. *The bird life of Great Salt Lake.* Univ. of Utah Press, Salt Lake City.

Behn, F., J. D. Goodall, A. W. Johnson, and R. A. Philippi. 1955. The geographic distribution of the blue-eyed shags, *Phalacrocorax albiventer* and *P. atriceps. Auk* 72:6–13.

Bell, B. D. 1986. The conservation status of New Zealand wildlife. New Zealand Wildl. Serv., Wellington. Occ. Publ. 12:1–103.

Bent, A. C. 1922. Life histories of North American petrels and pelicans and their allies. *U.S. Natl. Mus. Bull.* 121:1–341.

Bernstein, N. P., and S. J. Maxson. 1982. Behaviour of the Antarctic blue-eyed shag *Phalacrocorax atriceps bransfieldensis. Notornis* 29:197–207.

Berry, H. H. 1974. The crowned race of reed cormorant *Phalacrocorax africanus coronatus* breeding underneath Walvis Bay guano platform, South West Africa. *Madoqua* 8:59–62.

Berry, H. H. 1976. Physiological and behavioral ecology of the Cape cormorant *Phalacrocorax capensis. Madoqua* 9:5–55.

Berry, H. H. 1977. Seasonal fidelity of Cape cormorants to nesting areas. *Cormorant* 2:5–6.

Berry H. H., H. P. Stark, and A. S. van Vuuren. 1973. White pelicans *Pelecanus onocrotalus* breeding on the Etosha pan, South West Africa, during 1971. *Modoqua* 7:17–31.

Biderman, J. O., W. H. Drury, J. B. French, and S. Hinckley. 1978. Ecological studies in the northern Bering Sea: birds of coastal habitats on the south shore of the Seward Peninsula. Pp. 510–613, in: Environ. Assess. of the Alaskan Cont. Shelf, Ann. Repts. of Princ. Invest., NOAA, Boulder, Colo. vol. 2 (Birds).

Birkhead, M. E. 1978. Some aspects of the feeding ecology of the reed cormorant and darter in Lake Kariba, Rhodesia. *Ostrich* 49:1–7.

Blacklock, G. W., R. D. Slack, D. R. Blankenship, A. H. Chaney, K. A. King, J. C. Smith, and L. Mullins. 1979. *Texas colonial waterbird census, 1977–78.* Welder Wildlife Foundation, Sinton, Texas.

Blake, E. R. 1977. *Manual of Neotropical birds.* Vol. 1. Univ. of Chicago Press, Chicago.

Blakers, M., S. J. J. F. Davies, and P. N. Reilly. 1984. *The atlas of Australian birds.* Melbourne Univ. Press, Carlton, Vict., Australia.

Blankley, W. O. 1981. Marine foods of kelp gulls, lesser sheathbills, and imperial cormorants at Marion Island (subantarctic). *Cormorant* 9:77–84.

Bloekpoel, H., and W. C. Scharf. 1991. Status and conservation of seabirds nesting in the Great Lakes of North America. Pp. 17–42, in Croxall (1991).

Blomme, C. 1981. Status and breeding success of double-crested cormorant in two North Channel (Lake Huron) colonies in 1979. *Ont. Field Biol.* 35:70–78.

Blus, L. J., and J. A. Keahey. 1978. Variation in reproductivity with age in the brown pelican. *Auk* 95:128–34.

Boekelheide, R. J., and D. G. Ainley. 1989. Age, resource availability and breeding effort in Brandt's cormorant. *Auk* 106:389–401.

Boekelheide, R. J., D. G. Ainley, H. R. Huber, and T. J. Lewis. 1990. Pelagic cormorant and double-crested cormorant. Pp. 195–217, in: D. C. Ainley and R. J. Boekelheide (eds.), *Seabirds of the Farallon Islands: ecology, dynamics and structures of an upwelling-system community.* Stanford Univ. Press, Palo Alto.

Boudewijn, T. J., S. Dirksen, R. G. Mes, and B. L. K. Slager. 1989. (The cormorant: a useful guide to the quality of Netherlands' waters?). *Limosa* 62:96–97. (Dutch, English summary.)

Bowen, W., N. Gardiner, B. J. Harris, and J. D. Thomas. 1962. Communal nesting of *Phalacrocorax africanus*, *Bubulcus ibis*, and *Anhinga rufa* in southern Ghana. *Ibis* 104:246–47.

Bowmaker, A. P. 1963. Cormorant predation on two central African lakes. *Ostrich* 34:3–26.

Braithwaite, L. W., et al. 1985. *Tech. Mem. Div. Wildl. Rglds. Res., CSIRO Aust.* 21. (Not seen, cited in Marchant and Higgins, 1990.)

Brandt, C. A. 1984. Age and hunting success in the brown pelican: influences of skill and patch choice on foraging efficiency. *Oecologia* 62:132–37.

Brazil, M. A. 1991. *The birds of Japan.* Smithson. Inst. Press, Wash., D.C.

Brodkorb, P. 1963. Catalogue of fossil birds. Pt. 1 (Archaeopterygiiformes through Ardeiformes). *Bull. Fla. State Mus. Biol. Sci.* 7:179–293.

Brooke, R. K., J. Cooper, P. A. Shelton, and R. J. M. Crawford. 1982. Taxonomy, distribution, population size, breeding and conservation of the whitebreasted cormorant, *Phalacrocorax carbo*, on the southern African coast. *Gerfaut* 72:189–220.

Brothers, N. P. 1985. Breeding biology, diet and morphometrics of the king shag *Phalacrocorax albiventer purpurascens* at Macquarie Island. *Aust. Wildl. Res.* 12:81–94.

Brown, J. E. 1983. *The return of the brown pelican.* La. State Univ. Press, Baton Rouge.

Brown, L. H., and E. K. Urban. 1969. The breeding biology of the great white pelican *Pelecanus onocrotalus roseus* at Lake Shala, Ethiopia. *Ibis* 111:19–237.

Brown, L. H., E. K. Urban, and K. Newman (eds.). 1982. *The birds of Africa*, vol. 1. Academic Press, London.

Brown, R. G. B., D. N. Nettleship, P. Germain, C. E. Tull, and T. Davis. 1975. *Atlas of eastern Canadian seabirds.* Ottawa: Canadian Wildlife Service.

Browning, M. R. 1989. The correct name for the olivaceous cormorant, "maigue" of Piso (1658). *Wilson Bull.* 101:101–6.

Brun, E. 1979. Present status and trends in populations of seabirds in Norway. Pp. 289–301, in: Conservation of marine birds of northern North America, J. C. Bartonek and D. N. Nettleship (eds.). U.S. Fish & Wildl. Serv., Wild. Res. Rept. 11:1–319.

Bundy, G., R. J. Conner, and C. J. O. Harrison. 1989. *Birds of the eastern province of Saudi Arabia.* Witherby, London.

Burger, J., L. M. Miller, and D. C. Hahn. 1978. Behavior and sex roles of nesting anhingas at San Blas, Mexico. *Wilson Bull.* 90:359–75.

Burke, V. E. M., and L. H. Brown. 1970. Observations on the breeding of the pink-backed pelican. *Ibis* 112:449–512.

Campbell, R. W., N. K. Dawe, I. McTaggart-Cowan, J. M. Cooper, C. W. Kaiser, and M. C. E. McNall. 1990. *The birds of British Columbia.* Vol. 1. Non-passerines. Royal Brit. Col. Mus., Victoria.

Campo, J. J., B. Thompson, J. C. Barron, P. P. Durocher, and S. J. Gutreuter. 1988. Feeding habits of double-crested cormorants wintering in Texas. Tex. Parks & Wildl. Dept. Rept., Austin.

Carl, R. A. 1987. Age-class variation in foraging techniques by brown pelicans. *Condor* 89:525–33.

Carter, H. R., K. R. Hobson, and S. G. Sealy. 1984. Colony-site selection by pelagic cormorants (*Phalacrocorax pelagicus*) in Barkely Sound, British Columbia. *Colonial Waterbirds* 7:25–34.

Cash, K. J., and R. M. Evans. 1986. Brood reduction in the American white pelican (*Pelecanus erythrorhynchos*). *Behav. Ecol. Sociobiol.* 18:413–18.

Casler, C. L. 1973. The air-sac system and buoyancy of the anhinga and double-crested cormorant. *Auk* 90:324–40.

Cawkell, E. M., and J. E. Hamilton. 1961. The birds of the Falkland Islands. *Ibis* 103a:1–27.

Chandler A. 1916. A study of the structure of feathers, with reference to their taxonomic significance. *Univ. Calif. Publ. Zool.* 13:243–446.

Chapin, J., and D. Amadon. 1952. The roseate pelicans of Africa. *Ostrich* 23:123.

Chapman, B. R. 1988. History of the white pelican colonies in south Texas and northern Tamaulipas. *Colonial Waterbirds* 11:275–83.

Cheng Tso-hsin. 1987. *Synopsis of the avifauna of China*. Science Press, Beijing.

Clapp, R. B., R. C. Banks, D. Morgan-Jacobs, and W. A. Hoffman. 1982. Marine birds of the southeastern United States and Gulf of Mexico. Pt. 1. Gaviiformes through Pelecaniformes. U.S. Fish & Wildl. Serv., Off. Biol. Serv. FSW/OBS 82/01.

Clark, G. A., Jr. 1969. Spread-wing postures in Pelecaniformes, Ciconiiformes, and Falconiformes. *Auk* 86:136–39.

Close, D. H., J. M. Bonnin, M. H. Waterman, and D. J. Connell. 1982. Breeding waterbirds on the Salt Lagoon Islands, South Australia. *Corella* 6:25–36.

Coblentz, B. E. 1985. A possible reason for age-differential foraging success in brown pelicans. *J. Field Ornith.* 57:563–64.

Cobley, N. 1989. Aspects of the survival of blue-eyed shags (*Phalacrocorax atriceps* King). *Antarctic Spec. Top.*, 1989:93–96.

Coker, R. E. 1919. Habits and economic relations of the guano birds of Peru. *Proc. U.S. Nat. Mus.* 56:449–511.

Collar, N. J., and P. Andrew. 1988. Birds to watch. The ICBP world checklist of threatened birds. ICBP Tech. Pub. No. 8, Smithson. Inst. Press, Wash., D.C.

Collazo, J. A. 1986. Status and ecology of the brown pelican in the Greater Puerto Rican Bank region. Ph.D. diss., Iowa State Univ., Ames.

Conniff, P. 1991. Why catfish farmers want to throttle the crow of the sea. *Smithsonian* 22(4):44–55.

Conroy, J. W. H., and E. L. Twelves. 1972. Diving depths of the gentoo penguin (*Pygoscelis papua*) and the blue-eyed shag (*Phalacrocorax atriceps*) for the South Orkney Islands. *Brit. Antarct. Survey Bull.* 30:106–8.

Coomber, R. 1990. *A pictorial encyclopedia of birds*. Gallery Books, New York.

Cooper, J. 1980. Fatal sibling aggression in pelicans—a review. *Ostrich* 51:183–86.

Cooper, J. 1981. Biology of the bank cormorant. 1. Distribution, population size, movements and conservation. *Ostrich* 52:208–15.

Cooper, J. 1985a. Biology of the bank cormorant. 2. Morphometrics, plumage, bare parts and moult. *Ostrich* 56:79–85.

Cooper, J. 1985b. Biology of the bank cormorant. 3. Foraging behavior. *Ostrich* 56:86–95.

Cooper, J. 1985c. Foraging behavior of nonbreeding imperial cormorants at the Prince Edward Islands. *Ostrich* 56:96–100.

Cooper, J. 1986a. Biology of the bank cormorant. 4. Nest construction and characteristics. *Ostrich* 57:170–79.

Cooper, J. 1986b. Diving patterns of cormorants Phalacrocoracidae. *Ibis* 128:562–70.

Cooper, J. 1987. Biology of the bank cormorant. 5. Clutch size, eggs and incubation. *Ostrich* 58:1–8.

Cooper, J., R. K. Brooke, P. A. Shelton, and R. J. M. Crawford. 1982. Distribution, population size and conservation of the Cape cormorant *Phalacrocorax capensis*. *Fish. Bull. S. Afr.* 16:121–43.

Cott, H. B. 1961. Scientific results of an inquiry into the ecology and economic status of the Nile crocodile (*Crocodilus niloticus*) in Uganda and Northern Rhodesia. *Trans. Zool. Soc. London* 91:211–350.

Cottam, P. A. 1957. The pelecaniform characters of the shoebilled stork *Balaeniceps rex*. *Bull. Brit. Mus. Nat. Hist. (Zool).* 5:51–71.

Coues, E. 1894. *Key to North American birds*. 4th ed. Estes & Lauriat, Boston.

Cracraft, J. 1981. A phylogenetic classification of birds. *Auk* 98:681–714.

Cracraft, J. 1985. Monophyly and phylogenetic relationships of the Pelecaniformes: a numerical cladistic analysis. *Auk* 102:834–53.

Cramp, S., W. R. P. Bourne, and D. Saunders. 1974. *The seabirds of Britain and Ireland*. Collins, London.

Cramp, S., and K. E. L. Simmons. 1977. *The birds of the western Palearctic*. Vol. 1. Oxford Univ. Press, Oxford.

Craven, S. R., and E. Lev. 1987. Double-crested cormorants in the Apostle Islands, Wisconsin, USA: population trends, food habits and fishery depredations. *Colonial Waterbirds* 10:64–71.

Crawford, R. J. M., R. A. Cruickshank, P. A. Shelton, and I. Kruger. 1985. Partitioning of a goby resource amongst four avian predators and evidence for altered trophic flow in the pelagic community of an intense, perennial upwelling system. *S. Afr. J. Marine Res.* 3:215–28.

Crawford, R. J. M., P. A. Shelton, R. K. Brooke, and J. Cooper. 1982. Taxonomy, distribution, population size and conservation of the crowned cormorant. *Gerfaut* 72:3–30.

Crivelli, A. J. 1987. The ecology and behaviour of the Dalmatian pelican, *Pelecanus crispus* Bruch, a world-endangered species. Unpub. report, Comm. of the European Commun. & Stat. Biol. de la Tour de Valat.

Crivelli, A. J., G. Catsadorakis, H. Jerrentrup, D. Hatzilacos, and T. Mitchev. 1991. Conservation and management of pelicans nesting in the Palearctic. In ICBP Tech. Publication No. 12.

Crivelli, A. J., S. Focardi, C. Fossi, C. Leonzio, A. Massi, and A. Renzoni. 1989. Trace elements and chlorinated hydrocarbons in eggs of *Pelecanus crispus*, a world-endangered species nesting at Lake Mikri Prespa, north-western Greece. *Envir. Pollution* 61:235–47.

Crivelli, A. J., Y. Leshem, T. Mitchev, and H. Jerrentrup. 1991. Where do Palaearctic great white pelicans (*Pelecanus onocrotalus*) presently overwinter? *Rev. Ecol. (Terre Vie)* 46:145–71.

Crivelli, A. J., T. Mitchev, G. Catsadorakis, and V. Pomakov. 1991. Preliminary results on the wintering of the Dalmatian pelican, *Pelecanus crispus*, in Turkey. *Zool. Middle East* 5:11–20.

Crivelli, A. J., and R. W. Schreiber. 1984. Status of the Pelecanidae. *Biol. Cons.* 3:147–56.

Crivelli, A. J., and O. Vizi. 1981. The Dalmatian pelican *Pelecanus crispus* Bruch 1832, a recently world endangered species. *Biol. Cons.* 2:297–310.

Croxall, J. P. 1984. Seabirds. Pp. 533–619, in: R. M. Laws (ed.), *Antarctic ecology,* vol. 2. Academic Press, N.Y.

Croxall, J. P. (ed.). 1991. *Seabird status and conservation: a supplement.* Intern. Council for Bird Pres., Cambridge.

Croxall, J. P., P. G. H. Evans, and R. W. Schreiber (eds.). 1984. Status and conservation of the world's seabirds. Intern. Council for Bird Pres., Cambridge, Tech. Publ. No. 2.

Croxall, J. P., S. McInnes, and P. A. Prince. 1984. The status and conservation of seabirds at the Falkland Islands. Pp. 271–92, in: J. P. Croxall et al. (eds.), *Status and conservation of the world's seabirds.* ICBP, Cambridge.

Curry-Lindall, K. 1970. Spread-wing postures in Pelecaniformes and Ciconiiformes. *Auk* 87:371–72.

Danielson, F., and H. Skov. 1985. South-east Sumatra. *Interwader* 6:6–7.

Davies, D. H. 1956. The South African pilchard (*Sardinops ocellata*) and maasbanker (*Trachurus trachurus*). Bird predators, 1954–55. *Div. Fish. Un. S. Afr. Invest. Rept.* 23:1–40.

Debout, G. 1987. Le grande cormoran, *Phalacrocorax carbo,* en France: les populations nicheuses littorales. *Alauda* 55:35–54.

Debout, G. 1988. (Breeding biology of the great cormorant, *Phalacrocorax carbo,* in Normandy.) *Oiseau Rev. Franç. Ornith.* 58:1–17. (French, English summary.)

DeGange, A. R., and G. A. Sanger. 1986. Marine birds. Pp. 479–524, in: D. W. Hood and S. T. Zimmerman (eds.), *The Gulf of Alaska.* U.S. Dept. of Commerce, Springfield, Va.

de Juana, A. E., J. Varela, and H.-H. Witt. 1984. The conservation of seabirds at the Chafarinas Islands. Pp. 363–70, in: J. P. Croxall et al. (eds.), *Status and conservation of the world's seabirds.* ICBP, Cambridge.

Delacour, J., and E. Mayr. 1945. Notes on the taxonomy of the birds of the Philippines. *Zoologica* 30:105–7.

Dementiev, G. P., and N. A. Gladkov (eds.). 1951. (Birds of the Soviet Union.) Vol. 1. Sovetskya Nauka, Moscow. (In Russian. Translated in 1966 by the Israel Program for Scientific Translations, Jerusalem.)

Derenne, P., G. Mary, and J. L. Mougin. 1976. Le cormoran à ventre blanc, *Phalacrocorax albiventer melanogenis* (Blyth) de l'archipel Crozet. *Comité Natl. Français Recherches Antarctiques* 40:191–219.

DesGranges, J.-L., G. Chapdelaine, and P. Dupuis. 1984. (Nesting sites and population dynamics of the double-crested cormorant in Quebec.) *Can. J. Zool.* 62:1260–67. (French; English summary.)

Devillers, P., and J. A. Terschuren. 1978. Relationships between the blue-eyed shags of South America. *Gerfaut* 68:53–86.

Dewar, J. M. 1924. *The bird as a diver.* Witherby, London.

Dick, M. H., and L. S. Dick. 1971. The natural history of Cape Pierce and Nanvak Bay, Cape Newenham Natl. Wildl. Refuge, Alaska. Unpublished report, U.S. Bur. Sport Fish. & Wildl., Bethel, Alaska. (Not seen.)

Diem, K. L., and D. D. Condon. 1967. Banding studies of water birds on the Molly Islands, Yellowstone Lake, Wyoming. Yellowstone Library & Museum Assoc., Mammoth Hot Springs, Wyoming.

Din, N. A. 1979. *Ecology of pelicans in the Rwenzorie National Park, Uganda.* Starling Press, Tucson.

Din, N. A., and S. K. Eltringham. 1974a. Breeding of the pink-backed pelican *Pelecanus rufescens* in Ruwenzori National Park, Uganda, with notes on Marabou storks *Leptotilus crumeniferus. Ibis* 116:477–93.

Din, N. A., and S. K. Eltringham. 1974b. Ecological separation between white and pink-backed pelicans in the Ruwenzori National Park, Uganda. *Ibis* 116:28–43.

Din, N. A., and S. K. Eltringham. 1977. Weights and measurements of Ugandan pelicans with some seasonal variations. *East Afr. Wildl. J.* 15:317–26.

Dinsmore, J. J. 1974. White and brown pelicans feeding together. *Fla. Field Natl.* 2:11.

Dipper, F. 1991. Earth, air, fire, water, oil and war. *BBC Wildlife* 9(3):191–93.

Dolbeer, R. A. 1991. Migration patterns of double-crested cormorants east of the Rocky Mountains. *J. Field. Ornith.* 62:83–93.

Dorst, J., and J. L. Mougin. 1979. Order Pelecaniformes. Pp. 155–93, in: E. Mayr and G. W. Cottrell (eds.), *Check List of Birds of the World,* vol. 1. 2d ed. Museum of Comp. Zool., Cambridge, Mass.

Dorward, D. F. 1962. Comparative biology of the white booby and the brown booby, *Sula* spp., at Ascension. *Ibis* 103b:174–220.

Dostine, P. L., and S. R. Morton. 1988. Notes on the food and feeding habits of cormorants on a tropical floodplain. *Emu* 88:263–66.

Dostine, P. L., and S. R. Morton. 1989. Food of the darter, *Anhinga melanogaster,* in the Alligator Rivers region, Northern Territory. *Emu* 89:53–54.

Dowding, J. E., and M. J. Taylor. 1987. Genetics of polymorphism in the little shag. *Notornis* 34:51–57.

Downes, M. C., E. H. M. Ealey, A. M. Gwynn, and P. S. Young. 1959. The birds of Heard Island. *A.N.A.R.E. Sci. Rept.* (B)1:124–27. (Not seen.)

Draffan, R. D. W., S. T. Garnett, and G. J. Malone. 1983. Birds of the Torres Strait: an annotated list and biogeographical analysis. *Emu* 86:263–66.

Drent, R., and C. J. Guiguet. 1961. A catalogue of British Columbia sea-bird colonies. *Occ. Papers Brit. Col. Prov. Mus.* 12:1–173.

Drent, R., G. F. van Tets, F. Tompa, and K. Vermeer. 1964. The breeding birds of Mandarte Island, British Columbia. *Can. Field-Nat.* 78:208–61.

Drummond, H. 1987. A review of parent-offspring conflict and brood reduction in the Pelecaniformes. *Colonial Waterbirds* 10:1–15.

Duffy, D. C. 1980a. Comparative reproductive behavior and population regulation of seabirds of the Peruvian Coastal Current. Ph.D. diss., Princeton Univ., Princeton, N.J.

Duffy, D. C. 1980b. Patterns of piracy by Peruvian seabirds: a depth hypothesis. *Ibis* 122:521–25.

Duffy, D. C. 1983a. Competition for nesting space among Peruvian guano birds. *Auk* 100:680–88.

Duffy, D. C. 1983b. The ecology of tick parasitism on densely nesting Peruvian seabirds. *Ecology* 64:110–19.

Duffy, D. C. 1983c. The foraging ecology of Peruvian seabirds. *Auk* 100:800–810.

Duffy, D. C., W. E. Arntz, H. T. Serpa, P. D. Boersma, and R. L. Norton. 1988. A comparison of the effects of El Niño and the Southern Oscillation in Peru and the Atlantic Ocean. Pp. 1740–45, in: Proc. 19th Ornith. Congress, Ottawa, Canada, H. Ouellet (ed.), vol. 2. U. of Ottawa Press, Ottawa.

Duffy, D. C., C. Hays, and M. Plenge. 1984. The conservation status of Peruvian seabirds. Pp. 245–60, in J. P. Croxall et al. (eds.), *Status and conservation of the world's seabirds*. ICBP, Cambridge.

Duffy, D. C., and G. D. la Cock. 1985. Partitioning of nesting species among seabirds of the Benguela upwelling region. *Ostrich* 56:186–201.

Duffy D. C., R. P. Wilson, M.-P. Wilson, and C. Velasquez R. 1986. Plunge-diving by olivaceous cormorants in Chile. *Wilson Bull.* 98:607–8.

Dunbar, D. L. 1984. The breeding ecology and management of white pelicans at Stum Lake, British Columbia. B.C. Fish & Wildl. Report R-6, Victoria.

Dunn, E. H. 1975a. Caloric intake of nestling double-crested cormorants. *Auk* 92:553–65.

Dunn, E. H. 1975b. Growth, body components and energy content of nestling double-crested cormorants. *Condor* 77:431–38.

Dunn, E. H. 1976. Development of endothermy and existence energy of nestling double-crested cormorants. *Condor* 78:350–56.

Dunn, E. H. 1979. Time-energy use and life history strategies of northern seabirds. Pp. 141–66, in: J. C. Bartonek and D. N. Nettleship (eds.), *Conservation of marine birds of northern North America*. U.S. Fish & Wildl. Serv., Wild. Res. Bull. 11:1–319.

Dunning, J. B., Jr. 1984. Body weights of 686 species of North American birds. Western Bird Banding Assoc. Monogr. No. 1, Cave Creek, Ariz.

Egremont, P., and M. Rothschild. 1979. The calculating cormorants. *Biol. J. Linn. Soc.* 12(2):181–86.

Elliot, D. G. 1866–69. *The new and heretofore unfigured species of birds of North America*. Published by the author, New York.

Elliot, D. G. 1869. A monograph of the genus *Pelecanus*. *Proc. Zool. Soc. London* 1869, pp. 571–91.

Ellis, W. C. 1990. A Soviet sea lies dying. *Natl. Geog.* 177(2):73–92.

Elowson, A. M. 1984. Spread-wing postures and the water repellency of feathers: a test of Rijke's hypothesis. *Auk* 101:371–83.

Erskine, A. J. 1972. The great cormorants of eastern Canada. *Can. Wildl. Serv. Occas. Pap.* no. 14.

Espitalier-Noel, G., N. J. Adams, and N. T. Klages. 1988. Diet of the imperial cormorant *Phalacrocorax atriceps* at sub-Antarctic Marion Island. *Emu* 88:43–46.

Evans, P. G. H. 1984. The seabirds of Greenland: their status and conservation. Pp. 49–84, in: J. P. Croxall et al. (eds.), *Status and conservation of the world's seabirds*. ICBP, Cambridge.

Evans, R. M. 1969. Specific gravity of white pelican eggs. *Auk* 86:560–61.

Evans, R. M. 1972. Some effects of water level on the reproductive success of the white pelican at East Shoal Lake, Manitoba. *Can. Field-Nat.* 86:151–53.

Evans, R. M. 1984a. Development of thermoregulation in young white pelicans. *Can. J. Zool.* 65:808–13.

Evans, R. M. 1984b. Some causal and functional correlates of creching in young white pelicans. *Can. J. Zool.* 62:814–19.

Evans, R. M. 1988. Embryonic vocalizations and the removal of foot webs from pipped eggs in the American white pelican. *Condor* 190:721–23.

Evans, R. M. 1990a. Embryonic fine tuning of pipped egg temperature in the American white pelican. *Anim. Behav.* 40:963–68.

Evans, R. M. 1990b. Terminal egg-neglect in the American white pelican. *Wilson Bull.* 102:684–92.

Evans, R. M., and K. J. Cash. 1985. Early spring flights of American white pelicans: timing and functional role in attracting others to the breeding colony. *Condor* 87:252–55.

Everett, W. T., and D. W. Anderson, 1991. Status and conservation of the breeding seabirds on offshore Pacific Islands of Baja California and the Gulf of California. Pp. 115–40 in Croxall (1991).

Falla, R. A. 1933. King shags of Queen Charlotte Sound. *Emu* 33:44–48.

Falla, R. A. 1937. Birds. In: *British & New Zealand Antarctic Research Expedition, 1929–31*. 2B. Published by the Committee, Adelaide. (Not seen.)

Falla, R. A., R. B. Sibson, and E. G. Turbott. 1981. *The new guide to the birds of New Zealand*. Revised ed. Collins, Auckland.

Falla, R. A., and G. Stokell. 1945. Investigation of stomach contents of New Zealand fresh-water shags. *Trans. Proc. Roy. Soc. N.Z.* 74:320–31.

FAO Fisheries Department. 1981. *Atlas of the living resources of*

North Pacific shags, with a description of a new species. *U. of Kans. Mus. Nat. Hist. Occ. Pap.* 140:1–15.

Siegel-Causey, D., and G. L. Hunt, Jr. 1981. Colonial defense behavior in double-crested and pelagic cormorants. *Auk* 98:522–31.

Siegel-Causey, D., and G. L. Hunt, Jr. 1986. Breeding-site selection and colony formation in double-crested and pelagic cormorants. *Auk* 103:230–34.

Siegfried, W. R., A. J. Williams, P. G. H. Frost, and J. B. Kinahan. 1975. Plumage and ecology of cormorants. *Zool. Afr.* 10:183–92.

Silvius, M. 1986. South-east Sumatra. *Interwader* 7:1.

Simmons, G. 1974. Brown pelican on the brink. *Natl. Parks Conserv. Mag.* 48(12):21–23.

Simmons, K. E. L. 1964. Feather maintenance. Pp. 278–86, in: A. Landsborough-Thompson (ed.), *A new dictionary of birds.* McGraw-Hill, N.Y.

Simmons, K. E. L. 1972. Some adaptive features of seabird plumage types. *Brit. Birds* 65:465–79.

Sivak, J. G., W. R. Bobier, and B. Levy. 1978. The refractive significance of the nictitating membrane of the bird eye. *J. Comp. Physiol.* (A) 125:335–39.

Sivak, J. G., J. L. Lincer, and W. Bobier. 1977. Amphibious visual optics of the eyes of double-crested cormorant (*Phalacrocorax auritus*) and the brown pelican (*Pelecanus occidentalis*). *Can. J. Zool.* 55:782–88.

Skead, D. M. 1980. Dispersal, life expectancy, and annual mortality of whitebreasted cormorants *Phalacrocorax carbo* ringed as nestlings at Barberspan. *Cormorant* 8:73–80.

Sloan, N. M. 1973. Status of breeding colonies of white pelicans in the United States through 1972. *IBBA News* 45:83–86.

Sloan, N. M. 1982. Status of breeding colonies of white pelicans in the United States through 1979. *Am. Birds* 36:250–54.

Smith, M., T. Steinbach, and G. Pampush. 1984. Distribution, foraging relationships and colony dynamics of the American white pelican (*Pelecanus erythrorhynchos*) in southern Oregon and northeastern California. Nat. Conserv., Portland.

Smythies, B. E. 1968. *The birds of Borneo.* 2d ed. Oliver & Boyd, Edinburgh.

Snow, B. 1960. Breeding biology of the shag, *Phalacrocorax aristotelis* on the island of Lundy, Bristol Channel. *Ibis* 102:554–75.

Snow, B. 1963. Behaviour of the shag. *Brit. Birds* 56:77–103, 164–86.

Snow, B. 1966. Observations on the behaviour and ecology of the flightless cormorant *Nannopterum harrisi. Ibis* 108:265–80.

Sowls, A. L., A. R. DeGange, J. W. Nelson, and G. S. Lester. 1980. Catalog of California seabird colonies. U.S. Fish & Wildl. Serv., Off. Biol. Serv. FWS/OBS-80/37.

Sowls, A. L., S. A. Hatch, and C. J. Lensink. 1978. Catalog of Alaskan seabird colonies. U.S. Fish & Wildl. Serv., Off. Biol. Serv., FWS/OBS/78.

Speich, S. M., and T. R. Wahl. 1989. Catalog of Washington seabird colonies. U.S. Fish & Wildl. Serv., Biol. Serv. Prog. Rep. 88(6):1–510.

Spendelow, J. A., and S. R. Patton. 1988. National atlas of coastal waterbird colonies in the contiguous United States, 1976–82. U.S. Fish & Wildl. Serv., Biol. Serv. Prog. Rep. 88(5):1–326.

Spillner, W. 1972. Zum Baltz- und Paarungsverhalten des Kormorans. *Falke* 19:86–101.

Squibb, R., and G. L. Hunt, Jr. 1983. A comparison of nestledges used by seabirds at St. George Island. *Ecol.* 64:727–34.

Stejneger, L. 1889. Contribution to the history of the Pallas' cormorant. *Proc. U.S. Natl. Mus.* 12:83–88.

Steven, G. A. 1933. The foods consumed by shags and cormorants around the shores of Cornwall (England). *J. Mar. Biol. Asso. U.K.* 19:277–92.

Stiles, F. G., and A. F. Skutch. 1989. *A guide to the birds of Costa Rica.* Cornell Univ. Press, Ithaca.

Stonehouse, B. 1967. Feeding behavior and diving rhythms of some New Zealand shags, Phalacrocoracidae. *Ibis* 109:600–609.

Stoner, C. R. 1948. Fishing with the Indian darter in Assam. *J. Bombay Nat. Hist. Soc.* 47:746.

Storer, R. W. 1971. Classification of birds. Pp. 1–18, in: D. S. Farner and J. R. King (eds.), *Avian biology,* vol. 1. Academic Press, N.Y.

Strait, L. E. 1973. Population dynamics of a white pelican population, Chase Lake Wildlife Refuge, North Dakota. M.S. thesis, Mich. Tech. Univ., Houghton.

Strait, L. E., and N. F. Sloan. 1974. Life table analysis for the white pelican. *Bird-Banding News* 46:20–28.

Strait, L. E., and N. F. Sloan. 1975. Movements and mortality of juvenile white pelicans from North Dakota. *Wilson Bull.* 87:54–59.

Straka, U. 1990. (Observations on wintering pygmy cormorants at the Danube in lower Austria in the winter of 1989–90.) *Egretta* 33:77–85. (German, English summary.)

Stresemann, E. 1927–34. Aves. *Handbuch der Zoologie,* 7(2):1–899. W. Kükenthal and T. Krumbach (eds.). W. de Gruyter, Berlin.

Stresemann, E., and V. Stresemann. 1966. Die Mauser der Vogel. *J. Ornith.* (Sonderheft) 107:1–448.

Stuart, D. 1948. Vital statistics of the Mochrum cormorant colony. *Brit. Birds* 41:194–99.

Talent, L. 1984. Food habits of wintering Brandt's cormorants. *Wilson Bull.* 96:130–34.

Taylor, M. J. 1987. A colony of the little shag and the pied shag in which the plumage forms of the little shag freely interbreed. *Notornis* 34:41–50.

Texas Colonial Waterbird Society. 1982. An atlas and census

of Texas waterbird colonies, 1973–1980. Caesar Kleberg Wildl. Res. Inst., Texas A. & I. Univ., Kingsville.

Thompson, J. A., and N. W. Morley. 1966. Physiological correlates of habitat selection in Australian cormorants. *Emu* 66:17–26.

Ticehurst, C. D., and R. E. Cheesman. 1925. The birds of Jabrin, Jafura, and Hasa in central and eastern Arabia and of Bahrain Island, Persian Gulf. *Ibis* ser. 12 (vol. 1):1–31.

Ticehurst, C. D., P. Cox, and R. E. Cheesman. 1925. Birds of the Persian Gulf islands. *J. Bomb. Nat. Hist. Soc.* 30:725–33.

Tindle, R. 1984. The evolution of breeding strategies in the flightless cormorant (*Nannopterum harrisi*) of the Galapagos. *Biol. J. Linn. Soc.* 21:157–64.

Trayler, K. W., D. J. Brothers, and I. C. Potter. 1989. Opportunistic foraging by three species of cormorants in an Australian estuary. *J. Zool.* 218:87–98.

Trillmich, F., K. Trillmich, D. Limberger, and W. Arnold. 1983. The breeding season of the flightless cormorant *Nannopterum harrisi* at Cabo Hammond, Fernandina. *Ibis* 125:221–23.

Turbott, E. G. 1956. Notes on the plumages and breeding cycle of the spotted shag *Phalacrocorax (Stictocarbo) punctatus punctatus* (Sparrman, 1786). *Rec. Auckland (N.Z.) Inst.* 4:343–63.

Urban, E. K. 1979. Observations on the nesting biology of the great cormorant in Ethiopia. *Wilson Bull.* 91:461–63.

Urban, E. K., and T. G. Jefford. 1977. Movements of juvenile great white pelicans *Pelecanus onocrotalus* from Lake Shala, Ethiopia. *Ibis* 119:524–28.

Valle, C. A., and M. C. Coulter. 1987. Present status of the flightless cormorant, Galapagos penguin and greater flamingo populations in the Galapagos Islands, Ecuador, after the 1982–83 el Niño. *Condor* 89:276–81.

van der Veen, H. E. 1973. Some aspects of the breeding demography of the double-crested cormorant *Phalacrocorax auritus* on Mandarte Island. Ph.D. diss., Zool. Lab. der Rijksuniversiteit te Groningen, Netherlands.

van Dobben, W. H. 1952. The food of the cormorant in the Netherlands. *Ardea* 40:1–63.

van Mark, J. G., and K. H. Voous. 1988. The birds of Sumatra. British Ornithol. Union, B.O.U. Checklist No. 10.

van Tets, G. F. 1959. A comparative study of the reproductive behaviour and natural history of three sympatric species of cormorant (*Phalacrocorax auritus, Ph. pencillatus, Ph. pelagicus*) at Mandarte Island, B.C. M.A. thesis, Univ. Brit. Columbia, Vancouver.

van Tets, G. F. 1965. A comparative study of some social communication patterns in the Pelecaniformes. Am. Ornith. Union, *Ornith. Monogr.* No. 2.

van Tets, G. F. 1968. White-breasted cormorant swallows pebbles on land. *Emu* 67:224.

van Tets, G. F. 1976a. Australasia and the origin of shags

and cormorants, Phalacrocoracidae. Pp. 121–24, in: Proc. 16th Inter. Ornith. Congr., Canberra, Australia, 1974.

van Tets, G. F. 1976b. Further observations on the taking of pebbles by black-faced cormorants. *Emu* 76:151–52.

van Tets, G. F. 1980. (Observations on Campbell Island shag.) In: Prelim. Rept. Campbell Is. Exp. 1975–76, N.Z. Dept. Lands Surv. Reserve Ser. 7. (Not seen; cited in Marchant and Higgins, 1990.)

van Tets, G. F., P. V. Rich, and H. R. Marino-Hadiwardoyo. 1989. A reappraisal of *Protoplotus beauforti* from the early Tertiary of Sumatra and the basis for a new pelecaniform family. *Pub. Geol. Res. Div. Cent. Paleontol. Serv.* No. 5:57–75.

van Tets, G. F., M. H. Waterman, and D. Purchase. 1976. Dispersal patterns of cormorants banded in South Australia. *Aust. Bird Bander* 14:43–46.

Vaurie, C. 1965. *The birds of the Palearctic fauna.* Vol. 1 (Non-passeriformes). Witherby, London.

Vermeer, K. 1969. Colonies of double-crested cormorant and white pelican in Alberta. *Can. Field-Nat.* 83:36–39.

Vermeer, K. 1970a. Distribution in size of colonies of white pelican, *Pelecanus erythrorhynchos*, in Canada. *Can. J. Zool.* 48:1029–32.

Vermeer, K. 1970b. Some aspects of the nesting of double-crested cormorants at Cypress Lake, Saskatchewan, in 1969: a plea for protection. *Blue Jay* 28:11–13.

Vermeer, K. 1973. Great blue heron and double-crested cormorant colonies in the Prairie Provinces. *Can. Field-Nat.* 87:427–32.

Vermeer, K. 1977. Comparison of white pelican recoveries from colonies east and west of the Canadian Rocky Mountains. *Murrelet* 58:79–82.

Vermeer, K., K. H. Morgan, and C. E. J. Smith. 1988. Population trends and nesting habitat of double-crested and pelagic cormorants in the Strait of Georgia. Pp. 94–98, in K. Vermeer and R. W. Butler (eds.), *The ecology and status of marine and shoreline birds in the Strait of Georgia, British Columbia.* Can. Wildl. Serv., Ottawa.

Vermeer, K., and L. Rankin. 1984. Population trends in nesting double-crested and pelagic cormorants in Canada. *Murrelet* 65:1–9.

Vestjens, W. J. M. 1975. Breeding behaviour of the darter at Lake Cowal, NSW. *Emu* 75:121–31.

Vestjens, W. J. M. 1977a. Breeding behavior and ecology of the Australian pelican, *Pelecanus conspicillatus*, in New South Wales. *Aust. Wild. Res.* 4:37–58.

Vestjens, W. J. M. 1977b. Status, habitats and food of vertebrates at Lake Cowal, NSW. CSIRO Div. Wildl. Res., Tech. Memo 12.

Vestjens, W. J. M. 1983. Bird in the hand: Australian pelican *Pelecanus conspicillatus. Corella* 7:17–18.

Vogt, W. 1942. Aves guanera. *Boletin Compañía Administrador del Guano* 18:1–132.

Voisin, J. F. 1970. On the specific status of the Kerguelen shag and its affinities. *Notornis* 17:286–90.

Voisin, J. F. 1973. Notes on the blue-eyed shags (genus *Leucocarbo* Bonaparte). *Notornis* 20:262–71.

Voous, K. H. 1983. *Birds of the Netherlands Antilles.* de Walburg Pers, Utrecht. 2d ed.

Wanless, S., A. E. Burger, and M. P. Harris. 1991. Diving depths of shags, *Phalacrocorax aristotelis,* breeding on the Isle of May. *Ibis* 133:37–42.

Wanless, S., and M. P. Harris. 1991. Diving patterns of full-grown and juvenile rock shags. *Condor* 93:44–48.

Wanless, S., M. P. Harris, and J. A. Morris. 1991. Foraging range and feeding locations of shags, *Phalacrocorax aristotelis,* during chick rearing. *Ibis* 133:30–36.

Watanuki, Y., N. Kondo, and H. Nakagawa. 1988. (Status of seabirds breeding in Hokkaido.) *Jap. J. Ornith.* 37:17–32. (Japanese, English summary.)

Watson, G. E. 1975. *Birds of the Antartic and SubAntarctic.* Washington: Amer. Geophysical Union.

Watson, G. E., S. L. Olson, and J. R. Miller. 1991. A new subspecies of the double-crested cormorant, *Phalacrocorax auritus,* from San Salvador, Bahama Islands. *Proc. Biol. Soc. Wash.* 104:356–69.

Watt, J. P. C. 1975. Notes on Whero Island and other roosting and breeding stations of the Stewart Island shag (*Leucocarbo carunculatus chalconotus*). *Notornis* 22:265–72.

Wehle, D. H. S. 1978. Studies of marine birds on Ugaiushak Island. Pp. 208–312, in: Ann. Rept. Princ. Invest., Environ. Assess. Alaskan Cont. Shelf., NOAA, Envir. Res. Lab., Boulder, Colo. vol. 3 (Birds).

Wehle, D. H. S., E. P. Hoberg, and K. Powers. 1977. Studies of marine birds of Ugaiushak Island, Alaska. Pp. 155–92, in: Ann. Rept. Princ. Invest., Environ. Assess. Alaskan Cont. Shelf, NOAA, Envir. Res. Lab., Boulder, Colo. vol. 4 (Birds).

Weimerkirch, H., R. Zotier, and P. Jovetin. 1988. The avifauna of the Kerguelen Islands. *Emu* 89:15–29.

Weseloh, D. V., P. Mineau, S. M. Temple, G. B. McKeating, and S. Postupalsky. 1980. Improved quality of life parameters of double-crested cormorants in Canadian waters of the Great Lakes. *Pac. Seabird Group Bull.* 7:56. (Abstract.)

Wetmore, A. 1945. A review of the forms of the brown pelican. *Auk* 62:577–86.

Wetmore, A. 1960. A classification for the birds of the world. *Smithson. Misc. Coll.* 131(5):1–105.

Wetmore, A. 1981. The birds of the Republic of Panama. Pt. 1. *Smithsonian Misc. Coll.* 150:1–483.

Wheeler, W. R. 1946. Springtime observations at Fisherman's Bend, near Melbourne. *Emu* 46:192–94.

White, D. H., W. J. Fleming, and K. L. Ensor. 1988. Pesticide contamination and hatching success of waterbirds in Mississippi. *J. Wildl. Mgmt.* 52:724–29.

Whitfield, A. K., and S. J. M. Blaber. 1979. Feeding ecology of piscivorous birds at Lake St. Lucia. Pt. 3. Swimming birds. *Ostrich* 50:10–20.

Wilbur, S. R. 1987. *Birds of Baja California.* Univ. of Calif. Press, Berkeley.

Williams, A. J. 1987. New seabird breeding localities, and an extension of bank cormorant range, along the Namib coast of southern Africa. *Cormorant* 15:98–102.

Williams, A. J., and A. E. Burger. 1978. The ecology of the prey of Cape and bank cormorants. *Cormorant* 4:28–29.

Williams, A. J., and A. E. Burger. 1979. Aspects of the breeding biology of the imperial cormorant, *Phalacrocorax atriceps,* at Marion Island. *Gerfaut* 69:407–23.

Williams, A. J., and J. Cooper. 1983. The crowned cormorant: breeding biology, diet and offspring-reduction strategy. *Ostrich* 54:213–19.

Williams, L. 1942. Display and sexual behavior of the Brandt cormorant. *Condor* 41:85–104.

Williams, L. E., Jr., and T. Joanen. 1974. Age at first nesting in the brown pelican. *Wilson Bull.* 86:279–80.

Williams, S. O. 1978. Colonial waterbirds on the Mexican Plateau. Pp. 44–47, in: Proc. Colonial Waterbird Group Meeting, Dekalb, Ill., 20–23 Oct. 1977, W. E. Southern (ed.).

Winkler, H. 1983. The ecology of cormorants (genus *Phalacrocorax*). Pp. 193–99, in: F. Schiemer (ed.), *Limnology of Parakrama Samudra—Sri Lanka.* Junk, Der Haag.

Woods, R. W. 1975. *The birds of the Falkland Islands.* A. Nelson, London.

Yamamoto, H. 1967. (*Phalacrocorax capillatus* as a breeding bird on the Iwate Coast, Honshu.) *Misc. Rept. Yamashina Inst. Ornith. Zool.* 5:48–60. (Japanese, English summary.)

Yamashina Institute for Ornithology. 1987. Report of the bird migration research center, Feb. 1, 1986–Dec. 31, 1986. Yamashina Inst., Ornith., Abiko, Chiba, Japan.

Index

This index is limited to avian taxa, especially the genera, species, and subspecies of pelecaniform birds monographed in this book. It includes fossil taxa, which are indicated by an asterisk following their names. It follows the English and technical nomenclature used in the book; cross-referencing has also been provided for the more commonly encountered alternative English vernacular names. Complete indexing for each species is found under its primary English vernacular name, and the primary taxonomic accounts are printed in italics. The appendixes are not indexed.